Organizational Economics

━━━━━━━━━━━

Toward a New Paradigm
for Understanding and
Studying Organizations

Jay B. Barney
William G. Ouchi
Editors

Organizational Economics

 Jossey-Bass Publishers

San Francisco • London • 1986

ORGANIZATIONAL ECONOMICS
Toward a New Paradigm for Understanding and Studying Organizations
by Jay B. Barney and William G. Ouchi, Editors

Library of Congress Cataloging-in-Publication Data
Main entry under title:

Organizational economics.

(The Jossey-Bass management series) (The Jossey-Bass
social and behavioral science series)
Bibliography: p. 446
Includes index.
1. Managerial economics.   I. Barney, Jay B.
II. Ouchi, William G.   III. Series.   IV. Jossey-Bass
social and behavioral science series.
HD30.22.O74   1986   338.5   86–45622
ISBN 1-55542-015-X (alk. paper)

Manufactured in the United States of America

The paper in this book meets the guidelines for
permanence and durability of the Committee on
Production Guidelines for Book Longevity of the
Council on Library Resources.

JACKET DESIGN BY WILLI BAUM

FIRST EDITION

Code 8648

A joint publication in
The Jossey-Bass Management Series
and
The Jossey-Bass
Social and Behavioral Science Series

Consulting Editors
Organizations and Management

Warren Bennis
University of Southern California

Richard O. Mason
Southern Methodist University

Ian I. Mitroff
University of Southern California

Contents

ix

Preface

For us, organizational economics denotes the study of organizations and organizational phenomena using concepts taken from contemporary organization theory, organizational behavior, and microeconomics. Our approach is defined by the common focus of these three disciplines on organizations and draws on whatever concepts, ideas, and methods seem most useful in explaining and describing organizational phenomena, no matter what their disciplinary roots might be.

The history of research in organization theory is a history of borrowing from other disciplines. This borrowing began as early as the Hawthorne studies (Roethlisberger and Dickson, 1939), which borrowed from psychology and social psychology to establish what became known as the human relations school (Perrow, 1972). Later, concepts and a way of thinking were borrowed from sociology and political science to develop contingency and resource dependence theories (Miles, 1980). More recently, concepts from biology have been borrowed in the development of the population ecology model (Hannan and Freeman, 1977; McKelvey, 1982), and anthropology has been a source of concepts and a way of thinking for those studying organizational cultures (Jelinek, Smircich, and Hirsch, 1983).

With this strong interdisciplinary history, it is not surprising that organization theory is again beginning to borrow from a neighboring discipline. The discipline this time is microeconomics. It began slowly, with the work of Chandler (1962), Rumelt (1974), Ouchi (1980), Van de Ven (1982), and others. But now the list of works on this topic is growing, and its influence is being felt—both by those who embrace this new approach and by those who object to it.

Our own interest in this area began with Oliver Williamson's book *Markets and Hierarchies*, published in 1975, for in Williamson's arguments we saw the potential for addressing some of the most fundamental unanswered questions in organization theory: What is an organization? Why does it exist? What are its boundaries? Applying Williamson's framework has generated numerous insights for us, both in academic and applied settings.

As we began to move beyond *Markets and Hierarchies*, we discovered a rich and diverse body of knowledge in microeconomics concerning organizations and how they work. Unfortunately, much of this literature was difficult for a behavioral scientist to read because it employed unusual jargon and used mathematics liberally. Moreover, the sheer volume of this material was formidable. To read and analyze so much highly mathematical and technical material required an enormous commitment of time and energy. There were, and continue to be, few published guides to this literature. For this reason, we decided to bring together the materials in this book, to create a map to this economic literature that will help those in organization theory understand its implications for their work.

In *Organizational Economics*, we have gathered some of the most innovative work on the economics of organizations. An understanding of the substance of these collected papers will help noneconomists understand the implications economics has for their work on organizations and organizational phenomena.

As our own experience suggests, describing the implications of these recent developments in microeconomic theory for those who work in organization theory represents a special challenge, perhaps an even greater challenge than that of borrowing and explaining concepts from psychology, sociology, political science, anthropology, or even biology. The arguments, although they have important implications for organization theory, are written by economists for economists and rely on economic reasoning, assumptions, and iconography—all of which are unfamiliar to many organization theory researchers and teachers.

We have attempted to overcome this communication problem in three ways. First, we have chosen to include in the book only nonmathematical selections. Much of traditional microeconomics is expressed in mathematical form. The same holds true, albeit to a lesser extent, for the theoretical developments we consider here. While mathematical exposition can be extremely helpful in the rigorous and precise development of a theory, it is less useful for those being exposed to these ideas for the first time. Thus, we have limited ourselves to nonmathematical treatments.

Second, with a few exceptions, we have chosen to include only those selections that are attempts to develop broad theoretical statements. To this end, we have selected articles that are currently acknowledged to be, or seem likely to become, classics in organizational economics. Instead of focusing on important, but nonetheless limited, theoretical and empirical problems in traditional microeconomics, these articles focus on broader theoretical issues and thus offer a superior introduction to the general classes of problems currently interesting microeconomists and, by extension, organization theorists.

Finally, each set of readings is preceded by an introductory discussion that outlines the major features of the articles in that section and points out their major assumptions and ambiguities. Most important, we have attempted to illuminate the potential impact of each set of articles on the study of organizations.

The Audience for This Book

This collection of readings will be beneficial to three groups of scholars. First, organization theorists will be able to use the ideas presented here to focus and refine their research efforts. We neither expect, nor advocate, that the type of economics represented in this book will replace traditional organization theory. However, we do expect that some of the insights developed by organizational economists will help organizational theorists see their objects of study in new and fascinating ways and, in this sense, will continue the theoretical integration of these two fields.

Organizational behavior researchers, including social psychologists, will also find many of the ideas and concepts in this book interesting and suggestive. As becomes clear early on, the importance of productive teams in organizations is at the heart of many organizational economic models of the firm. Organizational economists, unlike organizational behavior theorists, have not focused their efforts on studying these teams, per se, but rather on studying the implications of teams for organizational action and structure. In this sense, many of the readings presented here suggest important implications for the study of groups in firms and represent a means through which the insights of organizational behavior can be extended to encompass the entire firm.

Finally, practicing (or studying) economists will find this collection of readings helpful, for the selection and organization of this work helps define the structure of what is still an emerging subdiscipline, organizational economics. Through the course of the book, distinct themes and points of view emerge, suggesting further research that needs to be done by trained organizational economists.

Overview of the Contents

The introductory chapter outlines the theoretical revolution that seems to be developing in microeconomics. It also discusses the apparent paradigmatic void in organization theory and suggests that organizational economics, because it is fundamentally multidisciplinary in character, may at least partly fill that void.

Chapter One presents the key concepts that underlie much of the economics of organizations, including such concepts as information and opportunism. Chapters Two and Three focus on theories of market failure, especially transaction-cost theory. Chapter Two presents that part of transaction-cost theory that focuses on alternative means of governing economic exchanges, including markets, bureaucracies, and other modes of governance. Here, the concepts of asymmetric information and opportunism are applied to explain why markets fail and what may replace them. In Chapter Three, the impact that organizational structure can have on transaction governance is explored. A typology of organization structures is presented, together with some empirical research that tests the efficiency of different structures.

Chapters Four, Five, and Six focus on theories concerning the impact of markets on firms. The theme developed throughout this part of the book is that markets, and the competition they represent, significantly constrain an organization's actions. In Chapter Four, the impact of capital markets on a firm is investigated through agency theory. Wherever delegation of responsibility takes place, possible conflicts of interest arise. But individuals cannot freely exploit the responsibility they receive, for they are constrained by market forces out of their control. How these forces shape the design and function of organizations is the focus of agency theory.

In Chapter Five, attention shifts to the evolutionary theory of the firm. Many of the constraints imposed by market forces cannot be anticipated, and thus enormous uncertainties and ambiguities arise concerning the appropriate responses to these forces. These uncertainties, in turn, suggest that a firm's performance can depend, at least in part, on its good fortune more than on its quality of management.

In Chapter Six, these ideas are extended to include the economics of the theory of strategy. Instead of passively accepting a foreordained fate, the firms described in this chapter recognize that organizations both shape and respond to market forces, and that a firm's actions and performance ultimately depend on this mix of action and response.

A concluding chapter summarizes many of the important themes presented throughout the book and discusses the impact of organizational economics on organization theory and organizational behavior and vice versa. Finally attention shifts to the future of organizational economics and to the issues and questions that still loom large in this field.

Taken together, these seven chapters represent what we think are the most important current areas of research in the economics of organizations. Future developments in the study of the economics of organizations seem likely to come from these areas of work, either alone or in combination. The readings presented here may form the basis of an integrated approach to organizational analysis, but they do not themselves provide that integration. For decades, leading scholars in organization theory, organizational behavior, and microeconomics have called for multidisciplinary theories of organizations and organizational phenomena (Simon, 1961). Only recently has it appeared that the potential for this type of integration exists. The readings in this book set the stage for what we believe will be the next wave of thinking about organizations through the 1990s.

Acknowledgments

The concepts and ideas developed in this book have formed the core of our research and teaching efforts for more than ten years. During this time, our thinking has been influenced in countless ways by both students and colleagues. However, as we began compiling the articles to form this collection, and as we began to develop the commentary to accompany these articles, several individuals made unusually important and helpful contributions. First, at the Graduate School of Management at the University of California at Los Angeles, our colleagues Richard Rumelt, William McKelvey, Chinu Balakrishnan, Mitchell Koza, Barbara Lawrence, Connie Gersick, Tom Copeland, Brad Cornell, Ron Masulis, and Sheriden Titman all provided thoughtful, and often skeptical, commentary on our efforts. Lynn Zucker and Marshal Meyer, participants in our meetings of the Organizations Interest Group, also helped refine many of the ideas developed here.

Several doctoral students also had an important influence on the development of this work, including Dave Ulrich and Wayne Brockbank (both now at the University of Michigan), Kathleen Reavis (at the Wharton School), Jim Kidney (at the University of Redlands), Maggi Philips, Todd Zenger, and Cynthia Beath. Indeed, much of this book was conceived and refined while Jay Barney was teaching a doctoral seminar on organizational economics that included many of these students.

Outside of this Southern California intellectual community, several individuals have influenced the development of this work, including Oliver Williamson and Sidney Winter (at the Yale School of Organization and Management), Andy Van de Ven and Ian

Maitland (at the University of Minnesota), Gordon Walker and Erin Anderson (both at the Wharton School), David Teece (at the University of California at Berkeley), Howard Aldrich (at the University of North Carolina), and Alan Wilkins (at Brigham Young University). This list, of course, only scratches the surface of those in the field who have influenced us.

One individual deserves special mention for his contributions: William Hesterly. Bill took on the assignment of preparing the articles for the publisher. This task included compiling the lengthy bibliography and tracking down obscure references on everything from the social life of lions and wolves to the history of guilds in the Middle Ages. Bill also read the entire manuscript and suggested several important substantive improvements. His efforts are one of the major reasons this work has come to fruition.

As every academic understands, the ability to write ultimately depends on sacrifices made by one's family. We hope that our wives, Kim and Carol, and our children understand how much we need and appreciate their support.

Los Angeles, California   Jay B. Barney
September 1986   William G. Ouchi

The Editors

Jay B. Barney is assistant professor of management at Texas A & M University. He received his B.S. degree (1975) from Brigham Young University and his M.A. (1979) and Ph.D. degrees (1982) from Yale University. From 1980 to 1986 he was assistant professor of management in the Graduate School of Management at the University of California at Los Angeles. Barney teaches courses in management and business strategy. His research focuses on integrating organization theory and organizational economics in the study of business strategy and in the study of the organization of capital acquisition.

William G. Ouchi is professor of management in the Graduate School of Management at the University of California at Los Angeles. He received his B.A. degree (1965) from Williams College, his M.B.A. degree (1967) from Stanford University, and his Ph.D. degree (1972) from the University of Chicago. He holds an honorary doctorate from Williams College. Ouchi teaches courses in management and business-government relations. His research focuses on applying organization theory and organizational economic concepts in these two areas. His first book, *Theory Z: How American Management Can Meet the Japanese Challenge* (1981), was on the best-seller list for five months. His second book, *The M-Form Society: How American Teamwork Can Recapture the Competitive Edge* (1984), reports on a three-year study by a team of sixteen researchers led by himself.

Organizational Economics

*Toward a New Paradigm
for Understanding and
Studying Organizations*

INTRODUCTION

The Search for New Microeconomic and Organization Theory Paradigms

Organizational Choices

Case 1. In the spring of 1978, a group vice-president in a large industrial organization met with his staff to evaluate the potential of a centralized manufacturing plant that would be shared by several profit center divisions in his group. The benefits and possible costs of the plan were listed. On the one hand, such a centralized facility would partially capture any synergies that existed among the business units in the group. It also would allow some of the business units to increase manufacturing efficiencies. Increased efficiency seemed particularly important since several highly efficient Japanese competitors were beginning just then to enter the U.S. market of one of the divisions. Without a more efficient manufacturing plant, this division could not hope to compete with the Japanese. Yet, on its own, the division could not afford these improvements. They could be made only by drawing on whatever economies of scale existed between profit center divisions in the group.

On the other hand, the culture of the firm did not facilitate interdivisional cooperation. Historically, division general managers had "run their own shop," and any attempt by the group vice-president to modify this tradition was certain to meet significant resistance. Moreover, all accounting and financing procedures in the company were profit center in orientation, making the possibility of developing cooperation less likely. Many of the division general managers did not trust the motives of the group vice-president. Was he really interested in the long-term financial per-

1

formance of divisions in the group, or was he only interested in implementing a highly visible program to enhance his personal promotability? After this group vice-president was gone, who would keep the centralized manufacturing facility running?

Case 2. In the summer of 1983, the founders of an entrepreneurial high technology firm located on the edge of Silicon Valley were considering their strategic and financial options. They had just negotiated a successful relationship with a venture capital firm, netting over $1 million dollars in working capital. They were currently drawing on this capital but wondered if they had given away too much of the company in this first round of financing.

Already, several engineers—the life blood of the firm—were talking about moving to a new firm in search of a greater opportunity to share in the equity of a start-up company. Would including these engineers among the equity holders in the firm entice them to stay, or were the engineer's complaints about a lack of equity only symptomatic of other problems more fundamental to that group? After all, bringing their first product to market had forced the firm to focus their normally freewheeling and free spirited attentions on the more mundane tasks of testing and customer service. Perhaps the research cycle of the engineering process was creating dissatisfaction among the engineers, and what was really needed was not more equity but another research project to sink their teeth into. In any case, how would the venture capitalists respond to the additional equity dilution that would come with including more engineers in the equity-holding group?

Case 3. In the summer of 1984, a highly respected U.S. manufacturer was struggling with a cost disadvantage of nearly 20 percent vis-à-vis its nearest competitor. Senior managers were perplexed. Unlike many firms in the industry, they had understood the importance of participative management and quality circles in improving productivity. In fact, they had long been enjoying the benefits of these programs. Their reputation in this area was nationwide, and they had been the subject of numerous research efforts attempting to establish an empirical correlation between participative management and productivity. And yet, their costs were way out of line with their major competitor.

The managers wondered if other characteristics of their competition, besides management style, might explain this differential. For example, their competitor had a higher debt-to-equity ratio than they did. Did the ability to rely on higher leverage benefit this firm? After all, interest payments are tax deductible. If this were the case, why would this competing firm's banks be willing to live with such a high debt-to-equity ratio? The managers were certain that their own bank would be very reluctant to continue funding them should they become that highly leveraged. In addition, this competitor was not as vertically integrated as they were, but instead had several suppliers that sold nearly all their output to them. Could these financial and structural attributes explain a 20 percent cost disadvantage?

General Management Decisions and Management Theory

Although each of these three real world situations is distinct in terms of detail, they share a characteristic common to virtually all general management decisions: they are simultaneously social and economic in character. In all these examples, the economic questions of strategy, manufacturing, and finance are intrinsically bound with social questions about organizational change, culture, and management style. If managers were to base decisions on the analysis of either the social or the economic aspects of these problems, but not both, they would run the risk of either implementing programs that were not economically viable, or of choosing economically powerful programs that could not be implemented.

While general managers constantly struggle with weighing economic imperatives against social and organizational realities, most of those who study or teach about organizations and organizational phenomena have conveniently avoided this difficult confrontation. Rather than treating the phenomena they study as an integrated package of social and economic issues, organization theorists and microeconomists have typically ignored those aspects of organizational phenomena that do not fit conveniently within their artificially narrow frameworks.

Organization theorists could help the group vice-president in the first example in implementing the centralized manufacturing facility but would have greater difficulty evaluating whether it was the strategically sound move. Microeconomists could assist the entrepreneurs in the second example in computing their cost of capital but would have relatively little input about the motivational problems of the engineers. Finally, while organization theorists might applaud the participative management style of the firm in the last example, only microeconomists would have much to say about the use of debt versus equity funding and the optimal degree of vertical integration.

Far too often, both microeconomists and organization theorists presume that because their models are not sufficiently general to incorporate both social and economic concepts, that these other aspects of organizational life are either nonexistent or independent of those organizational areas that they are studying. Of course, the truth is that most organizational phenomena are far from being separable into independent social and economic components, and, in fact, are both completely social and completely economic. Organizational reality does not fall neatly into arbitrary academic categories. It never has.

While the complexity of organizational phenomena cries out for theoretical and empirical integration across disciplines, historically the fields of microeconomics and organization theory have commingled neither theories nor findings, remaining fundamentally distinct in concept and approach. Most practitioners of organization theory have found microeconomic theory so abstract as to be almost devoid of reality and content. On the other hand, microeconomists have considered the less rigorous and less analytical field of organization theory as systematic common sense at best, and second rate journalism at worst. These fields have developed in isolation, each largely unaware of the insights the other was generating about their common focus of research: organizations and organizational actions.

Over the years, research in microeconomics and organization theory periodically overlapped, with results that suggested the great promise of theoretical and empirical integration. Yet, after Simon (1961) and March and Simon (1958) developed their insights into the decision-making process and bounded rationality, research in the two fields seemed to diverge and any interest in integration seemed to wane. Through the sixties and the seventies, the two fields continued to develop independently, each studying related phenomena, but within fundamentally unrelated theoretical frameworks.

Despite this historical lack of intellectual intercourse, recent developments in these two fields seem to suggest the possibility of an unprecedented level of theoretical and empirical integration. This possibility stems in part from a paradigmatic shift away from traditional theory in microeconomics, and in part from a paradigmatic void in organization theory.

Revolutionary Microeconomics

Thomas Kuhn (1970) has observed that knowledge accumulates in scientific disciplines in one of two ways. For long periods, a discipline will be dominated by one theoretical framework or paradigm. During this time, the paradigm defines the nature and the range of questions that scientists ask about the phenomena studied. The knowledge accumulated in this way tends to increase the field's understanding of the paradigm and its theoretical and empirical implications. Periodically, the normal activity of science is punctuated by revolutionary science. As a paradigm matures and becomes more fully tested, empirical anomalies begin to appear. At first, the old paradigm is twisted and bent in an attempt to fit the new data to an old model. Inevitably, the old paradigm is stretched too far, its inadequacies clear for all to see. Numerous contenders arise, all bidding to be the new paradigm for the field. Through the competitive process, a new general framework emerges. Typically, the new framework incorporates the insights of the older paradigm but stretches far beyond, not only to explain what were empirical anomalies, but to suggest whole new areas of research.

With the emergence of a new paradigm, a science enters a period of rapid progress characterized by great excitement as the theoretical and empirical implications of the new paradigm begin to be worked out. Over time, the field begins a shift back into a normal science state, accumulating enough knowledge until, inevitably, the groundwork for another paradigmatic shift is laid.

The occurrence of a true paradigmatic shift in a discipline is typically known with certainty only years after the fact. However, certain signs and activities within a discipline are the harbinger of a coming change. And while it is usually not possible to predict which theory among several contenders is likely to become the new paradigm, it is nevertheless possible to anticipate that change of some type is coming. In such disciplines, there tends to be a growing dissatisfaction with the received view, a frustration with the inability of the old paradigm to provide insights into empirical phenomena, and the emergence of numerous pretenders to the theoretical throne.

Microeconomics seems to have many of the attributes of a discipline approaching a paradigmatic shift. Since the publication of Adam Smith's *The Wealth of Nations* in 1776 and Alfred Marshall's *Principles of Economics* in 1891, positive microeconomics has been dominated by a paradigm that emphasizes supply and demand, equilibrium and optimization analyses, and perfect competition and monopoly (Hirshleifer, 1980). Taken together, this work forms what is known currently as microeconomic price theory. With few exceptions (Chamberlin, 1933; Robinson, 1933; Coase, 1937; Commons, 1934), work in microeconomics has focused on understanding the theoretical, empirical, and policy implications of this model.

Most microeconomists would agree that price theory is well suited to describing industries characterized by one of two extremes: perfect competition or perfect monopoly. Yet, there is a growing consensus that relatively few industries are characterized by these extreme models, and that the convenience of treating intermediate cases as deviations from these extremes, although mathematically tractable, does not generate theoretical or empirical insight. Emerging dissatisfaction with the traditional model has taken many forms. Citing the advantages of abstract modeling, some authors (Baumol, Panzar, and Willig, 1982) have continued theorizing with the use of very abstract idealized theories but have simplified the assumptions on which these theories are based. Other authors have suggested that most of the assumptions of the neoclassical framework, including supply and demand analysis, are misleading and must be replaced (Nelson and Winter, 1982). Still others have suggested that some of the insights and assumptions taken from the neoclassical paradigm should be carried over into a new and more powerful general theoretical framework (Jensen and Meckling, 1976a; Demsetz, 1967). These alternate views of how the current paradigm of microeconomics should be modified represent the contenders bidding to become that field's new paradigm. According to Kuhn (1970), they are to be expected in disciplines approaching a paradigmatic shift.

The Traditional Model of Perfect Competition

To comprehend the dissatisfaction with microeconomic price theory as it has developed, it is first necessary to understand something of this model. There is extensive literature addressing the limitations of monopoly theory (Baumol, Panzar, and Willig, 1982) and those of perfect competition theory. As a sample case, we will consider briefly the perfect competition model.

Probably hundreds of textbooks have been written about perfect competition theory, each with somewhat different characterizations of its assumptions and implications. Most authors would agree, however, that at least three basic assumptions underlie the perfect competition model, that (1) a market has a large number of buyers and sellers, (2) the product or service being exchanged is homogeneous, and (3) there are no costs to the activity of engaging in an exchange (Chamberlin, 1933; Williamson, 1975).

From these and related assumptions, most of the key implications of the perfect competition model can be derived. Implications key to this theory include the following. First, in perfectly competitive markets, there will be a tendency towards an equilibrium where the total supply of a good or service offered will approximately equal the total demand for that good or service. Second, the price of any good or service bought and sold at this equilibrium point implies that firms will obtain only normal profits from their exchanges, that is, profits just large enough to keep their assets engaged in their current activities. And finally, this equilibrium point is socially optimal in the sense that it will lead to an efficient allocation of resources in a given economy (Hirshleifer, 1980). These are strong theoretical conclusions. They also have important policy implications for how a market should or should not be regulated. Yet, despite these powerful conclusions, there is growing dissatisfaction with the perfect competition model.

Theoretical and Empirical Anomalies

Several authors (Williamson, 1975) have observed that few, if any, markets meet the stringent criteria of perfect competition. Some microeconomic theorists have turned aside such arguments by suggesting that as long as the behavior of industries generates patterns that appear to be derived from perfectly competitive markets, then the perfect competition models are useful (Friedman, 1953). Others have suggested that the perfect competition model, although unrealistic, is an excellent backdrop against which to compare actual market behavior. This assumes, of course, that the dimensions used to characterize perfect market competition are also relevant in characterizing imperfect competition (Robinson, 1933).

Despite these debates, there are some phenomena for which the application of the perfect competition model cannot be accomplished without stretching it beyond recognition. Consider just a few examples.

The Existence of Firms. As Coase initially observed in 1937, there is no explanation within traditional microeconomic theory of why firms exist. Indeed, rather than the traditional theory being a "theory of the firm," as it is often described, this model is really a theory of markets (Alchian, 1950). Instead of attempting to explain the existence of firms as a locus of economic activity, the traditional paradigm simply takes firms as a given and focuses attention on the market interactions of firms. Moreover, any attempted application of this framework to explain why firms exist leads one to the conclusion that indeed they should not. Under the assumption that the activity of engaging in economic exchanges has no costs, there should be no aggregate economic actors like firms. All transactions, including employment relations, should be carried out through markets, using explicit long- and short-term contracts, since the use of contracts would be less costly than organizational hierarchies. And yet, firms and organizations do exist and persist, suggesting, at the very least, that the assumption of zero costs when engaging in transactions is frequently violated. Several of the authors included in this volume focus on these kinds of questions.

Firm Heterogeneity. Not only do firms exist, they come in a wide variety of shapes and sizes. Even firms competing in the same market are rarely, if ever, identical. The perfect competition model offers little explanation for why such diversity develops and continues. Consider just two examples of a firm's heterogeneity: its organizational attributes and its product offerings.

Firms in a given industry may be organized according to function, in multiple divisions, or as a portfolio of different businesses (Williamson, 1975). Firms can be organized as corporations, as limited partnerships, or as sole proprietorships (Fama and Jensen, 1983a). Some firms adopt personnel policies consistent with the findings of organizational behavior; others do not (Ouchi, 1980). The variety of organizational forms within an industry is not consistent with the emphasis that the perfect competition model places on unique industry equilibria. In this state of equilibrium, competitive pressures are supposed to imply the existence of a unique set of optimal organizational strategies that should be common to most firms in an industry. Indeed, in the traditional model, firms are characterized as simple product-generating technologies that follow simple laws based on economies of scale. In the traditional approach, firms are the quintessential "black box." Implicit in this type of theorizing is the assumption that what goes on inside a firm is not relevant when predicting the aggregate behavior of markets. Microeconomists are now beginning to question this assumption. Organization theorists, of course, always have.

In addition to the organizational diversity of individual firms, the goods and services they offer vary from firm to firm. Rarely are markets characterized by the homogeneous products presumed in the perfect competition model. Differences in style, reputation, quality, and options differentiate product offerings along innumerable lines. Consumer choice is generally not restricted to choosing the identical product supplied by one of several identical firms. Yet despite this product differentiation, firms are still in direct competition for the goods and services they offer, as long as imperfect substitutes nevertheless remain partial substitutes for one another. As Chamberlin (1933) noted, because of product differentiation, most markets are characterized simultaneously by competition and monopoly, because consumers will insist on comparing products that cannot be perfectly compared. This type of heterogeneity provides a significant challenge to perfect competition reasoning.

Above-Normal Profits. A final anomaly can be cited. In the received view, firm profits are driven to a normal level in a perfect competition equilibrium. In this sense, a normal return is a return just large enough to keep the firm's assets engaged in their current activities. A firm that enjoys a greater than normal return is prospering. A firm with less than a normal return risks its survival. And a firm with a normal return simply survives. In the traditional theory, profits that persist above this normal level are attributable to one or a combination of three factors. One, such profits may be the manifestation of a temporary market disequilibrium. A firm that innovates may be able to enjoy some temporary advantages in a perfectly competitive world, but in the long run, this advantage will disappear as other firms imitate and increase competition. Two, sustained above-normal profits may reflect government interference, often in the form of regulatory or other protection. The traditional model suggests that without this protection, there would be no sustained superior performance. Finally, such performance can exist if there is either explicit or implicit anticompetitive, collusive behavior on the part of firms in the market. Firms can obtain sustained superior performance in this way, but such activities are illegal and carry with them the threat of significant legal sanctions.

While the traditional model can explain certain cases of sustained above-normal profits, there appear to be some organizations making above-normal profits for which none of the classical explanations apply. Porter (1980) and Peters and Waterman (1982) cite several examples of this type of firm, including IBM, Procter & Gamble, McDonald's, and Hewlett-Packard. Each of these firms seems to be very successful, enjoying sustained above-normal dealt with power and power relations. However, power structures, both as independent and dependent variables, did seem to dominate the field. Theoretical work by Weber (1947), Blau (1955), Crozier (1964), and Thompson (1967) seemed to set the stage for an enormous body of research on the structural and process implications of informal and formal power in organizations. The psychological implications of power within organizations were investigated by French and Raven (1960) and Hickson and others (1971) among numerous others. The study of power and power relations was extended to include interorganizational as well as intraorganizational phenomena. Much of this interorganizational work is summarized and integrated in Pfeffer and Salancik's 1978 book *The External Control of Organizations.*

The study of power within and between organizations continues and, periodically, additional insights are developed. But the theoretical gold mine that the power paradigm represented in the 1960s and 1970s appears to be running out. As is the case with the traditional microeconomic model, some of this waning of interest in theories about power within and between organizations stems from theoretical and empirical anomalies that are not well addressed in the power perspective. For example, the resource dependence model, as developed by Pfeffer and Salancik (1978), hypothesizes that firms typically manage the environmental uncertainty they face through some form of vertical integration. By bringing outside uncertainties under some degree of control, firms decrease the uncertainty they must face, a situation which—most power theorists would argue—enhances the survival possibilities of the firm (Ulrich and Barney, 1984). Whenever *any* environmental uncertainty faced a firm, the firm would adopt some form of vertical integration. Yet, within the theoretical framework of the power models, it is unclear why some form of vertical integration wouldn't always be in effect. The logical conclusion of this line of reasoning is that all industries characterized by any degree of uncertainty should be dominated by a relatively small number of vertically integrated organizations. Empirically, this simply is not the case.

While some empirical anomalies, vis-à-vis the power models, have been found, these anomalies do not seem to be the cause of reduced interest in this framework. Certainly, no studies have been

Introduction: The Search for New Paradigms

returns. Their success is too long-lasting to be an indicatio
temporary disequilibria. There appears to be little or no gove
ment protection from competition. And, there is little or no e
dence of anticompetitive behavior. The sustained success of the
and similar firms is a mystery within the context of the tradition
model.

The Contenders

(☆☆) Because of these and numerous other anomalies, many
microeconomists are ready to modify the traditional price theory
framework. This is not to suggest that shortly microeconomics will
abandon the received theory. Rather, the search is on for a more
general framework, a framework that will include the insights of
the traditional theory, but will place those insights in a context
that allows the theorist to explain a wider diversity of economic
and, particularly, organizational phenomena.

There are currently a large number of theoretical contenders,
all bidding to become the new dominant paradigm in the field if
and when traditional price theory is deposed. Most of these theories
are represented by chapters in this book, including transaction cost
theory, the evolutionary theory of the firm, agency theory, and
the theory of competitive strategy. At this stage, it is not possible
to predict which, if any, of these models will emerge as dominant,
or whether the revised microeconomic paradigm will be some as
yet undeveloped integration of several of these approaches. It could
be a new theory altogether. Whatever the outcome, the intellectual battle has been joined, and debate will go forward.

In Search of an Organizational Paradigm

Whereas microeconomics has many of the attributes of a
discipline approaching a paradigmatic shift, organization theory
has many of the attributes of a discipline in search of a paradigm.
Through the 1960s and 1970s, the dominant theoretical frameworks
in organization theory were drawn from sociology and social psychology and relied heavily on the concept of power (Williamson and
Ouchi, 1981). This is not to suggest that all work during this time

published that categorically refute the power models or their major implications. Rather, these models seem to have generated most of the theoretical and empirical insights that they are likely to. In short, they have simply run out of gas. In order to progress, organization theory has had to adopt ideas and concepts that, though not necessarily in contradiction with the power models, go beyond the scope of those models as they were developed in the sixties and seventies. For example, the population ecology (Hannan and Freeman, 1977; McKelvey, 1982) and institutional theories (Zucker, 1977; Meyer and Rowan, 1977) both seem to fit into a category of theories less concerned with the causes and implications of intra- and interorganizational power. The recent interest in organizational culture can be interpreted within a power framework (Riley, 1983) but can also be incorporated into theoretical models that have much less of a power focus (Wilkins and Ouchi, 1983; Jones, 1983).

With the waning of the power model, organization theory seems to have been set adrift in search of a new paradigm, a general framework with which to study organizations and organizational phenomena. All indications are that this search has not yet been resolved. To be generous, one could characterize organization theory as a multiparadigm field. Perhaps more realistically, it is a field without a paradigm.

Instead of developing and testing general theoretical paradigms, work in organization theory now seems to center on "topics." A new organizational topic seems to get "hot," generating an enormous amount of disjointed research effort, only to see this idea fade in the light of a new topic's growing popularity. Whether the topic is qualitative research methods, Japanese management techniques, or organizational culture, topical research is characterized by the application of a wide variety of theoretical frameworks to study one phenomenon; whereas, paradigm-driven research is characterized by the application of one general theoretical model in the study of a wide variety of organizational phenomena. Even a cursory review of the major journals in the field suggests the dominance of topical, not paradigmatic, research.

As in microeconomics, there are several theoretical rivals to the paradigmatic throne of organization theory, all bidding to replace or augment the power model. Some currently popular alternatives include the population ecology model, the organizational life cycle model, the institutionalization framework, organizational demographics, and the efficiency model (Ulrich and Barney, 1984). It is too early to predict which, if any, of these models will emerge as the new paradigm, or whether the new paradigm will combine aspects of all or several theories.

Intellectual Integration: Organizational Economics

With microeconomics poised to revamp traditional price theory, and with organization theory entering the debate to discover a new organizing framework, the stage is set for an unprecedented level of interaction and integration between these historically separate disciplines. Previously, organization theory could ignore microeconomic theory with its abstractions and unrealistic assumptions. However, this is no longer the case, since microeconomists are beginning to adopt assumptions and models very similar to those traditionally adopted by organization theorists. Moreover, microeconomists are beginning to ask questions about organizations and organizational phenomena that directly overlap the questions typically asked by organization theorists. Previously, microeconomists could dismiss organization theory as insufficiently rigorous to be of much use in their more formal theorizing. Now, however, these very microeconomists are beginning to adopt the same kinds of assumptions and concepts that organization theory has long accepted.

Moreover, each of the theoretical models contending for paradigmatic status in one of these two disciplines has theoretical parallels in the other. This parallelism is illustrated in Figure 1. The transaction-cost model (Chapter Three), for example, shares an interest in vertical integration with both resource dependence theory and the efficiency model. The transaction-cost model of organizational design and structure (Chapter Four) parallels much of the research on firm structure done by organization theorists. Research by organizational economists on the productive capabilities of teams (Chapters Two and Three) and their implications for organizational phenomena almost duplicates the widespread interest of organizational behavior researchers in team phenomena.

As Chapter Three will clarify, these arguments have important implications for the structure of organizations, as well. Organizational economic research on agency theory (Chapter Five) has important implications for the problem of cooperation within firms, and thus implications for research in organizational behavior, as well as very direct relevance for those studying the role of the board of directors in the modern corporation. Organization theory's population ecology model is very similar, both in approach and conclusion, to the evolutionary theory of the firm put forth by microeconomists (Chapter Six). And, finally, the overlap between the economics of strategy (Conclusion) and theories of strategy implementation is significant. These parallels will be discussed in more detail in the introduction to each chapter of readings.

**Figure 1. Parallel Theories in
Microeconomics and Organization Theory.**

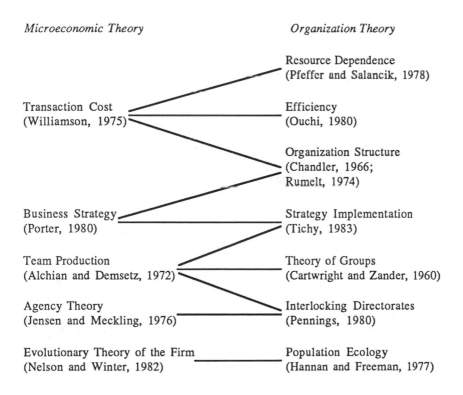

Microeconomic Theory	*Organization Theory*
	Resource Dependence (Pfeffer and Salancik, 1978)
Transaction Cost (Williamson, 1975)	Efficiency (Ouchi, 1980)
	Organization Structure (Chandler, 1966; Rumelt, 1974)
Business Strategy (Porter, 1980)	Strategy Implementation (Tichy, 1983)
Team Production (Alchian and Demsetz, 1972)	Theory of Groups (Cartwright and Zander, 1960)
Agency Theory (Jensen and Meckling, 1976)	Interlocking Directorates (Pennings, 1980)
Evolutionary Theory of the Firm (Nelson and Winter, 1982)	Population Ecology (Hannan and Freeman, 1977)

This parallelism is not all that surprising. Both microeconomists and organization theorists have been struggling to explain observed organizational phenomena. In this process, they have observed similar behavior within and between firms, which in turn, has led to the development of similar conceptual frameworks in an attempt to explain these phenomena. Although it has taken some time, the complexity of the common object of study of organization theory, organization behavior, and microeconomics—organizations—has finally brought these disciplines into a position where close intellectual interaction may take place. It may well be the case that a single paradigm may emerge to form the organizing framework of organization theory, organization behavior, and microeconomics. While differences in emphasis among these disciplines are likely to continue, differences in concept are likely to narrow.

Hoenack (1983, p. xi) puts it well in the introduction of his book *Economic Behavior Within Organizations:* "I have . . . concluded that when economic analysis and organization theory deal with the same issues, their results generally do not conflict. Although economic analysis has a different role in focusing on employees' choices in allocating resources, it does not emerge as a competing approach to organizations. I predict that further advances in our understanding of organizations will require economists to make use of insights provided by organization theorists and vice versa."

The purpose of this book is to facilitate the development of such an integrated framework. We have titled the book *Organizational Economics* in anticipation of this integrated theoretical framework. This integration is far from complete. Nevertheless, it is our belief that developments in organization theory, organization behavior, and microeconomics over the next decade or so will ultimately generate such an integrated framework and justify the title we have chosen.

Whatever the future of organization theory and microeconomics, the time when these disciplines could ignore one another without risk has passed. The insights that each discipline has developed separately, when joined together in a common intellectual framework, have too much theoretical and practical power to be ignored. In the future, competent researchers and teachers of organization theory will need to be capable of discussing the microeconomics of the firm, just as competent microeconomists will need to be capable of incorporating the behavioral insights of organization theory into their work. The object of study itself—organizations—demands such integrative efforts.

ONE

==== =====

Basic Concepts:
Information, Opportunism,
and Economic Exchange

Buying and selling is the fundamental process studied in economics. Traditional microeconomics has focused on that relatively narrow set of buying and selling exchanges where there are large numbers of buyers and sellers, where what is being exchanged is homogeneous across buyers and sellers, and where there are no search or other costs associated with buying and selling. Within this limited range of exchange, traditional microeconomics has a great deal to say about the amount of a good or service that will be produced, the price at which an exchange will go forward, the economic returns to parties in this exchange, and so on (Hirshleifer, 1980).

However, even casual observation suggests that only a relatively small number of the exchanges we each engage in every day are included within these narrow bounds. While this characterization might include, for example, buying and selling coffee beans, it certainly does not describe, say, going to a doctor and buying medical services, or buying one hundred thousand automobile transmissions, or buying a NASA spacecraft. It explicitly does not fit selling one's time, energy, and productive output to a firm as an employee, although it may describe the process of selling one's labor to a firm as an independent contractor.

Organizational economists have also recognized that most of the exchanges which characterize social life do not fit into the description of exchanges employed by traditional microeconomics. But observing that going to the doctor, buying a car, or obtaining an education are somehow different than buying food at the grocery store is not sufficient. What is also required is to specify how these exchanges differ and what implications these differences have for how these exchanges are organized.

⭐⭐ (The articles in this chapter serve as an introduction to two attributes of economic exchanges that many organizational economists believe differentiate simple exchanges like buying food from more complex exchanges like becoming an employee: asymmetric information and the possibility of opportunistic behavior. An information asymmetry exists in an economic exchange when one or more parties to the exchange enjoys some relevant informational advantage over other parties to the exchange. If, for example, one party knows more about the quality or value of the good or service being exchanged than others, then a condition of asymmetric information exists. Opportunistic behavior is any action engaged in by an exchange partner, enjoying an informational (or some other) advantage, to exploit that advantage to the economic detriment of others. In its crassest form, opportunism is "lying, stealing, and cheating" or other "self-disbelieved statements" (Williamson, 1975). In its more subtle forms, opportunism can be raising the price of your good or service once your customer has irreversibly committed to buy from you, lowering your quality in the same circumstances, or demanding other concessions when you enjoy some economic advantage.

(⭐⭐⭐) For Akerlof ("The Market for 'Lemons': Quality Uncertainty and the Market Mechanism"), information asymmetries exist because those who currently own a product know more about its quality characteristics than those who may buy it. For this reason, current owners may misrepresent their product as being of high quality, when it is in fact of low quality. This simple asymmetry in markets has surprisingly far reaching consequences for how exchanges can take place. Bad products drive out good products and threaten the very existence of markets, all because current owners know more about the quality of the item to be exchanged than do potential buyers.

Akerlof develops his model using the example of the used car market. When a line of new cars is manufactured, a certain percentage of them will turn out to be bad cars, or "lemons." When someone buys a new car, the price paid partly reflects the collective judgment of all car buyers concerning the probability that when you buy a new car, that car will end up being a lemon. If there were never any lemons, the price of new cars would be higher. Because there are at least some lemons, the price of all new cars is discounted, because the consumer cannot tell until after a car is purchased whether or not it is a lemon.

After the car is purchased, the owner comes to know with certainty whether it is a good car or a lemon. Suppose it is a good car, that after a few minor repairs it runs smoothly and gets good gas mileage. Also, suppose that for any of a variety of reasons, the current owner wants to sell this car, perhaps to acquire a larger or more luxurious model. While the current owner now knows that the car he bought is not a lemon, potential buyers do not have this information. Nor can the current owner convince potential buyers that the car he* is trying to sell is actually a good car, for everyone knows that if the car really were a lemon, the current owner would not admit this to potential buyers. To do so would jeopardize his ability to sell the car at a high price. Rather than frankly discussing the abysmal performance of a lemon, the current owner is more likely to lie or, at the very least, omit reference to some of the car's worst attributes. That is, exploiting an informational advantage, the current owner of a lemon will act opportunistically and misrepresent the lemon as a good car. Since everyone selling used cars will describe them as good cars—whether or not they are lemons—potential buyers will not be able to distinguish between good cars and lemons on the basis of the description of the current owners.

Now the person trying to sell a good used car has a problem. Since potential buyers cannot tell the difference between a good car and a lemon before they buy, the price of all used cars (at least within the same class) will be about the same. Once again, this price will reflect the buyer's perceptions of the probability of buying a lemon versus buying a good car. Thus, the price of a

---

*The use of the pronoun *he* has not yet been superseded by a convenient, generally accepted pronoun that means "either he or she." Therefore, we will continue to use *he* while acknowledging the inherent inequity of the traditional preference for the masculine pronoun.

good used car will be less than its true worth, because this price will reflect the probability that it is a lemon. But the current owner knows it is not a lemon. Thus, unless he is constrained to do so, the current owner probably will not bring a good used car to market, for he knows he will not receive the full value of this automobile. The result is clear: most of the cars left in the used car market will be lemons. Let the buyer beware.

This is what Akerlof calls the "Lemons Principle": When information asymmetries exist that create the possibility of opportunistic behavior, then bad products (lemons) will drive out the good, because sellers will not be able to obtain the full value of the good product. Akerlof's is a theoretical model. It does not necessarily imply that one should never buy used cars. It does suggest caution, however.

Akerlof applies his Lemons Principle to several other kinds of markets, including insurance, the labor market for minorities, the costs of dishonesty, and credit markets in underdeveloped countries. In all of these cases, good "products" are driven out to be replaced by bad, thereby jeopardizing the very existence of the market.

Akerlof's message is not completely pessimistic. While the Lemons Principle, left unchecked, can threaten market viability, several social and economic institutions can arise to effectively counter this tendency. Examples of such institutions include product guarantees, a product's brand name reputation, licensing practices, and chain ownership. Akerlof's observation that chain ownership (for example, Hilton Hotels, McDonald's) can reduce the impact of the Lemons Principle leads directly to our next selection, for Akerlof has begun to argue that different ways of organizing economic exchanges can help resolve the difficulties created by information asymmetry and opportunism.

This is one of the themes developed by Klein, Crawford, and Alchian ("Vertical Integration, Appropriable Rents, and the Competitive Contracting Process"). Klein, Crawford, and Alchian argue that whenever one party to an exchange depends on other parties to that exchange, then the dependent actors risk being economically exploited by those on whom they depend. Dependence exists when transaction specific investments are made. A transaction specific investment is any investment of money, time, or other valuable resources in a physical or human capital asset whose value in a particular transaction is higher than its value in alternative transactions. The more transaction specific the investment, the greater the difference between the value of the investment in the current transaction and the value of the investment in other transactions.

Klein, Crawford, and Alchian provide a series of excellent examples of transaction specific investments along with descriptions of what can happen to those who make such investments. Suppose two companies, one an oil refining company and one an oil pipeline company, agree to work together to build an oil refinery (owned by the refining company) supplied by a dedicated pipeline (owned by the pipeline company). Also, suppose that the refinery is to be built on the coast, thereby providing access for ocean-going oil tankers to supply the refinery. Now, has the oil refining company made an investment specific to the oil pipeline firm? The answer is no, because alternative oil sources (that is, ocean-going tankers) can keep the refinery supplied, probably at only a slightly higher price than the pipeline. Has the oil pipeline company made an investment specific to the refining company? The answer is yes, for if the refinery were to refuse to buy oil pumped through the pipeline, the value of the pipeline would tumble to almost nothing. Besides its value as scrap metal, the pipeline's only use would be as the world's largest enclosed water slide. Due to the asymmetric transaction specific investment, after the pipeline is in place, the oil refining company can make numerous demands on the pipeline company, including demanding a lower price, and can always threaten not to buy pipeline oil if its demands are not met. Klein, Crawford, and Alchian call this type of behavior ''opportunistic recontracting.'' Even if these firms have what appears to be an iron clad contractual agreement, the refining company could still make thousands of subtle demands that effectively reduce the price of its oil supply from the pipeline and that are difficult to detect and prove in court.

Whenever asymmetry transaction specific investments exist, dependence exists. Whenever dependence exists, there exists the

potential for opportunistic exploitation of those who are dependent. *In the SBE eg.*
the joint venture
Given no remedies, economic actors would not make transaction *Investor fin.*
specific investments. For in so doing, they would risk exploitation. *is not pursued.*
In the oil refining example, the pipeline would not be built.

  ✓   Like Akerlof, Klein, Crawford, and Alchian are able to suggest some remedies to the problems associated with dependence.
The first remedy they cite relies on what they call implicit contracts.
An implicit contract is usually an unwritten agreement between
partners to an exchange that is enforced, not through litigation
and the courts, but through the market for reputations—what behavioral scientists think of as normative control or socioeconomic
sanctions. For example, if one party to an exchange takes advantage of another party, the implicit contract may dictate that all
future business will be withdrawn from the offending party. Other
market forces that can come into play to enforce contracts include
the soiling of a firm's reputation and a diminishing of the brand
name value of its products. When a firm opportunistically exploits
its exchange partners, it risks these responses, all of which, in the
long run, can hurt the financial viability of the offending firm.

  ✓   The second remedy cited by Klein, Crawford, and Alchian
is vertical integration, a concept familiar to organization theorists.
When asymmetric transaction specific investments are high, then
vertical integration will be the only viable resolution to the problems of opportunism. This is very much the same prediction developed by resource dependence theorists in organization theory
(Thompson, 1967; Pfeffer and Salancik, 1978).

  ⚡★   Thus, both for Akerlof and for Klein, Crawford, and Alchian,
formal organization is one important mechanism through which
exchange problems that develop in markets with asymmetric information can be resolved. Implicitly, these authors are suggesting *Alamo*
that markets and firms are alternative ways of organizing economic *Contracting*
exchanges and that each of these mechanisms will emerge, depending on the objective properties of the exchange in question. In later
chapters, these arguments will be developed by other authors as
an explanation of the existence of hierarchical modes of exchange.

      The two readings in this chapter have other attributes in
common as well. In particular, both these papers continue to rely

on several assumptions taken from traditional microeconomics. Only one or two assumptions of the perfect competition model are modified, while the bulk of this theory remains intact. The tenor of these modifications is closer to theoretical "sensitivity analysis" than revolutionary theorizing. But the results of these modifications are revolutionary: bad products drive out good, the existence of markets is jeopardized, firms vertically integrate, and variables like reputation and brand names become important. Minor modifications that lead to revolutionary conclusions are characteristic of much of the work in organizational economics. Authors make what appear to be relatively minor alterations in the traditional theory, only to generate significantly different and sometimes surprising conclusions.

Implications for Organization Theory

Within the power framework that has dominated organization theory for at least the last two decades, the causes and consequences of resource dependence relations between economic actors have received a great deal of attention (Pfeffer and Salancik, 1978). Perhaps the most general conclusion of this research is that firms facing resource dependence must engage in some form of organizational elaboration in order to reduce that dependence (Thompson, 1967). Indeed, resource dependence has been presented as an important cause of vertical integration.

Research in organizational economics is not inconsistent with this conclusion. Indeed, as Klein, Crawford, and Alchian argue, vertical integration is one response to managing opportunistic recontracting that develops because of asymmetric transaction specific investments.

But vertical integration is not the only solution to dependence problems. The articles in this chapter propose at least two other classes of remedies: the use of market forces and the use of interpersonal relations. The market forces argument suggests that firms that do enjoy an advantage are not free to exploit that advantage however they like. If they do so, they are likely to gain a reputation that could foreclose opportunities for engaging in future business transactions. If a firm were to develop a reputation for exploiting partners in exchanges, consider how difficult it would be to obtain trading partners in the future.

Because firms are constrained in this manner, it may be possible to observe exchange relations characterized by high resource dependence that are very stable and efficient over time, in which relatively little exploitation of exchange partners takes place. This, of course, is inconsistent with most resource dependence arguments but is nevertheless consistent with organizational economic arguments. The stable relations between large firms in Japan and networks of dedicated suppliers seem to be consistent with these predictions (Ouchi, 1984), as is the reported relationship between Sears and its many suppliers, to cite another example.

The arguments of organizational economics also suggest that interpersonal relations can help resolve problems of opportunism associated with resource dependence. In the simplest case, this amounts to no more than recognizing that it is possible to buy a good used car from close friends or relatives, or that the development of close interpersonal relations can facilitate the exchange of goods and services between firms. Because of the potential impact of such relations, it again might be possible to observe highly asymmetrical exchanges that last over long periods.

Organization theorists have also recognized that interpersonal ties can help resolve conflicts in economic exchanges. But most often, there is an assumption that these relations are either themselves exploitative or conspiratorial in nature. Cooptation is a concept used to describe interpersonal relations that exploit one or more parties to an exchange, somehow neutralizing their ability to influence how the transaction will unfold (Selznick, [1949] 1966). Also, the enormous literature on overlapping boards of directors often presumes that these interpersonal ties somehow are inconsistent with the public interest (Pennings, 1980). While organizational economics admits the possibility that interpersonal ties can have these anticompetitive consequences, it also argues that these relations can sometimes have important implications for the economic efficiency with which economic exchanges are carried forward, and that this enhanced efficiency has positive social consequences.

The emphasis on interpersonal ties in resolving conflicts between exchange partners closely links organizational economics with work on the management of organizations. Indeed, relations among managers and workers within a firm are almost always characterized by high levels of specific investment in human capital, and thus represent an area in which the problems of resource and other dependencies can be very problematic (Becker, 1962). Management theorists have suggested that it is in precisely these circumstances that close interpersonal trust and teamwork are essential if firms are to be economically successful (Ouchi, 1981). In this sense, the existence of transaction specific investments becomes part of the explanation of management systems like Theory X and Theory Z (McGregor, 1960; Ouchi, 1981).

At the level of relations between firms, the significance of interpersonal ties in resolving exchange conflicts is similar in import to the work of the institutional school in organization theory (Zucker, 1977; Meyer and Rowan, 1977). While some of the literature of this school takes a conspiratorial view of the role of these interpersonal ties, it nevertheless admits the possibility that such relations are important in establishing the legitimacy of certain organizations in the absence of other mechanisms.

Finally, this work suggests that resource dependence, though perhaps one important source of exchange problems that can lead to vertical integration, is not the only source of such problems. Another source cited by Akerlof is asymmetric information. By asymmetric information, Akerlof does not mean information that one party to the exchange temporarily does not have. Rather, for Akerlof, this is information that a party to the exchange cannot obtain, expect at very high cost, until after the exchange in question is complete; in other words, until it is too late. In the chapters that follow, other authors will suggest still other sources of opportunism in economic exchanges, including the existence of cooperative teams in organizations (see Alchian and Demsetz reading, Chapter Two). In each case, the possible existence of opportunism creates problems for exchange partners that must be resolved through any of a large number of devices before a transaction can be initiated and completed.

The Market for "Lemons":
Quality Uncertainty and the Market Mechanism

George A. Akerlof

I. Introduction

This paper relates quality and uncertainty. The existence of goods of many grades poses interesting and important problems for the theory of markets. On the one hand, the interaction of quality differences and uncertainty may explain important institutions of the labor market. On the other hand, this paper presents a struggling attempt to give structure to the statement: "Business in underdeveloped countries is difficult"; in particular, a structure is given for determining the economic costs of dishonesty. Additional applications of the theory include comments on the structure of money markets, on the notion of "insurability," on the liquidity of durables, and on brand-name goods.

There are many markets in which buyers use some market statistic to judge the quality of prospective purchases. In this case there is incentive for sellers to market poor quality merchandise, since the returns for good quality accrue mainly to the entire group whose statistic is affected rather than to the individual seller. As a result there tends to be a reduction in the average quality of goods and also in the size of the market. It should also be perceived that in these markets social and private returns differ, and therefore, in some cases, governmental intervention may increase the welfare of all parties. Or private institutions may arise to take advantage of the potential increases in welfare which can accrue to all parties. By nature, however, these institutions are nonatomistic, and therefore concentrations of power—with ill consequences of their own—can develop.

The automobile market is used as a finger exercise to illustrate and develop these thoughts. It should be emphasized that this market

Note: The author would especially like to thank Thomas Rothenberg for invaluable comments and inspiration. In addition he is indebted to Roy Radner, Albert Fishlow, Bernard Saffran, William D. Nordhaus, Giorgio La Malfa, Charles C. Holt, John Letiche, and the referee for help and suggestions. He would also like to thank the Indian Statistical Institute and the Ford Foundation for financial support.

is chosen for its concreteness and ease in understanding rather than for its importance or realism.

II. The Model with Automobiles as an Example

The Automobile Market. The example of used cars captures the essence of the problem. From time to time one hears either mention of or surprise at the large price difference between new cars and those which have just left the showroom. The usual lunch table justification for this phenomenon is the pure joy of owning a "new" car. We offer a different explanation. Suppose (for the sake of clarity rather than reality) that there are just four kinds of cars. There are new cars and used cars. There are good cars and bad cars (which in America are known as "lemons"). A new car may be a good car or a lemon, and of course the same is true of used cars.

The individuals in this market buy a new automobile without knowing whether the car they buy will be good or a lemon. But they do know that with probability q it is a good car and with probability $(1 - q)$ it is a lemon; by assumption, q is the proportion of good cars produced and $(1 - q)$ is the proportion of lemons.

After owning a specific car, however, for a length of time, the car owner can form a good idea of the quality of this machine; i.e., the owner assigns a new probability to the event that his car is a lemon. This estimate is more accurate than the original estimate. An asymmetry in available information has developed: for the sellers now have more knowledge about the quality of a car than the buyers. But good cars and bad cars must still sell at the same price—since it is impossible for a buyer to tell the difference between a good car and a bad car. It is apparent that a used car cannot have the same valuation as a new car—if it did have the same valuation, it would clearly be advantageous to trade a lemon at the price of a new car, and buy another new car, at a higher probability q of being good and a lower probability of being bad. Thus the owner of a good machine must be locked in. Not only is it true that he cannot receive the true value of his car, but he cannot even obtain the expected value of a new car.

Gresham's law has made a modified reappearance. For most cars traded will be the "lemons," and good cars may not be traded at all. The "bad" cars tend to drive out the good (in much the same way that bad money drives out the good). But the analogy with Gresham's law is not quite complete: bad cars drive out the good because they sell at the same price as good cars; similarly, bad money drives out good because the exchange rate is even. But the bad cars sell at the same price as good cars since it is impossible for a buyer to tell the difference between a good and a bad car; only the seller knows. In Gresham's law, however, presumably both buyer and seller can tell the difference between good and bad money. So the analogy is instructive, but not complete.

B. *Asymmetrical Information.* It has been seen that the good cars may be driven out of the market by the lemons. But in a more continuous case with different grades of goods, even worse pathologies can exist. For it is quite possible to have the bad driving out the not-so-bad driving out the medium driving out the not-so-good driving out the good in such a sequence of events that no market exists at all.

One can assume that the demand for used automobiles depends most strongly upon two variables—the price of the automobile p and the average quality of used cars traded, μ, or $Q^d = D(p, \mu)$. Both the supply of used cars and also the average quality μ will depend upon the price, or $\mu = \mu(p)$ and $S = S(p)$. And in equilibrium the supply must equal the demand for the given average quality, or $S(p) = D(p, \mu(p))$. As the price falls, normally the quality will also fall. And it is quite possible that no goods will be traded at any price level.

Such an example can be derived from utility theory. Assume that there are just two groups of traders: groups one and two. Give group one a utility function

$$U_1 = M + \sum_{i=1}^{n} x_i$$

where M is the consumption of goods other than automobiles, x_i is the quality of the ith automobile, and n is the number of automobiles.

Similarly, let

$$U_2 = M + \sum_{i=1}^{n} 3/2x_i$$

where M, x_i, and n are defined as before.

Three comments should be made about these utility functions: (1) without linear utility (say with logarithmic utility) one gets needlessly mired in algebraic complication. (2) The use of linear utility allows a focus on the effects of asymmetry of information; with a concave utility function we would have to deal jointly with the usual risk-variance effects of uncertainty and the special effects we wish to discuss here. (3) U_1 and U_2 have the odd characteristic that the addition of a second car, or indeed a kth car, adds the same amount of utility as the first.

Again realism is sacrificed to avoid a diversion from the proper focus.

To continue, it is assumed (1) that both type one traders and type two traders are von Neumann-Morgenstern (1953) maximizers of expected utility; (2) that group one has N cars with uniformly distributed quality x, $0 \le x \le p$, and group two has no cars; (3) that the price of "other goods" M is unity.

Denote the income (including that derived from the sale of automobiles) of all type one traders as Y_1 and the income of all type two traders as Y_2. The demand for used cars will be the sum of the demands by both groups. When one ignores indivisibilities, the demand for automobiles by type one traders will be

$$D_1 = Y_1/p \qquad\qquad\qquad \mu/p > 1$$
$$D_1 = 0 \qquad\qquad\qquad\quad \mu/p < 1.$$

And the supply of cars offered by type one traders is

(1) $S_1 = pN/2 \qquad\qquad\qquad p \le 2$

with average quality

(2) $\mu = p/2$.

(To derive (1) and (2), the uniform distribution of automobile quality is used.)

Similarly the demand of type two traders is

$$D_2 = Y_2/p \qquad\qquad\qquad 3\mu/2 > p$$
$$D_2 = 0 \qquad\qquad\qquad\quad 3\mu/2 < p$$

and

$$S_2 = 0.$$

Thus total demand $D(p, \mu)$ is

$$D(p, \mu) = (Y_2 + Y_1)/p \qquad\qquad \text{if } p < \mu$$
$$D(p, \mu) = Y_2/p \qquad\qquad\qquad\; \text{if } \mu < p < 3\mu/2$$
$$D(p, \mu) = 0 \qquad\qquad\qquad\quad\;\; \text{if } p > 3\mu/2.$$

However, with price p, average quality is $p/2$ and therefore at no price will any trade take place at all: in spite of the fact that *at any given price* between 0 and 3 there are traders of type one who are willing to sell their automobiles at a price which traders of type two are willing to pay.

C. Symmetric Information. The foregoing is contrasted with the case of symmetric information. Suppose that the quality of all cars is uniformly distributed, $0 \le x \le 2$. Then the demand curves and supply curves can be written as follows:

Supply

$$S(p) = N \qquad\qquad p > 1$$
$$S(p) = 0 \qquad\qquad p < 1.$$

And the demand curves are

$$D(p) = (Y_2 + Y_1)/p \qquad\qquad p < 1$$
$$D(p) = (Y_2/p) \qquad\qquad 1 < p < 3/2$$
$$D(p) = 0 \qquad\qquad p > 3/2.$$

In equilibrium

(3) $p = 1$ if $Y_2 < N$

(4) $p = Y_2/N$ if $2Y_2/3 < N < Y_2$

(5) $p = 3/2$ if $N < 2Y_2/3$.

If $N < Y_2$ there is a gain in utility over the case of asymmetrical information of $N/2$. (If $N > Y_2$, in which case the income of type two traders
is insufficient to buy all N automobiles, there is a gain in utility of $Y_2/2$
units.)

Finally, it should be mentioned that in this example, if traders
of groups one and two have the same probabilistic estimates about the
quality of individual automobiles—though these estimates may vary from
automobile to automobile—(3), (4), and (5) will still describe equilibrium
with one slight change: p will then represent the expected price of one
quality unit.

III. Examples and Applications

A. Insurance. It is a well-known fact that people over 65 have great
difficulty in buying medical insurance. The natural question arises: why
doesn't the price rise to match the risk?

Our answer is that as the price level rises the people who insure
themselves will be those who are increasingly certain that they will need
the insurance; for error in medical check-ups, doctors' sympathy with
older patients, and so on make it much easier for the applicant to assess
the risks involved than the insurance company. The result is that the
average medical condition of insurance applicants deteriorates as the price
level rises—with the result that no insurance sales may take place at any
price.[1] This is strictly analogous to our automobiles case, where the
average quality of used cars supplied fell with a corresponding fall in
the price level. This agrees with the explanation in insurance textbooks:

> Generally speaking policies are not available at ages
> materially greater than sixty-five. . . . The term premiums
> are too high for any but the most pessimistic (which is to
> say the least healthy) insureds to find attractive. Thus there
> is a severe problem of adverse selection at these ages
> [Dickerson, 1959, p. 333].

The statistics do not contradict this conclusion. While demands for health insurance rise with age, a 1956 national sample survey of 2,809 families with 8,898 persons shows that hospital insurance coverage drops from 63 per cent of those aged 45 to 54, to 31 per cent for those over 65. And surprisingly, this survey also finds average medical expenses for males aged 55 to 64 of $88, while males over 65 pay an average of $77 (Anderson and Feldman, 1956). While noninsured expenditure rises from $66 to $80 in these age groups, insured expenditure declines from $105 to $70. The conclusion is tempting that insurance companies are particularly wary of giving medical insurance to older people.

The principle of "adverse selection" is potentially present in all lines of insurance. The following statement appears in an insurance text-book written at the Wharton School:

> There is potential adverse selection in the fact that
> healthy term insurance policy holders may decide to ter-
> minate their coverage when they become older and prem-
> iums mount. This action could leave an insurer with an
> undue proportion of below average risks and claims might
> be higher than anticipated. Adverse selection "appears (or
> at least is possible) whenever the individual or group in-
> sured has freedom to buy or not to buy, to choose the
> amount or plan of insurance, and to persist or to discon-
> tinue as a policy holder" [Denenberg, H. S., and others,
> 1964, p. 446].

Group insurance, which is the most common form of medical insurance in the United States, picks out the healthy, for generally adequate health is a precondition for employment. At the same time this means that medical insurance is least available to those who need it most, for the insurance companies do their own "adverse selection."

This adds one major argument in favor of medicare.[2] On a cost benefit basis medicare may pay off: for it is quite possible that every individual in the market would be willing to pay the expected cost of his medicare and buy insurance, yet no insurance company can afford to sell him a policy—for at any price it will attract too many "lemons." The welfare economics of medicare, in this view, is *exactly* analogous to the usual classroom argument for public expenditure on roads.

B. The Employment of Minorities. The Lemons Principle also casts light on the employment of minorities. Employers may refuse to hire members of minority groups for certain types of jobs. This decision may not reflect irrationality or prejudice—but profit maximization. For race may serve as a good *statistic* for the applicant's social background, quality of schooling, and general job capabilities.

Good quality schooling could serve as a substitute for this statistic; by grading students the schooling system can give a better indicator of quality than other more superficial characteristics. As T. W. Schultz (1964, p. 42) writes, "The educational establishment *discovers* and cultivates potential talent. The capabilities of children and mature students can never be known until *found* and cultivated." (Italics added.) An untrained worker may have valuable natural talents, but these talents must be certified by "the educational establishment" before a company can afford to use them. The certifying establishment, however, must be credible; the unreliability of slum schools decreases the economic possibilities of their students.

This lack may be particularly disadvantageous to members of already disadvantaged minority groups. For an employer may make a rational decision not to hire any members of these groups in responsible positions—because it is difficult to distinguish those with good job qualifications from those with bad qualifications. This type of decision is clearly what George Stigler had in mind when he wrote, "in a regime of ignorance Enrico Fermi would have been a gardener, Von Neumann a checkout clerk at a drugstore" (Stigler, 1962, p. 104).

As a result, however, the rewards for work in slum schools tend to accrue to the group as a whole—in raising its average quality—rather than to the individual. Only insofar as information in addition to race is used is there any incentive for training.

An additional worry is that the Office of Economic Opportunity is going to use cost-benefit analysis to evaluate its programs. For many benefits may be external. The benefit from training minority groups may arise as much from raising the average quality of the group as from raising the quality of the individual trainee; and, likewise, the returns may be distributed over the whole group rather than to the individual.

C. The Costs of Dishonesty. The Lemons model can be used to make some comments on the costs of dishonesty. Consider a market in which goods are sold honestly or dishonestly; quality may be represented, or it may be misrepresented. The purchaser's problem, of course, is to identify quality. The presence of people in the market who are willing to offer inferior goods tends to drive the market out of existence—as in the case of our automobile "lemons." It is this possibility that represents the major costs of dishonesty—for dishonest dealings tend to drive honest dealings out of the market. There may be potential buyers of good quality products and there may be potential sellers of such products in the appropriate price range; however, the presence of people who wish to pawn bad wares as good wares tends to drive out the legitimate business. The cost of dishonesty, therefore, lies not only in the amount by which the purchaser is cheated; the cost also must include the loss incurred from driving legitimate business out of existence.

Dishonesty in business is a serious problem in underdeveloped countries. Our model gives a possible structure to this statement and delineates the nature of the "external" economies involved. In particular, in the model economy described, dishonesty, or the misrepresentation of the quality of automobiles, costs 1/2 unit of utility per automobile; furthermore, it reduces the size of the used car market from N to 0. We can, consequently, directly evaluate the costs of dishonesty—at least in theory.

There is considerable evidence that quality variation is greater in underdeveloped than in developed areas. For instance, the need for quality control of exports and State Trading Corporations can be taken as one indicator. In India, for example, under the Export Quality Control and Inspection Act of 1963, "about 85 per cent of Indian exports are covered under one or the other type of quality control."[3] Indian housewives must carefully glean the rice of the local bazaar to sort out stones of the same color and shape which have been intentionally added to the rice. Any comparison of the heterogeneity of quality in the street market and the canned qualities of the American supermarket suggests that quality variation is a greater problem in the East than in the West.

In one traditional pattern of development the merchants of the pre-industrial generation turn into the first entrepreneurs of the next. The best-documented case is Japan (Levy, 1955), but this also may have been the pattern for Britain and America (Kindleberger, 1958, p. 86). In *our* picture the important skill of the merchant is identifying the quality of merchandise; those who can identify used cars in our example and can guarantee the quality may profit by as much as the difference between type two traders' buying price and type one traders' selling price. These people are the merchants. In production these skills are equally necessary—both to be able to identify the quality of inputs and to certify the quality of outputs. And this is one (added) reason why the merchants may logically become the first entrepreneurs.

The problem, of course, is that entrepreneurship may be a scarce resource; no development text leaves entrepreneurship unemphasized. Some treat it as central (Lewis, 1955, p. 196). Given, then, that entrepreneurship is scarce, there are two ways in which product variations impede development. First, the pay-off to trade is great for would-be entrepreneurs, and hence they are diverted from production; second, the amount of entrepreneurial time per unit output is greater, [and thus] the greater are the quality variations.

D. *Credit Markets in Underdeveloped Countries.* (1) Credit markets in underdeveloped countries often strongly reflect the operation of the Lemons Principle. In India a major fraction of industrial enterprise is controlled by managing agencies (according to a recent survey, these "managing agencies" controlled 65.7 per cent of the net worth of public limited companies and 66 per cent of total assets).[4] Here is a historian's account of the function and genesis of the "managing agency system":

> The management of the South Asian commercial scene remained the function of merchant houses, and a type of organization peculiar to South Asia known as the Managing Agency. When a new venture was promoted (such as a manufacturing plant, a plantation, or a trading venture), the promoters would approach an established managing agency. The promoters might be Indian or British, and they might have technical or financial resources or merely a concession. In any case they would turn to the agency because of its reputation, which would encourage confidence in the venture and stimulate investment [Tinker, 1966, p. 134].

In turn, a second major feature of the Indian industrial scene has been the dominance of these managing agencies by caste (or, more accurately, communal) groups. Thus firms can usually be classified according to communal origin.[5] In this environment, in which outside investors are likely to be bilked of their holdings, either (1) firms establish a reputation for "honest" dealing, which confers upon them a monopoly rent insofar as their services are limited in supply, or (2) the sources of finance are limited to local communal groups which can use communal—and possibly familial—ties to encourage honest dealing *within* the community. It is, in Indian economic history, extraordinarily difficult to discern whether the savings of rich landlords failed to be invested in the industrial sector (1) because of a fear to invest in ventures controlled by other communities, (2) because of inflated propensities to consume, or (3) because of low rates of return.[6] At the very least, however, it is clear that the British-owned managing agencies tended to have an equity holding whose communal origin was more heterogeneous than the Indian-controlled agency houses, and would usually include both Indian and British investors.

(2) A second example of the workings of the Lemons Principle concerns the extortionate rates which the local moneylender charges his clients. In India these high rates of interest have been the leading factor in landlessness; the so-called "Cooperative Movement" was meant to counteract this growing landlessness by setting up banks to compete with the local moneylenders.[7] While the large banks in the central cities have prime interest rates of 6, 8, and 10 per cent, the local moneylender charges 15, 25, and even 50 per cent. The answer to this seeming paradox is that credit is granted only where the granter has (1) easy means of enforcing his contract or (2) personal knowledge of the character of the borrower. The middleman who tries to arbitrage between the rates of the moneylender and the central bank is apt to attract all the "lemons" and thereby make a loss.

This interpretation can be seen in Sir Malcolm Darling's interpretation of the village moneylender's power:

> It is only fair to remember that in the Indian village the money-lender is often the one thrifty person amongst a generally thriftless people; and that his methods of business, though demoralizing under modern conditions, suit the happy-go-lucky ways of the peasant. He is always accessible, even at night; dispenses with troublesome formalities, asks no inconvenient questions, advances promptly, and if interest is paid, does not press for repayment of principal. He keeps in close personal touch with his clients, and in many villages shares their occasions of weal or woe. *With his intimate knowledge of those around him he is able, without serious risk, to finance those who would otherwise get no loan at all* [Darling, 1932, p. 204]. [Italics added.]

Or look at Barbara Ward's account:

> A small shopkeeper in a Hong Kong fishing village told me: "I give credit to anyone who anchors regularly in our bay; but if it is someone I don't know well, then I think twice about it unless I can find out all about him" [Ward, 1967, p. 142; see also Skinner, 1967, and Mintz, 1967].

Or, a profitable sideline of cotton ginning in Iran is the loaning of money for the next season, since the ginning companies often have a line of credit from Teheran banks at the market rate of interest. But in the first years of operation large losses are expected from unpaid debts—due to poor knowledge of the local scene.[8]

IV. Counteracting Institutions

Numerous institutions arise to counteract the effects of quality uncertainty. One obvious institution is guarantees. Most consumer durables carry guarantees to ensure the buyer of some normal expected quality. One natural result of our model is that the risk is borne by the seller rather than by the buyer.

A second example of an institution which counteracts the effects of quality uncertainty is the brand-name good. Brand names not only indicate quality but also give the consumer a means of retaliation if the quality does not meet expectations. For the consumer will then curtail future purchases. Often too, new products are associated with old brand names. This ensures the prospective consumer of the quality of the product.

Chains—such as hotel chains or restaurant chains—are similar to brand names. One observation consistent with our approach is the chain restaurant. These restaurants, at least in the United States, most often appear on interurban highways. The customers are seldom local. The reason is that these well-known chains offer a better hamburger than the *average* local restaurant; at the same time, the local customer, who knows his area, can usually choose a place he prefers.

Licensing practices also reduce quality uncertainty. For instance, there is the licensing of doctors, lawyers, and barbers. Most skilled labor carries some certification indicating the attainment of certain levels of proficiency. The high school diploma, the baccalaureate degree, the Ph.D., even the Nobel Prize, to some degree, serve this function of certification. And education and labor markets themselves have their own "brand names."

V. Conclusion

We have been discussing economic models in which "trust" is important. Informal written guarantees are preconditions for trade and production. Where these guarantees are indefinite, business will suffer— as indicated by our generalized Gresham's law. This aspect of uncertainty has been explored by game theorists, as in the Prisoner's Dilemma, but usually it has not been incorporated in the more traditional Arrow-Debreu approach to uncertainty (Radner, 1967). But the difficulty of distinguishing good quality from bad is inherent in the business world; this may indeed explain many economic institutions and may in fact be one of the more important aspects of uncertainty.

Notes

1. Arrow's (1963) fine article does not make this point explicitly. He emphasizes "moral hazard" rather than "adverse selection." In its strict sense, the presence of "moral hazard" is equally disadvantageous for both governmental and private programs; in its broader sense, which includes "adverse selection," "moral hazard" gives a decided advantage to governmental insurance programs.

2. The following quote, again taken from an insurance textbook, shows how far the medical insurance market is from perfect competition:

   . . . insurance companies must screen their applicants. Naturally it is true that many people will voluntarily seek adequate insurance on their own initiative. But in such lines as accident and health insurance, companies are likely to give a second look to persons who voluntarily seek insurance without being approached by an agent (Angell, 1957, pp. 8–9).

3. *The Times of India,* Nov. 10, 1967, p. 1.

4. *Report of the Committee on the Distribution of Income and Levels of Living,* Part I, Government of India, Planning Commission, Feb. 1964, p. 44.

5. The existence of the following table (and also the small per cent of firms under mixed control) indicates the communalization of the control of firms.

| | *Distribution of Industrial Control by Community* | | |
| | *1911* | *1931* | *1951* |
		(number of firms)	
British	281	416	382
Parsis	15	25	19
Gujratis	3	11	17
Jews	5	9	3
Muslims	—	10	3
Bengalis	8	5	20
Marwaris	—	6	96
Mixed control	28	28	79
Total	[340]	510	619

   Source: Mehta (1955, p. 314). Also, for the cotton industry see Fukuzawa (1965).

6. For the mixed record of industrial profits, see Buchanan (1966).

7. The following table may prove instructive:

	Secured Loans (percent)	Commonest Rates for Unsecured Loans (percent)	Grain Loans (percent)
Punjab	6 to 12	12 to 24 (18¾ commonest)	25
United Provinces	9 to 12	24 to 37½	25 (50 in Oudh)
Bihar		18¾	50
Orissa	12 to 18¾	25	25
Bengal	8 to 12	9 to 18 for "respectable clients" 18¾ to 37½ (the latter common to agriculturalists)	
Central Provinces	6 to 12	15 for proprietors 24 for occupancy tenants 37½ for ryots with no right of transfer	25
Bombay	9 to 12	12 to 25 (18 commonest)	
Sind		36	
Madras	12	15 to 18 (in insecure tracts 24 not uncommon	20 to 50

Source: From the leading authority on this subject, Sir Malcolm Darling (1932, p. 190).

8. Personal conversation with mill manager, April 1968.

Vertical Integration, Appropriable Rents, and the Competitive Contracting Process

Benjamin Klein
Robert G. Crawford
Armen A. Alchian

More than forty years have passed since Coase's fundamental insight that transaction, coordination, and contracting costs must be con-

Note: We wish to acknowledge useful comments on previous drafts by Harold Demetz, Stephen Friedberg, Victor Goldberg, Levis Kochin, Keith Leffler, Lynne Schneider, Earl Thompson, and participants at a seminar at the Center for the Study of American Business at Washington University and at Law and Economics Workshops at UCLA and the University of Chicago. Financial assistance was provided by a grant of the Lily Endowment Inc. for the study of property rights and by the Foundation for Research in Economics and Education. The authors are solely responsible for the views expressed and for the remaining errors.

sidered explicitly in explaining the extent of vertical integration (Coase, 1937). Starting from the truism that profit-maximizing firms will undertake those activities that they find cheaper to administer internally than to purchase in the market, Coase forced economists to begin looking for previously neglected constraints on the trading process that might efficiently lead to an intrafirm rather than an interfirm transaction. This paper attempts to add to this literature by exploring one particular cost of using the market system—the possibility of postcontractual opportunistic behavior.

Opportunistic behavior has been identified and discussed in the modern analysis of the organization of economic activity. Williamson, for example, has referred to effects on the contracting process of "*ex post* small numbers opportunism," (Williamson, 1975) and Teece has elaborated:

> Even when all of the relevant contingencies can be specified in a contract, contracts are still open to serious risks since they are not always honored. The 1970's are replete with examples of the risks associated with relying on contracts . . . [O]pen displays of opportunism are not infrequent and very often litigation turns out to be costly and ineffectual (Teece, 1976, p. 31).

The particular circumstance we emphasize as likely to produce a serious threat of this type of reneging on contracts is the presence of appropriable specialized quasi rents. After a specific investment is made and such quasi rents are created, the possibility of opportunistic behavior is very real. Following Coase's framework, this problem can be solved in two possible ways: vertical integration or contracts. The crucial assumption underlying the analysis of this paper is that, as assets become more specific and more appropriable quasi rents are created (and therefore the possible gains from opportunistic behavior increases), the costs of contracting will generally increase more than the costs of vertical integration. Hence, *ceteris paribus*, we are more likely to observe vertical integration.

I. Appropriable Quasi Rents of Specialized Assets

Assume an asset is owned by one individual and rented to another individual. The quasi-rent value of the asset is the excess of its value over its salvage value, that is, its value in its next best *use* to another renter. The potentially appropriable specialized portion of the quasi rent is that portion, if any, in excess of its value to the second highest-valuing *user*. If this seems like a distinction without a difference, consider the following example.

Imagine a printing press owned and operated by party A. Publisher B buys printing services from party A by leasing his press at a contracted rate of $5,500 per day. The amortized fixed cost of the printing press is $4,000 per day and it has a current salvageable value if moved elsewhere of $1,000 (daily rental equivalent). Operating costs are $1,500 and are paid by the printing-press owner, who prints final printed pages for the publisher. Assume also that a second publisher C is willing to offer at most $3,500 for daily service. The current quasi rent on the installed machine is $3,000 (= $5,500 − $1,500 − $1,000), the revenue minus the operating costs minus salvageable value. However, the daily quasi rent from publisher B relative to use of the machine for publisher C is only $2,000 (= $5,500 − $3,500). At $5,500 revenue daily from publisher B the press owner would break even on his investment. If the publisher were then able to cut his offer for the press from $5,500 down to almost $3,500, he would still have the press service available to him. He would be appropriating $2,000 of the quasi rent from the press owner. The $2,000 difference between his prior agreed-to daily rental of $5,500 and the next best revenue available to the press once the machine is purchased and installed is less than the quasi rent and therefore is potentially appropriable. If no second party were available at the present site, the entire quasi rent would be subject to threat of appropriation by an unscrupulous or opportunistic publisher.

Our primary interest concerns the means whereby this risk can be reduced or avoided. In particular, vertical integration is examined as a means of economizing on the costs of avoiding risks of appropriation of quasi rents in specialized assets by opportunistic individuals. This advantage of joint ownership of such specialized assets, namely, economizing on contracting costs necessary to insure nonopportunistic behavior, must of course be weighed against the costs of administering a broader range of assets within the firm.[1]

An appropriable quasi rent is not a monopoly rent in the usual sense, that is, the increased value of an asset protected from market entry over the value it would have had in an open market. An appropriable quasi rent can occur with no market closure or restrictions placed on rival assets. Once installed, an asset may be so expensive to remove or so specialized to a particular user that if the price paid to the owner were somehow reduced the asset's services to that user would not be reduced.

Thus, even if there were free and open competition for entry to the market, the specialization of the installed asset to a particular user (or more accurately the high costs of making it available to others) creates a quasi rent, but no "monopoly" rent. At the other extreme, an asset may be costlessly transferable to some other user at no reduction in value, while at the same time, entry of similar assets is restricted. In this case, monopoly rent would exist, but no quasi rent.

We can use monopoly terminology to refer to the phenomenon we are discussing as long as we recognize that we are not referring to the usual monopoly created by government restrictions on entry or referring to a single supplier or even highly concentrated supply. One of the fundamental premises of this paper is that monopoly power, better labeled "market power," is pervasive. Because of transaction and mobility costs, "market power" will exist in many situations not commonly called monopolies. There may be many potential suppliers of a particular asset to a particular user but once the investment in the asset is made, the asset may be so specialized to a particular user that monopoly or monopsony market power, or both, is created.

A related motive for vertical integration that should not be confused with our main interest is the optimal output and pricing between two successive monopolists or bilateral monopolists (in the sense of marginal revenue less than price). A distortion arises because each sees a distorted marginal revenue or marginal cost.[2] While it is true that this successive monopoly distortion can be avoided by vertical integration, the results of the integration could, for that purpose alone, be achieved by a long-term or a more detailed contract based on the true marginal revenue and marginal costs. Integrated ownership will sometimes be utilized to economize on such precontractual bargaining costs. However, we investigate a different reason for joint ownership of vertically related assets—the avoidance of postcontractual opportunistic behavior when specialized assets and appropriable quasi rents are present. One must clearly distinguish the transaction and information costs of reaching an agreement (discovering and heeding true costs and revenues and agreeing upon the division of profits) and the enforcement costs involved in assuring compliance with an agreement, especially one in which specialized assets are involved. It is this latter situation which we here explore as a motivation for intrafirm rather than interfirm transactions.

We maintain that if an asset has a substantial portion of quasi rent which is strongly dependent upon some other particular asset, both assets will tend to be owned by one party. For example, reconsider our printing press example. Knowing that the press would exist and be operated even if its owner got as little as $1,500, publisher B could seek excuses to renege on his initial contract to get the weekly rental down from $5,500 to close to $3,500 (the potential offer from publisher C, the next highest-valuing user at its present site). If publisher B could effectively announce he was not going to pay more than, say, $4,000 per week, the press owner would seem to be stuck. This unanticipated action would be opportunistic behavior (which by definition refers to unanticipated nonfulfillment of the contract) if the press owner had installed the press at a competitive rental price of $5,500 anticipating (possibly naively) good faith by the publisher. The publisher, for example, might plead that his newspaper business is depressed and he will be unable to continue unless rental terms are revised.

Alternatively, and maybe more realistically, because the press owner may have bargaining power due to the large losses that he can easily impose on the publisher (if he has no other source of press service quickly available), the press owner might suddenly seek to get a higher rental price than $5,500 to capture some newly perceived increase in the publisher's profits. He could do this by alleging breakdowns or unusually high maintenance costs. This type of opportunistic behavior is difficult to prove and therefore litigate.

As we shall see, the costs of contractually specifying all important elements of quality varies considerably by type of asset. For some assets it may be essentially impossible to effectively specify all elements of quality and therefore vertical integration is more likely. But even for those assets used in situations where all relevant quality dimensions can be unambiguously specified in a contract, the threat of production delay during litigation may be an effective bargaining device. A contract therefore may be clearly enforceable but still subject to postcontractual opportunistic behavior. For example, the threat by the press owner to break its contract by pulling out its press is credible even though illegal and possibly subject to injunctive action. This is because such an action, even in the very short run, can impose substantial costs on the newspaper publisher.[3]

This more subtle form of opportunistic behavior is likely to result in a loss of efficiency and not just a wealth-distribution effect. For example, the publisher may decide, given this possibility, to hold or seek standby facilities otherwise not worthwhile. Even if transactors are risk neutral, the presence of possible opportunistic behavior will entail costs as real resources are devoted to the attempt to improve posttransaction bargaining positions in the event such opportunism occurs. In particular, less specific investments will be made to avoid being "locked in."[4] In addition, the increased uncertainty of quality and quantity leads to larger optimum inventories and other increased real costs of production.

This attention to appropriable specialized quasi rents is not novel. In addition to Williamson's (1971, 1975) pathbreaking work in the area, Goldberg's (1976b) perceptive analysis of what he calls the "hold up" problem in the context of government regulation is what we are discussing in a somewhat different context. Goldberg indicates how some government regulation can usefully be considered a means of avoiding or reducing the threat of loss of quasi rent. (Goldberg treats this as the problem of providing protection for the "right to be served.") He also recognizes that this force underlies a host of other contractual and institutional arrangements such as stockpiling, insurance contracts, and vertical integration. Our analysis will similarly suggest a rationale for the existence of particular institutions and the form of governmental intervention or contractual provisions as alternatives to vertical integration in a wide variety of cases.

II. Contractual Solutions

The primary alternative to vertical integration as a solution to the general problem of opportunistic behavior is some form of economically enforceable long-term contract. Clearly a short-term (for example, one transaction, nonrepeat sale) contract will not solve the problem. The relevant question then becomes when will vertical integration be observed as a solution and when will the use of the market-contracting process occur. Some economists and lawyers have defined this extremely difficult question away by calling a long-term contract a form of vertical integration (e.g., Kessler and Stern, 1959). Although there is clearly a continuum here, we will attempt not to blur the distinction between a long-term rental agreement and ownership. We assume the opportunistic behavior we are concentrating on can occur only with the former.[5]

For example, if opportunism occurs by the owner-lessor of an asset failing to maintain it properly for the user-lessee and hence unexpectedly increasing the effective rental price, legal remedies (proving contract violation) may be very costly. On the other hand, if the user owned the asset, then the employee who failed to maintain the asset properly could merely be fired.[6] If the employee could still effectively cheat the owner-user of the asset because of his specific ability to maintain the asset, then the problem is that vertical integration of a relevant asset, the employee's human capital, has not occurred. For the moment, however, we will concentrate solely on the question of long-term rental versus ownership of durable physical assets.[7]

Long-term contracts used as alternatives to vertical integration can be assumed to take two forms: (1) an explicitly stated contractual guarantee legally enforced by the government or some other outside institution, or (2) an implicit contractual guarantee enforced by the market mechanism of withdrawing future business if opportunistic behavior occurs. Explicit long-term contracts can, in principle, solve opportunistic problems, but, as suggested already, they are often very costly solutions. They entail costs of specifying possible contingencies and the policing and litigation costs of detecting violations and enforcing the contract in the courts.[8] Contractual provisions specifying compulsory arbitration or more directly imposing costs on the opportunistic party (for example, via bonding) are alternatives often employed to economize on litigation costs and to create flexibility without specifying every possible contingency and quality dimension of the transaction.

Since every contingency cannot be cheaply specified in a contract or even known and because legal redress is expensive, transactors will generally also rely on an implicit type of long-term contract that employs a market rather than legal enforcement mechanism, namely, the imposition of a capital loss by the withdrawal of expected future business. This goodwill market-enforcement mechanism undoubtedly is a major element of the contractual alternative to vertical integration. Macaulay provides evidence that relatively informal, legally unenforceable contractual practices predominate in business relations and that reliance on explicit legal sanctions is extremely rare (Macaulay, 1963a). Instead, business firms are said to generally rely on effective extralegal market sanctions, such as the depreciation of an opportunistic firm's general goodwill because of the anticipated loss of future business, as a means of preventing nonfulfillment of contracts.

One way in which this market mechanism of contract enforcement may operate is by offering to the potential cheater a future "premium," more precisely, a price sufficiently greater than average variable (that is, avoidable) cost to assure a quasi-rent stream that will exceed the potential gain from cheating.[9] The present-discounted value of this future premium stream must be greater than any increase in wealth that could be obtained by the potential cheater if he, in fact, cheated and were terminated. The offer of such a long-term relationship with the potential cheater will eliminate systematic opportunistic behavior.[10]

The larger the potential one-time "theft" by cheating (the longer and more costly to detect a violation, enforce the contract, switch suppliers, and so forth) and the shorter the expected continuing business relationship, the higher this premium will be in a nondeceiving equilibrium. This may therefore partially explain both the reliance by firms on long-term implicit contracts with particular suppliers and the existence of reciprocity agreements among firms. The premium can be paid in seemingly unrelated profitable reciprocal business. The threat of termination of this relationship mutually suppresses opportunistic behavior.[11]

The premium stream can be usefully thought of as insurance payments made by the firm to prevent cheating.[12] As long as both parties to the transaction make the same estimate of the potential short-run gain from cheating, the quantity of this assurance that will be demanded and supplied will be such that no opportunistic behavior will be expected to occur.[13] If postcontractual reneging is anticipated to occur, either the correct premium will be paid to optimally prevent it or, if the premium necessary to eliminate reneging is too costly, the particular transaction will not be made.

We are not implicitly assuming here that contracts are enforced costlessly and cannot be broken, but rather that given our information-cost assumptions, parties to a contract know exactly when and how much a contract will be broken. An unanticipated broken contract, that is, opportunistic behavior, is therefore not possible in this particular equilibrium. In the context of this model, expected wealth maximization will yield some opportunistic behavior only if we introduce a stochastic element. This will alter the informational equilibrium state such that the potential cheater's estimate of the short-run gain from opportunistic behavior may be at times greater than the other firm's estimate. Hence, less than an optimal premium will be paid and opportunistic behavior will occur.

The firms collecting the premium payments necessary to assure fulfillment of contractual agreements in a costly information world may appear to be earning equilibrium "profits" although they are in a competitive market. That is, there may be many, possibly identical, firms available to supply the services of nonopportunistic performance of contractual obligations yet the premium will not be competed away if transactors cannot costlessly guarantee contractual performance. The assurance services, by definition, will not be supplied unless the premium is paid and the mere payment of this premium produces the required services.

Any profits are competed away in equilibrium by competitive expenditures on fixed (sunk) assets, such as initial specific investments (for example, a sign) with low or zero salvage value if the firm cheats, necessary to enter and obtain this preferred position of collecting the premium stream.[14] These fixed (sunk) costs of supplying credibility of future performance are repaid or covered by future sales on which a premium is earned. In equilibrium, the premium stream is then merely a normal rate of return on the "reputation," or "brand-name" capital created by the firm by these initial expenditures. This brand-name capital, the value of which is highly specific to contract fulfillment by the firm, is analytically equivalent to a forfeitable collateral bond put up by the firm which is anticipated to face an opportunity to take advantage of appropriable quasi rents in specialized assets.

While these initial specific investments or collateral bonds are sometimes made as part of the normal (minimum-cost) production process and therefore at small additional cost, transaction costs and risk considerations do make them costly.[15] We can generally say that the larger the appropriable specialized quasi rents (and therefore the larger the potential short-run gain from opportunistic behavior) and the larger the premium payments necessary to prevent contractual reneging, the more costly this implicit contractual solution will be. We can also expect the explicit contract costs to be positively related to the level of appropriable quasi rents since it will pay to use more resources (including legal services) to specify precisely more contingencies when potential opportunities for lucrative contractual reneging exist.

Although implicit and explicit contracting and policing costs are positively related to the extent of appropriable specialized quasi rents, it is reasonable to assume, on the other hand, that any internal coordination or other ownership costs are not systematically related to the extent of the appropriable specialized quasi rent of the physical asset owned. Hence we can reasonably expect the following general empirical regularity to be true: the lower the appropriable specialized quasi rents, the more likely that transactors will rely on a contractual relationship rather than common ownership. And conversely, integration by common or joint ownership is more likely, the higher the appropriable specialized quasi rents of the assets involved.

III. Example of Appropriable Specialized Quasi Rent

This section presents examples of specialized quasi rents where the potential for their appropriation serves as an important determinant of economic organization. A series of varied illustrations, some quite obvious and others rather subtle, will make the analysis more transparent and provide suggestive evidence for the relevance of the protection of appropriable quasi rents as an incentive to vertically integrate. It also suggests the direction of more systematic empirical work that obviously is required to assess the significance of this factor relative to other factors in particular cases. Where this force towards integration (that is, the economizing on contracting costs necessary to assure nonopportunistic behavior in the presence of appropriable quasi rents) does not appear to dominate, important insights regarding the determinants of particular contracting costs and contract provisions are thereby provided.[16]

A. *Automobile Manufacturing.* An illustrative example is the ownership by automobile-producing companies of the giant presses used for stamping body parts. The design and engineering specifications of a new automobile, for example Mustang for Ford, create value in Ford auto production. The manufacture of dies for stamping parts in accordance with the above specifications gives a value to these dies specialized to Ford, which implies an appropriable quasi rent in those dies. Therefore, the die owner would not want to be separate from Ford. Since an independent die owner may likely have no comparable demanders other than Ford for its product and to elicit supply requires payment to cover only the small operating costs once the large sunk fixed cost of the specific investment in the dies is made, the incentive for Ford to opportunistically renegotiate a lower price at which it will accept body parts from the independent die owner may be large. Similarly, if there is a large cost to Ford from the production delay of obtaining an alternative supplier of the specific body parts, the independent die owner may be able to capture quasi rents by demanding a revised higher price for the parts. Since the opportunity to lose the specialized quasi rent of assets is a debilitating prospect, neither party would invest in such equipment. Joint ownership of designs and dies removes this incentive to attempt appropriation.[17]

In this context, it is interesting to study in some detail the vertical merger that occurred in 1926 of General Motors with Fisher Body. The original production process for automobiles consisted of individually constructed open, largely wooden, bodies. By 1919 the production process began to shift towards largely metal closed body construction for which specific stamping machines became important. Therefore in 1919 General Motors entered a ten-year contractual agreement with Fisher Body for the supply of closed auto bodies.[18] In order to encourage Fisher Body to make the required specific investment, this contract had an exclusive dealing clause whereby General Motors agreed to buy substantially all its closed bodies from Fisher. This exclusive dealing arrangement significantly reduced the possibility of General Motors acting opportunistically by demanding a lower price for the bodies after Fisher made the specific investment in production capacity. Since exclusive dealing contractual conditions are relatively cheap to effectively specify and enforce, General Motor's postcontractual threat to purchase bodies elsewhere was effectively eliminated.

But large opportunities were created by this exclusive dealing clause for Fisher to take advantage of General Motors, namely to demand a monopoly price for the bodies. Therefore, the contract attempted to fix the price which Fisher could charge for the bodies supplied to General Motors. However, contractually setting in advance a "reasonable" price in the face of possible future changes in demand and production conditions is somewhat more difficult to effectively accomplish than merely "fixing" required suppliers. The price was set on a cost plus 17.6 per cent basis (where cost was defined exclusive of interest on invested capital). In addition, the contract included provisions that the price charged General Motors could not be greater than that charged other automobile manufacturers by Fisher for similar bodies nor greater than the average market price of similar bodies produced by companies other than Fisher and also included provisions for compulsory arbitration in the event of any disputes regarding price.

Unfortunately, however, these complex contractual pricing provisions did not work out in practice. The demand conditions facing General Motors and Fisher Body changed dramatically over the next few years. There was a large increase in the demand for automobiles and a significant shift away from open bodies to the closed body styles supplied by Fisher.[19] Meanwhile General Motors was very unhappy with the price it was being charged by its now very important supplier, Fisher. General Motors believed the price was too high because of a substantial increase in body output per unit of capital employed. This was an understandable development given the absence of a capital cost pass-through in the original contract.[20] In addition, Fisher refused to locate their body plants adjacent to General Motors assembly plants, a move General Motors claimed was necessary for production efficiency (but which required a large very specific and hence possibly appropriable investment on the part of Fisher).[21] By 1924, General Motors had found the Fisher contractual relationship intolerable and began negotiations for purchase of the remaining stock in Fisher Body, culminating in a final merger agreement in 1926.[22]

B. Petroleum Industry. Appropriable quasi rents exist in specialized assets of oil refineries, pipelines, and oil fields. This leads to common ownership to remove the incentive for individuals to attempt to capture the rents of assets owned by someone else.

Suppose several oil wells are located along a separately owned pipeline that leads to a cluster of independently owned refineries with no alternative crude supply at comparable cost. Once all the assets are in place (the wells drilled and the pipeline and refineries constructed) the oil-producing properties and the refineries are specialized to the

pipeline. The portion of their value above the value to the best alternative
user is an appropriable specialized quasi rent. The extent of the appropriable quasi rent is limited, in part, by the costs of entry to a potential parallel
pipeline developer. Since pipelines between particular oil-producing properties and particular refineries are essentially natural monopolies, the
existing pipeline owner may have a significant degree of market power.

These specialized producing and refining assets are therefore
"hostage" to the pipeline owner. At the "gathering end" of the pipeline,
the monopsonist pipeline could and would purchase all its oil at the same
well-head price regardless of the distance of the well from the refinery.
This price could be as low as the marginal cost of getting oil out of the
ground (or its reservation value for future use, if higher) and might not
generate a return to the oil-well owner sufficient to recoup the initial
investment of exploration and drilling. At the delivery-to-refinery end
of the pipeline, the pipeline owner would be able to appropriate the
"specialized-to-the-pipeline quasi rents" of the refineries. The pipeline
owner could simply raise the price of crude oil at least to the price of
alternative sources of supply to each refinery that are specialized to the
pipeline. Given the prospects of such action, if the pipeline owner were
an independent monopsonist facing the oil explorers and a monopolist
to the refinery owners, everyone (explorers and refiners) would know
in advance their vulnerability to rent extraction. Therefore oil-field owners
and refinery owners would, through shared ownership in the pipeline,
remove the possibility of subsequent rent extraction.[23]

The problem would not be completely solved if just the oil field
or the refineries (but not both) were commonly owned with the pipeline,
since the local monopoly (or monopsony) would persist vis-à-vis the other.
Prospectively, one would expect the common ownership to extend to
all three stages. If several refineries (or oil fields) were to be served by
one pipeline, all the refinery (or oil field) owners would want to jointly
own the pipeline. A common practice is a jointly owned company which
"owns" the pipeline with the shares by producers and refiners in the
pipeline company corresponding roughly to the respective shares of oil
to be transported.[24]

Consider other inputs in the production process. The oil tanker,
for example, is specialized to crude oil transportation. But since it is essentially equivalued by many alternative users, the appropriable quasi rent
is near zero. So we would expect oil tankers not to be extensively owned
by refiners or producers. Similarly, the assets used for refinery construction are not specialized to any single refiner or refinery and they should
also not be commonly owned with the refinery.

Preliminary examination of the development of the American petroleum industry in the nineteenth century reveals numerous examples that appear consistent with the hypothesis that as technological change leads to assets involved in production, transportation, refining, and marketing becoming more specialized to other specific assets, joint ownership became efficient as a means of preventing opportunistic behavior.

For example, Rockefeller recognized the importance of the pending technological change implied by the substitution of highly specific long-distance pipelines for the somewhat more general capital of the railroads as the efficient mode of transporting oil and took advantage of it. First, before long-distance pipelines were clearly economical, Rockefeller used his dominant oil-refining position to obtain a price reduction on oil he shipped by rail and also rebates from the railroads on oil shipped by competitive oil producers. We conjecture that Rockefeller obtained these price reductions by threatening to build a pipeline parallel to the railroad. He was therefore able to extract the appropriable quasi rents of the railroads. This explains why the rebates were solely a function of oil shipped and not related to nonoil products such as agricultural goods. It also explains why the discount and rebate to Rockefeller were often of the same magnitude. The payment should be a function of total demand for transporting oil.

The obvious question is why some small oil producer or even a nonoil-producing firm did not similarly threaten the railroads with building a pipeline early (before it was cheaper than rail transport) and demand a payment as a function of total oil shipped. The answer, we believe, is that only a dominant oil producer would have credible bargaining power with the railroads in this situation because only a dominant producer would be able to make such a highly specific investment. If a small producer or nonoil-producing firm made such an investment, it could easily be appropriated by the oil-producing firms, especially with an alternative means of transportation available. It was therefore necessary for Rockefeller to gain a dominant oil-producing and refining position in order to make a credible threat to the railroads. Appropriating the quasi rents of the railroads by discounts and rebates not only effectively metered the demand for oil transportation but also made it easier for Rockefeller to gain a monopolistic position in the industry without being forced to buy out rivals at prices that would completely reflect future-discounted monopoly profits.[25]

C. Specific Human Capital. The previous analysis has dealt with examples of physical capital. When specific human capital is involved, the opportunism problem is often more complex and, because of laws prohibiting slavery, the solution is generally some form of explicit or implicit contract rather than vertical integration.

For example, consider the following concrete illustration from the agricultural industry. Suppose someone owns a peach orchard. The ripened peaches, ready for harvest, have a market value of about $400,000. So far costs of $300,000 have been paid and the remaining harvesting and shipping costs will be $50,000 ($5,000 transport and $45,000 labor), leaving $50,000 as the competitive return on the owner's capital. Assume the laborers become a union (one party to whom the crop is now specialized) and refuse to pick unless paid $390,000. That would leave $5,000 for transport and only $5,000 for the owner of the peach orchard, instead of the $350,000 necessary to cover incurred costs and the cost of capital. If the union had power to exclude other pickers, it could extract all the appropriable quasi rent of that year's crop specialized to that particular labor union's service. The union would be extracting not just the usual monopoly rents involved in raising wages, but also the short-run appropriable quasi rents of the farmer's specific assets represented by the ripened peaches. This gain to the union is a one-period return because obviously the farmer will not make any additional specific investments in the future if he knows it will be appropriated by the union.

To reduce this risk of appropriation, the farmer may have a large clan family (or neighbors of similar farms) do his picking. Because of diseconomies of scale, however, this "cooperative" solution is not generally the lowest-cost arrangement and some reliance on market contracting will be necessary. The individual farmer, for example, may want the labor union to put up a forfeitable bond to compensate him in the event the union under threat of strike asks for more wages at harvest time. Alternatively, but equivalently, the collateral put up by the union could be the value of the brand-name capital of the union, a value which will depreciate if its leaders engage in opportunistic behavior. The farmer would then make a continuing brand-name payment to the union (similar to the premium payment noted above) for this collateral.[26]

The market value of the union's reputation for reliability of contract observance is the present-discounted value of these brand-name payments which will be greater than any short-run opportunistic gain to the union leaders that could be obtained by threats at harvest time. These payments which increase the cost to the union of opportunistic behavior would be substantial for a perishable product with a large appropriable quasi rent. It is therefore obvious why producers of highly perishable crops are so antagonistic to unionization of field labor. They would be especially hostile to unions without established reputations regarding fulfillment of contract and with politically motivated (and possibly myopic) leaders.[27]

In addition to implicit (brand-name) contracts, opportunistic union behavior may be prevented by use of explicit contracts, often with some outside arbitration as an element of the contract-enforcement mechanism. Although it is difficult for an outsider to distinguish between opportunistic behavior and good-faith modifications of contract, impartial arbitration procedures may reduce the necessity of explicitly specifying possible contingencies and thereby reduce the rigidity of the explicit long-term contract.[28]

When the problem is reversed and quasi rents of firm-specific human capital of employees may be opportunistically appropriated by the firm, implicit and explicit long-term contracts are also used to prevent such behavior. Because of economies of scale in monitoring and enforcing such contracts, unions may arise as a contract cost-reducing institution for employees with investments in specific human capital.[29]

In addition to narrow contract-monitoring economies of scale, a union creates a continuing long-term employment relationship that eliminates the last-period (or transient employee) contract-enforcement problem and also creates bargaining power (a credible strike threat) to more cheaply punish a firm that violates the contract. Even when the specific human-capital investment is made by the firm, a union of employees may similarly reduce the contract-enforcement costs of preventing individual-worker opportunism. There are likely to be economies of scale in supply credibility of contract fulfillment, including the long-term continuing relationship aspect of a union. The existence of a union not only makes it more costly for a firm to cheat an individual worker in his last period but also makes it more costly for an individual worker in his last period to cheat the firm, because the union has the incentive (for example, withholding pension rights) to prevent such an externality on the continuing workers. Therefore unions are more likely to exist when the opportunistic cheating problem is greater, namely, when there is more specific human capital present.[30]

The first Becker analysis of the specific human-capital problem (Becker, 1964) ignored opportunistic bargaining difficulties and implicitly assumed arbitrary contracting costs in particular situations to determine a solution. Becker initially assumed that the firm would cheat the employee if the employee made the specific investment. He then argued that the only reason the firm would not make the entire specific investment is because the quit rate of employees, which is a negative function of wages, would then be greater than optimal. Becker did not consider the completely reciprocal nature of the possibilities for cheating. The opportunistic behavior we are emphasizing suggests the possibility of the employee threatening to quit after the firm makes the specific investment unless the wage rate is readjusted upward. Becker's solution of a sharing of the costs and benefits of the specific investment via an initial lump-sum payment by the employee and a later higher-than-market wage does not eliminate the bilateral opportunistic bargaining problem because the employer may later decrease the wage back to the competitive level (or the employee may demand a higher wage to appropriate the partial specific investment by the employer). If it is assumed that employers will not cheat or break contracts in this way, then the efficient solution would be to merely have the employee make the entire specific investment (and therefore have the optimal quit rate) because the employer can costlessly "guarantee" (by assumption) a higher wage reflecting the increased productivity of the firm. But, more generally, to obtain an equilibrium solution to the problem, the costs of creating credibility of contract fulfillment and the costs of enforcing contracts must be explicitly considered.

One of the costs of using an explicit contract which relies on governmental or other outside arbitration for enforcement—rather than on an implicit contract which relies on depreciation of the value of a firm's brand-name (that is, the loss of future premium payments)—is the likely increase in rigidity. For example, the difficulty of specifying all contingencies in labor contracts and of adjusting to unanticipated conditions is likely to lead to wage rigidity. Because contractual changes tend to create suspicion regarding the purpose of the contract alteration and, in particular, raise the question of whether a firm is using the changed conditions as an opportunity to seize some of the specific quasi rents, long-term labor contracts may consist of rigid wages and layoff provisions. If in the face of declining demand, a firm must keep wages fixed and lay off workers rather than merely reduce wages, the incentive for it to opportunistically claim a false reduction in demand is substantially reduced.[31]

The fear of opportunistic behavior leads to price (and often also output) rigidity in all kinds of long-term explicit contracts where specific capital is present. This, in turn, leads to the creation of institutions to encourage increased flexibility in the face of changing market conditions. For example, the prime-rate convention, an announced benchmark in terms of which interest rates of corporate bank loans are stated, may be partially rationalized as a cheap means by which the bank can convey information to borrowers that the bank is not opportunistically raising interest fees to a particular customer. A corporate client who has made a specific investment in the supply of information to the bank regarding its credit worthiness (including its financial record of transactions with the bank) creates some appropriable quasi rents. However, when the price of the loan is stated as, say, prime plus one per cent, unless the bank decides to cheat all customers simultaneously and thereby limit new business, an individual customer can clearly distinguish between general market movements in interest rates and any changes the bank decides to make in the particular customer's credit rating. "Price protection" clauses in contracts, where a price decrease to any customer is guaranteed to be given to all customers, may be explained on similar grounds.

These information-cost-reducing institutions, including the use of impartial arbitrators, are highly imperfect. Therefore contracts involving specific assets, even where a price is not explicitly fixed long term, will consequently involve some price rigidity. The macroeconomic implications of this observation (for example, the employment effects of aggregate nominal demand shocks) are obvious.[32] But the interaction of macroeconomic considerations and industrial organization may not be that obvious. In particular, an increase in the variance of price-level movements, which increases the expected costs to both parties of price rigidity and thereby increases the acceptable degree of price flexibility, also makes it easier for a firm to cheat by opportunistically raising its price. Increased price uncertainty is therefore likely to lead to increased vertical integration.

Where more trust is present and implicit rather than explicit contracts are used, contract prices including wages are likely to be more flexible. If the variance of the price level increases—which makes it more difficult to detect opportunistic behavior and therefore the short-run gains from such cheating—the equilibrium implicit contract will imply a larger premium stream. The interesting question is what are the economic determinants of the implicit relative to explicit contracting costs which will in turn determine the degree of price flexibility.

One determinant of implicit contracting costs is the anticipated growth of demand for the firm's product. The more rapidly demand is expected to grow, the more likely a firm will rely on an implicit contract with its customers. Creating trust is cheaper for firms facing rapid demand growth compared to firms with stable or declining demand because the loss of future business by customer termination if the firm is found to be cheating implies a relatively larger cost. Therefore a smaller current premium payment is necessary to assure nonopportunistic behavior. Hence the higher the anticipated growth in demand for a firm, the lower the contracting cost of using implicit relative to explicit contracts and the more flexible prices and other contract terms set by the firm can be expected to be.[33]

The cost to a growing firm of cheating on laborers, for example, would be higher in terms of the future increased wages (of increased employment) it would have to pay if it cheated. The penalty for not relying on the firm's brand name is then more effective. This may explain why firms such as International Business Machines appear to have highly flexible labor compensation arrangements that are, in fact, quite similar to Japanese wage payments which consist of large, highly variable, biannual bonuses. Our analysis suggests that it is not because of different cultural values that Japanese labor relations rely on much trust, but because the high growth rate of future demand makes it relatively cheap for firms to behave in this way.[34]

D. Leasing Inputs and Ownership of the Firm. Examination of leasing companies should reveal that leases are less common (or too expensive) for assets with specialized quasi rents that could be appropriated by the lessee or lessor. Leasing does not occur in the obvious cases of elevators or the glass of windows in an office building where postinvestment bilaterally appropriable quasi rents are enormous, while the furniture in the building is often rented. In banks, the safe is owned by the bank, but computers (though not the memory discs) are sometimes rented.[35] Though this may seem like resorting to trivialities, the fact that such leasing arrangements are taken for granted merely corroborates the prior analysis.

The standard example of leasing arrangements occurs with transportation capital, such as the planes, trucks, or cars used by a firm. This capital is generally easily movable and not very specific. But leasing arrangements are far from universal because some of this capital can be quite specific and quasi rents appropriated. For example, early American steam locomotives were specialized to operating conditions such as high speed, hill climbing, short hauls, heavy loads, sharp corners, as well as types of coal for fuel. Slight differences in engines created significant differences in operating costs. High specialization made it desirable for the rail companies to own locomotives (as well as the land on which water was available for steam). The advent of the more versatile, less specialized, diesel locomotive enabled more leasing and equipment trust financing. Similarly, Swift, the meat packer and innovator of the refrigerator car for transporting slaughtered beef, owned the specialized refrigerator cars it used.[36]

On the other hand, some capital may be quite specific to other assets in a firm's productive process and yet leased rather than owned. These cases provide useful insights into the nature of the contracting costs underlying our analysis. For example, consider the fact that agricultural land, a highly specific asset, is not always owned but is often rented. Land rented for farming purposes is typically for annual crops, like vegetables, sugar beets, cotton, or wheat, while land used for tree crops, like nuts, dates, oranges, peaches, apricots, or grape vines—assets that are highly specialized to the land—is usually owned by the party who plants the trees or vines.[37] However, long-term rental arrangements even for these "specialized asset" crops are not entirely unknown.

It is instructive to recognize why land-rental contracts, rather than vertical integration, can often be used without leading to opportunistic behavior. The primary reason is because it is rather cheap to specify and monitor the relevant contract terms (the quality of the good being purchased) and to enforce this particular rental contract. In addition, the landowner generally cannot impose a cost on the farmer by pulling the asset out or reducing the quality of the asset during the litigation process. Note the contrast with labor rental where it is essentially impossible to effectively specify and enforce quality elements (for example, all working conditions and the effort expended by workers) and where the possibility of withdrawal by strike or lockout is real and costly. Therefore, we do observe firms making highly specific investments in, for example, trees or buildings on land they do not own but only rent long term.[38] This is because credible postcontractual opportunistic threats by the landowner are not possible. However, if the landowner can vary the quality of the land, for example, by controlling the irrigation system to the crops or the electricity supply to a building, then a significant possibility of postinvestment opportunistic behavior exists and we would therefore expect vertical integration.[39]

One specific asset that is almost always owned by the firm is its trade name or brand-name capital and, in particular, the logo it uses to communicate to customers. If this asset were rented from a leasing company, the problems would be obvious. The firm would be extremely hesitant to make any investments to build up its goodwill, for example, by advertising or by successful performance, because such investments are highly specific to that "name." The quasi rents could be appropriated by the leasing company through increases in the rental fee for the trade name. Not only would the firm not invest in this specific asset, but there would be an incentive for the firm to depreciate a valuable rented brand name. Although these problems seem insurmountable, rental of the capital input of a firm's brand name is not entirely unknown. In fact, franchisors can be thought of as brand-name leasing companies. A franchisee is fundamentally a renter of the brand-name capital (and logo) owned by the franchisor. Because of the specific capital problems noted above, direct controls are placed on franchisee behavior. The rental payment is usually some form of profit-sharing arrangement and, although the franchisee is legally considered to be an independent firm, the situation is in reality much closer to vertical integration than to the standard contractual relationship of the independent market.

Finally, the analysis throws light on the important question of why the owners of a firm (the residual claimants) are generally also the major capitalists of the firm.[40] As we have seen, owners may rent the more generalized capital, but will own the firm's specific capital. This observation has implications for recent discussions of "industrial democracy," which fail to recognize that although employees may own and manage a firm (say, through their union), they will also have to be capitalists and own the specific capital. It will generally be too costly, for example, for the worker-owners to rent a plant because such a specific investment could be rather easily appropriated from its owners after it is constructed. Therefore it is unlikely to be built. A highly detailed contractual arrangement together with very large brand-name premium payments by the laborers would be necessary to assure nonopportunistic behavior. This is generally too expensive an alternative and explains why capitalists are usually the owners of a firm.[41]

E. Social Institutions. Much of the previous analysis has dealt with tangible capital. Contractual arrangements involving such assets are often cheaper than complete vertical integration, even when the assets are highly specific (for example, the land-rental case.) As the discussion on human capital suggests, however, when the specific assets involved are intangible personal assets, the problems of contract enforcement become severe. In addition, when the number of individuals involved (or the extent of the specific capital) becomes very large, ownership arrangements often become extremely complex.

For example, consider country clubs. Golf country clubs are social, in addition to being golfing, organizations. Sociability of a country club involves substantial activities away from the golf course: dinners, dances, parties, cards, games, and general social activities with friends who are members of the club. However, some golf courses are operated with very few social activities for the set of members and their families. The social clubs (usually called "country clubs") are mutually owned by the members, whereas golf courses with virtually no off-course social activity often are privately owned with members paying daily golf fees without owning the golf course.

Mutual ownership is characteristic of the social country club because the specialized quasi rent of friendship is collected by each member whose friendship is specialized to the other members. The members' behavior toward one another constitutes an investment in forming valuable friendships, a congenial milieu, and rapport among the members. Each member has invested in creating that congenial milieu and atmosphere specialized to the other members. And its value could be stolen or destroyed by opportunistic behavior of a party authorized to admit new members.

To see how, suppose the club were owned by someone other than the members. Once the membership value is created by the interpersonal activities of the members, the owner of the club could then start to raise the fees for continuing members. Assuming some costs of the members moving away en masse and forming a new club, the owner could expropriate by higher fees some of the specialized quasi-rent value of the sociability created by the members' specialization to each other in their own group. Alternatively, the owner could threaten to break the implicit contract and destroy some of the sociability capital by selling admission to "undesirable" people who want to consort with the existing members.

Similarly, if the social country club were owned by the members as a corporation with each member owning a share of stock salable without prior approval of existing members (as is the case for the business corporation), a single member could, by threatening to sell to an "undesirable" potential member, extract some value of congeniality from the current members, as a payment for not selling.[42]

An extreme case of this general problem is a marriage. If each mate had a transferable share salable to a third party, there would be far fewer marriages with highly specific investments in affection and children. If a relationship is not one of specialized interest (specialized to a particular other party) or if it required no investment by any member, then the marriage relationship would be more like a corporation. As it is one of highly specific investments, marriages have historically been mutually owned entities, with permission of both parties generally required for alteration of membership. Government arbitration of this relationship to prevent postinvestment opportunistic behavior by either party can contribute toward lower bargaining costs and investments of resources (recoverable dowries) by both parties to improve their respective postinvestment bargaining positions, and, most importantly, create confidence that opportunistic behavior will not be successful. The legislative move-ment to "no-fault" divorce suggests that modern marriages may have less specific assets than formerly.[43]

The importance of mobility costs when many individuals in a group must jointly decide to take action, as in the case of an opportunistic country-club owner, and the importance of government intervention are clearly reflected in the case of the money-supply industry.[44] The decision regarding what is used as the dominant money (medium of exchange) in society, like many other social agreements and customs, entails a large degree of rigidity on the individual level. A decision to change a social institution, in this case what is used as money, must involve a large subset of the population to be effective. Given this natural monopoly, the cost to an individual or a new entrant of attempting change may be prohibi-tively costly. Therefore, once a dominant money supplier is established, the potential wealth gain that can be realized through opportunistic be-havior by the money issuer (that is, by unanticipated inflation) is enor-mous. The private implicit contractual solution would therefore entail an extremely high brand-name "premium" payment (seigniorage return) to guarantee that a wealth-maximizing, unregulated, private, dominant money supplier will not cheat by increasing the money supply faster than anticipated. Because this premium payment and therefore the rental price of money will be so high, it is unlikely that a private, implicit contractual solution is the cheapest arrangement.[45] Traditional vertical integration would also be extremely costly in this case of a consumer asset used by so many individuals (in fact it is difficult to even understand exactly what it would mean). Some form of government intervention is obviously likely, either in the form of regulation by enforcing an explicit contractual guar-antee, or in the form of outright nationalization. Government ownership of the monetary unit is actually close to what one may consider vertical integration on the part of consumers in this particular case.

IV. Concluding Comment

We should emphasize in conclusion that most business relation-ships are neither likely to be as simple as the standard textbook polar cases of vertical integration or market contract nor as easily explained as some of the above examples. When particular examples are examined in detail, business relationships are often structured in highly complex ways not represented by either a simple rental contract or by simple ver-tical integration. A timely example is the ownership rights of common services supplied in condominium or "new-town" projects. One solution often adopted is joint ownership of common assets, similar to the joint ownership by petroleum producers and refiners of oil pipeline as noted above. In the condominium case, however, the numbers of shareowners is sometimes equal to hundreds or even thousands of individuals and the resulting contractual arrangements are closer to a constitution for a local "government" than to the simple paradigm of a two-person market transaction. When governing costs are high, individuals have often opted for a long-term management contract (often with the builder of the housing project) for maintaining the common assets. The possible problems associated with the opportunistic appropriation by the manager of the quasi rents in specialized assets of the individual owners (including specific assets used to furnish each apartment such as carpeting and any specific "friendship capital" from association with other owner occupants) are obvious. The fact that there has been a great deal of litigation in this area is not surprising. The difficulty may be partially due to what appears to be significant economies of scale in supplying confidence concerning contract performance and diseconomies of scale in the actual production and management of housing. Some insurance or franchising arrangement may therefore evolve in this area.

There is continuing search in this difficult area using market and governmental (regulatory, legislative, and judicial) processes to produce institutional and private contractual innovation that will lead to more economical contractual relations and ownership rights. We have little idea why one solution appears to have been efficient for one condominium project and another solution for another project. This merely indicates that as we move toward more complex ownership relationships the problem of efficiently structuring the economic relationship, either within the firm or via contracts, also becomes highly complex. Stating that the world is complicated is another way of admitting our ignorance. However, explicitly recognizing that contracting costs are not zero, as they are often implicitly assumed to be in economic analysis, and explicitly considering the determinants of these costs (such as the presence of appropriable quasi rents) is the first step in explaining the large variety of contractual and ownership arrangements we observe in the real world.

More generally, we have seen that once we attempt to add empirical detail to Coase's fundamental insight that a systematic study of transaction costs is necessary to explain particular forms of economic organization, we find that his primary distinction between transactions made within a firm and transactions made in the marketplace may often be too simplistic. Many long-term contractual relationships (such as franchising) blur the line between the market and the firm. It may be more useful to merely examine the economic rationale for different types of particular contractual relationships in particular situations, and consider the firm as a particular kind or set of interrelated contracts.[46] Firms are therefore, by definition, formed and revised in markets and the conventional sharp distinction between markets and firms may have little general analytical importance. The pertinent economic question we are faced with is "What kinds of contracts are used for what kinds of activities, and why?"

Notes

1. Vertical integration does not completely avoid contracting problems. The firm could usefully be thought of as a complex nonmarket contractual network where very similar forces are present. Knight ([1933] 1964, p. 254) stressed the importance of this more than 50 years ago when he stated: "[T]he internal problems of the corporation, the protection of its various types of members and adherents against each other's predatory propensities, are quite as vital as the external problem of safeguarding the public interests against exploitation by the corporation as a unit."

2. This matter of successive and bilateral monopoly has long been known and exposited in many places. See, for example, Bork (1954); and the discussion in Machlup and Taber (1960), where the problem is dated back to Cournot's statement in 1838.

3. While newspaper publishers generally own their own presses, book publishers generally do not. One possible reason book publishers are less integrated may be because a book is planned further ahead in time and can economically be released with less haste. Presses located in any area of the United States can be used. No press is specialized to one publisher, in part because speed in publication and distribution to readers are generally far less important for books than newspapers, and therefore appropriable quasi rents are not created. Magazines and other periodicals can be considered somewhere between books and newspapers in terms of the importance of the time factor in distribution. In addition, because magazines are distributed nationally from at most a few plants, printing presses located in many different alternative areas are possible competitors for an existing press used at a particular location. Hence, a press owner has significantly less market power over the publisher of a magazine compared to a newspaper and we find magazines generally printed in nonpublisher-owned plants. (See Gustafson, 1959.) But while a magazine printing press may be a relatively less specific asset compared to a newspaper printing press, appropriable quasi rents may not be trivial (as possibly they are in the case of the book printing). The magazine printing contract is therefore unlikely to be of a short-term one-transaction form but will be a long-term arrangement.

4. The relevance for private investments in underdeveloped, politically unstable, that is, "opportunistic," countries is painfully obvious. The importance for

economic growth of predictable government behavior regarding the definition and enforcement of property rights has frequently been noted.

5. It is commonly held that users of assets that can be damaged by careless use and for which the damage is not easy to detect immediately are more likely to own rather than rent the assets. However, these efficient maintenance considerations apply to short-term contracts and are irrelevant if the length of the long-term rental contract coincides with the economic life of the asset. Abstracting from tax considerations, the long-term contract remains less than completely equivalent to vertical integration only because of the possibility of postcontractual opportunistic reneging. These opportunistic possibilities, however, may also exist within the firm; see note 1 above.

6. We are abstracting from any considerations of a firm's detection costs of determining proper maintenance. Ease of termination also analytically distinguishes between a franchisor-franchisee arrangement and a vertically integrated arrangement with a profit-sharing manager. If cheating occurs, it is generally cheaper to terminate an employee rather than a franchisee. (The law has been changing recently to make it more difficult to terminate either type of laborer.) But the more limited job-tenure rights of an employee compared to a franchisee reduce his incentive to invest in building up future business, and the firm must trade off the benefits and costs of the alternative arrangements. A profit-sharing manager with an explicit long-term employment contract would essentially be identical to a franchisee.

7. The problems involved with renting specific human capital are discussed below.

8. The recent Westinghouse case dealing with failure to fulfill uranium-supply contracts on grounds of "commercial impossibility" vividly illustrates these enforcement costs. Nearly three years after outright cancellation by Westinghouse of their contractual commitment, the lawsuits have not been adjudicated and those firms that have settled with Westinghouse have accepted substantially less than the original contracts would have entitled them to. A recent article by Joskow (1977) analyzes the Westinghouse decision to renege on the contract as anticipated risk sharing and therefore, using our definition, would not be opportunistic behavior. However, the publicity surrounding this case and the judicial progress to date are likely to make explicit long-term contracts a less feasible alternative to vertical integration in the situation we are analyzing.

9. The following discussion of the market enforcement mechanism is based upon the analysis of competitive equilibrium under costly quality information developed in Klein and Leffler (1981), which formally extends and more completely applies the analysis in Klein (1974). It is similar to the analysis presented in Becker and Stigler (1974) of insuring against malfeasance by an employer. This market-enforcement mechanism is used in Klein and McLaughlin (1978) to explain franchising arrangements and particular contractual provisions such as resale price maintenance, exclusive territories, initial specific investments, and termination clauses.

10. Formally, this arrangement to guarantee nonopportunistic behavior unravels if there is a last period in the relationship. No matter how high the premium, cheating would occur at the start of the last period. If transactors are aware of this, no transaction relying on trust (that is, the expectation of another subsequent trial) will be made in the penultimate period, because it becomes the last period, and so on. If some large lump-sum, final-period payment such as a pension as part of the market-enforcement scheme, as outlined by Becker and Stigler (1974), this last-period problem is obvious. One solution to this unrecognized last-period problem is the acceptance of some continuing third party (for example, escrow agents or government enforcers) to prevent reneging on the implicit contracts against reneging we are outlining. Alternatively, the potential loss of value of indefinitely long-lived salable brand-name assets can serve as deterrents to cheating even where the contract between two parties has a last period. If one party's reputation for nonopportunistic dealings can be sold and used in later transactions in an infinite-time-horizon economy, the firm that cheats in the "last" period to any one buyer from the firm experiences a capital loss. This may partially explain the existence of conglomerates and their use of identifying (not product-descriptive) brand names.

11. Although it may not always be in one's narrow self-interest to punish the other party in such a reciprocal relationship since termination may impose a cost on both, it may be rational for one to adopt convincingly such a reaction function to optimally prevent cheating. Trivers (1971) discusses similar mechanisms such as "moralistic aggression" which he claims have been genetically selected to protect reciprocating altruists against cheaters. Similarly, throughout the discussion we implicitly assume that cheating individuals can only cheat once and therefore earn the "competitive" rate of return. They may, however, be forced to earn less than the competitive wage if they are caught cheating, that is, take an extra capital loss (collusively, but rationally) imposed by other members of the group. This may explain why individuals may prefer to deal in business relations with their own group (for example, members of the same church or the same country club) where effective social sanctions can be imposed against opportunistic behavior. Reliance on such reciprocal business relationships and group enforcement mechanisms is more likely where governmental enforcement of contracts is weaker. Leff (1978), for example, documents the importance of such groups in less-developed countries. Industries supplying illegal products and services would likely be another example.

12. It is, of course, an insurance scheme that not only pools risks but also alters them.

13. As opposed to the analysis of Darby and Karni (1973), the equilibrium quantity of opportunistic behavior or "fraud" will be zero under our assumptions of symmetrical information.

14. A more complete analysis of market equilibrium by the use of specific capital in guaranteeing contract enforcement is developed in Klein and Leffler (1981).

15. An interesting example of the efficient creation of such a specific collateral investment is provided in *In re* Tastee-Freeze International, 82 F.T.C. 1195 (1973).

In this case the franchisor required the franchisee to purchase all the equipment to make soft ice cream except the final patented feeder mechanism which they would only rent at the nominal price of one dollar per month. This, we believe, served the function of substantially reducing the salvage value of the equipment upon termination and therefore was part of the enforcement mechanism to prevent cheating (for example, intentionally failing to maintain quality) by franchisees. If the feeder were sold, the equipment plus the feeder would have a substantial resale value and would not serve the purpose of assuring contract compliance. Similarly, if the equipment were rented along with the feeder the franchisee would not experience a capital loss if terminated. Since the assets of the franchisee are contractually made specific, a situation is created where the assets are now appropriable by an opportunistic franchisor. Generally, a franchisor will lose by terminating a franchisee without cause since that will produce poor incentives on the remaining franchisees to maintain quality and will make it more difficult for the franchisor to sell franchises in the future. But what prevents the franchisor from an unanticipated simultaneous termination of all franchisees, especially after growth of a chain is "complete"? This is logically equivalent to the last-period problem discussed at note 10 above and is restrained in part by its effects on the salable value of the brand name of the franchisor. While we do not know of any evidence of such systematic franchisor cheating, an analysis of this problem which merely asserts that franchisees voluntarily sign contracts with knowledge of these short-term termination provisions is certainly incomplete (see, for example, Rubin (1978)).

This example and much of this section of the paper is based upon a more complete theoretical and empirical analysis of actual contractual relationships developed for an ongoing study by Benjamin Klein of FTC litigation in the area of vertical-distribution arrangements.

16. It is important to recognize that not only will contracting and enforcement costs of constraining opportunistic behavior determine the form of the final economic arrangement adopted by the transacting parties, but they will also influence the firm's production function. That is, the level of specific investment and therefore the size of the potentially appropriable quasi rent is not an independent "technological" datum in each of these following cases, but is economically determined in part by transaction costs.

17. The argument also applies to die inserts which can be utilized to make slight modifications in original dies. The value of die inserts is largely an appropriable quasi rent, and so they will also be owned jointly with the designs and basic dies. Aside from the engineering design of the car, the engine blocks, the exterior shell (and possibly the crankshafts, camshafts, and gearing), no other part of the automobile would appear to possess specialized appropriable quasi rents and therefore necessarily be made exclusively by the automobile company. The integration of Ford into the manufacture of spark plugs—a part which seems to be easily standardizable among different autos—by their merger with Autolite, therefore must be explained on other grounds. See Ford Motor Co. v. United States, 405 U.S. 562 (1972).

18. The manufacturing agreement between General Motors and Fisher Body can

be found in the minutes of the Board of Directors of Fisher Body Corporation for November 7, 1919.

   In addition to this long-term contract General Motors also purchased a 60% interest in Fisher at this time. However, as demonstrated by future events, the Fisher brothers clearly seem to have maintained complete control of their company in spite of this purchase.

19. By 1924 more than 65% of automobiles produced by General Motors were of the closed body type. See *Sixteenth Annual Report* of the General Motors Corporation, year ended December 31, 1924.

20. Deposition of Alfred P. Sloan, Jr. in United States v. DuPont & Co., 366 U.S. 316 (1961), from complete set of briefs and trial records in custody of General Motors, 186–90 (April 28, 1952). Also see direct testimony of Alfred P. Sloan, Jr. in United States v. DuPont & Co., vol. 5 trial transcript, 2908–14 (March 17, 1953). (The government was attempting to demonstrate in this case that General Motors vertically integrated in order to get Fisher to purchase its glass requirements from DuPont.)

21. It is obvious that long-term exclusive dealing contracts are necessary if such investments are to be made by nonvertically integrated firms. See *In re* Great Lakes Carbon Corp., 82 F.T.C. 1529 (1973), for an example of the government's failure to understand this. Great Lakes Carbon Corporation built plants highly specific to particular refineries to process petroleum coke (a by-product of the refining process) for these refineries and was prosecuted for requiring long-term exclusive dealing contracts with refineries.

22. United States v. DuPont & Co., vol. 1, defendants trial exhibits numbers GM-32, GM-33, GM-34.

23. Our argument is distinct from the traditional argument in the oil-business literature that vertical integration occurs to achieve "assurance" of supplies or of markets in the face of implicitly or explicitly assumed disequilibrium conditions. See, for example, Frankel (1953); de Chazeau and Kahn (1959); and Canes (1976). Green (1974), similarly argues more formally that price inflexibility is an intermediate market which causes shortages and overproduction is an incentive for vertical integration.

   It is also important to distinguish between this risk-reducing reason for joint ownership (that is, the reduction in the risk of appropriation of user-associated specialized quasi rents) and the possible risk reduction from joint ownership when there is negative correlation of changes in values of nonappropriable generalized quasi rents. Joint ownership of assets whose value fluctuations are negatively correlated so that gains in one are offset by losses in the other is said to provide a form of insurance against total value changes of the resources used in the manufacturing process. These changes are not the result of any postcontractual opportunistic behavior but of general economic forces outside the control of the immediate parties. For example, a refinery and an oil-producing property fluctuate in value in opposite directions if a new oil field is discovered. The price of oil will fall but the price of refined products will not fall until additional refineries can process larger amounts of oil into more refined products at essentially constant production costs. Then, some of the oil-field owner's losses in value of crude oil are gained by his refinery. This reduces the fluctuation in values caused by factors unrelated to the efficiency of oil producing, refining, and distributing abilities.

However, diversification can also be achieved by methods other than vertical integration. One way is for the investor to buy stocks in the separate unintegrated firms—in effect integrating their ownership by joint holding of common stocks. Although individual action may not always be as cheap or effective as action through intermediaries, financial intermediaries are available such as mutual funds rather than direct diversification by integrated firms. One possible reason why negatively correlated assets could be worth more combined in a single firm is the reduction in the probability of bankruptcy and hence the probability of incurring bankruptcy costs (such as legal fees). An integrated firm with negatively correlated assets could increase its debt to equity ratio while keeping the probability of bankruptcy constant and therefore decrease the taxes on equity without any additional risk. This may be one of the gains of many conglomerate mergers.

24. Atwood and Kobrin (1977) find an extremely high positive correlation between a firm's crude production and its share of ownership in the pipeline. On the other hand, natural gas pipelines, although apparently economically similar in terms of potentially appropriable quasi rents, do not appear to be vertically integrated. Rather than joint-ownership arrangements with the gas producers, these pipelines are often independently owned. The difference may be due to more effective FPC (and now the Federal Energy Regulatory Commission) regulation (of the wellhead and citygate gas prices and the implied pipeline tariff) compared to the direct Interstate Commerce Commission regulation of oil pipelines as common carriers. Regulation of oil pipeline tariffs could, for example, be easily evaded by opportunistic decreases in the wellhead prices paid for oil. More complete government regulation of gas prices may effectively prevent opportunistic behavior by the natural gas pipeline owners, and thereby serve as an alternative to vertical integration. (See Goldberg, 1976b.) Edmund Kitch informs us that the evidence does indicate a much greater degree of vertical integration of natural gas pipelines in the period before the FPC regulation.

25. Although our preliminary investigation indicates that control of the transportation system and vertical integration of it with the oil fields and refineries were significant, there were many other factors in Rockefeller's success. For example, the unpredictability of the life of oil fields raised the risk of a substantial investment in an integrated pipeline transportation system from one field. That Rockefeller correctly or luckily surmised that the Bradford field in 1874 would be long-lived was surely a source of his success. Also his skill in discovering consumer-preferred retailing methods, achieving lower-cost refining, and correctly assessing the ability to refine sulphurous Ohio crude undoubtedly were additional factors. See, for example, Hidy and Hidy (1955); Nevins (1940); and Williamson and Daum (1959).

This oil-pipeline analysis of appropriable specific capital may be applicable in many other situations. It should hold, for example, for ore mines and refineries which are specialized to each other. We predict that copper smelters specialized to a single mine will tend to be jointly owned, as will a cement quarry and its nearby smelter (mill). Railroad spur lines (and the land on which the track runs) from ore mines to smelters should likewise be owned by the mine-smelter owner. In addition, we would expect television program producers in an area with a single transmitter tower to be joint owners of the tower.

26. If the premium is a payment to the union per unit time, then the arrangement is identical to a collateral-bond arrangement where the union collects the interest on the bond as long as no opportunistic behavior occurs. Because of possible legal difficulties of enforcing such an arrangement, however, the premium may be reflected in the price (that is, a higher wage).

27. It is interesting to note in this context that California grape farmers preferred the established Teamsters Union to the new, untried, and apparently more politically motivated fieldworkers union organized by Cesar Chavez.

    Since unions are not "owned," union leaders will not have the proper incentive to maximize the union's value; they will tend more to maximize returns during their tenure. If, however, union leadership (ownership) were salable, the leaders would have the optimal incentive to invest in and conserve the union's brand-name capital. They therefore would not engage in opportunistic actions that may increase current revenue while decreasing the market value of the union. "Idealistic" union leaders that do not behave as if they own the union may, in fact, produce less wealth-maximizing action than would "corrupt" leaders, who act as if they personally own the union. Alternatively, the current members of the union may have control, not in the sense of having directly salable shares, but in the sense that the valuable union asset can be transferred to their children or relatives. If government regulations force union members to give away these rights to future rents (for example, by forcing them to admit minorities and eliminate nepotism), we can expect them to intentionally depreciate or not create the reputation capital of the union by opportunistic strikes. See Klein (1974) where similar problems with regard to the supply of money by nonprivately owned, nonwealth-maximizing firms are discussed.

28. An interesting legal case in this area is Publishers' Ass'n v. Newspaper & Mail Del. Union, 114 N.Y.S.2d 401 (1952). The union authorized and sanctioned a strike against the New York Daily News although the collective bargaining agreement had "no-strike" and arbitration clauses. The Daily News took the union to arbitration, and the arbitrator found actual damages of $2,000 and punitive damages of $5,000 if the union again violated the contract. (The court, however, overturned the punitive damages for technical reasons.) See Feller (1973), for a discussion of the flexibility obtained with arbitration provisions in labor contracts.

29. We should explicitly note that we are not considering unions as cartelizing devices, the usually analyzed motivation for their existence. This force is obviously present in many cases (for example, interstate trucking) but is distinct from our analysis.

30. When allowing for this "reverse" effect of employee-specific capital, and therefore higher wages, on the formation of unions, the usual positive effect of unions on wages appears to vanish. See, for example, Ashenfelter and Johnson (1972); and Schmidt and Strauss (1976).

31. This argument is distinct from the recent argument for the existence of rigid long-term implicit labor contracts as a means of bearing risk. See, for example, Gordon (1974); and Azariadis (1975). We should also note that although Hashimoto (1975) has correctly argued that cyclically flexible wages are more likely when specific human capital is present because both workers and employers will want to minimize the likelihood of job separation and thereby protect future returns on the specific human-capital investment, he ignores the contrary effect of increased specific human capital increasing the potential for opportunistic cheating and therefore increasing wage rigidity. The net theoretical effect is indeterminate. One possible reason that high-ranking corporate executives with a great deal of specific human capital appear to have highly flexible wages is because of the large amount of information about the firm they possess and therefore the shorter lag in detecting opportunism.

32. The recent "rational-expectations" approach to business cycles, which relies on consumer and producer uncertainty regarding whether a particular demand shock is a relative or an aggregate shift (see, for example, Lucas (1973)), implicitly assumes economic agents do not observe current movements of money supply and price level. A more realistic assumption is that economic agents are not "fooled," especially over long periods, about the nature of the shock but rather are bound, either explicitly or implicitly, by long-term contracts that have previously fixed prices.

33. A crucial determinant of economic organization is therefore the anticipated demand growth compared to the actual demand growth, or the demand growth anticipated at the time of contract and the demand growth actually experienced and therefore anticipated at some later time. For example, one possible reason for the recent movement by oil-refining companies towards vertically integrated retail-marketing operations may be the increased cost of controlling franchised dealers due to the large decrease in the anticipated growth of demand for gasoline in the period since the large OPEC-initiated price increase of crude oil. With demand growing slower than originally anticipated, the initial equilibrium "premium" earned by dealers will now be less than necessary to assure their noncheating behavior. The anticipated decrease in the total number of dealers (that is, the fact that future demand is anticipated to be zero for many dealers in the new equilibrium) will create last-period problems for particular locations that can be largely avoided by employee-operated outlets. See Klein and Leffler (1981) for a more complete discussion of these issues.

34. Galenson and Odaka (1976); and Taira (1970), both documented the fact that this highly flexible wage feature of Japanese labor contracts did not become widespread until the postwar period, a time of extremely rapid growth.

35. In addition to computers being less specific and hence possessing smaller appro-

priable quasi rents than elevators, firms (for example, IBM) that supply computers generally possess extremely valuable brand names per unit of current sales due to a large anticipated growth in demand. Since there are some quasi rents associated with the use of a computer by a bank that could possibly be appropriated by threat of immediate removal, we would expect that if rental contracts existed they would more likely be with highly credible firms with high anticipated demand growth.

36. The great bulk of all refrigerator cars are not owned by the railroads, but rather by shipper-users such as packers and dairy companies. See Henry (1942).

37. While 25% of vegetable and melon farms in California in 1974 were fully owned by the farm operator, 82% of fruit and nut tree farms were fully owned, a significantly different ownership proportion at the 99% confidence interval. Similarly, the ownership proportions of cash grain and cotton farms were 40% and 39%, respectively, both also significantly different at the 99% confidence interval from the proportions of fruit and nut tree farm ownership. See 1 U.S. Dep't of Commerce, Bureau of the Census, 1974 Census of Agriculture, State and County Data, pt. 5 at tab. 28. Summary by Tenure of Farm Operator and Type of Organization, *id.,* 1974, California, pp. 1–29 to 1–30.

38. Rental terms may be related to sales of the firm using the land in order to share the risk of real-value changes and to reduce the risk of nominal land-value changes involved with a long-term contract.

39. Coase's example of a monopolist selling more of a durable good, say land, after initially selling a monopoly quantity at the monopoly price is analytically identical to the problem of postcontractual opportunistic behavior. Existing contractual relationships indicate, however, that the land case may be relatively easy to solve because it may not be expensive to make a credible contract regarding the remaining land. But, one of Coase's indicated solutions, the short-term rental rather than sale of the land is unlikely because it would discourage specific (to land) investments by the renter (such as building a house, developing a farm, and so forth) for fear of appropriation. See Coase (1972).

40. We are grateful to Earl Thompson for discerning this implication.

41. Alchian and Demsetz (1972), claim that if the owner of the firm also owns the firm's capital it supplies evidence that he can pay for rented inputs, including labor. This appears to be incorrect since the owner could supply credibility by using some of his assets completely unrelated to the production process, such as treasury bonds, for collateral. Jensen and Meckling (1977), emphasize the costs of monitoring managerial performance and the maintenance of rented capital, and the problems of efficiently allocating risks in a pure-rental firm. They also note that it is "impossible" for a firm to rent all the productive capital assets because many of them are intangible and therefore "it is impossible to repossess the asset if the firm refused to pay the rental fee" (Jensen and Meckling, 1977, p. 20). This argument is similar to our analysis of opportunistic behavior. However, rather than asserting that such rentals are impossible, we

would merely recognize the extremely high contracting costs generally present in such situations. More importantly, we claim that such an argument also extends to the rental of tangible specific capital.

42. The "free-rider" problems of bribing an opportunistic member to prevent sale to an "undesirable" member are obvious. This analysis could be applied to social clubs such as Elks, Masonic Order, and so forth.

43. Similarly, people whose work is highly specialized to each other will be partners (common ownership). For example, attorneys that have become highly specialized to their coattorneys will become partners, whereas new associates will at first be employees. A small team of performers (Laurel and Hardy, Sonny and Cher) who were highly specialized to each other would be "partners" (co-owners) rather than employee and employer. While it is still difficult to enforce such contracts and prevent postcontractual opportunistic behavior by either party, joint ownership creates an incentive for performance and specific investment not present in an easily terminable employer-employee contract that must rely solely on the personal brand-name reputation of contracting parties. Trust, including the reputation of certifying institutions such as theatrical agents, law schools, and so on, and the presence of social sanctions against opportunistic partners remain important.

44. The following discussion extends the analysis in Klein (1974).

45. The alternative cost of holding money will be significantly above the marginal cost of producing cash balances (where costs are defined exclusive of the costs necessary to guarantee nonopportunistic behavior), thereby leading to less than "the optimum" quantity of cash balances. See, for example, Friedman (1969) for the original statement of this supposed inefficiency.

   An alternative solution analytically equivalent to the "premium" solution would be the putting up by the dominant money supplier of a large forfeitable collateral bond equal to the value of the possible short-run wealth gain from cheating. This bond would be held in part by each of the demanders of the firm's money in proportion to each particular individual's money holdings and interest received on the bond by each individual would be paid to the firm if cheating did not occur. While this would not create any inefficiencies of price greater than marginal cost as implied by the premium solution, the transaction costs of enforcing such an arrangement among such a large and changing number of individuals would be extremely high. If the government acted as the consumers' agent, the solution would now be similar to a regulated industry, with the potential for opportunistic expropriation of the bond by the government.

46. If we think of firms as collections of interrelated contracts rather than the collection of goods operative in the contracts, the question of who "owns" the firm (the set of contracts) appears somewhat nonsensical. It may be useful to think solely of a set of claimants to various portions of the value consequences of the contractual coalition, with no "owner" of the firm.

TWO

Transaction-Cost Economics: Governing Economic Exchanges

Consider the organization of the long-haul moving industry (Barney, 1985). People being moved across the country by such firms will usually interact with three distinct types of workers. First, individuals who pack a family's belongings into boxes and load them into the truck are hired on a day by day basis, typically out of a union hiring hall. After a day's work, there may never be any further relationship between the moving company and these workers. The second group consists of those individuals who supervise the packing and loading of the truck and then drive the truck to its destination, where they supervise its unloading. These workers are typically independent contractors who maintain long-term contractual relations with the moving company. These explicit contracts are renegotiated periodically to reflect changes in the driver's costs, experience, and productivity. Finally, those individuals who manage the moving companies by developing marketing plans, acquiring franchise rights, engaging in litigation, and lobbying with the Federal Trade Commission, among other tasks, are typically regular full-time employees of the firm and draw a salary from its revenues.

Why is it that in the execution of what appears to be a single transaction (acquiring the services of a mover to change residences) one encounters so many different forms of governance? What is it about these various tasks that leads one individual to maintain a "spot market" relationship with the moving company, another to maintain a long-term contractual relationship, and still others to become employees?

These are the kinds of questions addressed by the transaction-cost framework in organizational economics. And because they

72

are questions about what kinds of transactions should and should not be brought inside a firm's boundary, they are also special cases of a much more general and basic question for those who study organizations: Why are there firms?

Neither traditional microeconomics or organization theory alone can answer this perhaps most fundamental of all theoretical questions in the study of organizations. The assumptions of microeconomics, when applied to the question of why there are firms, suggest that firms should not exist at all. Rather than explaining *why* firms exist, then, microeconomists on the whole have taken their existence as given, assumed away the relevance of all intraorganizational processes, and focused on aggregate market behavior.

For organization theory, the existential question never arises. Because organization theory typically includes no notion of market governance, the question of why firms exist, as opposed to other ways of organizing economic exchanges, is not an issue. Most organization theories take the existence of firms as given and then theorize about behavior within and between firms.

It was Coase's ("The Nature of the Firm") fundamental insight that firms exist because it is costly to use the price system to coordinate economic activity. In this one insight are locked most of the implications of what has come to be known as the transaction-cost model. Coase recognized that markets and firms are alternative ways of organizing economic exchanges and that uncertainty and opportunism increase the cost of using the price system. This perception led Coase to focus explicitly on the contracting process.

Although now widely acknowledged as extremely important, Coase's fundamental insights were largely ignored by the field of economics for thirty years. This was, perhaps, due to the powerful and universal results that were being obtained in traditional equilibrium microeconomic research (Hirshleifer, 1980). Coase (1972, p. 63) himself observed that his insights were often cited but seldom used. The resurgence of interest in the issues raised by Coase can be traced to the work of Simon, March, Cyert, Williamson, and others on decision-making processes and bounded rationality, done in the 1950s at Carnegie-Mellon University. Their concept of bounded rationality as a property of individuals is very closely related to Coase's analysis of the firm.

Work drawing on these insights led to a series of articles and books published during the 1960s and 1970s. These developments ultimately led to the publication of Williamson's (1975) *Markets and Hierarchies: Analysis and Antitrust Implications*. This book summarizes and integrates much of the previous work on transactions and transaction costs, and attempts to develop a systematic answer to the question of why firms exist. Williamson summarizes his model as follows (1975, p. 8; italics in the original):

> The general approach to economic organization employed here can be summarized compactly as follows: (1) Markets and firms are alternative instruments for completing a related set of transactions; (2) whether a set of transactions ought to be executed across markets or within a firm depends on the relative efficiency of each mode; (3) the costs of writing and executing complex contracts across a market *vary with the characteristics of the human decision makers who are involved with the transaction on the one hand, and the objective properties of the market on the other*; and (4) although the human and environmental factors that impede exchanges between firms (across a market) manifest themselves somewhat differently within the firm, the same set of factors apply to both.

For Williamson, the human characteristics that most affect the governance choice are bounded rationality and opportunism. The environmental characteristics that indicate market or hierarchical governance are uncertainty/complexity and small numbers. The existence of a small number of parties to an exchange increases the likelihood of opportunistic behavior, just as the existence of uncertainty/complexity makes bounded rationality operative, thus making it impossible for parties to an exchange to anticipate all possible future states in their relations. In such a setting, the costs of writing and enforcing a contract assuring all parties to an exchange of an outcome that all would deem as fair are high enough to be prohibitive. In this situation, a market would be an inefficient means of carrying forward a transaction, and it will be replaced by a hierarchy.

One of the criticisms of both Coase's and Williamson's work has been the unrealistic typology of transaction governance mechanisms they employ. While markets and hierarchies are alternative ways of organizing transactions, other options are also possible. Several authors (Ouchi, 1980; Barney and Ouchi, 1984) have suggested alternative typologies. In fact, Williamson himself has extended his earlier governance typology ("Transaction-Cost Economics: The Governance of Contractual Relations"). In so doing, he also modified his earlier characterization of the transaction attributes that raised the cost of employing simple mechanisms of market transaction governance. Drawing on the work of Klein, Crawford, and Alchian (1978), Williamson now emphasizes transaction specific investments as a key factor in explaining when markets will fail and be replaced by intermediate market or hierarchical governance mechanisms.

Alchian and Demsetz ("Production, Information Costs, and Economic Organization") also stress a type of transaction specific investment in developing their explanation of why firms exist. For Alchian and Demsetz, the reason for the existence of firms can ultimately be found in what they call team production. Team production exists when the collective output of a group of individuals is greater than the sum of the output of each of them separately, and where it is simultaneously difficult to discover each individual's contribution to the group's output. Individuals in these teams have firm specific skills—skills whose value is greater in combination with other members of the particular team than in other exchange contexts.

The productive efficiency of teams suggests that, setting any other difficulties aside, they should be quite common. However, the existence of productive teams does not, by itself, lead to hierarchical forms of organization. Teamwork only requires cooperation; it does not necessarily require an organizational hierarchy.

Alchian and Demsetz argue that the classical firm emerges because of the eventual need to monitor, or meter, the individuals that make up a productive team. Because it is difficult in a team to determine the individual contributions of each member, each member has an incentive to shirk. The possibility of shirking will deter high-output individuals from joining the team and may discourage customers and providers of capital as well. Team members, therefore, have an incentive to reduce the possibility of their own shirking. One way to reduce shirking is to provide for monitoring of the performance of each team member (Simon, 1959). A hierarchy thereby emerges, with some members assigned to evaluate others.

Yet problems remain. In particular, who will monitor the monitor? After all, this team member is no different from others, and has incentives to shirk unless incentives to the contrary exist. Alchian and Demsetz argue that the structuring of property rights can reduce the likelihood of shirking by a monitor by causing him or her to bear the costs of such behavior. These property rights include: (1) the right to the residual productivity of the team beyond that which is necessary to keep the team operating, (2) the right to observe the productive input of individuals on the team, (3) the right to monitor all contracts with sources of input into the team, and (4) the right to sell these rights. These property rights define the ownership of the firm. Clearly, the owner of the firm (that is, the owner of the team) has strong incentives not to shirk his monitoring responsibilities, since by doing so, he would not be maximizing his personal wealth.

Alchian and Demsetz go on to extend this relatively simple idea and explain why a variety of ownership schemes exist, such as profit-sharing firms, socialist firms, corporations, mutual and nonprofit firms, partnerships, employee unions. Throughout, the emphasis is on the metering problems associated with team production and how various forms of organization help alleviate these problems by creating incentives for certain members of the team to monitor the behavior of other team members.

Implications for Organization Theory

Perhaps the most fundamental implication of transaction-cost theory for organization theorists can be found in Coase's original insight that firms and markets are alternative means of organizing economic exchanges, and, thus, the theoretical task of explaining why firms exist is equivalent to explaining why markets do not exist for a particular transaction. It may be possible to disagree with Williamson's, Coase's, or Alchian and Demsetz's characterizations of the different mechanisms that can be used to govern economic transactions, and it may be possible to dispute their characterizations of the underlying transaction attributes that cause one of these mechanisms to be chosen over others, but the *form* of their reasoning remains compelling. The incorporation of market alternatives into organization theory's explanations of vertical integration, the influence of boards of directors, the stability of interorganizational exchange relations, and the structure of careers, to cite just a few important areas of research, represent a major conceptual challenge that needs to be addressed over the next several years by organization theorists.

The role of efficiency criteria in determining the appropriate governance mechanisms is closely linked with the idea that markets and hierarchies are alternative mechanisms for governing economic transactions. The efficiency criterion implies that, in order to remain competitive, firms must adopt the most efficient governance mechanism.

Competition is not a well-developed concept among organization theorists, and efficiency is only one of several criteria that have been used by organization theorists to judge the appropriateness of specific organizational forms. Of course, not all organizations face competitive constraints, and thus alternative criteria for judging the fitness of a firm will be useful in some circumstances. However, most organizations (Hoenack, 1983) and certainly most business firms do face competition that constrains their options to a small, efficient set of possibilities (Hirshleifer, 1980). Under competition, firms must do that which increases their survival potential; in other words, they must attempt to be efficient. Firms that constantly place themselves at a cost or other disadvantage, for example, by attempting to dominate customers or suppliers only to lose them to their competitors (Pfeffer and Salancik, 1978), cannot expect to survive in the long run.

A third set of implications of the transaction-cost model for organization theorists comes from the observation that the most fruitful level of analysis for organizational research is not the firm, but rather the transaction. In the transaction-cost framework, the effort is to analyze each economic transaction separately, to describe the objective characteristics of that transaction, and then to predict whether it will be organized across a market or within a hierarchy. This approach is incompatible with the typical analysis employed in organization theory in which the effort is to understand the impact of a firm's environment, taken as a whole, on firm behavior. For transaction-cost theorists, such contingency theories (Miles, 1980) lump together large numbers of transactions, each with somewhat different characteristics.

In this form of analysis, it makes no sense to summarize a firm's environment as complex, stable, or munificent. Rather, the transaction specific microenvironments that surround each economic exchange must be characterized separately. Some of these transactions will be complex; others will be simple; some will be subject to more uncertainty than others. Given such variation, aggregating these numerous transaction specific "environments" into a single measure of a firm's environment is clearly inappropriate. Like the mathematician who could not swim, but decided to cross a river that averaged only two feet deep, organization theorists can easily drown—on the average.

Employing the transaction as the unit of analysis also suggests an alternative way of thinking about the boundaries of firms (Barney and Ouchi, 1984). Typically, organization theorists have attempted first to define the boundaries of a firm according to some a priori criteria, for example, common goals, and then to examine relations between the entity thus defined and its environment. The transaction-cost approach suggests that the boundaries of a firm do not simply stem from some a priori commonality but must be discovered through a transaction-by-transaction analysis of the governance mechanisms employed. By determining how a transaction is governed—whether by a hierarchy, a market, or some intermediate governance mechanisms—one point in a firm's overall boundary can be specified. In this way, the boundary of an organization can be derived transaction by transaction. The transaction-cost approach has great power in discriminating between those firms that are more or less completely vertically integrated; it is a form of analysis that is not presently within the scope of organization theory but that has great implications for the study of all organizations and for the related study of strategy as well.

✦✦✦ Yet, this is a rather static notion of transaction governance, not completely consistent with the transaction-cost perspective. As technologies change, transaction characteristics change, efficient governance mechanisms change, and part of a firm's boundary changes. For example, with the wide distribution of personal computers, certain transactions that previously could be conducted only by bringing together a large group of people in face-to-face meetings can now be conducted by individuals connected through a common personal computer network. This new technology may simplify some transactions to the point at which they no longer need to be conducted within a hierarchy, but can be governed through market mechanisms, thereby changing the efficient boundary of the firm. Thus, instead of a static firm with well-defined limits, the transaction-cost model imagines a constantly shifting and changing entity, periodically taking transactions within its hierarchy, other times spinning a transaction off to be governed through markets. Rather than being similar to the traditional organization theory conception of firms, the transaction-cost view seems closer to the social psychological notions of organizations developed by Wcick (1969) and others.

Other well-known concepts in organization theory, besides the environment and the organizational boundary, take on whole new meanings—or become meaningless—when the transaction is taken as the unit of analysis. For example, with the transaction as the unit of analysis, it is possible to identify greater variety within a single firm: some transactions will be managed in a centralized way, others in a decentralized way; some will be managed autocratically, others participatively; some organically, others mechanistically. Despite the widely cited advantages of teamwork, the model will sometimes indicate that production should not take place through teams, but rather across markets.

At a more microanalytic level, these observations suggest that familiar injunctions to apply participative management (Ouchi, 1981; Peters and Waterman, 1982) in firms do not apply indiscriminantly within a firm but, rather, apply only where certain kinds of hierarchical governance mechanisms are appropriately employed. These ideas are explored in Ouchi's (1980) concept of markets, bureaucracies, and clans.

Finally, transaction-cost theory, and, in particular, Alchian and Demsetz's article, reaffirms the importance of the study of productive teams and teamwork in organizations. For Alchian and Demsetz, teams are not just interesting social-psychological phenomena—a laboratory to test theories developed in psychology and social psychology; rather, teams are the reason that firms exist. Those who study teams are studying the core of the firm. Improving their productive capacity, in this sense, is reaffirming the reason the firm exists. Those who create teams, whether they are academics or entrepreneurs, are in the business of creating firms.

The Nature of the Firm

R. H. Coase

Economic theory has suffered in the past from a failure to state clearly its assumptions. Economists in building up a theory have often omitted to examine the foundations on which it was erected. This examination is, however, essential not only to prevent the misunderstanding and needless controversy which arise from a lack of knowledge of the assumptions on which a theory is based, but also because of the extreme importance for economics of good judgment in choosing between rival sets of assumptions. For instance, it is suggested that the use of the word "firm" in economics may be different from the use of the term by the "plain man" (Robinson, 1932, p. 12). Since there is apparently a trend in economic theory towards starting analysis with the individual firm and not with the industry (Kaldor, 1934), it is all the more necessary not only that a clear definition of the word "firm" should be given but that its difference from a firm in the "real world," if it exists, should be made clear. Mrs. Robinson (1932, p. 6) has said that "the two questions to be asked of a set of assumptions in economics are: Are they tractable? and: Do they correspond with the real world ?" Though, as Mrs. Robinson points out, "more often one set will be manageable and the other realistic," yet there may well be branches of theory where assumptions may be both manageable and realistic. It is hoped to show in the following paper that a definition of a firm may be obtained which is not only realistic in that it corresponds to what is meant by a firm in the real world, but is tractable by two of the most powerful instruments of economic analysis developed by Marshall, the idea of the margin and that of substitution, together giving the idea of substitution at the margin (Keynes, 1933, pp. 223–224). Our definition must, of course, "relate to formal relations which are capable of being *conceived* exactly" (Robbins, 1932, p. 63).

I

It is convenient if, in searching for a definition of a firm, we first consider the economic system as it is normally treated by the economist. Let us consider the description of the economic system given by Sir Arthur Salter.[1] "The normal economic system works itself. For its current operation it is under no central control, it needs no central survey. Over the whole range of human activity and human need, supply is adjusted to demand, and production to consumption, by a process that is automatic, elastic and responsive." An economist thinks of the economic system as being co-ordinated by the price mechanism and society becomes not an organisation but an organism (Hayek, 1933). The economic system "works itself." This does not mean that there is no planning by individuals. These exercise foresight and choose between alternatives. This is necessarily so if there is to be order in the system. But this theory assumes that the direction of resources is dependent directly on the price mechanism. Indeed, it is often considered to be an objection to economic planning that it merely tries to do what is already done by the price mechanism (Hayek, 1933). Sir Arthur Salter's description, however, gives a very incomplete picture of our economic system. Within a firm, the description does not fit at all. For instance, in economic theory we find that the allocation of factors of production between different uses is determined by the price mechanism. The price of factor A becomes higher in X than in Y. As a result, A moves from Y to X until the difference between the prices in X and Y, except in so far as it compensates for other differential advantages, disappears. Yet in the real world, we find that there are many areas where this does not apply. If a workman moves from department Y to department X, he does not go because of a change in relative prices, but because he is ordered to do so. Those who object to economic planning on the grounds that the problem is solved by price movements can be answered by pointing out that there is planning within our economic system which is quite different from the individual planning mentioned above and which is akin to what is normally called economic planning. The example given above is typical of a large sphere

in our modern economic system. Of course, this fact has not been ignored by economists. Marshall introduces organisation as a fourth factor
of production; J. B. Clark gives the co-ordinating function to the entrepreneur; Professor Knight introduces managers who co-ordinate. As
D. H. Robertson points out, we find "islands of conscious power in this
ocean of unconscious co-operation like lumps of butter coagulating in
a pail of buttermilk" (Robertson, 1936, p. 85). But in view of the fact
that it is usually argued that co-ordination will be done by the price
mechanism, why is such organisation necessary? Why are there these
"islands of conscious power"? Outside the firm, price movements direct
production, which is co-ordinated through a series of exchange transactions on the market. Within a firm, these market transactions are eliminated and in place of the complicated market structure with exchange
transactions is substituted the entrepreneur-co-ordinator, who directs
production.[2] It is clear that these are alternative methods of co-ordinating
production. Yet, having regard to the fact that if production is regulated
by price movements, production could be carried on without any organisation at all, well might we ask, why is there any organisation?

Of course, the degree to which the price mechanism is superseded
varies greatly. In a department store, the allocation of the different sections
to the various locations in the building may be done by the controlling authority or it may be the result of competitive price bidding for space. In the
Lancashire cotton industry, a weaver can rent power and shop-room and
can obtain looms and yarn on credit. This co-ordination of the various
factors of production is, however, normally carried out without the intervention of the price mechanism. As is evident, the amount of "vertical" integration, involving as it does the supersession of the price
mechanism, varies greatly from industry to industry and from firm to firm.

It can, I think, be assumed that the distinguishing mark of the
firm is the supersession of the price mechanism. It is, of course, as Professor Robbins points out, "related to an outside network of relative prices
and costs" (Robbins, 1932, p. 71), but it is important to discover the
exact nature of this relationship. This distinction between the allocation
of resources in a firm and the allocation in the economic system has been
very vividly described by Mr. Maurice Dobb when discussing Adam
Smith's conception of the capitalist: "It began to be seen that there was
something more important than the relations inside each factory or unit
captained by an undertaker; there were the relations of the undertaker
with the rest of the economic world outside his immediate sphere. . . . the
undertaker busies himself with the division of labour inside each firm
and he plans and organises consciously," but "he is related to the much

larger economic specialisation, of which he himself is merely one specialised unit. Here, he plays his part as a single cell in a larger organism, mainly unconscious of the wider rôle he fills'' (1926, p. 20).

In view of the fact that while economists treat the price mechanism as a co-ordinating instrument, they also admit the co-ordinating function of the ''entrepreneur,'' it is surely important to enquire why co-ordination is the work of the price mechanism in one case and of the entrepreneur in another. The purpose of this paper is to bridge what appears to be a gap in economic theory between the assumption (made for some purposes) that resources are allocated by means of the price mechanism and the assumption (made for other purposes) that this allocation is dependent on the entrepreneur-co-ordinator. We have to explain the basis on which, in practice, this choice between alternatives is effected.[3]

II

Our task is to attempt to discover why a firm emerges at all in a specialised exchange economy. The price mechanism (considered purely from the side of the direction of resources) might be superseded if the relationship which replaced it was desired for its own sake. This would be the case, for example, if some people preferred to work under the direction of some other person. Such individuals would accept less in order to work under someone, and firms would arise naturally from this. But it would appear that this cannot be a very important reason, for it would rather seem that the opposite tendency is operating if one judges from the stress normally laid on the advantage of ''being one's own master.''[4] Of course, if the desire was not to be controlled but to control, to exercise power over others, then people might be willing to give up something in order to direct others; that is, they would be willing to pay others more than they could get under the price mechanism in order to be able to direct them. But this implies that those who direct pay in order to be able to do this and are not paid to direct, which is clearly not true in the majority of cases.[5] Firms might also exist if purchasers preferred commodities which are produced by firms to those not so produced; but even in spheres where one would expect such preferences (if they exist) to be of negligible importance, firms are to be found in the real world.[6] Therefore there must be other elements involved.

The main reason why it is profitable to establish a firm would seem to be that there is a cost of using the price mechanism. The most obvious cost of ''organising'' production through the price mechanism is that of discovering what the relevant prices are.[7] This cost may be reduced but it will not be eliminated by the emergence of specialists who will sell this information. The costs of negotiating and concluding a separate contract for each exchange transaction which takes place on a market must also be taken into account.[8] Again, in certain markets, e.g., produce exchanges, a technique is devised for minimising these contract costs; but they are not eliminated. It is true that contracts are not eliminated when there is a firm but they are greatly reduced. A factor of production (or the owner thereof) does not have to make a series of contracts with the factors with whom he is co-operating within the firm, as would be necessary, of course, if this co-operation were as a direct result of the working of the price mechanism. For this series of contracts is substituted one. At this stage, it is important to note the character of the contract into which a factor enters that is employed within a firm. The contract is one whereby the factor, for a certain remuneration (which may be fixed or fluctuating), agrees to obey the directions of an entrepreneur *within certain limits*.[9] The essence of the contract is that it should only state the limits to the powers of the entrepreneur. Within these limits, he can therefore direct the other factors of production.

There are, however, other disadvantages—or costs—of using the price mechanism. It may be desired to make a long-term contract for the supply of some article or service. This may be due to the fact that if one contract is made for a longer period, instead of several shorter ones, then certain costs of making each contract will be avoided. Or, owing to the risk attitude of the people concerned, they may prefer to make a long rather than a short-term contract. Now, owing to the difficulty of forecasting, the longer the period of the contract is for the supply of the commodity or service, the less possible, and indeed, the less desirable it is for the person purchasing to specify what the other contracting party is expected to do. It may well be a matter of indifference to the person supplying the service or commodity which of several courses of action is taken, but not to the purchaser of that service or commodity. But the purchaser will not know which of these several courses he will want the supplier to take. Therefore, the service which is being provided is expressed in general terms, the exact details being left until a later date. All that is stated in the contract is the limits to what the persons supplying the commodity or service is expected to do. The details of what the supplier is expected to do is not stated in the contract but is decided later by the purchaser. When the direction of resources (within the limits of the contract) becomes dependent on the buyer in this way, that relationship which I term a "firm" may be obtained.[10] A firm is likely therefore to emerge in those cases where a very short term contract would be unsatisfactory. It is obviously of more importance in the case of services—labour—than it is in the case of the buying of commodities. In the case of commodities, the main items can be stated in advance and the details which will be decided later will be of minor significance.

We may sum up this section of the argument by saying that the operation of a market costs something and by forming an organisation and allowing some authority (an "entrepreneur") to direct the resources, certain marketing costs are saved. The entrepreneur has to carry out his function at less cost, taking into account the fact that he may get factors of production at a lower price than the market transactions which he supersedes, because it is always possible to revert to the open market if he fails to do this.

The question of uncertainty is one which is often considered to be very relevant to the study of the equilibrium of the firm. It seems improbable that a firm would emerge without the existence of uncertainty. But those, for instance, Professor Knight, who make the *mode of payment* the distinguishing mark of the firm—fixed incomes being guaranteed to some of those engaged in production by a person who takes the residual, and fluctuating, income—would appear to be introducing a point which is irrelevant to the problem we are considering. One entrepreneur may sell his services to another for a certain sum of money, while the payment to his employees may be mainly or wholly a share in profits.[11] The significant question would appear to be why the allocation of resources is not done directly by the price mechanism.

Another factor that should be noted is that exchange transactions on a market and the same transactions organised within a firm are often treated differently by Governments or other bodies with regulatory powers. If we consider the operation of a sales tax, it is clear that it is a tax on market transactions and not on the same transactions organised within the firm. Now since these are alternative methods of "organisation"—by the price mechanism or by the entrepreneur—such a regulation would bring into existence firms which otherwise would have no *raison d'être*. It would furnish a reason for the emergence of a firm in a specialised exchange economy. Of course, to the extent that firms already exist, such a measure as a sales tax would merely tend to make them larger than they could otherwise be. Similarly, quota schemes, and methods of price control which imply that there is rationing, and which do not apply to firms producing such products for themselves, by allowing advantages to those who organise within the firm and not through the market, necessarily encourage the growth of firms. But it is difficult to believe that it is measures such as have been mentioned in this paragraph which have brought firms into existence. Such measures would, however, tend to have this result if they did not exist for other reasons.

These, then, are the reasons why organisations such as firms exist in a specialised exchange economy in which it is generally assumed that the distribution of resources is "organised" by the price mechanism. A firm, therefore, consists of the system of relationships which comes into existence when the direction of resources is dependent on an entrepreneur.

The approach which has just been sketched would appear to offer an advantage in that it is possible to give a scientific meaning to what is meant by saying that a firm gets larger or smaller. A firm becomes larger as additional transactions (which could be exchange transactions co-ordinated through the price mechanism) are organised by the entrepreneur and becomes smaller as he abandons the organisation of such transactions. The question which arises is whether it is possible to study the forces which determine the size of the firm. Why does the entrepreneur not organise one less transaction or one more? It is interesting to note that Professor Knight considers that:

> the relation between efficiency and size is one of the most serious problems of theory, being, in contrast with the relation for a plant, largely a matter of personality and historical accident rather than of intelligible general principles. But the question is peculiarly vital because the possibility of monopoly gain offers a powerful incentive to *continuous and unlimited* expansion of the firm, which force must be offset by some equally powerful one making for decreased efficiency (in the production of money income) with growth in size, if even boundary competition is to exist (Knight, [1933] 1964).

Professor Knight would appear to consider that it is impossible to treat scientifically the determinants of the size of the firm. On the basis of the concept of the firm developed above, this task will now be attempted.

It was suggested that the introduction of the firm was due primarily to the existence of marketing costs. A pertinent question to ask would appear to be (quite apart from the monopoly considerations raised by Professor Knight), why, if by organising one can eliminate certain costs and in fact reduce the cost of production, are there any market transactions at all?[12] Why is not all production carried on by one big firm? There would appear to be certain possible explanations.

First, as a firm gets larger, there may be decreasing returns to the entrepreneur function, that is, the costs of organising additional transactions within the firm may rise.[13] Naturally, a point must be reached where the costs of organising an extra transaction within the firm are equal to the costs involved in carrying out the transaction in the open market, or, to the costs of organising by another entrepreneur. Secondly, it may be that as the transactions which are organised increase, the entrepreneur fails to place the factors of production in the uses where their value is greatest, that is, fails to make the best use of the factors of production. Again, a point must be reached where the loss through the waste of resources is equal to the marketing costs of the exchange transaction in the open market or to the loss if the transaction was organised by another entrepreneur. Finally, the supply price of one or more of the factors of production may rise, because the ''other advantages'' of a small firm are greater than those of a large firm.[14] Of course, the actual point where the expansion of the firm ceases might be determined by a combination of the factors mentioned above. The first two reasons given most probably correspond to the economists' phrase of ''diminishing returns to management.''[15]

The point has been made in the previous paragraph that a firm will tend to expand until the costs of organising an extra transaction within the firm become equal to the costs of carrying out the same transaction by means of an exchange on the open market or the costs of organising in another firm. But if the firm stops its expansion at a point below the costs of marketing in the open market and at a point equal to the costs of organising in another firm, in most cases (excluding the case of ''combination''[16]), this will imply that there is a market transaction between these two producers, each of whom could organise it at less than the actual marketing costs. How is the paradox to be resolved? If we consider an example the reason for this will become clear. Suppose A is buying a product from B and that both A and B could organise this marketing transaction at less than its present cost. B, we can assume, is not organising one process or stage of production, but several. If A therefore wishes to avoid a market transaction, he will have to take over all the processes of production controlled by B. Unless A takes over all the processes of production, a market transaction will still remain, although it is a different product that is bought. But we have previously assumed that as each producer expands he becomes less efficient; the additional costs of organising extra transactions increase. It is probable that A's cost of organising the transactions previously organised by B will be greater than B's cost of doing the same thing. A therefore will take over the whole of

B's organisation only if his cost of organising *B*'s work is not greater than *B*'s cost by an amount equal to the costs of carrying out an exchange transaction on the open market. But once it becomes economical to have a market transaction, it also pays to divide production in such a way that the cost of organising an extra transaction in each firm is the same.

Up to now it has been assumed that the exchange transactions which take place through the price mechanism are homogeneous. In fact, nothing could be more diverse than the actual transactions which take place in our modern world. This would seem to imply that the costs of carrying out exchange transactions through the price mechanism will vary considerably as will also the costs of organising these transactions within the firm. It seems therefore possible that quite apart from the question of diminishing returns the costs of organising certain transactions within the firm may be greater than the costs of carrying out the exchange transactions in the open market. This would necessarily imply that there were exchange transactions carried out through the price mechanism, but would it mean that there would have to be more than one firm? Clearly not, for all those areas in the economic system where the direction of resources was not dependent directly on the price mechanism could be organised within one firm. The factors which were discussed earlier would seem to be the important ones, though it is difficult to say whether "diminishing returns to management" or the rising supply price of factors is likely to be the more important.

Other things being equal, therefore, a firm will tend to be larger:

a.   the less the costs of organising and the slower these costs rise with an increase in the transactions organised.
b.   the less likely the entrepreneur is to make mistakes and the smaller the increase in mistakes with an increase in the transactions organised.
c.   the greater the lowering (or the less the rise) in the supply price of factors of production to firms of larger size.

Apart from variations in the supply price of factors of production to firms of different sizes, it would appear that the costs of organising and the losses through mistakes will increase with an increase in the spatial distribution of the transactions organised, in the dissimilarity of the transactions, and in the probability of changes in the relevant prices.[17] As more transactions are organised by an entrepreneur, it would appear that the transactions would tend to be either different in kind or in different places. This furnishes an additional reason why efficiency will tend to decrease as the firm gets larger. Inventions which tend to bring factors of production nearer together, by lessening spatial distribution, tend to increase the size of the firm.[18] Changes like the telephone and the telegraph which tend to reduce the cost of organising spatially will tend to increase the size of the firm. All changes which improve managerial technique will tend to increase the size of the firm.[19,20]

It should be noted that the definition of a firm which was given above can be used to give more precise meanings to the terms "combination" and "integration."[21] There is a combination when transactions which were previously organised by two or more entrepreneurs become organised by one. This becomes integration when it involves the organisation of transactions which were previously carried out between the entrepreneurs on a market. A firm can expand in either or both of these two ways. The whole of the "structure of competitive industry" becomes tractable by the ordinary technique of economic analysis.

III

The problem which has been investigated in the previous section has not been entirely neglected by economists and it is now necessary to consider why the reasons given above for the emergence of a firm in a specialised exchange economy are to be preferred to the other explanations which have been offered.

It is sometimes said that the reason for the existence of a firm is to be found in the division of labour. This is the view of Professor Usher, a view which has been adopted and expanded by Mr. Maurice Dobb. The firm becomes "the result of an increasing complexity of the division of labour. . . . The growth of this economic differentiation creates the need for some integrating force without which differentiation would collapse into chaos; and it is as the integrating force in a differentiated economy that industrial forms are chiefly significant" (Usher, 1920, pp. 1–18). The answer to this argument is an obvious one. The "integrating force in a differentiated economy" already exists in the form of the price mechanism. It is perhaps the main achievement of economic science that it has shown that there is no reason to suppose that specialisation must lead to chaos.[22] The reason given by Mr. Maurice Dobb is therefore inadmissable. What has to be explained is why one integrating force (the entrepreneur) should be substituted for another integrating force (the price mechanism).

The most interesting reasons (and probably the most widely accepted) which have been given to explain this fact are those to be found

in Professor Knight's ([1933] 1964) *Risk, Uncertainty and Profit*. His views
will be examined in some detail.

Professor Knight starts with a system in which there is no uncertainty:

> [A]cting as individuals under absolute freedom but
> without collusion men are supposed to have organised
> economic life with the primary and secondary division of
> labour, the use of capital, etc., developed to the point famil-
> iar in present-day America. The principal fact which calls
> for the exercise of the imagination is the internal organi-
> sation of the productive groups or establishments. With
> uncertainty entirely absent, every individual being in pos-
> session of perfect knowledge of the situation, there would
> be no occasion for anything of the nature of responsible
> management or control of productive activity. Even mar-
> keting transactions in any realistic sense would not be
> found. The flow of raw materials and productive services
> to the consumer would be entirely automatic ([1933] 1964,
> p. 267).

Professor Knight says that we can imagine this adjustment as being "the result of a long process of experimentation worked out by trial-
and-error methods alone," while it is not necessary "to imagine every
worker doing exactly the right thing at the right time in a sort of 'pre-
established harmony' with the work of others. There might be managers,
superintendents, etc., for the purpose of co-ordinating the activities of
individuals," though these managers would be performing a purely
routine function, "without responsibility of any sort" (pp. 267–268).

Professor Knight then continues:

> With the introduction of uncertainty—the fact of
> ignorance and the necessity of acting upon opinion rather
> than knowledge—into this Eden-like situation, its character
> is entirely changed. . . . With uncertainty present doing
> things, the actual execution of activity, becomes in a real
> sense a secondary part of life; the primary problem or func-
> tion is deciding what to do and how to do it (p. 268).

This fact of uncertainty brings about the two most important
characteristics of social organisation.

In the first place, goods are produced for a market, on the basis of entirely impersonal prediction of wants, not for the satisfaction of the wants of the producers themselves. The producer takes the responsibility of forecasting the consumers' wants. In the second place, the work of forecasting and at the same time a large part of the technological direction and control of production are still further concentrated upon a very narrow class of the producers, and we meet with a new economic functionary, the entrepreneur. . . . When uncertainty is present and the task of deciding what to do and how to do it takes the ascendancy over that of execution the internal organisation of the productive groups is no longer a matter of indifference or a mechanical detail. Centralisation of this deciding and controlling function is imperative, a process of 'cephalisation' is inevitable (pp. 268–295).

The most fundamental change is:

the system under which the confident and venturesome assume the risk or insure the doubtful and timid by guaranteeing to the latter a specified income in return for an assignment of the actual results. . . . With human nature as we know it it would be impracticable or very unusual for one man to guarantee to another a definite result of the latter's actions without being given power to direct his work. And on the other hand the second party would not place himself under the direction of the first without such a guarantee. . . . The result of this manifold specialisation of function is the enterprise and wage system of industry. Its existence in the world is the direct result of the fact of uncertainty (p. 270).

These quotations give the essence of Professor Knight's theory. The fact of uncertainty means that people have to forecast future wants. Therefore, you get a special class springing up who direct the activities of others to whom they give guaranteed wages. It acts because good judgment is generally associated with confidence in one's judgment (pp. 269–270).

Professor Knight would appear to leave himself open to criticism on several grounds. First of all, as he himself points out, the fact that certain people have better judgment or better knowledge does not mean that they can only get an income from it by themselves actively taking part in production. They can sell advice or knowledge. Every business buys the services of a host of advisers. We can imagine a system where all advice or knowledge was bought as required. Again, it is possible to get a reward from better knowledge or judgment not by actively taking part in production but by making contracts with people who are producing. A merchant buying for future delivery represents an example of this. But this merely illustrates the point that it is quite possible to give a guaranteed reward providing that certain acts are performed without directing the performance of those acts. Professor Knight says that "with human nature as we know it it would be impracticable or very unusual for one man to guarantee to another a definite result of the latter's actions without being given power to direct his work." This is surely incorrect. A large proportion of jobs are done to contract, that is, the contractor is guaranteed a certain sum providing he performs certain acts. But this does not involve any direction. It does mean, however, that the system of relative prices has been changed and that there will be a new arrangement of the factors of production.[23] The fact that Professor Knight mentions that the "second party would not place himself under the direction of the first without such a guarantee" is irrelevant to the problem we are considering. Finally, it seems important to notice that even in the case of an economic system where there is no uncertainty Professor Knight considers that there would be co-ordinators, though they would perform only a routine function. He immediately adds that they would be "without responsibility of any sort," which raises the question by whom are they paid and why? It seems that nowhere does Professor Knight give a reason why the price mechanism should be superseded.

IV

It would seem important to examine one further point and that is to consider the relevance of this discussion to the general question of the "cost-curve of the firm."

It has sometimes been assumed that a firm is limited in size under perfect competition if its cost curve slopes upward (Kaldor, 1934; Robinson, 1933), while under imperfect competition, it is limited in size because it will not pay to produce more than the output at which marginal cost is equal to marginal revenue.[24] But it is clear that a firm may produce more than one product and, therefore, there appears to be no *prima facie* reason why this upward slope of the cost curve in the case of perfect competition or the fact that marginal cost will not always be below marginal revenue in the case of imperfect competition should limit the size of the firm.[25] Mrs. Robinson (1933) makes the simplifying assumption that only one product is being produced. But it is clearly important to investigate how the number of products produced by a firm is determined, while no theory which assumes that only one product is in fact produced can have very great practical significance.

It might be replied that under perfect competition, since everything that is produced can be sold at the prevailing price, then there is no need for any other product to be produced. But this argument ignores the fact that there may be a point where it is less costly to organise the exchange transactions of a new product than to organise further exchange transactions of the old product. This point can be illustrated in the following way. Imagine, following von Thunen, that there is a town, the consuming centre, and that industries are located around this central point in rings. These conditions are illustrated in the following diagram in which A, B and C represent different industries.

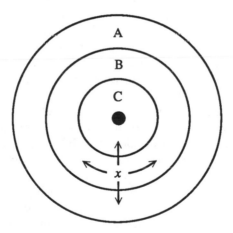

Imagine an entrepreneur who starts controlling exchange transactions from x. Now as he extends his activities in the same product (B), the cost of organising increases until at some point it becomes equal to that of a dissimilar product which is nearer. As the firm expands, it will therefore from this point include more than one product (A and C). This treatment of the problem is obviously incomplete,[26] but it is necessary to show that merely proving that the cost curve turns upwards does not give a limitation to the size of the firm. So far we have only considered the case of perfect competition; the case of imperfect competition would appear to be obvious.

To determine the size of the firm, we have to consider the marketing costs (that is, the costs of using the *rice* mechanism), and the costs of organising of different entrepreneurs and then we can determine how many products will be produced by each firm and how much of each it will produce. It would, therefore, appear that Mr.Shove[27] in his article on "Imperfect Competition" was asking questions which Mrs. Robinson's cost curve apparatus cannot answer. The factors mentioned above would seem to be the relevant ones.

V

Only one task now remains; and that is, to see whether the concept of a firm which has been developed fits in with that existing in the real world. We can best approach the question of what constitutes a firm in practice by considering the legal relationship normally called that of "master and servant" or "employer and employee."[28] The essentials of this relationship have been given as follows:

> (1) the servant must be under the duty of rendering personal services to the master or to others on behalf of the master, otherwise the contract is a contract for sale of goods or the like.
> (2) The master must have the right to control the servant's work, either personally or by another servant or agent. It is this right of control or interference, of being entitled to tell the servant when to work (within the hours of service) and when not to work, and what work to do and how to do it (within the terms of such service) which is the dominant characteristic in this relation and marks off the servant from an independent contractor, or from one employed merely to give to his employer the fruits of his labour. In the latter case, the contractor or performer is not under the employer's control in doing the work or effecting the service; he has to shape and manage his work so as to give the result he has contracted to effect (Batt, 1929, p. 6).

We thus see that it is the fact of direction which is the essence of the legal concept of "employer and employee," just as it was in the economic concept which was developed above. It is interesting to note that Professor Batt says further:

> That which distinguishes an agent from a servant is not the absence or presence of a fixed wage or the payment only of commission on business done, but rather the freedom with which an agent may carry out his employment (1929, p. 7).

We can therefore conclude that the definition we have given is one which approximates closely to the firm as it is considered in the real world.

Our definition is, therefore, realistic. Is it manageable? This ought to be clear. When we are considering how large a firm will be the principle of marginalism works smoothly. The question always is, will it pay to bring an extra exchange transaction under the organising authority? At the margin, the costs of organising within the firm will be equal either to the costs of organising in another firm or to the costs involved in leaving the transaction to be "organised" by the price mechanism. Business men will be constantly experimenting, controlling more or less, and in this way, equilibrium will be maintained. This gives the position of equilibrium for static analysis. But it is clear that the dynamic factors are also of considerable importance, and an investigation of the effect changes have on the cost of organising within the firm and on marketing costs generally will enable one to explain why firms get larger and smaller. We thus have a theory of moving equilibrium. The above analysis would also appear to have clarified the relationship between initiative or enterprise and management. Initiative means forecasting and operates through the price mechanism by the making of new contracts. Management proper merely reacts to price changes, rearranging the factors of production under its control. That the business man normally combines both functions is an obvious result of the marketing costs which were discussed above. Finally, this analysis enables us to state more exactly what is meant by the "marginal product" of the entrepreneur. But an elaboration of this point would take us far from our comparatively simple task of definition and clarification.

Notes

1. This description is quoted with approval by Robertson (1936, p. 85) and by Plant (1932).

2. In the rest of this paper I shall use the term entrepreneur to refer to the person

or persons who, in a competitive system, take the place of the price mechanism in the direction of resources.

3. It is easy to see when the State takes over the direction of an industry that, in planning it, it is doing something which was previously done by the price mechanism. What is usually not realised is that any business man in organising the relations between his departments is also doing something which could be organised through the price mechanism. There is therefore point in Mr. Durbin's answer to those who emphasise the problems involved in economic planning that the same problems have to be solved by business men in the competitive system. (See Durbin, 1936.) The important difference between these two cases is that economic planning is imposed on industry while firms arise voluntarily because they represent a more efficient method of organising production. In a competitive system, there is an "optimum" amount of planning!

4. See Dawes (1934, p. 86) who instances "the trek to retail shopkeeping and insurance work by the better paid of skilled men due to the desire (often the main aim in life of a worker) to be independent."

5. None the less, this is not altogether fanciful. Some small shopkeepers are said to earn less than their assistants.

6. Shove (1933, p. 116) points out that such preferences may exist, although the example he gives is almost the reverse of the instance given in the text.

7. According to Kaldor (1934), it is one of the assumptions of static theory that "All the relevant prices are known to all individuals." But this is clearly not true of the real world.

8. This influence was noted by Usher (1920, p. 13) when discussing the development of capitalism. He says: "The successive buying and selling of partly finished products were sheer waste of energy." But he does not develop the idea nor consider why it is that buying and selling operations still exist.

9. It would be possible for no limits to the powers of the entrepreneur to be fixed. This would be voluntary slavery. According to Batt (1929, p. 18) such a contract would be void and unenforceable.

10. Of course, it is not possible to draw a hard and fast line which determines whether there is a firm or not. There may be more or less direction. It is similar to the legal question of whether there is the relationship of master and servant or principal and agent. See the discussion of this problem below.

11. The views of Knight are examined below in more detail.

12. There are certain marketing costs which could only be eliminated by the abolition of "consumers' choice" and these are the costs of retailing. It is conceivable that these costs might be so high that people would be willing to accept rations because the extra product obtained was worth the loss of their choice.

13. This argument assumes that exchange transactions on a market can be considered as homogeneous; which is clearly untrue in fact. This complication is taken into account below.

14. For a discussion of the variation of the supply price of factors of production to firms of varying size, see Robinson (1932). It is sometimes said that the supply price of organising ability increases as the size of the firm increases because men prefer to be the heads of small independent businesses rather than the heads of departments in a large business. See Jones (1921, p. 531) and Macgregor (1906, p. 63). This is a common argument of those who advocate Rationalisation. It is said that larger units would be more efficient, but owing to the individualistic spirit of the smaller entrepreneurs, they prefer to remain independent, apparently in spite of the higher income which their increased efficiency under Rationalisation makes possible.

15. This discussion is, of course, brief and incomplete. For a more thorough discussion of this particular problem, see Kaldor (1934) and Robinson (1934).

16. A definition of this term is given below. [See note 21.]

17. This aspect of the problem is emphasized by Kaldor (1934). Its importance in this connection had been previously noted by Robinson (1932, pp. 83–106). This assumes that an increase in the probability of price movements increases the costs of organising within a firm more than it increases the cost of carrying out an exchange transaction on the market—which is probable.

18. This would appear to be the importance of the treatment of the technical unit by Robinson (1932, pp. 27–33). The larger the technical unit, the greater the concentration of factors and therefore the firm is likely to be larger.

19. It should be noted that most inventions will change both the costs of organising and the costs of using the price mechanism. In such cases, whether the invention tends to make firms larger or smaller will depend on the relative effect on these two sets of costs. For instance, if the telephone reduces the costs of using the price mechanism more than it reduces the costs of organising, then it will have the effect of reducing the size of the firm.

20. An illustration of these dynamic forces is furnished by Dobb (1926, p. 68): "With the passing of bonded labour the factory, as an establishment where work was organised under the whip of the overseer, lost its *raison d'être* until this was restored to it with the introduction of power machinery after 1846." It seems important to realise that the passage from the domestic system to the factory system is not a mere historical accident, but is conditioned by economic forces. This is shown by the fact that it is possible to move from the factory system to the domestic system, as in the Russian example, as well as *vice versa*. It is the essence of serfdom that the price mechanism is not allowed to operate. Therefore, there has to be direction from some organiser. When, however, serfdom passed, the price mechanism was allowed to operate. It was not until machinery drew workers into one locality that it paid to supersede the price mechanism and the firm again emerged.

21. This is often called "vertical integration," combination being termed "lateral integration."

22. See Clark (1899, p. 19) who speaks of the theory of exchange as being the "theory of the organisation of industrial society."

23. This shows that it is possible to have a private enterprise system without the existence of firms. Though, in practice, the two functions of enterprise, which actually influences the system of relative prices by forecasting wants and acting in accordance with such forecasts, and management, which accepts the system of relative prices as being given, are normally carried out by the same persons, yet it seems important to keep them separate in theory. This point is futher discussed below.

24. Robinson (1933) calls this the Imperfect Competition solution for the survival of the small firm.

25. Robinson's (1933, p. 249) conclusion would appear to be definitely wrong. He is followed by White (1936, p. 645). White states, "It is obvious that the size of the firm is limited in conditions of monopolistic competition."

26. As has been shown above, location is only one of the factors influencing the cost of organising.

27. In connection with an increase in demand in the suburbs and the effect on the price charged by suppliers, Shove (1933, p. 115) asks " . . . why do not the old firms open branches in the suburbs?" If the argument in the text is correct, this is a question which Mrs. Robinson's apparatus cannot answer.

28. The legal concept of "employer and employee" and the economic concept of a firm are not identical, in that the firm may imply control over another person's property as well as over their labour. But the identity of these two concepts is sufficiently close for an examination of the legal concept to be of value in appraising the worth of the economic concept.

Transaction-Cost Economics: The Governance of Contractual Relations

Oliver E. Williamson

The new institutional economics is preoccupied with the origins, incidence, and ramifications of transaction costs. Indeed, if transaction

Note: This paper has benefited from support from the Center for Advanced Study in the Behavioral Sciences, the Guggenheim Foundation, and the National Science Foundation. Helpful comments by Yoram Ben-Porath, Richard Nelson, Douglass North, Thomas Palay, Joseph Sax, David Teece, and Peter Temin and from the participants at seminars at the Yale Law School and the Institute for Advanced Study at Princeton are gratefully acknowledged. The paper was rewritten costs are negligible, the organization of economic activity is irrelevant, since any advantages one mode of organization appears to hold over another will simply be eliminated by costless contracting. But despite the growing realization that transaction costs are central to the study of economics,[1] skeptics remain. Stanley Fischer's complaint is typical: "Transaction costs have a well-deserved bad name as a theoretical device . . . [partly] because there is a suspicion that almost anything can be rationalized by invoking suitably specified transaction costs" (Fischer, 1977, p. 322). Put differently, there are too many degrees of freedom; the concept wants for definition.

Among the factors on which there appears to be developing a general consensus are: (1) opportunism is a central concept in the study of transaction costs;[2] (2) opportunism is especially important for economic activity that involves transaction-specific investments in human and physical capital;[3] (3) the efficient processing of information is an important and related concept;[4] and (4) the assessment of transaction costs is a comparative institutional undertaking (Dahlman, 1979). Beyond these general propositions, a consensus on transaction costs is lacking.

Further progress in the study of transaction costs awaits the identification of the critical dimensions with respect to which transaction costs differ and an examination of the economizing properties of alternative institutional modes for organizing transactions. Only then can the matching of transactions with modes be accomplished with confidence. This paper affirms the proposition that transaction costs are central to the study of economics, identifies the critical dimensions for characterizing transactions, describes the main governance structures of transactions, and indicates how and why transactions can be matched with institutions in a discriminating way.

I am mainly concerned with intermediate-product market transactions. Whereas previously I have emphasized the incentives to remove transactions from the market and organize them internally (vertical integration), the analysis here is symmetrical and deals with market, hier-

---

to advantage after reading Ben-Porath's discussion paper, "The F-Connection: Family, Friends, and Firms and the Organization of Exchange," and Temin's discussion paper, "Modes of Economic Behavior: Variations on Themes of J. R. Hicks and Herbert Simon."

archical, and intermediate modes of organization alike. The question of why there is so much vertical integration remains interesting, but no more so than the question of why there are so many market- (and quasi-market) mediated transactions. A discriminating analysis will explain which transactions are located where and give the reasons why. The overall object of the exercise essentially comes down to this: for each abstract description of a transaction, identify the most economical governance structure—where by governance structure I refer to the institutional framework within which the integrity of a transaction is decided. Markets and hierarchies are two of the main alternatives.

Some legal background to the study of transactions is briefly reviewed in Section I. Of the three dimensions for describing transactions that I propose, investment attributes are the least well understood and probably the most important. The special relevance of investments is developed in the context of the economics of idiosyncrasy in Section II. A general contracting schema is developed and applied to commercial contracting in Section III. Applications to labor, regulation, family transactions, and capital markets are sketched in Section IV. Major implications are summarized in Section V. Concluding remarks follow.

I. Some Contracting Background

Although there is widespread agreement that the discrete-transaction paradigm—"sharp in by clear agreement; sharp out by clear performance" (Macneil, 1974)—has served both law and economics well, there is increasing awareness that many contractual relations are not of this well-defined kind.[5] A deeper understanding of the nature of contract has emerged as the legal-rule emphasis associated with the study of discrete contracting has given way to a more general concern with the contractual purposes to be served.[6]

Ian Macneil, in a series of thoughtful and wide-ranging essays on contract, usefully distinguishes between discrete and relational transactions.[7] He further supplies twelve different "concepts" with respect to which these differ (1978, pp. 902–905; 1974, pp. 738–740). Serious problems of recognition and application are posed by such a rich classificatory apparatus. More useful for my purposes is the three-way classification of contracts that Macneil offers in his most recent article, where classical, neoclassical, and relational categories of contract law are recognized.

A. Classical Contract Law

As Macneil observes, any system of contract law has the purpose of facilitating exchange. What is distinctive about classical contract law is that it attempts to do this by enhancing discreteness and intensifying "presentiation" (1978, p. 862), where presentiation has reference to efforts to "make or render present in place or time; to cause to be perceived or realized at present" (1978, p. 863). The economic counterpart to complete presentiation is contingent-claims contracting—which entails comprehensive contracting whereby all relevant future contingencies pertaining to the supply of a good or service are described and discounted with respect to both likelihood and futurity.[8]

Classical contract law endeavors to implement discreteness and presentiation in several ways. For one thing, the identity of the parties to a transaction is treated as irrelevant. In this respect it corresponds exactly with the "ideal" market transaction in economics.[9] Second, the nature of the agreement is carefully delimited, and the more formal features govern when formal (for example, written) and informal (for example, oral) terms are contested. Third, remedies are narrowly prescribed such that, "should the initial presentiation fail to materialize because of nonperformance, the consequences are relatively predictable from the beginning and are not open-ended" (Macneil, 1978, p. 864). Additionally, third-party participation is discouraged (Macneil, 1978, p. 864). The emphasis, thus, is on legal rules, formal documents, and self-liquidating transactions.

B. Neoclassical Contract Law

Not every transaction fits comfortably into the classical-contracting scheme. In particular, long-term contracts executed under conditions of uncertainty are ones for which complete presentiation is apt to be prohibitively costly if not impossible. Problems of several kinds arise. First, not all future contingencies for which adaptations are required can be anticipated at the outset. Second, the appropriate adaptations will not be evident for many contingencies until the circumstances materialize. Third, except as changes in states of the world are unambiguous, hard contracting between autonomous parties may well give rise to veridical disputes when state-contingent claims are made. In a world where (at least some) parties are inclined to be opportunistic, whose representations are to be believed?

Faced with the prospective breakdown of classical contracting in these circumstances, three alternatives are available. One would be to forgo such transactions altogether. A second would be to remove these transactions from the market and organize them internally instead. Adaptive, sequential decision making would then be implemented under common ownership and with the assistance of hierarchical incentive and control systems. Third, a different contracting relation which preserves trading but provides for additional governance structure might be devised. This last brings us to what Macneil refers to as neoclassical contracting.

As Macneil observes, ''Two common characteristics of long-term contracts are the existence of gaps in their planning and the presence of a range of processes and techniques used by contract planners to create flexibility in lieu of either leaving gaps or trying to plan rigidly'' (1978, p. 865). Third-party assistance in resolving disputes and evaluating performance often has advantages over litigation in serving these functions of flexibility and gap filling. Lon Fuller's remarks on procedural differences between arbitration and litigation are instructive:

> . . . there are open to the arbitrator . . . quick methods of education not open to the courts. An arbitrator will frequently interrupt the examination of witnesses with a request that the parties educate him to the point where he can understand the testimony being received. This education can proceed informally, with frequent interruptions by the arbitrator, and by informed persons on either side, when a point needs clarification. Sometimes there will be arguments across the table, occasionally even within each of the separate camps. The end result will usually be a clarification that will enable everyone to proceed more intelligently with the case. There is in this informal procedure no infringement whatever of arbitrational due process (1963, pp. 11–12).

A recognition that the world is complex, that agreements are incomplete, and that some contracts will never be reached unless both parties have confidence in the settlement machinery thus characterizes neoclassical contract law. One important purposive difference in arbitration and litigation that contributes to the procedural differences described by Fuller is that, whereas continuity (at least completion of the contract) is presumed under the arbitration machinery, this presumption is much weaker when litigation is employed.[10]

C. Relational Contracting

The pressures to sustain ongoing relations "have led to the spin-off of many subject areas from the classical, and later the neoclassical, contract law system, e.g., much of corporate law and collective bargaining" (Macneil, 1978, p. 885). Thus, progressively increasing the "duration and complexity" of contract has resulted in the displacement of even neoclassical adjustment processes by adjustment processes of a more thoroughly transaction-specific, ongoing-administrative kind (Macneil, 1978, p. 901). The fiction of discreteness is fully displaced as the relation takes on the properties of "a minisociety with a vast array of norms beyond those centered on the exchange and its immediate processes" (Macneil, 1978, p. 901). By contrast with the neoclassical system, where the reference point for effecting adaptations remains the original agreement, the reference point under a truly relational approach is the "entire relation as it has developed . . . [through] time. This may or may not include an 'original agreement'; and if it does, may or may not result in great deference being given it" (Macneil, 1978, p. 890).

II. The Economics of Idiosyncrasy

Macneil's three-way discussion of contracts discloses that contracts are a good deal more varied and complex than is commonly realized.[11] It furthermore suggests that governance structures—the institutional matrix within which transactions are negotiated and executed—vary with the nature of the transaction. But the critical dimensions of contract are not expressly identified, and the purposes of governance are not stated. Harmonizing interests that would otherwise give way to antagonistic subgoal pursuits appears to be an important governance function, but this is not explicit in his discussion.

That simple governance structures should be used in conjunction with simple contractual relations and complex governance structures reserved for complex relations seems generally sensible. Use of a complex structure to govern a simple relation is apt to incur unneeded costs, and use of a simple structure for a complex transaction invites strain. But what is simple and complex in contractual respects? Specific attention to the defining attributes of transactions is evidently needed.

As developed in Section III, the three critical dimensions for characterizing transactions are (1) uncertainty, (2) the frequency with which transactions recur, and (3) the degree to which durable transaction-specific investments are incurred. Of these three, uncertainty is widely conceded to be a critical attribute;[12] and that frequency matters is at least plausible (Whinston, 1978). The governance ramifications of neither, however, have been fully developed—nor can they be until joined with the third critical dimension: transaction-specific investments. Inasmuch as a considerable amount of the "action" in the study of governance is attributable to investment differences, some explication is needed.

A. General

The crucial investment distinction is this: to what degree are transaction-specific (nonmarketable) expenses incurred. Items that are unspecialized among users pose few hazards, since buyers in these circumstances can easily turn to alternative sources, and suppliers can sell output intended for one order to other buyers without difficulty.[13] Nonmarketability problems arise when the *specific identity* of the parties has important cost-bearing consequences. Transactions of this kind will be referred to as idiosyncratic.

Occasionally the identity of the parties is important from the outset, as when a buyer induces a supplier to invest in specialized physical capital of a transaction-specific kind. Inasmuch as the value of this capital in other uses is, by definition, much smaller than the specialized use for which it has been intended, the supplier is effectively "locked into" the transaction to a significant degree. This is symmetrical, moreover, in that the buyer cannot turn to alternative sources of supply and obtain the item on favorable terms, since the cost of supply from unspecialized capital is presumably great.[14] The buyer is thus committed to the transaction as well.

Ordinarily, however, there is more to idiosyncratic exchange than specialized physical capital. Human-capital investments that are transaction-specific commonly occur as well. Specialized training and learning-by-doing economies in production operations are illustrations. Except when these investments are transferable to alternative suppliers at low cost, which is rare, the benefits of the set-up costs can be realized only so long as the relationship between the buyer and seller of the intermediate product is maintained.

Additional transaction-specific savings can accrue at the interface between supplier and buyer as contracts are successively adapted to unfolding events, and as periodic contract-renewal agreements are reached. Familiarity here permits communication economies to be realized: specialized language develops as experience accumulates and nuances are signaled and received in a sensitive way. Both institutional and personal trust relations evolve. Thus the individuals who are responsible for adapting the interfaces have a personal as well as an organizational stake in what transpires. Where personal integrity is believed to be operative, individuals located at the interfaces may refuse to be a part of opportunistic efforts to take advantage of (rely on) the letter of the contract when the spirit of the exchange is emasculated. Such refusals can serve as a check upon organizational proclivities to behave opportunistically.[15] Other things being equal, idiosyncratic exchange relations which feature personal trust will survive greater stress and display greater adaptability.

Idiosyncratic goods and services are thus ones where investments of transaction-specific human and physical capital are made and, contingent upon successful execution, benefits are realized. Such investments can and do occur in conjunction with occasional trades where delivery for a specialized design is stretched out over a long period (for example, certain construction contracts). The transactions that I wish to emphasize here, however, are exchanges of the recurring kind. Although large-numbers competition is frequently feasible at the initial award stage for recurring contracts of all kinds, idiosyncratic transactions are ones for which the relationship between buyer and supplier is quickly thereafter *transformed* into one of bilateral monopoly—on account of the transaction-specific costs referred to above. This transformation has profound contracting consequences.

Thus, whereas recurrent spot contracting is feasible for standardized transactions (because large-numbers competition is continuously self-policing in these circumstances), such contracting has seriously defective investment incentives where idiosyncratic activities are involved. By assumption, cost economies in production will be realized for idiosyncratic activities only if the supplier invests in a special-purpose plant and equipment or if his labor force develops transaction-specific skills in the course of contract execution (or both). The assurance of a continuing relation is needed to encourage investments of both kinds. Although the requisite incentives might be provided if long-term contracts were negotiated, such contracts are necessarily incomplete (by reason of bounded rationality). Appropriate state-contingent adaptations thus go unspecified. Intertemporal efficiency nevertheless requires that adaptations to changing market circumstances be made.

How to effect these adaptations poses a serious contracting dilemma, though it bears repeating that, absent the hazards of opportunism, the difficulties would vanish—since then the gaps in long-term, incomplete contracts could be faultlessly filled in an adaptive, sequential way. A general clause, to which both parties would agree, to the effect that "I will behave responsibly rather than seek individual advantage when an occasion to adapt arises," would, in the absence of opportunism, suffice. Given, however, the unenforceability of general clauses and the proclivity of human agents to make false and misleading (self-disbelieved) statements, the following hazard must be confronted: joined as they are in an idiosyncratic condition of bilateral monopoly, both buyer and seller are strategically situated to bargain over the disposition of any incremental gain whenever a proposal to adapt is made by the other party. Although both have a long-term interest in effecting adaptations of a joint profit-maximizing kind, each also has an interest in appropriating as much of the gain as he can on each occasion to adapt. Efficient adaptations which would otherwise be made thus result in costly haggling or even go unmentioned, lest the gains be dissipated by costly subgoal pursuit. Governance structures which attenuate opportunism and otherwise infuse confidence are evidently needed.

B. Examples

Some illustrations may help to motivate what is involved in idiosyncratic transactions. Specialized physical capital is relatively straightforward. Examples are (1) the purchase of a specialized component from an outside supplier or (2) the location of a specialized plant in a unique, proximate relation to a downstream processing stage to which it supplies vital input.

Thus assume (a) that special-purpose equipment is needed to produce the component in question (which is to say that the value of the equipment in its next-best alternative use is much lower), (b) that scale economies require that a significant, discrete investment be made, and (c) that alternative buyers for such components are few (possibly because of the organization of the industry, possibly because of special-design features). The interests of buyer and seller in a continuing exchange relation are plainly strong under these circumstances.

Plant-proximity benefits are attributable to transportation and related flow-process (inventory, thermal economy, and so on) economies. A specialized plant need not be implied, but long life and a unique location are. Once made, the investment preempts the unique location and is not thereafter moveable (except at prohibitive cost). Buyer and supplier again need to satisfy themselves that they have a workable, adaptable exchange agreement.[16]

Idiosyncratic investments in human capital are in many ways more interesting and less obvious than are those in physical capital. Polanyi's (1962) discussion of "personal knowledge" is illuminating:

> The attempt to analyze scientifically the established industrial arts has everywhere led to similar results. Indeed even in the modern industries the indefinable knowledge is still an essential part of technology. I have myself watched in Hungary a new, imported machine for blowing electric lamp bulbs, the exact counterpart of which was operating successfully in Germany, failing for a whole year to produce a single flawless bulb.

And he goes on to observe with respect to craftsmanship that:

> . . . an art which has fallen into disuse for the period of a generation is altogether lost. . . . It is pathetic to watch the endless efforts—equipped with microscopy and chemistry, with mathematics and electronics—to reproduce a single violin of the kind the half-literate Stradivarius turned out as a matter of routine more than 200 years ago (Polanyi, 1962, p. 53).

Polanyi's discussion of language also has a bearing on the argument advanced above that specialized code words or expressions can and do arise in the context of recurring transactions and that these yield economies. As he puts it, "Different vocabularies for the interpretation of things divide men into groups which cannot understand each other's way of seeing things and acting upon them" (1962, p. 112). And subsequently he remarks that:

> To know a language is an art, carried on by tacit judgments and the practice of unspecifiable skills. . . . Spoken communication is the successful application by two persons of the linguistic knowledge and skill acquired by such apprenticeship, one person wishing to transmit, the other to receive, information. Relying on what each has learnt, the speaker confidently utters words and the listener confidently interprets them, while they mutually rely on each other's correct use and understanding of these words. A true communication will take place if, and only if, these combined assumptions of authority and trust are in fact justified (1962, p. 206).

Babbage reports a remarkable example of transaction-specific value in exchange that occurred in the early 1800s. Although he attributes the continuing exchange in the face of adversity to values of "established character" (trust), I believe there were other specialized human and physical investments involved as well. In any event, the circumstance which he describes is the following:

> The influence of established character in producing confidence operated in a very remarkable manner at the time of the exclusion of British manufactures from the Continent during the last war. One of our largest establishments had been in the habit of doing extensive business with a house in the centre of Germany; but, on the closing of the continental ports against our manufacturers, heavy penalties were inflicted on all those who contravened the Berlin and Milan decrees. The English manufacturer continued, nevertheless, to receive orders, with directions how to consign them, and appointments for the time and mode of payment, in letters, the handwriting of which was known to him, but which were never signed, except by the Christian name of one of the firm, and even in some instances they were without any signature at all. These orders were executed; and in no instance was there the least irregularity in the payments (1832, pp. 220–221).

While most of these illustrations refer to technical and commercial transactions, other types of transactions also have an idiosyncratic quality. Justice Rehnquist (1978, p. 19) refers to some of these when speaking of the general class of cases where "the litigation of an individual's claim of deprivation of a right would bring parties *who must remain in a continuing relationship* into the adversarial atmosphere of a courtroom"[17]—which atmosphere he plainly regards as detrimental to the quality of the relationship. Examples that he offers include reluctance to have the courts mediate collective bargaining disputes (1978, pp. 11–13) and to allow children to bring suit against parents (1978, pp. 16–19).

But surely we must ask what is distinctive about these transactions. I submit that transaction-specific human capital is central to each. Why else would it take the Hungarians so long to operate the German light-bulb machine? And what else explains the loss of Stradivarius's craftsmanship? Likewise the understanding and trust which evolve between Babbage's transmitter and receiver are valued human assets which, once developed, will be sacrificed with reluctance. And the disruption of continuing relationships to which Justice Rehnquist refers occasions concern precisely because there are no adequate substitutes for these idiosyncratic relations.[18]

The general argument of this paper is that special governance structures supplant standard market-cum-classical contract exchange when transaction-specific values are great. Idiosyncratic commercial, labor, and family relationships are specific examples.

III. Commercial Contracting

The discussion of commercial contracting begins with a brief statement on economizing. The proposed schema for characterizing transactions and their governance is then developed, including the relation of the schema with Macneil's three-way classification of contract.

A. Economizing

The criterion for organizing commercial transactions is assumed to be the strictly instrumental one of cost economizing. Essentially this takes two parts: economizing on production expense and economizing on transaction costs.[19] To the degree that transaction costs are negligible, buying rather than making will normally be the most cost-effective means of procurement.[20] Not only can static scale economies be more fully exhausted by buying rather than making, but the supplier who aggregates uncorrelated demands can realize collective pooling benefits as well. Since external procurement avoids many of the bureaucratic hazards of internal procurement (which hazards, however, are themselves of a transaction-cost kind) (Williamson, 1975, pp. 117–131), external procurement is evidently warranted.[21]

As indicated, however, the object is to economize on the *sum* of production and transaction costs. To the degree production-cost economies of external procurement are small and/or the transaction costs associated with external procurement are great, alternative supply arrangements deserve serious consideration. Economizing on transaction costs essentially reduces to economizing on bounded rationality while simultaneously safeguarding the transactions in question against the hazards of opportunism. Holding the governance structure constant, these two objectives are in tension, since a reduction in one commonly results in an increase in the other.[22]

Governance structures, however, are properly regarded as part of the optimization problem. For some transactions, a shift from one structure to another may permit a simultaneous reduction in both the expense of writing a complex contract (which economizes on bounded rationality) and the expense of executing it effectively in an adaptive, sequential way (by attenuating opportunism). Indeed, this is precisely the attraction of internal procurement for transactions of a recurrent, idiosyncratic kind. Not only are market-aggregation economies negligible for such transactions—since the requisite investments are transaction-specific—but market trading in these circumstances is shot through with appropriable quasi-rent hazards. The issues here have been developed elsewhere.[23] The object of this paper is to integrate them into a larger contractual framework.

Note in this connection that the prospect of recovering the set-up costs associated with specialized governance structures varies with the frequency with which transactions recur. Specialized governance structures are much easier to justify for recurrent transactions than for identical transactions that occur only occasionally.

B. *Characterizing Transactions*

I asserted earlier that the critical dimensions for describing contractual relations are uncertainty, the frequency with which transactions recur, and the degree to which investments are idiosyncratic. To simplify the exposition, I will assume uncertainty exists in some intermediate degree and focus initially on frequency and the degree to which the expenses incurred are transaction-specific. The separate importance of uncertainty will then be developed in Section III.D. Three frequency and three investment categories will be recognized. Frequency can be characterized as one-time, occasional, and recurrent; and investments are classed as nonspecific, mixed, and idiosyncratic. To further simplify the argument, the following assumptions are made: (1) Suppliers intend to be in business on a continuing basis; thus the special hazards posed by fly-by-night firms can be disregarded. (2) Potential suppliers for any given requirement are numerous—which is to say that *ex ante* monopoly in ownership of specialized resources is assumed away. (3) The frequency dimension refers strictly to buyer activity in the market.[24] The investment dimension refers to the characteristics of investments made by suppliers.[25]

Although discrete transactions are intriguing—for example, purchasing local spirits from a shopkeeper in a remote area of a foreign

country to which one never again expects to visit nor to refer his friends—
few transactions have this totally isolated character. For those who do
not, the difference between one-time and occasional transactions is not
apparent. Accordingly, only occasional and recurrent frequency distinctions will be maintained. The two-by-three matrix shown in Figure 1
thus describes the six types of transactions to which governance structures need to be matched. Illustrative transactions appear in the cells.

Figure 1. Illustrative Commercial Transactions.

		Investment Characteristics		
		Nonspecific	Mixed	Idiosyncratic
Frequency	Occasional	Purchasing standard equipment	Purchasing customized equipment	Constructing a plant
	Recurrent	Purchasing standard material	Purchasing customized material	Site-specific transfer of intermediate product across successive stages

C. Governance Structures

Three broad types of governance structures will be considered:
nontransaction-specific, semi-specific, and highly specific. The market
is the classic nonspecific governance structure within which "faceless
buyers and sellers . . . meet . . . for an instant to exchange standardized
goods at equilibrium prices" (Ben-Porath, 1978, p. 7). By contrast, highly
specific structures are tailored to the special needs of the transaction.
Identity here clearly matters. Semi-specific structures, naturally, fall in
between. Several propositions are suggested immediately. (1) Highly standardized transactions are not apt to require specialized governance structure. (2) Only recurrent transactions will support a highly specialized
governance structure.[26] (3) Although occasional transactions of a nonstandardized kind will not support a transaction-specific governance struc-

ture, they require special attention nonetheless. In terms of Macneil's three-way classification of contract, classical contracting presumably applies to all standardized transactions (whatever the frequency), relational contracting develops for transactions of a recurring and nonstandardized kind, and neoclassical contracting is needed for occasional, nonstandardized transactions.

1. Market Governance: Classical Contracting. Market governance is the main governance structure for nonspecific transactions of both occasional and recurrent contracting. Markets are especially efficacious when recurrent transactions are contemplated, since both parties need only consult their own experience in deciding to continue a trading relationship, or, at little transitional expense, turn elsewhere. Being standardized, alternative purchase and supply arrangements are presumably easy to work out.

Nonspecific but occasional transactions are ones for which buyers (and sellers) are less able to rely on direct experience to safeguard transactions against opportunism. Often, however, rating services or the experience of other buyers of the same good can be consulted. Given that the good or service is of a standardized kind, such experience rating, by formal and informal means, will provide incentives for parties to behave responsibly.

To be sure, such transactions take place within and benefit from a legal framework. But such dependence is not great. As S. Todd Lowry puts it, "the traditional economic analysis of exchange in a market setting properly corresponds to the legal concept of *sale* (rather than contract), since sale presumes arrangements in a market context and requires legal support primarily in enforcing transfers of title" (1976, p. 12). He would thus reserve the concept of contract for exchanges where, in the absence of standardized market alternatives, the parties have designed "patterns of future relations on which they could rely" (Lowry, 1976, p. 13).

The assumptions of the discrete-contracting paradigm are rather well satisfied for transactions where markets serve as a main governance mode. Thus the specific identity of the parties is of negligible importance; substantive content is determined by reference to formal terms of the contract; and legal rules apply. Market alternatives are mainly what protect each party against opportunism by his opposite.[27] Litigation is strictly for settling claims; concentrated efforts to sustain the relation are not made because the relation is not independently valued.[28]

2. Trilateral Governance: Neoclassical Contracting. The two types of transactions for which trilateral governance is needed are occasional transactions of the mixed and highly idiosyncratic kinds. Once the principals to such transactions have entered into a contract, there are strong incentives to see the contract through to completion. Not only have specialized investments been put in place, the opportunity cost of which is much lower in alternative uses, but the transfer of these assets to a successor supplier would pose inordinate difficulties in asset valuation.[29] The interests of the principals in sustaining the relation are especially great for highly idiosyncratic transactions.

Market relief is thus unsatisfactory. Often the setup costs of a transaction-specific governance structure cannot be recovered for occasional transactions. Given the limits of classical contract law for sustaining these transactions, on the one hand, and the prohibitive cost of transaction-specific (bilateral) governance, on the other, an intermediate institutional form is evidently needed.

Neoclassical contract law has many of the sought-after qualities. Thus rather than resorting immediately to strict reliance on litigation—with its transaction-rupturing features—*third-party assistance* (arbitration) in resolving disputes and evaluating performance is employed instead. (The use of the architect as a relatively independent expert to determine the content of form construction contracts is an example) (Macneil, 1978, p. 866). Also, the expansion of the specific-performance remedy in past decades is consistent with continuity purposes—though Macneil declines to characterize specific performance as the "primary neoclassical contract remedy" (Macneil, 1978, p. 879). The section of the Uniform Commercial Code which permits the "seller aggrieved by a buyer's breach . . . unilaterally to maintain the relation" (Macneil, 1978, p. 880)[30] is yet another example.

3. Transaction-Specific Governance: Relational Contracting. The two types of transactions for which specialized governance structures are commonly devised are recurring transactions of the mixed and highly idiosyncratic kinds. The nonstandardized nature of these transactions makes primary reliance on market governance hazardous, while their recurrent nature permits the cost of the specialized governance structure to be recovered.

Two types of transaction-specific governance structures for intermediate-production market transactions can be distinguished: bilateral structures, where the autonomy of the parties is maintained, and unified structures, where the transaction is removed from the market and organized within the firm subject to an authority relation (vertical integration). Bilateral structures have only recently received the attention they deserve and their operation is least well understood.

(a) Bilateral Governance: Obligational Contracting. Highly idiosyncratic

transactions are ones where the human and physical assets required for production are extensively specialized, so there are no obvious scale economies to be realized through interfirm trading that the buyer (or seller) is unable to realize himself (through vertical integration). In the case, however, of mixed transactions, the degree of asset specialization is less complete. Accordingly, outside procurement for these components may be favored by scale-economy considerations.

As compared with vertical integration, outside procurement also is good in eliciting cost control for steady-state supply. Problems, however, arise when adaptability and contractual expense are considered. Whereas internal adaptations can be effected by fiat, outside procurement involves effecting adaptations across a market interface. Unless the need for adaptations has been contemplated from the outset and expressly provided for by the contract, which often is impossible or prohibitively expensive, adaptations across a market interface can be accomplished only by mutual, follow-on agreements. Inasmuch as the interests of the parties will commonly be at variance when adaptation proposals (originated by either party) are made, a dilemma is evidently posed.

On the one hand, both parties have an incentive to sustain the relationship rather than to permit it to unravel, the object being to avoid the sacrifice of valued transaction-specific economies. On the other hand, each party appropriates a separate profit stream and cannot be expected to accede readily to any proposal to adapt the contract. What is needed, evidently is some way for declaring admissible dimensions for adjustment such that flexibility is provided under terms in which both parties have confidence. This can be accomplished partly by (1) recognizing that the hazards of opportunism vary with the type of adaptation proposed and (2) restricting adjustments to those where the hazards are least. But the spirit within which adaptations are effected is equally important.[31]

Quantity adjustments have much better incentive-compatibility properties than do price adjustments. For one thing, price adjustments have an unfortunate zero-sum quality, whereas proposals to increase, decrease, or delay delivery do not. Also, except as discussed below, price-adjustment proposals involve the risk that one's opposite is contriving to alter the terms within the bilateral monopoly trading gap to his advantage. By contrast, a presumption that exogenous events, rather than strategic purposes, are responsible for quantity adjustments is ordinarily warranted. Given the mixed nature of the exchange, a seller (or buyer) simply has little reason to doubt the representations of his opposite when a quantity change is proposed.

Thus buyers will neither seek supply from other sources nor divert products obtained (at favorable prices) to other uses (or users)—because other sources will incur high setup costs and an idiosyncratic product is nonfungible across uses and users. Likewise, sellers will not withhold supply because better opportunities have arisen, since the assets in question have a specialized character. The result is that quantity representations for idiosyncratic products can ordinarily be taken at face value. Since inability to adapt both quantity and price would render most idiosyncratic exchanges nonviable, quantity adjustments occur routinely.

Of course, not all price adjustments pose the same degree of hazard. Those which pose few hazards will predictably be implemented. Crude escalator clauses which reflect changes in general economic conditions are one possibility. But since such escalators are not transaction-specific, imperfect adjustments often result when these escalators are applied to local conditions. We should therefore consider whether price adjustments that are more closely related to local circumstances are feasible. The issue here is whether interim price adjustments can be devised for some subset of conditions such that the strategic hazards described above do not arise. What are the preconditions?

Crises facing either of the parties to an idiosyncratic exchange constitute one class of exceptions. Faced with a viability crisis which jeopardizes the relationship, ad hoc price relief may be permitted. More relevant and interesting, however, is whether there are circumstances whereby interim price adjustments are made routinely. The preconditions here are two: first, proposals to adjust prices must relate to exogenous, germane, and easily verifiable events; and second, quantifiable cost consequences must be confidently related thereto. An example may help to illustrate. Consider a component for which a significant share of the cost is accounted for by a basic material (copper, steel). Assume, moreover, that the fractional cost of the components in terms of this basic material is well specified. An exogenous change in prices of materials would under these circumstances pose few hazards if partial but interim price relief were permitted by allowing pass-through according to formula. A more refined adjustment than aggregate escalators would afford thereby obtains.

It bears emphasis, however, that not all costs so qualify. Changes in overhead or other expenses for which validation is difficult and which, even if verified, bear an uncertain relation to the cost of the component will not be passed through in a similar way. Recognizing the hazards, the parties will simply forgo relief of this kind.

(b) Unified Governance: Internal Organization. Incentives for trading weaken as transactions become progressively more idiosyncratic. The

reason is that, as the specialized human and physical assets become more specialized to a single use, and hence less transferable to other uses, economies of scale can be as fully realized by the buyer as by an outside supplier.[32] The choice of organizing mode then turns on which mode has superior adaptive properties. As discussed elsewhere, vertical integration will invariably appear in these circumstances.[33]

The advantage of vertical integration is that adaptations can be made in a sequential way without the need to consult, complete, or revise interfirm agreements. Where a single ownership entity spans both sides of the transactions, a presumption of joint profit maximization is warranted. Thus price adjustments in vertically integrated enterprises will be more complete than in interfirm trading. And quantity adjustments, of course, will be implemented at whatever frequency serves to maximize the joint gain to the transaction.

Unchanging identity at the interface coupled with extensive adaptability in both price and quantity is thus characteristic of highly idiosyncratic transactions which are vertically integrated. Obligational contracting is supplanted by the more comprehensive adaptive capability afforded by administration.

The match of governance structures with transactions that results from these economizing efforts is shown in Figure 2.

Figure 2. Matching Governance Structures with Commercial Transactions.

		Investment Characteristics		
		Nonspecific	Mixed	Idiosyncratic
Frequency	Occasional	Market governance (classical contracting)	Trilateral governance (neoclassical contracting)	
	Recurrent		Bilateral governance	Unified governance
			(relational contracting)	

D. Uncertainty

Transactions conducted under certainty are relatively uninteresting. Except as they differ in the time required to reach an equilibrium-exchange configuration, any governance structure will do. More relevant are transactions where uncertainty is present to an intermediate or high degree. The foregoing has dealt with the first of these. The question here is how the governance of transactions is affected by increasing the degree of uncertainty.

Recall that nonspecific transactions are ones for which continuity has little value, since new trading relations are easily arranged. Increasing the degree of uncertainty does not alter this. Accordingly, market exchange continues and the discrete-contracting paradigm (classical contract law) holds across standardized transactions of all kinds, whatever the degree of uncertainty.

Matters are different with transaction-specific investments. Whenever investments are idiosyncratic in nontrivial degree, increasing the degree of uncertainty makes it more imperative that the parties devise a machinery to "work things out"—since contractual gaps will be larger and the occasions for sequential adaptations will increase in number and importance as the degree of uncertainty increases. This has special relevance for the organization of transactions with mixed investment attributes. Two possibilities exist. One would be to sacrifice valued design features in favor of a more standardized good or service. Market governance would then apply. The second would be to preserve the design but surround the transaction with an elaborated governance apparatus, thereby facilitating more effective adaptive, sequential decision making. Specifically, a more elaborate arbitration apparatus is apt to be devised for occasional, nonstandard transactions. And bilateral governance structures will often give way to unified ones as uncertainty is increased for recurrent transactions.

Reductions in uncertainty, of course, warrant shifting transactions in the opposite direction. To the extent that uncertainty decreases as an industry matures, which is the usual case, the benefits that accrue to integration presumably decline. Accordingly, greater reliance on obligational market contracting is commonly feasible for transactions of recurrent trading in mature industries.

IV. Other Applications

The three dimensions for describing transactions—frequency, investment idiosyncrasy, and uncertainty—apply to transactions of all kinds.

The same general considerations that apply to governance structures for commercial transactions carry over as well. The specific governance structures for organizing commercial transactions do not, however, apply without modification to the governance of other types of transactions. Applications of the framework to the study of labor markets, regulation, family law, and capital markets are briefly sketched here.

A. Labor

Occasional labor-market transactions typically take the form of repair or replacement services—the plumber, electrician, and so forth. Especially in older homes or structures, these transactions can take on an idiosyncratic quality. Although such transactions can be interesting, the transactions on which I want to focus are recurrent labor-market transactions of the nonspecific, mixed, and idiosyncratic kinds.

Clyde Summers's examination of collective agreements in relation to the law of contracts disclosed that, while the collective bargain differed greatly from the ordinary bargain of commerce, collective agreements are nonetheless a part of the "mainstream of contract" (1969, p. 527). He suggested that the study of contract proceed on two levels: the search for an underlying framework and, within that framework, an examination of the distinctive institutional attributes that distinguish each type of transaction. With respect to the first of these he conjectured that "the principles common to the whole range of contractual transactions are relatively few and of such generality and competing character that they should not be stated as legal rules at all" (1969, p. 568).

I am persuaded that Summers's two-part strategy for studying contract leads to a deeper understanding of the issues. And I believe that the framework set out in the preceding sections of this paper provides much of the underlying unity called for by Summers. What differs as one moves across various contracting activities is the institutional infrastructure.

(1) *Nonspecific Transactions.* Nonspecific labor-market transactions are ones where employer and employee are largely indifferent to the identity of each. Migrant farm labor is an example. Although an unchanging employment association between firm and worker may be observed to continue over long intervals for some of these employees, each party is essentially meeting bids in the spot market. A valuable ongoing relationship, in which specific training and on-the-job learning yield idiosyncratic benefits, is thus not implied. Both wages and employment are variable and market governance applies to transactions of this kind.

Consider, therefore, mixed and idiosyncratic labor-market transactions.

(2) *Mixed Transactions.* Probably the most interesting labor-market transactions are those where large numbers of workers acquire an intermediate degree of firm-specific skill. Note that, inasmuch as the degree of idiosyncrasy is a design variable, firms would presumably redesign jobs to favor more standardized operations if it were impossible to devise governance structures which prevented antagonistic bargaining relations from developing between firms and idiosyncratically skilled employees. Although least-cost production technologies would be sacrificed in the process, net gains might nevertheless be realized since incumbent workers would realize little strategic advantage over otherwise qualified but inexperienced outsiders.

Justice Rehnquist has observed that "Adjudicatory review of the decisions of certain institutions, while perhaps insuring a 'better' decision in some objective sense, can only disrupt on-going relationships within the institution and thereby hamper the institution's ability to serve its designated societal function" (1978, p. 4). Examples of adjudicatory review with respect to which he counsels caution include collective bargaining agreements.

The reasons for this are that adjudicatory review is not easily apprised of the special needs of the transaction and the prospect of such review impairs the incentive of the parties to devise bilateral governance structure. The *Vaca v. Stipes* holding, which Justice Rehnquist cites, is fully consistent with this interpretation. There the Court held that an individual could not compel his union to take his grievance to arbitration, since if the law were otherwise "the settlement machinery provided by the contract would be substantially undermined, thus . . . [introducing] the vagaries of independent and unsystematic negotiations."[34] Archibald Cox elaborates as follows:

> . . . giving the union control over all claims arising under the collective agreement comports so much better with the functional nature of a collective bargaining agreement. . . . Allowing an individual to carry a claim to arbitration whenever he is dissatisfied with the adjustment worked out by the company and the union . . . discourages the kind of day-to-day cooperation between company and union which is normally the mark of sound industrial relations—a relationship in which grievances are treated as problems to be solved and contracts are only guideposts in a dynamic human relationship. When . . . the individual's

> claim endangers group interests, the union's function is
> to resolve the competition by reaching an accommodation
> or striking a balance (1958, p. 24).

The practice described by Cox of giving the union control over arbitration claims plainly permits group interests—whence the concern for system viability—to supersede individual interests, thereby curbing small-numbers opportunism.

General escalator or predetermined wage adjustments aside, wages are unchanging under collective bargaining agreements.[35] Interim adaptations are nonetheless essential. These take three forms: (1) quantity adjustments, (2) assignment changes, and (3) refinement of working rules as a result of grievances.

Quantity adjustments are made in response to changing market opportunities. Either the level or the mix of employment is adjusted as economic events unfold. Given that valuable firm-specific training and learning reside in the workers, layoffs with a presumption of reemployment when conditions improve are common. Conformably, the degree to which the machinery governing access to jobs is elaborated ought to vary directly with the degree to which jobs in a firm are idiosyncratic. Thus promotion ladders in firms where a succession of interdependent jobs are highly idiosyncratic should be long and thin, with access mainly restricted to the bottom, whereas promotion ladders in nonidiosyncratic activities should be broadly structured (Wachter and Williamson, 1978, p. 567). Likewise, promotion on merit ought to be favored over promotion strictly by seniority in firms where jobs are more idiosyncratic.[36]

(3) *Highly Idiosyncratic Transactions.* Recall that idiosyncratic transactions involve not merely uniqueness but uniqueness of a transaction-specific kind. Also recall that our concern in this section is with recurring transactions. Thus, although there are many uniquely skilled individuals (artists, athletes, researchers, administrators), unique skills are rarely of a transaction-specific kind. On the contrary, most of these individuals could move to another organization without significant productivity losses.

The exceptions are those where the benefits which accrue to experience (inside knowledge) and/or team interaction effects are great. Whereas commercial transactions of a highly idiosyncratic nature are unified under a common ownership, limits on indenture foreclose this option for labor-market transactions. Instead of "merger," complex contracts designed to tie the interests of the individual to the organization on a long-term basis are negotiated. Severe penalties are provided should either party seek unilateral termination. Nonvested, long-term, contingent reward schemes are devised. More generally, transaction-specific infrastructure will be highly individuated for such transactions.

B. Regulation of Natural Monopoly

Again the argument is that specialized governance structure is needed to the degree efficient supply necessarily joins buyers and sellers in a bilateral trading relation of a continuing nature. And again, the object of governance is to (1) protect the interests of the respective parties and (2) adapt the relationship to changing circumstances.

Although differing in details, both Victor Goldberg (1979) and I (1975) have argued that specialized governance structure is needed for services for which natural monopoly features are great. Such structure presumably has the purpose of providing sellers (investors) and buyers with security of expectations, which is a protective function, while at the same time facilitating adaptive, sequential decision making. Rate-of-return regulation with periodic review has these features. To the extent, however, that such regulation is observed in conjunction with activities where transaction-specific investments are insubstantial (as, for example, in the trucking industry), the case for regulation is not at all apparent—or, if it is to be made, must appeal to arguments very different from those set out here.

C. Family Law

The issue here is whether the role of adjudication should be *expanded* to help govern family relationships. Granting that adjudication as ultimate relief can and often does serve a useful role for sustaining family relations, such relations are plainly idiosyncratic to an unusual degree and a specialized governance structure is surely the main mode of governance. As the role of adjudication is expanded, reliance upon internal structure is apt to be reduced. Therefore, except when individual rights are seriously threatened, withholding access to adjudication may be indicated.

Justice Rehnquist's remarks concerning the corrosive effects of adversary hearings on the family are apposite: "Any sort of adversary hearing which pits parent against child is bound to be disruptive, placing stresses and tensions on the intra-familial relationships which in turn weaken the family as an institution" (1978, p. 19). Whether, as this suggests, parent-child family relations are optimized where adjudication is zero or negligible is beyond the scope of this paper. It suffices for my purposes merely to note that valued family relations are recurrent and idiosyncratic and that a specialized, transaction-specific governance structure must be encouraged lest the parties withhold investing heavily in the institution.[37]

D. Capital Market Transactions

The ease of verification is critical to the operation of capital markets.[38] Where verification is easy, markets work well and additional governance is unnecessary. Where verification is difficult or very difficult, however, additional governance may be indicated. Occasional transactions are apt to benefit from third-party assistance, while recurring transactions are ones for which bilateral or unified governance will presumably be observed. Assessing capital-market transactions within the proposed framework is thus accomplished by substituting ''ease of verification'' for ''degree of transaction-specific investment.'' Once this is done, the governance structures appropriate to capital markets are broadly similar to those within which commercial transactions are organized.

V. Implications

Dimensionalizing transactions and examining the costs of executing different transactions in different ways generate a large number of institutional implications. Some of these are summarized here.

A. General

1. Nonspecific transactions, either occasional or recurrent, are efficiently organized by markets.
2. Occasional transactions that are nonstandardized stand most to benefit from adjudication.
3. A transaction-specific governance structure is more fully developed where transactions are (1) recurrent, (2) entail idiosyncratic investment, and (3) are executed under greater uncertainty.

B. Commercial Transactions

1. Optimization of commercial transactions requires simultaneous attention to (1) production economies, (2) transaction-cost economies, and (3) component design.
2. The reason why Macaulay (1963a) observes so few litigated cases

in business is because markets work well for nonspecific transactions, while recurrent, nonstandard transactions are governed by bilateral or unified structures.

3. As uncertainty increases, the obligational market-contracting mode will not be used for recurrent transactions with mixed investment features. Such transactions will either be standardized, and shifted to the market, or organized internally.

4. As generic demand grows and the number of supply sources increases, exchange that was once transaction-specific loses this characteristic and greater reliance on market-mediated governance is feasible. Thus vertical integration may give way to obligational market contracting, which in turn may give way to markets.

5. Where inventory and related flow-process economies are great, site-specific supply and transaction-specific governance (commonly vertical integration) will be observed. Generic demand here has little bearing.

6. The organization of the interface between manufacturing and distribution reflects similar investment considerations: goods and services that can be sold without incurring transaction-specific investment will be distributed through conventional marketing channels while those where such investments are great will be supported by specialized—mainly bilateral (for example, franchising) or unified (forward integration)—governance structures.

7. The governance of technical change poses special difficulties. The frequently noted limits of markets (Arrow, 1962) often give way to more complex governance relations, again for the same general reasons and along the same general lines as are set out here (Williamson, 1975, pp. 203–205).

C. Other Transactions

1. The efficiency benefits of collective organization are negligible for nonspecific labor. Accordingly, such labor will be organized late, often only with the assistance of the political process.

2. Internal labor markets become more highly individuated as jobs become more varied and idiosyncratic.

3. Regulation can be interpreted in part as a response to the transactional dilemma posed by natural monopoly.

4. A transaction-cost justification for regulating activities for which transaction-specific investments are lacking (for example, trucking) is not apparent. The possibility that politics is the driving consideration in such industries warrants consideration.

5. Adjudication should proceed with caution in the area of family law lest valued transaction-specific investments be discouraged.
6. Ease of verification is the capital-market counterpart of transaction-specific investments. Upon making this substitution, the organization of capital markets and intermediate-product markets is broadly similar.

VI. Concluding Remarks

Transaction-cost economics is an interdisciplinary undertaking that joins economics with aspects of organization theory and overlaps extensively with contract law. It is the modern counterpart of institutional economics and relies heavily on comparative analysis.[39] Frictionless ideals are useful mainly for reference purposes.

Although mathematical economics captures only a fraction of the transaction-cost phenomena of interest (Dahlman, 1979, pp. 144–147), this has not been the only obstacle. Headway with the study of transaction-cost issues has been impeded by lack of verbal definitions. Identifying the critical dimensions with respect to which transactions differ has been a significant omission.

This paper attempts to rectify this deficiency and identifies uncertainty, frequency of exchange, and the degree to which investments are transaction-specific as the principal dimensions for describing transactions. The efficient organization of economic activity entails matching governance structures with these transactional attributes in a discriminating way.

Although the main applications in this paper are to commercial contracting, the proposed approach generalizes easily to the study of labor contracts. It also has ramifications for understanding both public utility regulation and family relations. A unified approach to contract thus emerges.

The fact that the broad features of so many varied transactions fit within the framework is encouraging. The importance of transaction costs to the organization of economic activity is thus confirmed. But the world of contract is enormously complex (Klein, Crawford, and Alchian, 1978, p. 325), and the simple economizing framework proposed here cannot be expected to capture more than main features. Elaborating the framework to deal with microanalytic phenomena, however, should be feasible. And extending it to include additional or substitute dimensions (of which the ease of verification, in the case of capital-market transactions, is an example) may sometimes be necessary.

Notes

1. Ronald Coase has forcefully argued the importance of transaction costs at twenty-year intervals. See Coase (1937 and 1960). Much of my own work has been "preoccupied" with transaction costs during the past decade. See especially Williamson (1975). Other works in which transaction costs are featured include Calabresi (1968); Goldberg (1976b); Klein, Crawford, and Alchian (1978); and Dahlman (1979). For an examination of Pigou in which transaction costs are featured, see Goldberg (1979).

2. Opportunism is a variety of self-interest seeking but extends simple self-interest seeking to include self-interest seeking with guile. It is not necessary that all agents be regarded as opportunistic in identical degree. It suffices that those who are less opportunistic than others are difficult to ascertain ex ante and that, even among the less opportunistic, most have their price. For a more complete discussion of opportunism, see Williamson (1975, pp. 7–10, 26–30). For a recent application see Klein, Crawford, and Alchian (1978).

3. The joining of opportunism with transaction-specific investments (or what Klein, Crawford, and Alchian refer to as "appropriable quasi rents") is a leading factor in explaining decisions to vertically integrate. See Williamson (1971); Williamson (1975, pp. 16–19, 91–101) and Klein, Crawford, and Alchian (1978).

4. But for the limited ability of human agents to receive, store, retrieve, and process data, interesting economic problems vanish.

5. With respect to commercial contracts, see Llewellyn (1931); Havighurst (1961); Fuller (1963); Macaulay (1963a); Friedman (1965); Leff (1970); Macneil (1974, 1978); and Goldberg (1976a). Labor lawyers have made similar observations regarding contracts governing the employment relationship. See Cox (1958); Summers (1969); and Feller (1973).

6. The technical versus purposive distinction is made by Summers (1969). He distinguishes between "black letter law," on the one hand (pp. 539, 543, 548, 566) and a more circumstantial approach to law, on the other (pp. 549–51, 561, 566). "The epitome of abstraction is the *Restatement*, which illustrates its black letter rules by transactions suspended in mid-air, creating the illusion that contract rules can be stated without reference to surrounding circumstances and are therefore generally applicable to all contractual transactions" (p. 566). He observes that such a conception does not and cannot provide a "framework for integrating rules and principles applicable to all contractual transactions" (p. 566) but that this must be sought in a more affirmative view of the law in which effective governance relations are emphasized. Contract interpretation and completing contracts are among these affirmative functions.

7. See especially Macneil (1974); Macneil (1978) to related work of his cited therein.

8. For a discussion of complex contingent-claims contracting and its mechanics, see Arrow (1971); Meade (1971); and Williamson (1975, pp. 20–40).

9. As Telser and Higinbotham (1977, pp. 969–997) put it: "In an organized market the participants trade a standardized contract such that each unit of the contract is a perfect substitute for any other unit. The identities of the parties in any mutually agreeable transaction do not affect the terms of exchange. The organized market itself or some other institution deliberately creates a homogeneous good that can be traded anonymously by the participants or their agents."

10. As Friedman (1965, p. 205) observes, relationships are effectively fractured if a dispute reaches litigation.

11. To be sure, some legal specialists insist that all of this was known all along. There is a difference, however, between awareness of a condition and an understanding. Macneil's treatment heightens awareness and deepens the understanding.

12. For a recent study of contractual relations in which uncertainty is featured, see Temin (1979).

13. See Telser and Higinbotham (1977), also Ben-Porath (1978) and Barzel (1979). Note that Barzel's concern with standardization is mainly in connection with final-product markets, whereas I am more interested in nonstandard investments. The two are not unrelated, but identical quality can often be realized with a variety of inputs. I am concerned with specialized (transaction-specific) inputs.

14. This assumes that it is costly for the incumbent supplier to transfer specialized physical assets to new suppliers. On this, see Williamson (1976). Klein, Crawford, and Alchian (1978), use the term "appropriable quasi rent" to refer to this condition. Use versus user distinctions are relevant in this connection: "The quasi-rent value of the asset is the excess of its value over its salvage value, that is, its value in its next best *use* to another renter. The potentially appropriable specialized portion of the quasi rent is the portion, if any, in excess of its value to the second highest-valuing *user*" (Klein, Crawford, and Alchian, 1978, p. 298).

15. Veblen's ([1904] 1927) remarks on the distant relation of the head of a large enterprise to transactions are apposite. He observes that under these impersonal circumstances "The mitigating effect which personal conduct may have in dealings between man and man is . . . in great measured eliminated. . . . Business management [then] has a chance to proceed . . . untroubled by sentimental considerations of human kindness or irritation or of honesty." Veblen evidently assigns slight weight to the possibility that those to whom negotiating responsibilities are assigned will themselves invest the transactions with integrity.

16. The *Great Lakes Carbon* case is an example of the latter, 1970–1973 Trade Reg. Rep. Transfer Binder ¶ 19,848 (FTC Dkt No. 8805).

17. More recent examples of contracts wherein private parties can and evidently do "ignore" the law, even at some peril, when the law and the interests of the parties are at variance are offered by Macaulay (1963b, p. 16): "Requirements

contracts probably are not legally enforceable in Wisconsin and a few other States. Yet, chemicals, containers, and a number of other things are still bought and sold there on the basis of requirements contracts.

Decisions of the United States Court of Appeals for the Seventh Circuit indicate that a clause calling for a 'seller's price in effect at time and place of delivery' makes a contract unenforceable. The Wisconsin cases are not clear. Yet steel and steel products usually are sold in this way.''

18. As Ben-Porath (1978, p. 6) puts it, ''The most important characteristic of the family contract is that it is embedded in the identity of the partners without which it loses its meaning. It is thus specific and non-negotiable or nontransferable.''

19. More generally, the economizing problem includes choice between a special-purpose and a general-purpose good or service. A general-purpose item affords all of the advantages of market procurement, but possibly at the sacrifice of valued design or performance characteristics. A special-purpose item has the opposite features: valued differences are realized but market procurement here may pose hazards. For the purposes of this paper, intermediate-product characteristics are mainly taken as given and I focus principally on production and transaction-cost economies. A more general formulation would include product characteristics in the optimization.

20. This ignores transient conditions, such as temporary excess capacity. (In a zero-transaction-cost world, such excesses vanish as assets can be deployed as effectively by others as they can by the owner.)

21. Carlton (1979b) shows that economies of "vertical integration" can frequently be realized in a market where, absent integration, buyers and suppliers are randomly paired. As he defines vertical integration, however, this can be accomplished as effectively by long-term contract as it can by in-house production.

22. Thus a reduction in monitoring commonly gives rise to an increase in opportunism. Monitoring the employment relation, however, needs to be done with special care. Progressively increasing the intensity of surveillance can elicit resentment and have counterproductive (for example, work-to-rule) results. Such perversities are less likely for interfirm trading.

23. See note 14 above.

24. This seems reasonable for most intermediate-product market transactions.

25. Production aspects are thus emphasized. Investments in governance structure are treated separately.

26. Defense contracting may appear to be a counterexample, since an elaborate governance structure is devised for many of these. This reflects in part, however, the special disabilities of the government as a production instrument. But for this, many of these contracts would be organized in-house. Also, contracts that

are very large and of long duration, as many defense contracts are, do have a recurring character.

27. Although recurrent, standard transactions are ones for which an active spot market commonly exists, term contracting may also be employed—especially as planning economies are thereby realized by the parties. See Carlton (1979a). The duration of these contracts will not be long, however, since the assets in question can be employed in other uses and/or in the service of other customers. The result is that changing market circumstances will be reflected relatively quickly in both price and quantity and relatively stringent contracting attitudes may be said to prevail.

28. "Generally speaking, a serious conflict, even quite a minor one such as an objection to a harmlessly late tender of the delivery of goods, terminates the discrete contract as a live one and leaves nothing but a conflict over money damages to be settled by a lawsuit. Such a result fits neatly the norms of enhancing discreteness and intensifying . . . presentation" (Macneil, 1978, p. 877).

29. See the articles cited in note 14 above.

30. The rationale for this section of the Code is that "identification of the goods to the contract will, within limits, permit the seller to recover the price of the goods rather than merely damages for the breach. . . , ([where the] latter may be far less in amount and more difficult to prove)" (Macneil, 1978, p. 880).

31. As Macaulay (1963a, p. 61) observes, "Disputes are frequently settled without reference to the contract or to potential or actual legal sanctions. There is a hesitancy to speak of legal right or to threaten to sue in . . . negotiations" where continuing business is valued.

    The material which follows in this subsection was originally developed in connection with the study of inflation. See Wachter and Williamson (1978).

32. This assumes that factor prices paid by buyer and outside supplier are identical. Where this is not true, as in some unionized firms, buyers may choose to procure outside because of a differential wage rate. This is a common problem in the automobile industry, which has a very flat and relatively high wage scale.

33. See the references cited in note 3 above.

34. 386 U.S. 171, 191 (1967).

35. The reason, of course, is that it is very costly and apt to be unproductive to reopen wage bargaining during the period covered by a contract. Since to reopen negotiations for one type of job is to invite it for all, and as objective differences among jobs may be difficult to demonstrate, wage bargaining is foreclosed except at contract-renewal intervals.

36. Thus although both nonidiosyncratic and idiosyncratic jobs may be organized

collectively, the way in which the internal labor markets associated with each are organized should reflect objective differences between them. Additionally, the incentive to provide an orderly governance structure varies directly with the degree to which efficiencies are attributable thereto. *Ceteris paribus*, nonidiosyncratic jobs ought to be organized later and the governance structure less fully elaborated than for idiosyncratic jobs. Both propositions are borne out by the evidence.

37. For a more extensive discussion of family transactions, see Ben-Porath (1978, p. 4-7).

38. This feature was called to my attention by Sanford Grossman.

39. Reliance on comparative analysis has been repeatedly emphasized by Coase (1937, 1960).

Production, Information Costs, and Economic Organization

Armen A. Alchian
Harold Demsetz

The mark of a capitalistic society is that resources are owned and allocated by such nongovernmental organizations as firms, households, and markets. Resource owners increase productivity through cooperative specialization and this leads to the demand for economic organizations which facilitate cooperation. When a lumber mill employs a cabinetmaker, cooperation between specialists is achieved within a firm, and when a cabinetmaker purchases wood from a lumberman, the cooperation takes place across markets (or between firms). Two important problems face a theory of economic organization—to explain the conditions that determine whether the gains from specialization and cooperative production can better be obtained within an organization like the firm, or across markets, and to explain the structure of the organization.

It is common to see the firm characterized by the power to settle issues by fiat, by authority, or by disciplinary action superior to that available in the conventional market. This is delusion. The firm does not own all its inputs. It has no power of fiat, no authority, no disciplinary action any different in the slightest degree from ordinary market con-

Note: Acknowledgment is made for financial aid from the E. Lilly Endowment, Inc. grant to UCLA for research in the behavioral effects of property rights.

Reprinted in slightly adapted form from *American Economic Association*, 1972, *62* (5), 777–795. Used by permission of the authors and the American Economic Association.

tracting between any two people. I can "punish" you only by withholding future business or by seeking redress in the courts for any failure to honor our exchange agreement. That is exactly all that any employer can do. He can fire or sue, just as I can fire my grocer by stopping purchases from him or sue him for delivering faulty products. What then is the content of the presumed power to manage and assign workers to various tasks? Exactly the same as one little consumer's power to manage and assign his grocer to various tasks. The single consumer can assign his grocer to the task of obtaining whatever the customer can induce the grocer to provide at a price acceptable to both parties. That is precisely all that an employer can do to an employee. To speak of managing, directing, or assigning workers to various tasks is a deceptive way of noting that the employer continually is involved in renegotiation of contracts on terms that must be acceptable to both parties. Telling an employee to type this letter rather than to file that document is like my telling a grocer to sell me this brand of tuna rather than that brand of bread. I have no contract to continue to purchase from the grocer and neither the employer nor the employee is bound by any contractual obligations to continue their relationship. Long-term contracts between employer and employee are not the essence of the organization we call a firm. My grocer can count on my returning day after day and purchasing his services and goods even with the prices not always marked on the goods—because I know what they are—and he adapts his activity to conform to my directions to him as to what I want each day . . . he is not my employee.

Wherein then is the relationship between a grocer and his employee different from that between a grocer and his customers? It is in a *team* use of inputs and a centralized position of some party in the contractual arrangements of *all* other inputs. It is the *centralized contractual agent in a team productive process*—not some superior authoritarian directive or disciplinary power. Exactly what is a team process and why does it induce the contractual form, called the firm? These problems motivate the inquiry of this paper.

I. The Metering Problem

The economic organization through which input owners cooperate will make better use of their comparative advantages to the extent that it facilitates the payment of rewards in accord with productivity. If rewards were random, and without regard to productive effort, no incentive to productive effort would be provided by the organization; and if rewards were negatively correlated with productivity the organization would be subject to sabotage. Two key demands are placed on an economic organization—metering input productivity and metering rewards.[1]

Metering problems sometimes can be resolved well through the exchange of products across competitive markets, because in many situations markets yield a high correlation between rewards and productivity. If a farmer increases his output of wheat by 10 percent at the prevailing market price, his receipts also increase by 10 percent. This method of organizing economic activity meters the *output directly*, reveals the marginal product and apportions the *rewards* to resource owners in accord with that direct measurement of their outputs. The success of this decentralized, market exchange in promoting productive specialization requires that changes in market rewards fall on those responsible for changes in *output*.[2]

The classic relationship in economics that runs from marginal productivity to the distribution of income implicitly *assumes* the existence of an organization, be it the market or the firm, that allocates rewards to resources in accord with their productivity. The problem of economic organization, the economical means of metering productivity and rewards, is not confronted directly in the classical analysis of production and distribution. Instead, that analysis tends to assume sufficiently economic—or zero cost—means, as if productivity automatically created its reward. We conjecture the direction of causation is the reverse—the specific system of rewarding which is relied upon stimulates a particular productivity response. If the economic organization meters poorly, with rewards and productivity only loosely correlated, then productivity will be smaller; but if the economic organization meters well productivity will be greater. What makes metering difficult and hence induces means of economizing on metering costs?

II. Team Production

Two men jointly lift heavy cargo into trucks. Solely by observing the total weight loaded per day, it is impossible to determine each person's marginal productivity. With team production it is difficult, solely by observing total output, to either define or determine *each* individual's contribution to this output of the cooperating inputs. The output is yielded by a team, by definition, and it is not a *sum* of separable outputs of each of its members. Team production of Z involves at least two inputs, X_i and X_j, with $\partial^2 Z / \partial X_i \partial X_j \neq 0$.[3] The production function is *not* separable into two functions each involving only inputs X_i or only inputs X_j. Consequently there is no *sum* of Z of two separable functions to treat as the Z of the team production function. (An example of a *separable* case is $Z = aX_i^2 + bX_j^2$, which is separable into $Z_i = aX_i^2$ and $Z_j = bX_j^2$, and $Z = Z_i + Z_j$. This is not team production.) There exist production techniques in which the Z obtained is greater than if X_i and X_j had produced separable Z. Team production will be used if it yields an output enough larger than the sum of separable production of Z to cover the costs of organizing and disciplining team members—the topics of this paper.[4]

Usual explanations of the gains from cooperative behavior rely on exchange and production in accord with the comparative advantage specialization principle with separable additive production. However, as suggested above there is a source of gain from cooperative activity involving working as a *team*, wherein individual cooperating inputs do not yield identifiable, separate products which can be *summed* to measure the total output. For this cooperative productive activity, here called "team" production, measuring *marginal* productivity and making payments in accord therewith is more expensive by an order of magnitude than for separable production functions.

Team production, to repeat, is production in which (1) several types of resources are used and (2) the product is not a sum of separable outputs of each cooperating resource. An additional factor creates a team organization problem—(3) not all resources used in team production belong to one person.

We do not inquire into why all the jointly used resources are not owned by one person, but instead into the types of organization, contracts, and informational and payment procedures used among owners of teamed inputs. With respect to the one-owner case, perhaps it is sufficient merely to note that (a) slavery is prohibited, (b) one might assume risk aversion as a reason for one person's not borrowing enough to purchase all the assets or sources of services rather than renting them, and (c) the purchase-resale spread may be so large that costs of short-term ownership exceed rental costs. Our problem is viewed basically as one of organization among different people, not of the physical goods or services, however much there must be selection and choice of combination of the latter.

How can the members of a team be rewarded and induced to work efficiently? In team production, marginal products of cooperative team members are not so directly and separably (i.e., cheaply) observable. What a team offers to the market can be taken as the marginal product of the team but not of the team members. The costs of metering or ascertaining the marginal products of the team's members is what calls forth new organizations and procedures. Clues to each input's productivity can be secured by observing *behavior* of individual inputs. When lifting cargo into the truck, how rapidly does a man move to the next piece to be loaded, how many cigarette breaks does he take, does the item being lifted tilt downward toward his side?

If detecting such behavior were costless, neither party would have an incentive to shirk, because neither could impose the cost of his shirking on the other (if their cooperation was agreed to voluntarily). But since costs must be incurred to monitor each other, each input owner will have more incentive to shirk when he works as part of a team, than if his performance could be monitored easily or if he did not work as a team. If there is a net increase in productivity available by team production, net of the metering cost associated with disciplining the team, then team production will be relied upon rather than a multitude of bilateral exchange of separable individual outputs.

Both leisure and higher income enter a person's utility function.[5] Hence, each person should adjust his work and realized reward so as to equate the marginal rate of substitution between leisure and production of real output to his marginal rate of substitution in consumption. That is, he would adjust his rate of work to bring his demand prices of leisure and output to equality with their true costs. However, with detection, policing, monitoring, measuring or metering costs, each person will be induced to take more leisure, because the effect of relaxing on *his realized* (reward) rate of substitution between output and leisure will be less than the effect on the *true* rate of substitution. His realized cost of leisure will fall more than the true cost of leisure, so he "buys" more leisure (i.e., more nonpecuniary reward).

If his relaxation cannot be detected perfectly at zero cost, part of its effects will be borne by others in the team, thus making *his* realized cost of relaxation less than the true total cost to the team. The difficulty of detecting such actions permits the private costs of his actions to be less than their full costs. Since each person responds to his private realizable rate of substitution (in production) rather than the true total (i.e., social) rate, and so long as there are costs for other people to detect his shift toward relaxation, it will not pay (them) to force him to readjust completely by making him realize the true cost. Only enough efforts will be made to equate the marginal gains of detection activity with the marginal costs of detection; and that implies a lower rate of productive effort and more shirking than in a costless monitoring, or measuring, world.

In a university, the faculty use office telephones, paper, and mail for personal uses beyond strict university productivity. The university administrators could stop such practices by identifying *the* responsible person in each case, but they can do so only at higher costs than administrators are willing to incur. The extra costs of identifying each party (rather than merely identifying the presence of such activity) would exceed the savings from diminished faculty "turpitudinal peccadilloes." So the faculty is allowed some degree of "privileges, perquisites, or fringe benefits." And the total of the pecuniary wages paid is lower because of this irreducible (at acceptable costs) degree of amenity-seizing activity. Pay is lower in pecuniary terms and higher in leisure, conveniences, and ease of work. But still every person would prefer to see detection made more effective (if it were somehow possible to monitor costlessly) so that he, as part of the now more effectively producing team, could thereby realize a higher pecuniary pay and less leisure. If everyone could, at zero cost, have his reward-realized rate brought to the true production possibility real rate, all could achieve a more preferred position. But detection of the responsible parties is costly; that cost acts like a tax on work rewards.[6] Viable shirking is the result.

What forms of organizing team production will lower the cost of detecting "performance" (i.e., marginal productivity) and bring personally realized states of substitution closer to true rates of substitution? Market competition, in principle, could monitor some team production. (It already *organizes* teams.) Input owners who are not team members can offer, in return for a smaller share of the team's rewards, to replace excessively (i.e., overpaid) shirking members. Market competition among potential team members would determine team membership and individual rewards. There would be no team leader, manager, organizer, owner, or employer. For such decentralized organizational control to work, outsiders, possibly after observing each team's total output, can speculate about their capabilities as team members and, by a market competitive process, revised teams with greater productive ability will be formed and sustained. Incumbent members will be constrained by threats of replacement by outsiders offering services for lower reward shares or offering greater rewards to the other members of the team. Any team member who shirked in the expectation that the reduced output effect would not be attributed to him will be displaced if his activity is detected. Teams of productive inputs, like business units, would evolve in apparent spontaneity in the market—without any central organizing agent, team manager, or boss.

But completely effective control cannot be expected from individualized market competition for two reasons. First, for this competition to be completely effective, new challengers for team membership must know where, and to what extent, shirking is a serious problem, i.e., know they can increase net output as compared with the inputs they replace. To the extent that this is true it is probably possible for existing fellow team members to recognize the shirking. But, by definition, the detection of shirking by observing team output is costly for team production. Secondly, assume the presence of detection costs, and assume that in order to secure a place on the team a new input owner must accept a smaller share of rewards (or a promise to produce more). Then his incentive to shirk would still be at least as great as the incentives of the inputs replaced, because he still bears less than the entire reduction in team output for which he is responsible.

III. The Classical Firm

One method of reducing shirking is for someone to specialize as a monitor to check the input performance of team members.[7] But who will monitor the monitor? One constraint on the monitor is the aforesaid market competition offered by other monitors, but for reasons already given, that is not perfectly effective. Another constraint can be imposed on the monitor: give him title to the net earnings of the team, net of payments to other inputs. If owners of cooperating inputs agree with the monitor that he is to receive any residual product above prescribed amounts (hopefully, the marginal value products of the other inputs), the monitor will have an added incentive not to shirk as a monitor. Specialization in monitoring plus reliance on a residual claimant status will reduce shirking; but additional links are needed to forge the firm of classical economic theory. How will the residual claimant monitor the other inputs?

We use the term monitor to connote several activities in addition to its disciplinary connotation. It connotes measuring output performance, apportioning rewards, observing the input behavior of inputs as means of detecting or estimating their marginal productivity and giving assignments or instructions in what to do and how to do it. (It also includes, as we shall show later, authority to terminate or revise contracts.) Perhaps the contrast between a football coach and team captain is helpful. The coach selects strategies and tactics and sends in instructions about what plays to utilize. The captain is essentially an observer and reporter of the performance at close hand of the members. The latter is an inspector-steward and the former a supervisor manager. For the present all these activities are included in the rubric "monitoring." All these tasks are, in principle, negotiable across markets, but we are presuming that such market measurement of marginal productivities and job reassignments are not so cheaply performed for team production. And in particular our analysis suggests that it is not so much the costs of spontaneously negotiating contracts in the markets among groups for team production as it is the detection of the performance of individual members of the team that calls for the organization noted here.

The specialist *who receives the residual rewards* will be the monitor of the members of the team (i.e., will manage the use of cooperative inputs). The monitor earns his residual through the reduction in shirking that he brings about, not only by the prices that he agrees to pay the owners of the inputs, but also by observing and directing the actions or uses of these inputs. *Managing or examining the ways to which inputs are used in team production is a method of metering the marginal productivity of individual inputs to the team's output.*

To discipline team members and reduce shirking, the residual claimant must have power to revise the contract terms and incentives of *individual* members without having to terminate or alter every other input's contract. Hence, team members who seek to increase their productivity will assign to the monitor not only the residual claimant right but also the right to alter individual membership and performance on the team. Each team member, of course, can terminate his own membership (i.e., quit the team), but only the monitor may unilaterally terminate the membership of any of the other members without necessarily terminating the team itself or his association with the team; and he alone can expand or reduce membership, alter the mix of membership, or sell the right to be the residual claimant-monitor of the team. It is this entire bundle of rights: (1) to be a residual claimant; (2) to observe input behavior; (3) to be the central party common to all contracts with inputs; (4) to alter the membership of the team; and (5) to sell these rights, that defines the *ownership* (or the employer) of the *classical* (capitalist, free-enterprise) firm. The coalescing of these rights has arisen, our analysis asserts, because it resolves the shirking-information problem of team production better than does the noncentralized contractual arrangement.

The relationship of each team member to the *owner* of the firm (i.e., the party common to all input contracts *and* the residual claimant) is simply a "quid pro quo" contract. Each makes a purchase and sale. The employee "orders" the owner of the team to pay him money in the same sense that the employer directs the team member to perform certain acts. The employee can terminate the contract as readily as can the employer, and long-term contracts, therefore, are not an essential attribute of the firm. Nor are "authoritarian," "dictational," or "fiat" attributes relevant to the conception of the firm or its efficiency.

In summary, two necessary conditions exist for the emergence of the firm on the prior assumption that more than pecuniary wealth enter utility functions: (1) It is possible to increase productivity through team-oriented production, a production technique for which it is costly to directly measure the marginal outputs of the cooperating inputs. This makes it more difficult to restrict shirking through simple market exchange between cooperating inputs. (2) It is economical to estimate marginal productivity by observing or specifying input behavior. The simultaneous occurrence of both these preconditions leads to the contractual organization of inputs, known as the *classical capitalist firms* with (a) joint input production, (b) several input owners, (c) one party who is common to all the contracts of the joint inputs, (d) who has rights to renegotiate any input's contract independently of contracts with other input owners, (e) who holds the residual claim, and (f) who has the right to sell his central contractual residual status.[8]

Other Theories of the Firm. At this juncture, as an aside, we briefly place this theory of the firm in the contexts of those offered by Ronald Coase and Frank Knight.[9] Our view of the firm is not necessarily inconsistent with Coase's; we attempt to go further and identify refutable implications. Coase's penetrating insight is to make more of the fact that markets do not operate costlessly, and he relies on the cost of using markets to *form* contracts as his basic explanation for the existence of firms. We do not disagree with the proposition that, *ceteris paribus*, the higher is the cost of transacting across markets the greater will be the comparative advantage of organizing resources within the firm; it is a difficult proposition to disagree with or to refute. We could with equal ease subscribe to a theory of the firm based on the cost of managing, for surely it is true that, *ceteris paribus*, the lower is the cost of managing the greater will be the comparative advantage of organizing resources within the firm. To move the theory forward, it is necessary to know what is meant by a firm and to explain the circumstances under which the cost of "managing" resources is low relative to the cost of allocating resources through market transaction. The conception of and rationale for the classical firm that we propose takes a step down the path pointed out by Coase toward that goal. Consideration of team production, team organization, difficulty in metering outputs, and the problem of shirking are important to our explanation but, so far as we can ascertain, not in Coase's. Coase's analysis insofar as it had heretofore been developed would suggest open-ended contracts but does not appear to imply anything more—neither the residual claimant status nor the distinction between employee and subcontractor status (nor any of the implications indicated below). And it is not true that employees are generally employed on the basis of long-term contractual arrangements any more than on a series of short-term or indefinite length contracts.

The importance of our proposed additional elements is revealed, for example, by the explanation of why the person to whom the control monitor is responsible receives the residual, and also by our later discussion of the implications about the corporation, partnerships, and profit sharing. These alternative forms for organization of the firm are difficult to resolve on the basis of market transaction costs only. Our exposition also suggests a definition of the classical firm—something crucial that was heretofore absent.

In addition, sometimes a technological development will lower the cost of market transactions while, at the same time, it expands the role of the firm. When the "putting out" system was used for weaving, inputs were organized largely through market negotiations. With the development of efficient central sources of power, it became economical to perform weaving in proximity to the power source and to engage in team production. The bringing in of weavers surely must have resulted in a reduction in the cost of negotiating (forming) contracts. Yet, what we observe is the beginning of the factory system in which inputs are organized within a firm. Why? The weavers did not simply move to a common source of power that they could tap like an electric line, purchasing power while they used their own equipment. Now team production in the joint use of equipment became more important. The measurement of marginal productivity, which now involved interactions between workers, especially through their joint use of machines, became more difficult though contract negotiating cost was reduced, while managing the *behavior* of inputs became easier because of the increased centralization of activity. The firm as an organization expanded even though the cost of transactions was reduced by the advent of centralized power. The same could be said for modern assembly lines. Hence the emergence of central power sources expanded the scope of productive activity in which the firm enjoyed a comparative advantage as an organizational form.

Some economists, following Knight, have identified the bearing of risks of wealth changes with the director or central employer without explaining why that is a viable arrangement. Presumably, the more riskaverse inputs become employees rather than owners of the classical firm. Risk averseness and uncertainty *with regard to the firm's fortunes* have little, if anything, to do with our explanation although it helps to explain why all resources in a team are not owned by one person. That is, the role of risk taken in the sense of absorbing the windfalls that buffet the firm because of unforeseen competition, technological change, or fluctuations in demand are not central to our theory, although it is true that imperfect knowledge and, therefore, risk, in *this* sense of risk, underlie the problem of monitoring team behavior. We deduce the system of paying the manager with a residual claim (the equity) from the desire to have efficient means to reduce shirking so as to make team production economical and not from the smaller aversion to the risks of enterprise in a dynamic economy. We conjecture that "distribution-of-risk" is not a valid rationale for the *existence* and organization of the *classical* firm.

Although we have emphasized team production as creating a costly metering task and have treated team production as an essential (necessary?) condition for the firm, would not other obstacles to cheap metering also call forth the same kind of contractual arrangement here denoted as a firm? For example, suppose a farmer produces wheat in an easily ascertained quantity but with subtle and difficult to detect quality variations determined by how the farmer grew the wheat. A vertical integration could allow a purchaser to control the farmer's behavior in order to more economically estimate productivity. But this is not a case of joint or team production, unless "information" can be considered part of the product. (While a good case could be made for that broader conception of production, we shall ignore it here.) Instead of forming a firm, a buyer can contract to have his inspector on the site of production, just as home builders contract with architects to supervise building contracts; that arrangement is not a firm. Still, a firm might be organized in the production of many products wherein no team production or jointness of use of separately owned resources is involved.

This possibility rather clearly indicates a broader, or complementary, approach to that which we have chosen. (1) As we do in this paper, it can be argued that the firm is the particular policing device utilized when joint team production is present. If other sources of high policing costs arise, as in the wheat case just indicated, some other form of contractual arrangement will be used. Thus to each source of information cost there may be a different type of policing and contractual arrangement. (2) On the other hand, one can say that where policing is difficult across markets, various forms of contractual arrangements are devised, but there is no reason for that known as the firm to be uniquely related or even highly correlated with team production, as defined here. It might be used equally probably and viably for other sources of high policing cost. We have not intensively analyzed other sources, and we can only note that our current and readily revisable conjecture is that (1) is valid, and has motivated us in our current endeavor. In any event, the test of the theory advanced here is to see whether the conditions we have identified are necessary for firms to have long-run viability rather than merely births with high infant mortality. Conglomerate firms or collections of separate production agencies into one owning organization can be interpreted as an investment trust or investment diversification device—probably along the lines that motivated Knight's interpretation. A holding company can be called a firm, because of the common association of the word firm with any ownership unit that owns income sources. The term firm as commonly used is so turgid of meaning that we can not hope to explain every entity to which the name is attached in common or even technical literature. Instead, we seek to identify and explain a particular contractual arrangement induced by the cost of information factors analyzed in this paper.

IV. Types of Firms

A. Profit-Sharing Firms. Explicit in our explanation of the capitalist firm is the assumption that the cost of *managing* the team's inputs by a central monitor, who disciplines himself because he is a residual claimant, is low relative to the cost of metering the marginal outputs of team members.

If we look within a firm to see who monitors—hires, fires, changes, promotes, and renegotiates—we should find him being a residual claimant or, at least, one whose pay or reward is more than any others correlated with fluctuations in the residual value of the firm. They more likely will have options or rights or bonuses than will inputs with other tasks.

An implicit "auxiliary" assumption of our explanation of the firm is that the cost of team production is increased if the residual claim is not held entirely by the central monitor. That is, we assume that if profit sharing had to be relied upon for *all* team members, losses from the resulting increase in central monitor shirking would exceed the output gains from the increased incentives of other team members not to shirk. If the optimal team size is only two owners of inputs, then an equal division of profits and losses between them will leave each with stronger incentives to reduce shirking than if the optimal team size is large, for in the latter case only a smaller percentage of the losses occasioned by the shirker will be borne by him. Incentives to shirk are positively related to the optimal size of the team under an equal profit-sharing scheme.[10]

The preceding does not imply that profit sharing is never viable. Profit sharing to encourage self-policing is more appropriate for small teams. And, indeed, where input owners are free to make whatever contractual arrangements suit them, as generally is true in capitalist economies, profit sharing seems largely limited to partnerships with a relatively small number of *active*[11] partners. Another advantage of such arrangements for smaller teams is that it permits more effective reciprocal monitoring among inputs. Monitoring need not be entirely specialized.

Profit sharing is more viable if small team size is associated with situations where the cost of specialized management of inputs is large relative to the increased productivity potential in team effort. We conjecture that the cost of managing team inputs increases if the productivity of a team member is difficult to correlate with his behavior. In "artistic" or "professional" work, watching a man's activities is not a good clue to what he is actually thinking or doing with his mind. While it is relatively easy to manage or direct the loading of trucks by a team of dock workers where input activity is so highly related in an obvious way to output, it is more difficult to manage and direct a lawyer in the preparation and presentation of a case. Dock workers can be directed in detail without the monitor himself loading the truck, and assembly line workers can be monitored by varying the speed of the assembly line, but detailed direction in the preparation of a law case would require in much greater degree that the monitor prepare the case himself. As a result, artistic or professional inputs, such as lawyers, advertising specialists, and doctors, will be given relatively freer reign with regard to individual behavior. If the management of inputs is relatively costly, or ineffective, as it would seem to be in these cases, but, nonetheless if team effort is more productive than separable production with exchange across markets, then there will develop a tendency to use profit-sharing schemes to provide incentives to avoid shirking.[12]

B. Socialist Firms. We have analyzed the classical proprietorship and the profit-sharing firms in the context of free association and choice of economic organization. Such organizations need not be the most viable when political constraints limit the forms of organization that can be chosen. It is one thing to have profit sharing when professional or artistic talents are used by small teams. But if political or tax or subsidy considerations induce profit-sharing techniques when these are not otherwise economically justified, then additional management techniques will be developed to help reduce the degree of shirking.

For example, most, if not all, firms in Jugoslavia are owned by the employees in the restricted sense that all share in the residual. This is true for large firms and for firms which employ nonartistic, or nonprofessional, workers as well. With a decay of political constraints, most of these firms could be expected to rely on paid wages rather than shares in the residual. This rests on our auxiliary assumption that general sharing in the residual results in losses from enhanced shirking by the monitor that exceed the gains from reduced shirking by residual-sharing employees. If this were not so, profit sharing with employees should have occurred more frequently in Western societies where such organizations are neither banned nor preferred politically. Where residual sharing by employees is politically imposed, as in Jugoslavia, we are led to expect that some management technique will arise to reduce the shirking by the central monitor, a technique that will not be found frequently in Western societies since the monitor retains all (or much) of the residual in the West and profit sharing is largely confined to small, professional-artistic team production situations. We do find in the larger scale residual-sharing firms in Jugoslavia that there are employee committees that can recommend (to the state) the termination of a manager's contract (veto his continuance) with the enterprise. We conjecture that the workers' committee is given the right to recommend the termination of the manager's contract precisely because the general sharing of the residual increases "excessively" the manager's incentive to shirk.[13]

   C. *The Corporation.* All firms must initially acquire command over some resources. The corporation does so primarily by selling promises of future returns to those who (as creditors or owners) provide financial capital. In some situations resources can be acquired in advance from consumers by promises of future delivery (for example, advance sale of a proposed book). Or where the firm is a few artistic or professional persons, each can "chip in" with time and talent until the sale of services brings in revenues. For the most part, capital can be acquired more cheaply if many (risk-averse) investors contribute small portions to a large investment. The economies of raising large sums of equity capital in this way suggest that modifications in the relationship among corporate inputs are required to cope with the shirking problem that arises with profit sharing among large numbers of corporate stockholders. One modification is limited liability, especially for firms that are large relative to a stockholder's wealth. It serves to protect stockholders from large losses no matter how they are caused.

   If every stock owner participated in each decision in a corporation, not only would large bureaucratic costs be incurred, but many would shirk the task of becoming well informed on the issue to be decided, since the losses associated with unexpectedly bad decisions will be borne in large part by the many other corporate shareholders. More effective control of corporate activity is achieved for most purposes by transferring decision authority to a smaller group, whose main function is to negotiate with and manage (renegotiate with) the other inputs of the team. The corporate stockholders retain the authority to revise the membership of the management group and over major decisions that affect the structure of the corporation or its dissolution.

As a result a new modification of partnerships is induced—the right to sale of corporate shares without approval of any other stockholders. Any shareholder can remove his wealth from control by those with whom he has differences of opinion. Rather than try to control the decisions of the management, which is harder to do with many stockholders than with only a few, unrestricted salability provides a more acceptable escape to each stockholder from continued policies with which he disagrees.

Indeed, the policing of managerial shirking relies on across-market competition from new groups of would-be managers as well as competition from members within the firm who seek to displace existing management. In addition to competition from outside and inside managers, control is facilitated by the temporary congealing of share votes into voting blocs owned by one or a few contenders. Proxy battles or stock-purchases concentrate the votes required to displace the existing management or modify managerial policies. But it is more than a change in policy that is sought by the newly formed financial interests, whether of new stockholders or not. It is the capitalization of expected future benefits into stock prices that concentrates on the innovators the wealth gains of their actions if they own large numbers of shares. Without capitalization of future benefits, there would be less incentive to incur the costs required to exert informed decisive influence on the corporation's policies and managing personnel. Temporarily, the structure of ownership is reformed, moving away from diffused ownership into decisive power blocs, and this is a transient resurgence of the classical firm with power again concentrated in those who have title to the residual.

In assessing the significance of stockholders' power it is not the usual diffusion of voting power that is significant but instead the frequency with which voting congeals into decisive change. Even a one-man owned company may have a long term with just one manager—continuously being approved by the owner. Similarly a dispersed voting power corporation may be also characterized by a long-lived management. The question is the probability of replacement of the management if it behaves in ways not acceptable to a majority of the stockholders. The unrestricted salability of stock and the transfer of proxies enhances the probability of decisive action in the event current stockholders or any outsider believes that management is not doing a good job with the corporation. We are not comparing the corporate responsiveness to that of a single proprietorship; instead, we are indicating features of the corporate structure that are induced by the problem of delegated authority to manager-monitors.[14]

D. Mutual and Nonprofit Firms. The benefits obtained by the new management are greater if the stock can be purchased and sold, because this enables *capitalization* of anticipated future improvements into present *wealth* of new managers who bought stock and created a larger capital by their management changes. But in nonprofit corporations, colleges, churches, country clubs, mutual savings banks, mutual insurance companies, and "coops," the future consequences of improved management are not capitalized into present wealth of stockholders. (As if to make more difficult that competition by new would-be monitors, multiple shares of ownership in those enterprises cannot be bought by one person.) One should, therefore, find greater shirking in nonprofit, mutually owned enterprises. (This suggests that nonprofit enterprises are especially appropriate in realms of endeavor where more shirking is desired and where redirected uses of the enterprise in response to market-revealed values is less desired.)

E. Partnerships. Team production in artistic or professional intellectual skills will more likely be by partnerships than other types of team production. This amounts to market-organized team activity and to a nonemployer status. Self-monitoring partnerships, therefore, will be used rather than employer-employee contracts, and these organizations will be small to prevent an excessive dilution of efforts through shirking. Also, partnerships are more likely to occur among relatives or long-standing acquaintances, not necessarily because they share a common utility function, but also because each knows better the other's work characteristics and tendencies to shirk.

F. Employee Unions. Employee unions, whatever else they do, perform as monitors for employees. Employers monitor employees and similarly employees monitor an employer's performance. Are correct wages paid on time and in good currency? Usually, this is extremely easy to check. But some forms of employer performance are less easy to meter and are more subject to employer shirking. Fringe benefits often are in nonpecuniary, contingent form; medical, hospital, and accident insurance, and retirement pensions are contingent payments or performances partly in *kind* by employers to employees. Each employee cannot judge the character of such payments as easily as money wages. Insurance is a contingent payment—what the employee will get upon the contingent event may come as a disappointment. If he could easily determine what other employees had gotten upon such contingent events he could judge more accurately the performance by the employer. He could "trust" the employer not to shirk in such fringe contingent payments, but he would prefer an effective and economic monitor of those payments. We see a specialist monitor—the union employees' agent—hired by them and monitoring those aspects of employer payment most difficult for the employees to monitor. Employees should be willing to employ a specialist monitor to administer such hard-to-detect employer performance, even though their monitor has incentives to use pension and retirement funds not entirely for the benefit of employees.

V. Team Spirit and Loyalty

Every team member would prefer a team in which no one, not even himself, shirked. Then the true marginal costs and values could be equated to achieve more preferred positions. If one could enhance a common interest in nonshirking in the guise of a team loyalty or team spirit, the team would be more efficient. In those sports where team activity is most clearly exemplified, the sense of loyalty and team spirit is most strongly urged. Obviously the team is better, with team spirit and loyalty, because of the reduced shirking—not because of some other feature inherent in loyalty or spirit as such.[15]

Corporations and business firms try to instill a spirit of loyalty. This should not be viewed simply as a device to increase profits by *overworking* or misleading the employees, nor as an adolescent urge for belonging. It promotes a closer approximation to the employees' potentially available true rates of substitution between production and leisure and enables each team member to achieve a more preferred situation. The difficulty, of course, is to create economically that team spirit and loyalty. It can be preached with an aura of moral code of conduct—a morality with literally the same basis as the ten commandments—to restrict our conduct toward what we would choose if we bore our full costs.

VI. Kinds of Inputs Owned by the Firm

To this point the discussion has examined why firms, as we have defined them, exist? That is, why is there an owner-employer who is the common party to contracts with other owners of inputs in team activity? The answer to that question should also indicate the kind of the jointly used resources likely to be owned by the central-owner-monitor and the kind likely to be hired from people who are not team-owners. Can we identify characteristics or features of various inputs that lead to their being hired or to their being owned by the firm?

How can residual-claimant, central-employer-owner demonstrate ability to pay the other hired inputs the promised amount in the event of a loss? He can pay in advance or he can commit wealth sufficient to cover negative residuals. The latter will take the form of machines, land, buildings, or raw materials committed to the firm. Commitments of labor-wealth (i.e., human wealth) given the property rights in people, is less feasible. These considerations suggest that residual claimants—owners of the firm—will be investors of resalable capital equipment in the firm. The goods or inputs more likely to be invested, than rented, by the owners of the enterprise, will have higher resale values relative to the initial cost and will have longer expected use in a firm relative to the economic life of the good.

But beyond these factors are those developed above to explain the existence of the institution known as the firm—the costs of detecting output performance. When a durable resource is used it will have a marginal product and a depreciation. Its use requires payment to cover at least use-induced depreciation; unless that user cost is specifically detectable, payment for it will be demanded in accord with *expected* depreciation. And we can ascertain circumstances for each. An indestructible hammer with a readily detectable marginal product has zero user cost. But suppose the hammer were destructible and that careless (which is easier than careful) use is more abusive and causes greater depreciation of the hammer. Suppose in addition the abuse is easier to detect by observing the way it is used than by observing only the hammer after its use, or by measuring the output scored from a hammer by a laborer. If the hammer were rented and used in the absence of the owner, the depreciation would be greater than if the use were observed by the owner and the user charged in accord with the imposed depreciation. (Careless use is more likely than careful use—if one does not pay for the greater depreciation.) An absentee owner would therefore ask for a higher rental price because of the higher *expected* user cost than if the item were used by the owner. The expectation is higher because of the greater difficulty of observing specific user cost, by inspection of the hammer after use. Renting is therefore in this case more costly than owner use. This is the valid content of the misleading expressions about ownership being more economical than renting—ignoring all other factors that may work in the opposite direction, like tax provision, short-term occupancy and capital risk avoidance.

Better examples are tools of the trade. Watch repairers, engineers, and carpenters tend to own their own tools especially if they are portable. Trucks are more likely to be employee owned rather than other equally expensive team inputs because it is relatively cheap for the driver to police the care taken in using a truck. Policing the use of trucks by a nondriver owner is more likely to occur for trucks that are not specialized to one driver, like public transit busses.

The factor with which we are concerned here is one related to the costs of monitoring not only the gross product performance of an input but also the abuse or depreciation inflicted on the input in the course of its use. If depreciation or user cost is more cheaply detected when the owner can see its use than by only seeing the input before and after, there is a force toward owner use rather than renting. Resources whose user cost is harder to detect when used by someone else, tend on this count to be owner-used. Absentee ownership, in the lay language, will be less likely. Assume momentarily that labor service cannot be performed in the absence of its owner. The labor owner can more cheaply monitor any abuse of himself than if somehow labor-services could be provided without the labor owner observing its mode of use or knowing what was happening. Also his incentive to abuse himself is increased if he does not own himself.[16]

The similarity between the preceding analysis and the question of absentee landlordism and of sharecropping arrangements is no accident. The same factors which explain the contractual arrangements known as a firm help to explain the incidence of tenancy, labor hiring or sharecropping.[17]

VII. Firms as a Specialized Market Institution for Collecting, Collating, and Selling Input Information

The firm serves as a highly specialized surrogate market. Any person contemplating a joint-input activity must search and detect the qualities of available joint inputs. He could contact an employment agency, but that agency in a small town would have little advantage over a large firm with many inputs. The employer, by virtue of monitoring many inputs, acquires special superior information about their productive talents. This aids his *directive* (i.e., market hiring) efficiency. He "sells" his information to employee-inputs as he aids them in ascertaining good input combinations for team activity. Those who work as employees or who rent services to him are using him to discern superior combinations of inputs. Not only does the director-employer ''decide'' what each input will produce, he also estimates which heterogeneous inputs will work together jointly more efficiently, and he does this in the context of a privately owned market for forming teams. The department store is a firm and is a superior private market. People who shop and work in one town can as well shop and work in a privately owned firm.

This marketing function is obscured in the theoretical literature by the assumption of homogeneous factors. Or it is tacitly left for individuals to do themselves via personal market search, much as if a person had to search without benefit of specialist retailers. Whether or not the firm arose because of this efficient information service, it gives the director-employer more knowledge about the productive talents of the team's inputs, and a basis for superior decisions about efficient or profitable combinations of those heterogeneous resources.

In other words, opportunities for profitable team production by inputs already within the firm may be ascertained more economically and accurately than for resources outside the firm. Superior combinations of inputs can be more economically identified and formed from resources already used in the organization than by obtaining new resources (and knowledge of them) from the outside. Promotion and revision of employee assignments (contracts) will be preferred by a firm to the hiring of new inputs. To the extent that this occurs there is reason to expect the firm to be able to operate as a conglomerate rather than persist in producing a single product. Efficient production with heterogeneous resources is a result not of having *better* resources but in *knowing more accurately* the relative productive performances of those resources. Poorer resources can be paid less in accord with their inferiority; greater accuracy of knowledge of the potential and actual productive actions of inputs rather than having high productivity resources makes a firm (or an assignment of inputs) profitable.[18]

VIII. Summary

While ordinary contracts facilitate efficient specialization according to comparative advantage, a special class of contracts among a group of joint inputs to a team production process is commonly used for team production. Instead of multilateral contracts among all the joint inputs' owners, a central common party to a set of bilateral contracts facilitates efficient organization of the joint inputs in team production. The terms of the contracts form the basis of the entity called the firm—especially appropriate for organizing team production processes.

Team productive activity is that in which a union, or joint use, of inputs yields a larger output than the sum of the products of the separately used inputs. This team production requires—like all other production processes—an assessment of marginal productivities if efficient production is to be achieved. Nonseparability of the products of several differently owned joint inputs raises the cost of assessing the marginal productivities of those resources or services of each input owner. Monitoring or metering the productivities to match marginal productivities to costs of inputs and thereby to reduce shirking can be achieved more economically (than by across market bilateral negotiations among inputs) in a firm.

The essence of the classical firm is identified here as a contractual structure with: (1) joint input production; (2) several input owners; (3) one party who is common to all the contracts of the joint inputs; (4) who has rights to renegotiate any input's contract independently of contracts with other input owners; (5) who holds the residual claim; and (6) who has the right to sell his central contractual residual status. The central agent is called the firm's owner and the employer. No authoritarian control is involved; the arrangement is simply a contractual structure subject to continuous renegotiation with the central agent. The contractual structure arises as a means of enhancing efficient organization of team production. In particular, the ability to detect shirking among owners of jointly used inputs in team production is enhanced (detection costs are reduced) by this arrangement and the discipline (by revision of contracts) of input owners is made more economic.

Testable implications are suggested by the analysis of different types of organizations—nonprofit, proprietary for profit, unions, cooperatives, partnerships, and by the kinds of inputs that tend to be owned by the firm in contrast to those employed by the firm.

We conclude with a highly conjectural but possibly significant interpretation. As a consequence of the flow of information to the central party (employer), the firm takes on the characteristic of an efficient market in that information about the productive characteristics of a large set of specific inputs is now more cheaply available. Better recombinations or new uses of resources can be more efficiently ascertained than by the conventional search through the general market. In this sense inputs compete with each other within and via a firm rather than solely across markets as conventionally conceived. Emphasis on interfirm competition obscures intrafirm competition among inputs. Conceiving competition as the *revelation and exchange* of knowledge or information about qualities, potential uses of different inputs in different potential applications indicates that the firm is a device for enhancing competition among sets of input resources as well as a device for more efficiently rewarding the inputs. In contrast to markets and cities which can be viewed as publicly or nonowned market places, the firm can be considered a privately owned market; if so, we could consider the firm and the ordinary market as competing types of markets, competition between private proprietary markets and public or communal markets. Could it be that the market suffers from the defects of communal property rights in organizing and influencing uses of valuable resources?

Notes

1. Meter means to measure and also to apportion. One can meter (measure) output and one can also meter (control) the output. We use the word to denote both; the context should indicate which.

2. A producer's wealth would be reduced by the present capitalized value of the future income lost by loss of reputation. Reputation, i.e., credibility, is an asset, which is another way of saying that reliable information about expected performance is both a costly and a valuable good. For acts of God that interfere with contract performance, both parties have incentives to reach a settlement akin to that which would have been reached if such events had been covered by specific contingency clauses. The reason, again, is that a reputation for "honest" dealings—i.e., for actions similar to those that would probably have been reached had the contract provided this contingency—is wealth.

    Almost every contract is open-ended in that many contingencies are uncovered. For example, if a fire delays production of a promised product by A to B, and if B contends that A has not fulfilled the contract, how is the dispute settled and what recompense, if any, does A grant to B? A person uninitiated in such questions may be surprised by the extent to which contracts permit either party to escape performance or to nullify the contract. In fact, it is hard to imagine any contract, which, when taken solely in terms of its stipulations, could not be evaded by one of the parties. Yet that is the ruling, viable type of contract. Why? Undoubtedly the best discussion that we have seen on this question is by Stewart Macaulay [1963a].

    There are means not only of detecting or preventing cheating, but also for deciding how to allocate the losses or gains of unpredictable events or quality of items exchanged. Sales contracts contain warranties, guarantees, collateral, return privileges and penalty clauses for specific nonperformance. These are means of assignment of *risks* of losses of cheating. A lower price without warranty—an "as is" purchase—places more of the risk on the buyer while the seller buys insurance against losses of his "cheating." On the other hand, a warranty or return privilege or service contract places more risk on the seller with insurance being bought by the buyer.

3. The function is separable into additive functions if the cross partial derivative is zero, i.e., if $\partial^2 Z/\partial X_i \partial X_j = 0$.

4. With sufficient generality of notation and conception this team production function could be formulated as a case of the generalized production function interpretation given by our colleague, Thompson (1970).

5. More precisely: "if anything other than pecuniary income enters his utility function." Leisure stands for all nonpecuniary income for simplicity of exposition.

6. Do not assume that the sole result of the cost of detecting shirking is one form of payment (more leisure and less take home money). With several members of the team, each has an incentive to cheat against each other by engaging in more than the average amount of such leisure if the employer cannot tell at zero cost which employee is taking more than average. As a result the total productivity of the team is lowered. Shirking detection costs thus change the form of payment and also result in lower total rewards. Because the cross partial derivatives are positive, shirking reduces other people's marginal products.

7. What is meant by performance? Input energy, initiative, work attitude, perspiration, rate of exhaustion? Or output? It is the latter that is sought—the *effect* or output. But performance is nicely ambiguous because it suggests both input and output. It is *nicely* ambiguous because as we shall see, sometimes by inspecting a team member's input activity we can better judge his output effect, perhaps not with complete accuracy but better than by watching the output of the *team*. It is not always the case that watching input activity is the only or best means of detecting, measuring or monitoring output effects of each team member, but in some cases it is a useful way. For the moment the word performance glosses over these aspects and facilitates concentration on other issues.

8. Removal of (b) converts a capitalist proprietary firm to a socialist firm.

9. Recognition must also be made to the seminal inquiries by Silver and Auster (1969), and by Malmgren (1961).

10. While the degree to which residual claims are centralized will affect the size of the team, this will be only one of many factors that determine team size, so as an approximation, we can treat team size as exogenously determined. Under certain assumptions about the shape of the "typical" utility function, the incentive to avoid shirking with unequal profit sharing can be measured by the Herfindahl index.

11. The use of the word active will be clarified in our discussion of the corporation, which follows below.

12. Some sharing contracts, like crop sharing, or rental payments based on gross sales in retail stores, come close to profit sharing. However, it is gross output sharing rather than profit sharing. We are unable to specify the implications of the difference. We refer the reader to Cheung (1969).

13. Incidentally, investment activity will be changed. The inability to capitalize the investment value as "take-home" private property *wealth* of the members of

the firm means that the benefits of the investment must be taken as annual income by those who are employed at the time of the income. Investment will be confined more to those with shorter life and with higher rates or pay-offs if the alternative of investing is paying out the firm's income to its employees to take home and use as private property. For a development of this proposition, see the papers by Furobotn and Pejovich (1970), and by Pejovich (1969).

14. Instead of thinking of shareholders as joint *owners*, we can think of them as investors, like bondholders, except that the stockholders are more optimistic than bondholders about the enterprise prospects. Instead of buying bonds in the corporation, thus enjoying smaller risks, shareholders prefer to invest funds with a greater realizable return if the firm prospers as expected, but with smaller (possibly negative) returns if the firm performs in a manner closer to that expected by the more pessimistic investors. The pessimistic investors, in turn, regard only the bonds as likely to pay off.

     If the entrepreneur-organizer is to raise capital on the best terms to him, it is to his advantage, as well as that of prospective investors, to recognize these differences in expectations. The residual claim on earnings enjoyed by shareholders does not serve the function of enhancing their efficiency as monitors in the general situation. The stockholders are "merely" the less risk-averse or the more optimistic member of the group that finances the firm. Being more optimistic than the average and seeing a higher mean value future return, they are willing to pay more for a certificate that allows them to realize gain on their expectations. One method of doing so is to buy claims to the distribution of returns that "they see" while bondholders, who are more pessimistic, purchase a claim to the distribution that they see as more likely to emerge. Stockholders are then comparable to warrant holders. They care not about the voting rights (usually not attached to warrants); they are in the same position in so far as voting rights are concerned as are bondholders. The only difference is in the probability distribution of reward and the terms on which they can place their bets.

     If we treat bondholders, preferred and convertible preferred stockholders, and common stockholders and warrant holders as simply different classes of investors—differing not only in their risk averseness but in their beliefs about the probability distribution of the firm's future earnings, why should stockholders be regarded as "owners" in any sense distinct from the other financial investors? The entrepreneur-organizer, who let us assume is the chief operating officer and sole repository of control of the corporation, does not find his authority residing in common stockholders (except in the case of a take over). Does this type of control make any difference in the way the firm is conducted? Would it make any difference in the kinds of behavior that would be tolerated by competing managers and investors (and we here deliberately refrain from thinking of them as owner-stockholders in the traditional sense)?

     Investment old timers recall a significant incidence of nonvoting common stock, now prohibited in corporations whose stock is traded on listed exhanges. (Why prohibited?) The entrepreneur in those days could hold voting shares while investors held nonvoting shares, which in every other respect were identical. Nonvoting share holders were simply investors devoid of ownership connotations. The control and behavior of inside owners in such corporations has never, so far as we have ascertained, been carefully studied. For example, at the simplest level of interest, does the evidence indicate that nonvoting shareholders fared any worse because of not having voting rights? Did owners permit the non-voting holders the normal return available to voting shareholders? Though evidence is prohibitively expensive to obtain, it is remarkable that voting and nonvoting shares sold for essentially identical prices, even during some proxy battles. However, our casual evidence deserves no more than interest-initiating weight.

One more point. The facade is deceptive. Instead of nonvoting shares, today we have warrants, convertible preferred stocks all of which are solely or partly "equity" claims without voting rights, though they could be converted into voting shares.

In sum, is it the case that the stockholder-investor relationship is one emanating from the *division* of *ownership* among several people, or is it that the collection of investment funds from people of varying anticipations is the underlying factor? If the latter, why should any of them be thought of as the owners in whom voting rights, whatever they may signify or however exercisable, should reside in order to enhance efficiency? Why voting rights in any of the outside, participating investors?

Our initial perception of this possibly significant difference in interpreta tion was precipitated by Henry Manne [1965]. A reading of his paper makes it clear that it is hard to understand why an investor who wishes to back and "share" in the consequences of some new business should necessarily have to acquire voting power (i.e., power to change the manager-operator) in order to invest in the venture. In fact, we invest in some ventures in the hope that no other stockholders will be so "foolish" as to try to toss out the incumbent management. We want him to have the power to stay in office, and for the prospect of sharing in his fortunes we buy nonvoting common stock. Our willingness to invest is enhanced by the knowledge that we can act legally via fraud, embezzlement and other laws to help assure that we outside investors will not be "milked" beyond our initial discounted anticipations.

15. *Sports Leagues:* Professional sports contests among teams is typically conducted by a *league* of teams. We assume that sports consumers are interested not only in absolute sporting skill but also in skills *relative* to other teams. Being slightly better than opposing teams enables one to claim a major portion of the receipts; the inferior team does not release resources and reduce costs, since they were expected in the play of contest. Hence, absolute skill is developed beyond the equality of marginal investment in sporting skill with its true social marginal value product. It follows there will be a tendency to overinvest in training athletes and developing teams. "Reverse shirking" arises, as budding players are induced to overpractice hyperactively relative to the social marginal value of their enhanced skills. To prevent overinvestment, the teams seek an agreement with each other to restrict practice, size of teams, and even pay of the team members (which reduces incentives of young people to overinvest in developing skills). Ideally, if all the contestant teams were owned by one owner, overinvestment in sports would be avoided, much as ownership of common fisheries or underground oil or water reserve would prevent overinvestment. This hyperactivity (to suggest the opposite of shirking) is controlled by the league of teams, wherein the league adopts a common set of constraints on each team's behavior. In effect, the teams are no longer really owned by the team owners but are super-

vised by them, much as the franchisers of some product. They are not fullfledged owners of their business, including the brand name, and can not "do what they wish" as franchises. Comparable to the franchiser, is the league commissioner or conference president, who seeks to restrain hyperactivity, as individual team supervisors compete with each other and cause external diseconomies. Such restraints are usually regarded as anticompetitive, antisocial, collusive-cartel devices to restrain free open competition, and reduce players' salaries. However, the interpretation presented here is premised on an attempt to avoid hyperinvestment in team sports production. Of course, the team operators have an incentive, once the league is formed and restraints are placed on hyper-investment activity, to go further and obtain the private benefits of monopoly restriction. To what extent overinvestment is replaced by monopoly restriction is not yet determinable; nor have we seen an empirical test of these two competing, but mutually consistent interpretations. (This interpretation of league-sports activity was proposed by Thompson [1970] and formulated by Canes [1970].) Again, athletic teams clearly exemplify the specialization of monitoring with captains and coaches; a captain detects shirkers while the coach trains and selects strategies and tactics. Both functions may be centralized in one person.

16. Professional athletes in baseball, football, and basketball, where athletes having sold their source of service to the team owners upon entering into sports activity, are owned by team owners. Here the team owners must monitor the athletes' physical condition and behavior to protect the team owners' wealth. The athlete has *less* (not, *no*) incentive to protect or enhance his athletic prowess since capital value changes have less impact on his own wealth and more on the team owners. Thus, some athletes sign up for big initial bonuses (representing present capital value of future services). Future salaries are lower by the annuity value of the prepaid "bonus" and hence the athlete has *less* to lose by subsequent abuse of his athletic prowess. Any decline in his subsequent service value would in part be borne by the team owner who owns the player's future service. This does not say these losses of future salaries have no effect on preservation of athletic talent (we are not making a "sunk cost" error). Instead, we assert that the preservation is reduced, not eliminated, because the amount of loss of wealth suffered is smaller. The athlete will spend less to maintain or enhance his prowess thereafter. The effect of this revised incentive system is evidenced in comparisons of the kinds of attention and care imposed on the athletes at the "expense of the team owner" in the case where athletes' future services are owned by the team owner with that where future labor service values are owned by the athlete himself. Why athletes' future athletic services are owned by the team owners rather than being hired is a question we should be able to answer. One presumption is cartelization and monopsony gains to team owners. Another is exactly the theory being expounded in this paper—costs of monitoring production of athletes; we know not on which to rely.

17. The analysis used by Cheung (1969) in explaining the prevalence of sharecropping and land tenancy arrangements is built squarely on the same factors—the costs of detecting output performance of jointly used inputs in team production and the costs of detecting user costs imposed on the various inputs if owner used or if rented.

18. According to our interpretation, the firm is a specialized surrogate for a market for team use of inputs; it provides superior (i.e., cheaper) collection and collation of knowledge about heterogeneous resources. The greater the set of inputs about which knowledge of performance is being collated within a firm the greater are the present costs of the collation activity. Then, the larger the firm (market) the greater the attenuation of monitor control. To counter this force, the firm will be divisionalized in ways that economize on those costs—just as will the market be specialized. So far as we can ascertain, other theories of the reasons for firms have no such implications.

In Japan, employees by custom work nearly their entire lives with one firm, and the firm agrees to that expectation. Firms will tend to be large and conglomerate to enable a broader scope of input revision. Each firm is, in effect, a small economy engaging in "intranational and international" trade. Analogously, Americans expect to spend their whole lives in the United States, and the bigger the country, in terms of variety of resources, the easier it is to adjust to changing tastes and circumstances. Japan, with its lifetime employees, should be characterized more by large, conglomerate firms. Presumably, at some size of the firm, specialized knowledge about inputs becomes as expensive to transmit across divisions of the firms as it does across markets to other firms.

THREE

The Economics of
Organizational Structure

In many ways, the study of organizational structure marked the birth of organizational sociology. Beginning with Weber's (1946) analysis of the structure of bureaucracy and continuing with Blau's (1963) analysis of the structure of two government bureaus, this area of research has flourished over the years.

One of the most striking attributes of this line of research is that it has usually been conducted in a language that is foreign to managers. That is, while managers often talk in terms of functional departments and profit centers (Chandler, 1962), much of the study of organization structure has relied on concepts like differentiation, centralization, and integration (Lawrence and Lorsch, 1967).

The use of a specialized vocabulary to talk about organizational structure stands in marked contrast to work on structure done by organizational economists. While much of organizational economics is abstract and employs specialized vocabularies, research on structure has tended to be relatively applied in character, developed in a language familiar to management. In Chapter Two, for example, Alchian and Demsetz (1972) used the problems of metering associated with team production to suggest why firms exist as an alternative to markets for organizing economic transactions. They then went on to apply these ideas in explaining how different forms of ownership mitigate the metering problems that exist in team production. In doing so, Alchian and Demsetz implicitly developed a typology of organizational forms based on the structure of ownership rights. The categories of organization included in their typology are familiar to managers, including sole proprietorships, corporations, limited partnerships, and so on. For organizational economists like Alchian and Demsetz, firm structure is less a collection of abstract dimensions and more a set of discrete structural forms.

Williamson ("The Multidivisional Structure") continues this emphasis on discrete structural categories in his analysis of organizational structure. However, unlike Alchian and Demsetz, Williamson does not depend on the structure of ownership rights for his typology. Rather, Williamson relies on the informational properties of different organizational configurations.

Williamson's analysis suggests three basic organizational structures: the unitary, or U-form; the holding, or H-form; and the multidivisional, or M-form. Other organizational structures cited by Williamson are combinations of these three basic alternatives. U-form organizations are more commonly known as functional organizations. Groups within U-form organizations are organized around classic business functions, such as marketing, finance, and manufacturing. No one of these functions can conduct an entire business independently. The design, manufacture, and delivery of any product or service requires collaboration across all of the specialized units of the organization. Coordination among the units is provided through the direct intervention of the chief executive, who alone has access to multifunctional information and the potential for a companywide point of view.

Employing the chief executive of a U-form as the integrator and coordinator can work well as long as the firm is relatively small or in a relatively simple business. However, as a firm grows in size and complexity, it becomes difficult for one senior manager to provide the required direction and coordination. In these settings, U-form organizations begin to lose their efficiency.

Senior managers in successful entrepreneurial firms often report the consequences of this increase in size and complexity (Peters and Waterman, 1982). Chief executives in such organizations are usually unable to develop long-term strategic objectives. The top manager may try to redefine the total corporation in terms of the functional specialty he or she knows best. If their previous experience was in finance, for instance, these executives often focus on finance to the exclusion of other functions. If prior experience was in marketing, marketing gets companywide attention, while other functions suffer. Any such unbalanced focus will ultimately hurt the firm's performance.

The pure H-form company characteristically owns a large number of unrelated businesses. Each business is treated as a profit or investment center, and a general manager is given profit and loss responsibility for that center. In turn, each of the profit centers may be a U-form organization.

In an H-form organization, the role of the corporate staff is usually limited to evaluating financial performance, allocating corporate capital, and balancing the portfolio of businesses through acquisitions and divestitures. In this sense, the H-form organization is much like an internal capital market, with a business unit's financial performance determining the amount of capital it will receive and, ultimately, whether or not it will be kept or divested.

As an internal capital market, however, H-form organizations hold few advantages over external capital markets. For example, because H-form companies usually own all of the equity stock of their businesses, they have access, in principle at least, to information that is difficult for outside providers of capital to obtain. This information could enable the corporate staff in an H-form to make more informed capital allocation decisions than would be possible by the external capital market. However, in practice, the far-reaching diversification of H-form organizations makes it virtually impossible for the corporate staff to develop any but the most cursory understanding of the numerous businesses they own. Thus, potential information advantages are lost in the face of complexity from diversification.

Given this enormous complexity, corporate managers in H-form companies generally must rely on the simplest measures of financial performance, such as quarterly profits and sales, in making allocation decisions. These, of course, are precisely the same measures of firm performance used by the stock market to evaluate firms. In both the H-form and the stock market, such performance measures have the effect of emphasizing short-term performance, perhaps to the detriment of the long-term health and viability of the business (Hayes and Abernathy, 1980). Thus, in this crucial area, H-form companies, as an internal capital market, may not be superior to the external capital market, although empirical work in this area is not yet conclusive.

The underlying objective in owning a fully diversified portfolio of businesses, as is the case in a prototypical H-form, is to eliminate risk through diversification. The logic of diversification is straightforward: when some businesses are having a bad year, others will be having a good year, and the overall sales and profits of the corporation will be relatively stable over time. However, financial research in portfolio theory suggests that, without special information concerning the economic future of businesses in such a portfolio, the maximum expected rate of return on such a fully diversified portfolio of firms is a market rate of return (Copeland and Weston, 1979). That is, H-form companies can expect, on average, to perform no better than a well-managed, fully diversified portfolio of stocks.

Of course, some managers in H-form companies may not be satisfied with a market rate of return. Often, in an attempt to obtain a higher rate of return, corporate managers will try to exploit perceived opportunities in certain of their businesses. Unfortunately, because there are so many different businesses in an H-form, and because corporate managers cannot come to know any one of them intimately, more often than not, the result will be misinformed decision making and meddling. Thus, in seeking to improve performance beyond a market rate of return, corporate managers may end up unintentionally hurting the performance of both a particular business and the corporation as a whole.

Finally, in comparison to a fully diversified portfolio of stocks held by an individual stockholder, the portfolio of companies owned by an H-form is much less liquid. If, for any of a variety of reasons, an H-form decides to sell one of the businesses it controls, it must locate a potential buyer, convince that buyer that it has not stripped all assets from the company it is selling, and then negotiate a price. This is a selling situation where Akerlof's Lemons Principle (Chapter One) applies, since the H-form company selling a business knows a great deal more about that business than does a prospective buyer. Because buyers have a difficult time distinguishing between good and bad companies, the price of all companies being sold by H-forms reflects the probability that any one of them is bad. Thus, an H-form cannot expect to obtain the full value of a good company it is selling, which suggests that it will sell only bad companies, or perhaps that it will make a good company bad by stripping away all of its quality management and other assets. This reasoning suggests, at the very least, that H-forms may not be able to receive top dollar for the firms they decide to divest.

With all the problems of an H-form, one is forced to question why they exist at all. Although Williamson does not discuss this point in the article included here, it seems clear that H-forms are not unlike social experiments, which, for the most part, have not worked well. Indeed, recent evidence suggests that many of the H-form conglomerates created during the 1960s are currently selling off those businesses about which they know little in an attempt to focus on those businesses they know well (Leontiades, 1982). This more selective diversification of H-forms will leave many of these firms as M-form organizations.

This leads to Williamson's last primary structure, the M-form, or multidivisional structure. As the name implies, multidivisional organizations consist of a set of partially diversified business divisions. The degree of diversification in an M-form falls between that characteristic of a U-form and that of an H-form. Unlike the H-form case, there will exist several interdependencies or synergies between divisions in a typical M-form. One of the most important tasks of M-form corporate managers is to exploit these synergies.

As in the H-form, division general managers in an M-form are given profit and loss responsibility for their businesses. However, due to the interdependence between divisions, the profit and loss statement of each division is not perfectly unambiguous. The success of each business unit in an M-form depends, to some extent at least, on the use of shared business resources. For example, in many M-forms, several product divisions share common sales or research and development staffs. The success of each business unit depends, at least partly, on the success of these sales and research and development groups. As a result, the financial performance reported for each division will be an ambiguous measure of the underlying performance of a division considered individually.

Because of this interdependence, corporate managers must strike a careful balance in an M-form. On the one hand, they must encourage competition between divisions for capital and recognition. On the other hand, they must encourage cooperation in those areas where synergies exist between divisions in order to obtain higher overall levels of performance. M-forms that are able to strike this balance will outperform both large U-forms and all H-forms. This, in a nutshell, is Williamson's M-form hypothesis.

The M-form hypothesis is one of the most testable implications of the transaction cost model. Armour and Teece ("Organizational Structure and Economic Performance: A Test of the Multidivisional Hypothesis") attempt such a test using a sample of petroleum firms. The structure of Armour and Teece's analysis uses traditional microeconomic thinking and may be unfamiliar to many organization theorists. Within a microeconomic context, firms can obtain temporary superior financial performance by choosing and implementing a valuable organizational strategy. This implies that, in an industry where all firms are above some threshold in size and complexity, firms that innovate early and are one of the first to implement an M-form structure will enjoy a temporary performance advantage. Over time, as other firms in the industry imitate the M-form, these advantages will disappear, and performance will be approximately equal across firms, all other business factors being equal. The last few firms that implement the M-form structure should see their performance improve from below average to just average. In other words, while they will not realize an advantage from the M-form structure, they will no longer be at a disadvantage.

Armour and Teece use this diffusion logic to test the M-form hypothesis. While any empirical study can be criticized, these authors employ numerous relevant controls in their analysis, and apply widely accepted statistical methods. Their results are consistent with Williamson's predictions about the M-form structure.

Implications for Organization Theory

As was suggested earlier, research on organizational structure in organization theory focuses on underlying dimensions of structure like centralization, bureaucratization, differentiation (Lawrence and Lorsch, 1967; Hickson, Pugh, and Pheysey, 1969). One of the insights of Williamson's analysis is that the structure of an effective organization cannot be adequately described as a set of points on a number of independent dimensions. Structure in these firms is neither centralized, bureaucratic, and differentiated *or* decentralized, nonbureaucratic, and undifferentiated. Rather, the structure of firms, especially in the M-form case, is simultaneously centralized and decentralized, bureaucratic and nonbureaucratic, differentiated and undifferentiated. The nature of the structural relations between particular groups in a firm depends on the information necessary to conduct efficient transactions between groups. Where a great deal of local coordination and cooperation is needed, decentralized, nonbureaucratic, organic structures are appropriate. Where only minor local coordination and cooperation are required, centralized, bureaucratic, mechanistic, and even competitive structures are appropriate. This logic, not surprisingly, parallels exactly the logic of governance discussed in the previous chapter.

The challenge to senior managers in these firms, and again especially in M-form companies, is to harmonize these conflicting structures that exist within their operations. Balancing the degree of cooperation and competition in a firm is a task that is never solved once and for all. Rather, it is simply managed over time. Sometimes, there may be too much cooperation in the firm, at which time it might be necessary to increase the use of competitive structures. At other times, there may be too much competition, at which time it might be necessary to increase the use of cooperative structures. As technologies change, informational requirements change and organizational structures must change. The conception of organization structure presented here is not that structure is a static solution for a firm, but that a firm's structure defines the means through which constantly changing organizational requirements are isolated and met.

The Multidivisional Structure

Oliver E. Williamson

Starting with the assumption that in the beginning there were markets, progressively more ramified forms of internal organization have successively "evolved." First peer groups, then simple hierarchies, and finally the vertically integrated firm in which a compound hierarchy exists have appeared. As between alternative organizations of the compound hierarchy, the inside contracting system, which preserves considerable autonomy between the several functional parts and the center, was rejected in favor of an employment relation across all stages. What is referred to in Section 1, below, as the "unitary form" enterprise, has emerged.

The question addressed here is how ought the firm be organized as it continues to grow in size and complexity. Issues of both efficiency, with respect to a given goal, and effectiveness, with respect to the choice of goals, are posed. That a simple scaling up of the unitary form enterprise experiences problems that are greatly mitigated by a shift to the "multidivisional structure" illustrates the proposition that "the system cannot be derived from the parts; the system is an independent framework in which the parts are placed" (Angyal, 1969, p. 27)—which is to say once again that internal organization matters.

A discussion of some of the problems of the unitary form enterprise, as it takes on size and complexity, appears in Section 1. The displacement of the unitary form by the multidivisional structure is described and illustrated in Section 2. The distinctive properties of the multidivisional form in miniature capital market respects are examined in Section 3. Optimum divisionalization is discussed in Section 4. The "M-form hypothesis" and concluding remarks follow.

A major problem for testing the M-form hypothesis is that, if all divisionalized firms are classified as M-form firms without regard for the related internal decision-making and control apparatus, an overassignment to the M-form category will result. The internal controls in divisionalized firms are quite critical. A scheme for classifying firms according to internal structure is proposed in an Appendix.

Note: This chapter is a variant of a previously published paper on which Narottam Bhargava was a coauthor.

The Unitary Form Enterprise

1.1 Structural Attributes. As Chandler indicates (1962, Chap. 1), the late 1800s witnessed the emergence of the large, single-product, multifunctioned enterprise—in steel, meatpacking, tobacco, oil, and so forth. These firms were organized along functional lines and will be referred to as unitary form (or U-form) enterprises. The principal operating units in the U-form firm are the functional divisions—sales, finance, manufacturing—as shown in the organization chart in Figure 1. Specialization by function not only was then, but, in organizations of only moderate size at least, is now the "natural" way by which to organize multifunctional activities. In many respects, this is the vertical integration issue. Specialization by function permits both economies of scale and an efficient division of labor to be realized—provided that control over the various parts can also be realized (Ansoff and Brandenberg, 1971, pp. 718–720).

1.2 Consequences of Radial Expansion. The question to be addressed is what problems does the U-form enterprise experience when it expands, if the U-form (functional) basis for decomposing the enterprise remains in effect throughout? An answer that is both compelling and compact is not easy to provide. Mainly, what is involved is that radial expansion of the U-form enterprise (1) experiences cumulative "control loss" effects, which have internal efficiency consequences, and (2) eventually alters the character of the strategic decision-making process in ways that favor attending to other-than-profit objectives.[1] Chandler summarizes the defects of the large U-form enterprise in the following way (1966, pp. 382–383):

> The inherent weakness in the centralized, functionally departmentalized operating company . . . became critical only when the administrative load on the senior executives increased to such an extent that they were unable to handle their entrepreneurial responsibilities efficiently. This situation arose when the operations of the enterprise became too complex and the problems of coordination, appraisal, and policy formulation too intricate for a small number of top officers to handle both long-run, entrepreneurial, and short-run, operational administrative activities.

The ability of the management to handle the volume and complexity of the demands placed upon it became strained and even collapsed. Unable meaningfully to identify with or contribute to the realization of global goals, managers in each of the functional parts attended to what they perceived to be operational subgoals instead (Chandler, 1966, p. 156).

Figure 1. Unitary Form.

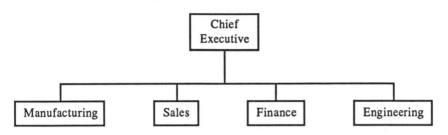

These are consequences of bounded rationality, although opportunism, coupled with information impactedness, may also be involved. Bounds on rationality give rise to finite spans of control, which in turn require that additional hierarchical levels be introduced as the U-form enterprise expands—whether the expansion is of the radial or vertical integration variety. Adding hierarchical levels can, if only for serial reproduction reasons, lead to an effective loss of control through incomplete or inaccurate transmittal of data moving up and instructions moving down the organizational hierarchy. Although various decoupling devices may be devised to reduce these transmission needs, these are costly and subject to diminishing returns. Decoupling merely alleviates, but does not overcome, the need for intrafunctional and peak coordination.

Information flows rarely take the form of simple serial reproduction, however, Rather, data are summarized and interpreted as they move forward, and instructions are operationalized as they move down (Arrow, 1974, pp. 53–54; Emery, 1969, p. 114; Beer, 1969, p. 407). Both processes provide additional opportunities for control losses to develop. These can occur in quite unintentional ways.

Continued expansion also eventually overcomes the capacity of the office of the chief executive to provide strategic planning and maintain effective control, which is another manifestation of bounded rationality. The usual means for augmenting this capacity has been to bring the heads of the functional divisions into the peak coordination process. The natural posture for these functional executives to take is one of advocacy in representing the interests of their respective operating units.

This change in the composition of the strategic decision-making unit produces a shift away from preferences characteristic of the office of the chief executive, which tend to be enterprise-wide in scope, in favor of partisan interests more closely associated with the functional divisions.

A persistent and collective pressure to provide more and better services is apt to develop; an expansionary bias in favor of staff expenditures easily obtains.

These bounded rationality consequences predictably result from the radial expansion of the U-form enterprise—even one in which the management is fully committed to conducting the affairs of the firm in a stewardship manner. If, however, managers perceive these stresses on the U-form structure as affording them with opportunities for discretion, because information is impacted to their advantage, and if, in addition, managers are given to behave opportunistically, further consequences obtain. Deliberate distortions will be introduced into the hierarchical information exchange process in support of subgoals. Permissive attitudes toward slack may also develop.

1.3 The Corporate Control Dilemma. In principle, competition in the product market and competition in the capital market will check discretionary outcomes. The resulting distortions and inefficiencies will not be viable where product market competition is extensive. Moreover, competition in the capital market fills the breach where product market competition breaks down: managers who fail to behave as neoclassical profit maximizers will be replaced at stockholder insistence. Two lines of defense thereby exist. If, however, the firms in question enjoy some degree of monopoly in their respective markets, and if, realistically, stockholders have insufficient knowledge or are otherwise indisposed to effect management displacement except where egregious distortions appear, a managerial discretion problem plainly exists.

Although they scarcely expressed the problem in this fashion, the corporate control dilemma perceived by Berle and Means can be interpreted in these terms. They noted that a separation in ownership from control existed and inquired: " . . . have we any justification for assuming that those in control of a modern corporation will also choose to operate it in the interests of the stockholders?" (Berle and Means, 1932, p. 121). The universe of firms with which they were concerned in the early 1930s was mainly large U-form enterprises, and many of these firms enjoyed monopoly power in their respective product markets. In consideration of the above-indicated effects on strategic decision-making and corporate goal pursuit that expansion of the U-form firm predictably has, Berle and Means' concern that stockholder objectives were possibly being sacrificed to favor managerial objectives was altogether appropriate.

Students of the large corporation who have succeeded Berle and Means have generally reached the same conclusion; to wit, the separation of ownership from control is extensive, and it is merely a matter of good fortune that the corporate sector performs as well as it does. In the background lurks the suspicion that one day these enclaves of private power will run amok (Mason, 1960, pp. 7–9). A search for substitute *external* controls has been set in motion on this account; solemn supplications on behalf of corporate responsibility have also been advanced. But the possibility that discretionary outcomes might be checked by *reorganizational* changes within the firm has been generally neglected. I submit, however, that organizational innovations, which in the 1930s were just getting underway, have mitigated capital market failures by transferring functions traditionally imputed to the capital market to the firm instead. Not only were the direct effects of substituting internal organization for the capital market beneficial, but the indirect effects served to renew the efficacy of capital market controls as well.

2. Organizational Innovation: The Multidivision Structure

2.1 General. Faced with the types of internal operating problems that emerge as the U-form enterprise increases in size and complexity, the DuPont Company, under the leadership of Pierre S. DuPont, and General Motors, under Alfred P. Sloan, Jr., devised what Chandler refers to as the multidivisional (or M-form) structure in the early 1920s. This organizational innovation involved substituting quasi-autonomous operating divisions (organized mainly along product, brand, or geographic lines) for the functional divisions of the U-form structure as the principal basis for dividing up the task and assigning responsibility. Inasmuch as each of these operating divisions is subsequently divided along functional lines (see Figure 2), one might characterize these operating divisions as scaled down, specialized U-form structures. Although this is a considerable oversimplification (for example, operating divisions may be further subdivided by product, geographic, or brand subdivisions before the final U-form structure appears), the observation has at least heuristic merit.

This simple change in the decomposition rules might not, by itself, appear to be all that significant. Indeed, for the reorganization to be fully effective really requires more. The peak coordinator's office (shown in Figure 2 as the general office) also has to undergo transformation and an elite staff needs to be supplied to assist the general office in its strategic decision-making (including control) responsibilities. Chandler characterizes the reasons for the success of the multidivision form as (1962, pp. 382–383):

The basic reason for its success was simply that it clearly removed the executives responsible for the destiny of the entire enterprise from the more routine operational activities, and so gave them the time, information, and even psychological commitment for long-term planning and appraisal. . . .

[The] new structure left the broad strategic decisions as to the allocation of existing resources and the acquisition of new ones in the hands of a top team of generalists. Relieved of operating duties and tactical decisions, a general executive was less likely to reflect the position of just one part of the whole.

More generally, the characteristics and advantages of the M-form innovation can be summarized in the following way (Williamson, 1970, pp. 120–121):

1. The responsibility for operating decisions is assigned to (essentially self-contained) operating divisions or quasifirms.
2. The elite staff attached to the general office performs both advisory and auditing functions. Both have the effect of securing greater control over operating division behavior.
3. The general office is principally concerned with strategic decisions, involving planning, appraisal, and control, including the allocation of resources among the (competing) operating divisions.
4. The separation of the general office from operations provides general office executives with the psychological commitment to be concerned with the overall performance of the organization rather than become absorbed in the affairs of the functional parts.
5. The resulting structure displays both rationality and synergy: the whole is greater (more effective, more efficient) than the sum of the parts.

In relation to the U-form organization of the same activities, the M-form organization of the large, complex enterprise served both to economize on bounded rationality and attenuate opportunism. Operating decisions were no longer forced to the top but were resolved at the divisional level, which relieved the communication load. Strategic decisions were reserved for the general office, which reduced partisan political input into the resource allocation process. And the internal auditing and control techniques, which the general office had access to, served to

Figure 2. Multidivision Form.

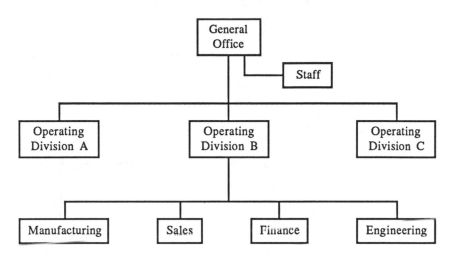

overcome information impactedness conditions and permit fine tuning controls to be exercised over the operating parts.

  2.2 An Illustration.[2] Suppose there are three activity stages: an early production stage, an intermediate stage in which production is completed, and a marketing stage. Assume that all products originate in a common first stage, that there are four distinct intermediate stage processes, and that there are five distinct final products. That there ought, under these circumstances, to be five divisions, one associated with each final product, is uncertain. For one thing, the economies of scale at the first stage may be sufficient to warrant that all production originate in a single, indecomposable plant. Second, if for some products economies of scale at the second stage are slight in relation to the size of the market, parallel divisionalization may be feasible. Third, even though products may be distinct, there may be interaction effects to consider. (For example, products may be complements.)

  Consider the situation shown in Figure 3. Here Q refers to first stage activity, I_i^j refers to intermediate stage processing, P_i^m refers to the final product, and the subscript refers to the process (product) type, while the superscript (if any) denotes replication. The proposed divisions are shown by the dotted lines.

  That it is generally inefficient for the early stage of a production process to transfer product to a later stage at a price that maximizes the profit of the early stage is well-known. Rather, in order to discourage

Figure 3. [The Stages of Production
and the Multidivisional Structure].

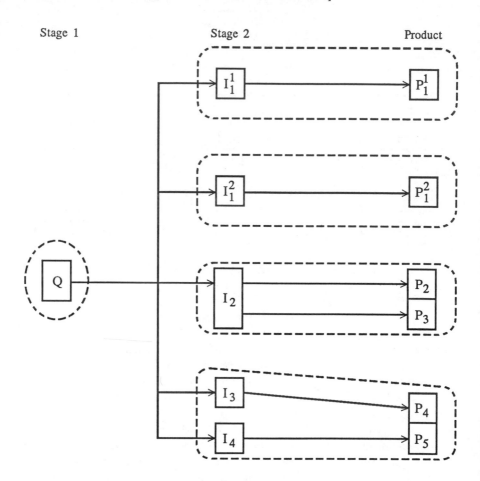

the use of inefficient factor proportions in the later stages and avoid the restriction of production, product should be transferred at its marginal cost. But then the early stage production divisions cannot, under these circumstances, be evaluated in profit center terms. Rather, Q becomes a cost center and its performance is assessed in least cost rather than net revenue terms.

Plants I_1^1 and I_1^2 are assumed to be identical and produce a common product (designated P_1^1 and P_1^2, respectively). Plant I_2 produces two distinct products, P_2 and P_3, while plants I_3 and I_4 produce the distinct products P_4 and P_5 respectively. Products P_4 and P_5, while manufactured by separate processes, are assumed to be complements.

The rationale for the divisionalization shown is as follows: First, Q is split off as a cost center since, for the reasons given above, it cannot efficiently be operated as a profit center, while to assign it to one of the later stages would place unaffiliated stages at a disadvantage,[3] and to combine several later stages leads to overaggregation (in that such aggregation impairs accountability with the result that internal control is sacrificed in the process) in relation to underlying "natural" decomposability conditions. Rules to insure efficient transactional relations between stages 1 and 2 are assumed to be feasible, whence the divisional standing accorded to Q.

A high degree of coordination between each intermediate stage and its corresponding marketing stage is assumed to exist and warrant the joining of each such pair of stages within a division. As indicated, I_1^1 and I_1^2 are replicated production facilities producing the common product P_1. A territorial market is set up for each plant, with the result that $I_1^1 - P_1^1$ and $I_1^2 - P_1^2$ are both profit centers. Territorialization serves to mitigate interdivisional competition in the product market, but interdivisional "competition," for performance comparison purposes, in other respects is possible.

Technological scale economies are assumed to be such that separate production facilities for P_2 and P_3 are uneconomical. Also, I_2 is assumed to bear a sole source relation to both P_2 and P_3. Since to split I_2 off as a separate division would require that it be operated as a cost center (given the sole source assumption) with the attendant difficulties that this poses, and as interstage coordination would be impaired in the process, a single profit center spanning I_2, P_2, and P_3 is set up instead.

I_3 and I_4 are separate plants between which there is no direct exchange relationship. They supply products P_4 and P_5 respectively. These products are assumed to be complements, however, for which a joint marketing effort is warranted. The resulting profit center spans I_3, I_4, P_4, and P_5.[4]

2.3 Diffusion. Imitation of the M-form innovation was at first rather slow. For one thing, however obvious its superior properties may have been to the innovators, others were naturally skeptical. As Brown puts it (1945, p. 295):

> To enterprises that have grown complex within themselves, . . . the resort to [divisionalization] may appear portentious and (since few relinquish without hesita-

tion the accustomed mode of life) uninviting. . . . [The]
dissolution of [a firm's] integrated state and the redistribution of responsibilities into multiple organization do present the aspect of a revolutionary rather than an evolutionary change.

Also in industries such as metal refining and forming, the divisionalized
structure was not as easy to create as in industries where distinct product or brand lines were readily established. In others, administrative inertia appears to have been substantial. Up through the 1930's, only a
handful of other firms had accomplished the transformation (Chandler,
1962, Chap. 7). A number of firms, which by 1940 had reorganizational
changes in the works postponed these with the onset of World War II.
Since 1945, however, the divisionalization of large firms (many of them
along M-form lines) has been extensive.

It is of some interest, moreover, to note that the multidivisional
structure has more recently been adopted by large European firms.
Franko reports that prior to 1968, most large European companies administered their domestic operations through U-form or holding company internal structures (1972, p. 342). With the advent of zero tariffs
within the European Economic Community on January 1, 1968, and
in the face of continuing penetration of European markets by American
firms, however, large European firms have felt compelled to adapt
(Franko, 1972, p. 358). A significant number of these firms have been
reorganized along multidivisional lines in the past several years.

3. Competition in the Capital Market

3.1 Frictionless Capital Markets

As the remarks of Bork (1969) and Bowman (1973) make clear,
advocates of received microtheory are loath to concede that capital markets
may fail to operate frictionlessly. Partly for this reason, the fiction that
managers operate firms in fully profit maximizing ways is maintained.
Any attempt by managers to opportunistically promote their own goals
at the expense of corporate profitability would occasion intervention
through the capital market. Effective control of the corporation would
be transferred to those parties who perceived the lapse; profit maximizing behavior would then be quickly restored.

Parties responsible for the detection and correction of deviant
behavior in the firm would, of course, participate in the greater profits

which the reconstituted management thereafter realized. This profit participation would not, however, be large. For one thing, incumbent managements, by assumption, have little opportunity for inefficiency or malfeasance because any tendency toward waywardness would be quickly detected and costlessly extinguished. Accordingly, the incremental profit gain occasioned by takeover is small. In addition, since competition among prospective takeover agents is presumably intensive, the gains mainly redound to the stockholders.

Peterson's sanguine views on corporate behavior are roughly of this kind. He characterizes the latitude of managers to disregard the profit goal as "small" (1965, p. 11) and goes on to observe: "Far from being an ordinary election, a proxy battle is a *catastrophic* event whose mere possibility is a threat, and one not remote when affairs are in *conspicuous* disarray." Indeed, even "stockholder suits . . . may be provoked by evidence of *serious* self-dealing." On the principle that the efficacy of legal prohibitions is to be judged "not by guilt discovered but by guilt discouraged," he concludes that such suits, albeit rare, may have accomplished much in helping to police the corporate system (Peterson, 1965, p. 21; emphasis added).

While I do not mean to suggest that such deterrence has been unimportant, Peterson's observations appear to me to be consistent with the proposition that traditional capital markets are beset by serious problems of information impactedness and incur nontrivial displacement costs if the incumbent management is disposed to resist the takeover effort. Why else the reference to catastrophic events, conspicuous disarray, and serious self-dealing? Systems that are described in these terms are not ones for which a delicately conceived control system can be said to be operating. As recent military history makes clear,[5] controls that involve a discrete shock to the system are appropriate only when an offense reaches egregious proportions. The limits of opportunism are accordingly wider than Peterson seems prepared to concede.

The reasons, I submit, why traditional capital market controls are relatively crude are because an information impactedness condition exists with respect to internal conditions in the firms and, because of sorting out difficulties, the risk of opportunism on the part of would-be takeover agents is great. Given information impactedness, outsiders can usually make confident judgements that the firm is not adhering to profit maximizing standards only at great expense. The large firm is a complex organization and its performance is jointly a function of exogenous economic events, rival behavior, and internal decisions. Causal inferences are correspondingly difficult to make, and hence, opportunism is costly to detect. Moreover, once detected, convincing interested stockholders that a displacement effort ought to be supported encounters problems. Inasmuch as time and analytical capacity on the part of stockholders are not free goods, which is to say that their information processing limits must be respected, the would-be takeover agent cannot simply display all of his evidence and expect stockholders to evaluate it and reach the "appropriate" conclusion. Rather, any appeal to the stockholders must be made in terms of highly digested interpretations of the facts. Although this helps to overcome the stockholder's bounded rationality problem, it poses another: How is the interested stockholder (or his agent) to distinguish between *bona fide* and opportunistic takeover agents.

The upshot of these remarks is that the transaction costs associated with *traditional* capital market processes for policing management, of the sort described by Peterson, are considerable. Correspondingly, the range of discretionary behavior open to incumbent managements is rather wider than Peterson and other supporters of the frictionlessness fiction concede.[6]

3.2 The M-Form Firm as a Miniature Capital Market

In a general sense, the most severe limitation of the capital market is that it is an *external* control instrument. It has limited constitutional powers to conduct audits and has limited access to the firm's incentive and resource allocation machinery. One should not, however, conclude that mere divisionalization, by itself, is sufficient to correct the inefficiencies and goal distortions that the large U-form firm develops. To emphasize this, the limits of the holding company form of organization are examined below. Attention is thereafter shifted to consider strategic controls of the sort appropriate to an M-form enterprise.

3.2.1 Holding Company. What is referred to here as a holding company form of organization is a loosely divisionalized structure in which the controls between the headquarters unit and the separate operating parts are limited and often unsystematic. The divisions thus enjoy a high degree of autonomy under a weak executive structure.[7]

Perhaps the least ambitious type of divisionalization to consider within the holding company classification is that in which the general office is essentially reduced to a clerical agency for the assembly and aggregation of earnings and other financial reports. The holding company in these circumstances serves as a risk-pooling agency, but in this respect is apt to be inferior to a mutual fund. The transaction costs associated with altering the composition of the portfolio of the holding company, by selling off existing divisions and acquiring new operating companies, will ordinarily exceed the costs that a mutual fund of comparable assets would incur by its trading of common stocks (or other securities) so as to adjust its portfolio. Little wonder that those academics who interpret the conglomerate as being a substitute mutual fund report that it has inferior diversification characteristics to mutual funds themselves (Smith and Schreiner, 1969; Westerfield, 1970).

Moreover, it is not clear that just a little bit of additional control from the general office will lead to results that are superior to those that would obtain were the various divisions of the holding company to be freestanding firms in their own right. Being part of a holding company rather than an independent business entity easily has umbrella effects. If the holding company serves as a collection agency for unabsorbed cash flows and uses these to shore up the ailing parts of the enterprise, the resulting insularity may encourage systematic distortions (of a managerial discretion sort) among the divisional managements. Being shielded from the effects of adversity in their individual product markets, slack behavior sets in.

This is not, of course, a necessary consequence. The general management might consciously refuse to reinvest earnings but mainly pay these out as dividends. Alternatively, it might scrutinize reinvestment decisions every bit as well as the unassisted capital market could. Indeed, because it enjoys an *internal* relationship to the divisions, with all of the constitutional powers that this affords, the general management might be prepared to assume risks that an *external* investor ought properly to decline. (Thus, the general management can ordinarily detect distortions and replace the divisional management at lower cost than can an external control agent similarly detect and change the management of a comparable, free standing business entity. The holding company, in this respect, is less vulnerable to the risks of what might be referred to as managerial moral hazard.) Given, however, that the holding company is *defined* to be a divisionalized firm in which the general office does not involve itself in strategic controls of the sort described below, it is unclear that the holding company form of organization is socially to be preferred to an arrangement in which the various divisions are each set up as fully independent enterprises instead. Holding companies certainly cannot be expected reliably to yield results that compare favorably with those which I impute to the M-form structure.

3.2.2 Strategic Controls in the M-Form Firm. If indeed the firm is to serve effectively as a miniature capital market, which in many respects is what the M-form structure ought to be regarded [as],[8] a more extensive internal control apparatus than the holding company form of organization possesses is required. This gets to the core issues. Manipulation of the incentive machinery, internal audits, and cash flow allocation each deserve consideration.

Closer adherence to the goals of the general management can be secured if the special incentive machinery to which internal organization uniquely has access to is consciously exercised to favor operating behavior that is consistent with the general management's objectives. Both pecuniary and nonpecuniary awards may be employed for this purpose.

That salaries and bonuses can be adjusted to reflect differential operating performance, assuming that such differentials exist and can be discerned, is a familiar application of the incentive machinery. That nonpecuniary rewards, especially status, can also be adjusted for this purpose should be evident from the [previous discussions].

Of course, sometimes a change of employment, or at least of position, may be altogether necessary. The division manager may not have the management capacities initially ascribed to him, conditions may change in ways that warrant the appointment of a manager with different qualities, or he may be managerially competent but uncooperative (given, for example, to aggressive subgoal pursuit in ways that impair overall performance). Changes made for either of the first two reasons reflect simple functional assessments of job requirements in relation to managerial skills. By contrast, to replace a division manager for the third reason involves the deliberate manipulation of the incentive machinery to produce more satisfactory results. The occasion to intervene in this way will presumably be rare, however, if the conditional nature of the appointment is recognized from the outset. Rather, the system becomes self-enforcing in this respect once it is clear that the general management is prepared to replace division managers who regularly defect from general management's goals.[9]

Although the general office does not ordinarily become directly involved in the exercise of the incentive machiney within the operating divisions, its indirect influence can be great. The decision to change (replace, rotate) a division manager is often made for the incentive effects this has on lower-level participants. Employment policies—including criteria for selection, internal training procedures, promotions, and so forth—can likewise be specified by the general office in ways that serve to ensure closer congruence between higher-level goals and the behavior of the operating parts. A more pervasive incentive impact on lower-level participants who are not directly subject to review by the general office can in these ways be effected.

Adjusting the incentive machinery in any fine tuning sense to achieve reliable results requires that the changes be made in an informed way. A backup internal audit that reviews divisional performance and attempts to attribute effects to the several possible causes—distinguishing especially between those outcomes that are due to changes in the condition of the environment from those that result from managerial decision-making—is useful for this purpose.[10] As Churchill, Cooper, and Sainsbury observe: ''. . . to be effective, an audit of historical actions should have, or at least be perceived as having, the power to go beneath the apparent evidence to determine what in fact did happen'' (1964, p. 258). Of particular importance in this connection is the recurrent nature of this auditing process. Thus, although current variations of actual from projected may sometimes be ''accounted for'' in plausible but inaccurate ways, a persistent pattern of performance failure can be explained only with difficulty.

The advantages of the general office over the capital market in auditing respects are of two kinds. First, division managers are subordinates; as such, both their accounting records and backup files are appropriate subjects for review. Stockholders, by contrast, are much more limited in what they can demand in the way of disclosure. Even relatively innocent demands for a list of the stockholders in the corporation, much less the details of internal operating performance, may be resisted by the management and disclosed only after a delay and by court order.

Second, the general office can expect knowledgeable parties to be much more cooperative than can an outsider. Thus, whereas disclosure of sensitive internal information to an outsider is apt to be interpreted as an act of treachery,[11] internal disclosure is unlikely to be regarded opprobriously. Rather, internal disclosure is affirmatively regarded as necessary to the integrity of the organization and is rewarded accordingly. Disclosure to outsiders, by contrast, commonly exposes the informant to penalties[12]—albeit that these may be subtle in nature.

Not only are internal audits useful for ascertaining causality, they also serve as a basis for determining when operating divisions could benefit from assistance. The general management may include on its staff what amounts to an internal management consulting unit—to be loaned or assigned to the operating divisions as the need arises. Partly the occasion for such an assignment may be revealed by the internal audit. Thus, although the general management ought not routinely to become involved in operating affairs,[13] having the capability to intervene prescriptively in an informed way under exceptional circumstances serves to augment its credibility as an internal control agent.[14] Self-regulatory behavior by the operating divisions is thereby encouraged.

In addition to the policing of internal efficiency matters, and thereby securing a higher level of adherence to profit maximization than the unassisted capital market could realize (at comparable cost), the general management and its support staff can perform a further capital market function—assigning cash flows to high yield uses. Thus, cash flows in the M-form firm are not automatically returned to their sources but instead are exposed to an internal competition. Investment proposals from the several divisions are solicited and evaluated by the general management. The usual criterion is the rate of return on invested capital.[15]

Moreover, because the costs of communicating and adapting internally are normally lower than would be incurred in making an investment proposal to the external capital market, it may be practicable to decompose the internal investment process into stages. A sequential decision process (in which additional financing is conditional on prior stage results and developing contingencies) may thus be both feasible and efficient as an internal investment strategy. The transaction costs of effectuating such a process through the capital market, by contrast, are apt to be prohibitive.

In many respects, *this assignment of cash flows to high yield uses is the most fundamental attribute of the M-form enterprise* in the comparison of internal with external control processes, albeit that the divisionalized firm is able to assign cash flows to only a fairly narrow range of alternatives at any one point in time. Even if the firm is actively acquiring new activities and divesting itself of old, its range of choice is circumscribed in relation to that which general investors, who are interested in owning and trading securities rather than managing real assets, have access to. What the M-form firm does is trade off breadth for depth in this respect.[16] In a similar context, Alchian and Demsetz explain: "Efficient production with heterogeneous resources is a result not of having *better* resources but in knowing more *accurately* the relative productive performances of those resources" (1972, p. 793).

4. Optimum Divisionalization

The M-form structure is thoroughly corrupted when the general management involves itself in the operating affairs of the divisions in an extensive and continuing way. The separation between strategic and operating issues is sacrificed in the process; the indicated internalization of capital market functions with net beneficial effects can scarcely be claimed. Accountability is seriously compromised; a substitution of enterprise expansion for profitability goals predictably obtains.

Effective divisionalization thus requires the general management to maintain an appropriate distance. Moreover, this holds for the support staff on which the general management relies for internal auditing and management consulting services. Overinvolvement upsets the rational allocation of responsibilities between short-run operating matters and longer-run planning and resource allocation activities. What March and Simon refer to as Gresham's Law of Planning—to wit, "Daily routine drives out planning" (1958, p. 185)—takes effect when operating and strategic functions are mixed. While the arguments here are familiar and their implications for organizational design reasonably clear, maintaining a separation between these two activities apparently poses severe strain on some managements. A desire to be comprehensively involved is evidently difficult to resist.

Optimum divisionalization thus involves: (1) the identification of separable economic activities within the firm; (2) according quasi-autonomous standing (usually of a profit center nature) to each; (3) monitoring the efficiency performance of each division; (4) awarding incentives; (5) allocating cash flows to high yield uses; and (6) performing strategic planning (diversification, acquisition, and related activities) in other respects. The M-form structure is one that *combines* the divisionalization concept with an internal control and strategic decision-making capability. The general management of the M-form usually requires the support of a specialized staff to discharge these functions effectively. It bears repeating, however, that care must be exercised lest the general management and its staff become overinvolved in operating matters and fail to perform the high-level planning and control functions on which the M-form enterprise relies for its continuing success.

Whether and how to divisionalize depends on firm size, functional separability, and the state of information technology (Emery, 1969). Also, it should be pointed out that the reference here to optimum is used in comparative institutional terms. As between otherwise comparable unitary or holding company forms of organization, the M-form structure would appear to possess significant advantages. It cannot, however, be established on the basis of the argument advanced here that the M-form structure is the best of all conceivable structures. Organizational innovations may even now be in the making that will obsolete it in part—but which academics will identify as noteworthy only after several years. A keener sensitivity to organizational innovations and their economic importance than has existed in the past should nevertheless help to avoid the long recognition lags that have transpired before the significance of the M-form structure and its conglomerate variant became apparent.

Lest, however, these remarks lead to an underevaluation of the merits of the M-form structure, I hasten to add that, while evolutionary change is to be expected, the hierarchical decomposition principles on which the M-form is based are very robust. In his discussion of adaptive corporate organization, Beer observes: "The notion of hierarchy is given in cybernetics as a necessary structural attribute of any viable organism. This is not surprising to us, although its theoretical basis is profound, because all viable systems do in fact exhibit hierarchical organizations" (1969, p. 399). Moreover, not only does Simon's review of the properties of complex biological, physical, and social systems reaffirm this, but he emphasizes that hierarchies commonly factor problems in such a way that "higher frequency dynamics are associated with the subsystems, the lower frequency dynamics with the larger systems, . . . [and] intra-component linkages are generally stronger than intercomponent linkages" (1962, p. 477). Hierarchical systems of this sort may be referred to as near-decomposable (Simon, 1962). It is not merely fortuitous that the M-form structure factors problems very much in this way.

5. The "M-Form Hypothesis" and Concluding Remarks

Although the M-form structure was initially devised and imitated as a means by which to correct local conditions of inefficiency and subgoal pursuit, it has subsequently had pervasive systems consequences. These systems effects are partly attributable to competition in the product market; unadapted firms have found it necessary, as a survival measure, to eliminate slack so as to remain viable. But the effects of takeover threats from the capital market are also important. The conglomerate variant on the M-form structure is of particular interest in this connection— which is the subject of the next chapter. Focusing, however, strictly on direct effects, which is sufficient for our purposes here, the argument comes down to this: *The organization and operation of the large enterprise along the lines of the M-form favors goal pursuit and least-cost behavior more nearly associated with the neoclassical profit maximization hypothesis than does the U-form organizational alternative.*[17]

But more than mere divisionalization is needed for these effects to be realized. It is also necessary that a separation of operating from strategic responsibilities be provided. The former are assigned to the operating divisions while the latter are made the focus of the general management. Moreover, such a partitioning does not, by itself, assure strategic effectiveness; for this to obtain requires that the general management develop an internal control apparatus, to assess the performance of the operating divisions, and an internal resource allocation capability, which favors the assignment of resources to high yield uses.

That divisionalized enterprises sometimes, and perhaps often, fail to meet these stipulations is suggested by Ansoff and Brandenberg, who observe that the performance potential in divisionalized firms frequently goes unrealized because general managements "either continue to be overly responsive to operating problems [that is, nonstrategic but interventionist] or reduce the size of the corporate office to a minimum level at which no capacity exists for strategic and structural decision making" (1971, p. 722). An effort to assess internal controls in divisionalized enterprises and to distinguish among the several types is accordingly indicated if tests of the M-form hypothesis are to be attempted. To facilitate such testing a six-way classification scheme is set out in the appendix.

Appendix: A Classification Scheme[18]

As noted, a major problem is posed for testing the M-form hypothesis in that, if all divisionalized firms are classified as M-form firms, without regard for the related internal decision-making and control apparatus, an overassignment to the M-form category will result. Some divisionalized firms are essentially holding companies, in that they lack the requisite control machinery, while others are only nominally divisionalized, with the general office maintaining extensive involvement in operating affairs. If indeed the M-form designation is to be reserved for those firms that *combine* the appropriate structural and internal operating attributes, information on both aspects is required.

The difficulty with this is threefold. First, information on internal operating procedures is less easy to come by than is that on divisionalization. Second, the appropriate degree of involvement by the general office in the affairs of the operating divisions varies with the nature of the factor or product market interdependencies that exist within the firm and thus need to be "harmonized." Divisions that are involved in the exchange of intermediate products (vertical integration) typically face different control needs than those in which such internal, crossdivisional transactions are absent. Similarly, the requisite product market controls are more extensive if operating divisions produce competitive products than when, by reason of product diversification, such interdependencies are absent.

The third problem is that reaching the M-form structure may require the firm to pass through a transitional stage during which the "optimum" control relationship, expressed in equilibrium terms, is violated.

An appreciation for the natural life cycle in the M-form enterprise is necessary if these transitional conditions are to be detected and an appropriate classification made.

Although experience with the scheme may disclose certain ambiguities, suggest better definitions, and reveal a need to devise still additional categories, it seems useful to get on with the assignment task and make the subsequent refinements. Surely enough is known about internal organization at this time to begin such an effort. The following classification scheme is accordingly proposed.

1. *Unitary (U-form)*. This is the traditional functionally organized enterprise. (It is still the appropriate structure in most small- to lower middle-sized firms. Some medium-sized firms, in which interconnections are especially rich, may continue to find this the appropriate structure.) A variant on this structure occasionally appears in which the enterprise is mainly of U-form character but where the firm has become diversified in slight degree and the incidental parts are given semi-autonomous standing. Unless such diversification accounts for at least a third of the firm's value added, such functionally organized firms will be assigned to the U-form category.

2. *Holding Company (H-form)*. This is the divisionalized enterprise for which the requisite internal control apparatus has not been provided. The divisions are often affiliated with the parent company through a subsidiary relationship.

3. *Multidivisional (M-form)*. This is the divisionalized enterprise in which a separation of operating from strategic decision-making is provided and for which the requisite internal control apparatus has been assembled and is systematically employed.

Two subcategories should be distinguished: type D_1, which denotes a highly integrated M-form enterprise, possibly with differentiated but otherwise common final products; and type D_2, which denotes the M-form enterprise with diversified final products or service. As between these two, a more extensive internal control apparatus to manage spillover effects is needed in the former.

4. *Transitional Multidivisional (M'-Form)*. This is the M-form enterprise that is in the process of adjustment. Organizational learning may be involved or newly acquired parts may not yet have been brought into a regular divisionalized relationship to the parent enterprise.[19]

5. *Corrupted Multidivisional (M̄-form)*. The M̄-form enterprise is a multidivisional structure for which the requisite control apparatus has been provided but in which the general management has become exten-

sively involved in operating affairs. The appropriate distance relation thus is missing, with the result that M-form performance, over the long-run, cannot reliably be expected.[20]

6. *Mixed (X-Form)*. Conceivably a divisionalized enterprise will have a mixed form in which some divisions will be essentially of the holding company variety, others will be M-form, and still others will be under the close supervision of the general management. Whether a mixed form is apt to be viable over the long run is perhaps to be doubted. Some exceptions might, however, survive simply as a matter of chance. The X-form classification thus might be included for completeness purposes and as a reminder that organizational survival is jointly a function of rational and chance processes. Over the long pull the rational structures should thrive, but aberrant cases will appear and occasionally persist.

That the X-form lacks for rationality properties, however, is probably too strong. For example, a large U-form firm that enjoys monopoly power in its main market may wish to restrict the reinvestment of cash flows back into this market. At the same time it may discover attractive opportunities to invest some part of these funds in unrelated business activities. Diversification could follow, but not in sufficient degree to warrant disestablishment of the main market from central office control. The diversified parts of the business thus might each be given divisional standing, but the main business retained, for the most part, under its earlier control relationship. Only if the main business itself could be efficiently divided (through product differentiation, geographic territorialization, or other lines), which eventually it may, might divisionalization of this part of the firm's activities be warranted.

Notes

1. For a more extensive discussion of these effects, see Williamson (1970, Chaps. 2, 3, and 7). The difficulties that the large, U-form enterprise experiences are there summarized in terms of indecomposability, incommensurability, nonoperational goal specification, and the confounding of strategic and operating decisions. Incommensurability makes it difficult to specify the goals of the functional divisions in ways which clearly contribute to higher-level enterprise objectives. Indecomposability makes it necessary to attempt more extensive coordination among the parts; for a given span of control, this naturally results in a high degree of control loss between hierarchical levels. Moreover, to the extent that efforts at coordination break down and the individual parts suboptimize, the intrinsic interconnectedness between them virtually assures that spillover costs will be substantial. The confounding of strategic and operating decisions serves further to compromise organizational purpose.

2. That the exercise is hypothetical and oversimple ought to be emphasized. If, however, it serves to better expose the issues, its purpose will have been realized.

3. This assumes that the later stages are about on a parity in terms of the volume and variety of demands placed on the early stage. If one stage were to be much larger than all of the others and to have special needs for coordinating with the early stage, a combination of these two stages might be warranted.

4. This is clearly arbitrary; a divisional separation between marketing and the prior production stage may sometimes be warranted.

5. Atomic weapons, with their catastrophic consequences, are ill-suited to support military campaigns involving even half a million men.

6. Smiley concludes his study of tender offers as follows (1973, pp. 124–125):

> Based on our most accurate estimating procedure, per share transaction costs are approximately 14% of the market value of the shares after a successful offer. We feel that this cost level is such as to inspire skepticism about the efficacy of the tender offer in constraining managers to act in the best interests of their shareholders. Another finding was that the equity of firms that have been tendered has lost half of its market value (in the 10 years prior to the tender offer) relative to what the equity would have been worth, had the management operated the firm in an optimal fashion.

7. That this is a somewhat special use of the term-holding company ought to be appreciated. (I considered referring to this as the federal form of organization but decided that that posed at least as many problems.) Essentially what I am after is a category which, for reference purposes, represents divisionalization of a very limited sort.

8. The argument is developed more extensively in Williamson (1970, pp. 138–150, 176–177). For somewhat similar views, see Drucker (1970), Heflebower (1960), and Weston (1970).

9. This assumes that there are no property rights (academic tenure, civil service, and so forth) associated with positions.

10. In principle, the superior inference capability of an internal audit, as compared with the relatively crude powers of the capital market in this respect, commends internal organization as a substitute for the capital market not merely because discretionary behavior may thereby be attenuated but also because division managers may be induced to accept risks which in a free-standing firm would be declined. Too often, as Luce and Raiffa observe: " . . . the strategist is evaluated in terms of the outcome of the adopted choice rather than in terms of the strategic desirability of the whole risk situation" (1957, p. 76). This tendency to rely on outcomes rather than assess the complex situation more

completely is especially to be expected of systems with low powers of inference. Managers of free-standing firms, realizing that outcomes rather than decision processes will be evaluated, are naturally reluctant to expose themselves to high variance undertakings. *Ceteris paribus*, the low cost access of internal organization to a wider range of sophisticated inference techniques encourages more aggressive risk-taking.

Whether the potential advantages of the divisional structure in auditing respects actually induce more aggressive risk-taking, however, is uncertain. Woods identified a strong conservative bias in the firms that he studied, where the companies were "rewarding the manager whose investment performance exceeds his original forecast and penalizing the one whose performance falls below the forecast" (1966, p. 93).

11. "Kings may vary in the tolerance they show to vices such as incompetence or laziness, but there is no tolerance of treason. Giving damaging information to the press or betraying plans to a rival are the actions of an enemy . . . ; these are unpardonable offenses" (Jay, 1971, p. 266). The disclosure of damaging inside information to the press or to a prospective takeover agent is regarded by the firm's leadership to be of this treacherous kind.

12. The disclosure of cost overruns on the C-5A by an employee of the Pentagon (A. Ernest Fitzgerald) resulted in his being fired. But for subsequent intervention by Senator Proxmire and others, his reemployment was unlikely. [See Mollenhoff (1973).] Such intervention is, of course, unusual and does not assure that the career expectations of the informant will be unimpaired.

13. The reasons for avoiding operating involvement have been given elsewhere. A recent comparative study by Allen of two divisionalized firms broadly supports the general argument. Allen observes that, of the two firms, the high-performing firm had a "fairly simple but highly selective set of organizational devices to maintain control over its divisions," while the management of the low-performing firm became "over-involved," in relation to its capacity, in the affairs of its operating divisions (1970, p. 28).

14. This internal management consulting unit would ordinarily be made available at the request of the operating divisions as well as at the behest of the general management. Such a unit would presumably possess scarce expertise of a high order. It would be uneconomical for each operating division to attempt to replicate such a capability.

15. For a discussion of a sophisticated internal resource allocation model in the International Utilities Corporation, see Hamilton and Moses (1973).

16. For a somewhat similar discussion of the internal resource allocation effects of M-form divisionalization, see Drucker (1970). Also of relevance in this connection are the treatments by Heflebower (1960) and Weston (1970). Certain work at the Harvard Business School also relates to these issues [see Bower (1971) and the references therein; also Allen (1970)].

17. It will be noted that the argument has been developed in comparative terms. It could, therefore, be as easily expressed instead as a U-form hypothesis; namely, the organization and operation of the large enterprise along the lines of the U-form favors goal pursuit and cost behavior more nearly associated with the managerial discretion hypothesis than does the M-form organizational alternative. This equivalent statement makes evident an underlying symmetry that some may find disconcerting: if one accepts the affirmative argument on behalf of the M-form organization advanced above, a tacit acceptance of managerial discretion theory (in the context of U-form organization) may also be implied. That is, if the M-form organization has, for the reasons given, the superior efficiency, motivational, and control properties that have been imputed to it, then presumably the organization and operation of the large enterprise along the lines of the traditional (U-form) structure contributes to control loss and utility-maximizing behavior of the sort described in Williamson (1964). To the extent, therefore, that the coincidence of large, unitary form structures and non-trivial opportunity sets (mainly by reason of favorable product market conditions) is observed in the economy, utility-maximizing behavior (and its attendant consequences) is to be expected.

18. The classification scheme independently proposed by Richard Rumelt [as reported by Scott (1973, pp. 138–139)] is somewhat similar to that suggested here, although he does not make the distinctions among M-form firms (as between M, M′, and M̄) that are suggested here and which I believe are important. For an illustrative use of the proposed scheme to a group of eight firms, see Williamson and Bhargava (1972).

19. Inasmuch as it may take some time for an organization to recognize the need for reorganization, to effect a major structural change, and then become adapted to its operational consequences (which is to say that organizational learning is involved), the period just prior to, during, and immediately following a reorganization along M-form lines is apt to be a disequilibrium interval. Some allowance for the difficulties of adjustment may be needed if the performance consequences of such a change are to be accurately evaluated.

    Similarly, the process of effectively integrating new acquisitions within an established M-form enterprise may take time. The incumbent managers of the newly acquired firm may have been able to negotiate, as a condition of support for the acquisition, that their division be accorded special autonomy. Only as this management is redeployed within the parent organization, reaches retirement, or is otherwise induced to accept a more normal divisionalized relationship can the M-form control apparatus be brought fully to bear. Indeed, as a transitional matter to hasten the divisionalization, the general management may, at its first "legitimate" opportunity, involve itself more actively in the operating affairs of the newly acquired parts than would, assessed in equilibrium terms, ordinarily be appropriate. The purpose of this effort, presumably, is to effect a more rapid conditioning of attitudes and transformation of procedures than would otherwise obtain—bringing both more nearly into congruence with those existing elsewhere in the firm. Such apparent overinvolvement ought not to be regarded a contradiction to M-form procedures unless the interference is long continued and widely practiced throughout the enterprise. Otherwise, it is merely a transitional condition and a violation of M-form operations is not implied.

20. It may be necessary to recognize a semicorrupted type of M-form organization. Thus, suppose that several M-form firms are combined and that the general offices of each are converted into group headquarters. If, now, the group vice-presidents not only head up their groups but also serve with the president in setting corporate policy, partisan representations are apt to reappear in the strategic decision-making process. Whether this mixed involvement of the group vice-presidents is of sufficient importance to warrant an additional classification is unclear at this time.

Organizational Structure and Economic Performance: A Test of the Multidivisional Hypothesis

Henry Ogden Armour
David J. Teece

1. Introduction

This paper attempts to assess the importance of internal organizational structure in determining firm performance. Its principal objective is to test empirically the validity of what Williamson (1975, chapter 8) refers to as the multidivisional form (*M*-form) hypothesis, which posits superior performance for those organizations adopting a particular kind of multidivisional structure. The investigation will focus on the relative performance characteristics of alternative organizational forms observed in a sample of petroleum industry firms during the period 1955–1973. As such, this paper represents an empirical exploration into the validity of the "Markets and Hierarchies" paradigm.

2. The multidivisional form hypothesis

Some Theoretical Issues. A common approach to the study of organizational form involves examining how a firm ought to organize as it grows in size and complexity. Chandler (1962), for instance, noted that in the early 1920s several of the larger functionally organized[1] American corporations developed multidivisional internal structures in response to increasingly complex administrative problems encountered as firm size increased, and along with it the diversity and magnitude of the firm's activities.[2] In extending Chandler's analysis, Williamson observed that two major problems were encountered by firms as they radially expanded: namely, cumulative control loss and the confounding of strategic and

Reprinted in slightly adapted form from the *Bell Journal of Economics*, 1978, *9* (1), 106–122 by permission of the publisher.

operating decisionmaking. The predicted result is a failure to achieve
least-cost profit-maximizing behavior (Williamson, 1970 and 1975). The
difficulties experienced by an expanding functionally organized enterprise can be expressed in terms of indecomposability, incommensurability,
nonoperational goal specification, and the confounding of strategic and
operating decisions.[3] Incommensurability makes it difficult to specify
the goals of the functional divisions in ways which clearly contribute to
higher-level enterprise objectives. Indecomposability makes it necessary
to attempt more extensive coordination among the parts; for a given
span of control, this naturally results in a high degree of control loss between hierarchical levels. Moreover, to the extent that efforts at coordination break down and the individual parts suboptimize, the intrinsic
interconnectedness between them virtually assures that spillover costs
will be substantial. The confounding of strategic and operating decisions
serves to further compromise organizational purpose (Williamson, 1975,
pp. 133–134).

A multidivisional organization is one response to such difficulties.
According to Williamson, a pure M-form involves control systems that
induce appropriate goal pursuit by divisions,[4] the separation of strategic
and operating decisionmaking, and superior internal information and
control techniques to those possessed by the external capital market. The
corollary is the M-form hypothesis (Williamson, 1975, p. 150):

> The organization and operation of the large enter-
> prise along the lines of the M-form favors goal pursuit and
> least-cost behavior more nearly associated with the neo-
> classical profit maximization hypothesis than does the U-
> form [functional] organizational alternative.

If this hypothesis is correct, then for a class of large complex firms
the adoption of the multidivisional organizational innovation will significantly affect their efficiency. Assuming that interfirm differences in
efficiency can exist at any given time and that such differences are reflected
in profitability, it follows that organizational form may be expected to
account for some part of the observed interfirm variation in profitability.

The M-form hypothesis raises several complex issues. First of all,
to observe the performance differential a degree of operating inefficiency
must be sustainable, at least transitionally. That is, if the hypothesis is
correct and large M-form firms do possess superior efficiency
characteristics, then presumably large functionally organized firms will
exhibit inferior efficiency characteristics (control loss and possibly subgoal

pursuit). To the extent that both types of organizational forms simultaneously exist in the economy when only the M-form organization is appropriate, then some form of transitional survival mechanism must exist to allow us to observe both types of firms. It is perhaps useful in this regard to think of the M-form organizational structure as an organizational innovation which is subject to a diffusion process. During the diffusion period when the M-form innovation is gradually replacing less efficient alternatives (e.g., functional forms) superior and inferior structures simultaneously exist, and it is possible to observe differential performance. However, once the innovation has been fully diffused, its superior efficiency attributes, as disclosed by superior performance, cease to be empirically observable in a competitive market. This suggests that an investigation should focus on a period which appears to be marked by the transitional adoption of the M-form structure and not on a period in which most firms have already adopted the structure.

Finally, to the extent that the M-form hypothesis is correct, it implies that previous empirical studies of firm profitability which have ignored internal structure may be subject to specification bias, and that this bias may be particularly serious if organizational form is correlated, as seems likely, with other variables (e.g., firm size) that are typically included in such studies. This potential error is of some concern in view of the implications for public policy relating to firm size and industrial structure issues.[5]

Sample Selection Considerations. The M-form hypothesis admits the simultaneous existence of optimally organized functional and multidivisional firms. This has important implications for the choice of a sample to test the hypothesis. For instance, suppose a sample which included firms whose optimal structure was of the functional form (e.g., firms in which cumulative control loss and the confounding of operating and strategic decisionmaking processes are not experienced) was chosen. Because some of the firms in the sample would have optimal functional forms, a simple comparison of the performance of M-form firms with the corresponding performance of functionally organized firms would contain an inherent bias against finding empirical support for the M-form hypothesis. However, if the sample selected were to consist of only those firms which will realize superior performance from the adoption of the M-form structure, the above bias vanishes, because only the M-form structure is optimal. An obvious problem is deciding whether a sample of firms includes optimally organized functional enterprises. The hypothesis does not specify the level of firm size and/or degree of task complexity for which the purported superior attributes of a multidivisional structure become apparent. Accordingly, one must resort to a somewhat arbitrary procedure for assigning optimal/nonoptimal classifications.[6]

Measurement of Firm Performance. The *M*-form hypothesis rests on the assumption that an optimally organized *M*-form firm will realize superior performance not only because the resource conversion process is more efficient (i.e., the firm is operating close to the production possibility frontier), but also because the strategic planning and decisionmaking processes allocate resources to high-yield opportunities more effectively. A performance measure that appears to be capable of reflecting superior performance is the rate of return on stockholders' equity (after-tax profits divided by stockholders' equity). The numerator of such a measure is appropriately defined as profits after tax, rather than before tax, since taxes might vary because of differing tax treatments and competitive entry should bring after tax profit rates (risk adjusted) toward equality under competition. The denominator of the measure is stockholders' equity and not total capital. This is the correct specification since it is what managers acting in the stockholders' best interest would seek to maximize (see Hall and Weiss (1967)).[7]

Model. The basic model posited in the present investigation can be expressed in its functional form as:[8]

$$\pi_{it} = f(SIZE_{it}, STRUCTURE_{it}, RISK_{it}, CAPUTIL_t, GROWTH_{it})$$

where

π_{it} = the rate of return on stockholders' equity (book value) associated with the ith firm in the tth period;

$SIZE_{it}$ = the size of the ith firm in the tth period as reflected in beginning period total assets (book value);[9]

$STRUCTURE_{it}$ = the organizational form corresponding to the ith firm in the tth period;

$RISK_{it}$ = the variability (variance) of the dependent variable associated with the ith firm in the tth period calculated on the basis of the observations in the five previous years;

$CAPUTIL_t$ = a measure of capacity utilization in the petroleum industry in period t; and

$GROWTH_{it}$ = the arithmetic average of the growth rates associated with the ith firm in the tth period in the five previous years.[10]

Firm size is included in the model to control for the possible effects of economies or diseconomies of scale. Moreover, the arguments made to support the M-form hypothesis suggest that a relationship may exist between firm size and organizational structure, and hence, if organizational form is a determinant of firm performance, it is likely that the size variable included in previous studies has been subjected to specification bias due to the exclusion of internal structure variables.

A growth variable is present to help correct for potential inflationary bias in the dependent variable. Given the arguments made above, a faster growing firm, *ceteris paribus*, will have an asset base whose value more closely approximates market values than will a slower growing firm. Accordingly, the performance of fast growing firms will be understated relative to that of slower growing firms. A measure of the rate of capacity utilization in the petroleum industry is included in the specification to account for the effect of industry-wide supply and demand conditions on firm profitability. The variable is defined as world refining runs divided by world refining capacity.[11] A risk variable is included, since economic theory suggests that the rate of return associated with a particular asset is a function of the risk inherent in the asset, and (assuming risk aversion) the greater the risk, the greater the expected return. The theoretical construct that is widely accepted as the foundation of modern capital market theory—the capital asset pricing model and subsequent derivative models (see Jensen (1972))—indicates that the measure of risk relevant to determining the requisite return on a security is the covariability of the security's return with the returns on all other securities. However, Beaver, Kettler and Scholes (1970) found that in attempting to predict the systematic risk of a firm's securities (the covariance of the securities' return with the return on all other securities) on the basis of financial statement information, earnings variability proved to be a more accurate predictor than earnings covariability. Accordingly, earnings variability has been selected for use as a measure of risk in this study. It is also interesting to note that of the 47 profitability studies reviewed by Weiss (1974), only one (Shepherd, 1972) included a measure of risk.

The organizational form variables to be used in the investigation consist of binary structural dummies. That is, a particular structural form variable will take the value of one in period t if the observation is associated with that structural form. Otherwise, the variable has a value of zero. The organizational structure classification scheme utilized includes the following categories: functional (F-form), functional with subsidiaries (FS-form), corrupted or degenerate divisionalized (C-form), holding company (H-form), transitional (T-form), and multidivisional (M-form). Lest one is tempted to interpret organizational structure solely in terms of the organizational chart, it is important to emphasize that internal control, planning, communication and coordination systems, and the degree of delegation of authority and responsibility represent equally (if not more) important dimensions of organizational structure. Although recent research has shown that consistent differences among the latter dimensions exist when categories are defined solely on the basis of organizational charts (Rumelt, 1974, pp. 33, 36), care must be taken to examine thoroughly the internal form of each sample firm to ensure that appropriate classification results.[12] Firms are assigned to the functional category (F-form) if they are organized along functional lines with the decision-making authority for both the development of long-run strategy and for daily operating tactics highly centralized.[13] Coordination of the functional areas is similarly centralized in these organizations. The functional with subsidiaries category (FS-form) refers to firms that are functionally organized with one or more divisions (which may or may not be legal subsidiaries) reporting to top management. These divisions are semi-autonomous in the sense that daily operating decisions are made within the divisions rather than by the centralized top management. The centralized management continues, however, to make operating decisions in the "nonsubsidiaries." The characteristics of a multidivisional firm (M-form) should be quite clear from the previous discussions. It has an internal structure in which operating and strategic decisionmaking is clearly separated and in which the requisite internal control systems exist and are systematically employed. A corrupted or degenerate divisionalized firm (C-form) is one in which a divisionalized structure and appropriate internal systems exist. In these firms, however, general management is highly involved in the operating decisionmaking process, a clear division between strategic and operating decisionmaking authority thus being absent. A holding company (H-form) structure possesses a centralized shell which is responsible for financial reporting but which has limited control over the operating division. Both strategic and tactical decision-making occur within the separate divisions. The holding company organizational structure is not necessarily associated with firms that are holding companies in a legal sense. A transitional classification (T-form) is assigned to all firms whose internal structure is in a state of flux as the firm moves from one internal border to another. Furthermore, this classification is assigned to all firms during the year immediately following a major organizational restructuring. The reason for this latter decision rule was to ensure that the observed firm performance following a reorganization was the result of the new internal form and not due to a Hawthorne effect.[14]

The above classification scheme . . . is quite similar to those proposed by Williamson and Bhargava (1972, pp. 125–128), by Chandler

(1962), and by Rumelt (1974, pp. 33–40). In the Williamson and Bhargava scheme the functional with subsidiaries and the transitional categories are combined. They have been separately defined in this study because it is believed that for some firms, particularly those with several business activities quite distinct from their basic or predominant business, the functional with subsidiaries structure may prove to be optimal. A transitional classification as defined above to reflect possible Hawthorne effects has not been previously proposed or used in the literature.

The proposed model is subject to the limitations of a single equation approach. We recognize that this performance equation is probably only one equation in a system of simultaneous equations in which performance, internal structure, size, and growth are jointly determined. However, as Cowling (1976, p. 1) has pointed out, it may be realistic to view such a system as being recursive. That is, although there may be feedbacks in the system, the associated lags are sufficiently long to allow us to pull out individual equations for separate treatment. In any case, this is what is done in the present investigation.

The Sample and the Data. The sample period runs 19 years from 1955 to 1973. 1955 was selected as the first year of the sample period since 1950 was the first year that data were available for many sample firms and since five previous annual observations on the dependent variable and on firm size were required to calculate the first observations on the risk and growth variables, respectively. Although data were available for 1974 and 1975, the sample period was defined to end in 1973 because of the effect that the Arab oil embargo and the quadrupling of crude oil prices by OPEC had on firm profitability in these years.[15] Were it the case that all sample firms were similarly affected by these events, a 1974–1975 dummy (binary) variable could be employed to isolate this effect. Unfortunately, this simply is not true. Since the effect the above events had on profitability operated primarily through inventory windfall gains, a variable that might adequately capture their influence would be the ratio of firm petroleum inventories to firm inventory capacity. Such data, however, are not publicly available, and the only recourse was to drop 1974 and 1975 from the sample period.

The sample was defined to include all petroleum industry firms in the 1975 Fortune 500.[16] There were 32 such firms, 28 of which participated in this study.[17] The organizational history of each of these firms was then traced back, when possible, to 1955. If a firm was involved in a significant merger during the 1955–1975 period, the merger partner was included in the sample in the premerger years if sufficient organizational information was available. For instance, Atlantic Refining Company and Richfield Oil Company are in the sample from 1955–1965 (adequate data being available for both firms) and Atlantic Richfield Company (ARCO) is in the sample from 1966–1975. However, the Pure Oil Company was not included in the sample prior to 1963 when it merged with Union Oil Company of California because there were insufficient data available on Pure.[18] Admittedly, the 1975 Fortune 500 is an arbitrary category from which to draw the sample. There certainly exists an inherent large firm bias. However, this is not troublesome in the present investigation because of the considerations mentioned earlier. Given that the purported superior attributes of the M-form can be realized only after a certain firm size/complexity is reached, it is appropriate to examine the performance of large firms such as the Fortune 500. Finally, by using the 1975 Fortune 500 rather than 1955 rankings, a surviving firm bias is introduced. To compensate for this the above-mentioned inclusion-of-merger-partners rule was adopted. The rationale for working from presently existing firms backwards in time (including earlier merger partners) rather than from 1955 firms forward was that there was a much larger organizational information data base for the former class of firms.

The procedure utilized in making the organizational form classifications and the resultant classifications are contained in the Appendix. Data on the dependent variable (the rate of return on stockholders' equity (book value)), firm size, risk, and growth were obtained from the 1950–1969 and 1956–1975 Compustat Annual Industrial tapes prepared by Investors Management Sciences, Denver, Colorado. World refining runs and refining capacity data from which the capacity utilization variable was calculated were obtained from the American Petroleum Institute (1975).

The Regression Model and Econometric Procedures. The regression model used in the investigation of the M-form hypothesis can be expressed in its most general form as:

$$\pi_{it} = \beta_0 + \beta_1 SIZE_{it} + \beta_2 MFORM_{it} + \beta_3 FSFORM_{it} + \beta_4 TFORM_{it}$$

$$+ \beta_5 CHFORM_{it} + \beta_6 RISK_{it} + \beta_7 CAPUTIL_t + \beta_8 GROWTH_{it} + e_{it},$$

where π_{it}, $SIZE_{it}$, $RISK_{it}$, $CAPUTIL_t$, and $GROWTH_{it}$ are as defined earlier in this section and

$$MFORM_{it} = \begin{cases} 1 \text{ if the } i\text{th firm in the } t\text{th period is characterized by an} \\ \quad M\text{-form internal structure,} \\ 0 \text{ otherwise;} \end{cases}$$

$$FSFORM_{it} = \begin{cases} 1 \text{ if the } i\text{th firm in the } t\text{th period is characterized by a functional with subsidiaries structure,} \\ 0 \text{ otherwise;} \end{cases}$$

$$TFORM_{it} = \begin{cases} 1 \text{ if the } i\text{th firm in the } t\text{th period is characterized by a structure of a transitional nature,} \\ 0 \text{ otherwise;} \end{cases}$$

$$CHFORM_{it} = \begin{cases} 1 \text{ if the } i\text{th firm in the } t\text{th period is characterized by either a corrupted divisionalized structure or a holding company internal form,} \\ 0 \text{ otherwise;} \end{cases}$$

$$e_{it} = \text{ a random disturbance term.}$$

The corrupted and holding company classifications are combined because of the relatively small number of observations associated with each structure. The merged category can be interpreted as representing nonoptimal divisionalized structures. Note that a functional form binary variable is excluded from the model. This is done to avoid singularity in the data matrix. β_0 thus represents the effect of a functional organizational form on profitability. The coefficients of the other organizational form variables reflect the differential performances associated with these forms as compared to the functional form. For example, suppose $\beta_0 = 0.10$ and $\beta_2 = 0.02$. This indicates that on average M-form firms realize a 12-percent rate of return on stockholders' equity, two percentage points above what the average functional form realizes.[19]

The econometric procedures used to estimate the above model are outlined in an appendix available from the authors. Briefly, the equation was first estimated with raw data by using ordinary least squares (OLS) techniques. Possible violation of the OLS assumption of nonautocorrelated error terms was then investigated (assuming an autoregressive scheme was constant across all firms). If significant autocorrelation was detected, an appropriate transformation of the data was made. Subsequently, the appropriateness of the OLS assumption of homoscedastic disturbance terms was assessed and another data transformation (designed to produce disturbances with homoscedastic properties) was performed if necessary.

Regressions were run on data from two subsample periods: 1955–1968 and 1969–1973. The reason for this was that the former period appeared to be one in which the M-form organizational innovation was being diffused, in which case it was possible that differential performance might be observable. The latter period appeared to be one characterized by close-to-full diffusion of the M-form, and so differential performance would be difficult to discern.[20] This diffusion process is made apparent by the data presented in Table 1 which reveal the percentage of M-form firms in the sample for each sample year. If the hypothesis advanced here is correct, we should expect the estimated coefficients to have the following indicated signs: $\hat{\beta}_1$ (no *a priori* hypothesis—positive (negative) if economies (diseconomies) of scale exist); $\hat{\beta}_2$ (positive on the basis of the M-form hypothesis, though perhaps only observable in the 1956–1968 period); $\hat{\beta}_3$ (unclear, depends on the efficiency ranking of the various organizational forms of which theory has little to say in this case); $\hat{\beta}_4$

Table 1. Percentage of Sample Firms in Each Category of Organizational Form.

	F	FS	T	H	C	M	Total Number of Sample Firms
1950	50	25	0	8	4	13	24
1951	50	25	0	8	4	13	24
1952	50	25	0	8	4	13	24
1953	52	24	0	8	4	12	25
1954	52	20	4	8	4	12	25
1955	52	20	0	8	4	16	25
1956	54	18	4	7	4	14	28
1957	50	18	7	7	4	14	28
1958	50	18	4	7	4	18	28
1959	48	14	10	7	0	21	29
1960	45	3	21	7	0	24	29
1961	45	3	14	7	0	31	29
1962	45	3	7	7	0	38	29
1963	41	3	7	7	0	41	29
1964	38	3	7	7	0	45	29
1965	38	3	7	7	0	45	29
1966	32	4	7	4	0	54	28
1967	29	7	4	4	0	57	28
1968	15	11	15	4	0	56	27
1969	11	11	11	4	0	63	27
1970	11	11	7	4	0	67	27
1971	11	11	4	4	0	70	27
1972	11	7	0	4	0	78	27
1973	11	7	4	0	0	78	27
1974	11	7	4	0	0	78	27
1975	7	7	7	0	0	78	27

Source: Appendix 1. Columns may not add to 100 percent due to rounding error.

(positive due to possible Hawthorne effects); $\hat{\beta}_5$ (unclear, though it should be less in value than $\hat{\beta}_2$); $\hat{\beta}_6$ (positive, assuming risk aversion); $\hat{\beta}_7$ (positive since a high capital utilization rate is associated with relatively strong demand conditions); and $\hat{\beta}_8$ (negative during inflationary periods because the asset bases of faster growing firms (as reflected in book values) will more closely reflect market values than will the asset bases of slower growing firms).

Results. The results are summarized in Table 2. We find strong statistical support for the *M*-form hypothesis. In the 1955–1968 period the multidivisional (*M*-form) structure significantly influenced (at better than the 99-percent level) the rate of return on stockholders' equity, raising it on average by about two percentage points ($\hat{\beta}_2 = 0.02079$) above the 7½ percent level ($\hat{\beta}_9 = 0.0767$) realized by the average functional form firm. Although firms in the transition between two organizational structures appear to have out-performed steady-state *M*-form firms ($\hat{\beta}_3 = 0.02337$), their performance is not significantly different from that of *M*-form firms at the 95-percent level.[21] That the transitional coefficient was insignificantly different from zero in the second period suggests that the Hawthorne phenomenon was relatively unimportant in this investigation. A plausible interpretation of the coefficient's initial period significance is simply that since most firms in the transitional category had just adopted an *M*-form structure, the coefficient actually reflected *M*-form performance (and hence was similar in magnitude to $\hat{\beta}_2$). Regardless, it certainly does not appear that the adoption of the *M*-form structure by a firm with an alternative previous structure is accompanied by any significant net adjustment costs.

Firms characterized by functional with subsidiaries or degenerate and holding company divisionalized structures do not appear to realize significantly different performance from an average functionally organized firm. The size of the degenerate and holding company coefficient relative to the *M*-form coefficient is as expected (indicating inferior relative performance).

Our results also indicate that observable superior multidivisional performance does not persist into the second sample period (1969–1973), a period characterized by close-to-full diffusion of the *M*-form structure. This is a reassuring result, implying that observable differential performance deriving from organizational form does not persist indefinitely. Nonoptimally organized firms are apparently faced with sufficiently strong competitive pressures to adopt the superior *M*-form structure and hence to eliminate the differential performance previously observed. Thus a plausible explanation for the unobserved superior performance in the

Table 2. Regression Coefficients, t-Statistics, and F-Tests in
Regression Equations to Explain the Rate of Return on Stockholders'
Equity Using Pooled Time Series-Cross Section Observations.

Independent Variable	1956–1968 (339 Observations)	1969–1973 (132 Observations)
C	0.767338×10^{-1}	-0.471747
	$(3.649)^{**}$	(-1.952)
SIZE	0.326463×10^{-6}	0.282800×10^{-5}
($ millions)	(0.371)	(1.569)
M-FORM	0.207939×10^{-1}	-0.172323×10^{-1}
	$(2.838)^{**}$	(-0.754)
T-FORM	0.235716×10^{-1}	-0.201286×10^{-1}
	$(3.254)^{**}$	(-0.561)
FS-FORM	0.125329×10^{-1}	-0.529042×10^{-1}
	(1.360)	(-1.703)
CH-FORM	-0.558522×10^{-1}	-0.322291×10^{-1}
	(-0.048)	(-0.744)
RISK	-0.274530	-0.353145
	(-1.571)	(-0.877)
CAP. UTIL.	0.342317×10^{-3}	0.610820
	(0.015)	$(2.278)^{*}$
GROWTH	0.279929	0.363157
	$(8.713)^{**}$	$(5.075)^{**}$
R^2	0.249	0.271
$\bar{R}^2$	0.231	0.224
F	13.686	5.721
D-W	1.774	1.776

*Significant at 95% level.
**Significant at 99% level.

Estimated autoregressive and heteroscedastic parameters are the following:

Equation	Estimated Autoregressive Parameter ($\hat{\rho}$)	Estimated Heteroscedastic Parameter ($\hat{\delta}$)*
1956–1968	0.631†	-0.566††
		(-6.012)
1969–1973	0.208†	-0.259
		(-1.822)

*Heteroscedastic parameter t-statistic in parentheses.

†Autoregressive transformation performed in reported regression equation (initial Durbin-Watson statistic indicating significant autocorrelation).

††Heteroscedastic transformation performed in reported regression equation (estimated heteroscedastic parameter being significantly different from zero at the 95% level).

second period is that the sample firms were, in general, appropriately organized. Support for this explanation lies in the observation that the six firms classified as *F-* or *FS-*form at any time in the 1969–1973 period were among the seven smallest sample firms.[22] The average asset size of these firms in 1969 was $247,530,000. In comparison, the average asset size of *M*-form firms in 1969 was $4,338,346,000. If one accepts the argument that the superior attributes of a multidivisional structure become increasingly relevant and important as firm size increases, the above observation can be interpreted as suggesting that firms whose characteristics in the second sample period were such that the *M*-form organizational structure would improve performance had in fact adopted the structure, while other firms remained appropriately organized as functional or functional with subsidiaries.

The positive sign of the capacity utilization coefficient is as expected in both sample periods. However, whereas the level of capacity utilization seems not to influence firm performance significantly in the 1955–1968 period, it does appear to do so in the 1969–1973 period. This effect in the latter period explains why the coefficient reflecting functional firm performance ($\hat{\beta}_0$) is negative, implying negative rates of return ($\hat{\beta}_0 = -0.4717$). When the average rate of capacity utilization in the 1969–1973 period (90 percent) is multiplied by the capacity utilization coefficient and the result added to $\hat{\beta}_0$, one sees that the average functionally organized firm (with average capacity utilization) in this period realized a rate of return on stockholders' equity of about 14 percent.

The coefficient associated with firm size is positive in both sample period regressions, though not significant at the 90 percent level. Thus, if there are any binding economies of scale associated with large firm size, they do not seem to be very important in determining overall firm performance.

The risk associated with a firm's performance, as measured by past variability in earnings, appears not to influence significantly current period rates of return on stockholders' equity in either sample period. The estimated coefficients are negative in sign, but they are not significantly different from zero at the 90 percent confidence level.

The average rate of growth experienced by the average firm in the five previous years significantly affects present period performance in a positive fashion. This is not in accord with the sign expected for this coefficient. It was postulated that in an inflationary period rapidly growing firms' asset bases would more nearly reflect current market values than would those of slower growing firms which have equal economic value (though lower book value), the performance of the former class of firms being relatively understated. A negative sign for this coefficient would hence be expected, though perhaps only in the latter sample period, since inflationary pressures were not serious prior to the late 1960s (and after the early 1950s). A possible explanation for this is that superior management is associated with fast growing firms, independent of any organizational form considerations. That is, it is possible that the managers of fast growing firms are more alert and aggressive, *ceteris paribus*, than the managers of corresponding slow growing firms with the result that the former firms tend to realize superior performance.

3. Conclusion

The results are broadly consistent with the M-form hypothesis. It certainly appears that there are characteristics associated with a multi-divisional form that lead to superior firm performance. That such superior performance is observed only in the 1955–1968 period and not in the 1969–1973 period is consistent with prior arguments made with respect to the diffusion of this organizational form. That is, one would expect to observe superior performance (if the attributes of the M-form exist as postulated) only while the organizational innovation was in the process of being diffused (i.e., when inferior substitutes simultaneously existed). Once the multidivisonal structure had displaced inferior internal forms, differential performance would not be observable, since the efficiency gains would have been passed on to consumers rather than having been impounded in profits.

The sample of firms used in the present investigation could have included firms which are optimally organized as functional forms, thereby creating a potential bias against positive empirical support for the M-form hypothesis.[23] In view of this, the results affirming the M-form hypothesis are particularly impressive. They imply not only that the efficacy of internal exchange is a function of organizational form (and hence that the appropriate division of economic activity between firms and markets is a function of organizational structure), but also that previous investigations of firm profitability may have been subject to specification bias as a result of the exclusion of organizational form considerations. Our findings suggest that past conclusions concerning the relationship between firm size and profitability may not be valid, since our results for the domestic petroleum industry suggest that such a relationship does not exist independent of organizational structure. Additional studies are needed to affirm the generality of this finding.

Notes

1. A functionally organized firm is characterized by the decisionmaking authority, for both the development of long-run strategy and for daily operating activities, residing in a centralized management group. Coordination of the functional areas (e.g., manufacturing, sales, engineering) is also carried out by the centralized management.

2. Chandler specifically focused on the DuPont Company (under the leadership of Pierre S. DuPont) and General Motors (under the leadership of Alfred P. Sloan, Jr.).

3. What in essence occurs is that operating decisions that require immediate attention displace management attention from less immediately critical strategic planning (capital allocation) decisions. Since there are always immediate operating decisions to be made, the strategic planning process is characteristically neglected.

4. There are several essential attributes associated with such control systems. First, there must be an explicit definition of an objective function, usually in terms of a profit or rate of return measure. Second, there must exist incentive machinery within the firm that induces division managers to maximize with respect to the specified objection function. The precise form of such machinery may vary considerably. Most obvious is the use of bonuses or raises which are tied to division performance. However, less formal devices may also be effective. For example, promotions (and the accompanying boost in status) or even more direct contact/communication with superiors following positive performance results; and/or demotions or transfers following unsatisfactory performance are frequently cited as alternative effective motivational machinery (particularly for management personnel). Regardless of the exact form of the incentive devices, a key factor in assuring their effectiveness is the continuous management (through internal information audits) of division performance by the centralized executive management (which itself may be an effective informal control system) with corrective actions being taken when results dictate. (See Williamson (1975, pp. 145–146).) The existence of these control systems serves the purpose of attenuating the internal control loss encountered by the management of a functionally organized firm as it expands.

5. In an extensive review of 47 prominent (and not so prominent) profitability studies made by Weiss, not a single investigation included an organizational form variable. See Weiss (1974, pp. 184–233).

6. The above discussion does, however, suggest the following research strategy: As has been pointed out, when a sample is selected, it is not known for sure whether it includes optimally organized functional firms. Hence it is not clear whether a comparison of functional firm performance with multidivisional firm performance is biased against the M-form hypothesis. If a statistical test is

conducted and results consistent with the hypothesis are found, one can be fairly confident of the results, since, if a bias was in fact present (and it may not have been), it would operate against such a finding. With this outcome subjective optimal/nonoptimal structural classifications are avoided. Unfortunately, if the results are not affirmative and one cannot reject the M-form hypothesis, it is necessary to resort to subjective classification assignments. The implications for research are clear. First, compare the performances of multidivisional and functional firms. If findings consistent with the hypothesis are revealed, they can be confidently accepted. If the results do not support the hypothesis, proceed to make necessarily subjective judgments regarding the optimal/nonoptimal nature of the structures involved and undertake a second performance comparison on the basis of the new classifications.

7. There is still the question of whether the above performance measure should reflect market or book values. The desirability of using a book value measure can be illustrated as follows. Consider a firm which has identified and pursued a market opportunity yielding a return disproportionate with the risk involved (e.g., a product or process innovation, or a superior internal control system). Assume that this above normal return is effectively isolated from competitive pressure for an extended period of time (e.g., due to patent protection or to a significant lead time for competitive entry into the relevant market). The return on the equity invested in the endeavor, as measured by appropriate book values, will continue to reflect the disproportionate return realized by the firm until competitive entry has effectively eliminated it, or until the firm is sold and its assets are revalued, with the above normal returns being fully capitalized into the selling price. The capitalization of these returns into the value of the firm's securities will occur, however, at a much more rapid pace, since as soon as investors learn of the disproportionate return associated with the underlying assets, the price of the securities will be bid up to the point where the associated capital market return just compensates for the inherent risk. Furthermore, it is extremely difficult to identify exactly when such capitalization will occur. Consequently, it seems that in an analysis of the efficiency characteristics of the firm, the use of a book value profit rate measure is appropriate.

   There are, however, several problems inherent in the use of a book value profit rate measure. We now identify two of the most important. First, the return required on a capital investment depends upon the risk inherent in the investment. Thus the return on the assets of two firms of equal efficiency may differ if the riskiness associated with the firms' assets differs. Second, in the presence of inflation the historical cost of a firm's assets as reported on its balance sheet will underestimate real asset values. In addition, reported profits, through undervalued depreciation and raw material charges, are likely to be overstated. Consequently, the rates of return to two firms (calculated on the basis of unadjusted book values) identical in all respects save that the capital structure of one is more recent (though of equal economic value) may erroneously suggest that the newer (or faster growing) firm is inferior with respect to firm performance. For a more complete and thorough discussion of these issues, see Stigler (1968).

8. Note that this specification omits the market structure variables that permeate other profitability studies. The reason for this is quite simple. Past studies have

characteristically been interindustry investigations in which market structure varied widely across industries. The present investigation focuses on a single industry, the market structure of which has not significantly changed over the sample period. Accordingly, it seems reasonable to omit consideration of the prevailing market structure.

9. The size variable is defined to be beginning period size rather than end of period size to avoid a simultaneity problem between firm size and the dependent variable. That is, the increase in firm size during the year (as measured by book values) is clearly a function of the year's profits unless all such profits are distributed to shareholders.

10. That is, GROWTH = $\{[(SIZE_{-1}/SIZE_{-2}) + (SIZE_{-2}/SIZE_{-3}) + (SIZE_{-3}/SIZE_{-4}) + (SIZE_{-4}/SIZE_{-5}) + (SIZE_{-5}/SIZE_{-6})]5\} - 1$.

11. The variable excludes Sino-Soviet bloc data. This capacity utilization measure was chosen because it is believed to reflect general economic conditions throughout the industry (i.e., in the crude oil market, the transportation market, and the refined products market). This is true because crude oil itself (which is obviously required to produce refined products—with the minor exception of wellhead gas) can rarely be used without being somewhat refined. That crude production over crude reserves was not used as the capacity variable stems from the much more reliable refining capacity data than the crude reserves data. The minor difference between crude production and refining runs is almost totally the result of changes in year-end crude inventories.

12. Williamson (1975, p. 151) suggests that such an examination of the internal systems and interactions of the firm is required in order to avoid misleading classification assignments. This is particularly important when empirically assessing the performance implications associated with alternative organizational structures.

13. The primary functional areas in the petroleum industry are: crude oil exploration and production, refining, transportation, and marketing.

14. A Hawthorne effect in the present context can be defined as improved performance (following a structural reorganization) which results not from characteristics of the new structure, but rather from the novelty of a new system or from heightened workers' interest (and hence productivity) in the system. For a more complete discussion, see Luthans (1973, pp. 23–32).

15. Although the embargo took place late in 1973, significant effects on petroleum firms' profitability did not occur until 1974.

16. Firms were defined "petroleum firms" if more than 50 percent of total firm revenues were derived from petroleum industry activities. Two additional reasons for using the Fortune 500 are as follows. First, a preliminary information search revealed that organization data for smaller firms were not widely available. Second, classification of the organizational structures of the firm in the 1970 Fortune 500 (and earlier merger partners) itself was a considerable large task.

17. Crown Central Petroleum, Tesoro Petroleum, Pennzoil Company, and Amerada Hess did not participate in the research project.

18. A list of the firms and the years they were included in the sample is available from the authors.

19. For a discussion of binary variable models, see Kmenta (1971, pp. 409–429).

20. Arguments in support of this split sample procedure were outlined above.

21. The relevant t-statistic for testing the significance of the difference in the T-Form and M-Form estimated coefficients has a value of 0.478.

22. The six firms were: American Petrofina, Clark Oil & Refining, Commonwealth Oil Refining, Murphy Oil, Superior Oil, and United Refining.

23. Other sources of statistical bias against the M-Form Hypothesis exist because of our focus on surviving firms (inefficient functionally organized enterprises could have been eliminated) and because superior management may be able to sustain functional firms beyond their appropriate life cycle. It often appears that organizational change is associated with the introduction of a new group of top managers after the retirement of senior executives who have made the functional structure perform through the application of Herculian management efforts.

FOUR

▭▭▭▭▭▭▭▭▭

Agency Theory:
How Market Forces Affect
the Management of a Firm

Up to this point in the text, most of the readings and arguments presented have been "market failures" arguments. That is, the authors so far have attempted to specify the conditions under which market forms of governance will become prohibitively expensive, and thus will be replaced by hierarchical forms of governance.

The discussion of agency theory, the focus of the current chapter, represents a shift in emphasis from market failures to a discussion of how market forces can affect a firm. In most of the chapters that follow, the authors presented will not attempt to explain why firms exist as an alternative to markets but will take the existence of both markets and firms as a given and will study the interaction between these two modes of governance.

This change in emphasis, although fundamental, often carries subtle implications in the models presented here. Arguments about the relationship between markets and firms can easily be confused with arguments about market failures. This is particularly the case in agency theory, which has traditionally been applied to study the relationship between a firm and its capital markets. Many of its most important implications depend on subtle modifications of traditional microeconomic assumptions about managerial interests and incentives. For example, instead of assuming that managers are simple utility maximizers, most agency theorists adopt the assumption that managers are boundedly rational and that they may act opportunistically. These are, of course, the same assumptions employed by transaction-cost theorists, and thus agency theory could easily be confused with a market failure argument.

However, while agency theory adopts these transaction-cost assumptions about managers, the primary theoretical "engine" driving agency theory is not capital market failure but, rather, capital market efficiency. Indeed, according to agency theory, whatever impact capital markets have on firm behavior exists, not despite capital market efficiency, but because of it. Because it requires that markets do not fail, agency theory is quite distinct from transaction-cost and related arguments.

Because the readings in this and subsequent chapters evaluate the impact of market forces on firms, they begin to point to ways in which one of the major deficiencies in organization theory, alluded to earlier, can be resolved. Namely, organization theory has placed relatively little emphasis on the competitive setting facing firms. Competition in this sense refers to the concrete actions of other firms in response to, or perhaps even in anticipation of, the strategic actions of a given firm. More frequently, organization theorists have discussed either the impact of a firm's environment on firm behavior or the impact of bilateral relations between a firm and one actor in its environment. Neither of these formulations of competition focuses on the concrete actions of the network of interdependent and independent actors in a firm's environment, and how such actions can constrain and affect organizational behavior. We now begin to consider these competitive market forces.

The Acquisition of Capital

As was suggested earlier, in the discipline of finance, much of agency theory has developed in an attempt to understand relationships between the firm and its capital markets. This focus is not unlike the focus of resource dependence and other organization theorists on the acquisition of a broad range of resources required by firms (Pfeffer and Salancik, 1978). Indeed, the relationship between firms and suppliers of labor and management (March and Simon, 1958), raw materials (Pfeffer and Salancik, 1978, p. 114), political influence (Selznick, [1949] 1966), and funding in the not-for-profit sector (Pfeffer and Leong, 1977; Selznick, [1949] 1966) have all been studied by organization theorists. Studies done by agency theorists on the relationship between firms and their sources of capital can be seen as a continuation of this research tradition.

One of the major differences between this organization theory work and work in agency theory, however, is that agency theorists have generally adopted the view that capital markets are efficient. The efficiency characteristics of factor markets facing firms has not been of primary concern in organization theory.

Given the importance of efficient capital markets in agency theory, it is appropriate to briefly review this concept. In its simplest form, the assertion that capital markets are efficient is no more or no less than asserting that outside investors in a firm are not foolish when making their investment decisions and, in particular, that they will take whatever information they have about the value of the firm into consideration when pricing a firm's debt and equity. Fama (1970a) has presented a more formal analysis of the efficient capital market concept in which he has isolated three distinct versions of market efficiency: strong-form efficiency, semistrong efficiency, and weak-form capital market efficiency. Strong-form capital market efficiency asserts that the prices of a firm's assets fully and instantaneously reflect all information, no matter what its source, concerning the value of those assets. Semistrong capital market efficiency asserts that the prices of a firm's assets fully and instantaneously reflect all publicly available information concerning the value of those assets. Such public information includes, for example, a firm's audited and anticipated financial performance, past and anticipated announcements, street rumors, and the previous performance of a firm's securities. Finally, in its weak form, capital market efficiency asserts only that all historically available information concerning the value of a firm's assets is reflected in their current price.

While theoretical arguments can be developed to justify each of these forms of capital market efficiency, most empirical work seems to suggest that real capital markets are not efficient in the strong form, but that they are efficient in both the semistrong and weak forms (Copeland and Weston, 1979). Moreover, most agency theorists have adopted the semistrong form of capital market efficiency in developing their arguments.

Capital Structure

Among the first financial economists to adopt the efficient capital market assumptions were Modigliani and Miller (1958, 1963). They argued that if capital markets are efficient (and if there are no corporate income taxes), then a firm's capital structure will have no impact on its market value. In its simplest form, this conclusion asserts that a firm's debt-to-equity ratio (or, the percentage of its outside funding that is debt divided by the percentage of this funding that is equity) will not have an impact on a firm's cost of obtaining debt or equity. This was a bold assertion that swept aside much of the common sense of finance popular at the time. It also suggested that there is no such thing as an "optimal capital structure," that is, a mixture of different forms of debt and equity funding that will optimally reduce a firm's cost of debt and equity.

A significant amount of research since Modigliani and Miller has focused on developing a rationale for an optimal capital structure consistent with efficient capital markets. Two possibilities have received a great deal of attention: the tax deductibility of interest payments on debt (Modigliani and Miller, 1963), and the costs of bankruptcy (Copeland and Weston, 1979; Stiglitz, 1972). Jensen and Meckling ("Theory of the Firm: Managerial Behavior, Agency Costs, and Ownership Structure") suggest a third possible explanation of why an optimal capital structure might exist, an explanation that depends on the belief that managers will not make decisions that maximize the wealth of outside debt and equity holders.

The Agency Relation

To develop their argument, Jensen and Meckling employ the concept of an agency relationship. In general, an agency relationship is "a contract under which one or more persons (the principal(s)) engage another person (the agent) to perform some service on their behalf which involves delegating some decision-making authority to the agent'' (Jensen and Meckling, 1976a, p. 308). One obvious example is the relationship between a firm's outside investors and managers. Here, outside investors may turn over the day-to-day managing of their investment to managers in the firm who may or may not hold a debt or equity position in the firm.

Jensen and Meckling explore the implications of agency relations of this type by focusing on the incentives that motivate managers who hold less than a 100 percent debt and/or equity interest in a firm. They are able to show that, in a wide variety of circumstances, these managers have incentives to make decisions that are inconsistent with the interests of ''outsiders'' (such as outside stockholders) in order to maximize their personal wealth and utility. For example, a manager might approve the purchase of a corporate jet. This manager may enjoy 100 percent of the benefit of the aircraft, but he does not bear its full costs. Instead, some of these costs are borne by other debt and equity holders. If a manager has no debt or equity holdings in a firm, then he will bear none of these costs directly. In this situation, managers clearly face an incentive to make decisions that are contrary to the best, wealth-maximizing interests of outside investors.

Of course, outside investors may engage in a wide variety of activities to monitor the activities and decisions of managers. In principle, such monitoring increases the likelihood that the managers will make decisions consistent with the self-interests of outside investors. To go further, managers can bond themselves to outside investors by designing arrangements that will penalize them as individuals should they make decisions that violate the interests of outside investors. However, according to Jensen and Meckling, no matter what monitoring and bonding mechanisms are employed, at least some conflict of interest between outside investors and managers will generally continue.

These continuing conflicts, together with the monitoring and bonding mechanisms designed to reduce them, are costly. Jensen and Meckling call the sum of these costs agency costs. Total agency costs are made up of (1) monitoring expenditures made by the principal to regulate and monitor the behavior of the agent, (2) bonding expenditures made by the agent to reassure principals, and

(3) residual agency costs, or costs due to unresolved conflicts of interests between agent and principals.

Jensen and Meckling then question who bears these agency costs. They develop the answer that, in efficient capital markets, the agent, or manager, bears the total wealth effects of total agency costs. In efficient capital markets, investors will anticipate the total agency costs of their agency relations with managers and will discount the price they are willing to pay for a firm's securities by these anticipated costs. Thus, in their attempt to raise capital, managers bear the anticipated wealth effects of total agency costs of debt and equity. In an imaginary world without agency costs, outside equity investors would be willing to pay a price, P, for a firm's equity. However, because they anticipate total agency costs, A, these outsiders will discount the value of the firm's equity, and will pay only a price, $P - A$. In this way, managers, in their attempt to raise funds from outside sources, bear all the economic burden of the agency costs. Similar logic can be applied for the agency costs of debt.

Jensen and Meckling use these conclusions to investigate the possibility of an optimal capital structure for a firm. Since managers bear all agency costs in their attempt to raise capital, they have a strong incentive to choose the capital structure that minimizes total agency costs. In this way, they reduce their cost of capital. Because each investment situation is likely to generate different agency costs for debt and equity, firms in different situations are likely to choose various combinations of debt and equity. These situation-specific combinations of debt and equity are the optimal capital structures that Jensen and Meckling seek to explain in the article included here.

Agency Theory and Firm Structure

In their development of an agency theory of an optimal capital structure, Jensen and Meckling propose a definition of what constitutes a firm. In their view, the firm is a legal fiction that serves as a nexus of contracts among various factors of production. This definition of the firm is not dissimilar to the definition developed by transaction-cost theorists. Recall that for transaction-cost theorists, the boundaries of a firm are defined through an aggregation process, transaction by transaction, by considering the nature and character of transaction governance mechanisms. In agency theory, these governance mechanisms are various forms of contracts, ranging in character from formal to informal, explicit to implicit, and objective to subjective.

Fama and Jensen ("Separation of Ownership and Control") develop this same theme in their work. These authors begin by generalizing the discussion of the agency relationship from the specific example of the relationship between outside investors and managers to the study of the relationship between any two stages of the decision-making and implementing process. In particular, Fama and Jensen suggest that any decision-making process can be broken down into a series of stages and that, under a wide variety of conditions, different individuals or groups will specialize in one or another of these stages. Such specialization enhances the skill with which particular parts of a decision are executed but creates important agency problems. These problems arise because those specializing in the early stage of the decision-making process must depend on others to implement or to monitor their decisions, whereas those who specialize in the later stages of the decision-making process must depend on others to collect the appropriate information and make decisions that can, in principle, be implemented.

Fama and Jensen go on to note that a wide variety of organizational structures and processes can emerge to reduce these agency problems. The set of organizational responses that emerges depends on the characteristics of the agency problems and the stages of the decision-making process that are involved. In presenting their arguments, Fama and Jensen imply yet another typology of organizational forms based on the nature and type of agency problems that exist. The typology suggested by these authors is distinct from the empirical typologies developed by organizational theorists (Blau, 1955; Hickson, Pugh, and Pheysey, 1969) and the transaction-cost typology developed by Williamson (1975), although it is quite similar to the typology suggested by Alchian and Demsetz (1972).

Implications for Organization Theory

In the Introduction to this book, it was suggested that organization theory cannot explain why firms exist because it includes no concept of a market, as an alternative to an organization, for governing economic exchanges. The market failures arguments presented in Chapters Two and Three of this book partially address this omission. In this chapter, we suggest that markets might need to play yet another role in organization theory. Not only are markets an alternative to firms for governing exchanges, but markets have a significant impact on firm behavior. Markets largely define the opportunities and constraints that firms face. They can rarely, if ever, be avoided completely. Theories that purport to explain the behavior of organizations must certainly include some conception of markets.

Without a conception of market-caused organizational effects in models of organizational behavior, the organization theorist is likely to mistakenly specify the exogenous sources of influence on organizations. For example, without efficient markets impinging on them and constraining and disciplining their behavior, firms facing uncertainty from sources in their environment may simply appear to dominate that source, either politically or economically (Pfeffer and Salancik, 1978). The message of agency theory is not that such domination never occurs, but that market disciplines generally dictate the attachment of a cost to such actions. In many circumstances, firms cannot profitably do what they would like to do because of these market disciplines. In agency theory, the efficient markets that surround a firm cannot be denied for long.

These simple conclusions help to resolve one of the anomalies of the power model suggested in the Introduction. There, we briefly argued that if firms attempting to minimize their environmentally induced uncertainty employ some form of vertical integration to reduce that uncertainty (as is implied by most power models), then most industries would be dominated by a small number of highly vertically integrated firms. However, by recognizing that firms may act in markets that modify and constrain their behavior, it becomes clear that vertical integration to reduce uncertainty is not costless. Sometimes, perhaps under conditions of very high uncertainty, the cost of integration will be worth the benefit, but in many circumstances this simply will not be the case. Yet, until the costs of these strategies are included in this model, that is, until it incorporates some concept of markets and market-driven behavior, explanations of dependence and dependence minimization will remain incomplete.

In addition to focusing attention on the role of competitive markets in constraining firm behavior, agency theory points to an important connection between the more psychological analysis of processes within firms and organizational economics. Jensen and Meckling suggest that wherever cooperation exists, agency problems are likely to exist. Fama and Jensen discuss the decision-making process as it unfolds in firms, noting that making and implementing decisions requires just the kind of cooperation that gives rise to agency problems. When these observations are combined with Alchian and Demsetz's argument that the reason firms exist is because of the metering problems associated with team production, it becomes clear that one of the most important organizational processes that needs to be studied is cooperation among employees within a firm. Williamson's (1975) discussion of cooperation in an M-form organization is also consistent with this observation.

A close connection between the voluminous research on groups and group processes (Cartwright and Zander, 1960) and organizational economics seems imminent, but it has yet to be clearly established. Ouchi (1980) and Barney and Ouchi (1984) have recognized the importance of this connection in the concept of clans and clan-assisted markets. For Ouchi (1980), a clan is a type of transaction governance mechanism that relies on shared values and trust developed over long periods to resolve exchange conflicts.

But the concept of a clan only scratches the surface of the potential relationship between organizational economics and organization behavior research on cooperation in firms. One of the major challenges of organizational economics over the next decade will be to take the numerous insights from this research tradition and incorporate them into organizational economic models.

Theory of the Firm: Managerial Behavior, Agency Costs, and Ownership Structure

Michael C. Jensen
William H. Meckling

This paper integrates elements from the theory of agency, the theory of property rights and the theory of finance to develop a theory of the ownership structure of the firm. We define the concept of agency costs, show its relationship to the "separation and control" issue, investigate the nature of the agency costs generated by the existence of debt and outside equity, demonstrate who bears these costs and why, and investigate the Pareto optimality of their existence. We also provide a new definition of the firm, and show how our analysis of the factors influencing the creation and issuance of debt and equity claims is a special case of the supply side of the completeness of markets problem.

> The directors of such [joint-stock] companies, however, being the managers rather of other people's money than of their own, it cannot well be expected, that they should watch over it with the same anxious vigilance with which the partners in a private copartnery frequently watch over their own. Like the stewards of a rich man, they are apt to consider attention to small matters as not for their master's honour, and very easily give themselves a dispensation from having it. Negligence and profusion, therefore, must always prevail, more or less, in the management of the affairs of such a company.
> —Adam Smith, *An Inquiry into the Nature and Causes of the Wealth of Nations*, 1776, Cannan Edition (Modern Library, New York, 1937) p. 700.

Note: An earlier version of this paper was presented at the Conference on Analysis and Ideology, Interlaken, Switzerland, June 1974, sponsored by the Center for Research in Government Policy and Business at the University of Rochester, Graduate School of Management. We are indebted to F. Black, E. Fama, R. Ibbotson, W. Klein, M. Rozeff, R. Weil, O. Williamson, an anonymous referee, and to our colleagues and members of the Finance Workshop at the University of Rochester for their comments and criticisms, in particular G. Benston, M. Canes, D. Henderson, K. Leffler, J. Long, C. Smith, R. Thompson, R. Watts and J. Zimmerman.

Reprinted in slightly adapted form from the *Journal of Financial Economics,* 1976, *3* (4), 305–360. Used by permission of North-Holland Publishing Company.

1. Introduction and Summary

1.1. Motivation of the Paper

In this paper we draw on recent progress in the theory of (1) property rights, (2) agency, and (3) finance to develop a theory of ownership structure[1] for the firm. In addition to tying together elements of the theory of each of these three areas, our analysis casts new light on and has implications for a variety of issues in the professional and popular literature such as the definition of the firm, the "separation of ownership and control," the "social responsibility" of business, the definition of a "corporate objective function," the determination of an optimal capital structure, the specification of the content of credit agreements, the theory of organization, and the supply side of the completeness of markets problem.

Our theory helps explain:

1. why an entrepreneur or manager in a firm which has a mixed financial structure (containing both debt and outside equity claims) will choose a set of activities for the firm such that the total value of the firm is *less* than it would be if he were the sole owner and why this result is independent of whether the firm operates in monopolistic or competitive product or factor markets;

2. why his failure to maximize the value of the firm is perfectly consistent with efficiency;

3. why the sale of common stock is a viable source of capital even though managers do not literally maximize the value of the firm;

4. why debt was relied upon as a source of capital before debt financing offered any tax advantage relative to equity;

5. why preferred stock would be issued;

6. why accounting reports would be provided voluntarily to creditors and stockholders, and why independent auditors would be engaged by management to testify to the accuracy and correctness of such reports;

7. why lenders often place restrictions on the activities of firms to whom they lend, and why firms would themselves be led to suggest the imposition of such restrictions;

8. why some industries are characterized by owner-operated firms whose sole outside source of capital is borrowing;

9. why highly regulated industries such as public utilities or banks will

have higher debt equity ratios for equivalent levels of risk than the average non-regulated firm;

10.   why security analysis can be socially productive even if it does not increase portfolio returns to investors.

1.2. Theory of the Firm: An Empty Box?

While the literature of economics is replete with references to the "theory of the firm", the material generally subsumed under that heading is not a theory of the firm but actually a theory of markets in which firms are important actors. The firm is a "black box" operated so as to meet the relevant marginal conditions with respect to inputs and outputs, thereby maximizing profits, or more accurately, present value. Except for a few recent and tentative steps, however, we have no theory which explains how the conflicting objectives of the individual participants are brought into equilibrium so as to yield this result. The limitations of this black box view of the firm have been cited by Adam Smith and Alfred Marshall, among others. More recently, popular and professional debates over the "social responsibility" of corporations, the separation of ownership and control, and the rash of reviews of the literature on the "theory of the firm" have evidenced continuing concern with these issues.[2]

A number of major attempts have been made during recent years to construct a theory of the firm by substituting other models for profit or value maximization; each attempt motivated by a conviction that the latter is inadequate to explain managerial behavior in large corporations.[3] Some of these reformulation attempts have rejected the fundamental principle of maximizing behavior as well as rejecting the more specific profit maximizing model. We retain the notion of maximizing behavior on the part of all individuals in the analysis to follow.[4]

1.3. Property Rights

An independent stream of research with important implications for the theory of the firm has been stimulated by the pioneering work of Coase, and extended by Alchian, Demsetz and others.[5] A comprehensive survey of this literature is given by Furobotn and Pejovich (1972). While the focus of this research has been "property rights,"[6] the subject matter encompassed is far broader than that term suggests. What is important for the problems addressed here is that specification of individual rights determines how costs and rewards will be allocated among the participants in any organization. Since the specification of rights is generally effected through contracting (implicit as well as explicit), individual behavior in organizations, including the behavior of managers, will depend upon the nature of these contracts. We focus in this paper on the behavioral implications of the property rights specified in the contracts between the owners and managers of the firm.

1.4. Agency Costs

Many problems associated with the inadequacy of the current theory of the firm can also be viewed as special cases of the theory of agency relationships in which there is a growing literature.[7] This literature has developed independently of the property rights literature even though the problems with which it is concerned are similar; the approaches are in fact highly complementary to each other.

We define an agency relationship as a contract under which one or more persons (the principal(s)) engage another person (the agent) to perform some service on their behalf which involves delegating some decision making authority to the agent. If both parties to the relationship are utility maximizers there is good reason to believe that the agent will not always act in the best interests of the principal. The *principal* can limit divergences from his interest by establishing appropriate incentives for the agent and by incurring monitoring costs designed to limit the aberrant activities of the agent. In addition in some situations it will pay the *agent* to expend resources (bonding costs) to guarantee that he will not take certain actions which would harm the principal or to ensure that the principal will be compensated if he does take such actions. However, it is generally impossible for the principal or the agent at zero cost to ensure that the agent will make optimal decisions from the principal's viewpoint. In most agency relationships the principal and the agent will incur positive monitoring and bonding costs (non-pecuniary as well as pecuniary), and in addition there will be some divergence between the agent's decisions[8] and those decisions which would maximize the welfare of the principal. The dollar equivalent of the reduction in welfare experienced by the principal due to this divergence is also a cost of the agency relationship, and we refer to this latter cost as the "residual loss." We define *agency costs* as the sum of:

1. the monitoring expenditures by the principal,[9]
2. the bonding expenditures by the agent,
3. the residual loss.

Note also that agency costs arise in any situation involving co-operative effort (such as the co-authoring of this paper) by two or more people even though there is no clear cut principal-agent relationship. Viewed in this light it is clear that our definition of agency costs and their importance to the theory of the firm bears a close relationship to the problem of shirking and monitoring of team production which Alchian and Demsetz (1972) raise in their paper on the theory of the firm.

Since the relationship between the stockholders and manager of a corporation fit the definition of a pure agency relationship it should be no surprise to discover that the issues associated with the "separation of ownership and control" in the modern diffuse ownership corporation are intimately associated with the general problem of agency. We show below that an explanation of why and how the agency costs generated by the corporate form are born leads to a theory of the ownership (or capital) structure of the firm.

Before moving on, however, it is worthwhile to point out the generality of the agency problem. The problem of inducing an "agent" to behave as if he were maximizing the "principal's" welfare is quite general. It exists in all organizations and in all cooperative efforts—at every level of management in firms,[10] in universities, in mutual companies, in cooperatives, in governmental authorities and bureaus, in unions, and in relationships normally classified as agency relationships such as are common in the performing arts and the market for real estate. The development of theories to explain the form which agency costs take in each of these situations (where the contractual relations differ significantly), and how and why they are born will lead to a rich theory of organizations which is now lacking in economics and the social sciences generally. We confine our attention in this paper to only a small part of this general problem—the analysis of agency costs generated by the contractual arrangement between the owners and top management of the corporation.

Our approach to the agency problem here differs fundamentally from most of the existing literature. That literature focuses almost exclusively on the normative aspects of the agency relationship; that is how to structure the contractual relation (including compensation incentives) between the principal and agent to provide appropriate incentives for the agent to make choices which will maximize the principal's welfare given that uncertainty and imperfect monitoring exist. We focus almost entirely on the positive aspects of the theory. That is, we assume individuals solve these normative problems and given that only stocks and bonds can be issued as claims, we investigate the incentives faced by each of the parties and the elements entering into the determination of the equilibrium contractual form characterizing the relationship between the manager (i.e., agent) of the firm and the outside equity and debt holders (i.e., principals).

1.5. Some General Comments on the Definition of the Firm

Ronald Coase (1937) in his seminal paper on ''The Nature of the Firm'' pointed out that economics had no positive theory to determine the bounds of the firm. He characterized the bounds of the firm as that range of exchanges over which the market system was suppressed and resource allocation was accomplished instead by authority and direction. He focused on the cost of using markets to effect contracts and exchanges and argued that activities would be included within the firm whenever the costs of using markets were greater than the costs of using direct authority. Alchian and Demsetz (1972) object to the notion that activities within the firm are governed by authority, and correctly emphasize the role of contracts as a vehicle for voluntary exchange. They emphasize the role of monitoring in situations in which there is joint input or team production.[11] We sympathize with the importance they attach to monitoring, but we believe the emphasis which Alchian–Demsetz place on joint input production is too narrow and therefore misleading. Contractual relations are the essence of the firm, not only with employees but with suppliers, customers, creditors, etc. The problem of agency costs and monitoring exists for all of these contracts, independent of whether there is joint production in their sense; i.e., joint production can explain only a small fraction of the behavior of individuals associated with a firm. A detailed examination of these issues is left to another paper.

It is important to recognize that most organizations are simply *legal fictions*[12] *which serve as a nexus for a set of contracting relationships among individuals.* This includes firms, non-profit institutions such as universities, hospitals and foundations, mutual organizations such as mutual savings banks and insurance companies and cooperatives, some private clubs, and even governmental bodies such as cities, states and the Federal government, government enterprises such as TVA, the Post Office, transit systems, etc.

The private corporation or firm is simply one form of *legal fiction which serves as a nexus for contracting relationships and which is also characterized*

*by the existence of divisible residual claims on the assets and cash flows of
the organization which can generally be sold without permission of the other
contracting individuals.* While this definition of the firm has little substantive content, emphasizing the essential contractual nature of firms
and other organizations focuses attention on a crucial set of questions—why particular sets of contractual relations arise for various
types of organizations, what the consequences of these contractual
relations are, and how they are affected by changes exogenous to
the organization. Viewed this way, it makes little or no sense to try
to distinguish those things which are "inside" the firm (or any other
organization) from those things that are "outside" of it. There is
in a very real sense only a multitude of complex relationships (i.e.,
contracts) between the legal fiction (the firm) and the owners of labor,
material and capital inputs and the consumers of output.[13]

Viewing the firm as the nexus of a set of contracting relationships
among individuals also serves to make it clear that the personalization
of the firm implied by asking questions such as "what should be the objective function of the firm," or "does the firm have a social responsibility" is seriously misleading. *The firm is not an individual.* It is a legal
fiction which serves as a focus for a complex process in which the conflicting objectives of individuals (some of whom may "represent" other
organizations) are brought into equilibrium within a framework of contractual relations. In this sense the "behavior" of the firm is like the
behavior of a market; i.e., the outcome of a complex equilibrium process. We seldom fall into the trap of characterizing the wheat or stock
market as an individual, but we often make this error by thinking about
organizations as if they were persons with motivations and intentions.[14]

1.6. An Overview of the Paper

We develop the theory in stages. Sections 2 and 4 provide analyses
of the agency costs of equity and debt respectively. These form the major
foundation of the theory. Section 3 poses some unanswered questions
regarding the existence of the corporate form of organization and examines the role of limited liability. Section 5 provides a synthesis of the
basic concepts derived in sections 2–4 into a theory of the corporate ownership structure which takes account of the tradeoffs available to the entrepreneur-manager between inside and outside equity and debt. Some
qualifications and extensions of the analysis are discussed in section 6,
and section 7 contains a brief summary and conclusions.

2. The Agency Costs of Outside Equity

2.1. Overview

In this section we analyze the effect of outside equity on agency costs by comparing the behavior of a manager when he owns 100 percent of the residual claims on a firm to his behavior when he sells off a portion of those claims to outsiders. If a wholly owned firm is managed by the owner, he will make operating decisions which maximize his utility. These decisions will involve not only the benefits he derives from pecuniary returns but also the utility generated by various non-pecuniary aspects of his entrepreneurial activities such as the physical appointments of the office, the attractiveness of the secretarial staff, the level of employee discipline, the kind and amount of charitable contributions, personal relations ("love," "respect," etc.) with employees, a larger than optimal computer to play with, purchase of production inputs from friends, etc. The optimum mix (in the absence of taxes) of the various pecuniary and non-pecuniary benefits is achieved when the marginal utility derived from an additional dollar of expenditure (measured net of any productive effects) is equal for each non-pecuniary item and equal to the marginal utility derived from an additional dollar or after tax purchasing power (wealth).

If the owner-manager sells equity claims on the corporation which are identical to his (i.e., share proportionately in the profits of the firm and have limited liability) agency costs will be generated by the divergence between his interest and those of the outside shareholders, since he will then bear only a fraction of the costs of any non-pecuniary benefits he takes out in maximizing his own utility. If the manager owns only 95 percent of the stock, he will expend resources to the point where the marginal utility derived from a dollar's expenditure of the firm's resources on such items equals the marginal utility of an additional 95 cents in general purchasing power (i.e., *his* share of the wealth reduction) and not one dollar. Such activities, on his part, can be limited (but probably not eliminated) by the expenditure of resources on monitoring activities by the outside stockholders. But as we show below, the owner will bear the entire wealth effects of these expected costs so long as the equity market anticipates these effects. Prospective minority shareholders will realize that the owner-manager's interests will diverge somewhat from theirs, hence the price which they will pay for shares will reflect the monitoring costs and the effect of the divergence between the manager's interest and theirs. Nevertheless, ignoring for the moment the possibility of borrowing against his wealth, the owner will find it desirable to bear these costs as long as the welfare increment he experiences from converting his claims on the firm into general purchasing power[15] is large enough to offset them.

As the owner-manager's fraction of the equity falls, his fractional claim on the outcomes falls and this will tend to encourage him to appropriate larger amounts of the corporate resources in the form of perquisites. This also makes it desirable for the minority shareholders to expend more resources in monitoring his behavior. Thus, the wealth costs to the owner of obtaining additional cash in the equity markets rise as his fractional ownership falls.

We shall continue to characterize the agency conflict between the owner-manager and outside shareholders as deriving from the manager's tendency to appropriate perquisites out of the firm's resources for his own consumption. However, we do not mean to leave the impression that this is the only or even the most important source of conflict. Indeed, it is likely that the most important conflict arises from the fact that as the manager's ownership claim falls, his incentive to devote significant effort to creative activities such as searching out new profitable ventures falls. He may in fact avoid such ventures simply because it requires too much trouble or effort on his part to manage or to learn about new technologies. Avoidance of these personal costs and the anxieties that go with them also represent a source of on the job utility to him and it can result in the value of the firm being substantially lower than it otherwise could be.

2.2. A Simple Formal Analysis of the Sources of Agency Costs of Equity and Who Bears Them

In order to develop some structure for the analysis to follow we make two sets of assumptions. The first set (permanent assumptions) are those which shall carry through almost all of the analysis in sections 2–5. The effects of relaxing some of these are discussed in section 6. The second set (temporary assumptions) are made only for expositional purposes and are relaxed as soon as the basic points have been clarified.

Permanent Assumptions

(P.1)   All taxes are zero.
(P.2)   No trade credit is available.
(P.3)   All outside equity shares are non-voting.

(P.4) No complex financial claims such as convertible bonds or preferred stock or warrants can be issued.

(P.5) No outside owner gains utility from ownership in a firm in any way other than through its effect on his wealth or cash flows.

(P.6) All dynamic aspects of the multiperiod nature of the problem are ignored by assuming there is only one production-financing decision to be made by the entrepreneur.

(P.7) The entrepreneur-manager's money wages are held constant throughout the analysis.

(P.8) There exists a single manager (the peak coordinator) with ownership interest in the firm.

Temporary Assumptions

(T.1) The size of the firm is fixed.

(T.2) No monitoring or bonding activities are possible.

(T.3) No debt financing through bonds, preferred stock, or personal borrowing (secured or unsecured) is possible.

(T.4) All elements of the owner-manager's decision problem involving portfolio considerations induced by the presence of uncertainty and the existence of diversifiable risk are ignored.

Define:

X = $\{x_1, x_2, \ldots, x_n\}$ = vector of quantities of all factors and activities within the firm from which the manager derives non-pecuniary benefits;[16] the x_i are defined such that his marginal utility is positive for each of them;

$C(X)$ = total dollar cost of providing any given amount of these items;

$P(X)$ = total dollar value to the firm of the productive benefits of X;

$B(X)$ = $P(X) - C(X)$ = net dollar benefit to the firm of X ignoring any effects of X on the equilibrium wage of the manager.

Ignoring the effects of X on the manager's utility and therefore on his equilibrium wage rate, the optimum levels of the factors and activities X are defined by X^* such that

$$\frac{\delta B(X^*)}{\delta X^*} = \frac{\delta P(X^*)}{\delta X^*} - \frac{\delta C(X^*)}{\delta X^*} = 0.$$

Thus for any vector $X \geq X^*$ (i.e., where at least one element of X is greater than its corresponding element of X^*), $F \equiv B(X^*) - B(X) > 0$ measures the dollar cost to the firm (net of any productive effects) of providing the increment $X - X^*$ of the factors and activities which generate utility to the manager. We assume henceforth that for any given level of cost to the firm, F, the vector of factors and activities on which F is spent are those, $\hat{X}$, which yield the manager maximum utility. Thus $F \equiv B(X^*) - B(\hat{X})$.

We have thus far ignored in our discussion the fact that these expenditures on X occur through time and therefore there are tradeoffs to be made across time as well as between alternative elements of X. Furthermore, we have ignored the fact that the future expenditures are likely to involve uncertainty (i.e., they are subject to probability distributions) and therefore some allowance must be made for their riskiness. We resolve both of these issues by defining C, P, B, and F to be the *current market values* of the sequence of probability distributions on the period by period cash flows involved.[17]

Given the definition of F as the current market value of the stream of manager's expenditures on non-pecuniary benefits we represent the constraint which a single owner-manager faces in deciding how much non-pecuniary income he will extract from the firm by the line $\overline{V}F$ in Figure 1. This is analogous to a budget constraint. The market value of the firm is measured along the vertical axis and the market value of the manager's stream of expenditures on non-pecuniary benefits, F, are measured along the horizontal axis. $0\overline{V}$ is the value of the firm when the amount of non-pecuniary income consumed is zero. By definition $\overline{V}$ is the maximum market value of the cash flows generated by the firm for a given money wage for the manager when the manager's consumption of non-pecuniary benefits are zero. At this point all the factors and activities within the firm which generate utility for the manager are at the level X^* defined above. There is a different budget constraint $\overline{V}F$ for each possible scale of the firm (i.e., level of investment, I) and for alternative levels of money wage, W, for the manager. For the moment we pick an arbitrary level of investment (which we assume has already been made) and hold the scale of the firm constant at this level. We also assume that the manager's money wage is fixed at the level W^* which represents the current market value of his wage contract[18] in the optimal compensation package which consists of both wages, W^*, and non-pecuniary benefits, F^*. Since one dollar of current value of non-pecuniary benefits withdrawn from the firm by the manager reduces the market value of the firm by $\$1$, by definition, the slope of $\overline{V}F$ is -1.

The owner-manager's tastes for wealth and non-pecuniary benefits is represented in Figure 1 by a system of indifference curves, U_1, U_2, etc.[19] The indifference curves will be convex as drawn as long as the

Figure 1. The value of the firm (V) and the level of non-pecuniary benefits consumed (F) when the fraction of outside equity is $(1 - \alpha)V$, and U_j ($j = 1,2,3$) represents owner's indifference curves between wealth and non-pecuniary benefits.

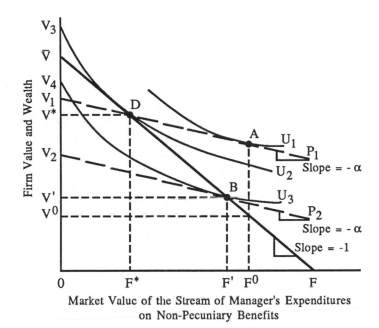

Market Value of the Stream of Manager's Expenditures
on Non-Pecuniary Benefits

owner-manager's marginal rate of substitution between non-pecuniary benefits and wealth diminishes with increasing levels of the benefits. For the 100 percent owner-manager, this presumes that there are not perfect substitutes for these benefits available on the outside, i.e., to some extent they are job specific. For the fractional owner-manager this presumes the benefits cannot be turned into general purchasing power at a constant price.[20]

When the owner has 100 percent of the equity, the value of the firm will be V^* where indifference curve U_2 is tangent to VF, and the level of non-pecuniary benefits consumed is F^*. If the owner sells the entire equity but remains as manager, and if the equity buyer can, at zero cost, force the old owner (as manager) to take the same level of non-pecuniary benefits as he did as owner, then V^* is the price the new owner will be willing to pay for the entire equity.[21]

In general, however, we would not expect the new owner to be able to enforce identical behavior on the old owner at zero costs. If the old owner sells a fraction of the firm to an outsider, he, as manager, will no longer bear the full cost of any non-pecuniary benefits he consumes. Suppose the owner sells a share of the firm, $1 - \alpha$, $(0 < \alpha < 1)$ and retains for himself a share, α. If the prospective buyer believes that the owner-manager will consume the same level of non-pecuniary benefits as he did as full owner, the buyer will be willing to pay $(1 - \alpha)V^*$ for a fraction $(1 - \alpha)$ of the equity. Given that an outsider now holds a claim to $(1 - \alpha)$ of the equity, however, the *cost* to the owner-manager of consuming \$1 of non-pecuniary benefits in the firm will no longer be \$1. Instead, it will be $\alpha \times \$1$. If the prospective buyer actually paid $(1 - \alpha)V^*$ for his share of the equity, and if thereafter the manager could choose whatever level of non-pecuniary benefits he liked, his budget constraint would be V_1P_1 in Figure 1 and has a slope equal to $-\alpha$. Including the payment the owner receives from the buyer as part of the owner's post-sale wealth, his budget constraint, V_1P_1, must pass through D, since he can if he wishes have the same wealth and level of non-pecuniary consumption he consumed as full owner.

But if the owner-manager is free to choose the level of perquisites, *F*, subject only to the loss in wealth he incurs as a part owner, his welfare will be maximized by increasing his consumption of non-pecuniary benefits. He will move to point A where V_1P_1 is tangent to U_1 representing a higher level of utility. The value of the firm falls from V^*, to V^0, i.e., by the amount of the cost to the firm of the increased non-pecuniary expenditures, and the owner-manager's consumption of non-pecuniary benefits rises from F^* to F^0.

If the equity market is characterized by rational expectation the buyers will be aware that the owner will increase his non-pecuniary consumption when his ownership share is reduced. If the owner's response function is known or if the equity market makes unbiased estimates of the owner's response to the changed incentives, the buyer will not pay $(1 - \alpha)V^*$ for $(1 - \alpha)$ of the equity.

Theorem. For a claim on the firm of $(1 - \alpha)$ the outsider will pay only $(1 - \alpha)$ times the value he expects the firm to have given the induced change in the behavior of the owner-manager.

Proof. For simplicity we ignore any element of uncertainty introduced by the lack of perfect knowledge of the owner-manager's response function. Such uncertainty will not affect the final solution if the equity market is large as long as the estimates are rational (i.e., unbiased) and the errors are independent across firms. The latter condition assures that this risk is diversifiable and therefore equilibrium prices will equal the expected values.

Let W represent the owner's total wealth after he has sold a claim equal to $1 - \alpha$ of the equity to an outsider. W has two components. One is the payment, S_o, made by the outsider for $1 - \alpha$ of the equity; the rest, S_i, is the value of the owner's (i.e., insider's) share of the firm, so that W, the owner's wealth, is given by

$$W = S_o + S_i = S_o + \alpha V(F, \alpha),$$

where $V(F, \alpha)$ represents the value of the firm given that the manager's fractional ownership share is α and that he consumes perquisites with current market value of F. Let V_2P_2, with a slope of $-\alpha$ represent the tradeoff the owner-manager faces between non-pecuniary benefits and his wealth after the sale. Given that the owner has decided to sell a claim $1 - \alpha$ of the firm, his welfare will be maximized when V_2P_2 is tangent to some indifference curve such as U_3 in Figure 1. A price for a claim of $(1 - \alpha)$ on the firm that is satisfactory to both the buyer and the seller will require that this tangency occur along $\overline{V}F$, i.e., that the value of the firm must be V'. To show this, assume that such is not the case— that the tangency occurs to the left of the point B on the line $\overline{V}F$. Then, since the slope of V_2P_2 is negative, the value of the firm will be larger than V'. The owner-manager's choice of this lower level of consumption of non-pecuniary benefits will imply a higher value both to the firm as a whole and to the fraction of the firm $(1 - \alpha)$ which the outsider has acquired; that is, $(1 - \alpha)V' > S_o$. From the owner's viewpoint, he has sold $1 - \alpha$ of the firm for less than he could have, given the (assumed) lower level of non-pecuniary benefits he enjoys. On the other hand, if the tangency point B is to the right of the line $\overline{V}F$, the owner-manager's higher consumption of non-pecuniary benefits means the value of the firm is less than V', and hence $(1 - \alpha)V(F, \alpha) < S_o = (1 - \alpha)V'$. The outside owner then has paid more for his share of the equity than it is worth. S_o will be a mutually satisfactory price if and only if $(1 - \alpha)V' = S_o$. But this means that the owner's post-sale wealth is equal to the (reduced) value of the firm V', since

$$W = S_o + \alpha V' = (1 - \alpha)V' + \alpha V' = V'.$$

Q.E.D.

The requirement that V' and F' fall on $\overline{V}F$ is thus equivalent to requiring that the value of the claim acquired by the outside buyer be equal to the amount he pays for it and conversely for the owner. *This means that the decline in the total value of the firm* $(V^* - V')$ *is entirely imposed on the owner-manager.* His total wealth after the sale of $(1 - \alpha)$ of the equity is V' and the decline in his wealth is $V^* - V'$.

The distance $V^* - V'$ is the reduction in the market value of the firm engendered by the agency relationship and is a measure of the "residual loss" defined earlier. In this simple example the residual loss represents the total agency costs engendered by the sale of outside equity because monitoring and bonding activities have not been allowed. The welfare loss the owner incurs is less than the residual loss by the value to him of the increase in non-pecuniary benefits $(F' - F^*)$. In Figure 1 the difference between the intercepts on the Y axis of the two indifference curves U_2 and U_3 is a measure of the owner-manager's welfare loss due to the incurrence of agency costs,[22] and he would sell such a claim only if the increment in welfare he achieves by using the cash amounting to $(1 - \alpha)V'$ for other things was worth more to him than this amount of wealth.

2.3. Determination of the Optimal Scale of the Firm

The Case of All Equity Financing. Consider the problem faced by an entrepreneur with initial pecuniary wealth, W, and monopoly access to a project requiring investment outlay, I, subject to diminishing returns to scale in I. Figure 2 portrays the solution to the optimal scale of the firm taking into account the agency costs associated with the existence of outside equity. The axes are as defined in Figure 1 except we now plot on the vertical axis the total wealth of the owner, i.e., his initial wealth, W, plus $V(I) - I$, the net increment in wealth he obtains from exploitation of his investment opportunities. The market value of the firm, $V = V(I, F)$, is now a function of the level of investment, I, and the current market value of the manager's expenditures of the firm's resources on non-pecuniary benefits, F. Let $\overline{V}(I)$ represent the value of the firm as a function of the level of investment when the manager's expenditures on non-pecuniary benefits, F, are zero. The schedule with intercept labeled $W + [\overline{V}(I^*) - I^*]$ and slope equal to -1 in Figure 2 represents the locus of combinations of post-investment wealth and dollar cost to the firm of non-pecuniary benefits which are available to the manager when investment is carried to the value maximizing point, I^*. At this point $\Delta \overline{V}(I) - \Delta I = 0$. If the manager's wealth were large enough to cover the investment required to reach this scale of operation, I^*, he would consume F^* in non-pecuniary benefits and have pecuniary wealth with value $W + V^* - I^*$. However, if outside financing is required to cover the investment he will not reach this point if monitoring costs are non-zero.[23]

Figure 2. Determination of the optimal scale of the firm in the case where no monitoring takes place. Point C denotes optimum investment, I^*, and non-pecuniary benefits, F^*, when investment is 100% financed by entrepreneur. Point D denotes optimum investment, I', and non-pecuniary benefits, F, when outside equity financing is used to help finance the investment and the entre-preneur owns a fraction α' of the firm. The distance A measures the gross agency costs.

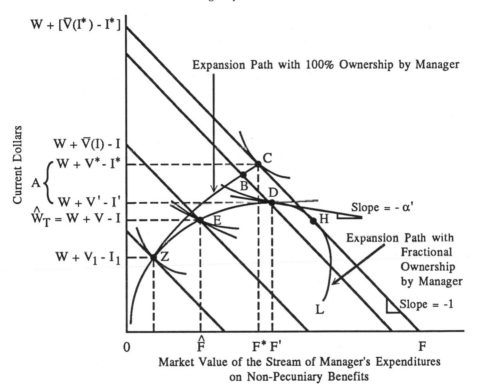

The expansion path $OZBC$ represents the equilibrium combinations of wealth and non-pecuniary benefits, F, which the manager could obtain if he had enough personal wealth to finance all levels of invest-ment up to I^*. It is the locus of points such as Z and C which represent the equilibrium position for the 100 percent owner-manager at each possi-ble level of investment, I. As I increases we move up the expansion path to the point C where $V(I) - I$ is at a maximum. Additional investment beyond this point reduces the net value of the firm, and as it does the equilibrium path of the manager's wealth and non-pecuniary benefits retraces (in the reverse direction) the curve $OZBC$. We draw the path as a smooth concave function only as a matter of convenience.

If the manager obtained outside financing and if there were zero costs to the agency relationship (perhaps because monitoring costs were zero) the expansion path would also be represented by *OZBC*. Therefore, this path represents what we might call the "idealized" solutions, i.e., those which would occur in the absence of agency costs.

Assume the manager has sufficient personal wealth to completely finance the firm only up to investment level I_1 which puts him at point Z. At this point $W = I_1$. To increase the size of the firm beyond this point he must obtain outside financing to cover the additional investment required, and this means reducing his fractional ownership. When he does this he incurs agency costs, and the lower is his ownership fraction the larger are the agency costs he incurs. However, if the investments requiring outside financing are sufficiently profitable his welfare will continue to increase.

The expansion path *ZEDHL* in Figure 2 portrays one possible path of the equilibrium levels of the owner's non-pecuniary benefits and wealth at each possible level of investment higher than I_1. This path is the locus of points such as E or D where (1) the manager's indifference curve is tangent to a line with slope equal to $-\alpha$ (his fractional claim on the firm at that level of investment), and (2) the tangency occurs on the "budget constraint" with slope = -1 for the firm value and non-pecuniary benefit tradeoff at the same level of investment.[24] As we move along *ZEDHL* his fractional claim on the firm continues to fall as he raises larger amounts of outside capital. This expansion path represents his complete opportunity set for combinations of wealth and non-pecuniary benefits given the existence of the costs of the agency relationship with the outside equity holders. Point D, where this opportunity set is tangent to an indifference curve, represents the solution which maximizes his welfare. At this point, the level of investment is I', his fractional ownership share in the firm is α', his wealth is $W + V' - I'$, and he consumes a stream of non-pecuniary benefits with current market value of F'. The gross agency costs (denoted by A) are equal to $(V^* - I^*) - (V' - I')$. Given that no monitoring is possible, I' is the socially optimal level of investment as well as the privately optimal level.

We can characterize the optimal level of investment as that point, I', which satisfies the following condition for small changes:

$$\Delta V - \Delta I + \alpha' \Delta F = 0.$$

$\Delta V - \Delta I$ is the change in the net market value of the firm, and $\alpha' \Delta F$ is the dollar value to the manager of the incremental fringe benefits he consumes (which cost the firm ΔF dollars).[25] Furthermore, recognizing that $V = \overline{V} - F$, where $\overline{V}$ is the value of the firm at any level of investment when $F = 0$, we can substitute into the optimum condition to get

$$(\Delta \bar{V} - \Delta I) - (1 - \alpha')\Delta F = 0$$

as an alternative expression for determining the optimum level of investment.

The idealized or zero agency cost solution, I^*, is given by the condition $(\Delta \bar{V} - \Delta I) = 0$, and since ΔF is positive the actual welfare maximizing level of investment I' will be less than I^*, because $(\Delta \bar{V} - \Delta I)$ must be positive at I' if (3) is to be satisfied. Since $-\alpha'$ is the slope of the indifference curve at the optimum and therefore represents the manager's demand price for incremental non-pecuniary benefits, ΔF, we know that $\alpha'\Delta F$ is the dollar value to him of an increment of fringe benefits costing the firm ΔF dollars. The term $(1 - \alpha')\Delta F$ thus measures the dollar ''loss'' to the firm (and himself) of an additional ΔF dollars spent on non-pecuniary benefits. The term $\Delta \bar{V} - \Delta I$ is the gross increment in the value of the firm ignoring any changes in the consumption of non-pecuniary benefits. Thus, the manager stops increasing the size of the firm when the gross increment in value is just offset by the incremental ''loss'' involved in the consumption of additional fringe benefits due to his declining fractional interest in the firm.

2.4. The Role of Monitoring and Bonding Activities in Reducing Agency Costs

In the above analysis we have ignored the potential for controlling the behavior of the owner-manager through monitoring and other control activities. In practice, it is usually possible by expending resources to alter the opportunity the owner-manager has for capturing non-pecuniary benefits. These methods include auditing, formal control systems, budget restrictions, and the establishment of incentive compensation systems which serve to more closely identify the manager's interests with those of the outside equity holders, etc. Figure 3 portrays the effects of monitoring and other control activities in the simple situation portrayed in Figure 1. Figures 1 and 3 are identical except for the curve BCE in Figure 3 which depicts a ''budget constraint'' derived when monitoring possibilities are taken into account. Without monitoring, and with outside equity of $(1 - \alpha)$, the value of the firm will be V' and non-pecuniary expenditures F'. By incurring monitoring costs, M, the equity holders can restrict the manager's consumption of perquisites to amounts less than F'. Let $F(M, \alpha)$ denote the maximum perquisites the manager can consume for alternative levels of monitoring expenditures, M, given his ownership share α. We assume that increases in monitoring reduce F, and reduce it at a decreasing rate, i.e., $\delta F/\delta M < 0$ and $\delta^2 F/\delta M^2 < 0$.

Since the current value of expected future monitoring expenditures by the outside equity holders reduce the value of any given claim on the firm to them dollar for dollar, the outside equity holders will take this into account in determining the maximum price they will pay for any given fraction of the firm's equity. Therefore, given positive monitoring activity the value of the firm is given by $V = \overline{V} - F(M, \alpha) - M$ and the locus of these points for various levels of M and for a given level of α lie on the line BCE in Figure 3. The vertical difference between the $\overline{V}F$ and BCE curves is M, the current market value of the future monitoring expenditures.

If it is possible for the outside equity holders to make these monitoring expenditures and thereby to impose the reductions in the owner-manager's consumption of F, he will voluntarily enter into a contract with the outside equity holders which gives them the rights to restrict

Figure 3. The value of the firm (V) and level of non-pecuniary benefits (F) when outside equity is ($1 - \alpha$), U_1, U_2, U_3 represent owner's indifference curves between wealth and non-pecuniary benefits, and monitoring (or bonding) activities impose opportunity set BCE as the tradeoff constraint facing the owner.

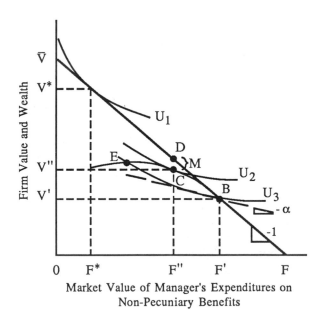

Market Value of Manager's Expenditures on
Non-Pecuniary Benefits

his consumption of non-pecuniary items to F''. He finds this desirable because it will cause the value of the firm to rise to V''. Given the contract, the optimal monitoring expenditure on the part of outsiders, M, is the amount $D - C$. The entire increase in the value of the firm that accrues will be reflected in the owner's wealth, but his welfare will be increased by less than this because he forgoes some non-pecuniary benefits he previously enjoyed.

If the equity market is competitive and makes unbiased estimates of the effects of the monitoring expenditures on F and V, potential buyers will be indifferent between the following two contracts:

(i)   Purchase of a share $(1 - \alpha)$ of the firm at a total price of $(1 - \alpha)V'$ and no rights to monitor or control the manager's consumption of perquisites.

(ii) Purchase of a share $(1 - \alpha)$ of the firm at a total price of $(1 - \alpha)V''$ and the right to expend resources up to an amount equal to $D - C$ which will limit the owner-manager's consumption of perquisites to F.

Given contract (ii) the outside shareholders would find it desirable to monitor to the full rights of their contract because it will pay them to do so. However, if the equity market is competitive the total benefits (net of the monitoring costs) will be capitalized into the price of the claims. Thus, not surprisingly, the owner-manager reaps all the benefits of the opportunity to write and sell the monitoring contract.[27]

An Analysis of Bonding Expenditures. We can also see from the analysis of Figure 3 that it makes no difference who actually makes the monitoring expenditures—the owner bears the full amount of these costs as a wealth reduction in all cases. Suppose that the owner-manager could expend resources to guarantee to the outside equity holders that he would limit his activities which cost the firm F. We call these expenditures "bonding costs," and they would take such forms as contractual guarantees to have the financial accounts audited by a public accountant, explicit bonding against malfeasance on the part of the manager, and contractual limitations on the manager's decision making power (which impose costs on the firm because they limit his ability to take full advantage of some profitable opportunities as well as limiting his ability to harm the stockholders while making himself better off.)

If the incurrence of the bonding costs were entirely under the control of the manager and if they yielded the same opportunity set BCE for him in Figure 3, he would incur them in amount $D - C$. This would limit his consumption of perquisites to F'' from F', and the solution is exactly the same as if the outside equity holders had performed the monitoring. The manager finds it in his interest to incur these costs as long as the net increments in his wealth which they generate (by reducing the agency costs and therefore increasing the value of the firm) are more valuable than the perquisites given up. This optimum occurs at point C in both cases under our assumption that the bonding expenditures yield the same opportunity set as the monitoring expenditures. In general, of course, it will pay the owner-manager to engage in bonding activities and to write contracts which allow monitoring as long as the marginal benefits of each are greater than their marginal cost.

   Optimal Scale of the Firm in the Presence of Monitoring and Bonding Activities. If we allow the outside owners to engage in (costly) monitoring activities to limit the manager's expenditures on non-pecuniary benefits and allow the manager to engage in bonding activities to guarantee to the outside owners that he will limit his consumption of F we get an expansion path such as that illustrated in Figure 4 on which Z and G lie. We have assumed in drawing Figure 4 that the cost functions involved in monitoring and bonding are such that some positive levels of the activities are desirable, i.e., yield benefits greater than their cost. If this is not true the expansion path generated by the expenditure of resources on these activities would lie below ZD and no such activity would take place at any level of investment. Points Z, C, and D and the two expansion paths they lie on are identical to those portrayed in Figure 2. Points Z and C lie on the 100 percent ownership expansion path, and points Z and D lie on the fractional ownership, zero monitoring and bonding activity expansion path.

   The path on which points Z and G lie is the one given by the locus of equilibrium points for alternative levels of investment characterized by the point labeled C in Figure 3 which denotes the optimal level of monitoring and bonding activity and resulting values of the firm and non-pecuniary benefits to the manager given a fixed level of investment. If any monitoring or bonding is cost effective the expansion path on which Z and G lie must be above the non-monitoring expansion path over some range. Furthermore, if it lies anywhere to the right of the indifference curve passing through point D (the zero monitoring-bonding solution) the final solution to the problem will involve positive amounts of monitoring and/or bonding activities. Based on the discussion above we know that as long as the contracts between the manager and outsiders are unambiguous regarding the rights of the respective parties the final solution will be at that point where the new expansion path is just tangent to

Figure 4. Determination of optimal scale of the firm allowing for monitoring and bonding activities. Optimal monitoring costs are M'' and bonding costs are b'' and the equilibrium scale of the firm, manager's wealth and consumption of non-pecuniary benefits are at point G.

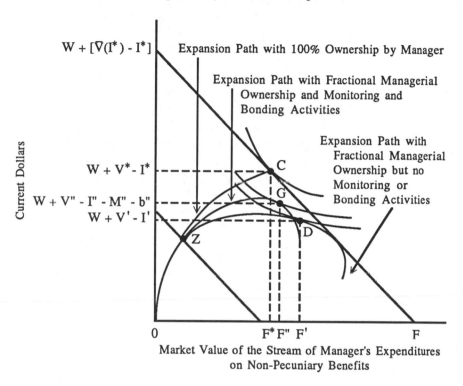

the highest indifference curve. At this point the optimal level of monitoring and bonding expenditures are M'' and b''; the manager's post-investment-financing wealth is given by $W + V'' - I'' - M'' - b''$ and his non-pecuniary benefits are F''. The total gross agency costs, A, are given by $A(M'', b'', \alpha'', I'') = (V^* - I^*) - (V'' - I'' - M'' - b'')$.

2.5. Pareto Optimality and Agency Costs in Manager-Operated Firms

In general we expect to observe both bonding and external monitoring activities, and the incentives are such that the levels of these activities will satisfy the conditions of efficiency. They will not, however, result in the firm being run in a manner so as to maximize its value. The difference between V^*, the efficient solution under zero monitoring and bonding costs (and therefore zero agency costs), and V'', the value of the firm given positive monitoring costs, are the total gross agency costs defined earlier in the introduction. These are the costs of the "separation of ownership and control" which Adam Smith focused on in the passage quoted at the beginning of this paper and which Berle and Means (1932) popularized 157 years later. The solutions outlined above to our highly simplified problem imply that agency costs will be positive as long as monitoring costs are positive—which they certainly are.

The reduced value of the firm caused by the manager's consumption of perquisites outlined above is "non-optimal" or inefficient only in comparison to a world in which we could obtain compliance of the agent to the principal's wishes at zero cost or in comparison to a *hypothetical* world in which the agency costs were lower. But these costs (monitoring and bonding costs and "residual loss") are an unavoidable result of the agency relationship. Furthermore, since they are borne entirely by the decision maker (in this case the original owner) responsible for creating the relationship he has the incentives to see that they are minimized (because he captures the benefits from their reduction). Furthermore, these agency costs will be incurred only if the benefits to the owner-manager from their creation are great enough to outweigh them. In our current example these benefits arise from the availability of profitable investments requiring capital investment in excess of the original owner's personal wealth.

In conclusion, finding that agency costs are non-zero (i.e., that there are costs associated with the separation of ownership and control in the corporation) and concluding therefrom that the agency relationship is non-optimal, wasteful or inefficient is equivalent in every sense to comparing a world in which iron ore is a scarce commodity (and therefore costly) to a world in which it is freely available at zero resource cost, and concluding that the first world is "non-optimal"—a perfect example of the fallacy criticized by Coase (1964) and what Demsetz (1969) characterizes as the "Nirvana" form of analysis.[28]

2.6. Factors Affecting the Size of the Divergence from Ideal Maximization

The magnitude of the agency costs discussed above will vary from firm to firm. It will depend on the tastes of managers, the ease with which they can exercise their own preferences as opposed to value maximization in decision making, and the costs of monitoring and bonding activities.[29] The agency costs will also depend upon the cost of measuring the manager's (agent's) performance and evaluating it, the cost of devising and applying an index for compensating the manager which correlates with the owner's (principal's) welfare, and the cost of devising and enforcing specific behavioral rules or policies. Where the manager has less than a controlling interest in the firm, it will also depend upon the market for managers. Competition from other potential managers limits the costs of obtaining managerial services (including the extent to which a given manager can diverge from the idealized solution which would obtain if all monitoring and bonding costs were zero). The size of the divergence (the agency costs) will be directly related to the cost of replacing the manager. If his responsibilities require very little knowledge specialized to the firm, if it is easy to evaluate his performance, and if replacement search costs are modest, the divergence from the ideal will be relatively small and vice versa.

The divergence will also be constrained by the market for the firm itself, i.e., by capital markets. Owners always have the option of selling their firm, either as a unit or piecemeal. Owners of manager-operated firms can and do sample the capital market from time to time. If they discover that the value of the future earnings stream to others is higher than the value of the firm to them given that it is to be manager-operated, they can exercise their right to sell. It is conceivable that other owners could be more efficient at monitoring or even that a single individual with appropriate managerial talents and with sufficiently large personal wealth would elect to buy the firm. In this latter case the purchase by such a single individual would completely eliminate the agency costs. If there were a number of such potential owner-manager purchasers (all with talents and tastes identical to the current manager) the owners would receive in the sale price of the firm the full value of the residual claimant rights including the capital value of the eliminated agency costs plus the value of the managerial rights.

Monopoly, Competition and Managerial Behavior. It is frequently argued that the existence of competition in product (and factor) markets will constrain the behavior of managers to idealized value maximization, i.e., that monopoly in product (or monopsony in factor) markets will permit larger divergences from value maximization.[30] Our analysis does not support this hypothesis. The owners of a firm with monopoly power have the same incentives to limit divergences of the manager from value maximization (i.e., the ability to increase their wealth) as do the owners of competitive firms. Furthermore, competition in the market for managers will generally make it unnecessary for the owners to share rents with the manager. The owners of a monopoly firm need only pay the supply price for a manager.

Since the owner of a monopoly has the same wealth incentives to minimize managerial costs as would the owner of a competitive firm, both will undertake that level of monitoring which equates the marginal cost of monitoring to the marginal wealth increment from reduced consumption of perquisites by the manager. Thus, the existence of monopoly will not increase agency costs.

Furthermore the existence of competition in product and factor markets will not eliminate the agency costs due to managerial control problems as has often been asserted [cf. Friedman (1970)]. If my competitors all incur agency costs equal to or greater than mine I will not be eliminated from the market by their competition.

The existence and size of the agency costs depends on the nature of the monitoring costs, the tastes of managers for non-pecuniary benefits and the supply of potential managers who are capable of financing the entire venture out of their personal wealth. If monitoring costs are zero, agency costs will be zero or if there are enough 100 percent owner-managers available to own and run all the firms in an industry (competitive or not) then agency costs in that industry will also be zero.[31]

3. Some Unanswered Questions Regarding the Existence of the Corporate Form

3.1 The Question

The analysis to this point has left us with a basic puzzle: Why, given the existence of positive costs of the agency relationship, do we find the usual corporate form of organization with widely diffuse ownership so widely prevalent? If one takes seriously much of the literature regarding the ''discretionary'' power held by managers of large corporations, it is difficult to understand the historical fact of enormous growth in equity in such organizations, not only in the United States, but throughout the world. Paraphrasing Alchian (1968): How does it happen that millions of individuals are willing to turn over a significant fraction of their wealth to organizations run by managers who have so little interest in their welfare? What is even more remarkable, why are they willing to make these commitments purely as residual claimants, i.e., on the anticipation that managers will operate the firm so that there will be earnings which accrue to the stockholders?

There is certainly no lack of alternative ways that individuals might invest, including entirely different forms of organizations. Even if consideration is limited to corporate organizations, there are clearly alternative ways capital might be raised, i.e., through fixed claims of various sorts, bonds, notes, mortgages, etc. Moreover, the corporate income tax seems to favor the use of fixed claims since interest is treated as a tax deductible expense. Those who assert that managers do not behave in the interest of stockholders have generally not addressed a very important question: Why, if non-manager-owned shares have such a serious deficiency, have they not long since been driven out by fixed claims?[32]

3.2 Some Alternative Explanations of the Ownership Structure of the Firm

The Role of Limited Liability. Manne (1967) and Alchian and Demsetz (1972) argue that one of the attractive features of the corporate form vis-a-vis individual proprietorships or partnerships is the limited liability feature of equity claims in corporations. Without this provision each and every investor purchasing one or more shares of a corporation would be potentially liable to the full extent of his personal wealth for the debts of the corporation. Few individuals would find this a desirable risk to accept and the major benefits to be obtained from risk reduction through diversification would be to a large extent unobtainable. This argument, however, is incomplete since limited liability does not eliminate the basic risk, it merely shifts it. The argument must rest ultimately on transactions costs. If all stockholders of GM were liable for GM's debts, the maximum liability for an individual shareholder would be greater than it would be if his shares had limited liability. However, given that many other stockholders also existed and that each was liable for the unpaid claims in proportion to his ownership it is highly unlikely that the maximum payment each would have to make would be large in the event of GM's bankruptcy since the total wealth of those stockholders would also be large. However, the existence of unlimited liability would impose incentives for each shareholder to keep track of both the liabilities of GM and the wealth of the other GM owners. It is easily conceivable that the costs of so doing would, in the aggregate, be much higher than simply paying a premium in the form of higher interest rates to the creditors of GM in return for their acceptance of a contract which grants limited liability to the shareholders. The creditors would then bear the risk of any non-payment of debts in the event of GM's bankruptcy.

It is also not generally recognized that limited liability is merely a necessary condition for explaining the magnitude of the reliance on equities, not a sufficient condition. Ordinary debt also carries limited liability.[33] If limited liablity is all that is required, why don't we observe large corporations, individually owned, with a tiny fraction of the capital supplied by the entrepreneur, and the rest simply borrowed?[34] At first this question seems silly to many people (as does the question regarding why firms would ever issue debt or preferred stock under conditions where there are no tax benefits obtained from the treatment of interest or preferred dividend payments[35]). We have found that oftentimes this question is misinterpreted to be one regarding why firms obtain capital. The issue is not why they obtain capital, but why they obtain it through the particular forms we have observed for such long periods of time. The fact is that no well articulated answer to this question currently exists in the literature of either finance or economics.

The "Irrelevance" of Capital Structure. In their pathbreaking article on the cost of capital, Modigliani and Miller (1958) demonstrated that in the absence of bankruptcy costs and tax subsidies on the payment of interest the value of the firm is independent of the financial structure. They later (1963) demonstrated that the existence of tax subsidies on interest payments would cause the value of the firm to rise with the amount of debt financing by the amount of the capitalized value of the tax subsidy. But this line of argument implies that the firm should be financed almost entirely with debt. Realizing the inconsistence with observed behavior Modigliani and Miller (1963, p. 442) comment:

> [I]t may be useful to remind readers once again that the existence of a tax advantage for debt financing . . . does not necessarily mean that corporations should at all times seek to use the maximum amount of debt in their capital structures. . . . there are as we pointed out, limitations imposed by lenders . . . as well as many other dimensions (and kinds of costs) in real-world problems of financial strategy which are not fully comprehended within the framework of static equilibrium models, either our own or those of the traditional variety. These additional considerations, which are typically grouped under the rubric of "the need for preserving flexibility," will normally imply the maintenance by the corporation of a substantial reserve of untapped borrowing power.

Modigliani and Miller are essentially left without a theory of the determination of the optimal capital structure, and Fama and Miller (1972, p. 173) commenting on the same issue reiterate this conclusion:

> And we must admit that at this point there is little in the way of convincing research, either theoretical or

empirical, that explains the amounts of debt that firms do
decide to have in their capital structure.

The Modigliani–Miller theorem is based on the assumption that
the probability distribution of the cash flows to the firm is independent
of the capital structure. It is now recognized that the existence of positive
costs associated with bankruptcy and the presence of tax subsidies on
corporate interest payments will invalidate this irrelevance theorem precisely because the probability distribution of future cash flows changes
as the probability of the incurrence of the bankruptcy costs changes, i.e.,
as the ratio of debt to equity rises. We believe the existence of agency
costs provide stronger reasons for arguing that the probability distribution of future cash flows is *not* independent of the capital or ownership
structure.

While the introduction of bankruptcy costs in the presence of tax
subsidies leads to a theory which defines an optimal capital structure,[36]
we argue that this theory is seriously incomplete since it implies that
no debt should ever be used in the absence of tax subsidies if bankruptcy
costs are positive. Since we know debt was commonly used prior to the
existence of the current tax subsidies on interest payments this theory
does not capture what must be some important determinants of the corporate capital structure.

In addition, neither bankruptcy costs nor the existence of tax subsidies can explain the use of preferred stock or warrants which have no
tax advantages, and there is no theory which tells us anything about what
determines the fraction of equity claims held by insiders as opposed to
outsiders which our analysis in section 2 indicates is so important. We
return to these issues later after analyzing in detail the factors affecting
the agency costs associated with debt.

4. The Agency Costs of Debt

In general if the agency costs engendered by the existence of outside owners are positive it will pay the absentee owner (i.e., shareholders)
to sell out to an owner-manager who can avoid these costs.[37] This could
be accomplished in principle by having the manager become the sole
equity holder by repurchasing all of the outside equity claims with funds
obtained through the issuance of limited liability debt claims and the
use of his own personal wealth. This single-owner corporation would
not suffer the agency costs associated with outside equity. Therefore there
must be some compelling reasons why we find the diffuse-owner corporate
firm financed by equity claims so prevalent as an organizational form.

An ingenious entrepreneur eager to expand, has open to him the opportunity to design a whole hierarchy of fixed claims on assets and earnings, with premiums paid for different levels of risk.[38] Why don't we observe large corporations individually owned with a tiny fraction of the capital supplied by the entrepreneur in return for 100 percent of the equity and the rest simply borrowed? We believe there are a number of reasons: (1) the incentive effects associated with highly leveraged firms, (2) the monitoring costs these incentive effects engender, and (3) bankruptcy costs. Furthermore, all of these costs are simply particular aspects of the agency costs associated with the existence of debt claims on the firm.

4.1. The Incentive Effects Associated with Debt

We don't find many large firms financed almost entirely with debt type claims (i.e., non-residual claims) because of the effect such a financial structure would have on the owner-manager's behavior. Potential creditors will not loan $100,000,000 to a firm in which the entrepreneur has an investment of $10,000. With that financial structure the owner-manager will have a strong incentive to engage in activities (investments) which promise very high payoffs if successful even if they have a very low probability of success. If they turn out well, he captures most of the gains, if they turn out badly, the creditors bear most of the costs.[39]

To illustrate the incentive effects associated with the existence of debt and to provide a framework within which we can discuss the effects of monitoring and bonding costs, wealth transfers, and the incidence of agency costs, we again consider a simple situation. Assume we have a manager-owned firm with no debt outstanding in a world in which there are no taxes. The firm has the opportunity to take one of two mutually exclusive equal cost investment opportunities, each of which yields a random payoff, $\tilde{X}_j$, T periods in the future ($j = 1,2$). Production and monitoring activities take place continuously between time 0 and time T, and markets in which the claims on the firm can be traded are open continuously over this period. After time T the firm has no productive activities so the payoff $\tilde{X}_j$ includes the distribution of all remaining assets. For simplicity, we assume that the two distributions are log-normally distributed and have the same expected total payoff, $E(\tilde{X})$, where $\tilde{X}$ is defined as the logarithm of the final payoff, The distributions differ only by their variances with $\sigma_1^2 < \sigma_2^2$. The systematic or covariance risk of each of the distributions, β_j, in the Sharpe (1964)–Lintner (1965) capital asset pricing model, is assumed to be identical. Assuming that asset prices are determined according to the capital asset pricing model, the preceding assumptions imply that the total market value of each of these distributions is identical, and we represent this value by V.

If the owner-manager has the right to decide which investment program to take, and if after he decides this he has the opportunity to sell part or all of his claims on the outcomes in the form of either debt or equity, he will be indifferent between the two investments.[40]

However, if the owner has the opportunity to *first* issue debt, then to decide which of the investments to take, and then to sell all or part of his remaining equity claim on the market, he will not be indifferent between the two investments. The reason is that by promising to take the low variance project, selling bonds and then taking the high variance project he can transfer wealth from the (naive) bondholders to himself as equity holder.

Let X^* be the amount of the "fixed" claim in the form of a non-coupon bearing bond sold to the bondholders such that the total payoff to them, $R_j(j = 1,2)$, denotes the distribution the manager chooses), is

$$R_j = X^*, \quad \text{if} \quad \tilde{X}_j \geqq X^*,$$
$$= X_j, \quad \text{if} \quad \tilde{X}_j \leqq X^*.$$

Let B_1 be the current market value of bondholder claims if investment 1 is taken, and let B_2 be the current market value of bondholders claims if investment 2 is taken. Since in this example the total value of the firm, V, is independent of the investment choice and also of the financing decision we can use the Black–Scholes (1973) option pricing model to determine the values of the debt, B_j, and equity, S_j, under each of the choices.[41]

Black–Scholes derive the solution for the value of a European call option (one which can be exercised only at the maturity date) and argue that the resulting option pricing equation can be used to determine the value of the equity claim on a levered firm. That is the stockholders in such a firm can be viewed as holding a European call option on the total value of the firm with exercise price equal to X^* (the face value of the debt), exercisable at the maturity date of the debt issue. More simply, the stockholders have the right to buy the firm back from the bondholders for a price of X^* at time T. Merton (1973, 1974) shows that as the variance of the outcome distribution rises the value of the stock (i.e., call option) rises, and since our two distributions differ only in their variances, $\sigma_2^2 < \sigma_1^2$, the equity value S_1 is less than S_2. This implies $B_1 > B_2$, since $B_1 = V - S_1$ and $B_2 = V - S_2$.

Now if the owner-manager could sell bonds with face value X^* under the conditions that the potential bondholders believed this to be a claim on distribution 1, he would receive a price of B_1. After selling the bonds, his equity interest in distribution 1 would have value S_1. But we know S_2 is greater than S_1 and thus the manager can make himself better off by changing the investment to take the higher variance distribution 2, thereby redistributing wealth from the bondholders to himself. All this assumes of course that the bondholders could not prevent him from changing the investment program. *If the bondholders cannot do so, and if they perceive that the manager has the opportunity to take distribution 2 they will pay the manager only B_2 for the claim X^*, realizing that his maximizing behavior will lead him to choose distribution 2.* In this event there is no redistribution of wealth between bondholders and stockholders (and in general with rational expectations there never will be) and no welfare loss. It is easy to construct a case, however, in which these incentive effects do generate real costs.

Let cash flow distribution 2 in the previous example have an expected value, $E(X_2)$, which is lower than that of distribution 1. Then we know that $V_1 > V_2$, and if ΔV, which is given by

$$\Delta V = V_1 - V_2 = (S_1 - S_2) + (B_1 - B_2),$$

is sufficiently small relative to the reduction in the value of the bonds the value of the stock will increase.[42] Rearranging the expression for ΔV we see that the difference between the equity values for the two investments is given by

$$S_2 - S_1 = (B_1 - B_2) - (V_1 - V_2),$$

and the first term on the RHS, $B_1 - B_2$, is the amount of wealth "transferred" from the bondholders and $V_1 - V_2$ is the reduction in overall firm value. Since we know $B_1 > B_2$, $S_2 - S_1$ can be positive even though the reduction in the value of the firm, $V_1 - V_2$, is positive.[43] Again, the bondholders will not actually lose as long as they accurately perceive the motivation of the equity owning manager and his opportunity to take project 2. They will presume he will take investment 2, and hence will pay no more than B_2 for the bonds when they are issued.

In this simple example the reduced value of the firm, $V_1 - V_2$, is the agency cost engendered by the issuance of debt[44] and it is borne by the owner-manager. If he could finance the project out of his personal wealth, he would clearly choose project 1 since its investment outlay was assumed equal to that of project 2 and its market value, V_1, was greater. This wealth loss, $V_1 - V_2$, is the "residual loss" portion of what we have defined as agency costs and it is generated by the cooperation required to raise the funds to make the investment. Another important part of the agency costs are monitoring and bonding costs and we now consider their role.

4.2. The Role of Monitoring and Bonding Costs

In principle it would be possible for the bondholders, by the inclusion of various covenants in the indenture provisions, to limit the managerial behavior which results in reductions in the value of the bonds. Provisions which impose constraints on management's decisions regarding such things as dividends, future debt issues,[45] and maintenance of working capital are not uncommon in bond issues.[46] To completely protect the bondholders from the incentive effects, these provisions would have to be incredibly detailed and cover most operating aspects of the enterprise including limitations on the riskiness of the projects undertaken. The costs involved in writing such provisions, the costs of enforcing them and the reduced profitability of the firm (induced because the covenants occasionally limit management's ability to take optimal actions on certain issues) would likely be non-trivial. In fact, since management is a continuous decision making process it will be almost impossible to completely specify such conditions without having the bondholders actually perform the management function. All costs associated with such covenants are what we mean by monitoring costs.

The bondholders will have incentives to engage in the writing of such covenants and in monitoring the actions of the manager to the point where the "nominal" marginal cost to them of such activities is just equal to the marginal benefits they perceive from engaging in them. We use the word nominal here because debtholders will not in fact bear these costs. As long as they recognize their existence, they will take them into account in deciding the price they will pay for any given debt claim,[47] and therefore the seller of the claim (the owner) will bear the costs just as in the equity case discussed in section 2.

In addition the manager has incentives to take into account the costs imposed on the firm by covenants in the debt agreement which directly affect the future cash flows of the firm since they reduce the market value of his claims. Because both the external and internal monitoring costs are imposed on the owner-manager it is in his interest to see that the monitoring is performed in the lowest cost way. Suppose, for example, that the bondholders (or outside equity holders) would find it worthwhile to produce detailed financial statements such as those contained in the usual published accounting reports as a means of monitoring the manager. If the manager himself can produce such information at lower costs than they (perhaps because he is already collecting much of the data they desire for his own internal decision making purposes), it would pay him to agree in advance to incur the cost of providing such reports and to have their accuracy testified to by an independent outside auditor. This is an example of what we refer to as bonding costs.[48],[49]

4.3. Bankruptcy and Reorganization Costs

We argue in section 5 that as the debt in the capital structure increases beyond some point the marginal agency costs of debt begin to dominate the marginal agency costs of outside equity and the result of this is the generally observed phenomenon of the simultaneous use of both debt and outside equity. Before considering these issues, however, we consider here the third major component of the agency costs of debt which helps to explain why debt doesn't completely dominate capital structures—the existence of bankruptcy and reorganization costs.

It is important to emphasize that bankruptcy and liquidation are very different events. The legal definition of bankruptcy is difficult to specify precisely. In general, it occurs when the firm cannot meet a current payment on a debt obligation,[50] or one or more of the other indenture provisions providing for bankruptcy is violated by the firm. In this event the stockholders have lost all claims on the firm,[51] and the remaining loss, the difference between the face value of the fixed claims and the market value of the firm, is borne by the debtholders. Liquidation of the firm's assets will occur only if the market value of the future cash flows generated by the firm is less than the opportunity cost of the assets, i.e., the sum of the values which could be realized if the assets were sold piecemeal.

If there were no costs associated with the event called bankruptcy the total market value of the firm would not be affected by increasing the probability of its incurrence. However, it is costly, if not impossible, to write contracts representing claims on a firm which clearly delineate the rights of holders for all possible contingencies. Thus even if there were no adverse incentive effects in expanding fixed claims relative to equity in a firm, the use of such fixed claims would be constrained by the costs inherent in defining and enforcing those claims. Firms incur obligations daily to suppliers, to employees, to different classes of investors, etc. So long as the firm is prospering, the adjudication of claims is seldom a problem. When the firm has difficulty meeting some of its obligations, however, the issue of the priority of those claims can pose serious problems. This is most obvious in the extreme case where the firm is forced into bankruptcy. If bankruptcy were costless, the reorganization would be accompanied by an adjustment of the claims of various parties and the business, could, if that proved to be in the interest of the claimants, simply go on (although perhaps under new management).[52]

In practice, bankruptcy is not costless, but generally involves an adjudication process which itself consumes a fraction of the remaining value of the assets of the firm. Thus the cost of bankruptcy will be of concern to potential buyers of fixed claims in the firm since their existence will reduce the payoffs to them in the event of bankruptcy. These are examples of the agency costs of cooperative efforts among individuals (although in this case perhaps "non-cooperative" would be a better term) The price buyers will be willing to pay for fixed claims will thus be inversely related to the probability of the incurrence of these costs, i.e., to the probability of bankruptcy. Using a variant of the argument employed above for monitoring costs, it can be shown that the total value of the firm will fall, and the owner-manager equity holder will bear the entire wealth effect of the bankruptcy costs as long as potential bondholders make unbiased estimates of their magnitude at the time they initially purchase bonds.[53]

Empirical studies of the magnitude of bankruptcy costs are almost non-existent. Warner (1975) in a study of 11 railroad bankruptcies between 1930 and 1955 estimates the average costs of bankruptcy[54] as a fraction of the value of the firm three years prior to bankruptcy to be 2.5% (with a range of 0.4% to 5.9%). The average dollar costs were $1.88 million. Both of these measures seem remarkably small and are consistent with our belief that bankruptcy costs themselves are unlikely to be the major determinant of corporate capital structures. It is also interesting to note that the annual amount of defaulted funds has fallen significantly since 1940. [See Atkinson (1967).] One possible explanation for this phenomenon is that firms are using mergers to avoid the costs of bankruptcy. This hypothesis seems even more reasonable, if, as is frequently the case, reorganization costs represent only a fraction of the costs associated with bankruptcy.

In general the revenues or the operating costs of the firm are not independent of the probability of bankruptcy and thus the capital structure of the firm. As the probability of bankruptcy increases, both the operating costs and the revenues of the firm are adversely affected, and some of these costs can be avoided by merger. For example, a firm with a high probability of bankruptcy will also find that it must pay higher salaries to induce executives to accept the higher risk of unemployment. Furthermore, in certain kinds of durable goods industries the demand function for the firm's product will not be independent of the probability of bankruptcy. The computer industry is a good example. There, the buyer's welfare is dependent to a significant extent on the ability to maintain the equipment, and on continuous hardware and software development. Furthermore, the owner of a large computer often receives benefits from the software developments of other users. Thus if the manufacturer leaves the business or loses his software support and development experts because of financial difficulties, the value of the equipment to his users will decline. The buyers of such services have a continuing interest in the manufacturer's viability not unlike that of a bondholder, except that their benefits come in the form of continuing services at lower cost rather than principal and interest payments. Service facilities and spare parts for automobiles and machinery are other examples.

In summary then the agency costs associated with debt[55] consist of:

1. the opportunity wealth loss caused by the impact of debt on the investment decisions of the firm,
2. the monitoring and bonding expenditures by the bondholders and the owner-manager (i.e., the firm),
3. the bankruptcy and reorganization costs.

4.4. Why Are the Agency Costs of Debt Incurred?

We have argued that the owner-manager bears the entire wealth effects of the agency costs of debt and he captures the gains from reducing them. Thus, the agency costs associated with debt discussed above will tend, in the absence of other mitigating factors, to discourage the use of corporate debt. What are the factors that encourage its use?

One factor is the tax subsidy on interest payments. (This will not explain preferred stock where dividends are not tax deductible.)[56] Modigliani and Miller (1963) originally demonstrated that the use of riskless perpetual debt will increase the total value of the firm (ignoring the agency costs) by an amount equal to τB, where τ is the marginal and average corporate tax rate and B is the market value of the debt. Fama and Miller (1972, chapter 4) demonstrate that for the case of risky debt the value of the firm will increase by the market value of the (uncertain) tax subsidy on the interest payments. Again, these gains will accrue entirely to the equity and will provide an incentive to utilize debt to the point where the marginal wealth benefits of the tax subsidy are just equal to the marginal wealth effects of the agency costs discussed above.

However, even in the absence of these tax benefits, debt would be utilized if the ability to exploit potentially profitable investment opportunities is limited by the resources of the owner. If the owner of a project cannot raise capital he will suffer an opportunity loss represented by the increment in value offered to him by the additional investment opportunities. Thus even though he will bear the agency costs from selling debt, he will find it desirable to incur them to obtain additional capital as long as the marginal wealth increments from the new investments projects are greater than the marginal agency costs of debt, and these agency costs are in turn less than those caused by the sale of additional equity discussed in section 2. Furthermore, this solution is optimal from the social viewpoint. However, in the absence of tax subsidies on debt these projects must be unique to this firm[57] or they would be taken by other competitive entrepreneurs (perhaps new ones) who possessed the requisite personal wealth to fully finance the projects[58] and therefore able to avoid the existence of debt or outside equity.

5. A Theory of the Corporate Ownership Structure

In the previous sections we discussed the nature of agency costs associated with outside claims on the firm—both debt and equity. Our purpose here is to integrate these concepts into the beginnings of a theory of the corporate ownership structure. We use the term "ownership structure" rather than "capital structure" to highlight the fact that the crucial variables to be determined are not just the relative amounts of debt and equity but also the fraction of the equity held by the manager. Thus, for a given size firm we want a theory to determine three variables:[59]

S_i : inside equity (held by the manager),
S_o: outside equity (held by anyone outside of the firm),
B : debt (held by anyone outside of the firm).

The total market value of the equity is $S = S_i + S_o$, and the total market value of the firm is $V = S + B$. In addition, we also wish to have a theory which determines the optimal size of the firm, i.e., its level of investment.

5.1. Determination of the Optimal Ratio of Outside Equity to Debt

Consider first the determination of the optimal ratio of outside equity to debt, S_o/B. To do this let us hold the size of the firm constant. V, the actual value of the firm for a given size, will depend on the agency costs incurred, hence we use as our index of size V^*, the value of the firm at a given scale when agency costs are zero. For the moment we also hold the amount of outside financing $(B + S_o)$, constant. Given that a specified amount of financing $(B + S_o)$ is to be obtained externally our problem is to determine the optimal fraction $E^* \equiv S_o^*/(B + S_o)$ to be financed with equity.

We argued above that: (1) as long as capital markets are efficient (i.e., characterized by rational expectations) the price of assets such as debt and outside equity will reflect unbiased estimates of the monitoring costs and redistributions which the agency relationship will engender, and (2) the selling owner-manager will bear these agency costs. Thus from the owner-manager's standpoint the optimal proportion of outside funds to be obtained from equity (versus debt) *for a given level of internal equity* is that E which results in minimum total agency costs.

Figure 5 presents a breakdown of the agency costs into two separate components: Define $A_{So}(E)$ as the total agency costs (a function of E) associated with the "exploitation" of the outside equity holders by the owner-manager, and $A_B(E)$ as the total agency costs associated with the presence of debt in the ownership structure. $A_T(E) = A_{So}(E) + A_B(E)$ is the total agency cost.

Consider the function $A_{So}(E)$. When $E \equiv S_o/(B + S_o)$ is zero, i.e., when there is no outside equity, the manager's incentives to exploit the outside equity is at a minimum (zero) since the changes in the value of the *total* equity are equal to the changes in *his* equity.[60] As E increases to 100 percent his incentives to exploit the outside equity holders increase and hence the agency costs $A_{So}(E)$ increase.

The agency costs associated with the existence of debt, $A_B(E)$ are composed mainly of the value reductions in the firm and monitoring costs caused by the manager's incentive to reallocate wealth from the bondholders to himself by increasing the value of his equity claim. They are at a maximum where all outside funds are obtained from debt, i.e., where $S_o = E = 0$. As the amount of debt declines to zero these costs also go to zero because as E goes to 1, his incentive to reallocate wealth from the bondholders to himself falls. These incentives fall for two reasons: (1) the total amount of debt falls, and therefore it is more difficult to reallocate any given amount away from the debtholders, and (2) his share

Figure 5. Total agency costs, $A_T(E)$, as a function of the ratio of outside equity, to total outside financing, $E \equiv S_o(B + S_o)$, for a given firm size V^* and given total amounts of outside financing $(B + S_o)$. $A_{So}(E) \equiv$ agency costs associated with outside equity, $A_B(E) \equiv$ agency costs associated with debt, B. $A_T(E^*) =$ minimum total agency costs at optimal fraction of outside financing E^*.

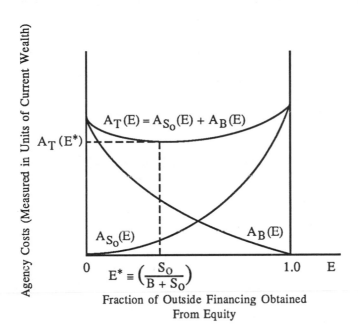

Fraction of Outside Financing Obtained
From Equity

of any reallocation which is accomplished is falling since S_o is rising and therefore $S_i/(S_o + S_i)$, his share of the total equity, is falling.

The curve $A_T(E)$ represents the sum of the agency costs from various combinations of outside equity and debt financing, and as long as $A_{So}(E)$ and $A_B(E)$ are as we have drawn them the minimum total agency cost for [a] given size firm and outside financing will occur at some point such as $A_T(E^*)$ with a mixture of both debt and equity.[61]

A Caveat. Before proceeding further we point out that the issue regarding the exact shapes of the functions drawn in Figure 5 and several others discussed below is essentially an open question at this time. In the end the shape of these functions is a question of fact and can only be settled by empirical evidence. We outline some a priori arguments which we believe can lead to some plausible hypotheses about the behavior of the system, but confess that we are far from understanding the many

conceptual subtleties of the problem. We are fairly confident of our arguments regarding the signs of the first derivatives of the functions, but the
second derivatives are also important to the final solution and much more
work (both theoretical and empirical) is required before we can have much
confidence regarding these parameters. We anticipate the work of others
as well as our own to cast more light on these issues. Moreover, we suspect
the results of such efforts will generate revisions to the details of what
follows. We believe it is worthwhile to delineate the overall framework
in order to demonstrate, if only in a simplified fashion, how the major
pieces of the puzzle fit together into a cohesive structure.

5.2 Effects of the Scale of Outside Financing

In order to investigate the effects of increasing the amount of outside financing, $B + S_o$, and therefore reducing the amount of equity held
by the manager, S_i, we continue to hold the scale of the firm, V^*, constant. Figure 6 presents a plot of the agency cost functions, $A_{So}(E)$, $A_B(E)$
and $A_T(E) = A_{So}(E) + A_B(E)$, for two different levels of outside financing.
Define an index of the amount of outside financing to be

$$K = (B + S_o)/V^*,$$

and consider two different possible levels of outside financing K_o and
K_1 for a given scale of the firm such that $K_o < K_1$.

As the amount of outside equity increases, the owner's fractional
claim on the firm, α, falls. He will be induced thereby to take additional
non-pecuniary benefits out of the firm because his share of the cost falls.
This also increases the marginal benefits from monitoring activities and
therefore will tend to increase the optimal level of monitoring. Both of
these factors will cause the locus of agency costs $A_{So}(E; K)$ to shift upward as the fraction of outside financing, K, increases. This is depicted
in Figure 6 by the two curves representing the agency costs of equity,
one for the low level of outside financing, $A_{So}(E; K_o)$, the other for the
high level of outside financing, $A_{So}(E; K_1)$. The locus of the latter lies
above the former everywhere except at the origin where both are 0.

The agency costs of debt will similarly rise as the amount of outside financing increases. This means that the locus of $A_B(E; K_1)$ for high
outside financing, K_1, will lie above the locus of $A_B(E; K_o)$ for low outside financing, K_o because the total amount of resources which can be
reallocated from bondholders increases as the total amount of debt increases. However, since these costs are zero when the debt is zero for

Figure 6. Agency cost functions and optimal outside equity as a fraction of total outside financing, $E^*(K)$, for two different levels of outside financing, K, for a given size firm, V^*: $K_1 > K_0$.

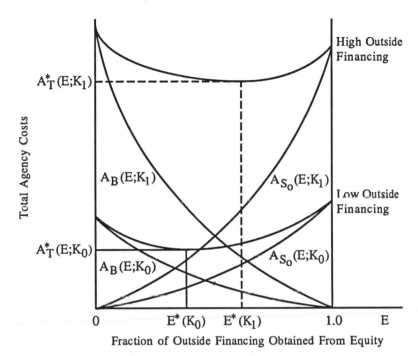

Fraction of Outside Financing Obtained From Equity

both K_0 and K_1 the intercepts of the $A_B(E; K)$ curves coincide at the right axis.

The net effect of the increased use of outside financing given the cost functions assumed in Figure 6 is to: (1) increase the total agency costs from $A_T(E^*; K_0)$ to $A_T(E^*; K_1)$, and (2) to increase the optimal fraction of outside funds obtained from the sale of outside equity. We draw these functions for illustration only and are unwilling to speculate at this time on the exact form of $E^*(K)$ which gives the general effects of increasing outside financing on the relative quantities of debt and equity.

The locus of points, $A_T(E^*; K)$ where agency costs are minimized (not drawn in Figure 6), determines $E^*(K)$, the optimal proportions of equity and debt to be used in obtaining outside funds as the fraction of outside funds, K, ranges from 0 to 100 percent. The solid line in Figure 7 is a plot of the minimum total agency costs as a function of the amount

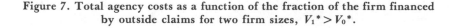

Figure 7. Total agency costs as a function of the fraction of the firm financed by outside claims for two firm sizes, $V_1^* > V_0^*$.

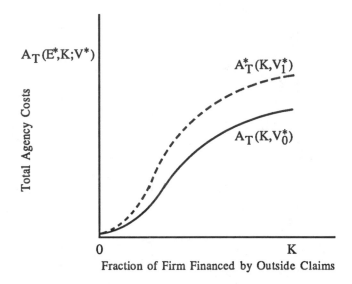

of outside financing for a firm with scale V_0^*. The dotted line shows the total agency costs for a larger firm with scale $V_1^* > V_0^*$. That is, we hypothesize that the larger the firm becomes the larger are the total agency costs because it is likely that the monitoring function is inherently more difficult and expensive in a larger organization.

5.3 Risk and the Demand for Outside Financing

The model we have used to explain the existence of minority shareholders and debt in the capital structure of corporations implies that the owner-manager, if he resorts to any outside funding, will have his entire wealth invested in the firm. The reason is that he can thereby avoid the agency costs which additional outside funding impose. This suggests he would not resort to outside funding until he had invested 100 percent of his personal wealth in the firm—an implication which is not consistent with what we generally observe. Most owner-managers hold personal wealth in a variety of forms, and some have only a relatively small fraction of their wealth invested in the corporation they manage.[62] Diversification on the part of owner-managers can be explained by risk aversion and optimal portfolio selection.

If the returns from assets are not perfectly correlated an individual can reduce the riskiness of the returns on his portfolio by dividing his wealth among many different assets, i.e., by diversifying.[63] Thus a manager who invests all of his wealth in a single firm (his own) will generally bear a welfare loss (if he is risk averse) because he is bearing more risk than necessary. He will, of course, be willing to pay something to avoid this risk, and the costs he must bear to accomplish this diversification will be the agency costs outlined above. He will suffer a wealth loss as he reduces his fractional ownership because prospective shareholders and bondholders will take into account the agency costs. Nevertheless, the manager's desire to avoid risk will contribute to his becoming a minority stockholder.

5.4 Determination of the Optimal Amount of Outside Financing, K^*

Assume for the moment that the owner of a project (i.e., the owner of a prospective firm) has enough wealth to finance the entire project himself. The optimal scale of the corporation is then determined by the condition that, $\Delta V - \Delta I = 0$. In general if the returns to the firm are uncertain the owner-manager can increase his welfare by selling off part of the firm either as debt or equity and reinvesting the proceeds in other assets. If he does this with the optimal combination of debt and equity (as in Figure 6) the total wealth reduction he will incur is given by the agency cost function, $A_T(E^*, K; V^*)$ in Figure 7. The functions $A_T(E^*, K; V^*)$ will be S shaped (as drawn) if total agency costs for a given scale of firm increase at an increasing rate at low levels of outside financing, and at a decreasing rate for high levels of outside financing as monitoring imposes more and more constraints on the manager's actions.

Figure 8 shows marginal agency costs as a function of K, the fraction of the firm financed with outside funds assuming the total agency cost function is as plotted in Figure 7, and assuming the scale of the firm is fixed. The demand by the owner-manager for outside financing is shown by the remaining curve in Figure 8. This curve represents the marginal value of the increased diversification which the manager can obtain by reducing his ownership claims and optimally constructing a diversified portfolio. It is measured by the amount he would pay to be allowed to reduce his ownership claims by a dollar in order to increase his diversification. If the liquidation of some of his holdings also influences the owner-manager's consumption set, the demand function plotted in Figure 8 also incorporates the marginal value of these effects. The intersection of these two schedules determines the optimal fraction of the firm to be

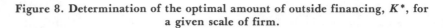

Figure 8. Determination of the optimal amount of outside financing, K^*, for a given scale of firm.

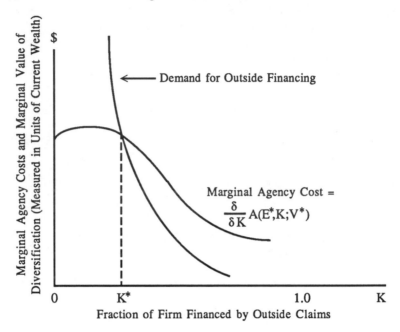

held by outsiders and this in turn determines the total agency costs borne by the owner. This solution is Pareto optimal; there is no way to reduce the agency costs without making someone worse off.

5.5. Determination of the Optimal Scale of the Firm

While the details of the solution of the optimal scale of the firm are complicated when we allow for the issuance of debt, equity and monitoring and bonding, the general structure of the solution is analogous to the case where monitoring and bonding are allowed for the outside equity example (see Figure 4).

If it is optimal to issue any debt, the expansion path taking full account of such opportunities must lie above the curve ZG in Figure 4. If this new expansion path lies anywhere to the right of the indifference curve passing through point G debt will be used in the optimal financing package. Furthermore, the optimal scale of the firm will be determined by the point at which this new expansion path touches the highest indifference curve. In this situation the resulting level of the owner-manager's welfare must therefore be higher.

6. Qualifications and Extensions of the Analysis

6.1. Multiperiod Aspects of the Agency Problem

We have assumed throughout our analysis that we are dealing only with a single investment-financing decision by the entrepreneur and have ignored the issues associated with the incentives affecting future financing-investment decisions which might arise after the initial set of contracts are consumated between the entrepreneur-manager, outside stockholders and bondholders. These are important issues which are left for future analysis.[64] Their solution will undoubtedly introduce some changes in the conclusions of the single decision analysis. It seems clear for instance that the expectation of future sales of outside equity and debt will change the costs and benefits facing the manager in making decisions which benefit himself at the (short-run) expense of the current bondholders and stockholders. If he develops a reputation for such dealings he can expect this to unfavourably influence the terms at which he can obtain future capital from outside sources. This will tend to increase the benefits associated with "sainthood" and will tend to reduce the size of the agency costs. Given the finite life of any individual, however, such an effect cannot reduce these costs to zero, because at some point these future costs will begin to weigh more heavily on his successors and therefore the relative benefits to him of acting in his own best interests will rise.[65] Furthermore, it will generally be impossible for him to fully guarantee the outside interests that his successor will continue to follow his policies.

6.2. The Control Problem and Outside Owner's Agency Costs

The careful reader will notice that nowhere in the analysis thus far have we taken into account many of the details of the relationship between the part owner-manager and the outside stockholders and bondholders. In particular we have assumed that all outside equity is non-voting. If such equity does have voting rights then the manager will be concerned about the effects on his long-run welfare of reducing his fractional ownership below the point where he loses effective control of the corporation. That is, below the point where it becomes possible for the outside equity holders to fire him. A complete analysis of this issue will require a careful specification of the contractual rights involved on both sides, the role of the board of directors, and the coordination (agency) costs borne by the stockholders in implementing policy changes. This latter point involves consideration of the distribution of the outside ownership claims. Simply put, forces exist to determine an equilibrium distribution of outside ownership. If the costs of reducing the dispersion of ownership are lower than the benefits to be obtained from reducing the agency costs, it will pay some individual or group of individuals to buy shares in the market to reduce the dispersion of ownership. We occasionally witness these conflicts for control which involve outright market purchases, tender offers and proxy fights. Further analysis of these issues is left to the future.

6.3. A Note on the Existence of Inside Debt and Some Conjectures on the Use of Convertible Financial Instruments

We have been asked[66] why debt held by the manager (i.e., "inside debt") plays no role in our analysis. We have as yet been unable to incorporate this dimension formally into our analysis in a satisfactory way. The question is a good one and suggests some potentially important extensions of the analysis. For instance, it suggests an inexpensive way for the owner-manager with both equity and debt outstanding to eliminate a large part (perhaps all) of the agency costs of debt. If he binds himself contractually to hold a fraction of the total debt equal to his fractional ownership of the total equity he would have no incentive whatsoever to reallocate wealth from the debt holders to the stockholders. Consider the case where

$$B_i/S_i = B_o/S_o,$$

where S_i and S_o are as defined earlier, B_i is the dollar value of the inside debt held by the owner-manager, and B_o is the debt held by outsiders. In this case if the manager changes the investment policy of the firm to reallocate wealth between the debt and equity holders, the net effect on the total value of his holdings in the firm will be zero. Therefore, his incentives to perform such reallocations are zero.[67]

Why then don't we observe practices or formal contracts which accomplish this elimination or reduction of the agency costs of debt? Maybe we do for smaller privately held firms (we haven't attempted to obtain this data), but for large diffuse owner corporations the practice does not seem to be common. One reason for this we believe is that in some respects the claim that the manager holds on the firm in the form of his wage contract has some of the characteristics of debt.[68] If true, this implies that even with zero holdings of formal debt claims he still has positive holdings of a quasi-debt claim and this may accomplish the satisfaction of condition (4). The problem here is that any formal analysis of this issue requires a much deeper understanding of the relationship between formal debt holdings and the wage contract; i.e., how much debt is it equivalent to?

This line of thought also suggests some other interesting issues. Suppose the implicit debt characteristics of the manager's wage contract result in a situation equivalent to

$$B_i/S_i = B_o/S_o.$$

Then he would have incentives to change the operating characteristics of the firm (i.e., reduce the variance of the outcome distribution) to transfer wealth from the stockholders to the debt holders which is the reverse of the situation we examined in section 4. Furthermore, this seems to capture some of the concern often expressed regarding the fact that managers of large publicly held corporations seem to behave in a risk averse way to the detriment of the equity holders. One solution to this would be to establish incentive compensation systems for the manager or to give him stock options which in effect give him a claim on the upper tail of the outcome distribution. This also seems to be a commonly observed phenomenon.

This analysis also suggests some additional issues regarding the costs and benefits associated with the use of more complicated financial claims such as warrants, convertible bonds and convertible preferred stock which we have not formally analyzed as yet. Warrants, convertible bonds and convertible preferred stock have some of the characteristics of non-voting shares although they can be converted into voting shares under some terms. Alchian–Demsetz (1972) provide an interesting analysis regarding the use of non-voting shares. They argue that some shareholders with strong beliefs in the talents and judgements of the manager will want to be protected against the possibility that some other shareholders will take over and limit the actions of the manager (or fire him). Given that the securities exchanges prohibit the use of non-voting shares by listed firms the use of option type securities might be a substitute for these claims.

In addition warrants represent a claim on the upper tail of the distribution of outcomes, and convertible securities can be thought of as securities with non-detachable warrants. It seems that the incentive effects of warrants would tend to offset to some extent the incentive effects of the existence of risky debt because the owner-manager would be sharing part of the proceeds associated with a shift in the distribution of returns with the warrant holders. Thus, we conjecture that potential bondholders will find it attractive to have warrants attached to the risky debt of firms in which it is relatively easy to shift the distribution of outcomes to expand the upper tail of the distribution to transfer wealth from bondholders. It would also then be attractive to the owner-manager because of the reduction in the agency costs which he would bear. This argument also implies that it would make litte difference if the warrants were detachable (and therefore saleable separately from the bonds) since their mere existence would reduce the incentives of the manager (or stockholders) to increase the riskiness of the firm (and therefore increase the probability of bankruptcy). Furthermore, the addition of a conversion privilege to fixed claims such as debt or preferred stock would also tend to reduce the incentive effects of the existence of such fixed claims and therefore lower the agency costs associated with them. The theory predicts that these phenomena should be more frequently observed in cases where the incentive effects of such fixed claims are high than when they are low.

6.4. Monitoring and the Social Product of Security Analysis

One of the areas in which further analysis is likely to lead to high payoffs is that of monitoring. We currently have little which could be glorified by the title of a ''Theory of Monitoring'' and yet this is a crucial building block of the analysis. We would expect monitoring activities to become specialized to those institutions and individuals who possess comparative advantages in these activities. One of the groups who seem to play a large role in these activities is composed of the security analysts employed by institutional investors, brokers and investment advisory services as well as the analysis performed by individual investors in the normal course of investment decion making.

A large body of evidence exists which indicates that security prices incorporate in an unbiased manner all publicly available information and much of what might be called ''private information.''[69] There is also a large body of evidence which indicates that the security analysis activities of mutual funds and other institutional investors are not reflected in portfolio returns, i.e., they do not increase risk adjusted portfolio returns over a naive random selection buy and hold strategy.[70] Therefore some have been tempted to conclude that the resources expended on such research activities to find under- or over-valued securities is a social loss. Jensen (1974) argues that this conclusion cannot be unambiguously drawn because there is a large consumption element in the demand for these services.

Furthermore, the analysis of this paper would seem to indicate that to the extent that security analysis activities reduce the agency costs associated with the separation of ownership and control they are indeed socially productive. Moreover, if this is true we expect the major benefits of the security analysis activity to be reflected in the higher capitalized value of the ownership claims to corporations and *not* in the period to period portfolio returns of the analyst. Equilibrium in the security analysis industry requires that the private returns to analysis (i.e., portfolio returns) must be just equal to the private costs of such activity,[71] and this will not reflect the social product of this activity which will consist of larger output and higher *levels* of the capital value of ownership claims. Therefore, the argument implies that if there is a non-optimal amount of security analysis being performed it is too much[72] not too little (since the shareholders would be willing to pay directly to have the "optimal" monitoring performed), and we don't seem to observe such payments.

6.5. Specialization in the Use of Debt and Equity

Our previous analysis of agency costs suggests at least one other testable hypothesis: i.e., that in those industries where the incentive effects of outside equity or debt are widely different, we would expect to see specialization in the use of the low agency cost financing arrangement. In industries where it is relatively easy for managers to lower the mean value of the outcomes of the enterprise by outright theft, special treatment of favored customers, ease of consumption of leisure on the job, etc. (for example, the bar and restaurant industry) we would expect to see the ownership structure of firms characterized by relatively little outside equity (i.e., 100 percent ownership of the equity by the manager) with almost all outside capital obtained through the use of debt.

The theory predicts the opposite would be true where the incentive effects of debt are large relative to the incentive effects of equity. Firms like conglomerates, in which it would be easy to shift outcome distributions adversely for bondholders (by changing the acquisition or divestiture policy) should be characterized by relatively lower utilization of debt. Conversely in industries where the freedom of management to take riskier projects is severely constrained (for example, regulated industries such as public utilities) we should find more intensive use of debt financing.

The analysis suggests that in addition to the fairly well understood role of uncertainty in the determination of the quality of collateral there is at least one other element of great importance—the ability of the owner of the collateral to change the distribution of outcomes by shifting either the mean outcome or the variance of the outcomes. A study of bank lending policies should reveal these to be important aspects of the contractual practices observed there.

6.6. Application of the Analysis to the Large Diffuse Ownership Corporation

While we believe the structure outlined in the proceeding pages is applicable to a wide range of corporations it is still in an incomplete state. One of the most serious limitations of the analysis is that as it stands we have not worked out in this paper its application to the very large modern corporation whose managers own little or no equity. We believe our approach can be applied to this case but space limitations preclude discussion of these issues here. They remain to be worked out in detail and will be included in a future paper.

6.7. The Supply Side of the Incomplete Markets Question

The analysis of this paper is also relevant to the incomplete market issue considered by Arrow (1964b), Diamond (1967), Hakansson (1974a, b), Rubinstein (1974), Ross (1974a) and others. The problems addressed in this literature derive from the fact that whenever the available set of financial claims on outcomes in a market fails to span the underlying state space [see Arrow (1964b) and Debreu (1959)] the resulting allocation is Pareto inefficient. A disturbing element in this literature surrounds the fact that the inefficiency conclusion is generally drawn without explicit attention in the analysis to the costs of creating new claims or of maintaining the expanded set of markets called for to bring about the welfare improvement.

The demonstration of a possible welfare improvement from the expansion of the set of claims by the introduction of new basic contingent claims or options can be thought of as an analysis of the demand conditions for new markets. Viewed from this perspective, what is missing in the literature on this problem is the formulation of a positive analysis of the supply of markets (or the supply of contingent claims). That is, what is it in the maximizing behavior of individuals in the economy that causes them to create and sell contingent claims of various sorts?

The analysis in this paper can be viewed as a small first step in the direction of formulating an analysis of the supply of markets issue which is founded in the self-interested maximizing behavior of individuals. We have shown why it is in the interest of a wealth maximizing entrepreneur to create and sell claims such as debt and equity. Furthermore, as we have indicated above, it appears that extensions of these arguments will lead to a theory of the supply of warrants, convertible bonds and convertible preferred stock. We are not suggesting that the specific analysis offered above is likely to be sufficient to lead to a theory of the supply of the wide range of contracts (both existing and merely potential) in the world at large. However, we do believe that framing the question of the completeness of markets in terms of the joining of both the demand and supply conditions will be very fruitful instead of implicitly assuming that new claims spring forth from some (costless) wellhead of creativity unaided or unsupported by human effort.

7. Conclusions

The publicly held business corporation is an awesome social invention. Millions of individuals voluntarily entrust billions of dollars, francs, pesos, etc., of personal wealth to the care of managers on the basis of a complex set of contracting relationships which delineate the rights of the parties involved. The growth in the use of the corporate form as well as the growth in market value of established corporations suggests that at least, up to the present, creditors and investors have by and large not been disappointed with the results, despite the agency costs inherent in the corporate form.

Agency costs are as real as any other costs. The level of agency cost depends among other things on statutory and common law and human ingenuity in devising contracts. Both the law and the sophistication of contracts relevant to the modern corporation are the products of a historical process in which there were strong incentives for individulas to minimize agency costs. Moreover, there were alternative organizational forms available, and opportunities to invent new ones. Whatever its shortcomings, the corporation has thus far survived the market test against potential alternatives.

Notes

1. We do not use the term "capital structure" because that term usually denotes the relative quantities of bonds, equity, warrants, trade credit, etc., which represent the liabilities of a firm. Our theory implies there is another important dimension to this problem—namely the relative amounts of ownership claims held by insiders (management) and outsiders (investors with no direct role in the management of the firm).

2. Reviews of this literature are given by Peterson (1965), Alchian (1965, 1968), Machlup (1967), Shubik (1970), Cyert and Hedrick (1972), Branch (1973), Preston (1975).

3. See Williamson (1964, 1970, 1975), Marris (1964), Baumol (1959), Penrose (1958), and Cyert and March (1963). Thorough reviews of these and other contributions are given by Machlup (1967) and Alchian (1965).

   Simon (1955) developed a model of human choice incorporating information (search) and computational costs which also has important implications for the behavior of managers. Unfortunately, Simon's work has often been misinterpreted as a denial of maximizing behavior, and misused, especially in the marketing and behavioral science literature. His later use of the term "satisficing" [Simon (1959)] has undoubtedly contributed to this confusion because it suggests rejection of maximizing behavior rather than maximization subject to costs of information and of decision making.

4. See Meckling (1976) for a discussion of the fundamental importance of the assumption of resourceful, evaluative, maximizing behavior on the part of individuals in the development of theory. Klein (1976) takes an approach similar to the one we embark on in this paper in his review of the theory of the firm and the law.

5. See Coase (1937, 1959, 1960), Alchian (1965, 1968), Alchian and Kessel (1962), Demsetz (1967), Alchian and Demsetz (1972), Monsen and Downs (1965), Silver and Auster (1969), and McManus (1975).

6. Property rights are of course human rights, i.e., rights which are possessed by human beings. The introduction of the wholly false distinction between property rights and human rights in many policy discussions is surely one of the all time great semantic flimflams.

7. Cf. Berhold (1971), Ross (1973, 1974a), Wilson (1968, 1969), and Heckerman (1975).

8. Given the optimal monitoring and bonding activities by the principal and agent.

9. As it is used in this paper the term monitoring includes more than just measuring or observing the behavior of the agent. It includes efforts on the part of the principal to "control" the behavior of the agent through budget restrictions, compensation policies, operating rules etc.

10. As we show below the existence of positive monitoring and bonding costs will result in the manager of a corporation possessing control over some resources which he can allocate (within certain constraints) to satisfy his own preferences. However, to the extent that he must obtain the cooperation of others in order to carry out his tasks (such as divisional vice presidents) and to the extent that he cannot control their behavior perfectly and costlessly they will be able to appropriate some of these resources for their own ends. In short, there are agency costs generated at every level of the organization. Unfortunately, the analysis of these more general organizational issues is even more difficult than that of the "ownership and control" issue because the nature of the contractual obligations and rights of the parties are much more varied and generally not as well specified in explicit contractual arrangements. Nevertheless, they exist and we believe that extensions of our analysis in these directions show promise of producing insights into a viable theory of organization.

11. They define the classical capitalist firm as a contractual organization of inputs in which there is "(a) joint input production, (b) several input owners, (c) one party who is common to all the contracts of the joint inputs, (d) who has rights to renegotiate any input's contract independently of contracts with other input owners, (e) who holds the residual claims, and (f) who has the right to sell his contractual residual status."

12. By legal fiction we mean the artificial construct under the law which allows certain organizations to be treated as individuals.

13. For example, we ordinarily think of a product as leaving the firm at the time it is sold, but implicitly or explicitly such sales generally carry with them continuing contracts between the firm and the buyer. If the product does not perform as expected the buyer often can and does have a right to satisfaction. Explicit evidence that such implicit contracts do exist is the practice we occasionally observe of specific provision that "all sales are final."

14. This view of the firm points up the important role which the legal system and the law play in social organizations, especially, the organization of economic activity. Statutory laws sets bounds on the kinds of contracts into which individuals and organizations may enter without risking criminal prosecution. The police powers of the state are available and used to enforce performance of contracts or to enforce the collection of damages for non-performance. The courts adjudicate conflicts between contracting parties and establish precedent which form the body of common law. All of these government activities affect both the kinds of contracts executed and the extent to which contracting is relied upon. This in turn determines the usefulness, productivity, profitability and viability of various forms of organization. Moreover, new laws as well as court decisions often can and do change the rights of contracting parties ex post, and they can and do serve as a vehicle for redistribution of wealth. An analysis of some of the implications of these facts is contained in Jensen and Meckling (1976b) and we shall not pursue them here.

15. For use in consumption, for the diversification of his wealth, or more importantly, for the financing of "profitable" projects which he could not otherwise

finance out of his personal wealth. We deal with these issues below after having developed some of the elementary analytical tools necessary to their solution.

16. Such as office space, air conditioning, thickness of the carpets, friendliness of employee relations, etc.

17. And again we assume that for any given market value of these costs, F, to the firm the allocation across time and across alternative probability distributions is such that the manager's current expected utility is at a maximum.

18. At this stage when we are considering a 100% owner-managed firm the notion of a ''wage contract'' with himself has no content. However, the 100% owner-managed case is only an expositional device used in passing to illustrate a number of points in the analysis, and we ask the reader to bear with us briefly while we lay out the structure for the more interesting partial ownership case where such a contract does have substance.

19. The manager's utility function is actually defined over wealth and the future time sequence of vectors of quantities of non-pecuniary benefits, X_t. Although the setting of his problem is somewhat different, Fama (1970b, 1972) analyzes the conditions under which these preferences can be represented as a derived utility function defined as a function of the money value of the expenditures (in our notation F) on these goods conditional on the prices of goods. Such a utility function incorporates the optimization going on in the background which define $\hat{X}$ discussed above for a given F. In the more general case where we allow a time series of consumption, $\hat{X}_t$, the optimization is being carried out across both time and the components of X_t for fixed F.

20. This excludes, for instance, (a) the case where the manager is allowed to expend corporate resources on anything he pleases in which case F would be a perfect substitute for wealth, or (b) the case where he can ''steal'' cash (or other marketable assets) with constant returns to scale—if he could the indifference curves would be straight lines with slope determined by the fence commission.

21. Point D defines the fringe benefits in the optimal pay package since the value to the manager of the fringe benefits F^* is greater than the cost of providing them as is evidenced by the fact that U_2 is steeper to the left of D than the budget constraint with slope equal to -1.

    That D is indeed the optimal pay package can easily be seen in this situation since if the conditions of the sale to a new owner specified that the manager would receive no fringe benefits after the sale he would require a payment equal to V_3 to compensate him for the sacrifice of his claims to V^* and fringe benefits amounting to F^* (the latter with total value to him of $V_3 - V^*$). But if $F = 0$, the value of the firm is only V. Therefore, if monitoring costs were zero the sale would take place at V^* with provision for a pay package which included fringe benefits of F^* for the manager.

    This discussion seems to indicate there are two values for the ''firm,'' V_3 and V^*. This is not the case if we realize that V^* is the value of the right to be the residual claimant on the cash flows of the firm and $V_3 - V^*$ is the value of the managerial rights, i.e., the right to make the operating decisions which include access to F^*. There is at least one other right which has value which plays no formal role in the analysis as yet—the value of the control right. By control right we mean the right to hire and fire the manager and we leave this issue to a future paper.

22. The distance $V^* - V'$ is a measure of what we will define as the gross agency costs. The distance $V_3 - V_4$ is a measure of what we call net agency costs, and it is this measure of agency costs which will be minimized by the manager in the general case where we allow investment to change.

23. I^* is the value maximizing and Pareto Optimum investment level which results from the traditional analysis of the corporate investment decision if the firm operates in perfectly competitive capital and product markets and the agency cost problems discussed here are ignored. See Debreu (1959, ch. 7), Jensen and Long (1972), Long (1972), Merton and Subrahmanyam (1974), Hirshleifer (1958, 1970), and Fama and Miller (1972).

24. Each equilibrium point such as that at E is characterized by $(\hat{a}, \hat{F}, \hat{W}_T)$ where $\hat{W}_T$ is the entrepreneur's post-investment financing wealth. Such an equilibrium must satisfy each of the following four conditions:

(1)
$$\hat{W}_T + F = V(I) + W - I = V(I) - K,$$

where $K - I$ W is the amount of outside financing required to make the investment I. If this condition is not satisfied there is an uncompensated wealth transfer (in one direction or the other) between the entrepreneur and outside equity buyers.

(2)
$$U_F(\hat{W}_T, \hat{F})/U_{wT}(\hat{W}_T, \hat{F}) = \hat{a},$$

where U is the entrepreneur's utility function on wealth and perquisites, U_F and U_{wT} are marginal utilities and $\hat{a}$ is the manager's share of the firm.

(3)
$$(1 - \hat{a})V(I) = (1 - \hat{a})[V(I) - \hat{F}] \geq K,$$

which says the funds received from outsiders are at least equal to K, the minimum required outside financing.

(4) Among all points $(\hat{a}, \hat{F}, \hat{W}_T)$ satisfying conditions (1)–(3), (α, F, W_T) gives the manager highest utility. This implies that $(\hat{a}, \hat{F}, \hat{W}_T)$ satisfy condition (3) as an equality.

25. *Proof.* Note that the slope of the expansion path (or locus of equilibrium points) at any point is $(\Delta V - \Delta I)/\Delta F$ and at the optimum level of investment this must be equal to the slope of the manager's indifference curve between wealth and market value of fringe benefits, F. Furthermore, in the absence of monitoring, the slope of the indifference curve, $\Delta W/\Delta F$, at the equilibrium point, D, must be equal to $-\alpha'$. Thus,

$$(\Delta V - \Delta I)/\Delta F = -\alpha' \qquad (2)$$

is the condition for the optimal scale of investment and this implies condition (1) holds for small changes at the optimum level of investment, I'.

26. Since the manager's indifference curves are negatively sloped we know that the optimum scale of the firm, point D, will occur in the region where the expansion path has negative slope, i.e., the market value of the firm will be declining and the *gross* agency costs, A, will be increasing and thus, the manager will not minimize them in making the investment decision (even though he will minimize them for any *given* level of investment). However, we define the *net* agency cost as the dollar equivalent of the welfare loss the manager experiences because of the agency relationship evaluated at $F = 0$ (the vertical distance between the intercepts on the Y axis of the two indifference curves on which points C and D lie). The optimum solution, I', does satisfy the condition that net agency costs are minimized. But this simply amounts to a restatement of the assumption that the manager maximizes his welfare.

    Finally, it is possible for the solution point D to be a corner solution and in this case the value of the firm will not be declining. Such a corner solution can occur, for instance, if the manager's marginal rate of substitution between F and wealth falls to zero fast enough as we move up the expansion path, or if the investment projects are "sufficiently" profitable. In these cases the expansion path will have a corner which lies on the maximum value budget constraint with intercept $V(I^*) - I^*$, and the level of investment will be equal to the idealized optimum, I^*. However, the market value of the residual claims will be less than V^* because the manager's consumption of perquisites will be larger than F^*, the zero agency cost level.

27. The careful reader will note that point C will be the equilibrium point only if the contract between the manager and outside equity holders specifies with no ambiguity that they have the right to monitor to limit his consumption of perquisites to an amount no less than F''. If any ambiguity regarding these rights exists in this contract then another source of agency costs arises which is symmetrical to our original problem. If they could do so the outside equity holders would monitor to the point where the net value of *their* holdings, $(1 - \alpha)V - M$, was maximized, and this would occur when $(\delta V/\delta M)(1 - \alpha) - 1 = 0$ which would be at some point between points C and E in Figure 3. Point E denotes the point where the value of the firm net of the monitoring costs is at a maximum, i.e., where $\delta V/\delta M - 1 = 0$. But the manager would be worse off than in the zero monitoring solution if the point where $(1 - \alpha)V - M$ was at a maximum were to the left of the intersection between BCE and the indifference curve U_3 passing through point B (which denotes the zero monitoring level of welfare). Thus if the manager could not eliminate enough of the ambiguity in the contract to push the equilibrium to the right of the intersection of the curve BCE with indifference curve U_3 he would not engage in any contract which allowed monitoring.

28. If we could establish the existence of a feasible set of alternative institutional arrangements which would yield net benefits from the reduction of these costs

we could legitimately conclude the agency relationship engendered by the corporation was not Pareto optimal. However, we would then be left with the problem of explaining why these alternative institutional arrangements have not replaced the corporate form of organization.

29. The monitoring and bonding costs will differ from firm to firm depending on such things as the inherent complexity and geographical dispersion of operations, the attractiveness of perquisites available in the firm (consider the mint), etc.

30. "Where competitors are numerous and entry is easy, persistent departures from profit maximizing behavior inexorably leads to extinction. Economic natural selection holds the stage. In these circumstances, the behavior of the individual units that constitute the supply side of the product market is essentially routine and uninteresting and economists can confidently predict industry behavior without being explicitly concerned with the behavior of these individual units.

    When the conditions of competition are relaxed, however, the opportunity set of the firm is expanded. In this case, the behavior of the firm as a distinct operating unit is of separate interest. Both for purposes of interpreting particular behavior within the firm as well as for predicting responses of the industry aggregate, it may be necessary to identify the factors that influence the firm's choices within this expanded opportunity set and embed these in a formal model" [Williamson (1964, p. 2)].

31. Assuming there are no special tax benefits to ownership nor utility of ownership other than that derived from the direct wealth effects of ownership such as might be true for professional sports teams, race horse stables, firms which carry the family name, etc.

32. Marris (1964, pp. 7 9) is the exception, although he argues that there exists some "maximum leverage point" beyond which the chances of "insolvency" are in some undefined sense too high.

33. By limited liability we mean the same conditions that apply to common stock. Subordinated debt or preferred stock could be constructed which carried with it liability provisions; i.e., if the corporation's assets were insufficient at some point to pay off all prior claims (such as trade credit, accrued wages, senior debt, etc.) and if the personal resources of the "equity" holders were also insufficient to cover these claims the holders of this "debt" would be subject to assessments beyond the face value of their claim (assessments which might be limited or unlimited in amount).

34. Alchian–Demsetz (1972, p. 709) argue that one can explain the existence of both bonds and stock in the ownership structure of firms as the result of differing expectations regarding the outcomes to the firm. They argue that bonds are created and sold to "pessimists" and stocks with a residual claim with no upper bound are sold to "optimists."

    As long as capital markets are perfect with no taxes or transactions costs and individual investors can issue claims on distributions of outcomes on the same terms as firms, such actions on the part of firms cannot affect their values.

The reason is simple. Suppose such "pessimists" did exist and yet the firm issues only equity claims. The demand for those equity claims would reflect the fact that the individual purchaser could on his own account issue "bonds" with a limited and prior claim on the distribution of outcomes on the equity which is exactly the same as that which the firm could issue. Similarly, investors could easily unlever any position by simply buying a proportional claim on both the bonds and stocks of a levered firm. Therefore, a levered firm could not sell at a different price than an unlevered firm solely because of the existence of such differential expectations. See Fama and Miller (1972, chap. 4) for an excellent exposition of these issues.

35. Corporations did use both prior to the institution of the corporate income tax in the U.S. and preferred dividends have, with minor exceptions, never been tax deductible.

36. See Kraus and Litzenberger (1972) and Lloyd-Davies (1975).

37. And if there is competitive bidding for the firm from potential owner-managers the absentee owner will capture the capitalized value of these agency costs.

38. The spectrum of claims which firms can issue is far more diverse than is suggested by our two-way classification—fixed vs. residual. There are convertible bonds, equipment trust certificates, debentures, revenue bonds, warrants, etc. Different bond issues can contain different subordination provisions with respect to assets and interest. They can be callable or non-callable. Preferred stocks can be "preferred" in a variety of dimensions and contain a variety of subordination stipulations. In the abstract, we can imagine firms issuing claims contingent on a literally infinite variety of states of the world such as those considered in the literature on the time–state-preference models of Arrow (1964b), Debreu (1959) and Hirshleifer (1970).

39. An apt analogy is the way one would play poker on money borrowed at a fixed interest rate, with one's own liability limited to some very small stake. Fama and Miller (1972, pp. 179–180) also discuss and provide a numerical example of an investment decision which illustrates very nicely the potential inconsistency between the interests of bondholders and stockholders.

40. The portfolio diversification issues facing the owner-manager are brought into the analysis in section 5 below.

41. See Smith (1976) for a review of this option pricing literature and its applications and Galai and Masulis (1976) who apply the option pricing model to mergers, and corporate investment decisions.

42. While we used the option pricing model above to motivate the discussion and provide some intuitive understanding of the incentives facing the equity holders, the option pricing solutions of Black and Scholes (1973) do not apply when incentive effects cause V to be a function of the debt/equity ratio as it is in general and in this example. Long (1974) points out this difficulty with respect to the

usefulness of the model in the context of tax subsidies on interest and bankruptcy cost. The results of Merton (1974) and Galai and Masulis (1976) must be interpreted with care since the solutions are strictly incorrect in the context of tax subsidies and/or agency costs.

43. The numerical example of Fama and Miller (1972, pp. 172–180) is a close representation of this case in a two-period state model. However, they go on to make the following statement on p. 180:

> From a practical viewpoint, however, situations of potential conflict between bondholders and shareholders in the application of the market value rule are probably unimportant. In general, investment opportunities that increase a firm's market value by more than their cost both increase the value of the firm's shares and strengthen the firm's future ability to meet its current bond commitments.

This first issue regarding the importance of the conflict of interest between bondholders and stockholders is an empirical one, and the last statement is incomplete—in some circumstances the equity holders could benefit from projects whose net effect was to reduce the total value of the firm as they and we have illustrated. The issue cannot be brushed aside so easily.

44. Myers (1975) points out another serious incentive effect on managerial decisions of the existence of debt which does not occur in our simple single decision world. He shows that if the firm has the option to take future investment opportunities the existence of debt which matures after the options must be taken will cause the firm (using an equity value maximizing investment rule) to refuse to take some otherwise profitable projects because they would benefit only the bondholders and not the equity holders. This will (in the absence of tax subsidies to debt) cause the value of the firm to fall. Thus (although he doesn't use the term) these incentive effects also contribute to the agency costs of debt in a manner perfectly consistent with the examples discussed in the text.

45. Black-Scholes (1973) discuss ways in which dividend and future financing policy can redistribute wealth between classes of claimants on the firm.

46. Black, Miller and Posner (1974) discuss many of these issues with particular reference to the government regulation of bank holding companies.

47. In other words, these costs will be taken into account in determining the yield to maturity on the issue. For an examination of the effects of such enforcement costs on the nominal interest rates in the consumer small loan market, see Benston (1977).

48. To illustrate the fact that it will sometimes pay the manager to incur "bonding" costs to guarantee the bondholders that he will not deviate from his promised behavior let us suppose that for an expenditure of $$b$ of the firm's resources he can guarantee that project 1 will be chosen. If he spends these resources and

takes project 1 the value of the firm will be $V_1 - b$ and clearly as long as $(V_1 - b) > V_2$, or alternatively $(V_1 - V_2) > b$ he will be better off, since his wealth will be equal to the value of the firm minus the required investment, I (which we assumed for simplicity to be identical for the two projects).

On the other hand, to prove that the owner-manager prefers the lowest cost solution to the conflict let us assume he can write a covenant into the bond issue which will allow the bondholders to prevent him from taking project 2, if they incur monitoring costs of \$$m$, where $m < b$. If he does this his wealth will be higher by the amount $b - m$. To see this note that if the bond market is competitive and makes unbiased estimates, potential bondholders will be indifferent between:

    i. a claim X^* with no covenant (and no guarantees from management) at a price of B_2,
    ii. a claim X^* with no covenant (and no guarantees from management, through bonding expenditures by the firm of \$$b$, that project 1 will be taken) at a price of B_1, and
    iii. a claim X^* with a covenant and the opportunity to spend m on monitoring (to guarantee project 1 will be taken) at a price of $B_1 - m$.

The bondholders will realize that (i) represents in fact a claim on project 2 and that (ii) and (iii) represent a claim on project 1 and are thus indifferent between the three options at the specified prices. The owner-manager, however, will not be indifferent between incurring the bonding costs, b, directly, or including the covenant in the bond indenture and letting the bondholders spend m to guarantee that he take project 1. His wealth in the two cases will be given by the value of his equity plus the proceeds of the bond issue less the required investment, and if $m < b < V_1 - V_2$, then his post-investment-financing wealth, W, for the three options will be such that $W_i < W_{ii} < W_{iii}$. Therefore, since it would increase his wealth, he would voluntarily include the covenant in the bond issue and let the bondholders monitor.

49. We mention, without going into the problem in detail, that similar to the case in which the outside equity holders are allowed to monitor the owner-manager, the agency relationship between the bondholders and stockholders has a symmetry if the rights of the bondholders to limit actions of the manager are not perfectly spelled out. Suppose the bondholders, by spending sufficiently large amounts of resources, could force management to take actions which would transfer wealth from the equity holder to the bondholders (by taking sufficiently less risky projects). One can easily construct situations where such actions could make the bondholders better off, hurt the equity holders and actually lower the total value of the firm. Given the nature of the debt contract the original owner-manager might maximize his wealth in such a situation by selling off the equity and keeping the bonds as his ''owner's'' interest. If the nature of the bond contract is given, this may well be an inefficient solution since the total agency costs (i.e., the sum of monitoring and value loss) could easily be higher than the alternative solution. However, if the owner-manager could strictly limit the rights of the bondholders (perhaps by inclusion of a provision which expressly reserves all rights not specifically granted to the bondholder for the equity holder), he would find it in his interest to establish the efficient contractual arrangement

since by minimizing the agency costs he would be maximizing his wealth. These issues involve the fundamental nature of contracts and for now we simply assume that the ''bondholders'' rights are strictly limited and unambiguous and all rights not specifically granted them are reserved for the ''stockholders''; a situation descriptive of actual institutional arrangements. This allows us to avoid the incentive effects associated with ''bondholders'' potentially exploiting ''stockholders.''

50. If the firm were allowed to sell assets to meet a current debt obligation, bankruptcy would occur when the total market value of the future cash flows expected to be generated by the firm is less than the value of a current payment on a debt obligation. Many bond indentures do not, however, allow for the sale of assets to meet debt obligations.

51. We have been told that while this is true in principle, the actual behavior of the courts appears to frequently involve the provision of some settlement to the common stockholders even when the assets of the company are not sufficient to cover the claims of the creditors.

52. If under bankruptcy the bondholders have the right to fire the management, the management will have some incentives to avoid taking actions which increase the probability of this event (even if it is in the best interest of the equity holders) if they (the management) are earning rents or if they have human capital specialized to this firm or if they face large adjustment costs in finding new employment. A detailed examination of this issue involves the value of the control rights (the rights to hire and fire the manager) and we leave it to a subsequent paper.

53. Kraus and Litzenberger (1972) and Lloyd-Davies (1975) demonstrate that the total value of the firm will be reduced by these costs.

54. These include only payments to all parties for legal fees, professional services, trustees' fees and filing fees. They do not include the costs of management time or changes in cash flows due to shifts in the firm's demand or cost functions discussed below.

55. Which, incidentally, exist only when the debt has some probability of default.

56. Our theory is capable of explaining why in the absence of the tax subsidy on interest payments, we would expect to find firms using both debt and preferred stock—a problem which has long puzzled at least one of the authors. If preferred stock has all the characteristics of debt except for the fact that its holders cannot put the firm into bankruptcy in the event of nonpayment of the preferred dividends, then the agency costs associated with the issuance of preferred stock will be lower than those associated with debt by the present value of the bankruptcy costs.

However, these lower agency costs of preferred stock exist only over some range if as the amount of such stock rises the incentive effects caused by their existence impose value reductions which are larger than that caused by debt (including the bankruptcy costs of debt). There are two reasons for this. First, the equity holder's claims can be eliminated by the debtholders in the event of bankruptcy, and second, the debtholders have the right to fire the management in the event of bankruptcy. Both of these will tend to become more important as an advantage to the issuance of debt as we compare situations with large amounts of preferred stock to equivalent situations with large amounts of debt because they will tend to reduce the incentive effects of large amounts of preferred stock.

57. One other condition also has to hold to justify the incurrence of the costs associated with the use of debt or outside equity in our firm. If there are other individuals in the economy who have sufficiently large amounts of personal capital to finance the entire firm, our capital constrained owner can realize the full capital value of his current and prospective projects and avoid the agency costs by simply selling the firm (i.e., the right to take these projects) to one of these individuals. He will then avoid the wealth losses associated with the agency costs caused by the sale of debt or outside equity. If no such individuals exist, it will pay him (and society) to obtain the additional capital in the debt market. This implies, incidentally, that it is somewhat misleading to speak of the owner-manager as the individual who bears the agency costs. One could argue that it is the project which bears the costs since, if it is not sufficiently profitable to cover all the costs (including the agency costs), it will not be taken. We continue to speak of the owner-manager bearing these costs to emphasize the more correct and important point that he has the incentive to reduce them because, if he does, his wealth will be increased.

58. We continue to ignore for the moment the additional complicating factor involved with the portfolio decisions of the owner, and the implied acceptance of potentially diversifiable risk by such 100% owners in this example.

59. We continue to ignore such instruments as convertible bonds and warrants.

60. Note, however, that even when outsiders own none of the equity the stockholder-manager still has some incentives to engage in activities which yield him non-pecuniary benefits but reduce the value of the firm by more than he personally values the benefits if there is any risky debt outstanding. Any such actions he takes which reduce the value of the firm, V, tend to reduce the value of the bonds as well as the value of the equity. Although the option pricing model does not in general apply exactly to the problem of valuing the debt and equity of the firm, it can be useful in obtaining some qualitative insights into matters such as this. In the option pricing model $\delta S/\delta V$ indicates the rate at which the stock value changes per dollar change in the value of the firm (and similarly for $\delta B/\delta V$). Both of these terms are less than unity [cf. Black and Scholes (1973)]. Therefore, any action of the manager which reduces the value of the firm, V, tends to reduce the value of both the stock and the bonds, and the larger is the total debt/equity ratio the smaller is the impact of any given change in V on the value of the equity, and therefore, the lower is the cost to him of consuming non-pecuniary benefits.

61. This occurs, of course, not at the intersection of $A_{So}(E)$ and $A_B(E)$, but at the

point where the absolute value of the slopes of the functions are equal, i.e., where $A'_{So}(E) + A'_B(E) = 0$.

62. On the average, however, top managers seem to have substantial holdings in absolute dollars. A recent survey by Wytmar (*Wall Street Journal*, Aug. 13, 1974, p. 1) reported that the median value of 826 chief executive officers' stock holdings in their companies at year end 1973 was $557,000 and $1.3 million at year end 1972.

63. These diversification effects can be substantial. Evans and Archer (1968) show that on the average for New York Stock Exchange securities approximately 55% of the total risk (as measured by standard deviation of portfolio returns) can be eliminated by following a naive strategy of dividing one's assets equally among 40 randomly selected securities.

64. The recent work of Myers (1975) which views future investment opportunities as options and investigates the incentive effects of the existence of debt in such a world where a sequence of investment decisions is made is another important step in the investigation of the multiperiod aspects of the agency problem and the theory of the firm.

65. Becker and Stigler (1972) analyze a special case of this problem involving the use of non-invested pension rights to help correct for this end game play in the law enforcement area.

66. By our colleague David Henderson.

67. This also suggests that *some* outside debt holders can protect themselves from "exploitation" by the manager by purchasing a fraction of the total equity equal to their fractional ownership of the debt. All debt holders, of course, cannot do this unless the manager does so also. In addition, such an investment rule restricts the portfolio choices of investors and therefore would impose costs if followed rigidly. Thus the agency costs will not be eliminated this way either.

68. Consider the situation in which the bondholders have the right in the event of bankruptcy to terminate his employment and therefore to terminate the future returns to any specific human capital or rents he may be receiving.

69. See Fama (1970a) for a survey of this "efficient markets" literature.

70. See Jensen (1969) for an example of this evidence and references.

71. Ignoring any pure consumption elements in the demand for security analysis.

72. Again ignoring the value of the pure consumption elements in the demand for security analysis.

Separation of Ownership and Control

Eugene F. Fama
Michael C. Jensen

I. Introduction

Absent fiat, the form of organization that survives in an activity is the one that delivers the product demanded by customers at the lowest price while covering costs.[1] Our goal is to explain the survival of organizations characterized by separation of "ownership" and "control"—a problem that has bothered students of corporations from Adam Smith to Berle and Means and Jensen and Meckling (Smith, [1776] 1937; Berle and Means, 1932; Jensen and Meckling, 1976a). In more precise language, we are concerned with the survival of organizations in which important decision agents do not bear a substantial share of the wealth effects of their decisions.

We argue that the separation of decision and risk-bearing functions observed in large corporations is common to other organizations such as large professional partnerships, financial mutuals, and nonprofits. We contend that separation of decision and risk-bearing functions survives in these organizations in part because of the benefits of specialization of management and risk bearing but also because of an effective common approach to controlling the agency problems caused by separation of decision and risk-bearing functions. In particular, our hypothesis is that the contract structures of all of these organizations separate the ratification and monitoring of decisions from initiation and implementation of the decisions.

Note: This paper is a revision of parts of our earlier paper (Fama and Jensen, 1980). In the course of this work we have profited from the comments of R. Antle, R. Benne, F. Black, F. Easterbrook, A. Farber, W. Gavett, P. Hirsch, R. Hogarth, C. Holderness, R. Holthausen, C. Horne, J. Jeuck, R. Leftwich, S. McCormick, D. Mayers, P. Pashigian, M. Scholes, C. Smith, G. Stigler, R. Watts, T. Whisler, R. Yeaple, J. Zimmerman, and especially A. Alchian, W. Meckling, and C. Plosser. Financial support for Fama's participation is from the National Science Foundation. Jensen is supported by the Managerial Economics Research Center of the University of Rochester.

II. Residual Claims and Decision Processes

An organization is the nexus of contracts, written and unwritten, among owners of factors of production and customers (Jensen and Meckling, 1976a). These contracts or internal "rules of the game" specify the rights of each agent in the organization, performance criteria on which agents are evaluated, and the payoff functions they face. The contract structure combines with available production technologies and external legal constraints to determine the cost function for delivering an output with a particular form of organization (Jensen and Meckling, 1979). The form of organization that delivers the output demanded by customers at the lowest price, while covering costs, survives.

The central contracts in any organization specify (1) the nature of residual claims and (2) the allocation of the steps of the decision process among agents. These contracts distinguish organizations from one another and explain why specific organizational forms survive. We first discuss the general characteristics of residual claims and decision processes. We then present the major hypotheses about the relations between efficient allocations of residual claims and decision functions. The analysis focuses on two broad types of organizations—those in which risk-bearing and decision functions are separated and those in which they are combined in the same agents. We analyze only private organizations that depend on voluntary contracting and exchange.

A. Residual Claims

The contract structures of most organizational forms limit the risks undertaken by most agents by specifying either fixed promised payoffs or incentive payoffs tied to specific measures of performance. The residual risk—the risk of the difference between stochastic inflows of resources and promised payments to agents—is borne by those who contract for the rights to net cash flows. We call these agents the residual claimants or residual risk bearers. Moreover, the contracts of most agents contain the implicit or explicit provision that, in exchange for the specified payoff, the agent agrees that the resources he provides can be used to satisfy the interests of residual claimants.

Having most uncertainty borne by one group of agents, residual claimants, has survival value because it reduces the costs incurred to monitor contracts with other groups of agents and to adjust contracts for the changing risks borne by other agents. Contracts that direct decisions toward the interests of residual claimants also add to the survival value of organizations. Producing outputs at lower cost is in the interests of residual claimants because it increases net cash flows, but lower costs also contribute to survival by allowing products to be delivered at lower prices.

The residual claims of different organizational forms contain different restrictions. For example, the least restricted residual claims in common use are the common stocks of large corporations. Stockholders are not required to have any other role in the organization; their residual claims are alienable without restriction; and, because of these provisions, the residual claims allow unrestricted risk sharing among stockholders. We call these organizations *open* corporations to distinguish them from *closed* corporations that are generally smaller and have residual claims that are largely restricted to internal decision agents.[2]

B. The Decision Process

By focusing on entrepreneurial firms in which all decision rights are concentrated in the entrepreneur, economists tend to ignore analysis of the steps of the decision process. However, the way organizations allocate the steps of the decision process across agents is important in explaining the survival of organizations.

In broad terms, the decision process has four steps:

1. *initiation*—generation of proposals for resource utilization and structuring of contracts;
2. *ratification*—choice of the decision initiatives to be implemented;
3. *implementation*—execution of ratified decisions; and
4. *monitoring*—measurement of the performance of decision agents and implementation of rewards.

Because the initiation and implementation of decisions typically are allocated to the same agents, it is convenient to combine these two functions under the term *decision management*. Likewise, the term *decision control* includes the ratification and monitoring of decisions. Decision management and decision control are the components of the organization's decision process or decision system.

III. Fundamental Relations Between Risk-Bearing and Decision Processes

We first state and then elaborate the central complementary hypotheses about the relations between the risk-bearing and decision processes of organizations.

1. Separation of residual risk bearing from decision management leads to decision systems that separate decision management from decision control.
2. Combination of decision management and decision control in a few agents leads to residual claims that are largely restricted to these agents.

A. The Problem

Agency problems arise because contracts are not costlessly written and enforced. Agency costs include the costs of structuring, monitoring, and bonding a set of contracts among agents with conflicting interests. Agency costs also include the value of output lost because the costs of full enforcement of contracts exceed the benefits.[3]

Control of agency problems in the decision process is important when the decision managers who initiate and implement important decisions are not the major residual claimants and therefore do not bear a major share of the wealth effects of their decisions. Without effective control procedures, such decision managers are more likely to take actions that deviate from the interests of residual claimants. An effective system for decision control implies, almost by definition, that the control (ratification and monitoring) of decisions is to some extent separate from the management (initiation and implementation) of decisions. Individual decision agents can be involved in the management of some decisions and the control of others, but separation means that an individual agent does not exercise exclusive management and control rights over the same decisions.

The interesting problem is to determine when separation of decision management, decision control, and residual risk bearing is more efficient than combining these three functions in the same agents. We first analyze the factors that make combination of decision management, decision control, and residual risk bearing efficient. We then analyze the factors that make separation of these three functions efficient.

B. Combination of Decision Management,
  Decision Control, and Residual Risk Bearing

Suppose the balance of cost conditions, including both technology and the control of agency problems, implies that in a particular activity the optimal organization is noncomplex. For our purposes, *noncomplex* means that specific information relevant to decisions is concentrated in one or a few agents. (Specific information is detailed information that is costly to transfer among agents.)[4] Most small organizations tend to be noncomplex, and most large organizations tend to be complex, but the correspondence is not perfect. For example, research oriented universities, though often small in terms of assets or faculty size, are nevertheless complex in the sense that specific knowledge, which is costly to transfer, is diffused among both faculty and administrators. On the other hand, mutual funds are often large in terms of assets but noncomplex in the sense that information relevant to decisions is concentrated in one or a few agents. We take it as given that optimal organizations in some activities are noncomplex. Our more limited goal is to explain the implications of noncomplexity for control of agency problems in the decision process.

If we ignore agency problems between decision managers and residual claimants, the theory of optimal risk bearing tells us that residual claims that allow unrestricted risk sharing have advantages in small as well as in large organizations.[5] However, in a small noncomplex organization, specific knowledge important for decision management and control is concentrated in one or a few agents. As a consequence, it is efficient to allocate decision control as well as decision management to these agents. Without separation of decision management from decision control, residual claimants have little protection against opportunistic actions of decision agents, and this lowers the value of unrestricted residual claims.

A feasible solution to the agency problem that arises when the same agents manage and control important decisions is to restrict residual claims to the important decision agents. In effect, restriction of residual claims to decision agents substitutes for costly control devices to limit the discretion of decision agents. The common stocks of closed corporations are this type of restricted residual claim, as are the residual claims in proprietorships and partnerships. The residual claims of these organizations (especially closed corporations) are also held by other agents whose special relations with decision agents allow agency problems to be controlled without separation of the management and control of decisions. For example, family members have many different dimensions of exchange with one another over a long horizon and therefore have advantages in monitoring and disciplining related decision agents. Business associates whose goodwill and advice are important to the organization are also potential candidates for holding minority residual claims of organizations that do not separate the management and control of decisions.[6]

Restricting residual claims to decision makers controls agency problems between residual claimants and decision agents, but it sacrifices the benefits of unrestricted risk sharing and specialization of decision functions. The decision process suffers efficiency losses because decision agents must be chosen on the basis of wealth and willingness to bear risk as well as for decision skills. The residual claimants forgo optimal risk reduction through portfolio diversification so that residual claims and decision making can be combined in a small number of agents. Forgone diversification lowers the value of the residual claims and raises the cost of risk-bearing services.

Moreover, when residual claims are restricted to decision agents, it is generally rational for the residual claimant–decision makers to assign lower values to uncertain cash flows than residual claimants would in organizations where residual claims are unrestricted and risk bearing can be freely diversified across organizations. As a consequence, restricting residual claims to agents in the decision process leads to decisions (for example, less investment in risky projects that lower the costs of outputs) that tend to penalize the organization in the competition for survival.[7]

However, because contracts are not costlessly written and enforced, all decision systems and systems for allocating residual claims involve costs. Organizational survival involves a balance of the costs of alternative decision systems and systems for allocating residual risk against the benefits. Small noncomplex organizations do not have demands for a wide range of specialized decision agents; on the contrary, concentration of specific information relevant to decisions implies that there are efficiency gains when the rights to manage and control decisions are combined in one or a few agents. Moreover, the risk-sharing benefits forgone when residual claims are restricted to one or a few decision agents are less serious in a small noncomplex organization than in a large organization, because the total risk of net cash flows to be shared is generally smaller in small organizations. In addition, small organizations do not often have large demands for wealth from residual claimants to bond the payoffs promised to other agents and to purchase risky assets. As a consequence, small noncomplex organizations can efficiently control the agency problems caused by the combination of decision management and control in one or a few agents by restricting residual claims to these agents. Such a combination of decision and risk-bearing functions is efficient in small noncomplex organizations because the benefits of unrestricted risk sharing and specialization of decision functions are less than the costs that would be incurred to control the resulting agency problems.

The proprietorships, partnerships, and closed corporations observed in small scale production and service activities are the best examples of classical entrepreneurial firms in which the major decision makers are also the major residual risk bearers. These organizations are evidence in favor of the hypothesis that combination of decision management and decision control in one or a few agents leads to residual claims that are largely restricted to these agents.

We analyze next the forces that make separation of decision management, decision control, and residual risk bearing efficient—in effect, the forces that cause the classical entrepreneurial firm to be dominated by organizational forms in which there are no decision makers in the classical entrepreneurial sense.

C. Separation of Decision Management, Decision Control, and Residual Risk Bearing

Our concern in this section is with the organizational forms characterized by separation of decision management from residual risk bearing—what the literature on open corporations calls, somewhat imprecisely, separation of ownership and control. Our hypothesis is that all such organizations, including large open corporations, large professional partnerships, financial mutuals, and nonprofits, control the agency problems that result from separation of decision management from residual risk bearing by separating the management (initiation and implementation) and control (ratification and monitoring) of decisions. Documentation of this hypothesis takes up much of the rest of the paper.

1. Specific Knowledge and Diffusion of Decision Functions. Most organizations characterized by separation of decision management from residual risk bearing are *complex* in the sense that specific knowledge relevant to different decisions—knowledge which is costly to transfer across agents— is diffused among agents at all levels of the organization. Again, we take it as given that the optimal organizations in some activities are complex. Our theory attempts to explain the implications of complexity for the nature of efficient decision processes and for control of agency problems in the decision process.

Since specific knowledge in complex organizations is diffused among agents, diffusion of decision management can reduce costs by delegating the initiation and implementation of decisions to the agents with valuable relevant knowledge. The agency problems of diffuse decision management can then be reduced by separating the mangement (initiation and implementation) and control (ratification and monitoring) of decisions.

In the unusual cases where residual claims are not held by important decision managers but are nevertheless concentrated in one or a few residual claimants, control of decision managers can in principle be direct and simple, with the residual claimants ratifying and monitoring important decisions and setting rewards (Alchian and Demsetz, 1972). Such organizations conform to our hypothesis, because top-level decision control is separated from top-level decision managers and exercised directly by residual claimants.

However, in complex organizations valuable specific knowledge relevant to decision control is diffused among many internal agents. This generally means that efficient decision control, like efficient decision management, involves delegation and diffusion of decision control as well as separation of decision management and control at different levels of the organization. We expect to observe such delegation, diffusion, and separation of decision management and control below the top level of complex organizations, even in those unusual complex organizations where residual claims are held primarily by top-level decision agents.

2. Diffuse Residual Claims and Delegation of Decision Control. In the more common complex organizations, residual claims are diffused among many agents. Having many residual claimants has advantages in large complex organizations because the total risk of net cash flows to be shared is generally large and there are large demands for wealth from residual claimants to bond the payoffs promised to a wide range of agents and to purchase risky assets. When there are many residual claimants, it is costly for all of them to be involved in decision control and it is efficient for them to delegate decision control. For example, some delegation of decision control is observed even in the large professional partnerships in public accounting and law, where the residual claimants are expert internal decision agents. When there are many partners it is inefficient for each to participate in ratification and monitoring of all decisions.

Nearly complete separation and specialization of decision control and residual risk bearing is common in large open corporations and financial mutuals where most of the diffuse residual claimants are not qualified for roles in the decision process and thus delegate their decision control rights to other agents. When residual claimants have no role in decision control, we expect to observe separation of the management and control of important decisions at all levels of the organization.

Separation and diffusion of decision management and decision control—in effect, the absence of a classical entrepreneurial decision maker—limit the power of individual decision agents to expropriate the interests of residual claimants. The checks and balances of such decision systems have costs, but they also have important benefits. Diffusion and separation of decision management and control have benefits because they allow valuable knowledge to be used at the points in the decision process where it is most relevant and they help control the agency problems of diffuse residual claims. In complex organizations, the benefits of diffuse residual claims and the benefits of separation of decision functions from residual risk bearing are generally greater than the agency costs they generate, including the costs of mechanisms to separate the management and control of decisions.

3. *Decision Control in Nonprofits and Financial Mutuals.* Most organizations characterized by separation of decision management from residual risk bearing are complex. However, separation of the management and control of decisions contributes to the survival of any organization where the important decision managers do not bear a substantial share of the wealth effects of their decisions—that is, any organization where there are serious agency problems in the decision process. We argue below that separation of decision management and residual risk bearing is a characteristic of nonprofit organizations and financial mutuals, large and small, complex and noncomplex. Thus, we expect to observe separation of the management and control of important decisions even in small noncomplex nonprofits and financial mutuals where, ignoring agency problems in the decision process, concentrated and combined decision management and control would be more efficient.

4. *Common General Features of Decision Control Systems.* Our hypothesis about the decision systems of organizations characterized by separation of decision management and residual risk bearing gets support from the fact that the major mechanisms for diffusing and separating the management and control of decisions are much the same across different organizations.

Decision Hierarchies. A common feature of the diffuse decision management and control systems of complex organizations (for example, large nonprofit universities as well as large open corporations) is a formal decision hierarchy with higher level agents ratifying and monitoring the decision initiatives of lower level agents and evaluating their performance (Weber, 1946; Simon, 1962; Blau, 1956; Williamson, 1975; Chandler, 1977; Chandler and Daems, 1980). Such hierarchical partitioning of the decision process makes it more difficult for decision agents at all levels of the organization to take actions that benefit themselves at the expense of residual claimants. Decision hierarchies are buttressed by organizational rules of the game, for example, accounting and budgeting systems, that monitor and constrain the decision behavior of agents and specify the performance criteria that determine rewards.[8]

Mutual Monitoring Systems. The formal hierarchies of complex organizations are also buttressed by information from less formal mutual monitoring among agents. When agents interact to produce outputs, they acquire low-cost information about colleagues, information not directly available to higher level agents. Mutual monitoring systems tap this information for use in the control process. Mutual monitoring systems derive their energy from the interests of agents to use the internal agent markets of organizations to enhance the value of human capital (Fama, 1980). Agents choose among organizations on the basis of rewards offered and potential for development of human capital. Agents value the competitive interaction that takes place within an organization's internal agent market because it enhances current marginal products and contributes to human capital development. Moreover, if agents perceive that evaluation of their performance is unbiased (that is, if they cannot systematically fool their evaluators) then they value the fine tuning of the reward system that results from mutual monitoring information, because it lowers the uncertainty of payoffs from effort and skill. Since the incentive structures and diffuse decision control systems that result from the interplay of formal hierarchies and less formal mutual monitoring systems are also in the interests of residual claimants, their survival value is evident.

    Boards of Directors. The common apex of the decision control systems of organizations, large and small, in which decision agents do not bear a major share of the wealth effects of their decisions is some form of board of directors. Such boards always have the power to hire, fire, and compensate the top-level decision managers and to ratify and monitor important decisions. Exercise of these top-level decision control rights by a group (the board) helps to ensure separation of decision management and control (that is, the absence of an entrepreneurial decision maker) even at the top of the organization.[9]

IV. The Spectrum of Organizations

A. Introduction

    Organizations in which important decision agents do not bear a major share of the wealth effects of their decisions include open corporations, large professional partnerships, financial mutuals, and nonprofits. We are concerned now with analyzing the data each of these organizations provides to test the hypothesis that separation of decision management functions from residual risk bearing leads to decision systems that separate the management and control of decisions.

To motivate the discussion of specific organizational forms, we also outline a set of more specialized propositions to explain the survival value of the special features of their residual claims. These more specialized hypotheses about the survival of specific organizational forms in specific activities are developed in our paper "Agency Problems and Residual Claims" (Fama and Jensen, 1983a).

B. Open Corporations

1. Unrestricted Common Stock Residual Claims. Most large nonfinancial organizations are open corporations. The common stock residual claims of such organizations are unrestricted in the sense that stockholders are not required to have any other role in the organization, and their residual claims are freely alienable. As a result of the unrestricted nature of the residual claims of open corporations, there is almost complete specialization of decision management and residual risk bearing. Even managers who own substantial blocs of stock, and thus are residual risk bearers, may elect to sell these shares.

Unrestricted common stock is attractive in complicated risky activities where substantial wealth provided by residual claimants is needed to bond the large aggregate payoffs promised to many other agents. Unrestricted common stock, with its capacity for generating large amounts of wealth from residual claimants on a permanent basis, is also attractive in activities more efficiently carried out with large amounts of risky assets owned within the organization rather than rented. Moreover, since decision skills are not a necessary consequence of wealth or willingness to bear risk, the specialization of decision management and residual risk bearing allowed by unrestricted common stock enhances the adaptability of a complex organization to changes in the economic environment. The unrestricted risk sharing and diversification allowed by common stock also contributes to survival by lowering the cost of risk-bearing services.

2. Control of the Agency Problems of Common Stock. Separation and specialization of decision management and residual risk bearing leads to agency problems between decision agents and residual claimants. This is the problem of separation of ownership and control that has long troubled students of corporations. For example, potential exploitation of residual claimants by opportunistic decision agents is reflected in the arguments leading to the establishment of the Securities and Exchange Commission and in the concerns of the modern corporate governance movement. Less well appreciated, however, is the fact that the unrestricted nature of common stock residual claims also allows special market and organizational mechanisms for controlling the agency problems of specialized risk bearing.

The Stock Market. The unrestricted alienability of the residual claims of open corporations gives rise to an external monitoring device unique to these organizations—a stock market that specializes in pricing common stocks and transferring them at low cost. Stock prices are visible signals that summarize the implications of internal decisions for current and future net cash flows. This external monitoring exerts pressure to orient a corporation's decision process toward the interests of residual claimants.

The Market for Takeovers. External monitoring from a takeover market is also unique to the open corporation and is attributable to the unrestricted nature of its residual claims.[10] Because the residual claims are freely alienable and separable from roles in the decision process, attacking managers can circumvent existing managers and the current board to gain control of the decision process, either by a direct offer to purchase stock (a tender offer) or by an appeal for stock holder votes for directors (a proxy fight).

Expert Boards. Internal control in the open corporation is delegated by residual claimants to a board of directors. Residual claimants generally retain approval rights (by vote) on such matters as board membership, auditor choice, mergers, and new stock issues. Other management and control functions are delegated by the residual claimants to the board. The board then delegates most decision management functions and many decision control functions to internal agents, but it retains ultimate control over internal agents—including the rights to ratify and monitor major policy initiatives and to hire, fire, and set the compensation of top level decision managers. Similar delegation of decision management and control functions, at the first step to a board and then from the board to internal decision agents, is common to other organizations, such as financial mutuals, nonprofits, and large professional partnerships, in which important decision agents do not bear a major share of the wealth effects of their decisions.

However, the existence of the stock market and the market for takeovers, both special to open corporations, explains some of the special features of corporate boards, in particular: (1) why inside manager board members are generally more influential than outside members, and (2) why outside board members are often decision agents in other complex organizations (Herman, 1981).

Since the takeover market provides an external court of last resort for protection of residual claimants, a corporate board can be in the hands of agents who are decision experts. Given that the board is to be composed of experts, it is natural that its most influential members are internal managers since they have valuable specific information about the organization's activities. It is also natural that when the internal decision control system works well, the outside members of the board are nominated by internal managers. Internal managers can use their knowledge of the organization to nominate outside board members with relevant complementary knowledge: for example, outsiders with expertise in capital markets, corporate law, or relevant technology who provide an important support function to the top managers in dealing with specialized decision problems.

However, the board is not an effective device for decision control unless it limits the decision discretion of individual top managers. The board is the top-level court of appeals of the internal agent market (Fama, 1980), and as such it must be able to use information from the internal mutual monitoring system. To accomplish this and to achieve effective separation of top-level decision management and control, we expect the board of a large open corporation to include several of the organization's top managers. The board uses information from each of the top managers about his decision initiatives and the decision initiatives and performance of other managers. The board also seeks information from lower level managers about the decision initiatives and performance of top managers.[11] This information is used to set the rewards of the top managers, to rank them, and to choose among their decision initiatives. To protect information flows to the board, we expect that top managers, especially those who are members of the board, can effectively be fired only with consent of the board and thus are protected from reprisals from other top managers.

The decision processes of some open corporations seem to be dominated by an individual manager, generally the chief executive officer. In some cases, this signals the absence of separation of decision management and decision control, and, in our theory, the organization suffers in the competition for survival. We expect, however, that the apparent dominance of some top managers is more often due to their ability to work with the decision control systems of their organizations than to their ability to suppress diffuse and separate decision control. In any case, the financial press regularly reports instances where apparently dominant executives are removed by their boards.

Corporate boards generally include outside members, that is, members who are not internal managers, and they often hold a majority of seats (Herman, 1981). The outside board members act as arbiters in disagreements among internal managers and carry out tasks that involve serious agency problems between internal managers and residual claimants, for example, setting executive compensation or searching for replacements for top managers.

Effective separation of top-level decision management and control means that outside directors have incentives to carry out their tasks and do not collude with managers to expropriate residual claimants. Our hypothesis is that outside directors have incentives to develop reputations as experts in decision control. Most outside directors of open corporations are either managers of other corporations or important decision agents in other complex organizations (Herman, 1981). The value of their human capital depends primarily on their performance as internal decision managers in other organizations. They use their directorships to signal to internal and external markets for decision agents that (1) they are decision experts, (2) they understand the importance of diffuse and separate decision control, and (3) they can work with such decision control systems. The signals are credible when the direct payments to outside directors are small, but there is substantial devaluation of human capital when internal decision control breaks down and the costly last resort process of an outside takeover is activated.

C. Professional Partnerships

1. Mutual Monitoring, Specific Knowledge, and Restricted Residual Claims. The residual claims of professional partnerships in activities such as law, public accounting, medicine, and business consulting are restricted to the major professional agents who produce the organization's services. This restriction increases the incentives of agents to monitor each other's actions and to consult with each other to improve the quality of services provided to customers. Such mutual monitoring and consulting are attractive to the professional agents in service activities where responsibility for variation in the quality of services is easily assigned and the value of professional human capital is sensitive to performance. The monitoring and consulting are likely to be effective when professional agents with similar specialized skills agree to share liability for the actions of colleagues.

In both large and small partnerships, individuals or small teams work on cases, audits, and so forth. Because of the importance of specific knowledge about particular clients and circumstances, it is efficient for the teams to make most decisions locally. At this level, however, decision management and decision control are not separate. To control the resulting agency problems, the residual claims in professional partnerships, large and small, are restricted to the professional agents who have the major decision-making roles. This is consistent with our hypothesis that combination of decision management and control functions leads to restriction of residual claims to the agents who both manage and control important decisions.

2. *Large Professional Partnerships*. The partners in large professional partnerships are diffuse residual claimants whose welfare depends on the acts of agents they do not directly control. Thus, these organizations provide a test of our hypothesis that separation of residual risk bearing and decision management induces decision systems that separate the management and control of important decisions. The major decision control devices of large professional partnerships are similar to those of other organizations with diffuse residual claims. For example, residual claimants in large partnerships delegate to boards the ratification and monitoring of important decisions above the level of individual cases and audits. Moreover, the sharing of liability and residual cash flows among important decision agents (the partners) ensures that large partnerships have strong versions of the mutual monitoring systems that we contend are common to the decision control systems of complex organizations.

The boards of large partnerships have special features that relate to the restriction of the residual claims to important internal agents. The residual claimants are experts in the organization's activities, and they observe directly the effects of actions taken by the board of managing partners. Thus, unlike the stockholders of open corporations, the residual claimants in large partnerships have little demand for outside experts to protect their interests, and their boards are composed entirely of partners.

The board is involved in decisions with respect to the management of the partnership, for example, where new offices should be opened, who should be admitted to the partnership, and who should be dismissed. The board is also involved in renegotiating the shares of the partners. Here, as in other decisions, the boards of large partnerships combine the valuable specific knowledge available at the top level with information from partner–residual claimants. The role of the board is to develop acceptable consensus decisions from this information. Thus, the boards of large professional partnerships are generally called committees of managing partners rather than boards of directors. The idea is that such committees exist to manage agency problems among partners and to study and determine major policy issues in a manner that is less costly than when performed jointly by all partners.

Since the residual claims in a large professional partnership are not alienable, unfriendly outside takeovers are not possible. Inside takeovers by dissident partners are possible, however, because the managing boards of these organizations are elected by the partner–residual claimants.

D. Financial Mutuals

A common form of organization in financial activities is the mutual. An unusual characteristic of mutuals is that the residual claimants are customers, for example, the policyholders of mutual insurance companies, the depositors of mutual savings banks, and the shareholders of mutual funds. Like the diffuse stockholders of large nonfinancial corporations, most of the diffuse depositors, policyholders, and mutual fund shareholders of financial mutuals do not participate in the internal decision process. Thus, financial mutuals provide another test of our hypothesis that substantial separation of decision management and residual risk bearing leads to decision systems that separate the management and control of decisions.

1. The Control Function of Redeemable Claims. For the purpose of decision control, the unique characteristic of the residual claims of mutuals is that they are redeemable on demand. The policyholder, depositor, or shareholder can, on demand, turn in his claim at a price determined by a prespecified rule. For example, the shareholder of an open-end mutual fund can redeem his claim for the market value of his share of the fund's assets, while the whole life or endowment insurance policyholder, like the shareholder of a mutual savings bank, can redeem his claim for its specified value plus accumulated dividends.

The decision of the claim holder to withdraw resources is a form of partial takeover or liquidation which deprives management of control over assets. This control right can be exercised independently by each claim holder. It does not require a proxy fight, a tender offer, or any other concerted takeover bid. In contrast, customer decisions in open nonfinancial corporations and the repricing of the corporation's securities in the capital market provide signals about the performance of its decision agents. Without further action, however, either internal or from the market for takeovers, the judgments of customers and of the capital market leave the assets of the open nonfinancial corporation under the control of the managers.

2. The Board of Directors. Like other organizations characterized by substantial separation between decision management and residual risk bearing, the top-level decision control device in financial mutuals is a board of directors. Because of the strong form of diffuse decision control inherent in the redeemable residual claims of financial mutuals, however, their boards are less important in the control process than the boards of open nonfinancial corporations. The reduced role of the board is especially evident in mutual savings banks and mutual funds, which are not complex even though often large in terms of assets. Moreover, the residual claimants of mutuals show little interest in their boards and often do not have the right to vote for board members.[12] Outside board members are generally chosen by internal managers. Unlike open corporations, the boards of financial mutuals do not often impose changes in managers. The role of the board, especially in the less complex mutuals, is largely limited to monitoring agency problems against which redemption of residual claims offers little protection, for example, fraud or outright theft of assets by internal agents.

E. Nonprofit Organizations

When an organization's activities are financed in part through donations, part of net cash flows is from resources provided by donors. Contracts that define the share of residual claimants in net cash flows are unlikely to assure donors that their resources are protected from expropriation by residual claimants. In a nonprofit organization, however, there are no agents with alienable rights in residual net cash flows and thus there are residual claims. We argue in ''Agency Problems and Residual Claims'' that the absence of such residual claims in nonprofits avoids the donor–residual claimant agency problem and explains the dominance of nonprofits in donor-financed activities (Fama and Jensen, 1983a; Hansmann, 1980).

The absence of residual claims in nonprofits avoids agency problems between donors and residual claimants, but the incentives of other internal agents to expropriate donations remain. These agency problems between donors and decision agents in nonprofits are similar to those in other organizations where important decision managers do not bear a major share of the wealth effects of their decisions. Our hypothesis predicts that, like other organizations characterized by separation of decision management from residual risk bearing, nonprofits have decision systems that separate the management (initiation and implementation) and control (ratification and monitoring) of decisions. Such decision systems survive in donor nonprofits because of the assurance they provide that donations are used effectively and are not easily expropriated.

1. Nonprofit Boards. In small nonprofits delegation of decision management to one or a few agents is generally efficient. For example,

in nonprofit cultural performing groups, an artistic director usually chooses performers, does the primary monitoring of their outputs, and initiates and implements major decisions. Nevertheless, the important decision agents in these organizations are chosen, monitored, and evaluated by boards of directors. Boards with similar decision control rights are common to other small nonprofits characterized by concentrated decision management, such as charities, private museums, small private hospitals, and local Protestant and Jewish congregations. Boards are also observed at the top of the decision control systems of complex nonprofits, such as private universities, in which both decision management and decision control are diffuse.

Although their functions are similar to those of other organizations, nonprofit boards have special features that are due to the absence of alienable residual claims. For example, because of the discipline from the outside takeover market, boards of open corporations can include internal decision agents, and outside board members can be chosen for expertise rather than because they are important residual claimants. In contrast, because a nonprofit lacks alienable residual claims, the decision agents are immune from ouster (via takeover) by outside agents. Without the takeover threat or the discipline imposed by residual claimants with the right to remove members of the board, nonprofit boards composed of internal agents and outside experts chosen by internal agents would provide little assurance against collusion and expropriation of donations. Thus, nonprofit boards generally include few if any internal agents as voting members, and nonprofit boards are often self-perpetuating, that is, new members are approved by existing members. Moreover, nonprofit board members are generally substantial donors who serve without pay. Willingness to provide continuing personal donations of wealth and time is generally an implicit condition for membership on nonprofit boards. Acceptance of this condition certifies to other donors that board members are motivated to take their decision control task seriously.

2. The Roman Catholic Church. To our knowledge the only nonprofit organization that is financed with donations but lacks a board of important continuing donors with effective decision control rights is the Roman Catholic church. Parish councils exist in local Catholic churches, but unlike their Protestant and Jewish counterparts, they are only advisory. The clerical hierarchy controls the allocation of resources, and the papal system does not seem to limit the discretion of the Pope, the organization's most important decision agent.

Other aspects of the contracts of the Catholic clergy in part substitute for the control of expropriation of donations that would be provided by more effective donor-customer constraints on decisions. For example, the vows of chastity and obedience incorporated into the contracts of the Catholic clergy help to bond against expropriation of donations by avoiding conflicts between the material interests of a family and the interests of donor-customers. In addition, the training of a Catholic priest is organization-specific. For example, it involves a heavy concentration on (Catholic) theology, whereas the training of Protestant ministers places more emphasis on social service skills. Once certified, the Catholic priest is placed by the hierarchy. He cannot offer his services on a competitive basis. In exchange for developing such organization-specific human capital, the Catholic priest, unlike his Protestant and Jewish counterparts, gets a lifetime contract that promises a real standard of living. The organization-specific nature of the human capital of the Catholic clergy and the terms of the contract under which it is employed act as a bond to donor-customers that the interests of the Catholic clergy are closely bound to the survival of the organization and thus to the interests of donor-customers.

Although Protestantism arose over doctrinal issues, the control structures of Protestant sects—in particular, the evolution of lay councils with power to ratify and monitor resource allocation decisions—can be viewed as a response to breakdowns of the contract structure of Catholicism, that is, expropriation of Catholic donor-customers by the clergy. The evolution of Protestantism is therefore an example of competition among alternative contract structures to resolve an activity's major agency problem—in this case monitoring important agents to limit expropriation of donations.

There is currently pressure to allow Catholic priests to marry, that is, to drop the vow of chastity from their contracts. We predict that if this occurs, organizational survival will require other monitoring and bonding mechanisms, for example, control over allocation of resources by lay councils similar to those observed in Protestant and Jewish congregations.

3. The Private University and Decision Systems in Complex Nonprofits. In complex nonprofits we observe mechanisms for diffuse decision control similar to those of other complex organizations. For example, large private universities, like large open corporations, have complicated decision hierarchies and active internal agent markets with mutual monitoring systems that generate information about the performance of agents. Again, however, the decision control structures of complex nonprofits have special features attributable to the absence of alienable residual claims.

For example, a university's trustees are primarily donors rather than experts in the details of education or research. In ratifying and monitoring decision initiatives presented by internal decision agents (presidents, chancellors, provosts, etc.), and in evaluating the agents themselves, boards rely on information from the internal diffuse decision system—for example, reports from faculty senates and appointments committees—and on external peer reviews.

Moreover, the structure of internal diffuse decision control systems is a more formal part of a university's contract structure (its charter or bylaws) than in large for-profit organizations such as open corporations. For example, unlike corporate managers, university deans, department heads, provosts, and presidents are generally appointed for fixed terms. The end of a contract period activates a process of evaluation, with search committees chosen according to formal rules and with rules for passing their recommendations on to the board. A more formal structure of diffuse decision management and control is helpful to trustees who do not have specialized knowledge about a university's activities. It also helps to assure donors that the absence of discipline from an outside takeover market is compensated by a strong system for internal decision control.

V. Summary

The theory developed in this paper views an organization as a nexus of contracts (written and unwritten). The theory focuses on the contracts that (1) allocate the steps in an organization's decision process, (2) define residual claims, and (3) set up devices for controlling agency problems in the decision process. We focus on the factors that give survival value to organizational forms that separate what the literature imprecisely calls ownership and control.

A. The Central Hypotheses

An organization's decision process consists of decision management (initiation and implementation) and decision control (ratification and monitoring). Our analysis produces two complementary hypotheses about the relations between decision systems and residual claims:

1. Separation of residual risk bearing from decision management leads to decision systems that separate decision management from decision control.
2. Combination of decision management and decision control in a few agents leads to residual claims that are largely restricted to these agents.

B. Combination of Decision Management and Control

When it is efficient to combine decision management and control functions in one or a few agents, it is efficient to control agency problems between residual claimants and decision makers by restricting residual claims to the decision makers. This proposition gets clear support from the proprietorships, small partnerships, and closed corporations observed in small-scale production and service activities. These organizations are all characterized by concentrated decision systems and residual claims that are restricted to decision agents.

C. Separation of Residual Risk Bearing from Decision Management

1. The Role of Specific Knowledge. In contrast, most of the organizations characterized by separation of residual risk bearing from decision management are complex in the sense that specific information valuable for decisions is diffused among many agents throughout the organization. Thus in a complex organization separation of residual risk bearing from decision management arises in part because efficient decision systems are diffuse. Benefits from better decisions can be achieved by delegating decision functions to agents at all levels of the organization who have relevant specific knowledge, rather than allocating all decision management and control to the residual claimants. Control of the agency problems of such diffuse decision systems is then achieved by separating the ratification and monitoring of decisions (decision control) from initiation and implementation (decision management). The efficiency of such decision systems is buttressed by incentive structures that reward agents both for initiating and implementing decisions and for ratifying and monitoring the decision management of other agents.

2. The Role of Diffuse Residual Claims. In most complex organizations, residual claims are diffused among many agents. When there are many residual claimants, it is costly for all of them to be involved in decision control. As a consequence there is separation of residual risk bearing from decision control, and this creates agency problems between residual claimants and decision agents. Separation of decision management and decision control at all levels of the organization helps to control these agency problems by limiting the power of individual agents to expropriate the interests of residual claimants. Thus diffusion and separation of decision management and control have survival value in complex organizations both because they allow valuable specific knowledge to be used at the points in the decision process where it is most relevant and because they help control the agency problems of diffuse residual claims.

3. Common Features of Decision Control Systems. What we call separation of residual risk bearing from decision management is the separation of ownership and control that has long bothered students of open corporations. We argue that separation of decision and risk bearing functions is also common to other organizations like large professional partnerships, financial mutuals, and nonprofits. Moreover, our central hypothesis about control of the agency problems caused by separation of residual risk bearing from decision management gets support from the fact that the major mechanisms for separating decision management and decision control are much the same across organizations.

The common central building blocks of the diffuse decision control systems of complex organizations of all types are formal decision hierarchies in which the decision initiatives of lower level agents are passed on to higher level agents, first for ratification and then for monitoring. Such decision hierarchies are found in large open corporations, large professional partnerships, large financial mutuals, and large nonprofits. Formal decision hierarchies are buttressed by less formal mutual monitoring systems that are a by-product of interaction that takes place to produce outputs and develop human capital.

The common apex of the decision control systems of organizations, large and small, in which decision agents do not bear a major share of the wealth effects of their decisions is a board of directors (trustees, managing partners, etc.) that ratifies and monitors important decisions and chooses, dismisses, and rewards important decision agents. Such multiple-member boards make collusion between top-level decision management and control agents more difficult, and they are the mechanism that allows separation of the management and control of the organization's most important decisions.

Notes

1. Alchian (1950) is an early proponent of the use of natural selection in economic analysis. For a survey of general issues in the analysis of organizations, see Jensen (1983).

2. The terms ''public corporation'' and ''close corporation,'' which are common in the legal literature, are not used here. ''Closed corporation'' seems more descriptive than ''close corporation.'' The term ''public corporation'' best describes government-owned corporations such as Amtrak and the TVA. In contrast, what we call ''open corporations'' are private organizations.

3. This definition of agency costs comes from Jensen and Meckling (1976a).

4. Specific information is closely related to the notions of "information impactedness" and "bounded rationality" discussed in Williamson (1975, 1981). Hayek (1945) uses specific information to discuss the role of markets in complex economies. See also Sowell (1980). Our analysis of the relations between specific information and efficient decision processes owes much to ongoing work with William Meckling.

5. See, for example, Arrow (1964b); or Fama (1976).

6. In contrast, the analysis predicts that when venture equity capital is put into a small entrepreneurial organization by outsiders, mechanisms for separating the management and control of important decisions are instituted.

7. These propositions are developed in Fama and Jensen (1983b).

8. The separation of decision management from decision control that we emphasize is reflected in the auditing profession's concern with allocating operating and accounting responsibility to different agents. For instance, it is recommended that an agent with responsibility for billing should not have a role in receiving or recording customer payments. See, for example, Horngren (1982); or Stettler (1977).

9. Decision functions can be delegated in two general ways: (1) joint delegation to several agents (as in a committee), or (2) partitioning and delegation of the parts to different agents. Boards of directors are examples of the former approach; decision hierarchies are examples of the latter.

10. Monitoring from the takeover market is emphasized in Manne (1965).

11. For example, Horngren (1982, p. 911), describes the role of the audit committee of the board (generally composed of outside board members) as a collector and conduit of information from the internal mutual monitoring system: "The objective of the audit committee is to oversee the accounting controls, financial statements, and financial affairs of the corporation. The committee represents the full board and provides personal contact and communication among the board, the external auditors, the internal auditors, the financial executives, and the operating executives."

12. See Herman (1969), for documentation of such lack of interest. For example, he describes situations where in more than a decade only four depositors in total attended the annual meeting of two savings and loan associations and other situations where management did not even bother to collect proxies.

FIVE

Evolutionary Theory:
Questioning Managerial
Impact on Firm Performance

At the heart of much organization research and practice is the often implicit assumption that managers and the decisions they make can have a major impact on the destiny of firms. This point of view appears most clearly in the research on general management conducted at Harvard University over the last several decades (Christensen and others, 1982) which describes the ability of an individual manager to turn a firm from disaster to success. The importance of the organizational entrepreneur—the manager who can make a difference—is also trumpeted loudly in the popular business press (Iacocca and Novak, 1984).

The belief that managerial actions can greatly affect a firm's fortunes is also seen, albeit somewhat more subtly, in much of organization theory. Peters and Waterman (1982), for example, studied excellent firms in an attempt to describe a management system that, if employed by other firms, would improve their performance. Works by McGregor (1960), Vroom and Yetton (1973), and many others all fit into this category. Although he concluded that it was bounded in some important ways, Simon's (1961) initial focus on managerial decision making nevertheless reaffirmed the managerial decision as the center point of research on effective organizations.

More recently, this apparently self-evident assertion has come to be questioned, both in organizational economics and in organization theory. The strongest contrary view expressed to date has been that of McKelvey (1982) who argues that managers have no impact on a firm's potential for survival in the long run.

299

The readings in this chapter present some of the earliest work in organizational economics concerning the question of the impact of managerial actions on firm performance. This work began by questioning a whole raft of common sense assumptions about managers and organizations. No assumption seemed to be above examination. Some researchers asked whether the assumption of profit maximization, so commonly used in traditional microeconomics, corresponds to the actual decision-making patterns of managers in firms. Others asked what managers are doing when they make business decisions if not acting as profit maximizers? Still others wondered whether the objectives of managers are at all significant when describing and predicting the behavior of individual firms. Do different assumptions about the motives of managers generate different predictions about organizational behavior?

Early Work

These are the questions asked by a group of organizational economists who have come to be known as evolutionary theorists. Their answers to these questions have often been surprising, rarely consistent with managerial common sense, and almost always controversial. Some of these authors have suggested that knowledge of the motivations of managers is irrelevant, that the focus of concern should be on actual economic performance, no matter what the original motivation for making a decision might have been (Alchian, 1950). Others have suggested that managers employ highly simplified "rules of thumb" when making decisions, and that these standard operating procedures tend to resist change over time, even when more traditional and perhaps more rational economic analyses would suggest that they should change (Winter, 1975; Nelson and Winter, 1982). No matter what assumptions these authors make about the motives of managers, they are unanimous in their emphasis on the importance of a firm's environment acting as a selection mechanism in determining the current behavior and evolution of a firm and industry.

One of the first authors to consider these issues explicitly was Alchian ("Uncertainty, Evolution, and Economic Theory").

Alchian begins by considering whether or not profit maximizing makes any sense whatsoever as a theoretical assumption to explain the action and behavior of firms. Alchian employs the concepts of bounded rationality and uncertainty to argue that it does not. The reasoning is straightforward. Under conditions of uncertainty, specific decisions made by managers typically do not have a single possible outcome. On the contrary, before a decision is actually implemented, a whole range of possible outcomes exist. These outcomes can be arranged in a distribution. Any two separate decisions may have outcome distributions that overlap. That is, under uncertainty, two separate decisions may each generate the same results. In this setting, it clearly does not make sense to talk about managers making decisions that maximize profits, since any number of different choices may each result in profit-maximizing outcomes. If decision A leads to a profit-maximizing outcome and decision B leads to the same profit-maximizing outcome, then the managerial motivation to maximize profits cannot be used to explain why decision A was made, as opposed to decision B. In this sense, Alchian concludes, the assumption that managers are motivated by profit maximization considerations in their decision making is meaningless under conditions of uncertainty.

If, under conditions of uncertainty, profit maximization is a useless concept, what motivation for managerial decision making does make sense? Alchian's answer to this question is truly revolutionary, for he suggests that it does not matter what the motivation for making a decision might be. All that is relevant is the actual pattern of financial performance that results. One could imagine, for example, a manager making decisions in an attempt to maximize sales rather than profits, but, in a world of uncertainty, see these decisions end up maximizing profits instead.

But Alchian goes even further, by arguing that it is not the observed pattern of absolute maximum profits that is key to organizational survival, but the observed pattern of relative profits. For Alchian, any firm that enjoys returns that are "normal" or better will survive; that is, any firm whose returns are greater than or equal to those needed to keep its assets employed in its current activity is a viable firm. The concept of greater than normal returns is a relative one, one that requires for survival that a firm's returns only be greater than a given minimum, not necessarily as great as possible. Thus, firms with realized positive profits will survive, regardless of the motivations behind the decisions leading to those profits.

To emphasize his point that it is outcomes rather than motivations which are crucial to understanding actual organizational behavior, Alchian develops a model of complete uncertainty, one in which managers make decisions but have little or no ability to predict the outcomes of their decisions. Accordingly, their motivations for making decisions are irrelevant. If managerial motivations in decision making are irrelevant, then the quality of management—at least as it has been traditionally defined—is irrelevant when predicting which firms will succeed and which will fail. Under this kind of uncertainty, Alchian is able to show that, within a certain probability, some firms will end up enjoying greater than normal returns or positive profits. Of course, which firms end up enjoying these returns depends on pure chance. It is Alchian's argument that, under conditions of uncertainty, luck will play a significant role in determining which firms will succeed and which will fail.

For Alchian, the incorporation of uncertainty and imperfect information into a microanalytic economic model represents a fundamental shift from the traditional model, a shift away from focusing on the individual actors in an economy to a focus on the environments that surround and mold the behavior of those actors.

Hirshleifer ("Economics from a Biological Viewpoint") builds on this perspective in his work. Hirshleifer begins by noting several conceptual similarities between microeconomics and sociobiology. By way of analogy, he suggests that the concept of competition in biology and economics is very similar and that economics has a great deal to learn from the form of reasoning used by biologists.

After noting these numerous biological and economic analogies, Hirshleifer moves beyond any of his predecessors and begins to explore some of the biological underpinnings of economic behavior. For Hirshleifer, biology and economics not only deserve comparison as interesting analogies, but they should be partially integrated, with biology providing a conceptual base on which economics can build. In particular, Hirshleifer considers the biological validity of economic concepts such as profit maximizing and utility maximizing, which happen to be key assumptions in traditional microeconomics. While acknowledging that much behavior can be understood as a manifestation of this traditional logic, he observes that among lower forms of life, altruism exists and is well documented. By reviewing the studies of biologists attempting to explain altruistic behavior, Hirshleifer is suggesting that economic theory could be much more widely applicable, providing it could be more flexible in its underlying assumptions. Suggested areas of application include the theory of family structure and the theory of communities, among others.

Implications for Organization Theory

Many of the issues addressed by evolutionary organizational economists directly parallel views developed by population ecologists in organization theory. Indeed, Hannan and Freeman (1977) and McKelvey (1982) all explore the biological analogy in their work and agree that the impact of managers and managerial decision making has been overstated in traditional organization theory.

The issues raised by these authors present several problems for traditional work in organization theory. If managers can have little impact on a firm's performance, why are there consultants, why do we have business schools, and why is so much effort expended in improving the management skills of managers in firms? Are all these efforts foolhardy?

More recent work in this area (Lippman and Rumelt, 1982; Barney, forthcoming (b)) suggests that both managerial luck and skill must be included in explaining the performance of firms. This argument turns on the observation that two types of environmentally induced uncertainty face most firms: reducible and irreducible uncertainty. Reducible uncertainty refers to that uncertainty about decision outcomes that can be reduced by focused managerial efforts at data collection and analysis. Examples of this type of uncertainty might include uncertainty about customer preferences (which can be reduced through collecting information from market surveys), uncertainty about the actions of competitors (which can be reduced by hiring away managers from competitors and by direct observation of their activities), and uncertainty about the actions of suppliers (which can be reduced by maintaining close relations with suppliers) (Porter, 1980).

On the other hand, irreducible uncertainty is simply that uncertainty about decision outcomes that cannot be overcome, to any great extent, by managerial efforts. Examples of this type of uncertainty include so-called acts of God (earthquakes and other natural disasters), accidents, revolutionary technological break-throughs, and other completely unexpected environmental events. While managers may attempt to reduce this source of uncertainty in their decision making, they can never completely remove it.

In a decision context characterized by only irreducible uncertainty, the quality of managers is irrelevant in explaining firm performance. No matter how good managers might be, they cannot reduce this type of uncertainty. Successful firms and managers in this setting are merely lucky. Unsuccessful firms and managers are merely unlucky.

At the other extreme, in decision situations characterized only by reducible uncertainty, the quality of management in reducing this uncertainty will explain most of the difference in performance between different firms. However, in this setting, luck can still play a role in generating high levels of performance for a poorly managed firm that happens by chance to make a correct decision.

Of course, most decision situations are not characterized by either of these two extremes, and thus a mix of luck and managerial skill at reducing decision-making uncertainty must be employed in explaining the level of firm performance. However, because the quality of management can have an impact on firm performance, there continues to be an important role for consulting, business schools, and management training in developing higher levels of management skill designed to reduce the uncertainty firms face when making and implementing decisions.

There are few areas in organizational economics that share as many concepts and conclusions with organization theory as the evolutionary theory of the firm and the evolutionary or population ecology model of organizations. Any serious student of either approach will find conceptual and empirical clarity and reaffirmation in considering research coming from the other discipline. Perhaps just as important, this convergence in theory and concept in organizational economics and organization theory presents a significant challenge to those organization theorists who would reject the environmental and evolutionary approaches. The evolutionary approach gains credibility if for no other reason than through a form of theoretical triangulation which has led separate students of organizational action to come to similar conclusions. Moreover, concepts taken from the economic evolutionary theory of the firm, because they provide an alternative yet supportive view, buttress many of the concepts and conclusions that organizational theorists might otherwise be tempted to reject prematurely.

Uncertainty, Evolution, and Economic Theory

Armen A. Alchian

A modification of economic analysis to incorporate incomplete information and uncertain foresight as axioms is suggested here. This approach dispenses with "profit maximization"; and it does not rely on the predictable, individual behavior that is usually assumed, as a first approximation, in standard textbook treatments. Despite these changes, the analytical concepts usually associated with such behavior are retained because they are not dependent upon such motivation or foresight. The suggested approach embodies the principles of biological evolution and natural selection by interpreting the economic system as an adoptive mechanism which chooses among exploratory actions generated by the adaptive pursuit of "success" or "profits." The resulting analysis is applicable to actions usually regarded as aberrations from standard economic behavior as well as to behavior covered by the customary analysis. This wider applicability and the removal of the unrealistic postulates of accurate anticipations and fixed states of knowledge have provided motivation for the study.

Note: I am indebted to Dr. Stephen Enke for criticism and stimulation leading to improvements in both content and exposition.

The exposition is ordered as follows: First, to clear the ground, a brief statement is given of a generally ignored aspect of "profit maximization," that is, where foresight is uncertain, "profit maximization" is *meaningless* as a guide to specifiable action. The constructive development then begins with an introduction of the element of environmental adoption by the economic system of a posteriori most appropriate action according to the criterion of "realized positive profits." This is illustrated in an extreme, random-behavior model without any individual rationality, foresight, or motivation whatsoever. Even in this extreme type of model, it is shown that the economist can predict and explain events with a modified use of his conventional analytical tools.

This phenomenon—environmental adoption—is then fused with a type of individual motivated behavior based on the pervasiveness of uncertainty and incomplete information. Adaptive, imitative, and trial-and-error behavior in the pursuit of "positive profits" is utilized rather than its sharp contrast, the pursuit of "maximized profits." A final section discusses some implications and conjectures.

I. "Profit Maximization" Not a Guide to Action

Current economic analysis of economic behavior relies heavily on decisions made by rational units customarily assumed to be seeking perfectly optimal situations.[1] Two criteria are well known—profit maximization and utility maximization.[2] According to these criteria, appropriate types of action are indicated by marginal or neighborhood inequalities which, if satisfied, yield an optimum. But the standard qualification usually added is that nobody is able really to optimize his situation according to these diagrams and concepts because of uncertainty about the position and, sometimes, even the slopes of the demand and supply functions. Nevertheless, the economist interprets and predicts the decisions of individuals in terms of these diagrams, since it is alleged that individuals use these concepts implicitly, if not explicitly.

Attacks on this methodology are widespread, but only one attack has been really damaging, that of G. Tinter (1941a, 1941b, 1942). He denies that profit maximization even makes any sense where there is uncertainty. Uncertainty arises from at least two sources: imperfect foresight and human inability to solve complex problems containing a host of variables even when an optimum is definable. Tinter's proof is simple. Under uncertainty, by definition, each action that may be chosen is identified with a *distribution* of potential outcomes, not with a unique outcome. Implicit in uncertainty is the consequence that these distributions of potential outcomes are overlapping.[3] It is worth emphasis that each possible action has a *distribution* of potential outcomes, only one of which will materialize if the action is taken, and that one outcome cannot be foreseen. Essentially, the task is converted into making a decision (selecting an action) whose potential outcome *distribution* is preferable, that is, choosing the action with the *optimum distribution*, since there is no such thing as a *maximizing* distribution.

For example, let each of two possible choices be characterized by its subjective distribution of potential outcomes. Suppose one has the higher "mean" but a larger spread, so that it might result in larger profits or losses, and the other has a smaller "mean" and a smaller spread. Which one is the maximum? This is a nonsensical question; but to ask for the optimum distribution is not nonsense. In the presence of uncertainty—a necessary condition for the existence of profits—there is no meaningful criterion for selecting the decision that will "maximize profits." The maximum-profit criterion is not meaningful as a basis *for selecting* the action which will, in fact, result in an outcome with higher profits than any other action would have, unless one assumes nonoverlapping potential outcome distributions. It must be noticed that the meaningfulness of "maximum profits—a realized outcome which is the largest that could have been realized from the available actions"—is perfectly consistent with the meaninglessness of "profit maximization"—a criterion for selecting among alternative lines of action, the potential outcomes of which are describable only as distributions and not as unique amounts.

This crucial difficulty would be avoided by using a preference function as a criterion for selecting most preferred distributions of potential outcomes, but the search for a criterion of rationality and choice in terms of preference functions still continues. For example, the use of the mean, or expectation, completely begs the question of uncertainty by disregarding the variance of the distribution, while a "certainty equivalent" assumes the answer. The only way to make "profit maximization" a specifically meaningful action is to postulate a model containing certainty. Then the question of the predictive and explanatory reliability of the model must be faced.[4]

II. Success Is Based on Results, Not Motivation

There is an alternative method which treats the decisions and criteria dictated by the economic *system* as more important than those made by the individuals in it. By backing away from the trees—the optimization calculus by individual units—we can better discern the forest of impersonal market forces.[5] This approach directs attention to the inter-relationships of the environment and the prevailing types of economic behavior which appear through a process of economic natural selection. Yet it does not imply that individual foresight and action do not affect the nature of the existing state of affairs.

In an economic system the realization of profits is the criterion according to which successful and surviving firms are selected. This decision criterion is applied primarily by an impersonal market system in the United States and may be completely independent of the decision processes of individual units, of the variety of inconsistent motives and abilities, and even of the individual's awareness of the criterion. The reason is simple. Realized positive profits, not *maximum* profits, are the mark of success and viability. It does not matter through what process of reasoning or motivation such success was achieved. The fact of its accomplishment is sufficient. This is the criterion by which the economic system selects survivors: those who realize *positive profits* are the survivors; those who suffer losses disappear.

The pertinent requirement—positive profits through relative efficiency—is weaker than "maximized profits," with which, unfortunately, it has been confused. Positive profits accrue to those who are better than their actual competitors, even if the participants are ignorant, intelligent, skilful, etc. The crucial element is one's aggregate position relative to actual competitors, not some hypothetically perfect competitors. As in a race, the award goes to the relatively fastest, even if all the competitors loaf. Even in a world of stupid men there would still be profits. Also, the greater the uncertainties of the world, the greater is the possibility that profits would go to venturesome and lucky rather than to logical, careful, fact-gathering individuals.

The preceding interpretation suggests two ideas. First, success (survival) accompanies relative superiority; and, second, it does not require proper motivation but may rather be the result of fortuitous circumstances. Among all competitors, those whose particular conditions happen to be the most appropriate of those offered to the economic system for testing and adoption will be "selected" as survivors. Just how such an approach can be used and how individuals happen to offer these appropriate forms for testing are problems to which we now turn.[6]

III. Chance or Luck Is One Method of Achieving Success

Sheer chance is a substantial element in determining the situation selected and also in determining its appropriateness or viability. A second element is the ability to adapt one's self by various methods to an appropriate situation. In order to indicate clearly the respective roles of luck and conscious adapting, the adaptive calculcus will, for the moment, be completely removed. All individual rationality, motivation, and foresight will be temporarily abandoned in order to concentrate upon the ability of the environment to *adopt* "appropriate" survivors even in the absence of any adaptive behavior. This is an apparently unrealistic, but nevertheless very useful, expository approach in establishing the attenuation between the ex post survival criterion and the role of the individual's adaptive decision criterion. It also aids in assessing the role of luck and chance in the operation of our economic system.

Consider, first, the simplest type of biological evolution. Plants "grow" to the sunny side of buildings not because they "want to" in awareness of the fact that optimum or better conditions prevail there but rather because the leaves that happen to have more sunlight grow faster and their feeding systems become stronger. Similarly, animals with configurations and habits more appropriate for survival under prevailing conditions have an enhanced viability and will with higher probability be typical survivors. Less appropriately acting organisms of the same general class having lower probabilities of survival will find survival difficult. More common types, the survivors, may appear to be those having *adapted* themselves to the environment, whereas the truth may well be that the environment has *adopted* them. There may have been no motivated individual adapting but, instead, only environmental adopting.

A useful, but unreal, example in which individuals act without any foresight indicates the type of analysis available to the economist and also the ability of the system to "direct" resources despite individual ignorance. Assume that thousands of travelers set out from Chicago, selecting their roads completely at random and without foresight. Only our "economist" knows that on but one road are there any gasoline stations. He can state categorically that travelers will *continue* to travel only on that road; those on other roads will soon run out of gas. Even though each one selected his route at random, we might have called those travelers who were so fortunate as to have picked the right road wise, efficient, foresighted, etc. Of course, we would consider them the lucky ones. If gasoline supplies were now moved to a new road, some formerly luckless travelers again would be able to move; and a new pattern of travel would be observed, although none of the travelers had changed his particular path. The really possible paths have changed with the changing environment. All that is needed is a set of varied, risk-taking (adoptable) travelers. The correct direction of travel will be established. As circumstances

(economic environment) change, the analyst (economist) can select the
types of participants (firms) that will now become successful; he may
also be able to diagnose the conditions most conducive to a greater probability of survival.[7]

IV. Chance Does Not Imply
Nondirected, Random Allocation of Resources

These two examples do not constitute an attempt to base all analysis on adoptive models dominated by chance. But they do indicate that
collective and individual random behavior does not per se imply a nihilistic
theory incapable of yielding reliable predictions and explanations; nor
does it imply a world lacking in order and apparent direction. It might,
however, be argued that the facts of life deny even a substantial role
to the element of chance and the associated adoption principle in the
economic system. For example, the long lives and disparate sizes of
business firms and hereditary fortunes may seem to be reliable evidence
of consistent foresighted motivation and nonrandom behavior. In order
to demonstrate that consistent success cannot be treated as prima facie
evidence against pure luck, the following chance model of Borél, the
famous French mathematician, is presented.

Suppose two million Parisians were paired off and set to tossing
coins in a game of matching. Each pair plays until the winner on the
first toss is again brought to equality with the other player. Assuming
one toss per second for each eight-hour day, at the end of ten years there
would still be, on the average, about a hundred-odd pairs; and if the
players assign the game to their heirs, a dozen or so will still be playing
at the end of a thousand years! The implications are obvious. Suppose
that some business had been operating for one hundred years. Should
one rule out luck and chance as the essence of the factors producing the
long-term survival of the enterprise? No inference whatever can be drawn
until the number of original participants is known; and even then one
must know the size, risk, and frequency of each commitment. One can
see from the Borél illustration the danger in concluding that there are
too many firms with long lives in the real world to admit an important
role to chance. On the contrary, one might insist that there are actually
too few!

The chance postulate was directed to two problems. On the one
hand, there is the actual way in which a substantial fraction of economic
behavior and activity is effected. On the other, there is the method of
analysis which economists may use in their predictions and diagnoses.

Before modifying the extreme chance model adding adaptive behavior, some connotations and implications of the incorporation of chance elements will be elaborated in order to reveal the richness which is really inherent in chance. First, even if each and every individual acted in a haphazard and nonmotivated manner, it is possible that the variety of actions would be so great that the resulting collective set would contain actions that are best, in the sense of perfect foresight. For example, at a horse race with enough bettors wagering strictly at random, someone will win on all eight races. Thus individual random behavior does not eliminate the likelihood of observing "appropriate" decisions.[8]

Second, and conversely, individual behavior according to some foresight and motivation does not necessarily imply a collective pattern of behavior that is different from the collective variety of actions associated with a random selection of actions. Where there is uncertainty, people's judgments and opinions, even when based on the best available evidence, will differ; no one of them may be making his choice by tossing coins; yet the aggregate *set* of actions of the entire group of participants may be indistinguishable from a set of individual actions, each selected at random.[9]

Third, and fortunately, a chance-dominated model does not mean that an economist cannot predict or explain or diagnose. With a knowledge of the economy's realized requisites for survival and by a comparison of alternative conditions, he can state what types of firms or behavior relative to other possible types will be more viable, even though the firms themselves may not know the conditions or even try to achieve them by readjusting to the changed situation if they do know the conditions. It is sufficient if all firms are slightly different so that in the new environmental situation those who have their fixed internal conditions closer to the new, but unknown, optimum position now have a greater probability of survival and growth. They will grow relative to other firms and become the prevailing type, since survival conditions may push the observed characteristics of the set of survivors toward the unknowable optimum by either (1) repeated trials or (2) survival of more of those who happened to be near the optimum—determined ex post. If these new conditions last "very long," the dominant firms will be different ones from those which prevailed or would have prevailed under other conditions. Even if environmental conditions cannot be forecast, the economist can compare for given alternative potential situations the types of behavior that would have higher probability of viability or adoption. If explanation of past results rather than prediction is the task, the economist can diagnose the particular attributes which were critical in facilitating survival, even though individual participants were not aware of them.[10]

Fourth, the bases of prediction have been indicated in the preceding paragraph, but its character should be made explicit. The prediction will not assert that every—or, indeed, any—firm necessarily changes its characteristics. It asserts, instead, that the characteristics of the new *set* of firms, or possibly a set of new firms, will change. This may be characterized by the "representative firm," a purely statistical concept— a vector of "averages," one dimension for each of the several qualities of the population of firms. A "representative firm" is not typical of any one producer but, instead, is a set of statistics summarizing the various "modal" characteristics of the population. Surely, this was an intended use of Marshall's "representative firm."

Fifth, a final implication drawn from consideration of this extreme approach is that empirical investigations via questionnaire methods, so far used, are incapable of evaluating the validity of marginal productivity analysis. This is true because productivity and demand analyses are essential in evaluating relative viability, even though uncertainty eliminates "profit maximization" and even if price and technological changes were to have no consciously redirecting effect on the firms. To illustrate, suppose that, in attempting to predict the effects of higher real wage rates, it is discovered that every businessman says he does not adjust his labor force. Nevertheless, firms with a lower labor-capital ratio will have relatively lower cost positions and, to that extent, a higher probability of survival. The force of competitive survival, by eliminating higher-cost firms, reveals a population of remaining firms with a new average labor-capital ratio. The essential point is that individual motivation and foresight, while sufficient, are not necessary. Of course, it is not argued here that therefore it is absent. All that is needed by economists is their own awareness of the survival conditions and criteria of the economic system and a group of participants who submit various combinations and organizations for the system's selection and adoption. Both these conditions are satisfied.[11]

As a consequence, only the method of use, rather than the usefulness, of economic tools and concepts is affected by the approach suggested here; in fact, they are made more powerful if they are not pretentiously assumed to be necessarily associated with, and dependent upon, individual foresight and adjustment. They are tools for, at least, the diagnosis of the operation of an economic system, even if not also for the internal business behavior of each firm.

V. Individual Adapting via Imitation and Trial and Error

Let it again be noted that the preceding extreme model was designed to present in purest form only one element of the suggested approach. It is not argued that there is no purposive, foresighted behavior present in reality. In adding this realistic element—adaptation by individuals with some foresight and purposive motivation—we are expanding the preceding extreme model. We are not abandoning any part of it or futilely trying to merge it with the opposite extreme of perfect foresight and "profit maximization."

Varying and conflicting objectives motivate economic activity, yet we shall here direct attention to only one particular objective—the sufficient condition of realized positive profits. There are no implications of "profit maximization," and this difference is important. Although the latter is a far more extreme objective when definable, only the former is the sine qua non of survival and success. To argue that, with perfect competition, the two would come to the same thing is to conceal an important difference by means of a very implausible assumption. The pursuit of profits, and not some hypothetical undefinable perfect situation, is the relevant objective whose *fulfilment* is rewarded with survival. Unfortunately, even this proximate objective is too high. Neither perfect knowledge of the past nor complete awareness of the current state of the arts gives sufficient foresight to indicate profitable action. Even for this more restricted objective, the pervasive effects of uncertainty prevent the ascertainment of actions which are supposed to be optimal in achieving profits. Now the consequence of this is that modes of behavior replace optimum equilibrium conditions as guiding rules of action. Therefore, in the following sections two forms of conscious adaptive behavior are emphasized.

First, wherever successful enterprises are observed, the elements common to these observable successes will be associated with success and copied by others in their pursuit of profits or success. "Nothing succeeds like success." Thus the urge for "rough-and-ready" imitative rules of behavior is accounted for. What would otherwise appear to be merely customary "orthodox," nonrational rules of behavior turns out to be codified imitations of observed success, e.g., "conventional" markup, price "followship," "orthodox" accounting and operating ratios, "proper" advertising policy, etc. A conventionally employed type of behavior pattern is consistent with the postulates of the analysis employed, even though the reasons and justifications for the particular conventions are not.[12]

Many factors cause this motive to imitate patterns of action observable in past successes. Among these are: (1) the absence of an identifiable criterion for decision-making, (2) the variability of the environment, (3) the multiplicity of factors that call for attention and choice, (4) the uncertainty attaching to all these factors and outcomes, (5) the awareness that superiority relative to one's competitors is crucial, and (6) the non-availability of a trial-and-error process converging to an optimum position.

In addition, imitation affords relief from the necessity of really making decisions and conscious innovations, which, if wrong, become "inexcusable." Unfortunately, failure or success often reflects the willingness to depart from rules when conditions have changed; what counts, then, is not only imitative behavior but the willingness to abandon it at the "right" time and circumstances. Those who are different and successful "become" innovators, while those who fail "become" reckless violators of tried-and-true rules. Although one may deny the absolute appropriateness of such rules, one cannot doubt the existence of a strong urge to create conventions and rules (based on observed success) and a willingness to use them for action as well as for rationalizations of inaction. If another untried host of actions might have been even more successful, so much the worse for the participants who failed, and even for those who missed "perfect success."

Even innovation is accounted for by imitation. While there certainly are those who consciously innovate, there are those who, in their imperfect attempts to imitate others, unconsciously innovate by unwittingly acquiring some unexpected or unsought unique attributes which under the prevailing circumstances prove partly responsible for the success. Others, in turn will attempt to copy the uniqueness, and the imitation-innovation process continues. Innovation is assured, and the notable aspects of it here are the possibility of unconscious pioneering and leadership.

The second type of conscious adaptive behavior, in addition to imitation, is "trial and error." This has been used with "profit maximization," wherein, by trial and ensuing success or failure, more appropriate actions are selected in a process presumed to converge to a limit of "profit maximization" equilibrium. Unfortunately, at least two conditions are necessary for convergence via a trial-and-error process, even if one admits an equilibrium situation as an admissible limit. First, a trial must be classifiable as a success or failure. The position achieved must be comparable with results of other potential actions. In a static environment, if one improves his position relative to his former position, then the action taken is better than the former one, and presumably one could continue by small increments to advance to a local optimum. An analogy is pertinent. A nearsighted grasshopper on a mound of rocks can crawl to the top of a particular rock. But there is no assurance that he can also get to the top of the mound, for he might have to descend for a while or hop to new rocks. The second condition then, for the convergence via trial and error is the continual rising toward some *optimum optimorum* without intervening descents. Whether decisions and actions in economic life satisfy these two conditions cannot be proved or disproved here, but the available evidence seems overwhelmingly unfavorable.

The above convergence conditions do not apply to a changing environment, for there can be no observable comparison of the result of an action with any other. Comparability of resulting situations is destroyed by the changing environment. As a consequence, the measure of goodness of actions in anything except a tolerable-intolerable sense is lost, and the possibility of an individual's converging to the optimum activity via a trial-and-error process disappears. Trial and error becomes survival or death. It cannot serve as a basis of the *individual's* method of convergence to a "maximum" or optimum position. Success is discovered by the economic system through a blanketing shotgun process, not by the individual through a converging search.

In general, uncertainty provides an excellent reason for imitation of observed success. Likewise, it accounts for observed uniformity among the survivors, derived from an evolutionary, adopting, competitive system employing a criterion of survival, which can operate independently of individual motivations. Adapting behavior via imitation and venturesome innovation enlarges the model. Imperfect imitators provide opportunity for innovation, and the survival criterion of the economy determines the successful, possibly because imperfect, imitators. Innovation is provided also by conscious wilful action, whatever the ultimate motivation may be, since drastic action is motivated by the hope of great success as well as by the desire to avoid impending failure.

All the preceding arguments leave the individual economic participant with imitative, venturesome, innovative, trial-and-error adaptive behavior. Most conventional economic tools and concepts are still useful, although in a vastly different analytical framework—one which is closely akin to the theory of biological evolution. The economic counterparts of genetic heredity, mutations, and natural selection are imitation, innovation, and positive profits.

VI. Conclusion and Summary

I shall conclude with a brief reference to some implications and conjectures.

Observable patterns of behavior and organization are predictable in terms of their relative probabilities of success or viability *if* they are tried. The observed prevalence of a type of behavior depends upon both this probability of viability and the probability of the different types being submitted to the economic system for testing and selecting. One is the probability of appearance of a certain type of organization (mutation), and the other is the probability of its survival or viability, once it appears (natural selection). There is much evidence for believing that these two probabilities are interrelated. But is there reason to suppose that a high probability of viability implies a high probability of an action's being taken, as would be implied in a system of analysis involving some "inner directed urge toward perfection"? If these two probabilities are not highly correlated, what predictions of types of action can the economist make? An answer has been suggested in this paper.

While it is true that the economist can define a profit maximization behavior by assuming *specific* cost and revenue conditions, is there any assurance that the conditions and conclusions so derivable are not too perfect and absolute? If profit maximization (certainty) is not ascertainable, the confidence about the predicted effects of changes, e.g., higher taxes or minimum wages, will be dependent upon how close the formerly existing arrangement was to the formerly "optimal" (certainty) situation. What really counts is the various actions actually tried, for it is from these that "success" is selected, not from some set of perfect actions. The economist may be pushing his luck too far in arguing that actions in response to changes in environment and changes in satisfaction with the existing state of affairs will converge as a result of adaptation or adoption toward the optimum action that should have been selected, if foresight had been perfect.[13]

In summary, I have asserted that the economist, using the present analytical tools developed in the analysis of the firm under certainty, can predict the more adoptable or viable types of economic interrelationships that will be induced by environmental change even if individuals themselves are unable to ascertain them. That is, although individual participants may not know their cost and revenue situations, the economist can predict the consequences of higher wage rates, taxes, government policy, etc. Like the biologist, the economist predicts the effects of environmental changes on the surviving class of living organisms; the economist need not assume that each participant is aware of, or acts according to, his cost and demand situation. These are concepts for the economist's use and not necessarily for the individual participant's, who may have other analytic or customary devices which, while of interest to the economist, serve as data and not as analytic methods.

An alternative to the rationale of individual profit maximization has been presented without exorcising uncertainty. Lest isolated arguments be misinterpreted, let it be clearly stated that this paper does not argue that purposive objective-seeking behavior is absent from reality, nor, on the other hand, does it indorse the familiar thesis that action of economic units cannot be expressed within the marginal analysis. Rather, the contention is that the precise role and nature of purposive behavior in the presence of uncertainty and incomplete information have not been clearly understood or analyzed.

It is straightforward, if not heuristic, to start with complete uncertainty and nonmotivation and then to add elements of foresight and motivation in the process of building an analytical model. The opposite approach, which starts with certainty and unique motivation, must abandon its basic principles as soon as uncertainty and mixed motivations are recognized.[14] The approach suggested here is intellectually more modest and realistic, without sacrificing generality. It does not regard uncertainty as an aberrational exogenous disturbance, as does the usual approach from the opposite extreme of accurate foresight. The existence of uncertainty and incomplete information is the foundation of the suggested type of analysis; the importance of the concept of a class of "chance" decisions rests upon it; it permits of various conflicting objectives; it motivates and rationalizes a type of adaptive imitative behavior; yet it does not destroy the basis of prediction, explanation, or diagnosis. It does not base its aggregate description on individual optimal action; yet it is capable of incorporating such activity where justified. The formalization of this approach awaits the marriage of the theory of stochastic processes and economics—two fields of thought admirably suited for union. It is conjectured that the suggested modification is applicable to a wide class of events and is worth attempts at empirical verification.[15]

Notes

1. See, e.g., Robinson (1933, p. 6) for a strong statement of the necessity of such optimal behavior. Standard textbooks expound essentially the same idea. See also Samuelson (1946).

2. In the following we shall discuss only profit maximization, although everything said is applicable equally to utility maximization by consumers.

3. Thus uncertainty is defined here to be the phenomenon that produces overlapping distributions of potential outcomes.

4. Analytical models in all sciences postulate models abstracting from some realities in the belief that derived predictions will still be relevant. Simplifications are necessary, but continued attempts should be made to introduce more realistic assumptions into a workable model with an increase in generality and detail (see M. Friedman and L. Savage, 1948).

5. In effect, we shall be reverting to a Marshallian type of analysis combined with the essentials of Darwinian evolutionary natural selection.

6. Also suggested is another way to divide the general problem discussed here. The process and rationale by which a unit chooses its actions so as to optimize its situation is one part of the problem. The other is the relationship between changes in the environment and the consequent observable results, i.e., the decision process of the economic *society*. The classification used in the text is closely related to this but differs in emphasizing the degree of knowledge and foresight.

7. The undiscerning person who sees survivors corresponding to changes in environment claims to have evidence for the "Lysenko" doctrine. In truth, all he may have is evidence for the doctrine that the environment, by competitive conditions, selects the most viable of the various phenotypic characteristics for perpetuation. Economists should beware of economic "Lysenkoism."

8. The Borél gamblers analogue is pertinent to a host of everyday situations.

9. Of course, the economic units may be going through a period of soul-searching, management training, and research activity. We cannot yet identify mental and physical activity with a process that results in sufficient information and foresight to yield uniquely determinate choices. To do so would be to beg the whole question.

10. It is not even necessary to suppose that each firm acts as if it possessed the conventional diagrams and knew the analytical principles employed by economists in deriving optimum and equilibrium conditions. The atoms and electrons do not know the laws of nature; the physicist does not impart to each atom a wilful scheme of action based on laws of conservation of energy, etc. The fact that an economist deals with human beings who have sense and ambitions does not *automatically* warrant imparting to these humans the great degree of foresight and motivations which the economist may require for his customary analysis as an outside observer or "oracle." The similarity between this argument and Gibbsian statistical mechanics, as well as biological evolution, is *not* mere coincidence.

11. This approach reveals how the "facts" of Lester's dispute with Machlup can be handled with standard economic tools.

12. These constructed rules of behavior should be distinguished from "rules" which, in effect, do no more than define the objective being sought. Confusion between objectives which motivate one and rules of behavior are commonplace. For example, "full-cost pricing" is a "rule" that one cannot really follow. He can

try to, but whether he succeeds or fails in his objective of survival is not controllable by following the "rule of full-cost pricing." If he fails in his objective, he must, of necessity, fail to have followed the "rule." The situation is parallel to trying to control the speed of a car by simply setting by hand the indicator on the speedometer.

13. An anomalous aspect of the assumption of perfect foresight is that it nearly results in tautological and empty statements. One cannot know everything, and this is recognized by the addendum that one acts within a "given state and distribution of the arts." But this is perilously close, if not equivalent, to saying either that action is taken only where the outcome is accurately foreseen or that information is always limited. The qualification is inserted because one might contend that it is the "*constancy* of the state and distribution of arts" that is necessary as a *ceteris paribus*. But even the latter is no solution. A large fraction of behavior in a world of incomplete information and uncertainty is necessarily directed at increasing the state of arts and venturing into an unknown sphere. While it is probably permissible to start with a prescribed "distribution of the knowledge of the arts," holding it constant is too restrictive, since a large class of important and frequent actions necessarily involves changes in the state and distribution of knowledge. The modification suggested here incorporates this search for more knowledge as an essential foundation.

14. If one prefers, he may believe that the suggestions here contain reasons why the model based on certainty may predict outcomes, although individuals really cannot try to maximize profits. But the dangers of this have been indicated.

15. Preliminary study in this direction has been very convincing, and, in addition, the suggested approach appears to contain important implications relative to general economic policy; but discussions of these are reserved for a later date.

Economics from a Biological Viewpoint

J. Hirshleifer

I. Economics and Biology

The field variously called population biology, sociobiology, or ecology is concerned to explain the observed interrelations among the

Note: Thanks for comments and suggestions, far too numerous and important to be fully responded to here, are due to: Armen Alchian, Shmuel Amir, Edward C. Banfield, Gary Becker, Eric L. Charnov, Ronald Cohen, Harold Demsetz, Michael Ghiselin, Joel Guttman, Bruce Herrick, Gertrude Himmelfarb, David Levine, John G. Riley, Vernon L. Smith, Robert Trivers, and James Weinrich.

various forms of life—organisms, species, and broader groupings and communities—and between forms of life and their external environments. The subject includes both material aspects of these interrelations (the geographical distributions of species in relation to one another, their respective numbers, physical properties like size differences between the sexes) and behavioral aspects (why some species are territorial while others flock, why some are monogamous and others polygamous, why some are aggressive and others shy).

From one point of view, the various social sciences devoted to the study of mankind, taken together, constitute but a subdivision of the all-encompassing field of sociobiology (E. O. Wilson, 1975; 1977). The ultimately biological subject matter of economics in particular has been recognized by some of our leading thinkers.[1] There is however a special link between economics and sociobiology over and above the mere fact that economics studies a subset of the social behavior of one of the higher mammals. *The fundamental organizing concepts of the dominant analytical structures employed in economics and in sociobiology are strikingly parallel* (Rapport and Turner, 1977). What biologists study can be regarded as "Nature's economy" (Ghiselin, 1974). Oswald Spengler perceived (and regarded it as a serious criticism) that Darwin's contribution represented "the application of economics to biology" (Himmelfarb, 1959, p. 396). Fundamental concepts like scarcity, competition, equilibrium, and specialization play similar roles in both spheres of inquiry. And terminological pairs such as species/industry, mutation/innovation, evolution/progress, mutualism/exchange have more or less analogous denotations.

Regarded more systematically, the isomorphism between economics and sociobiology involves the intertwining of two levels of analysis. On the first level, acting units or entities choose strategies or develop techniques that promote success in the struggle or *competition* for advantage in given environments. The economist usually calls this process "optimizing," the biologist, "adapting." The formalizations involved are equations of constrained maximization. The second, higher level of analysis examines the social or aggregate resultant of the interaction of the striving units or agents. The formalizations here take the form of equations of equilibrium. (In more general versions, the static solutions may be embedded in "dynamic" equations showing the time paths of approach to solution states.) The solutions on the two levels are of course interdependent. The pursuit of advantage on the part of acting units takes place subject to opportunities and constraints that emerge from the social context, while the resulting social configuration (constituting at least part of the environment for each separate agent) depends in turn upon the strategies employed by the advantage-seeking entities.

Among the methodological issues that might arise at this point are two with somewhat opposed thrusts: (1) Given the validity of a sociobiological outlook on human behavior, are we not claiming too much for economics? What role is there left for the other social sciences if economics can be regarded as essentially coextensive with the sociobiology of human behavior? (2) But alternatively, are we not claiming too little for economics (and a fortiori for the other social sciences) in adopting the reductive interpretation of human behavior implicit in the sociobiological approach? May it not be the case that the cultural evolution of the human species has carried it into a realm where biological laws are determinative of only a minor fraction of behavioral phenomena? (Or perhaps economics is the discipline that regards mankind as merely sociobiological in nature, while the other social sciences treat of the higher aspects of human culture?)

Consideration of the second group of questions will be reserved for the concluding sections of this paper. With regard to the first—a seeming claim that the domain of economics is coextensive with the total sphere of all the social sciences together—a unified social-science viewpoint is adopted here, in which economics and other social studies are regarded as interpenetrating rather than compartmentalized. The traditional core area of compartmentalized economics is characterized by models that: (a) postulate rational self-interested behavior on the part of individuals with given preference for material goods and services, and (b) attempt to explain those interactions among such individuals that take the form of market exchanges, under a fixed legal system of property and free contract. That only a very limited portion of human behavioral association could be adequately represented under such self-imposed analytical constraints has often been pointed out to economists by other social scientists. In recent years economics has begun to break through these self-imposed barriers, to take as subject matter all human activity that can be interpreted as goal-directed behavior constrained to and yet, in the aggregate, determinative of resultant social configurations. Significant innovative instances of the application of techniques of economic analysis to broader social issues include Schelling and Boulding's works on conflict and warfare, Downs and Buchanan and Tullock on political choice, and Becker on crime and marriage (Schelling, 1960; Boulding, 1962; Downs, 1957; Buchanan and Tullock, 1962; Becker, 1968, 1973). And each of these efforts has been followed by a growing literature, in which both economists and other social scientists have participated.[2] The upshot is that (at least in their properly scientific aspect) the social sciences generally can be regarded as in the process of coalescing. As economics ''imperialistically'' employs its tools of analysis over a wider range of social issues, it will *become* sociology and anthropology and political science. But correspondingly, as these other disciplines grow increasingly rigorous, they will not merely resemble but will *be* economics. It is in this sense that ''economics'' is taken here as broadly synonymous with ''social science.'' [3]

One of the obvious divergences between economics and sociobiology, it might appear, is that men can consciously optimize—or so we often like to think—whereas, for all but a few higher animals, the concepts of ''choice'' or ''strategy'' are only metaphorical. What happens in the biological realm is that, given a sufficiently long run, *natural selection* allows survival only of entities that have developed successful strategies in their respective environments. So the result is sometimes (though not always, as we shall see) *as if* conscious optimization were taking place. The idea that selective pressure of the environment can do the work of conscious optimizing (thus freeing us of any need to postulate a ''rational'' economic agent) has also received some controversial discussion in the economics literature. This topic will be reviewed in Section III.

After these preliminaries, the central portion of the paper will survey some of the main parallels and divergences in economic and sociobiological reasoning. Since this is written by an economist with only an amateur interest in the biological sciences, attention will be devoted to ''what message sociobiology has for economics'' rather than to ''how we can set the biologists straight.''

II. Some Mutual Influences

The most famous example of the influence of an economist upon biological thought is of course the impact of Malthus upon Darwin and Wallace. The codiscoverers of evolution each reported that Malthus' picture of the unremitting pressure of human population upon subsistence provided the key element leading to the idea of evolution by natural selection in the struggle for life.[4] Malthusian ideas of compounded growth also play a role in modern biological theory. The ''Malthusian parameter,'' as defined by biologists, represents the exponential rate at which a population will grow as limited by its genetic capabilities and constrained by the environment.[5]

In the very recent period a number of biologists have come to make significant use of tools and approaches of economics. Michael T. Ghiselin (1974) has urged fellow biologists to adopt the ''methodological individualism'' of economics in preference to the open or disguised "teleologism" of assuming optimizing behavior on the part of higher-level groupings and species (Demsetz, 1975). A few instances of recent biological optimization studies that seem to be consciously modelled upon economic analytical techniques can be cited: (1) Rapport (1971) showed that the extent of "predator switching" from one prey species to another in response to changes in relative abundance could be expressed in terms of shapes of the predator's indifference curves and opportunity frontier; (2) Gadgil and Bossert (1970) interpreted various characteristics of organisms' life histories—such as the timing and scale of reproductive effort and the determination of survival probabilities at various ages—as the resultant of a balance between "profit" (that is, gain) and "cost" (that is, foregone gain or opportunity cost) in choosing strategies to maximize the Malthusian parameter of population growth. (3) Trivers (1972) demonstrated that several aspects of parental behavior, in particular the differing extent in various species of male versus female "investment" in care of offspring, could be explained in terms of differences in the selectional return on investment to the male and female parents (that is, in terms of the comparative propagation of their respective genetic endowments); (4) Cody (1974) examined the conditions determining the relative competitive advantages of "generalist" versus "specialist" strategies in the exploitation of a mixed-resource environment. (5) E. O. Wilson (1975) employed linear programming models to determine the optimal number and proportion of castes in the division of labor among social insects. (6) Charnov (1976) develops an optimality theorem for foraging animals, in which the forager terminates exploitation of a given food patch when the marginal energy intake falls to equality with the average return from the habitat.

But the more significant intellectual influence has been in the other direction, from biology to social science. The success of theories of evolution and natural selection in the biological realm led quickly to the body of thought called "Social Darwinism"—the most characteristic figures being the philosopher Herbert Spencer in England and the economist William Graham Sumner in America. On the scientific level Social Darwinism represented an attempt to explain patterns of social stratification as the consequence of the selection of superior human types and forms of organization through social competition. To a considerable extent, its exponents went on to draw the inference that such existing stratification was therefore ethically *justified*. The political unpalatability of this conclusion has led to an exceptionally bad press for Social Darwinism—at the hands of other social scientists, jurists, and philosophers, as economists after Sumner have scarcely discussed the question. The

Social Darwinists, or some of them at least, did confuse descriptive with moral categories so as to attribute excessive beneficence to natural selection on the human level. In the real world, we know, success *may* sometimes be the reward of socially functional behavior, but also sometimes of valueless or disruptive activities like monopolization, crime, or most of what is carried on under the heading of politics.

It would be incorrect to assume that Darwinism is necessarily conservative in its social implications. The implications would seem to be radical or conservative according as emphasis is placed upon the necessity and importance of mutability and change (*evolution*) or upon final states of harmonious adaptation as a result of selection (*equilibrium*) (Lewontin, 1968). Similarly, racist and imperialist theories, on the one hand, and pacifist and universalist theories, on the other hand, could both be founded on Darwinian ideas (Hofstadter, 1955; Himmelfarb, 1959). The first would emphasize the role of ongoing struggle, and the latter the role of social instinct and mutual aid, in promoting selection of human type. And even among those for whom the key lesson of Darwinism is the competitive struggle for survival, there are a variety of interpretations, ranging from individualistic versions of Spencer and Sumner to a number of collectivist versions: the idea of superior or fitter social classes (Karl Marx), or systems of law and government (Bagehot, 1875), or of course racial groups.[6]

> In the spectrum of opinion that went under the name of social Darwinism almost every variety of belief was included. In Germany, it was represented chiefly by democrats and socialists; in England by conservatives. It was appealed to by nationalists as an argument for a strong state, and by the proponents of laissez-faire as an argument for a weak state. It was condemned by some as an aristocratic doctrine designed to glorify power and greatness, and by others, like Nietzsche, as a middle-class doctrine appealing to the mediocre and submissive. Some socialists saw in it the scientific validation of their doctrine; others the negation of their moral and spiritual hopes. Militarists found in it the sanction of war and conquest, while pacifists saw the power of physical force transmuted into the power of intellectual and moral persuasion (Himmelfarb, 1959, p. 407).

But the too-total rejection of Social Darwinism has meant a lack of appreciation of its valid core of scientific insights: (1) that individuals, groups, races, and even social arrangements (democracy versus dictatorship, capitalism versus socialism, small states versus large) are in never-ending competition with one another, and while the results of this competition have no necessary correlation with moral desert, the competition itself is a fact with explanatory power for social phenomena; (2) that the behavior of mankind is strongly influenced by the biological heritage of the species, and that the forces tending toward either cooperation or conflict among men are in large part identical with phenomena observable in the biological realm.

The sweeping rejection of biological categories for the explanation of human phenomena, on the part of social scientists, is strikingly evidenced by the concluding paragraph of Hofstadter's influential and penetrating study:

> Whatever the course of social philosophy in the future, however, a few conclusions are now accepted by most humanists: that such biological ideas as the "survival of the fittest," whatever their doubtful value in natural science, are utterly useless in attempting to understand society; that the life of man in society, while it is incidentally a biological fact, has characteristics that are not reducible to biology and must be explained in the distinctive terms of a cultural analysis; that the physical well-being of men is a result of their social organization and not vice versa; that social improvement is a product of advances in technology and social organization, not of breeding or selective elimination; that judgements as to the value of competition between men or enterprises or nations must be based upon social and not allegedly biological consequences; and, finally, that there is nothing in nature or a naturalistic philosophy of life to make impossible the acceptance of moral sanctions that can be employed for the common good (1955, p. 204).

This statement is on solid ground in rejecting attempts to draw moral claims from biological premises. But it promotes confusion in confounding these claims with—and therefore rejecting out of hand—the entirely scientific contention that man's biological endowment has significant implications for his social behavior.

Following Nicholson (1960), Darwinian evolution involves four main factors: the occurrence of *variations*, some mechanism of *inheritance* to preserve variations, the Malthusian tendency to *multiplication* (leading sooner or later to *competition* among organisms), and finally environmental *selection*. From this broad point of view it is clear that there may be cultural evolution even apart from any biological change. Hofstadter seems to regard the forms of human association and the patterns of human social and cultural change as almost entirely free of biological determinants— apart, presumably, from permanent human characteristics like degree of intelligence which determine and constrain the *possibilities* of cultural advance. In contrast, the sociobiological point of view is that cultural and biological change cannot be so totally dichotomized; cultural tracking of environmental change is a group-behavioral form of adaptation, which interacts in a variety of ways with genetic and populational responses (E. O. Wilson, 1975, p. 145). There is cultural evolution even in the nonhuman sphere, as animals discover successful patterns of behavior which then spread by learning and imitation. Apart from the direct implications for population composition (those individuals who succeed in learning more efficient behavior survive in greater numbers), there may be genetic consequences in that the behavioral changes may modify the conditions of selection among genetic mutations and recombinations (Mayr, 1960).

Along this line, the anthropologist Alland (1967) emphasizes that culture itself should be regarded as a kind of biological adaptation. And there is a long tradition among biologists which encourages attention to the implications of human biological origins for social behavior and institutions. Among the important recent instances are J. Huxley (1958), Fisher (1958), Dobzhansky (1962), Lorenz (1966), Tiger and Fox (1971), and of course E. O. Wilson (1975). On the more popular level are such works as Ardrey (1961; 1970) and Morris (1967). But these ideas have won relatively little acceptance among social scientists.

Turning now to economics, the relevance of quasi-biological (selectional) models has been the topic of controversial discussion since Alchian's paper in 1950. Alchian argued that environmental selection (''adoption'') could replace the traditional analysis premised upon rational profit-maximizing behavior (''adaptation'') as a source of verifiable predictions about visible characteristics of business firms. This discussion, which has interesting parallels within biology proper, will be reviewed next.

III. Biological Models of the Firm: Optimization Versus Selection

Alchian contended that optimization on the part of the business firm (profit maximization in the traditional formulation) was an unnecessary and even unhelpful idea for purposes of scientific explanation and prediction. While profit is undoubtedly the firm's goal, the substantive content of profit *maximization* as a guiding rule erodes away when it is realized that any actual choice situation always involves profit as a probability distribution rather than as a deterministic variable (1950, p. 212). And even if firms never attempted to *maximize profit* but behaved purely randomly, the environment would nevertheless select ("adopt") relatively correct decisions in the sense of meeting the *positive realized profit* condition of survival (1950, p. 217). Without assuming profit maximization, therefore, the economist can nevertheless predict that relatively correct (viable) adaptations or decisions will tend to be the ones observed—for example, the employment of low-skilled workers becomes less viable a practice after imposition of a minimum-wage law.

Enke (1951) expanded on Alchian's discussion, with a significant shift in point of view. He suggested that, *given sufficient intensity of competition,* all policies save the optimum would in time fail the survival test. As firms pursuing successful policies expand and multiply, absorbing a larger fraction of the market, a higher and higher standard of behavior becomes the minimum criterion for competitive survival. *In the long run, viability dictates optimality.* Consequently, for long-run predictive purposes (under conditions of intense competition), the analyst is entitled to assume that firms behave "as if" optimizing.

"As if" optimization is of course what the biologist ordinarily has in mind in postulating that organisms (or, sometimes, genes or populations) "choose" strategies leading to evolutionary success. Two levels of the optimization metaphor in biology may be distinguished. First, there are axes along which the organism can be regarded as having a degree of actual choice (what size of territory to defend, how much effort to devote to the struggle for a mate, what intensity of parental care to confer upon offspring). Here we speak only of "as if" optimizing because we do not credit the animal with the intelligence necessary for true (nonmetaphorical) optimization. Secondly, there are axes along which the organism cannot exercise choice in any meaningful sense at all (whether or not to be an unpalatable insect, whether or not to be a male or female). Nevertheless, such is the power of selection that the optimization metaphor often seems workable for "choice" of biological characters even on this second level.

There is, however, a serious problem here not yet adequately treated in either economics or biology. If, as applies in almost all interesting cases, the strategic choice is *among probability distributions,* what is the "optimum"? According to what criterion does natural selection select when strategies have uncertain outcomes?

In evolutionary theory, the "as if" criterion of success (the maximand) is generally postulated to be *fitness:* the ratio of offspring numbers to parent numbers at corresponding points in the generational life cycle (Fisher, 1958). In a deterministic situation, no doubt it is better adaptive strategy to choose higher fitness over lower. (Or, translating from metaphorical to literal language, in the long run the environment will be filled by those types of organisms who have developed and passed on to descendants traits permitting higher multiplication ratios.) But what if the situation is not deterministic, so that some or all of the strategies available generate probability distributions rather than definite deterministic numbers for the fitness ratio? In such circumstances the strategy that is optimal in terms of *mean* fitness—that yields the highest mathematical expectation of offspring per parent—might be quite different from the strategy that rates highest in terms of viability (that minimizes the probability of extinction). Where such a conflict arises, some biologists have suggested that viability considerations dominate over mean fitness (Williams, 1966).

No solution to this general problem in evolution theory will be offered here.[7] The point to be underlined is that Enke envisaged a situation where the outcome of each alternative policy option for the firm is *objectively* deterministic, although *subjectively* uncertain from the point of view of the firm's decision-maker (acting under limited information). Under these conditions there really does exist an objectively optimum course of action leading to maximum profit, which intense competition (even in the absence of knowledge) ultimately enforces—in Enke's view—upon all surviving firms. Alchian (1950, p. 212) sometimes seems to have the same idea. In saying that *maximum* realized profits is meaningful while *maximizing* profit is not, he means that one cannot "maximize" a probability distribution representing subjective uncertainty about profit, but there is nevertheless a deterministic or objective "maximum" of profit that could be attained if the knowledge were available. Usually, however, Alchian seems to have in mind the quite different case in which the outcomes are intrinsically or *objectively* probabilistic, rather than merely subjectively uncertain because of imperfect knowledge. Here there does not exist any unequivocal optimum, and Enke's argument does not apply. For Alchian, it is in such an environment that viability (positive realized profit) becomes the relevant success criterion.

Independent of Alchian's introduction of the viability argument, but parallel in its implications, was Herbert A. Simon's (1955, 1959) contention that firms are better regarded as "satisficing" than as optimizing. Starting from a psychological rather than evolutionary orientation, Simon contended that decision-makers are conservative about modifying established routines yielding satisfactory results—unless forced to do so by exogenous changes that threaten unacceptable outcomes. The reason given was informational: the decision-maker who recognizes the inadequacy of his knowledge, or the costs of performing the computations necessary for determining optimality even if he had all the relevant data, does not find that it pays even to attempt to optimize.[8] Simon did allow for a long-run approach toward optimization under stationary conditions in the form of a gradual shift of the decision-maker's "aspiration level" toward the best outcome attainable. But, he emphasized, business decisions take place in a context of ever-recurring change; the process of gradual approximation of optimality can never progress very far before being confounded by events. Thus, for Simon as for Alchian, the environment primarily plays a selective role in rewarding choice of *viable* strategies. Simon, in contrast with Alchian, chooses to emphasize how this process has in effect been internalized into the psychology of decision-makers.

A closely related aspect of the optimizing-selection process is the question of "perfection." It is possible in evolutionary models alternatively to emphasize the *achieved state of adaptation*, or the *process of adaptive change* toward that state. In the biological realm a high state of perfection on the organismic level has been attained: " . . . organisms in general are, in fact, marvellously and intricately adapted, both in their internal mechanisms, and in their relations to external nature" (Fisher, 1958, p. 44). The high degree of perfection is evidenced by the fact that the vast majority of mutations, which follow a random law, are harmful to the organism rather than beneficial. An important and less obvious consequence of the high degree of perfection is that the environment, as it changes under a variety of random influences, is always (from the organism's viewpoint) tending to deteriorate. So even relatively well-adapted organisms, or particularly such organisms, require the ability to track environmental changes. In the economic sphere, in contrast, we do not—though perhaps we should—think in terms of a very high degree of perfection in the adaptations of individuals or firms.[9] The argument in terms of perfection has been at the heart of much of the critical discussion of the biological model in economics.

Penrose (1952, 1953) criticized Alchian by contending, in effect, that the achieved state of economic adaptation is generally *too perfect* to be accounted for by merely random behavior on the part of businessmen. Although high states of adaptation are indeed attained in the biological sphere even without rational optimizing, that is due, she argued, to the extreme intensity of competition forced by organisms' innate urge to multiply—the Malthusian principle. This urge being lacking in the economic sphere, and competition therefore less intense, the business-man's purposive drive to make money is required to supply the analogous driving force (Penrose, 1952, p. 812).

Of course, the *desire* to make money is not enough. The key point of the Penrose criticism is that this desire must, for the most part, be realized. Businessmen must expect to be successful if they are to enter the competitive arena. And any such expectation would be too regularly refuted to persist if actual outcomes realized were no better than would ensue from random action. So the Penrose image is one of a changing environment (else there would not be much in the way of profit oppor-tunities) very effectively tracked by rationally optimizing businessmen.

The selectional processes of Nature, driven by random variation and Malthusian competition, are profligately wasteful of life and energy (Haldane, 1957; Feller, 1967). An implication of the Penrose thesis is that the wastage cost of economic selection should be considerably less than that of biological selection.[10] Quantitative estimates of the selec-tional wastage cost (bankruptcies, abandonments, etc.) would be of in-terest, therefore, in providing some measure of the prevalence and suc-cess of rational optimization.[11]

While Penrose argued that the observed degree of adaptation in the economy is *too perfect* to be accounted for by blind environmental selection, Winter's (1964, 1971, 1975) critique is based on the opposite contention—that the state of adaptation is *too imperfect* to be accounted for by a process that leads to the same outcomes ''as if'' firms actually optimized. His argument is therefore directed against Enke's extension of the selectional model, against the idea that in the long run viability requires optimality, rather than against Alchian's original version. The main evidence of imperfection cited by Winter (1971, p. 241) is the prevalence in business practice of conventional rules of thumb (for ex-ample, a pricing policy of fixed percentage markups) even where seem-ingly in conflict with profit-maximizing behavior.

Winter contributed interesting suggestions about the nature of *inheritance* and *variation* in economic selectional models. For Alchian (1950, p. 216), the inherited aspect of the firm was described as ''fixed internal conditions''—in effect, simple inertia due to the fact that the firm is more or less the same from one day to the next. Variation was attributed to imitation of successful firms,[12] or simply to trial-and-error exploration. For Winter, the inherited element, analogous to the biological genotype, is represented by certain more permanent aspects of the firm (its "decision rule"). This is to be distinguished from the specific decision made in a given context, which is analogous to the biological phenotype. What the environment selects is the correct action, even though it be the chance result of a rather inferior decision rule. In natural selection as well, well-adapted and less well-adapted genotypes might be represented at a given moment by the same phenotype. But, over a number of generations, natural selection working together with the Mendelian laws of inheritance will tend to fix the superior genotype in the population.[13] The economic mechanism of repeated trials is somewhat different, as no genetic recombination is involved. But surely we can expect that, as a variety of selectional tests are imposed over time, those firms providing a merely lucky action-response to a particular environmental configuration will tend to be selected against as compared with those following a more correct decision rule.[14]

In his first article Winter employed the term "organization form" for what his later papers call "decision rule" or "rule of action." While the intended referent is the same, and is indeed better described by the words "decision rule" or "rule of action," the initial term had interesting implications that might well have been pursued. "Organization form" would ordinarily be understood to mean something like corporation or partnership, large firm or small, etc. This is a more visible and operational concept than "decision rule." Since even the best decision rule (in the usual sense of that term) might not make possible survival of a firm with an ill-adapted organizational form, we should really think of three levels of selection—action, decision rule, and organization form.[15]

The broadly similar views of Alchian and Winter represent, it might be noted, a Lamarckian evolutionary model. Lamarck believed (as did Darwin) that acquired characters can be inherited, and also that variations tend to appear when needed. Failure-stimulated search for new rules of action (Winter), taking in particular the form of imitation of observed success (Alchian), is—if the results are assumed to be heritable—certainly in the spirit of Lamarck. The Lamarckian model is inapplicable to inheritance and variation (whether somatic or behavioral) mediated by the *genetic* mechanism, but it seems to be broadly descriptive of *cultural* evolution in general, and of economic responses in particular.[16]

Perhaps Winter's most important contribution in this area is his actual modelling of possible *selectional equilibrium* situations. Space does not permit adequate exposition or review of these formulations here, but the following summary may be suggestive:

Those organization forms which have the lowest zero growth price are viable, others are not. Or, to put the matter another way, price will tend to the lowest value at which some firm's organization form still yields non-negative growth. Firms whose organization forms result in decline at that price will approach zero scale as time goes on, leaving the firms which have the minimum zero growth price to share the market (Winter, 1964, p. 253).

This language suggests the "long run zero-profit equilibrium" of the competitive industry, reinterpreted in terms of the biologists' population equilibrium condition of zero growth. But Winter is at pains to show that even a firm with the lowest possible zero-growth price (lowest minimum of Average Total Cost curves) might—as a result of using an inappropriate decision rule—not actually be a survivor in selectional equilibrium. So the traditional competitive equilibrium might not be generated, or, once generated, might not respond in the standard way to changes in exogenous determinants.[17] One reason for this divergence from the traditional result, however, is that Winter's model is limited to the single adjustment mechanism of *firm growth*. Among the factors not considered, *entry pressure* on the part of new firms and (a more surprising omission in view of the previous emphasis) *failure-stimulated search* on the part of unsuccessful existing firms would tend to force a progressively higher state of adaptation upon survivors.

In his 1971 article Winter (1971, p. 247) indicates that in order to achieve the optimality properties of the standard competitive model an "innovating remnant" is needed. This category consists of firms that are, for unexplained reasons, inveterate searchers who will ultimately hit upon any as-yet-undiscovered superior decision rules. But new entrants, upon whom standard theory relies to discipline firms already in the industry, can also serve this exploratory role. A fruitful approach, consistent with biological observation, would be to recognize that one of the many possible survival strategies adopted by organisms (firms) is a tendency to search—and at any moment of time there will be a balance between organisms searching for new niches and organisms adapting to existing ones. (This point will come up again when competitive strategies are discussed below.)

It is a rather odd accident that biological models entered into economic thought in connection with the theory of the *business firm*—a highly specialized and consciously contrived "cultural" grouping. To some extent, as just seen, evolution theory is applicable to firms: inheritance, variation, competition, selection, adaptation—all play roles in explaining the observed patterns of survivorship and activity. Still, if biological models were being explored afresh for possible relevance to economic behavior, one's first target for consideration would naturally be the *individual* together with the *family*—entities of direct biological significance. Without any preconceived limitation of attention to the business firm, several aspects of economic theorizing will now be examined from a biological orientation: the nature and provenance of preferences; the evolution of patterns of competition, cooperation, and conflict; and resulting tendencies toward equilibrium, cycles, and progressive change.

IV. Elements of Economic Theorizing:
A Biological Interpretation

The contention here is that the social processes studied by economics, or rather by the social sciences collectively, are not mere analogs but are rather *instances* of sociobiological mechanisms—in the same sense in which chemical reactions have been shown to be a special class of processes following the laws of physics (Alland, 1967; Wilson, 1977). For this to be in any way a useful idea, it remains to be shown that a more general sociobiological outlook can in fact provide social scientists with a deeper and more satisfactory explanation of already-known results, or better still can generate new ones.[18]

A. Utility, Fitness, and the Provenance of Preferences—Especially, Altruism. Modern neoclassical economics has forsworn any attempt to study the source and content of preferences, that is, the goals that motivate men's actions. It has regarded itself as the logic of choice under conditions of "given tastes." But many of the great and small social changes in history have stemmed from *shifts* in people's goals for living. The very terminology used by the economist—preferences, wants, tastes—tends not only to trivialize these fundamental aims and values, but implies that they are arbitrary or inexplicable (*de gustibus non est disputandum*). Nor have the other social sciences, to whom the economists have unilaterally delegated the task of studying preferences, made much progress in that regard. The healthy aggrandizing tendency of modern economics requires us, therefore, to overstep this boundary like so many others.

No doubt there is a large arbitrary element in the determination of wants. Individuals are idiosyncratic, and even socially influenced preferences may reflect chance accidents in the histories of particular societies. But it is equally clear that not all preferences for commodities represent "mere taste." When we learn that Alabamans like cooling drinks more than Alaskans do, it is not hard to decipher the underlying physiological explanation for such differences in "tastes." Unfortunately, the refusal of modern economics to examine the biological functions of preferences[19] has meant that the bridge between human physiology and social expressions of desire has been studied by no one (except, perhaps, by practitioners of empirical "human engineering").

On a very abstract level, the concept of *homeostasis* has been put forward as the foundation of wants: the individual is postulated as acting to maintain vital internal variables within certain limits necessary for optimum functioning, or at least for survival (Day, 1975). But homeostasis is too limited a goal to describe more than very short-run human adaptations. And in any case, the internal "production function" connecting these internal variables with external social behavior has somehow fallen outside the domain of any established field of research.

Of more critical importance to social science than tastes for ordinary commodities are preferences taking the form of attitudes toward other humans. Anger and envy are evidently antisocial sentiments, while benevolence and group identification promote socialization. Socially relevant attitudes differ from culture to culture: in some societies hierarchical dominance is a prime motive for action, in others not; in some, marital partners value fidelity highly, in others promiscuity is regarded as normal; in some cultures people cluster closely together, in others they avoid personal contact. The programmatic contention here is that such preference patterns, despite seemingly arbitrary elements, have survived because they are mainly adaptive to environmental conditions. (No strong emphasis will be placed upon the issue of whether such adaptations are cultural or genetic in origin, in line with the argument above that the ability to evolve cultural traits is itself a kind of genetic adaptation.) This contention will surely not be always found to hold; in the biology of plants and animals as well, it is often unclear whether a particular morphological or behavioral trait is truly adaptive or merely an accidental variation. Nature is unceasingly fertile in producing random modifications. But if a trait has survived, as a working hypothesis the biologist looks for an adaptive function.[20]

As a nice example, in a famous passage in *The Descent of Man* Darwin asserted that for hive bees the instinct of maternal hatred rather than maternal love serves an adaptive function. He went on to generalize that, for animals in general (and not excluding mankind), "sentiments" or social attitudes are but a mechanism of adaptation (Ghiselin, 1974). The anthropologist Ronald Cohen (1972) has similarly pointed to variations among cultures in degrees of "affect" (that is, of interpersonal emotional attachment) as adaptive responses to environmental circumstances.

The biological approach to preferences, to what economists call the utility function, postulates that all such motives or drives or tastes represent proximate aspects of a single underlying goal—fitness. Preferences are governed by the all-encompassing *drive for reproductive survival*. This might seem at first absurd. That all humans do not solely and totally regard themselves as children-making machines seems evidenced by phenomena such as birth control, abortion, and homosexuality. Or, if these be considered aberrations, by the large fractions of income and effort devoted to human aims that compete with child-rearing—among them entertainment, health care beyond the childbearing age, personal intellectual advancement, etc. Yet, all these phenomena might still be indirectly instrumental to fitness. Birth control may be a device leading *on net balance* to more descendants rather than fewer; health care beyond the childbearing age may more effectively promote the survival and vigor of children or grandchildren. And, as we shall see shortly, even a childlessness strategy *may* be explicable in fitness terms!

In any attempt to broaden the application of economic reasoning, to make it a general social science, a key issue is the problem of altruism (the "taste" for helping others): its extent, provenance, and determinants. Old-fashioned, narrow economics was often criticized for employing the model of economic man—a selfish, calculating, and essentially nonsocial being.[21] Of course, it was impossible to postulate such a man in dealing with that essential social grouping, *the family*. Neoclassical economics avoided the difficulty by abandoning attempts to explain intrafamily interactions! Some economists formalized this evasion by taking the household rather than the individual as the fundamental *unit* of economic activity; in effect, they postulated total altruism within and total selfishness outside the family.

Modern economic "imperialists" have been dissatisfied both with the excessively restrictive postulate of individual selfishness and with the exclusion of intrafamily behavior from the realm of economic analysis. The modern view postulates a generalized preference of utility function in which selfishness is only the midpoint of a spectrum ranging from benevolence at one extreme to malevolence at the other (Becker, 1974).[22] But, standing alone, this is really an empty generalization. Where any individual happens to lie on the benevolence-malevolence scale with regard to other individuals still remains a merely arbitrary "taste." And yet we all know that patterns of altruism are not merely arbitrary. That a parent is more benevolent to his own child than to a stranger's is surely capable of explanation.

From the evolutionary point of view the great analytical problem of altruism is that, in order to survive the selectional process, altruistic behavior must be profitable in fitness terms. It must somehow be the case that being generous (at least sometimes, to some beneficiaries) is selectively more advantageous than being selfish!

A possible semantic confusion arises here. If altruism were defined simply as accepting injury to self in order to help others, without counter-vailing benefit of any kind, then indeed natural selection would quickly eliminate altruist behavior. When biologists speak of altruism they do not mean to rule out offsetting or redeeming mechanisms making unselfish behavior profitable in some sense; indeed, their analysis requires that such exist.[23]

The redeeming mechanisms identified by biologists seem to fall into two main categories. In the first, altruistic behavior survives because, despite initial appearances, a fuller analysis shows that *the preponderance of benefit or advantage is really conferred on the self*. We may, though paradox-ically, call such behavior "selfish altruism"; being ultimately selfish, such altruism does not require compensation or reciprocity to be viable. In the second class of redeeming mechanism compensation does take place; Trivers (1971) has termed such behavior "reciprocal altruism." Recip-rocal altruism, apart from motivation, approaches what economists would of course call *exchange*. It will be discussed, in connection with that topic, in Section B following.

The clearest cases of selfish altruism, of behavior only seemingly selfish, stem from the fact that *in the biological realm there are two levels of self*. On one level is the morphological and physiological constitution of the organism (the phenotype); on the other level the organism's genetic endowment (the genotype). The genetic constitution may contain reces-sive genes that are not expressed in the phenotype; perhaps even more important, the phenotype is subjected to and modified by environmental influences that leave the genotype unaffected. "Unselfish" action defined as behavior that injures the organism's phenotypical well-being may yet tend to propagate the organism's genotype. Indeed, since all living beings eventually die, ultimately the only way to achieve a payoff in fitness terms is to help certain other organisms—most notably, of course, one's off-spring—carry one's genetic endowment beyond the death barrier.

The mechanism rewarding this type of altruist behavior is called *kin selection* (Hamilton, 1964). Maximization of fitness from the point of view of the genotype often dictates a degree of altruism from the point of view of the phenotype—not only to offspring, but more generally to close relatives. Setting aside a number of qualifications, we might say that any individual should be willing to give his life to save two of his brothers (since full sibs have at least half their genes in common), or four half-brothers, or eight cousins, etc. Put another way, the "as if" maximand governing choice of evolutionary strategy is not the organism's *own* fitness but its *inclusive* fitness—the reproductive survival, with appropriate discounting for distance of relationship, of all those organisms sharing its genetic endowment.

Before proceeding to draw out some of the implications of altruism motivated by kin selection, a word of caution: actual behavior always represents the *interaction* of two determining factors—on the one side preferences, on the other side opportunities (constraints). We cannot directly infer altruistic preferences from cooperative behavior; in some environments the limited opportunities available may dictate that even enemies cooperate in the interests of selfish survival. Nor can we directly infer malevolence from hostile behavior; in some environments even brothers may be impelled to fight one another for survival.

Compare parent-to-offspring altruism with sib-to-sib altruism. Parental altruism is behaviorally much the more evident, and yet the degree of kinship (proportion of shared genes) in the two cases is exactly the same! The reason for the difference is that brothers and sisters are ordinarily in much closer *competition* with one another than parents are with children.[24] Why then the famed maternal hatred and sisterly altruism among ants? The explanation is remarkable. Due to the unusual method of sex determination called haplodiploidy (Trivers and Hare, 1976), sisters in ant colonies (the queen and worker castes) are more closely related to one another than they are to their own offspring (or would be, if they had offspring)! The notoriously lazy male drones, on the other hand, have only the ordinary degree of kiship with other colony members.

Yet it must not be assumed that parents and offspring never compete. Each offspring's selfish interest lies in having its parents' full devotion. But the parent aiming at reproductive survival strives for an optimal allocation of care and protection over *all* his or her offspring—past, present, and future. One nice implication is described by Trivers (1974). Intergenerational conflict occurs during the period when additional parental care, still desirable from the offspring's point of view, is no longer optimal for the parent (who must consider his opportunity cost in the form of the potential fitness gain in caring for a new batch of offspring). But the *intensity* of such "weaning conflict" is a function of the offspring's expected degree of relationship with his sibs of the later batch. If an offspring in a promiscuous species foregoes maternal care, his sacrifice will probably operate to the benefit of more half-sibs; in permanently mating species, to the benefit of full sibs. Hence the prediction, which is in fact confirmed, that offspring will be somewhat less "selfish" (weaning conflict will be less intense) in species following the stable-family pattern.[25]

Another point of interest: why are parents generally more altruistic to offspring than offspring to parents—since the degree of relationship is the same? The reason turns on their disparate *opportunities* for helping one another. The offspring may initially require care simply in order to survive, while the parents usually have energy available over their own immediate survival needs. As the offspring develop self-sustaining capacity over time, parental devotion diminishes. Still another factor is the asymmetry in time. In terms of fitness comparisons, offspring generally have greater "reproductive value," that is, offspring are more efficient at producing future descendants for parents than parents are in producing future relatives (sibs and their descendants) for offspring (Fisher, 1958, pp. 27–30). This is of course clearest when parents have entirely completed their reproductive activity. And, as seen above, the sibs are likely anyway to be pretty close competitors. Yet, in appropriate biological environments, offspring sometimes do curtail personal reproduction to help parents rear sibs (E. O. Wilson, 1975, p. 125).

What of altruism *within* the parental pair? From the biological viewpoint, alas, the parental partner is just a means to the end of selfish reproductive survival. He or she is undoubtedly to be valued, but only as a kind of specialized livestock! Trivers (1972) has explored in detail the mixed cooperative-competitive incentives for parents. Each requires the other to achieve reproductive survival, yet each is motivated to load on to the other a disproportionate share of the burden. The relatively smaller male investment in germ cells (sperm vs. egg) tends to lead to desertion, promiscuity, or to polygyny as ways for males to maximize numbers of descendants. The female, having already made a substantial somatic commitment in each reproductive episode, is less well placed than her mate to refuse additional parental commitment. (Females sometimes have means of cheating through cuckoldry, however.) The actual expression of one or more of these nonaltruistic tendencies depends upon the specific opportunities provided by the environmental situations of each species. There are situations in which parental pairs are models of mutual devotion, most notably in difficult environments where the survival of offspring requires full concentrated teamwork on the part of both parents (E. O. Wilson, 1975, p. 330).

Let us now go beyond the kin-selection mechanism favoring altruism directed at close relatives. Wynne-Edwards (1962) propounded the broader view that altruistic behavior may be favorably selected because it promotes the good of the species as a whole even though adverse to individual fitness—an example being voluntary restriction of number of offspring in times of food scarcity. Or, more generally, it has been argued that in environments where within-group altruism strongly promotes group success (as will often be the case), altruism tends to evolve through a process of *group selection*. For example, ant colonies that cooperate more efficiently will thrive and multiply, in comparison with colonies whose altruism is not so fully developed.

But biologists recognize a serious difficulty here, equivalent to what economists call a ''free-rider problem.'' To wit, the bearer of a gene dictating altruistic behavior tends to be negatively selected *within* his group as against fellow group members who are nonaltruists. Thus, *individual* selection opposes *group* selection; the altruistic groups may thrive, but always tend to become less and less altruistic while doing so. Even if the altruist groups drive all others to extinction, they themselves tend to end up nonaltruistic.

One important consideration might make it appear, at first sight, that the argument for selection of *kin-directed* altruism (that it is really selfish behavior, genotypically speaking) extends with almost equal force to broader within-group altruism—and indeed, even to cooperation on the level of the species as a whole. There is a strong degree of relationship (in the sense of correlation of genetic endowments) even among ''unrelated'' members of the same species. At many, or even the great majority of loci, genes are *fixed* in any given species (Fisher, 1958, p. 137); everyone has both genes in common at any such locus. So even individuals chosen at random in a species may well share 70 or 80 per cent of their genetic endowments.

This fact would seem to imply a very heavy ''selfish'' payoff, genotypically speaking, for altruistic behavior toward any conspecifics whatsoever. (And, of course, the correlation will tend to be closer, and so the payoff greater, within localized groupings having any degree of inbreeding.) The flaw in this argument is that group selection for altruistic behavior is not governed by *overall* correlations of genetic endowments, but by the presence or absence of the *specific* gene or genes determining altruist behavior. The ''free-rider problem'' operates equally effectively to favor noncarriers of the altruist gene, whether or not the individuals concerned otherwise have high or low correlations of genetic endowments. The altruist gene, metamorphically speaking, only ''wants'' to help *its* close relatives—organisms likely to be bearing the same specific gene. Given that the altruist gene is initially rare, it is highly unlikely that both parents carry it. Thus there is only a 50 per cent chance that one's full brother is a fellow carrier, and essentially no chance that a random conspecific is.

Still, it remains true that, from the point of view of the organism's overall genotype, altruism has a higher value for promoting fitness the higher the genetic correlation with the beneficiary. The mechanism governing the spread of the specific altruist gene might be thought of as the "supply" factor, with the overall genotypical benefit as the "demand" factor, in the process. The idea is that the free-rider problem is more likely to be overcome the greater the benefit from doing so.[26]

Two different types of process for overcoming the free-rider problem seem to have been identified by biologists: genetic drift, and group dispersal-reassortment. Genetic drift refers to variation of gene frequencies due simply to random fluctuations in the process of genetic recombination associated with mating. It may so happen that, despite the free-rider factor acting systematically to reduce within-group frequency of the altruist gene, by sheer random fluctuation the gene may nevertheless become fixed in the group (Smith, 1964). Once every member of the mating group possesses *only* altruist genes, there can be no within-group selection against altruists (unless the nonaltruist gene is reintroduced by mutation or by entry of outsiders). Such a development is highly improbable, unless the group is very small. And yet, Nature's experiments over time have been so unimaginably numerous that the improbable does happen from time to time. The improbability is sharply reduced for colonial species that "bud off" mating pairs to found new colonies (Lewontin, 1970). Here the altruist gene need only become fixed from time to time in a minimally-sized group—a mating pair. Such a pair may then found a colony which will be favorably group-selected in competition with other colonies. With successive "buddings off" from such a thriving colony, the altruist genes may spread and eventually preponderate.

The second process, often mixed with the first, involves regular dispersal and reassortment of groups having larger and smaller proportions of altruist genes (D. S. Wilson, 1975). *Within* each of the two classes of groups, prevalence of the altruist gene is progressively reduced by individual selection. Yet, if the collective advantage of altruist behavior is sufficiently large, it may be that groups with larger altruist representation increase in numbers so much relative to the others that the *overall* representation of the altruist gene increases in the population at large. If the groups regularly disperse and reassort themselves at some stage in the life cycle, this process can continue. (Failing dispersal and reassortment, on the other hand, individual selection will ultimately tend to drive out the altruist genes.)

A quite different sort of altruistic behavior, not necessarily involving close kin or even fellow carriers of the altruist gene, still falls into the selfish category. An instance appears in the development of alarm calls in birds (Trivers, 1971, pp. 43–44). A caller who alerts the flock to a predator, it is hypothesized, is thereby subjected to a higher risk (by attracting attention to itself). This behavior can be viable in fitness terms in certain circumstances, provided that it is only *comparatively* (not absolutely) disadvantageous to the caller. Thus, the altruism is merely *incidental* to selfish behavior. (The alarm may discourage the predator entirely or at least reduce his efficiency, so that the caller benefits on balance.) Still, under such "incidental altruism" even the *comparative* disadvantage tends to lead to elimination of the altruistic caller types by natural selection in favor of other group members (free riders). The saving feature here is that flocks are fluid, ever-changing aggregations. The caller gets only a small benefit, but gets it every time; the noncaller occasionally gets a big benefit from a free ride, but otherwise loses by refraining from calling. This tends to lead to an interior solution with a mixed population of callers and noncallers, for as the callers increase in numbers, the marginal advantage of being a noncaller (receiving more free rides) increases (Charnov and Krebs, 1975).

Incidental altruism of the alarm-call type is an instance of what economists would term the *private provision of a public good*. Olson (1965) argues that such a provision is more likely to be found in small groups, and particularly so where there are size or taste disparities within the group. (The larger members, or of course the more desirous ones, are the most motivated to provide the public good; the smaller, or the less desirous, are more likely be the free riders.) Buchanan (1968) has a somewhat different analysis, showing that substantial amounts of the public good might be provided even without such disparities. For Buchanan the main factor is the wealth enhancement that each group member derives from the purchase of the public good by others. On the one hand such purchases by others impel him to cut back his own purchases (the free-rider effect), but on the other hand the wealth enhancement stops him from cutting back all the way to zero (income effect).

Summing up, we have seen how altruistic behavior may prove to be viable in selectional terms even in the absence of any reciprocation. Over the course of human and pre-human evolutionary development, drives or instincts promoting such behavior have evolved and ultimately taken the form that the economist so inadequately calls preferences. And what is true for the specific "taste for altruism" holds in considerable degree for preferences in general—that these are not arbitrary or accidental, but rather the resultants of systematic evolutionary processes. This does not mean that such attitudes are now immutable. On the contrary, the inbuilt drives themselves contain the capability of expressing themselves in diverse ways depending upon environmental circumstances, which will in turn be modified by cultural evolution. The main lesson to be drawn, therefore, is not that preferences are biologically determined in any complete way—but rather, that they are scientifically analyzable and even in principle predictable in terms of the inheritance of past genetic and cultural adaptations together with the new adjustments called for by current environmental circumstances.

   B. *Exchange and Other Competitive Strategies.* Exchange, the sole form of social interaction traditionally studied by economists, is a particular competitive strategy in the great game of life—one involving a mutually beneficial relation among two or more organisms. It fits into the more general category called "mutualism" by biologists, of which there are both interspecific and intraspecific examples. Among the former are the symbiosis of alga and fungus that constitutes a lichen, the pollination-nectar exchange between bees and flowers, the presence of nitrogen-fixing bacteria on the roots of leguminous plants, and the resident protozoa in the gut of the termite that facilitate digestion of cellulose. Particularly interesting are the complementary associations among somewhat higher animals, which can be regarded as involving a degree of consciousness and discretionary choice. Here mutualism approaches the economic concept of exchange.

   In the absence of legal enforcement of compensation for acts conferring advantages on others, such patterns of mutual aid in the biological realm may represent instances of altruism on the part of one or more of the participants.[27] A nice example of what Trivers (1971) called reciprocal altruism is the interaction wherein certain fish species feed by grooming other, larger species—who in return refrain from eating their cleaners.[28]

   The key question for the selectional advantage of such reciprocal aid (in economic terms, for the viability of a pattern of exchange or "market") is control of cheating. As Trivers points out, this is a Prisoner's Dilemma—a special case of the more general public-good situation. However great the advantage jointly to the trading pair of establishing a reciprocal relationship, it pays each member to cheat if he can. The big fish, once having been properly groomed, would seem to be in a position to profit by snapping up his helper. (The little cleaner fish often does his work actually within the mouth of the client.) On the other side of the transaction, mimics have evolved that imitate the characteristic markings of the true cleaners. Upon being permitted to approach the big fish, the mimic takes a quick bite and then escapes!

The problem here is essentially the same as the cheating, sale of "lemons," or "moral hazard" that arises in a number of market contexts (Akerlof, 1970; Darby and Karni, 1973). While these phenomena threaten market viability, given the mutual advantage of trade the market can tolerate *some* slippage through cheating, provided it is kept within bounds (Zeckhauser, 1972). A number of devices have evolved, in both market and biological contexts, to limit the degree of slippage. The market cheater may be punished by law, the mimic cleaner fish by being (with some probability) caught and eaten. Noncheaters in markets establish personal reputations and brand names, while cleaner fish develop (so it is claimed) a regular clientele of satisfied customers.

Mutually advantageous exchange is facilitated by altruistic motivations; the emotions of affection and sympathy have evolved, Trivers contends, because they provide a better guarantee of reciprocity than any mere calculated advantage of doing so. Put another way, altruism economizes on costs of policing and enforcing agreements (Kurz, 1975).

Becker (1976) has contended that sympathetic motivation may be required *only on one side* of reciprocal-altruism interactions. The other party can be quite selfish in his aims, yet may still find cooperative behavior advantageous. Consider a selfish beneficiary of a parent's benevolence: a "rotten kid." The key proposition is that the rotten kid may still act benevolently toward the parent, simply in order to maximize the latter's capacity to bestow benefits upon him. And, in these circumstances, the mutual advantage of cooperative behavior may be such that even the "unselfish" parent ends up *selfishly* better off than he would if he were not altruistic! Consequently, in biological terms, no loss of fitness on either side is involved. This altruistic "contagiousness"— unselfish motivation on one side breeding cooperative behavior on the other side—would seem to promote the evolution of mutual aid patterns. Let one party be so motivated, for whatever reason (for example, altruism on the part of the parent could evolve simply from kin selection), and we will tend to observe reciprocity and mutual aid.[29]

More generally, Trivers argues that human evolution has developed a balance between the abilities to engage in and to detect and suppress subtle cheating while participating in reciprocal interactions. The sense of justice, what Trivers calls "moralistic aggression," is an emotion that involves third parties as additional enforcers to punish cheaters. Finally, the selectional advantage of these emotions has led to evolution of the ability to stimulate or mimic them—to hypocrisy. Note once again how these emotional qualities, absent from the makeup of "economic man," turn out to have an important place in the biological economy of human relationships. Economics can, as the economic imperialists allege, deal with the whole human being, and indeed *must* do so even to explain the phenomena in its traditional domain of market behavior.

The chief biological example of *intraspecific* exchange is of course mating interaction. Here vying for trading partners, sexual competition, not only has market parallels but is of course an important economic phenomenon in its own right. In some human societies marriage partners are explicitly sold, but more generally the marriage relationship constitutes a form of "social exchange."[30] The competition for mates in the biological realm displays many familiar and some unexpected parallels with market phenomena.

Health and vigor in sexual partners are obviously desirable qualities, correlated with the probability of generating and rearing viable offspring. As a means of demonstrating these qualities (that is, of advertising), sexual displays, combats, and rituals have developed.[31] There is a nice analogy here with recent economic theories of "competitive signalling" (Spence, 1974b; Stiglitz, 1975; Riley, 1976). Some characteristics may be acquired by economic agents not because they *confer* competitive superiority, but only because they *demonstrate* a preexisting superiority (in potential for mutually advantageous exchange). Just as success in display or combat, even in cases where biologically useless in itself, may signal sexual vigor—so educational attainment, even where of itself useless in contributing to productivity, may yet be a signal of useful qualities like intelligence.

Another desirable quality in a mate is possession of territory, generally by the male.[32] This is advertised in birds by the call. Presumably it is not the artistic excellence of the male's call that attracts the female, but the mere announcement effect—since the quality of the product (of the territory) is evident on inspection.[33] But for goods whose quality can be determined only by experience, the main message conveyed by advertising is simply that the product is worth the effort of advertising (Nelson, 1970, 1974)! Sexual displays seem to fall in this category.

Sexual competition also provides parallels with what is sometimes called "excessive" or "destructive" competition for trade. Cheating is once again a factor, as it pays males to mimic vigor by convincing displays even if they do not actually possess it. (The "coyness" of the female is said to have evolved to prevent premature commitment of her limited reproductive capacity to males with only a superficially attractive line (E. O. Wilson, 1975, p. 320).) Sexual combats may go beyond mere demonstration and actually harm the vanquished party, or sometimes the victor as well. Biologists have devoted considerable attention to cases like the peacock, where the extreme development of sexual ornaments appears to be disfunctional to the species or even to the individual. The explanation seems to be that positive *sexual selection* can to a degree overcome a disadvantage in terms of *natural selection*—the peacock with a splendid tail does not survive so well or so long but is more likely to find a mate. Such a development requires that male ornamentation and female preference evolve in parallel, which when carried to an extreme degree may represent a rather unstable equilibrium (Fisher, 1958).

In economic exchange, another mechanism of competition is *entry and exit*—variation of numbers to equalize on the margin the net advantages of the various types of activity. This also operates in sexual competition; the sex ratio varies to equalize the advantage of being a male or a female! Other things equal the equilibrium male/female sex ratio is 1/1. Taking any offspring generation, exactly half its genetic endowment is provided by male parents and half by female parents. Hence, if one sex were scarcer than the other in the parent generation at mating age, its *per capita* representation in the offspring generation's genes (genetic fitness) would be greater. If the disproportion persisted, it would pay in fitness terms to have offspring of the scarcer sex, and an adaptive response in this direction would correct the disparity. Even such practices as disproportionate infanticide of females will not affect the equilibrium 1/1 ratio. (This outcome displays the power of individual as opposed to group selection, since a 1/1 ratio is not the most "efficient" from the point of view of species growth. In terms of group selection it would generally be much more desirable to have a larger proportion of females.)

One factor that does distort the equilibrium sex ratio has been described by Trivers and Willard (1973). It is nearly universal among mammals that male parents have a higher *variance* in number of offspring than female parents. (A single male can father hundreds or even thousands of offspring, but the female's reproductive capacity is much more severely limited.) Also, healthy, vigorous parents tend to have healthy, vigorous offspring and physically weak parents, weak offspring. Taken together, these two considerations imply that it pays stronger parents to have *male* offspring; strong male children will tend to engender a relatively larger number of descendants. Conversely, it pays weaker parents to have *female* offspring, to minimize exposure to variance. Thus an explanation is provided for the otherwise mysterious tendency of the human male/female sex ratio to rise with socioeconomic status (Shapiro, Schlesinger, and Nesbitt, 1968) (since status tends to be correlated with health and vigor).

More generally, the normally higher early male mortality is explained. Prenatal and postnatal mechanisms discriminating against males permit stronger parents (who will suffer relatively less early mortality among their offspring) to end up with relatively more male children and weaker parents with relatively more female children.

Even *interest*, Trivers (1971) suggests, ultimately has a biological origin. *Reproductive value* (the average number of offspring an organism will engender in the future) declines with age in the childbearing life phase. A loan today involves a cost to the lender in fitness terms; since his reproductive value upon repayment will be less, the repayment would have to be proportionately greater to make up the difference.

So exchange in a variety of forms, and with many familiar implications, exists in the biological realm. But what does seem to be a specifically human invention is the *organized* market, a form of exchange involving "middlemen" specialized to trading activity. This must have been what Adam Smith really had in mind in his otherwise too-sweeping assertion that "the propensity to truck, barter, and exchange" is specifically associated with the human species.[34] Sexual competition and cleaning symbioses provide sufficient evidence to the contrary. And associations such as pack membership also undoubtedly involve "social exchange."

But competition for trading partners remains only one very special type of biological competition. The more general concept used by biologists is illustrated in Figure 1.[35] Let N_G and N_H signify numbers of two populations G and H. Then if $\dot{N}_G$, the time-derivative of N_G, is a negative function of N_H, and N_H of N_G, the two populations are called competitors. In the diagram we can draw for population G what the economist would call a "reaction curve" showing the population levels for which $\dot{N}_G = 0$, and similarly for population H. Since the populations are competitors, the reaction curves have negative slope. Their intersection will be a state of equilibrium. (Whether the equilibrium is stable or unstable depends upon the relative slopes at the point of intersection— as will be explored further in the next section.) If the reaction curves are *positively* sloped as in Figure 2, the two populations are complementary rather than competitive. (Again, depending upon the relative slopes, the intersection point may be stable or unstable.) Finally, there is a mixed case, typified by predator-prey interactions, where the reaction curve of the predator has $\dot{N}_G$ as an increasing function of the prey population N_H, while N_H is a falling function of N_G. (Again the equilibrium at the intersection may or may not be stable.)

Figure 1. Two Competitive Populations, Stable Coexistence Equilibrium.

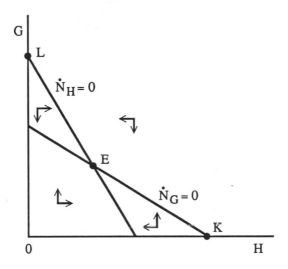

Competition in the general sense exists because some resource of relevance for two or more organisms is in scarce supply. The consequent *universality of competition* (the "struggle for existence") was of course the main message Darwin drew from Malthus. The ecologists speak of an organism's "fundamental niche" as the volume of abstract resource space in which it can exist—and of the "realized niche" as the volume which it actually occupies. Where niches overlap, there is competition. These considerations have one very essential implication: *that competition is generally more severe the more similar the organism.* The more similar the organisms, the greater the niche overlap. In particular, *intra*species competition tends to be more intense than *inter*species competition (Darwin, 1859).[36] For example, territorial birds exclude conspecifics but to a greater or lesser extent tolerate birds of other species. And, we have seen, competition tends to be particularly severe within families and especially among litter-mates; the high correlation of genetic endowments and of positions in the generational life cycle, plus physical proximity, make for near identity of resource requirements (niches).

There are two opposing forces which together constitute what might be called the "dilemma of sociality." On the one hand, altruistic preferences or motivations stem mainly from degree of relationship (from correlation of genetic endowments), not only among close kin but extend-

Figure 2. Two Complementary Populations, Stable Coexistence Equilibrium.

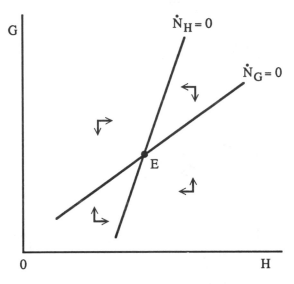

ing to more distant relatives. And even, perhaps, to a degree over the entire species. (Other things equal, a man's genes would tell him to favor his fellowman fighting with a bear.) This is the main socializing force. On the other hand, competition, which opposes socialization, tends to be most intense precisely where degree of relationship is closest. (The other man will often be a closer competitor than the bear.) In consequence, as organisms strike some balance between cooperative and competitive strategies, there is an element of instability in the outcome. The degree of conflict or of social cooperation is not a simple function of closeness of relationship, but depends upon the specific details of kinship as related to the environmental situation.

Competition-limiting strategies range over a spectrum, from minimal patterns of "holding back" to full cooperation. "Holding back" means that the economic unit or biological organism merely competes somewhat less intensely for resources than short-run selfish interest would dictate. An obvious economic example is cartelization, but more praiseworthy forms of holding back—for example, refraining from blowing up your competitor's premises—also fall into this category. In human societies the institutions of government and law provide reinforcers for what might otherwise be the too-frail force of altruism in limiting the extent of destructive forms of competition. Unfortunately, as evidenced most strikingly by the phenomenon of war, human genetic and cultural evolution have not progressed as far in this direction as might be desired.

Limits on competition have also evolved in the biological realm. In what is called "exploitation competition" organisms scramble to utilize resources but ignore competitors, whereas, in "interference competition," they gain resources precisely by hampering competitors (McNaughton and Woolf, 1973; E. O. Wilson, 1975). Interference may take the milder form, as in territoriality, of fighting only as necessary to deny a limited zone of resource access to others. But more aggressive versions also exist, of direct attack upon conspecifics—even of cannibalism, where the competitor himself is converted into a resource. This is relatively rare, however. Presumably, extreme forms of interference strategies have mainly proved disfunctional to the groups or species evolving them, and have therefore been selected against. (*Group* selection need not be involved here, as there is a fitness loss to the individual to the extent that his own descendants are inclined to eat one another up.) Biologists have observed that interference competition is more likely to evolve when resource limitations are particularly severe. In economic affairs as well, "cut-throat competition" is a product of hard times. When organisms are occupying unfilled environments, on the other hand, or firms are interacting in a growing market, competition takes place mainly through the externality of resource depletion (in economic terms, bidding up prices of inputs or driving down prices of products).

Another important means of limiting competition is *specialization*. It is useful to distinguish the specialization that results from competitive pressure, on the one hand, from the kind of cooperative specialization more properly called *the division of labor*. Unfortunately, there has been some confusion on this score. The valuable pioneering study on biology and economics by Houthakker (1956) confounds the two categories. The very important analysis by the biologist Ghiselin (1974), on the other hand, distinguishes what he calls the *competitive* division of labor (represented by the subdivision of ecological niches in the biological sphere, corresponding to product or locational differentiation in the economy) from the *cooperative* division of labor. In the former case (which, preferably, ought to be termed simply competitive specialization) there is no mutual dependence or complementarity among the entities. Each would be better off if the others were to vanish. The latter type of differentiation, the division of labor proper, is associated with true alliance—to achieve a common end, or at least for mutual benefit where a degree of complementarity exists.

In competitive specialization in the biological realm, each of the contending species is forced away from the zone of resource overlap—

not only in locational terms, but in the form of divergent evolution of characters. This process of character displacement, resulting in an equilibrium *separation distance* between the species (McNaughton and Woolf, 1973), is completely parallel to the economic mechanisms described in our textbooks under the heading of product-differentiation competition and locational competition ("monopolistic competition"). But on the other hand, the biologists emphasize, such specialization is constrained by the possibility that a generalist of intermediate character might outcompete the set of specialist types (Cody, 1974). Relative abundance and certainty of resources favor specialists; relative scarcity and unpredictability favor generalists.

Biologists, having developed a more subtle and elaborate approach to this question of specialization/generalization strategies than economists, recognize a variety of different dimensions of "generalist" competition against specialists. Individuals of a species might tend to a common intermediate character, able to make tolerably good use of a range of resources. Or the *individuals* might be specialized, yet the *species* show enough interindividual variety to generalize its command over resources. Still another form of generalization is *plasticity*, whereby the species is enabled to change its character in response to environmental shifts (Stigler, 1966). Such plasticity might be genetically determined if the population maintains a reserve of variety in the form of a largely heterozygotic genetic composition. Or failing this, it may have evolved a high mutation rate as a way of tracking the environment. Finally, even with a fixed genetic constitution the capability for learning and *behavioral* adaptation may exist to a greater or lesser extent. The human species, of course, has concentrated upon becoming a generalist of this last type.

Turning now to cooperation in the true sense, we arrive at what is properly called the division of labor. Since competition is most intense when organisms are all attempting to do the *same* thing (to occupy the same niche, to use the same resources), one way out is for individuals or groups to cooperate by doing *different* things. For the group, or rather for each member thereof, command over resources is thereby extended.

The division of labor in Nature penetrates profoundly into the deepest aspects of the differentiation of living matter. In multicelled organisms the parts unselfishly cooperate to serve the whole, which is of course warranted by the fact that all the cells of an individual organism are genetically identical (save the germ cells, of course). Sexual differentiation also represents an evident instance of the cooperative division of labor in the interests of reproductive survival. Here altruism is less perfect, in that each member of the parental team is altruistic toward the other only to the extent necessary for promoting the reproductive survival of his or her own genetic endowment (Trivers, 1972). Nevertheless, the mechanism works well enough to have won out, for the most part, over asexual reproduction. Going beyond this most elemental social unit—the male-female pair—the *family* involves a related type of role differentiation: that associated with the generational life cycle. This provides a temporal division of labor; each generation plays its role, in due course, in promoting the reproductive survival of the parent-offspring chain. While altruism between generations is by no means unlimited, as seen above, the differentiation of tasks ties together the interests of the family group.

For larger cooperative associations, necessarily among more remotely related organisms, specialization through the division of labor with its concomitant of social exchange must, to be viable, become compensatingly productive as the force of altruism is diluted. Traditional economies, epitomized by Adam Smith, demonstrated the economic advantage of the division of labor even for a group of entirely selfish individuals. The sociologist Durkheim (1933), in contrast, claimed that the division of labor generates a kind of superorganismic "solidarity." He argued that the economic benefits of the division of labor are picayune compared to this solidarity, a union not only of interests but of sentiments (as in the case of friends or mates). As so often occurs in social analysis, however, Durkheim fails to distinguish properly between desires (preferences) and opportunities. If there is any superorganismic tie among individuals, it can only be (according to the hypothesis accepted here) their sharing of genetic endowments. Yet in many important instances of the division of labor (for example, bees and flowers) there is no genetic association at all. The cooperative division of labor in such cases is no more than an alliance for mutual benefit. With genetic sharing it is no doubt easier for cooperation to evolve, but superorganismic ties are not sufficient causes and certainly not necessary consequences of the division of labor.

The human species, of course, has carried the division of labor to extraordinary lengths. The extent to which this represents genetic versus cultural evolution is not a simple matter to resolve. The regulation of cheating, necessary to make exchange and therefore the division of labor possible, has, as we have seen, been achieved in Nature to some degree. Even emotional supports for exchange, like the sense of justice ("moralistic aggression") may represent genetically evolved characters. On the other hand, human culture has evolved institutional supports for exchange and the division of labor—property, law, and government.

Analysis on the part of economists of the determinants of the division of labor has gone little beyond Smith's (1937, pp. 17–21) famous proposition: " . . . That the division of labour is limited by the extent of the market." Houthakker (1956), taking the standpoint of the individual, views him as the potential beneficiary of a number of activities some or all of which may however be disharmonious if undertaken together. The choice to be made is for individuals either to act as nonspecialists and incur costs of internal coordination, or else to separate and distribute the activities via a division of labor that entails costs of external coordination. Here Smith's "extent of the market" is taken as the inverse of inter-individual transaction costs, the absence of which would facilitate specialization with external coordination. Stigler's (1951) analysis is fundamentally similar, though concentrating on firms as decision units rather than individuals. Again, there are a number of activities, all desirable or even essential in the production of output, but diverging mainly in offering economies or diseconomies of *scale*. The firms would do better to divest themselves of at least the increasing-returns activities, if a specialized external supplier were available. As the *industry* expands, such specialized suppliers become economically viable entities. Thus, for Stigler, "extent of the market" signifies *aggregate* scale of output.

The discussion by the biologist Ghiselin (1974) provides many apt illustrations: for example, that an insect colony must reach a certain size before it pays to have a specialized soldier caste. But Ghiselin is inclined to stress that there are important advantages of nonspecialization, such as the existence of complementarities among certain activities (for example, teaching and research). In addition, there may be sequential rather than individual specialization, as when members of an ant colony all progress through a common series of different productive roles in the course of the life cycle.

Following up a suggestion by Ghiselin, it might really be better to think in terms of "combination of labor" rather than "division of labor." Division is the first step; it is the combination (external coordination) that produces the result. Apart from the division of labor as a form of *complementary combination* of individuals undertaking different specialized tasks, there is also the possibility of *supplementary combination* whereby individuals reinforce one another in performing the *same* task. A simple example would be men tugging on a rope to move a load; such "threshold phenomena" are quite important and widespread. Wherever scale economies for a given activity dictate a minimum efficient size greater than the full output of a single individual, we would expect to see a mixture of complementation and supplementation, of specialization and multiplication of numbers, in the general process of cooperation through the combination of labor.

A number of other dimensions of choice have been explored by biologists. One such is between "K-strategies" and "r-strategies." K symbolizes the carrying capacity of the environment, that is, the species number N^* at which the time-rate of change $N = O$. The symbol r signifies the maximum rate of Malthusian growth, which obtains under conditions where the environment is not constraining. The r-strategists are opportunist species, who pioneer and settle new unfilled environments. The K-strategists are solider citizens, who compete by superior effectiveness in utilizing the resources of relatively saturated environments. The r-strategists thus make their living from the recurrence of disequilibrium situations (entrepreneurial types, we would say). But their success can only be transient; ultimately they will be displaced by the more efficient K-strategist species. The r-strategists tend to be characterized by high early mortality, as they must continually disperse and take long chances of finding new unsaturated habitats. A high birth rate is therefore a necessity. Among other tendencies are rapid maturity, small body size, early reproduction, and short life. K-strategists, in contrast, tend to develop more slowly, have larger body size, and longer life (E. O. Wilson, 1975). Their inclination is to produce a smaller number of more carefully optimized offspring (Becker, 1960, 1974).

Analogs in the world of business exist for a number of these strategies. In the high-fashion industry we observe high birth rates and death rates of firms, in public utilities the reverse. In general, pioneering strategies tend to be more suitable for small firms—which survive better in highly changeable environments.

But as applied to *firms*, as emphasized previously, biological reasoning is only a metaphor. In particular, firms do not follow the reproductive laws of biology: small firms do not give birth to other small firms, and firms of one "species" (industry) may transfer to another. By way of contrast, human individuals, families, races, etc. *are* biological entities which may be regarded as choosing competitive strategies. Martial races may concentrate on success through politics, conflict, or violence ("interference strategy"); others may have proliferated and extended their sway through high birth rates; others through lower birth rates but superior efficiency in utilizing resources ("exploitation strategy"). The r-strategist pioneering human type was presumably selected for in the early period of American history—a period long enough for genetic evolution, though cultural adaptation may have been more important. This type was not entirely antisocial; altruist "pioneer" virtues such as mutual defense and sharing in adversity can emerge under r-selection. In the present more crowded conditions the preferred forms of altruism represent "urban" virtues of a negative rather than positive sort: tolerance, nonaggressiveness, and reproductive restraint (E. O. Wilson, 1975). Even today it seems likely that a suitable comparison of populations in environments like Alaska on the one hand and New York City on the other would reveal differential genetic (over and beyond merely cultural) adaptations.[37]

   C. The Results of Social Interaction—Equilibrium Versus Change. Equilibrium in biology has one striking feature with no close counterpart in economics: a dualism between processes taking place simultaneously on the level of *organisms* and on the level of *genes*.

   In dealing with the interactions of *organisms* the biologist generally uses a partial-equilibrium model, taking genetic compositions as fixed. He then asks such questions as: (1) For a given species G, what will be the limiting population number in a particular environment (the "carrying capacity" of the environment for that species)? (2) Or, with two or more interacting populations, G and H, what will be their respective equilibrium numbers N_G and N_H. And, in particular, will one drive the other to extinction, or might they even *both* become extinct? (The last possibility may seem surprising. Yet a predator might conceivably be so efficient as ultimately to wipe out its prey, in which case its own extinction may follow.) (3) Where new species may enter an environment by migration, thus offsetting loss of species from extinction, what is the equilibrium number of distinct species, and how do the species partition the total biomass?

   To take up the second of these three questions, it was remarked above that the intersection of the two reaction curves of Figure 1 (two competitive populations) might be a stable or an unstable equilibrium point. It will be evident, by consideration of the nature of the interaction (as illustrated by the arrows showing the directions of change of the two populations from any N_G, N_H point in the positive quadrant), that the intersection equilibrium as shown is stable. Thus, we have here a coexistence solution at point E. If the labels on the reaction curves were reversed, however, it may be verified (by making appropriate changes in the arrows showing the directions of change) that the coexistence equilibrium would be unstable. Depending upon the initial situation, population H would drive G to extinction at point K, or population G would drive H to extinction at point L.

   A similar analysis of the complementary populations in Figure 2 will show that the coexistence equilibrium at point E is again stable. But if the labels on the reaction curves were reversed, the populations would jointly (depending upon the starting point) either decay toward zero or explode toward infinity. (Of course, in the latter case another branch of at least one of the reaction curves would eventually be encountered, beyond which the rate of change of population would again become negative.)

The arrows of directional change in the predator-prey diagram of Figure 3 show that a kind of spiral or cobweb exists around the intersection point E. Depending upon the slopes of the curve, the cobweb could: (a) repeat itself indefinitely, (b) converge to the coexistence equilibrium at E, or (c) oscillate explosively. In the latter case the result may be extinction of the predator (if the spiral first hits the prey axis, since the prey can continue to survive without the predator), or the extinction of both (if the spiral first hits the predator axis, in the case where the predator cannot continue to survive without prey). The theoretical tendency of predator-prey interactions toward cycles in population numbers has in fact been confirmed in empirical observations (McNaughton and Woolf, 1973).

These models have rather direct analogies with a number of processes in the realm of the human sciences. The reaction-curve format closely parallels Lewis F. Richardson's (1948) models of arms races (Rapoport, 1960; Boulding, 1962, 1950) and Lanchester's (1916) equations of combat (Morse and Kimball, 1951). Economists will of course recognize the duopoly solutions associated with Cournot (Allen, 1938).

Figure 3. Predator-Prey Interaction.

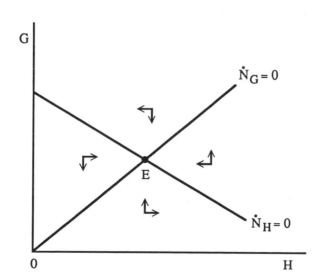

Biological models of equilibrium on the *genetic* level are again of a partial-equilibrium nature, since they typically involve only processes within a single population. The simplest version of such models is known as the Hardy-Weinberg Law. If at a particular gene locus two alleles A and a exist, under sexual reproduction there are three possible genotypes: AA, Aa, and aa. With random mating, if selective and other pressures determine the proportions p and q (where $p + q = 1$) for the prevalence of alleles A and a respectively, then the equilibrium proportions for the genotypes will be p^2 for AA, $2pq$ for Aa, and q^2 for aa. This equilibrium is reached extremely rapidly, in fact—apart from random fluctuations—in the first filial generation (Feller, 1950).

The proportions p and q will not in general remain stable, however. They are affected by mutation (A may change into a, and vice versa), by gene flow due to migration, by random fluctuation ("genetic drift"), and most importantly by natural and sexual selection associated with differing fitnesses of the three genotypes.

Selection operates on the gene proportions through differential survival of the phenotypes. A *dominant* deleterious (low-fitness) gene will tend to be extinguished relatively rapidly, in terms of generational time. But a *recessive* deleterious allele expresses itself as a phenotype only in the case of the aa genotype, and so tends to be eliminated only slowly. There may be other complicating features. For example, the allele causing human sickle-cell anemia is a recessive lethal in the homozygote (aa) form, but tends to confer a degree of immunity against malaria in the heterozygote (Aa) form. Where malaria is a serious cause of reduced fitness, the a-type allele will not be eliminated (Wilson and Bossert, 1971).

"Genetic drift" occurs because the actual numbers of the phenotypes AA, Aa, and aa will differ stochastically to a greater or lesser degree from the respective mean values p^2, $2pq$, and q^2. The most important consequence is a tendency toward the loss of heterozygosity, that is, genetic drift tends ultimately to fix a single allele in the population. Genetic drift operates more powerfully upon smaller populations, of course, and elimination obviously is much more likely to occur for an allele that is already rare. Note that even a superior-fitness allele, if sufficiently rare, might well be eliminated by stochastic fluctuations. (It was genetic drift that was called on above to explain the occasional fixing of low-individual-fitness "altruist" genes in some populations.)

Somewhat tenuous analogies exist between genes and ideas, between mutation and invention, etc. (Boulding, 1950, p. 7). A human population might increase fitness by "mutations" like a new form of social organization or the invention of a new tool or weapon. And ideas, like genes, are subject to the selectional test of competition. But the laws of the generation and propagation of ideas are so different from those of genes that the comparison does not really seem fruitful.

Some broader parallels might still be of interest, however. Sexual reproduction may be interpreted as a device that (among other things) provides populations with a *reserve of variability of characters*. Heterozygosity makes a range of different phenotypes available for selection in each generation, thus permitting the tracking of environmental shifts while delaying the loss of potential characters that might turn out to be useful in the future. Asexual organisms, lacking this reserve of variability, are more vulnerable to environmental shifts. In effect, sexual reproduction provides species with "memory," though at the cost of some loss of efficiency. In each generation, as was seen above, each of the combinations AA, Aa, and aa will generally be "recalled" and tried again—so long as $0 < p < 1$. And in actuality, more than two alleles are often "stored" at a given locus, and in addition there may exist other, more complex forms of genetic recombination or recall. The widened opportunities provided by sexual reproduction are related to the issue of satisficing versus optimizing discussed at several points previously. In the absence of "memory" of alternative possibilities, a biological entity could not successfully stray very far from any current combination that leads to even minimally satisfactory outcomes—since it cannot remember anything old, it can scarcely afford to learn something new. The mental development of the human species, culminating in speech and writing, has permitted the vast development of *cultural* memory independent of genetic storage of variability, thus widening the ability to explore alternatives and approach closer to true optimization.

Another feature that operates to store variety in the economic system is *the law of diminishing returns*, in its various forms. Rising marginal cost tends to lead to interior or coexistence solutions; entities or forms of organization that are favored by environmental changes tend to increase in prevalence, but not ordinarily so totally as to drive out all others. Thus, a capacity for rapid response to change tends to be preserved.[38] The concept corresponding to diminishing returns in biology is called "density dependence," though biologists tend to call upon this mainly to explain why single populations do not increase without limit (Wilson and Bossert, 1971). With respect to competing populations the biologists have a proposition that seems to run counter to diminishing returns in economics—Gause's Exclusion Principle. The idea is that no two species that fill the same ecological niche can permanently coexist (Wilson and Bossert, 1971, pp. 156–158). Here, at least, it would seem that the biologists can learn from us. Because of diminishing returns to any form of expansion (density-dependent effects), coexistence equilibria in the same niche should be perfectly possible. Ultimately, the same forces preventing a single *organism* from monopolizing a niche against conspecifics also tends to control the expansion of the species as a whole against its competitors.[39]

Biologists, as compared with economists, seem to devote relatively more effort to the description of processes of ongoing *change* as opposed to processes leading to *equilibrium* in the sense of stationary states. This is historically understandable, in that modern biology was faced at the outset with the great polemical problem of winning public acceptability for the fact of evolutionary change. In consequence, perhaps, biologists do not seem to have developed (or at any rate do not pay much attention to) concepts of *general* equilibrium. They do not seem, to cite one example, to have felt the need for integrating the two partial-equilibrium developments described above—one on the level of population numbers, the second on the level of genetic composition. On the other hand, they have developed models showing the working of a rich variety of mechanisms of change—mutation and recombination, selection and migration, learning, genetic drift, etc.—as well as useful generalizations concerning the extent and prevalence of certain patterned responses to change such as mimicry, convergence, character release, speciation, and the like.

Related to the intellectual problem of the relative importance of equilibrium versus change is an issue that has concerned both disciplines—the question that biologists call teleology. In Panglossian terms, is this the best of all possible worlds? Or, if not the best just yet, does our world at least progress toward such a desirable goal?

In biology, the teleological theme seems to underlie the concluding sentence of *The Origin of Species* (Darwin, 1859):

> Thus, from the war of nature, from famine and death, the most exalted object which we are capable of conceiving, namely, the production of the higher animals, directly follows. There is grandeur in this view of life, with its several powers having been originally breathed by the Creator into a few forms or into one; and that, whilst this planet has gone cycling on according to the fixed law of gravity, from so simple a beginning endless forms most beautiful and most wonderful have been, and are being evolved.

Darwin's language suggests, though it does not quite say, that evolution is directed by some higher force and that its results represent in some sense progress. Herbert Spencer and others went further to develop an evolutionist ethics—moral conduct is *defined* as that which contributes to better adaptation and progress toward higher forms. T. H. Huxley, Darwin's great supporter, declared: "The absolute justice of the system of things is as clear to me as any scientific fact."[40]

The alternative mechanistic view, that evolution is an entirely undirected process, is almost universally and emphatically postulated by modern biologists.[41] Ghiselin (1974) contends further that hidden teleology lurks wherever adaptation is explained in such terms as "the good of the species" or "the good of the community." But this accusation does not seem warranted. The scientific question is simply whether the mechanistic processes of evolution can lead to the emergence of characters benefiting larger groups although harming the individual bearer. That this is at least possible, as in the devotion of parents to offspring, can scarcely be denied. More generally, the genetic-relationship argument for altruism (kin selection) shades gradually in diluted form to groups up to the level of the species, and possibly beyond. Since Nature does select simultaneously on both the organism and the gene level—and on higher population and community levels as well—and since groups of genes or groups of individuals may become coadapted in a variety of ways and so coselected, it would seem that some of Nature's productions could validly be interpreted as responding to "the good of the group" rather than solely of the organism (or the gene).

Yet, it is evident, the argument of "perfection" does not hold with any force above the organism level. The many forms of destructive competition in Nature—from sexual combats within species to predation between species—preclude any inference of a universal harmonious adaptation to the nonliving environment (Tullock, 1971). Still, it seems that there may be at least some slow long-run pressure in this direction (Frech, 1973).[42]

A related question is the degree to which *cultural* evolution, which necessarily concerns group rather than individual traits, is adaptive. Again, one can hardly make any strong arguments for perfection of cultural adaptation. And yet, selection processes are certainly at work which tend to destroy societies that have somehow evolved seriously maladapted cultures (Alland, 1967; E. O. Wilson, 1975; Cohen, 1972; Durham, 1976).

The main classical tradition in economics has similarly been subjected to criticism on grounds of teleology. Adam Smith's view,[43] that under laissez-faire an "invisible hand" leads to a kind of *harmony* of private interests, has been attacked as apologetics for the capitalist system—as a tendentious attempt to prove that what exists is indeed the best of all possible worlds. Setting questions of motivation aside, it is indeed true that much of the intellectual effort of modern theorizing has gone into proving social optimality—in the very special sense of *Pareto-optimality*—of idealized versions of the laissez-faire capitalist economy. (Or, in some cases, of the welfare-state or even the socialist economy!) More specifically, what has been shown is that the equilibrium outcome under an unregulated economy with fully defined property rights is a social optimum in the sense that it would not be possible to improve the situation of any individual (in his own eyes) without harming one or several individuals (in their own eyes).

However, these results might equally well be interpreted as anti-apologetics. For, the idealized conditions necessary to make them valid evidently do not fully apply to any actual capitalist (or welfare-state or socialist) economy. And in fact, economists have devoted major energy to examination of forces leading to failures of Pareto-optimality—natural monopoly, oligopoly, externalities, and public goods being leading examples.

The lack of the institution of *property*—founded, in turn, upon the larger institutions of *law* and *government*—in the economy of Nature is an important element explaining the "imperfection" of social adaptations in the biological realm. Some observers have regarded animal *territoriality* as closely analogous to property, but this is incorrect. Territory in Nature is held only so long as it is continuously and effectively defended by the force of its possessor. Property does sometimes need to be defended by force, but what makes it property is the availability of impersonal enforcement through the law of the community.[44] To the extent that the property system is effective, a degree of progressive cultural adaptation tends to take place over time. Individuals need not expend energy in combat or other contests for possession, but are instead motivated to search out mutually advantageous ways of employing property so as to achieve a more complete division of labor. In particular, they are motivated to find ways around the failures of Pareto-optimality mentioned above (Coase, 1960).

Yet, lest this seem too unguardedly hopeful, it must be pointed out that the institutions of law and government are powerful mechanisms that may be employed to achieve many private or group ends quite apart

from Pareto-optimality. Law and government may destroy some individuals for the benefit of others, may penalize rather than promote
the division of labor, may undermine rather than support the institution of property. Nor can we say on scientific grounds that law and
government "ought not" do so. But to the extent that they do not, the
progress of adaptation to the environment will be hampered or even
reversed.

V. Points of Comparison—A Tabular View

Tables 1 and 2 have been designed as a way of pulling together,
without undue repetition, the strands of the preceding discussions. The
first table is an attempt to systematize, in a comparative way, the entities or units of action as viewed by biologists and by economists. The
second table is intended to display, again in a comparative way, the processes of action and interaction involving these entities.

For the economist the fundamental acting unit or agent is of course
the *individual*. Individuals organize into many types of composite units
for purposes of joint action—these are the "Cooperative Groups" in
Table 1. A useful though somewhat rough distinction can be made between "unselfish" groupings, whose dominant feature is the existence
of altruistic preference functions connecting the goals of the members,
and "selfish" aggregations where cooperative action is motivated only
by mutual anticipation of selfish gain.

The family is of course the standard example of a supposedly
"unselfish" grouping. As explained at length above, some or all participating family members may actually be motivated to a greater or lesser
degree by considerations of personal advantage rather than by other-
regarding love and concern. But for the most part, family associations
respond to supra-individual goals (kin selection). A variety of other communal associations ("brotherhoods")—social, religious, and the like—also
exist, at least purportedly, to unite the members thereof in unselfish
fellowship.

Economics, in contrast with other social sciences, has concentrated
attention upon the "selfish" associations in the next line of the Table.
These include *alliances* of all sorts: the firm in the realm of economics,
the gang for criminal activity, political parties and other associations
for achieving or exercising power. "Exchange associations" are links
in the division of labor. Just as the "unselfish" associations are in fact
not completely so, similarly the "selfish" combinations typically have
and may indeed require a certain social cement in the form of feelings

Table 1. Acting Entities, Units, and Groups.

	Economic System	Biological System A	Biological System B
Agents	Individuals	Organisms	Genes
Cooperative Groups			
"Unselfish"	Families, "brotherhoods"	Reproductive associations	(None)
"Selfish"	Firms, parties and other political associations, gangs, exchange associations	Packs, mutualists	Organisms, chromosomes and other gene linkages
Competitive Clusters	Industries, crafts and professions, other contending sets (of gangs, parties, nations, etc.)	Sexes, species, set of niche competitors	Set of alleles, of genotypes
Universal Group	Society	Biota	Gene pool

of fraternity and community (altruism). This cement is perhaps least binding in the case of exchange associations, but even there at least a simulation of uncalculated fellowship between the parties may be essential for good business. While the state or polity falls into the "selfish" grouping, its survival in the face of military competition probably requires a high degree of unselfish patriotic sentiment.

The next major heading represents "Competitive Clusters." The term, for lack of a better, is intended to represent aggregations of units that are mainly *striving against* rather than *cooperating with* one another. Here there may be no sense of actual association on the part of the participants, the cluster being merely a discrete *classification* as viewed by an observer. Such an aggregate of closely competing firms we call an industry, of competing workers a craft or profession, etc. We lack accepted single words for clusters of competing gangs, of competing parties and political associations, of competing nations, etc. (Sometimes we refer to them as the players in the political game, the diplomatic game, and so forth.) The members of cooperating groups may do *different* things, so as to complement one another; or they do the same thing, where scale economies make supplementation a more advantageous cooperation technique than complementation. But members of competitive clusters are trying to do the same thing in a rivalrous sense, in a context where the success of one entity to some extent precludes that of others.

Here again, the distinction is not always so sharp. Contending groups or individuals generally have some mutual interest in limiting at least the degree of competition. They are better able to find this opportunity for mutual gain if an element of "brotherhood" is thought to exist among the competitors. Trade unions (often actually called "brotherhoods") call on class sentiment to limit the competition among workers.

Finally, at the bottom line we have the "Universal Group"—society itself. Society as an entirety is a complex structure of cooperating and competing elements.

In the biological realm, as was indicated earlier, there are two interwoven *systems* of thinking—here simply denoted A and B. In A the organism is the fundamental unit, in B it is the gene. In system A the egg serves to reproduce the chicken, in system B the chicken is the means of reproducing the egg (that is, the gene). Genes are chemical units that have somehow evolved ways of reproducing themselves. (Not that they "want" to do so, of course, but rather that once self-reproduction somehow came about it tended to be selected by Nature for survival.) In system A there are "unselfish" (kin-selected) cooperative groupings like the family, here more abstractly called reproductive associations. But in system B there are no "unselfish" genes!

Now consider the "selfish" cooperative groupings of individual organisms in system A—packs or other alliances (within or between species) whose members gain by mutual association in feeding or defense or reproduction. The leading analog in system B is the *organism* itself. That is, the individual organism represents a kind of alliance of the various genes making up its genetic endowment! As a rather less important point, study of the details of the process of genetic reproduction reveals that the genes are themselves not isolated but are organized into chromosomes and other linkages whose prospects for reproduction are connected in various ways.

The most obvious instance of the "Competitive Cluster" category in system A is the species itself—regarded as the aggregate of its competing individual members. While competition is severest within a species, interspecific competition also occurs where the potential niches of different species overlap. Each *sex* also represents a competitive cluster (that is, all males compete against one another, as do all females) within a sexually reproducing species. In system B the set of competing alleles at a given locus, and the set of alternative genotypes, are instances of competitive clusters. Finally, the "Universal Group" is the entire biota in system A. In system B the gene pool represents the universe in which various forms of cooperation and competition may take place.

In Table 2 the chief point of interpretation to be emphasized is that the biological processes and mechanisms represent more general classes into which the economic ones fall as particular instances. Where standard economics takes the satisfaction of preferences as the primitive objective or "utility function" of the acting individuals, biological theory suggests that what seems like mere preference or taste evolves out of the objective dictates of reproductive survival. As to the principle of action or behavior, the process of calculated optimization postulated in standard economics can be regarded as a special instance of the uncalculated "as if" optimization dictated by the selective forces of Nature. The thrust of the "satisficing" controversy in descriptive economics is that, even in the economic sphere, explicit optimization cannot always serve as the principle of action.

The *opportunities* available to organisms in the biological realm can be categorized in ways that seem familiar to the economist. Exploitation of resources is akin to production; mutualism corresponds to exchange; predation and war have obvious analogs in human society. Biology's emphasis on reproduction corresponds to the range of choices involved in family formation in the social context.

In terms of selective processes at work, the biological environment chooses for superior fitness, the analog being superior economic efficiency in the processes studied by standard economics. However, since economic efficiency is not propagated by mechanisms closely analogous to inheritance in biology, the processes of competition in the two areas are not closely comparable.

Economics distinguishes three levels of equilibrium: (1) short-run exchange equilibrium (market-clearing); (2) long-run entry/exit equilibrium, in which there is no longer any net advantage from redirection of resources (zero-profit condition); and (3) a hypothetical very-long-run stationary state where there is no longer any advantage to the formation of new resources (by accumulation). There seems to be no close analog in biology to the short-run concept. The equivalent of the long-run equilibrium condition of economics can be taken to be the biological situation where each type of population (on the organism level) or each type of allele (on the genetic level) has a reproductive ratio ("fitness") equal to unity. And one can also imagine a hypothetical very-long-run

Table 2. Processes and Relationships.

	Economic System	Biological System
Objective Function	Subjective preferences ("tastes")	Reproductive survival ("fitness")
Principle of Action	Optimization [alternatively, "satisficing"]	"As if" optimization
Opportunities	Production Exchange via market Crime, war Family formation	Exploitation of resources Mutualism Predation, war Reproduction
Principle of Competitive Selection	Economic efficiency	Superior "fitness"
Principles of Equilibrium a. Short-run b. Long-run c. Very long-run	Markets cleared Zero-profit Stationary state	? Reproductive ratio = 1 Saturated environment
"Progress"	Accumulation, technological advance	Evolution: improved adaptation via mutation, recombination, migration, drift, and behavioral adjustment
Social Optimality Concepts	Pareto-optimality	None (?)

equilibrium condition in which the environment is so totally saturated as to leave no niche for the formation of new life entities.

"Progress" takes place in the economy in two main ways: accumulation of resources by saving and technological advance. In biology the analogous process is of course *evolution*, the improvement of adaptation to environment by a variety of processes.

Finally, we have the question of social optimality. In biology, the standard mechanistic view seems to leave no room for such a concept. In economics we have the one rather debatable, and in any case highly limited, criterion of Pareto-optimality. While Pareto-optimality is usually regarded as a normative concept, it does have positive content in one respect—that there is at least a weak tendency in the competitive economy to move toward Pareto-optimal outcomes. Despite the "teleological" ring of the argument, it is conceivable that a similar tendency, toward solving the Prisoner's Dilemma by arriving at cooperative rather than conflictual outcomes, may be operating, however weakly, in the biological realm.

VI. Economy, Biology, and Society

I have tried here to trace some of the implications of Alfred Marshall's view that economics is a branch of biology. Or, in more sweeping terms, of the contention that the social sciences generally can fruitfully be regarded as the sociobiology of the human species (E. O. Wilson, 1975). Yet, at the same time, it was suggested, we might well claim that certain laws of the economizing process—optimization on the individual level, and equilibrium on the societal level—apply to biology as well (Cody, 1974; Rapport and Turner, 1977). Viewed this way, economics can be regarded as the general field, whose two great subdivisions consist of the natural economy studied by the biologists and the political economy studied by economists proper (Ghiselin, 1974). Considerable light has been shed, I believe, upon many of the questions and results of the social sciences. These involve broad issues like the provenance of tastes (including, what is particularly essential for social processes, individuals' "taste" for *altruism*), the balance between optimization and selection in governing social outcomes, the forces favoring cooperation versus conflict as competitive strategies in social interaction, and the determinants of specialization in human productive activities. And some specific phenomena as well: the correlation of the male/female sex ratio with socioeconomic status, the recent tendency to have smaller numbers of "higher-quality" children, the predominance of small firms in transient economic environments, positive interest or time-preference, and minimum separation distances in locational or product-differentiation situations.

It was not very debatable, perhaps, that the sociobiological approach does have *some* utility for social science purposes. But how much? The central question is whether or not the human species has entered a new domain of experience where general biological laws will have only negligible relevance or have even been abolished by the unique developmental advances achieved by mankind. Among such might be included: (1) the transcending importance of cultural as opposed to genetic change; (2) the degree of intelligence and awareness, suggesting that man can henceforth regulate and control the evolutionary process by deliberate cultural and even genetic modifications of the human material itself—

quite apart from operations on the environment; (3) the invention of weapons of intraspecies competition that threaten the survival of all mankind; and (4) what might hopefully be a countervailing factor, man's possession of moral, spiritual, and ethical values.

At this point it is possible only to pose the question, not to answer it. In terms of the proximate goal of research strategy, perhaps it is sufficient to say that the sociobiological approach holds out great hope for breaking down not only the "vertical" discontinuity between the sciences of human behavior and more fundamental studies of life but also the "horizontal" barriers among the various social studies themselves.

Notes

1. "But economics has no near kinship with any physical science. It is a branch of biology broadly interpreted." Marshall (1891). See also Boulding (1950). Also relevant, of course, are the famous passages in The Wealth of Nations where Adam Smith ([1776] 1937) attributed the emergence of the division of labor among mankind, and its failure to develop among animal species, to a supposedly innate human "propensity to truck, barter, and exchange."

2. In the earlier "classical" era the compartmentalization of economics within such narrow boundaries had not yet taken place. Adam Smith in particular discussed law, government, psychology, and the biological instincts promoting and hindering social cooperation—as well as economics in the narrow sense—throughout his works. See Coase (1976); Billet (1976). In a sense, then, economics is in the process of returning to the classical view of the whole man.

3. Marx's "economic interpretation of history" can be regarded as an earlier instance of intellectual imperialism of economics, but its connection with this modern development is limited. Marx's economic interpretation was a *materialistic* one. He contended that the essentially autonomous progress of the methods and organizations of material production was decisive for shaping the entirety of social relationships in every era. True or false, this is a *substantive* proposition essentially independent of the *methodological* stance of modern economic imperialists. The latter analyze marriage, fertility, crime, law, revolution, etc., with the tools of economic analysis without necessarily asserting that these patterns of social interaction are determined by "materialistic" considerations (such as the ownership of the means of production) as contended by Marx.

4. Oddly enough, this example is not really a valid one, for the borrowing was already from biology to economics in Malthus' own thought! Malthus drew his ideas about human populations from a biological generalization attributed to Benjamin Franklin on the first page of the Essay on the Principles of Population: "It is observed by Dr. Franklin that there is no bound to the prolific nature of plants or animals but what is made by their crowding and interfering with each other's means of subsistence." See Himmelfarb (1959, chap. 7)

5. The classical definition by Fisher (1958) as applied by him to a population of mixed ages, corresponds to what the economist would call the *internal rate of return* on investment (the growth rate of invested capital). Fisher, in fact, uses the metaphor of a business loan to explain the concept.

6. Himmelfarb (1959, p. 407). The subtitle of the Origin of Species is ''The Preservation of Favoured Races in the Struggle for Life,'' and there is no doubt that Darwin himself applied this conception to the competition among races of mankind.

7. A number of the complex issues involved may be briefly alluded to. In balancing extinction probability against multiplication ratio, a long-term (multi-generational) point of view must be taken. In any such long-term comparison there will be some prospect of changes in the external environment and even in the genetic constitution of the organism's descendants over time. Even if a high-mean-fitness strategy pays off, the extinction risk being avoided, eventually diminishing-returns constraints (what the biologists call ''density-dependent effects'') are likely to be encountered—so that the one-generation high-multiplication ratio cannot be indefinitely maintained. On both these grounds the probability distribution for ''fitness'' measured in terms of a *single* generation's multiplication ratio may give misleading results. A high extinction probability is more acceptable if descendants will spread into a number of different environments or otherwise diversify so that the extinction risks have a degree of independence of one another. In this case, while many lines of descent may be extinguished, others are likely to survive and multiply. Finally, flexibility is an important consideration; a very advantageous strategy might include a capacity to mutate between high-mean-fitness and low-extinction-probability characters over time.

8. Of course, behavior might be optimized *subject to these informational constraints*. While it seems possible to adopt such an interpretation, there may be operational or even logical difficulties in calculating ''the optimal amount of departure from optimality.'' See Winter (1975).

9. But note that a high degree of such ''selfish'' adaptation, on the part of private economic agents, need not imply optimality of the Invisible-Hand variety on the *social* level. Similarly in the biological domain, perfection on the level of the organism does not imply that the entire biota, or even smaller aggregates like single species, have been optimally adapted to the environment. See Tullock (1971); Ghiselin (1974). This point will be discussed further below.

10. Not all biological adaptive mechanisms are random in their working, however. Mutations and genetic combinations are completely random, but patterns of activity (for example, feeding, mating) often are not. Even lower animals display simple purposive behavior, such as escape maneuvers when threatened. And there is a great deal of adaptive *learning* on the nonhuman level.

11. To some extent, market experiments—while failing to capture the full richness and variety of economic environments—do provide insights as to the rapidity of convergence to optimal solutions. Smith (1976), in surveying such experiments

is generally quite impressed by the ability of experimental subjects to approximate optimal (rather than merely viable) behavior. Experiments on economic choices even on the part of animals provide evidence of a considerable degree of "rationality". Kagel and others (1975).

12. And "innovation" to imperfect imitation that happens to be successful!

13. Suppose a dominant allele A at a certain gene locus is the superior type, and the recessive allele a is inferior. Then the heterozygote Aa will be represented by the same phenotype (and so be subjected in the current generation to the same selection) as the homozygote AA. But in the next and succeeding generations, the descendants of AA will on the average do better than those of Aa—ultimately extinguishing the inferior allele.

14. Winter (1971, p. 97; 1964, pp. 257–258) appears to doubt this.

15. Stigler (1958) employed, though without placing any emphasis upon biological analogies, a selectional model called *the survivor principle* to draw inferences about efficient plant and firm sizes in a variety of industries. The same method could evidently be applied to other firm characteristics that could be described as "organizational forms."

16. Since behavioral changes, by modifying the conditions of selection, may *lead* to changes in genetic compositions of populations, to a degree Lamarckism plays a role even in the modern theory of genetic evolution. See Waddington (1961).

17. In a more recent work, Nelson and Winter (1974) have developed simulation models of growth in which firms and industries evolve over time by a selectional process, one not describable as a path of moving equilibrium.

18. And, of course, it is possible that the more general science of sociobiology might benefit from results independently achieved in the special fields of the human sciences.

19. Recent reformulations of consumer theory by Lancaster (1966) and Becker (1965) treat commodities as packages of more fundamental characteristics which constitute the true desired entities. But without a biological interpretation, this reformulation merely pushes the arbitrariness of tastes one step farther back.

20. Though whether the function is adaptive to the individual only, or alternatively to some larger social group to which he belongs, may remain subject to controversy.

21. Michael T. Ghiselin (1974, pp. 218–219). Adam Smith, it might be noted, argued that the desires (or passions, appetites, or sentiments) driving men have been implanted (as by a wise Providence) to promote the survival of the species. See R. H. Coase (1937).

22. A criticism quite inapplicable, as already observed, to Adam Smith's view of man (1937).

23. Still another semantic difficulty is suggested by a remark like the following: "If an individual's utility function has the well-being of another party as argument, there need be no conflict between (selfishly) maximizing utility and (unselfishly) helping the other." Here maximizing utility is taken as the *definition* of selfish behavior, a verbal device that only evades the real substantive issue: to explain *how* it is that aiding others can viably enter an individual's utility function.

24. For many species, the struggle for food or shelter among members of a litter is a matter of life or death.

25. In human polygamous families, full sibs reputedly display greater mutual altruism than half-sibs. But I am unaware of any hard evidence on this point.

26. I am indebted to Joel Guttman for this point.

27. But even in human interactions, exchange very often takes place without legally enforceable contracts. This is true not only for trading among primitive peoples, but for highly sophisticated transactions under the most modern conditions. Macaulay (1963a). And in the sphere of "social exchange" among humans (Homans, 1958) legal enforcement is ordinarily out of the question.

28. Trivers also classes alarm calls in birds under reciprocal altruism. But, as argued above (and in line with his detailed analysis), the benefit to the calling bird in no way depends upon reciprocation in the form of self-sacrificing behavior on the part of other birds. Alarm calls appear to represent incidental altruism, under the more general heading called "selfish altruism" in the previous section.

29. There is one important limitation, however. The benevolent party must be in a position to have the last word, the last move in the interaction. If "rotten kid" has the last free choice of action, he may ruthlessly destroy his parent (Shakespeare's Regan and Goneril in relation to King Lear), so that the interaction would not be viable in selectional terms. See Hirshleifer (1977a).

30. An economic analysis quantifying some of the determinants of polygynous marriages appears in Grossbard (1976).

31. "Advertising" is also observed in some interspecific exchanges, for example, showy flowers and fragrances designed to attract the attention of pollinating insects.

32. While the most obvious illustrations of sexual competition involve male competition for females, females compete for males as well. This is reasonably evident in the human species.

33. It seems, however, that there may be some selection for excellence in the call. The reason appears to be that well-developed calls are correlated with age which is a good indicator of ability in birds. (Personal communication from M. Cody).

34. "It is common to all men, and to be found in no other race of animals, which

seem to know neither this nor any other species of contracts" (Smith, [1776] 1937, pp. 15–18). Simmel, who adopted a broad view of exchange as equivalent to *compromise*, also regarded the process as a human invention. Simmel (1955). But compromise surely occurs in nonhuman interactions.

35. These curves have already been expounded and analyzed in the economic literature by Boulding (1950) and (1962).

36. In exceptional cases, however, as when population density is held down by other forces such as predation, intraspecies competition may not be very severe.

37. Many such associations of human genetic types with historical and geographical determinants are elaborated in Huntington (1945). While his work remains highly controversial, and not all of his instances are convincing, that some racial characters are indeed adaptive (for example, the dark skin of Africans, the body shape of Eskimos) is evident.

38. On the other hand, the less stringent inheritance process in economics—the ability of a "mutation" to spread by mere imitation—means that storage of alternative productive techniques or forms of organization is not so vital.

39. While the law of diminishing returns makes coexistence equilibrium *possible*, corner solutions are not necessarily ruled out.

40. Quoted in Himmelfarb (1959, p. 382). Huxley was later to totally reverse his position, going on to argue that ethical progress required *combating* the natural tendency of the cosmic processes (Himmelfarb, p. 385).

41. Mechanism is not, any more than its opposite (the postulate of design or purposiveness) a scientifically provable proposition. It is a working hypothesis.

42. One possible instance is the tendency of disease parasites to evolve in the direction of reduced virulence (E. O. Wilson, 1975). It is sometimes contended that the beneficial bacteria living within our bodies have evolved from harmful ones.

43. "By pursuing his own interest he frequently promotes that of the society more effectually than when he really intends to promote it" (Smith, 1937, p. 423).

44. Fredlund (1976) claims to have found that property in this sense does exist, at least in primitive form, in some animal communities.

SIX

The Economics of
Business Strategy

Research in strategy is usually aimed at developing normative theories that managers can apply in choosing strategies to generate a high return on investment (Porter, 1980; Henderson, 1979). Much of this research rests on the observation that the nature and character of the competitive conditions facing a firm determines a firm's strategic opportunities, as well as the return potential of exploiting those opportunities. This emphasis on the strategic implications of competition suggests a close link between the development of normative theories of strategy and organizational economics. Of all the social sciences, microeconomics is linked most closely with the study of competition and competitive behavior among firms (Hirshleifer, 1980).

The concept of competition is used by different microeconomists in subtly different and interdependent ways. In this chapter, we look at three ways that the concept of competition is used by microeconomists and consider the implications that these different usages might have for theories of strategy.

While the concept of competition is used by a large number of microeconomists in a variety of ways, most usages of this concept that either have already been used by strategy theorists or appear likely to be used in the near future seem to reflect one of three broad research traditions in microeconomics: industrial organization (IO) economics (Mason, 1939; Bain, 1956, 1968), Chamberlinian economics (Chamberlin, 1933), and Schumpeterian economics (Schumpeter, 1934, 1950; Nelson and Winter, 1982). Of these three conceptions of competition, the IO economic version has been incorporated most completely into currently popular theories of

372

strategy. This integration has been accomplished by Porter (1974b, 1980), Caves (1980), Caves and Porter (1977), and Spence (1977, 1979), among others. However, both Chamberlinian and Schumpeterian notions of competition represent logical and empirical alternatives to the more widely applied IO concept of competition. Indeed, these two research traditions may help overcome many of the limitations of the IO model, cited even by IO proponents (Porter, 1981), in developing normative theories of strategy.

Industrial Organization Competition

The concept of competition in industrial organization economics and its implications for normative theories of strategy is reviewed in this chapter by Porter ("The Contributions of Industrial Organization to Strategic Management"). Porter suggests that the basic concept of competition employed in IO economics has not changed fundamentally since this model was first developed by Mason (1939) and Bain (1956, 1968). In this model, returns to firms are determined by the structure of the industry within which a firm finds itself. The key attributes of an industry's structure that are thought to have an impact on firm returns include the existence and value of barriers to entry (Bain, 1956), the number and relative size of firms, the existence and degree of product differentiation in the industry, and the overall elasticity of demand for the industry (Porter, 1980, p. 23). Industries with extensive barriers to entry, a small number of firms, and a high degree of product differentiation or high demand elasticity characteristically are made up of firms earning higher returns than firms in industries without these attributes. Mason and Bain's insights into the relationship between the structural characteristics of industries and firm performance have come to be known collectively as the structure, conduct, and performance paradigm, since firm conduct (i.e., strategy) and performance are presumed to follow directly from an industry's structural attributes.

The IO model was originally developed to assist government policy makers in formulating economic policy. By focusing on the structural characteristics of industries, policy makers could anticipate those industries in which firm returns would be greater than a socially optimal, fully competitive level (Hirshleifer, 1980). With a list of the structural attributes that reduce competition in an industry, policy makers can design regulations and other remedies that will result in socially optimal levels of intraindustry competition. Given this strong policy orientation, it is not surprising that much of the research in IO microeconomics has focused, first, on testing the empirical validity of the structure, conduct, and performance paradigm and, second, on understanding the policy implications of this theoretical approach (Caves, 1980).

In their attempt to use IO thinking to develop a normative theory of competitive strategy, strategy theorists have turned the original policy objectives of this model upside down. Instead of assisting policy makers in reducing firm returns to a fully competitive level, strategy theorists have sought to develop models to help firms obtain higher than normal economic returns on their business investments (Porter, 1980).

Within the context of the structure, conduct, and performance paradigm, the appropriate focus of firms seeking to obtain higher than normal economic returns is apparent. In order to obtain high returns on their strategic investments, these firms should focus on creating and/or modifying the structural characteristics of their industry to favor high returns. Accordingly, such firms should attempt to create high barriers to entry, reduce the number of firms in their industry, and increase product differentiation or modify demand elasticity (Porter, 1980). Firms that successfully accomplish one or several of these tasks will find themselves protected from return-reducing competitive entry, and can enjoy sustained periods of superior financial performance.

Chamberlinian Competition

A second, but related, type of competition used by some organizational economists can be traced to the work of Chamberlin and Associates ("Monopolistic Competition"). Whereas IO economics begins with the assumption of homogeneous firms within an industry or group, Chamberlinian economics begins with the assumption that firms are heterogeneous. Indeed, Chamberlin and his contemporaries (Robinson, 1933) developed their models in reaction to the strong assumptions of homogeneity characteristic of most neoclassical microeconomics (Hirshleifer, 1980). For Chamberlin (1933), competition in industries *always* goes forward between firms with different though perhaps overlapping resources and characteristics. Certain of these resources and asset differences may allow some firms to implement high-return strategies that cannot be implemented by other firms. For this reason, firm heterogeneity can represent an important source of competitive advantage for firms (Demsetz, 1973; Barney, forthcoming (c)).

Chamberlin (1933) cites some of the key differences between firms that can lead to differences in firm performance, including differences in technical "know-how," reputation, brand awareness, and the ability of managers to work together. Patents and trademarks are the two differences between firms analyzed most closely by Chamberlin.

Because firms in an industry or group typically have unique but overlapping resources and capabilities, competition within an industry has many of the characteristics of perfect competition, as it has been described in neoclassical microeconomics (Hirshleifer, 1980), as well as many of the characteristics of a monopoly. Chamberlin called this type of competition monopolistic competition.

Chamberlin was able to show that industries characterized by monopolistic competition will also be characterized by competitive equilibria in which there will be a distribution of economic returns to firms. In other words, at least some firms in these industries can obtain sustained periods of superior financial performance. This result of Chamberlin's work suggests an important connection between monopolistic competition and the theory of strategy, since the objective of normative theories of strategy is to specify ways by which firms can obtain this level of economic performance (Porter, 1980).

Notice that Chamberlin's view of competition in an industry, especially as it is translated into normative theories of strategy, does not contradict the view developed in IO economics. Indeed, Chamberlinian differences between firms can be seen as one of the structural traits of an industry that defines that industry's return potential. Also, the IO model, developed by Bain (1956) and Mason (1939), can be thought of as suggesting which categories of strategy a firm should implement—barriers to entry or product differentiation, for instance—whereas, the Chamberlinian model suggests which particular strategies within those broad categories a firm should choose to implement, strategies that exploit a firm's unique skills, resources, and distinctive competencies. Thus, an application of Chamberlin's logic would assist firms in deciding, for example, which particular barrier to entry it should implement.

Schumpeterian Competition

While both IO and Chamberlinian conceptions of competition have been applied, to some extent at least, in the development of normative theories of strategy, the concept of competition contained in Schumpeterian ("The Process of Creative Destruction") economics has resisted such translation. This is not because Schumpeterian competition is somehow a less "real" form of economic competition than either IO or Chamberlinian competition. Rather, IO and Chamberlinian economics have been translated into theories of strategy because both these models presume a level of stability in the competitive dynamics facing a firm sufficient to allow a firm to anticipate competitive threats and opportunities, and to respond to these opportunities appropriately. These are models in which strategic planning and other strategic management efforts are entirely appropriate. Competition, as it is characterized by Schumpeter, is not as stable and certainly less predictable. Though classic strategic management techniques can be applied in responding to and anticipating Schumpeterian competition, such efforts are likely to be less directly applicable and their results less predictable.

Schumpeter's (1934, 1950) original objective was to describe the process of economic development in western economics. In this effort, Schumpeter came to focus on major revolutionary technological and product market shifts and to dismiss, as relatively unimportant in the long run, price and other competitive actions of firms in a relatively stable industry. This was not to suggest that such competition did not exist, but rather that it was of secondary importance when describing the evolution of an economy through history.

For Schumpeter, revolutionary innovations in product, market, or technology can be anticipated only imperfectly by firms. Sometimes firms in an industry may survive a revolutionary innovation to become important actors in a succeeding industry. It may even be the case that investments made by a currently successful firm will themselves generate a Schumpeterian revolution. Other times, a revolutionary innovation will have the effect of displacing all currently competing firms. Moreover, in the competitive setting envisioned by Schumpeter, when major innovations do appear, their ultimate impact may not be known for some time, at which point it may be too late for older firms with older technologies and skills to compete in new markets requiring new skills. On the other hand, guessing too early that a given innovation will become dominant may jeopardize a firm's long-term survival by betting on a technology or market that ultimately is not dominant.

Although it is difficult to cull straightforward strategic implications from the Schumpeterian model, it nevertheless represents a point of view that should be integrated with more traditional IO and Chamberlinian concepts in the development of a normative theory of strategy. The similarities between Schumpeterian competition and evolutionary theories of the firm discussed in a previous chapter reaffirm the difficulty of deriving strategic management implications from this approach to competition.

The last article in this chapter, by Demsetz ("Industry Structure, Market Rivalry, and Public Policy"), is in many ways an integration of IO, Chamberlinian, and Schumpeterian forms of competition into a single model. Demsetz attempts to explain how it is that some firms can apparently enjoy relatively long periods of superior financial performance. He suggests that such performance is attributable to one or a combination of two factors: special insights into the competitive future of an industry (Chamberlinian competition) that a firm holds or a firm's good fortune and luck to be in the right place at the right time when a Schumpeterian revolution occurs in product or market (Schumpeterian competition). In addition, Demsetz argues that market structure could also be a source of such performance (IO competition).

Just as these previously cited economists do, Demsetz uses his analysis in an attempt to understand its implications for the structure and behavior of industries as a whole. In particular, he argues that sustained superior financial performance may be a manifestation of economic efficiency, rather than an indication of the inefficient allocation of economic resources, as is usually implied in IO reasoning. In Demsetz's argument, firms discover what unique and valuable insights and skills they might control and choose strategies that exploit those attributes. Because each firm attempts to implement strategies for which it is unusually well suited, superior financial performance is a manifestation of a firm choosing a strategy that efficiently exploits its abilities.

Implications for Organization Theory

There are few areas in which the overlap between organization theory and organizational economics is as complete as in the area of strategy. Perhaps the only major difference between these two approaches lies in the emphasis that many organization theorists place on strategy implementation, while many organizational economists focus on the design of strategies. But even these apparent differences disappear in the face of Chamberlin's logic, which suggests that firms should attempt to implement only those strategies for which they have a comparative advantage in implementation. In this context, an essential part of the process by which firms choose strategies to implement is the analysis of a firm's unique skills and capabilities. The techniques and skills of organization development seem likely to assist managers in these discovery efforts.

Where strategy implementation and strategic choice are brought together through Chamberlin's observation that different firms can implement different strategies, the strategic implications of the population ecology model and the evolutionary theory of the firm are highlighted through Schumpeter's and Demsetz's analysis of industry evolution and revolution. All of these models posit a level of irreducible uncertainty facing firms that can have an impact on firm performance. Because of this uncertainty, firm performance depends, at least in part, on managerial good fortune. When the ultimate determinants of a firm's success are at least partly beyond managerial control, outcomes become indeterminant and luck becomes a major factor in explaining competitive outcomes.

Finally, the role of industrial organizational economics in defining the competitive context facing firms is in many ways an elaboration of research on interorganizational relations by organization theorists. Pfeffer and Salancik (1978) suggest that firms can enhance their survival potential by dominating suppliers and customers. Porter (1980) goes beyond to suggest that firms should seek to dominate their suppliers and customers, not only to enhance their survival potential, but to obtain greater than normal economic performance. But Porter sees the performance of firms constrained by other factors as well, including the potential of new entrants, the potential of new substitute products, and the number and degree of rivalry among current competitors. In this way, Porter is suggesting an integration of traditional resource dependence logic with its emphasis on interorganizational relations, with logic taken from the study of the impact of a firm's total environment on firm behavior.

The three types of competition discussed by organizational economists also suggest a life cycle model of the competitive forces that shape and mold firms (Barney, forthcoming (c)). In this view, industries begin as a result of Schumpeterian revolutions in markets, technologies, or consumer demands. The sources of a Schumpeterian revolution cannot, by definition, be perfectly anticipated, though after the fact they can usually be described. This revolutionary change defines the character of competition in an industry by defining the technological and market bases of competition, the organizational resources and assets that are strategically valuable, and the organizational resources and assets that are strategically irrelevant. By defining the skills and abilities that are strategically valuable, a Schumpeterian revolution also defines which firms are likely to be successful early on, which firms must modify their resource base to become successful, and which firms are least likely to survive.

If it were possible to anticipate a Schumpeterian revolution with certainty, then most firms would be able to plan to respond accordingly by acquiring the appropriate resources and implementing the necessary strategies. However, Schumpeterian revolutions can be anticipated only imperfectly, even by firms whose innovations in product or technology turn out to create them. Because they can be anticipated only imperfectly, the effects of Schumpeterian revolutions in defining some organizations' abilities and assets as newly valuable, while simultaneously defining other organizations' abilities and assets as no longer valuable, are at least partly stochastic in nature.

After a Schumpeterian revolution has defined the competitive bases of a new industry, including which firms do and do not control strategically valuable assets and abilities, IO and Chamberlinian competition become analytically more relevant, although Schumpeterian shocks that affect but do not displace an industry are also important features of the competitive landscape. Normatively, the IO model suggests that firms should attempt to implement barriers to entry, product differentiation, and other steps to protect or to create niches within which they can obtain above normal economic returns. The Chamberlinian model suggests that these strategies should be implemented by exploiting the unique strategically relevant skills and resources controlled by firms, those aspects that make up a firm's distinctive competence. Firms without strategically valuable skills must either acquire such skills or face extinction.

Interfirm rivalry, as described by Porter (1980), will continue within these industries, perhaps for relatively long periods. Firms will continue to jockey for positions that capitalize on their competitive advantages. This will continue as long as the bases for competition defined originally by the Schumpeterian revolution remain stable or evolve predictably. In general, however, neither IO or Chamberlinian strategies will protect firms from Schumpeterian revolutions, which cannot be anticipated completely and have the effect of redefining the fundamental bases of competition in an industry. If and when these revolutions occur, what were viable IO and Chamberlinian strategies may become suddenly irrelevant.

The Contributions of Industrial
Organization to Strategic Management

Michael E. Porter

The traditional Bain/Mason paradigm of industrial orga-
nization (IO) offered strategic management a systematic model for
assessing competition within an industry, yet the model was seldom
used in the business policy (BP) field. IO and BP differed in their
frames of reference (public vs. private), units of analysis (industry
vs. firm), views of the decision maker and stability of structure,
and in other significant respects. Development of IO theory during
the 1970s has narrowed the gap between the two fields, to the ex-
tent that IO should now be of central concern to policy scholars.

The majority of economists studying industrial organization (or industrial economics) and strategic management researchers have, over the years, mostly viewed each other with suspicion—if they knew each other existed. With few exceptions, industrial organization had little effect on the business policy concept of strategy, and business policy had little effect on industrial organization, despite the increasingly clear evidence that much promise for cross-fertilization existed. Why these ships have passed in the night is an intriguing question. Some of the reasons reflect subtle, deep-rooted suspicions and even the type of training that scholars in both fields traditionally received. But many of the reasons reflect real underlying differences in the purposes, frame of reference, unit of analysis, and research values that each field has traditionally embraced.

It is becoming recognized today that industrial organization can offer much to the analysis of strategic choices by firms within industries, and the contribution is growing rapidly as new research breaks down the differences to which I have alluded. In addition to analytical techniques, industrial organization is bringing a new methodological tradition to bear in research on strategic management, one that holds promise

Note: I wish to thank R. E. Caves, Malcolm Salter, and K. R. Andrews for their comments on earlier versions of this article. This article represents a revision of a paper presented at the annual meeting of the Academy of Management, Atlanta, August 1979.

of contributing to the development of the policy field in a way quite distinct from the purely conceptual. And the benefits are clearly flowing in both directions—exposure to business policy concepts is having a decidedly positive influence on industrial organization research and, recently, on microeconomic theory.

In this article, I will examine some existing and potential contributions of industrial organization to strategic management, especially to the formulation of competitive strategy in individual industries. I will take a quasi-historical approach, in order to examine why the traditional industrial organization paradigm, while offering a valuable tool, made relatively few inroads into the policy field. Making the reasons for this explicit will highlight some of the conceptual underpinnings and assumptions of both fields and provide a framework for seeing why new industrial organization research is having an impact. The reasons will also provide an agenda for where future progress must be made if the true promise of industrial organization is to be realized.

Most of my attention will be addressed to strategy for competing in an individual industry or at the so-called strategic business unit level, because this is where industrial organization can have the greatest impact. When considering the contribution of industrial organization to strategy formulation at the level of the diversified firm as a whole, I will clearly note the shift in frame of reference.

The Promise of the Industrial Organization Paradigm

The traditional industrial organization paradigm has long held tantalizing promise for strategy formulation. This is clear when one examines the Learned, Christensen, Andrews, and Guth (LCAG) framework that has become the foundation of business policy (1969; Andrews, 1971). LCAG defined strategy as how a firm attempts to compete in its environment, encompassing key choices about goals, products, markets, marketing, manufacturing, and so on. The goals of the firm were broadly conceived to encompass both economic and noneconomic considerations, such as social obligations, treatment of employees, and organizational climate. Effective strategy formulation from a normative standpoint, according [to] the LCAG, entailed relating the four key elements shown in Figure 1.

The successful firm had to match its internal competencies and values to its external environment, and LCAG offered a series of general but logically compelling consistency tests that could help a firm probe its strategy to see if it truly related these elements. These consistency

Figure 1. The Four Key Elements of Effective Strategy Formulation.

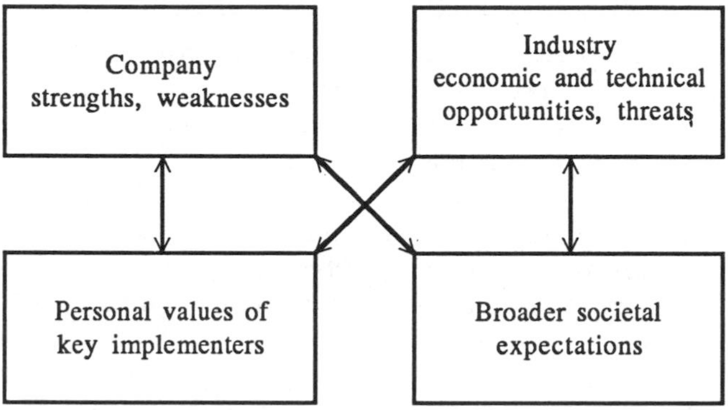

tests stressed the need for a firm's policies in each functional area to be interrelated as well as the need for the entire group of functional policies to make sense, given the environment. The high-performing (high return on investment) firm in LCAG's framework was one that had found or created a position in its industry where such consistency was present. However, LCAG offered no help in assessing the "contents" of each of the boxes in Figure 1 in a particular situation. This was left to the practitioner.

The concept of strategy emerged from the need to help the practitioner (particularly the general manager) transform the daily chaos of events and decisions into an orderly way of sizing up the firm's position in its environment. As a result, the early policy literature on strategy formulation subsequent to LCAG was largely process oriented, translating the basic LCAG paradigm and extensions of it into a sequence of logical (and very general) analytical steps (e.g., Ansoff, 1965). Recently, quite a bit of research has sought to identify broad categories of factors that might be considered in assessing the contents of each box in Figure 1 and has offered generalized strategic alternatives and some of their pros and cons (Cannon, 1968; Hofer and Schendel, 1978; Uyterhoeven, Ackerman, and Rosenblum, 1977). Another recent thread of research has been examining the social, political, and organizational processes by which strategic choices are actually made (Bower, 1970; MacMillan, 1978).

Empirical research on the substance of strategy formulation in individual industries (as distinguished from the administrative processes by which firms arrive at strategies) has been rather limited until recently. This is no doubt in part because the broad concerns of policy researchers have encompassed the complex role of the general manager, of which strategy formulation is but a part. Much policy research attention has been given to the more administrative dimensions of the general manager's job, such as relating organizational arrangements to strategy, resource allocation processes, strategic planning systems, and the like.

In the backdrop of the LCAG paradigm and subsequent work, the traditional Bain/Mason industrial organization (IO) paradigm of the 1950s and 1960s held obvious promise at one level. The essence of this paradigm is that a firm's performance in the marketplace depends critically on the characteristics of the industry environment in which it competes. This is expressed in the familiar structure-conduct-performance framework shown in Figure 2.

Figure 2. The Traditional Bain/Mason Industrial Organization Paradigm.

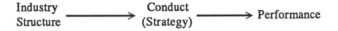

Industry structure determined the behavior or conduct of firms, whose joint conduct then determined the collective performance of the firms in the marketplace (Bain, 1968; Mason, 1939). *Performance* was defined broadly and in the economist's sense of social performance, encompassing dimensions such as allocative efficiency (profitability), technical efficiency (cost minimization), and innovativeness. *Conduct* was the firm's choice of key decision variables such as price, advertising, capacity, and quality. Thus, in policy terms, conduct could be viewed as the economic dimensions of firm strategy. Finally, *industry structure* was defined as the relatively stable economic and technical dimensions of an industry that provided the context in which competition occurred (Bain, 1972). The primary elements of structure identified as important to performance in the early IO research were barriers to entry (Bain, 1956), the number and size distribution of firms, product differentiation, and the overall elasticity of demand (Bain, 1968). A final crucial aspect of the Bain/Mason paradigm was the view that because structure determined conduct (strategy), which in turn determined performance, we could ignore conduct and look directly at industry structure in trying to explain performance. Conduct merely reflected the environment.

An important branch of IO research was so-called oligopoly theory, or the study of the outcome of competitive interactions in markets where one firm's actions affect its rivals (for a survey, see Scherer, 1970).

Oligopoly theory sought to specify the link between industry structure and firm-to-firm rivalry, providing a rich set of determinants of the difficulty firms face in coordinating their actions in the marketplace (for the classic analysis, see Fellner, [1949] 1985). It filled a gaping hole for the analysis of real markets that had been left by economists' traditional exclusive focus on the polar cases of pure competition and pure monopoly. Game theory, born at nearly the same time as the Bain/Mason paradigm itself, introduced a potentially rich framework for examining competitive interaction (Schelling, 1960; von Neumann and Morgenstern, 1953). Game theory took its place in IO as a part of oligopoly theory.

The early Mason approach of identifying many structural factors that were important in influencing conduct and performance soon gave way to the Bain-initiated focus on a few key aspects of structure. Bain also pioneered an empirical tradition of statistical studies relating aspects of industry structure to conduct and performance (usually profitability). Literally hundreds of studies of this form, drawn from large sample of industries all over the world, have formed the backbone of IO literature.

The Bain/Mason paradigm of IO (enriched with oligopoly theory) is a useful contribution to strategy formulation in an industry, though it has been a little-used one. It offers a systematic model for assessing the nature of competition in an industry—one aspect of the four-part LCAG framework: industry opportunity and threats. Identifying the "structure" of the industry in IO terms casts the spotlight on the crucial aspects of the firm's industry environment, and illuminates such critical concepts as barriers to entry and demand elasticity. The model also allows an analysis of the performance a firm could hope to achieve in its industry. It reinforces the important point that not all industries are equal in terms of their potential profitability. Thus the model can help firms predict a level of performance that can reasonably be expected. Unlike the ad hoc approach to industry analysis embodied in most policy literature, Bain/Mason is potentially a systematic and relatively rigorous one backed by empirical tests. Bain/Mason does *not* help the strategist with the other three key elements identified by LCAG, but it clearly helps with one.

The Limitations of the Bain/Mason Paradigm

Faced with this clear promise, why didn't strategy teachers and practitioners stumble over each other to embrace the new IO paradigm? A number of the reasons relate less to the substance of the paradigm than to the scholarly traditions in the IO and BP fields. Many policy scholars were not aware of developments going on in IO, a different, self-contained discipline with its own jargon. Some policy scholars also seemed to be innately suspicious of economists' work, possibly because of their exposure to microeconomics at the introductory level, where it is laced with assumptions and normative premises that practitioners cannot live with. And there was little cross-fertilization between people; either one was an economist, or one was a business teacher or practitioner.

However, these reasons may have been only reflections of more fundamental, substantive reasons why well-informed policy practitioners *should have been* skeptical of IO. Some important ones are outlined below:

There were translation problems owing to different frames of reference. Policy practitioners were interested in improving a firm's performance from a private viewpoint, which meant increasing return on investment (ROI). IO researchers were motivated to improve performance from a social viewpoint—which could mean *reducing* ROI to the purely competitive level. IO was historically oriented toward informing public policy, and the literature was written from this frame of reference.

As I have argued, the IO explanation of industry competition and performance could clearly be applied to *either* purpose—private or social. For example, public policymakers could use their knowledge of the sources of entry barriers to lower them, whereas business strategists could use theirs to raise barriers, within the rules of the game set by antitrust policy. However, this fundamental difference in the frame of reference meant that IO theory had to be translated before it appeared compatible with the private perspective and thereby recognizably useful to policy practitioners. This translation was not made in the literature.

Policy teachers and practitioners also had a different definition of their task. Policy aimed at understanding the multiple functions and multiple objectives of the general manager, only some of which were purely economic. IO theory focused much more narrowly on the economic bases of competition.

IO differs in its unit of analysis and related assumptions. Policy practitioners have been vitally interested in the problems of the individual company, and have viewed each firm as a unique entity with unique strengths and problems. Terms such as "distinctive competence" are hallmarks of the policy field in defining the bases on which firm strategies should be set. Simple observation clearly revealed that firms differed a great deal in performance even though they competed in the same industry.

Conversely, the IO theory of the 1950s and 1960s took the *industry* as the unit of analysis. Mason's early work showed a strong interest in firm conduct but this was largely lost when Bain's influence came to be felt. That it was lost made sense from the traditional IO frame of reference, since it is collective industry performance and not one firm's performance that determines the quality of resource allocation in the economy and hence social performance. Furthermore, IO theory implicitly assumed that all firms in an industry are identical in an economic sense, except for differences in their size; the other differences are random noise. As a result, there was little room for stable differences in the performance of firms in the same industry. Therefore, while IO is useful for determining the likely average profitability of an industry, in its traditional form it clearly is not very useful for sorting out the different performances of different companies.

IO and BP have different views of the decision maker. IO, by and large, viewed the firm as a single decision-making unit making choices based on economic objectives. Some IO literature recognized that firms were really collections of individuals (Cyert and March, 1963), and there was some discussion of objectives other than profit maximization, but these isolated efforts were hardly integrated into mainstream theory. Policy practitioners, on the other hand, placed great stress on how the personality of the leader, political processes within the firm, and a broad range of possible firm objectives have a major impact on a firm's actual behavior in the market place (a good illustration is Bower, 1970). Also, BP has always stressed the difficulty leaders have in correctly perceiving environmental change, and the long-standing assumptions that often create strategic myopia. The human dimension was central in BP; no humans were visible in IO.

IO views the firm as a free-standing entity. IO has implicitly viewed the firm as a free-standing entity competing in a single business, and the IO literature on diversification is largely distinct from the literature on competitive outcomes in oligopolistic markets. Yet policy practitioners have long recognized that the individual business unit is often but one part of a diversified firm's "portfolio" of businesses, and that the needs of the corporation as a whole often strongly affect the objectives of the unit as well as the resources made available to it. All this can strongly influence market outcomes. Furthermore, manufacturing, marketing, distribution, and research costs are often shared among related business units in a firm even though they are in distinct industries from the viewpoint of conventional approaches to industry definition. For exmple, a firm might manufacture motors it then uses to manufacture such disparate products as hair dryers and cooling fans. Its costs in motor manufacturing, a key part of its end-product costs, are thus in part determined by the total sales of these essentially unrelated products. To handle such shared costs, many firms must formulate strategy both at the individual business unit level and for the entire group of related business units.

Related to the failure to see the business unit as part of a centrally managed corporate portfolio is the failure of much IO research to recognize the simultaneous determination of firm behavior in such areas as advertising, research, and vertical integration. The concept of strategy stresses the need to interrelate these individual functional policies. IO research has tended to look at each function in a piecemeal fashion.

IO had a static perspective. The Bain/Mason paradigm of the 1950s and 1960s was a static, cross-sectional one that sought to explain the industry performance that resulted from a given industry structure. Structure was definitionally stable. Although the static model is a useful one as far as it goes, policy practitioners are used to having to cope with changes in structure. Concentration rises and falls, as do entry barriers and the other measures of structure identified in the IO paradigm. It is these structural changes that seem to raise the most fundamental strategic problems for firms in competition. A key question from the policy viewpoint, unanswered in Bain/Mason, was what made structure what it was, and what did one do about changes in structure from a strategic standpoint?

Determinism was an element of IO theory. Traditional IO theory took industry structure as exogenously given, and held that the firm's strategy and performance were fully determined by this structure. Thus the firm was stuck with the structure of its industry and had no latitude to alter the state of affairs. Policy practitioners, on the other hand, have long observed that firms can fundamentally *change* the structure of their industries through their actions. The policy field has a long tradition of emphasizing the insight, creativity, and even vision that some firms have exhibited in finding unique ways to change the rules of the game in their industries.

However, firms cannot always change industry structure, and thus understanding industry structure in the traditional IO sense is crucial. Furthermore, one must know what the key elements of structure are before one knows what to change, so that the traditional IO model is an important place for firms to start in formulating strategies that change the rules of competition. Nevertheless, the determinism in the traditional IO paradigm was a limitation to weigh against these benefits.

IO was too limited. IO theory identified a relatively few, critical aspects of structure, such as the distribution of firm sizes (particularly concentration) and entry barriers. Policy practitioners, on the other hand, could easily think of examples of other, unmentioned variables that were crucial to strategy in individual industries. This difference was partly a result of BP and IO having different academic traditions. Economists are prone to set forth general categories without fully articulating the subcategories. For example, the concept of entry barriers encompasses a myriad of specific factors, many of which are not elucidated in the usual IO accounts. Policy practitioners are more interested in the "long list" than in the generality of various items. But the problem was more than just stylistic: many relevant structural variables were undiscovered in the IO theory of the 1950s and 1960s.

IO and BP had different loss functions. IO researchers were interested in uncovering structure/performance relationships that generally held true, even if they did not hold in every industry and even if they explained only some of the variation in performance. The desire to advance public policy made such generalization palatable. Uncovering a few statistically robust relationships that could improve competition policy was more important than the risk that a given relationship might not hold or might be unimportant in a particular situation.

Policy practitioners, on the other hand, have always been vitally concerned with each firm's unique situation. It was not acceptable, from their viewpoint, for a particular firm to be the exception and for the hypothesized relationship therefore not to apply. If anything, the focus in policy has been on what makes a particular firm exceptional or unique and thus what might provide the basis for a unique strategy. In statistical terms, then, the loss functions or weights attached to making different kinds of errors in developing theory have been fundamentally different for policy practitioners and IO researchers.

Oligopoly theories were abstract and needed to be translated. A general theory of oligopoly eluded (and still eludes) IO researchers, and established models of oligopoly were built on grossly unrealistic assumptions such as mechanical reaction functions, identical cost and demand functions among competitors, and the like. Game theory, which promised to overcome the deficiencies of using marginal analysis in an oligopoly setting, was articulated using examples not directly taken from industry competition: nuclear war, labor negotiations, or tactical pricing decisions. Game theory therefore required translation to be readily applied to real markets, and suffered from its own set of uncomfortable assumptions, such as the heroic amounts of information utilized by all parties, simplistic strategy options, and one-time games. Testing of oligopoly and game theory concepts was undertaken almost entirely in abstract experimental situations and not actual industries (for a survey of some of the experimental evidence, see Scherer, 1970).

These reasons and others rightly made policy practitioners uncomfortable about embracing IO, but my own view is that even the IO research of the 1950s and 1960s could be highly useful in strategy formulation in industries, provided the translation of the setting and frame of reference is made, and provided it is recognized and accepted that IO is *not* an answer to the broader concern of BP about the general management function. IO offers at least a start toward a systematic understanding of the industry environment, which can always be supplemented with particularistic analysis. IO encompasses some extraordinarily powerful concepts, and game theory offers a framework that can be applied to firm-to-firm warfare. IO does not go all the way, for the reasons discussed, but it goes some of the way.

The New Promise of Industrial Organization

The limitations of IO for strategy formulation that I have discussed are inherent in the classic IO paradigm as personified by Bain/Mason. It is probably accurate to call this a creature of the 1950s and 1960s. Yet IO as a field has continued to develop, aided by increasing exposure to the policy field. In fact, some of the reservations of policy practitioners turned up, not surprisingly, in self-criticisms of the IO field by its own practitioners.

During the 1970s, particularly the last five years or so, IO has been enriched by addressing, at least in a partial way, many of the limitations I have described. Too often IO is criticized as if Bain/Mason were the current state of theory or as if IO consisted solely of Galbraith. As a result of new developments, IO has moved from being a useful tool to consider in strategy formulation to being a field that should take a central place among the conceptual frameworks used in the policy field. Let us review the progress of IO against the limitations of Bain/Mason identified earlier. I must hasten to add that this does *not* purport to be a comprehensive survey, but rather an attempt to provide an overview along with examples of specific research. As one who has been working in the intersection of these two fields, I will undoubtedly err in drawing my examples too heavily from work going on at Harvard.

Translation. Although they are still relatively few, extensions of the IO paradigm to the perspective of strategy formulation are now in the literature. An early effort was my ''Note on the Structural Analysis of Industries,'' originally written in 1974. A modified version appears as Chapter 1 in my 1980 book, a larger study of the IO/strategy link. In addition, mentions of IO concepts have appeared in other recent books and papers on strategy analysis (Hofer and Schendel, 1978; Kasper, 1979; Thorelli, 1977). There is a course at Harvard that applies contemporary IO concepts to problems of developing competitive strategy, and similar courses have started or are starting elsewhere.

Unit of Analysis. In the past decade, work in IO has shifted the unit of analysis to *both* the firm and the industry. Empirical researchers began to examine the performance of firms as well as industries (Demsetz, 1973; Gale, 1972; Shepherd, 1972), though lacking clear theoretical models of firm performance. The beginnings of a model have emerged in the concept of *strategic groups*, a term coined by Hunt (1972). I have made efforts at generalizing this concept (Porter, 1973, 1976a, 1979a, 1980), and Newman (1973, 1978) has artfully examined an important subcase. The concept of strategic groups is that firms within industries can be clustered according to their strategies, and that their reactions to disturbances and the pattern of rivalry will be determined by the configuration of groups.

On the heels of the notion of strategic groups came the generalization of entry barriers to the concept of "mobility barriers" (Caves and Porter, 1977; Porter, 1973). The argument is that the difficulty of entry into an industry depends on the strategic position the firm seeks to adopt (or on its strategic group). Mobility barriers are deterrents to a shift in strategic position of firms within an industry, deterrents that give some firms stable advantages over others. Thus, mobility barriers provide an explanation of differences in performance by firms in the same industry, and provide a conceptual basis for positioning a firm within its industry.

Mobility barriers, the configuration of strategic groups in the industry, industry-wide structural traits, and aspects of a firm's position within its strategic group have been combined into a theory of the strategic position of firms in their industry and their resulting profitability (Porter, 1978, 1979b). I have recently tested the theory's implications for the profitability of differently situated firms (Porter, 1979b), and the theory's premises have been supported in work by Hatten (1974), Hatten and Schendel (1976) and Stonebreaker (1976).

The strategic group/mobility barrier extension of IO has additional benefits for strategic analysis. One is that it constitutes the beginning of a systematic way to determine what a firm's strengths and weaknesses are. This is one of the things that much of the literature has left practitioners to handle unaided. Thus the extension promises to increase the scope of IO's contribution to strategic analysis, by enabling it to contribute to the analysis of the upper left box in the LCAG quadrangle (Figure 1). In addition, the strategic group/mobility barrier concept is a starting point for the dynamic modeling of industry evolution, in which firms with different strategies and different objectives make investments in improving their strategic position.

Free-Standing Entity. IO research is beginning to explore the interrelation between business units and their corporate siblings in modeling industry outcomes. The interrelation is embodied in the theory of strategic groups, and Newman (1973) has explored one aspect of the relationship in some detail. Spence and I have built the relationship into a model of capacity expansion in oligopoly (Porter and Spence, 1978; see also Porter, 1980, Chap. 3). Recent work on so-called economies of scope has explored some implications of shared costs. Removing the assumption of a free-standing entity is a high-priority area for continued IO research.

Static Tradition. Increasingly, IO research is beginning to encompass dynamic models of industry evolution, some framed from the point of view of the strategic decision facing the individual firm. Numerous studies have investigated the determinants of changes in industry concentration (e.g., Mueller and Hamm, 1974; Orr, 1974) and some have investigated the determinants of entry. The work of the Boston Consulting Group has stimulated a number of rigorous models of learning curve phenomena (e.g., Spence, 1981). A number of models have explored additional aspects of firm investment and innovation in a dynamic context. Michael Spence and I, for example, have modeled the dynamic capacity expansion problem facing the firm in growing oligopoly using data drawn from a comprehensive case study of the corn-milling industry. The model exposes the critical role of uncertainty early in an industry's life for the subsequent structural evolution, among other variables. I have also explored the dynamic forces underlying industry change (Porter, 1980; Porter and Spence, 1978). These and other efforts (e.g., Flaherty, 1976; Kamien and Schwartz, 1972; Spence, 1979) at dynamic modeling are far from fully satisfactory, but they are beginning to yield some important implications for how firms should compete in evolving industries.

Determinism. The Bain view that strategic choices do not have an important influence on industry structure is nearly dead. It is now recognized that there are feedback effects of firm conduct (strategy) on market structure, as depicted in Figure 3. For example, firm innovations can enhance or diminish entry and mobility barriers. Some authors have gone a step further to propose and test models in which past performance affects the strategic options available to firms—hence the dotted line in Figure 3 (e.g., Comanor and Wilson, 1974, Chap. 6). Recognition of both feedback loops has led to the increasing adoption of simultaneous

Figure 3. An Updated Version of the Industrial Organization Paradigm.

equation models to test IO propositions (Caves, Porter, and Spence, 1980; Comanor and Wilson, 1974, Chap. 6). Some recent articles have demonstrated how firms can affect or even deter entry into their industries by carefully choosing their strategies (Porter, 1980; Salop, 1979; Schmalensee, 1978; Spence, 1979).

The view is developing that there are some fundamental structural parameters of an industry dictated by the basic product characteristics and technology, but that within those parameters industry evolution can take many paths, depending on such factors as the luck of the draw in terms of the identity of industry rivals and uncertain events, as well as on the strategic choices firms actually make that follow from their unique objective functions. By articulating these factors, IO offers rich insights into strategy formulation.

Completeness. IO researchers have identified an increasingly rich set of elements of industry structure that are important to competitive interaction. Richard Caves and I have articulated the concept of exit barriers, such as specialized assets and fixed costs of exit (Caves and Porter, 1977; Porter, 1976b, 1980). Harrigan (1979) has applied the exit barrier and other IO concepts to the study of competitive interaction in eight declining industries. The study of industry structure has moved beyond looking at the conditions of supply to examine vertical bargaining relations with suppliers and buyers. Lustgarten (1975) and others have examined buyer power in producer goods industries and I have explored manufacturer/retailer bargaining in consumer goods industries and other aspects of the buyer's effect on strategy (Porter, 1974a, 1980). Labor is being shown to be a competitor for firm profits (see Caves, Porter, and Spence, 1980, for a survey).

International trade and competition is being built into IO models of industry competition, and this work is showing how obsolete the view is that all industries are domestic (Caves, Porter, and Spence, 1980; Pugel, 1978). Linkages between the capital markets and industry competition are receiving attention, reflecting the view that capital market conditions can affect the ability of differently situated firms to compete and that financial strategy can be a competitive weapon (Fruhan, 1979; Hurdle,

1974). Topics such as vertical integration and franchising have been explored in detail in the IO literature (Caves and Murphy, 1976). Although there are further frontiers to be explored, IO has already achieved a richness that makes it of great utility in a broad array of strategy formulation problems.

Loss Function. IO researchers are stretching for still richer models that recognize interfirm and interindustry differences. In part because of contact with the policy literature, they are no longer satisfied with broad conclusions, even for public policy purposes—although the constraints of empirical data may force them to live with such conclusions.

Oligopoly Theory. Some strides have been made in applying oligopoly and game theory to real market conditions, although difficulties remain with this aspect of IO theory. Fruhan (1972) applied game theoretic concepts to competition in the domestic airline industry and Sultan (1974) to the electrical equipment industry. Aharoni (1966) applied game theory to foreign direct investment decisions. Schelling's (1960) rich qualitative theory of games has stressed concepts that can be applied to market settings, such as commitment, credibility, and focal points (Porter, 1980). Knickerbocker (1973) has applied oligopoly theory and other IO concepts to the establishment of foreign subsidiaries by multinational firms. The ideas in all this literature could substantially enhance the subtlety with which firms can make and respond to competitive moves.

These developments have pushed IO theory squarely toward the heart of the policy field. The IO framework for analyzing industry structure and evolution, firm position within industries, and competitive interaction and strategic moves is increasingly rich and motivated by values close to those driving the policy practitioner. Many frontiers remain, to be sure, but IO has come of age for contributing substantively to strategy analysis.

My discussion has focused exclusively on strategy formulation at the business unit level, but recently IO research has begun to offer some intriguing possibilities for the study of diversification strategy and strategy implementation. IO-style models of the relation between diversification strategy, industry structure, and firm performance are beginning to appear (Caves, Porter, and Spence, 1980, Chap. 12; Grinyer, Yasai-Ardekani, and Al-Bazzaz, 1980; Rumelt, 1974). Williamson (1975) and others, reflecting a long tradition dating back to Herbert Simon (1961), are exploring the factors that influence the scope of the firm, or the trade-off between using market and administrative transactions. Williamson identifies contractual failures that prevent certain types of market transactions from taking place. This sort of analysis can be fruitfully applied to questions of vertical integration, joint ventures, and organizational design. Another thread of research views organizational structure as a cost/benefit calculation, weighing coordination costs against the benefits of autonomy (Caves, 1980).

The Methodological Promise

I have been arguing the promise of IO for strategy analysis (and vice versa) in substantive terms. It seems important to consider its possible methodological contribution as well. IO research has developed a strong empirical tradition built around the statistical analysis of populations of firms and industries. Research on strategy is now using such methods to supplement the in-depth case studies that have been the bread and butter of policy research; the PIMS Program is a particularly ambitious example (Buzzell, Gale, and Sultan, 1976). Recently a hybrid research design has emerged, using a series of mini-case studies to test richer hypotheses than can be feasibly tested in big samples (Harrigan, 1979; Newman, 1978).

The biggest block to further methodological diversity in strategy research is the availability of data. The PIMS Program of the Strategic Planning Institute has made some strides through the collection of an extensive data base that is unique in revealing some aspects of strategic choice. A new effort is underway at Harvard—the Program for Industry and Company Analysis, which is assembling an industry-centered data base designed explicitly for strategy research. The Federal Trade Commission's business-reporting efforts should also yield major benefits in terms of data availability. Recognition by policy practitioners of the potential of cross-sectional and time series research methods will, one hopes, further stimulate data collection of a richness and firm-specificity responsive to policy concerns, aided by the increasing disclosure requirements being placed on public firms.

Concluding Remarks

Most of the areas I have identified as limitations of IO theory still remain as frontiers for IO research and thus they provide a research agenda for IO. Another intriguing frontier for IO research is the development of a model of the competitive interaction among multibusiness firms with business units in partly overlapping markets. Such overlapping complicates coordination among firms, but offers possibilities for threats, deterrence, and side payments that go beyond those possible when competition is on a market-by-market basis. In view of the prevalence of large, diversified firms in many markets, this avenue of research seems to hold great interest.

Despite the long agenda, I am confident that the research frontiers of IO will be pushed back because of the shared research motivations in IO and BP, and the fact that both economists and business scholars are participating.

Frontiers aside, it should be clear that there is gold to mine in applying IO concepts to strategy formulation, just as there has been much gold mined (with much more still in the seam) by employing a policy perspective in IO research. If this article stimulates more cross-fertilization, then it will have served what I believe is a useful purpose. I am confident that, with or without this article, more cross-fertilization is going to occur.

Monopolistic Competition

E. H. Chamberlin

1. The Meaning of Differentiation

The interplay of monopolistic and competitive forces now to be considered is of a different sort from that described [previously]. It arises from what we shall call the differentiation of the product. This chapter introduces the subject by explaining what differentiation means, and how and in what relationship it involves both monopoly and competition.

A general class of product is differentiated if any significant basis exists for distinguishing the goods (or services) of one seller from those of another. Such a basis may be real or fancied, so long as it is of any importance whatever to buyers, and leads to a preference for one variety of the product over another. Where such differentiation exists, even though it be slight, buyers will be paired with sellers, not by chance and at random (as under pure competition), but according to their preferences.

Differentiation may be based upon certain characteristics of the product itself, such as exclusive patented features; trade-marks; trade names; peculiarities of the package or container, if any; or singularity in quality, design, color, or style. It may also exist with respect to the conditions surrounding its sale. In retail trade, to take only one instance, these conditions include such factors as the convenience of the seller's location, the general tone or character of his establishment, his way of doing business, his reputation for fair dealing, courtesy, efficiency, and all the personal links which attach his customers either to himself or to those employed by him. In so far as these and other intangible factors vary from seller to seller, the "product" in each case is different, for buyers take them into account, more or less, and may be regarded as purchasing them along with the commodity itself. When these two aspects of differentiation are held in mind, it is evident that virtually all products are differentiated, at least slightly, and that over a wide range of economic activity differentiation is of considerable importance.

In explanation of the adjustment of economic forces over this field, economic theory has offered (*a*) a theory of competition, and (*b*) a theory of monopoly. If the product is fairly individual, as the services of an electric street railway, or if it has the legal stamp of a patent or a copyright, it is usually regarded as a monopoly. On the other hand, if it stands out less clearly from other "products" in a general class, it is grouped with them and regarded as part of an industry or field of economic activity which is essentially competitive. Thus, although patents are usually classed as monopolies, trade-marks are more often looked upon as conferring a lesser degree of individuality to a product, and hence as quite compatible with competition (sometimes even as requisite to it). By this dispensation, the value of patented goods is explained in terms of the monopolist's maximizing his total profit within the market which he controls, whereas that of trade-marked goods is described in terms of an equilibrium between demand and supply over a much wider field. All value problems are relegated to one category or the other according to their predominant element; the partial check exerted by the other is ignored.

This procedure has led to a manner of thinking which goes even further and denies the very existence of the supposedly minor element. Monopoly and competition are very generally regarded, not simply as antithetical, but as mutually exclusive. To demonstrate competition is to prove the absence of monopoly, and vice versa. Indeed, to many the very phrase "monopolistic competition" will seem self-contradictory— a juggling of words. This conception is most unfortunate. Neither force excludes the other, and more often than not both are requisite to an intelligible account of prices.

2. Patents and Trade-Marks

The general case for a theory which recognizes both elements concurrently may be presented by inquiring into a particular problem: does any basis really exist for distinguishing between patents and trade-marks? Patents (and copyrights) are ordinarily considered as monopolies. They are granted under the authority vested in Congress by the United States Constitution to secure "for limited times, to authors and inventors, exclusive rights to their respective writings and discoveries." The privilege granted is *exclusive*—the inventor has the sole right to manufacture and sell his invention for seventeen years. The monopoly nature of this privilege is generally recognized both in the literature of patents and in that of general economics (Elfreth, 1918; Prindle, 1908; Mill, 1884; Ely, 1930; Garver and Hansen, 1928). To be sure, the issue is usually not sharply drawn, but one gains the impression that here are instances where the principles of monopoly value are true without qualification.

On the other hand, the competitive element has been pointed out, and it has even been claimed that patents are, in their essence, competitive rather than monopolistic. Vaughn (1927, p. 26) argues that "Patented products may be in competition both with patented and unpatented goods. In fact, the patent law is conducive to competition in that it stimulates individual initiative and private enterprise." Seager (1917, p. 414) points out that "a large number of them [patents] are for the protection of rival processes and serve to stimulate rather than to diminish competition among those employing the different methods." The Committee on Patents in the House of Representatives reported in 1912 that before the era of trusts and combinations in restraint of trade "the monopoly granted by the patent law, limited as it was, in time tended to stimulate competition. It incited inventors to new effort, and capitalists and business men were encouraged to develop inventions. Under these conditions a patent, while granting a monopoly in a specific article, had rarely a tendency to monopolize any branch of the trade, because few inventions were so fundamental in character as to give the owner of the patent a monopoly in any branch of the trade, and every great financial success arising from an individual patent was sure to result in rival inventions" (Vaughn, 1927, p. 27). The report goes on to demonstrate the competition normally present if patents are separately held, in the following words: "Capital seeking to control industry through the medium of patents proceeds to buy up all important patents pertaining to the particular field. The effect of this is to shut out competition that would be inevitable if the various patents were separately and adversely held" (Vaughn, 1927, p. 5). Evidently, when they are so held, the fact that they are monopolies does not preclude their being in competition with each other. Every patented article is subject to the competition of more or less imperfect substitutes.

It is the same with copyrights. Copyrighted books, periodicals, pictures, dramatic compositions, are monopolies; yet they must meet the competition of similar productions, both copyrighted and not. The individual's control over the price of his own production is held within fairly narrow limits by the abundance and variety of substitutes. Each copyrighted production is monopolized by the holder of the copyright; yet it is also subject to the competition which is present over a wider field.

Let us turn to trade-marks. Their monopolistic nature has not been entirely ignored. Says Johnson (1909, pp. 246–247), "Somewhat analogous to the profits arising from a patent are the profits arising from the use of a trade-mark or from the 'good-will' of a concern." These returns "fall under the general head of monopoly profits." The tone of hesitancy should, however, be noted, for it is characteristic. These profits are not *the same* as those arising from a patent; they are only "somewhat analogous." Ely (1917, p. 43) classifies trade-marks as "general welfare monopolies," and, although "it may be questioned whether they ought to be placed here," he argues that they should be. "They give the use or monopoly of a certain sign or mark to distinguish one's own productions. . . . Of course, another person may build up another class of goods, and may establish value for another trade-mark." He therefore concludes that "it is a monopoly only in a certain line, marking off the goods of one manufacturer." Veblen ([1904] 1927, p. 55) speaks of monopolies "resting on custom and prestige" as "frequently sold under the name of goodwill, trade-marks, brands, etc." Knight (1921, p. 185) puts "in the same category of monopoly . . . the use of trade-marks, trade names, advertising slogans, etc., and we may include the services of professional men with established reputations (whatever their real foundation)." The list might be extended further.

On the other hand, trade-marks and brands are commonly regarded in the business world as a means of enabling one seller to compete more effectively with another—as congruous with and even necessary to competition. The view is implicitly sanctioned in economic literature by a common failure to take any cognizance of trade-marks whatever. They are simply taken for granted as a part of the essentially competitive régime. Frequently patents and copyrights alone are mentioned as monopolies; the implication is that the trade-marks are not. A positive stand is taken by the late Professor Young in Ely, *Outlines of Economics*, where the elaborate classification found in Ely, *Monopolies and Trusts*, is reproduced with the significant change that trade-marks are omitted. "Trade-marks, like patents, are monopolies in the strictly legal sense that no one else may use them. But, unlike patents, they do not lead to a monopoly in the economic sense of giving exclusive control of one sort of business." By means of a trade-mark a successful business man "may be able to lift himself a little above the 'dead level' of competition . . . he is able to obtain what might be called a quasi-monopoly. But because his power to control the price of his product is in general much more limited than that of the true monopolist, and because competition limits and conditions his activities in other ways, his business is more properly called competitive than monopolistic" (Ely, 1930, pp. 562–563). Against this position it may be urged, first, that single patents, as has been shown, do not ordinarily give exclusive control of one sort of business and do not confer a monopoly in this sense of the term; and secondly, that, even granting that patents do give *more* control, this is simply a matter of degree, reducible to relative elasticity of demand. Both patents and trade-marks may be conceived of as monopoly elements of the goods to which they are attached; the competitive elements in both cases are the similarities between these goods and others. To neglect either the monopoly element in trade-marks or the competitive element in patents by calling the first competitive and the second monopolistic is to push to opposite extremes and to represent as *wholly* different two things which are, in fact, essentially alike.

An uncompromising position as to the competitive nature of trade-marks is found in Rogers (1914), *Goodwill, Trade-Marks and Unfair Trading.* "These things [patents and copyrights] are monopolies created by law. . . . A trade-mark is quite a different thing. There is no element of monopoly involved at all. . . . A trade-mark precludes the idea of monopoly. It is a means of distinguishing one product from another; it follows therefore that there must be others to distinguish from. If there are others there is no monopoly, and if there is a monopoly there is no need for any distinguishing" (pp. 50–52). Here explicitly is the dialectic behind the attitude widely prevalent in economic and legal thinking, to which reference has already been made, that monopoly and competition must be regarded as alternatives. Evidently, it applies equally well to patents, for, to paraphrase the argument, no matter how completely the patented article may be different from others, there are always others, and therefore no monopoly. Monopoly becomes, by this reasoning, a possibility only if there is but one good in existence. What is the difficulty? Assuredly, two things may be alike in some respects and different in others. To center attention upon either their likeness or their unlikeness is, in either case, to give only half of the picture. Thus, if a trademark distinguishes, that is, marks off one product as different from another, it gives the seller of that product a monopoly, from which we might argue, following Rogers, that there is no competition. Indeed, Rogers himself falls into the trap and refutes his own argument a few pages further on, where, speaking of a buyer's assumed preference for "Quaker Oats," he says, "It is a habit pure and simple, and it is a *brand* habit, a *trade-mark* habit that we and others like us have, and that habit is worth something to the producer of the goods to whose use we have become habituated. It *eliminates competition*, for to us there is nothing 'just as good.'" If trade-marks "preclude monopoly" and "eliminate competition," one may well ask the nature of the remainder.

Are there any bases, after all, for distinguishing between patents and trade-marks? Each makes a product unique in certain respects; this is its monopolistic aspect. Each leaves room for other commodities almost but not quite like it; this is its competitive aspect. The differences between them are only in degree, and it is doubtful if a significant distinction may be made even on this score. It would ordinarily be supposed that the degree of monopoly was greater in the case of patents. Yet the huge prestige value of such names as "Ivory," "Kodak," "Uneeda," "Coca-Cola," and "Old Dutch Cleanser," to cite only a few, is sufficient at least to make one skeptical. It would be impossible to compute satisfactorily for comparison the value of the monopoly rights granted by the United States Government in the form of patents and copyrights, and the value of those existing in the form of trade-marks, trade names, and good-will. The insuperable difficulty would be the definition (for purposes of deduction from total profits) of "competitive" returns, and of profits attributable to other monopoly elements. Allowance would also have to be made for the difference in duration of patents and trade-marks, for the enhanced value of patents in many cases by combination, and for other factors. But merely to suggest such a comparison is to raise serious doubts as to whether the monopoly element in patents is even quantitatively as important as that in trade-marks.

Let us apply the reasoning to the second phase of differentiation mentioned above,—that with respect to the conditions surrounding a product's sale. An example is the element of location in retail trade. The availability of a commodity at one location rather than at another being of consequence to purchasers, we may regard these goods as differentiated spatially and may apply the term "spatial monopoly" to that control over supply which is a seller's by virtue of his location. A retail trader has complete and absolute control over the supply of his "product" when this is taken to include the advantages, to buyers, of his particular location. Other things being equal, those who find his place of business most convenient to their homes, their habitual shopping tours, their goings and comings from business or from any other pursuit, will trade with him in preference to accepting more or less imperfect substitutes in the form of identical goods at more distant places; just as, in the case of trade-marked articles and of goods qualitatively differentiated, buyers are led to prefer one variety over another by differences in their personal tastes, needs, or incomes.

In this field of "products" differentiated by the circumstances surrounding their sale, we may say, as in the case of patents and trade-marks, that both monopolistic and competitive elements are present. The field is commonly regarded as competitive, yet it differs only in degree from others which would at once be classed as monopolistic. In retail trade, each "product" is rendered unique by the individuality of the establishment in which it is sold, including its location (as well as by trade-marks, qualitative differences, etc.); this is its monopolistic aspect. Each is subject to the competition of other "products" sold under different circumstances and at other locations; this is its competitive aspect. Here, as elsewhere in the field of differentiated products, both monopoly and competition are always present.

Speaking more generally, if we regard monopoly as the antithesis of competition, its extreme limit is reached only in the case of control of the supply of all economic goods, which might be called a case of pure monopoly in the sense that all competition of substitutes is excluded by definition. At the other extreme is pure competition, where, large classes of goods being perfectly standardized, every seller faces a competition of substitutes for his own product which is perfect. Between the two extremes there are all gradations, but both elements are always present, and must always be recognized. To discard either competition or monopoly is to falsify the result, and in a measure which may be far out of proportion to the apparent importance of the neglected factor.

Hence the theory of pure competition falls short as an explanation of prices when the product is (even slightly) differentiated. By eliminating monopoly elements (i.e., by regarding the product as homogeneous) it ignores the upward force which they exert, and indicates an equilibrium price which is below the true norm. The analogy of component forces, although not exact, is helpful. Actual prices no more approximate purely competitive prices than the actual course of a twin-screw steamship approximates the course which would be followed if only one propeller were in operation. Pure competition and pure monopoly are extremes, just as the two courses of the ship, when propelled by either screw separately, are extremes. Actual prices tend towards neither, but towards a middle position determined with reference to the relative strength of the two forces in the individual case. A purely competitive price is not a normal price; and except for those few cases in the price system where competition is actually pure, there is no tendency for it to be established.

It might seem that the theory of monopoly would offend equally in the opposite sense by excluding the competitive elements. This would be true, however, only in the case of *pure* monopoly, as defined above— control of the supply of all economic goods by the same person or agency. The theory of monopoly has never been interpreted in this way. It applies to particular goods, and as such always admits competition between the product concerned and others. Indeed, we may go so far as to say that the theory *seems* fully to meet the essential requirement of giving due recognition to both elements, and the interesting possibility is at once suggested of turning the tables and describing economic society as perfectly monopolistic instead of as (almost) perfectly competitive. Subsequent chapters will carry the refutation of this view. Meanwhile the issues are clarified by displaying the large element of truth it contains. Let us see upon what grounds it may *not* be refuted.

3. The Economic Order as Perfectly Monopolistic

The essence of monopoly is control over supply.[1] May not the entire field of differentiated product therefore be described in terms of perfect monopolies, one for each seller?

The first objection which may be made is that substitutes exist for many products which are, in fact, virtually the same product; whence it would appear that the element of monopoly, instead of being absolute and perfect, is almost non-existent.

Now, of course, the owner of a trade-mark does not possess a monopoly or any degree of monopoly over the broader field in which this mark is in competition with others. A monopoly of "Lucky Strikes" does not constitute a monopoly of cigarettes, for there is no degree of control whatever over the supply of other substitute brands. But if, in order to possess a perfect monopoly, control must extend to substitutes, the only perfect monopoly conceivable would be one embracing the supply of everything, since all things are more or less imperfect substitutes for each other. There is no reason to stop with the supply of cigarettes any more than with the supply of cigarettes within a certain quality or price range (which would be narrower) or with that of tobacco in all forms (which would be broader). The term "monopoly" is meaningless without reference to the thing monopolized. A monopoly of diamonds is not a monopoly of precious stones, nor, to go still further, of jewelry. Differentiation implies gradations, and it is compatible with *perfect* monopoly of one product that control stop short of some more general class of which this product is a part, and within which there is competition.

Although the idea has never been developed into a hybrid theory of value, it represents, so far, no departure from currently accepted doctrine. Two writers only need be cited. According to Taussig, "Copyrights and patents supply the simplest cases of absolute monopoly by law" (1921, p. 114). Yet he is explicit that "the holder of such a monopoly must reckon with the competition of more or less available substitutes, and thus is compelled to abate his prices and enlarge his supplies more than he would otherwise do." Ely (1917, p. 35) points out that "the use of substitutes is consistent with monopoly, and we nearly always have them. For almost anything we can think of, there is some sort of a substitute more or less perfect, and the use of substitutes furnishes one of the limits to the power of the monopolist. In the consideration of monopoly we have to ask, what are the substitutes, and how effective are they?"

To the conception of economic society as perfectly monopolistic it may be objected, secondly, that, if differentiation is slight, even perfect control over *supply* may give a control over *price* which is negligible or nonexistent. This is the ground upon which Professor Young, choosing between alternatives, preferred to call trade-marks competitive rather than monopolistic (Ely, 1917, p. 60). Seager (1917, p. 213) also makes control over price an important element in his definition of monopoly. Now a monopolist's control over price may be limited for either of two reasons: first, because his control over the supply is only partial, or secondly, because the demand for his product is highly elastic. If control over the supply is not complete, clearly the monopoly is not perfect, and control over price is only partial. But a highly elastic demand is a limitation of another sort. A monopolist's control over price is never complete in the sense that he can set it without regard for the conditions of demand for his product. It is to his advantage that the demand be inelastic, to be sure, but it is not in accord with general usage to measure the perfection of his monopoly by the degree of its elasticity.

The demand for a good may be so elastic that the seller's best price is little different from that of others selling products almost identical. It may be lower instead of higher, or it may conform to a commonly accepted price for the general class of goods. But the fact that all the producers set the same price does not indicate absence of monopoly, for, as will be shown later, this price will be higher than it would be if the commodity were perfectly homogeneous and sold under conditions of pure competition. Of course, prices might be higher yet if, instead of a monopoly of each different brand, there existed a monopoly of the entire class of product. The more substitutes controlled by any one seller, the higher he can put his price. But that is another matter. As long as the substitutes are to any degree imperfect, he still has a monopoly of his own product and control over its price within the limits imposed upon any monopolist—those of the demand.[2]

Thirdly, it may be objected that distinctive features often give profits which are not excessive, unreasonable, or above the "competitive level." This is, of course, true, but it has no bearing on the question. Most patents come to nothing; but they are not for this reason competitive. They are worthless monopolies—things nobody wants. Many copyrighted books are unsuccessful, and others, although sold at prices higher than they would be under pure competition, are sold in such small volume that the profits are nominal or wholly absent. It is quite possible for the preferences of buyers to be distributed with rough uniformity among the products of a number of competing sellers, so that all have about the same profits. Monopoly necessarily involves neither a price higher than that of similar articles nor profits higher than the ordinary rate.

In summary, wherever products are differentiated, the theory of monopoly *seems* adequately to describe their prices. Competition is not eliminated from the explanation; it is fully taken into account by the recognition that substitutes affect the elasticity of demand for each monopolist's product.

4. Monopolistic Competition

It may now be asked in what respect monopolistic competition differs from this. Is it anything more than a new name, designed to soften a much wider application of the theory of monopoly than has heretofore been made? And if it is more, wherein lies the deficiency of the theory of monopoly, which has just been defended as adequate?

The answers to these questions are fully developed in the chapters to follow. Monopolistic competition is evidently a different thing from either *pure* monopoly or *pure* competition. As for monopoly, *as ordinarily conceived and defined,* monopolistic competition embraces it and takes it as a starting point. It is possible to do this where it would not be possible to take competition as a starting point, for the reason which has just been set forth at such length: that the theory of monopoly at least recognizes both elements in the problem, whereas the theory of competition, by regarding monopoly elements as "imperfections," eliminates them.

The theory of monopoly, although the opening wedge, is very soon discovered to be inadequate. The reason is that it deals with the isolated monopolist, the demand curve for whose product is given. Although such a theory may be useful in cases where substitutes are fairly remote, in general the competitive interrelationships of groups of sellers preclude taking the demand schedule for the product of any one of them as given. It depends upon the nature and prices of the substitutes with which it is in close competition. Within any group of closely related products (such as that ordinarily included in one imperfectly competitive market) the demand and cost conditions (and hence the price) of any one are defined only if the demand and cost conditions with respect to the others are taken as given. Partial solutions of this sort, yielded by the theory of monopoly, contribute nothing towards a solution of the whole problem, for each rests upon assumptions with respect to the others. Monopolistic competition, then, concerns itself not only with the problem of an *individual* equilibrium (the ordinary theory of monopoly), but also with that of a *group* equilibrium (the adjustment of economic forces within a group of competing monopolists, ordinarily regarded merely as a group of competitors). In this it differs both from the theory of competition and from the theory of monopoly.

The matter may be put in another way. It has already been observed that, when products are differentiated, buyers are given a basis for preference, and will therefore be paired with sellers, not in random fashion (as under pure competition), but according to these preferences. Under pure competition, the market of each seller is perfectly merged with those of his rivals; now it is to be recognized that each is in some measure isolated, so that the whole is not a single large market of many sellers, but a network of related markets, one for each seller. The theory brings into the foreground the monopoly elements arising from ubiquitous partial independence. These elements have received but fragmentary recognition in economic literature, and never have they been allowed as a part of the general explanation of prices, except under the heading of "imperfections" in a theory which specifically excludes them.[3] It is now proposed to give due weight to whatever degree of isolation exists by focusing attention on the market of the individual seller. A study of "competition" from this point of view gives results which are out of harmony with accepted competitive theory.

Notes

1. An able defense of a broader definition of monopoly to include all cases of scarcity appears in Dobb (1926, p. 105), together with references to prove that such a definition has "the sanction of usage." To the writer this seems misleading and dangerous. Mr. Dobb distinguishes three kinds of monopoly (scarcity)—natural, institutional, and deliberate, the latter referring to control of the supply by one person or group of persons. Clearly the third type must be distinguished from the other two, and even though qualifying adjectives are employed, the distinction is weakened and confused analysis invited by broadening the definition to include all cases of "restriction," or scarcity. The Greek derivation of the word ($\mu\acute{o}\nu os$, alone $+$ $\pi\omega\lambda\epsilon\hat{\iota}\nu$, to sell), as well as the *preponderance* of economic usage, is definitely against such extension.

2. There is an apparent difficulty in the case where, the differences between products being very slight, the seller might be unable to dispose of anything at all above the generally accepted price for that type of goods, the demand schedule for his product being perfectly elastic—the horizontal line which has been identified with pure competition. Buyers might prefer his goods at the same price, whereas they would go *en masse* to his competitors if there were the slightest difference.

   The difficulty would not appear if the monetary unit were infinitely divisible. For if buyers had a preference for one product over another at the same price, it would require at least a slight divergence in price to eliminate it. The amount of this divergence would vary with individual buyers, and hence, if there were many of them the demand schedule for each product would be continuous and tipped slightly from the horizontal. Actually, however, let it be granted that, at the next price above the one asked, sales may fall to zero. Monopoly is not thereby eliminated, for profits may be high through a large volume of sales as well as through a high price. Where this is the case, extra profits must be attributed to differentiation, for if the product were perfectly homogeneous, buyers would have no basis whatever for choice and would trade with different sellers at random, giving them each approximately the same volume of sales. Any excess of actual profits over what they would be under pure competition must be regarded as due to monopoly.

3. Several instances of fragmentary mention given to the idea of a separate market for each seller may be cited. Fisher (1912, p. 323) points out that "the slight undercutting of prices by one grocer will not ruin the trade of another in another part of the same town for the reason that the two are not absolutely in the same market. Each has a sphere which the other can only partially reach, not only because of distance, but also because each has his own 'custom,' i.e., the patronage of people, who, from habit or from other reasons, would not change grocers merely because of a slight difference in price." Marshall (1891, p. 458) speaks of "industries in which each firm is likely to be confined more or less to its own particular market," but seems to regard this as entirely a short time phenomenon. The particular demand curve of the producer's own special market, he thinks, "will generally be very steep," probably on this account. No doubt it will be less elastic for a short period than for a long period, but,

the differentiation of product remaining, it will never become horizontal, as under pure competition. The following passage is found in Dobb (1926, p. 88): "In any fairly-established line of business . . . each firm will probably possess a 'private market' of its own, composed of a fairly regular clientele which in various ways it has attached to itself."

J. M. Clark (1923, p. 418), in explaining his conception of a qualified monopoly as necessary to competition, says that "to a limited extent, each producer has his own individual market, connected more or less closely with those of his competitors, so that discrepancies are limited in amount and in duration, becoming narrower and briefer in proportion to the standardized character of the goods." But he develops the idea no further, and thinks of competition as taking place in one large market. A. B. Wolfe (1924, p. 50) points out the fallacy of treating retail merchants in different cities as if they were in the same market, and finds that even in the same city there are "distinct, though not absolutely independent, markets, defined by location and by class of custom." But he never reaches the logical conclusion of the argument—a "distinct, though not absolutely independent," market for each seller. To him, "each town or locality constitutes a market," though with many qualifications and adequate recognition of its imperfections. F. H. Knight (1921, p. 332) states clearly the case for applying the theory of monopoly rather than that of competition to the "partial monopoly" resulting from differentiated products. Actually, however, he has shown no inclination to modify his fundamental position that "economic theory" is simply the theory of perfect competition. See my comment (1946, p. 93).

It is unnecessary to extend the list further.

The Process of Creative Destruction

J. A. Schumpeter

The theories of monopolistic and oligopolistic competition and their popular variants may in two ways be made to serve the view that capitalist reality is unfavorable to maximum performance in production. One may hold that it always has been so and that all along output has been expanding in spite of the secular sabotage perpetrated by the managing bourgeoisie. Advocates of this proposition would have to produce evidence to the effect that the observed rate of increase can be accounted for by a sequence of favorable circumstances unconnected with the mechanism of private enterprise and strong enough to overcome the latter's resistance. This is precisely the question which we shall discuss in Chapter IX. However, those who espouse this variant at least avoid the trouble about historical fact that the advocates of the alternative proposition have to face. This avers that capitalist reality once tended to favor maximum productive performance, or at all events productive performance so considerable as to constitute a major element in any serious appraisal of the system; but that the later spread of monopolist structures, killing competition, has by now reversed that tendency.

First, this involves the creation of an entirely imaginary golden age of perfect competition that at some time somehow metamorphosed itself into the monopolistic age, whereas it is quite clear that perfect competition has at no time been more of a reality than it is at present. Secondly, it is necessary to point out that the rate of increase in output did not decrease from the nineties from which, I suppose, the prevalence of the largest-size concerns, at least in manufacturing industry, would have to be dated; that there is nothing in the behavior of the time series of total output to suggest a "break in trend"; and, most important of all, that the modern standard of life of the masses evolved during the period of relatively unfettered "big business." If we list the items that enter the modern workman's budget and from 1899 on observe the course of their prices not in terms of money but in terms of the hours of labor that will buy them—i.e., each year's money prices divided by each year's hourly wage rates—we cannot fail to be struck by the rate of the advance which, considering the spectacular improvement in qualities, seems to have been greater and not smaller than it ever was before. If we economists were given less to wishful thinking and more to the observation of facts, doubts would immediately arise as to the realistic virtues of a theory that would have led us to expect a very different result. Nor is this all. As soon as we go into details and inquire into the individual items in which progress was most conspicuous, the trail leads not to the doors of those firms that work under conditions of comparatively free competition but precisely to the doors of the large concerns—which, as in the case of agricultural machinery, also account for much of the progress in the competitive sector—and a shocking suspicion dawns upon us that big business may have had more to do with creating that standard of life than with keeping it down.

The conclusions alluded to at the end of the preceding chapter are in fact almost completely false. Yet they follow from observations and theorems that are almost completely[1] true. Both economists and popular writers have once more run away with some fragments of reality they happened to grasp. These fragments themselves were mostly seen correctly. Their formal properties were mostly developed correctly. But no conclusions about capitalist reality as a whole follow from such fragmentary analyses. If we draw them nevertheless, we can be right only by accident. That has been done. And the lucky accident did not happen.

The essential point to grasp is that in dealing with capitalism we are dealing with an evolutionary process. It may seem strange that anyone can fail to see so obvious a fact which moreover was long ago emphasized by Karl Marx. Yet that fragmentary analysis which yields the bulk of our propositions about the functioning of modern capitalism persistently neglects it. Let us restate the point and see how it bears upon our problem.

Capitalism, then, is by nature a form or method of economic change and not only never is but never can be stationary. And this evolutionary character of the capitalist process is not merely due to the fact that economic life goes on in a social and natural environment which changes and by its change alters the data of economic action; this fact is important and these changes (wars, revolutions and so on) often condition industrial change, but they are not its prime movers. Nor is this evolutionary character due to a quasi-automatic increase in population and capital or to the vagaries of monetary systems of which exactly the same thing holds true. The fundamental impulse that sets and keeps the capitalist engine in motion comes from the new consumers' goods, the new methods of production or transportation, the new markets, the new forms of industrial organization that capitalist enterprise creates.

As we have seen in the preceding chapter, the contents of the laborer's budget, say from 1760 to 1940, did not simply grow on unchanging lines but they underwent a process of qualitative change. Similarly, the history of the productive apparatus of a typical farm, from the beginnings of the rationalization of crop rotation, plowing and fattening to the mechanized thing of today—linking up with elevators and railroads—is a history of revolutions. So is the history of the productive apparatus of the iron and steel industry from the charcoal furnace to our own type of furnace, or the history of the apparatus of power production from the overshot water wheel to the modern power plant, or the history of transportation from the mailcoach to the airplane. The opening up of new markets, foreign or domestic, and the organizational development from the craft shop and factory to such concerns as U.S. Steel illustrate the same process of industrial mutation—if I may use that biological term—that incessantly revolutionizes[2] the economic structure *from within*, incessantly destroying the old one, incessantly creating a new one. This process of Creative Destruction is the essential fact about capitalism. It is what capitalism consists in and what every capitalist concern has got to live in. This fact bears upon our problem in two ways.

First, since we are dealing with a process whose every element takes considerable time in revealing its true features and ultimate effects, there is no point in appraising the performance of that process *ex visu* of a given point of time; we must judge its performance over time, as it unfolds through decades or centuries. A system—any system, economic or other—that at *every* given point of time fully utilizes its possibilities to the best advantage may yet in the long run be inferior to a system that does so at *no* given point of time, because the latter's failure to do so may be a condition for the level or speed of long-run performance.

Second, since we are dealing with an organic process, analysis of what happens in any particular part of it—say, in an individual concern or industry—may indeed clarify details of mechanism but is inconclusive beyond that. Every piece of business strategy acquires its true significance only against the background of that process and within the situation created by it. It must be seen in its role in the perennial gale of creative destruction; it cannot be understood irrespective of it or, in fact, on the hypothesis that there is a perennial lull.

But economists who, *ex visu* of a point of time, look for example at the behavior of an oligopolist industry—an industry which consists of a few big firms—and observe the well-known moves and countermoves within it that seem to aim at nothing but high prices and restrictions of output are making precisely that hypothesis. They accept the data of the momentary situation as if there were no past or future to it and think that they have understood what there is to understand if they interpret the behavior of those firms by means of the principle of maximizing profits with reference to those data. The usual theorist's paper and the usual government commission's report practically never try to see that behavior, on the one hand, as a result of a piece of past history and, on the other hand, as an attempt to deal with a situation that is sure to change presently—as an attempt by those firms to keep on their feet, on ground that is slipping away from under them. In other words, the problem that is usually being visualized is how capitalism administers existing structures, whereas the relevant problem is how it creates and destroys them. As long as this is not recognized, the investigator does a meaningless job. As soon as it is recognized, his outlook on capitalist practice and its social results changes considerably.[3]

The first thing to go is the traditional conception of the *modus operandi* of competition. Economists are at long last emerging from the stage in which price competition was all they saw. As soon as quality competition and sales effort are admitted into the sacred precincts of theory, the price variable is ousted from its dominant position. However, it is still competition within a rigid pattern of invariant conditions, methods of production and forms of industrial organization in particular, that practically monopolizes attention. But in capitalist reality as distinguished from its textbook picture, it is not that kind of competition which counts but the competition from the new commodity, the new technology, the new source of supply, the new type of organization (the largest-scale unit of control for instance)—competition which commands a decisive cost or quality advantage and which strikes not at the margins of the profits and the outputs of the existing firms but at their foundations and their very lives. This kind of competition is as much more effective than the other as a bombardment is in comparison with forcing a door, and so much more important that it becomes a matter of comparative indifference whether competition in the ordinary sense functions more or less promptly; the powerful lever that in the long run expands output and brings down prices is in any case made of other stuff.

It is hardly necessary to point out that competition of the kind we now have in mind acts not only when in being but also when it is merely an ever-present threat. It disciplines before it attacks. The businessman feels himself to be in a competitive situation even if he is alone in his field or if, though not alone, he holds a position such that investigating government experts fail to see any effective competition between him and any other firms in the same or a neighboring field and in consequence conclude that his talk, under examination, about his competitive sorrows is all make-believe. In many cases, though not in all, this will in the long run enforce behavior very similar to the perfectly competitive pattern.

Many theorists take the opposite view which is best conveyed by an example. Let us assume that there is a certain number of retailers in a neighborhood who try to improve their relative position by service and ''atmosphere'' but avoid price competition and stick as to methods to the local tradition—a picture of stagnating routine. As others drift into the trade that quasi-equilibrium is indeed upset, but in a manner that does not benefit their customers. The economic space around each of the shops having been narrowed, their owners will no longer be able to make a living and they will try to mend the case by raising prices in tacit agreement. This will further reduce their sales and so, by successive pyramiding, a situation will evolve in which increasing potential supply will be attended by increasing instead of decreasing prices and by decreasing instead of increasing sales.

Such cases do occur, and it is right and proper to work them out. But as the practical instances usually given show, they are fringe-end cases to be found mainly in the sectors furthest removed from all that is most characteristic of capitalist activity.[4] Moreover, they are transient by nature. In the case of retail trade the competition that matters arises not from additional shops of the same type, but from the department store, the chain store, the mail-order house and the supermarket which are bound to destroy those pyramids sooner or later.[5] Now a theoretical construction which neglects this essential element of the case neglects all that is most typically capitalist about it; even if correct in logic as well as in fact, it is like *Hamlet* without the Danish prince.

Notes

1. As a matter of fact, those observations and theorems are not completely satisfactory. The usual expositions of the doctrine of imperfect competition fail in particular to give due attention to the many and important cases in which, even as a matter of static theory, imperfect competition approximates the results of perfect competition. There are other cases in which it does not do this, but offers compensations which, while not entering any output index, yet contribute to what the output index is in the last resort intended to measure—the cases in which a firm defends its market by establishing a name for quality and service for instance. However, in order to simplify matters, we will not take issue with that doctrine on its own ground.

2. Those revolutions are not strictly incessant; they occur in discrete rushes which are separated from each other by spans of comparative quiet. The process as a whole works incessantly however, in the sense that there always is either revolution or absorption of the results of revolution, both together forming what are known as business cycles.

3. It should be understood that it is only our appraisal of economic performance and not our moral judgment that can be so changed. Owing to its autonomy, moral approval or disapproval is entirely independent of our appraisal of social (or any other) results, unless we happen to adopt a moral system such as utilitarianism which makes moral approval and disapproval turn on them *ex definitione*.

4. This is also known by a theorem we frequently meet with in expositions of the theory of imperfect competition, viz., the theorem that, under conditions of imperfect competition, producing or trading businesses tend to be irrationally small. Since imperfect competition is at the same time held to be an outstanding characteristic of modern industry we are set to wondering what world these theorists live in, unless, as stated above, fringe-end cases are all they have in mind.

5. The mere threat of their attack cannot, in the particular conditions, environmental and personal, of small-scale retail trade, have its usual disciplining influence, for the small man is too much hampered by his cost structure and, however well he may manage within his inescapable limitations, he can never adapt himself to the methods of competitors who can afford to sell at the price at which he buys.

Industry Structure, Market Rivalry, and Public Policy

Harold Demsetz

I. Introduction

Quantitative work in industrial organization has been directed mainly to the task of searching for monopoly even though a vast number of other interesting topics have been available to the student of economic organization. The motives for this preoccupation with monopoly are numerous, but important among them are the desire to be policy-relevant and the ease with which industrial concentration data can be secured. This paper takes a critical view of contemporary doctrine in this area and presents data which suggest that this doctrine offers a dangerous base upon which to build a public policy toward business.

II. Concentration Through Competition

Under the pressure of competitive rivalry, and in the apparent absence of effective barriers to entry, it would seem that the concentration of an industry's output in a few firms could only derive from their superiority in producing and marketing products or in the superiority of a structure of industry in which there are only a few firms. In a world in which information and resource mobility can be secured only at a cost, an industry will become more concentrated under competitive conditions only if a differential advantage in expanding output develops in some firms. Such expansion will increase the degree of concentration at the same time that it increases the rate of return that these firms earn. The cost advantage that gives rise to increased concentration may be reflected in scale economies or in downward shifts in positively sloped marginal cost curves, or it may be reflected in better products which satisfy demand at a lower cost. New efficiencies can, of course, arise in other ways. Some firms might discover ways of lowering cost that require that firms become smaller, so that spinoffs might be in order. In such cases, smaller firms will tend to earn relatively high rates of

Note: The author wishes to thank the Research Program in Competition and Public Policy at U.C.L.A. for assisting in the preparation of this article.

return. Which type of new efficiency arises most frequently is a question of fact.

Such profits need not be eliminated soon by competition. It may well be that superior competitive performance is unique to the firm, viewed as a team, and unobtainable to others except by purchasing the firm itself. In this case the return to superior performance is in the nature of a gain that is completely captured by the owner of the firm itself, not by its inputs.[1] Here, although the industry structure may change because the superior firm grows, the resulting increase in profit cannot easily serve to guide competitors to similar success. The firm may have established a reputation or goodwill that is difficult to separate from the firm itself and which should be carried at higher value on its books. Or it may be that the members of the employee team derive their higher productivity from the knowledge they possess about each other in the environment of the particular firm in which they work, a source of productivity that may be difficult to transfer piecemeal. It should be remembered that we are discussing complex, large enterprises, many larger (and more productive) than entire nations. One such enterprise happens to "click" for some time while others do not. It may be very difficult for these firms to understand the reasons for this difference in performance or to know to which inputs to attribute the performance of the successful firm. It is not easy to ascertain just why G.M. and I.B.M. perform better than their competitors. The complexity of these organizations defies easy analysis, so that the inputs responsible for success may be undervalued by the market for some time. By the same token, inputs owned by complex, unsuccessful firms may be overvalued for some time. The success of firms will be reflected in higher returns and stock prices, not higher input prices, and lack of success will be recorded in lower returns and stock prices, not lower input prices.

Moreover, inputs are acquired at historic cost, but the use made of these inputs, including the managerial inputs, yields only uncertain outcomes. Because the outcomes of managerial decisions are surrounded by uncertainty and are specific to a particular firm at a particular point in its history, the acquisition cost of inputs may fail to reflect their value to the firm at some subsequent time. By the time their value to the firm is recognized, they are beyond acquisition by other firms at the same historic cost, and, in the interim, shareholders of the successful or lucky firm will have enjoyed higher profit rates. When nature cooperates to make such decisions correct, they can give rise to high accounting returns for several years or to a once and for all capital gain if accountants could value *a priori* decisions that turn out to be correct *ex post*. During the period when such decisions determine the course of events, output will tend to be concentrated in those firms fortunate enough to have made the correct decisions.

None of this is necessarily monopolistic (although monopoly may play some role). Profit does not arise because the firm creates "artificial scarcity" through a reduction in its output. Nor does it arise because of collusion. Superior performance can be attributed to the combination of great uncertainty plus luck or atypical insight by the management of a firm. It is not until the experiments are actually tried that we learn which succeed and which fail. By the time the results are in, it is the shareholder that has captured (some of) the value, positive or negative, of past decisions. Even though the profits that arise from a firm's activities may be eroded by competitive imitation, since information is costly to obtain and techniques are difficult to duplicate, the firm may enjoy growth and a superior rate of return for some time.

Superior ability also may be interpreted as a competitive basis for acquiring a measure of monopoly power. In a world in which information is costly and the future is uncertain, a firm that seizes an opportunity to better serve customers does so because it expects to enjoy some protection from rivals because of their ignorance of this opportunity or because of their inability to imitate quickly. One possible source of some monopoly power is superior entrepreneurship. Our patent, copyright, and trademark laws explicitly provide as a reward for uncovering new methods (and for revealing these methods), legal protection against free imitation, and it may be true in some cases that an astute rival acquires the exclusive rights to some resource that *later* becomes valuable. There is no reason to suppose that competitive behavior never yields monopoly power, although in many cases such power may be exercised not by creating entry barriers, but through the natural frictions and ignorance that characterize any real economy. If rivals seek better ways to satisfy buyers or to produce a product, and if one or a few succeed in such endeavors, then the reward for their entrepreneurial efforts is likely to be some (short term) monopoly power and this may be associated with increased industrial concentration. To destroy such power when it arises may very well remove the incentive for progress. This is to be contrasted with a situation in which a high rate of return is obtained through a successful *collusion* to restrict output; here there is less danger to progress if the collusive agreement is penalized. Evidence presented below suggests that there are definite dangers of decreasing efficiency through the use of deconcentration or anti-merger policies.

III. Inefficiency Through Anti-Concentration Public Policy

The discussion in part II noted that concentration may be brought about because a workable system of incentives implies that firms which better serve buyers will tend to grow relative to other firms. One way in which a firm could better serve buyers is by seizing opportunities to exploit scale economies, although if scale economies are the main cause of concentration, it is difficult to understand why there is no significant trend toward one-firm industries; the lack of such a trend seems to suggest that superiority results in lower but *positively* sloped cost curves in the relevant range of large firm operations. This would set limits to the size of even the successful firms. Successful firms thus would seem to be more closely related to the ''superior land'' of classical economic rent analysis than to the single firm of natural monopoly theory. Whether or not superiority is reflected in scale economies, deconcentration may have the total effect of promoting inefficiency even though it also may reduce some monopoly-caused inefficiencies.[2]

The classic portrayal of the inefficiency produced by concentration through the exercise of monopoly power is that of a group of firms cooperating somehow to restrict entry and prevent rivalrous price behavior. Successfully pursued, this policy results in a product price and rate of return in excess of that which would have prevailed in the absence of collusion. However, if all firms are able to produce at the same cost, then the rate of return to successfully colluding firms should be independent of the particular sizes adopted by these firms to achieve low cost production. One firm may require a small scale, and hence have a smaller investment, while another may require a large scale, and corresponding large investment. At any given collusive price, the absolute amounts of monopoly profits will be proportional to output, but capital investment also will be proportionate to output, so we can expect the rate of return to be invariant with respect to size of firm.

If one size of firm earns a higher rate of return than another size, given any collusive price, then there must exist differences in the cost of production which favor the firm that earns the higher rate of return. Alternatively, if there is no single price upon which the industry agrees, but, rather a range of prices, then one firm can earn a higher rate of return if it produces a superior product and sells it at a higher price without thereby incurring proportionately higher costs; here, also, the firm that earns the higher rate of return can be judged to be more efficient because it delivers more value per dollar of cost incurred.

A deconcentration or antimerger policy is more likely to have benign results if small firms in concentrated industries earn the same or higher rates of return than large firms, for, then, deconcentration may reduce collusion,[3] if it is present, while simultaneously allocating larger shares of industry output to smaller firms which are no less efficient than larger firms. But if increased concentration has come about because of the superior efficiency of those firms that have become large, then a deconcentration policy, while it may reduce the ease of colluding, courts the danger of reducing efficiency either by the penalties that it places on innovative success or by the shift in output to smaller, higher cost firms that it brings about. This would seem to be a distinct possibility if large firms in concentrated industries earn higher rates of return than small firms.

The problem posed is how to organize data to shed light on the probability that deconcentration will promote inefficiency. Correlating industry rate of return with concentration will not be enlightening for this problem, for even if concentrated industries exhibit higher rates of return, it is difficult to determine whether it is efficiency or monopoly power that is at work. Similarly, large firms would tend to earn high profit rates in concentrated industries either because they are efficient or because they are colluding. However, partitioning industry data by size of firm does suggest that there exists a real danger from a deconcentration or anti-merger public policy, for the rates of return earned by small firms give no support to the doctrine relating collusion to concentration. A successful collusion is very likely to benefit the smaller firms, and this suggests that there should be a positive correlation between the rate of return earned by small firms and the degree to which the industry is concentrated. By the same token, if efficiency is associated with concentration, there should be a positive correlation between concentration and the difference between the rate of return earned by large firms and that earned by small firms; that is, large firms have become large because they are more efficient than other firms and are able to earn a higher rate of return than other firms.

Tables 1 and 2 show 1963 rates of return based on internal revenue data partitioned by size of firm and industry concentration for 95 three digit industries. In these tables, C_{63} designates the four firm concentration ratio measured on industry sales; R_1, R_2, R_3, and R_4, respectively, measure accounting rates of return (profit plus interest)/total assets, for firms with asset value less than \$500,000, \$500,000 to \$5,000,000, \$5,000,000 to \$50,000,000 and over \$50,000,000. Table 1 is calculated by assigning equal weight to all industries. It is based, therefore, on the assumption

Table 1. Rates of Return by Size and Concentration (Unweighted).

C_{63}	Number of Industries	R_1	R_2	R_3	R_4	$\bar{R}$
10–20%	14	6.7%	9.0%	10.8%	10.3%	9.2%
20–30	22	4.5	9.1	9.7	10.4	8.4
30–40	24	5.2	8.7	9.9	11.0	8.7
40–50	21	5.8	9.0	9.5	9.0	8.3
50–60	11	6.7	9.8	10.5	13.4	10.1
over 60	3	5.3	10.1	11.5	23.1	12.5

Table 2. Rates of Return by Size and Concentration (Weighted by Assets).

C_{63}	Number of Industries	R_1	R_2	R_3	R_4	$\bar{R}$
10–20%	14	7.3%	9.5%	10.6%	8.0%	8.8%
20–30	22	4.4	8.6	9.9	10.6	8.4
30–40	24	5.1	9.0	9.4	11.7	8.8
40–50	21	4.8	9.5	11.2	9.4	8.7
50–60	11	0.9	9.6	10.8	12.2	8.4
over 60	3	5.0	8.6	10.3	21.6	11.3

that each industry, regardless of size, offers an equally good observational unit for comparing the efficiency and monopolistic aspects of industry structure. Table 2 presents the same basic data with accounting rates of return weighted by asset value. Hence, an industry with many assets owned by small firms receives a larger weight in calculating the small firm rate of return for a given interval of concentration ratios.

Both tables fail to reveal the beneficial effects to small firms that we would expect from an association of collusion and industry concentration. The rate of return earned by firms in the smallest asset size does not increase with concentration. This seems to be true for the next two larger asset size classifications also, although in Table 1 the 11.5 per cent earned by R_3 firms in industries with concentration ratios higher than 60 per cent offers some indication of a larger rate of return than in less concentrated industries.[4] The data do not seem to support the notion that concentration and collusion are closely related, and, therefore, it is difficult to remain optimistic about the beneficial efficiency effects of a deconcentration or anti-merger public policy. On the contrary, the data suggest that such policies will reduce efficiency by impairing the survival of large firms in concentrated industries, for these firms do seem better able to produce at lower cost than their competitiors.[5] Both tables indicate that R_4 size firms in industries with concentration ratios greater than 50 per cent produce at lower average cost.

Since a larger fraction of industry output is produced by larger firms in the more concentrated industries, these industries may exhibit higher rates of return than other industries. That this is so can be seen from the unweighted row averages given by column $\bar{R}$. Industries with $C_{63} > 50$ per cent seem to have earned higher rates of return than less concentrated industries. But this result, which is consistent with some earlier studies, may be attributed to the superior performance of the larger firms and not to collusive practices. Table 2 reveals this pattern even more clearly. Because the rates of return of smaller firms receive a larger weight (by total assets) in Table 2, industry rates of return are reduced even for concentrated industries in which large firms continue to perform well.

The general pattern of these data can be seen in Table 3. The results of regressing differences in profit rates on concentration ratios are shown in this table.

Table 3. [Profit Rates and Concentration Ratios.]

$R_4 - R_1 = -1.4 + .21^*C_{63}$	$r^2 = .09$
$(.07)$	
$R_4 - R_2 = -2.6 + .12^{**}C_{63}$	$r^2 = .04$
$(.06)$	
$R_4 - R_3 = -3.1 + .10^{**}C_{63}$	$r^2 = .04$
$(.05)$	

Notes: *, **, significant at the 1% and 5% levels respectively. Standard errors are shown in parenthesis.

These regressions reveal a significant positive relationship between concentration and differences in rates of return, especially when comparing the largest and smallest firms in an industry.[6] The three regressions taken together indicate a nonlinear, decreasing impact of concentration on relative rates of return as the size of the smaller firms is increased from R_1 to R_3.

The competitive view of industry structure suggests that rapid changes in concentration are brought about by changed cost conditions and not by alterations in the height of entry barriers. Industries experiencing rapid increases in concentration should exhibit greater disparities between large and small rates of return because of the more significant cost of differences which are the root cause of rapid alternations in industry structure. The monopoly view of concentration does not imply such a relationship, for if an industry is rapidly achieving workable collusive practices there is no reason to suppose that the difference between large and small firm profit rates should increase. At the time of writing, matching data on concentration were available for both 1963 and 1967. This time span is too short to reveal much variation in concentration ratios, and so we cannot be very confident about evidence gained by regressing differences in profit rates on changes in concentration ratios. However, the persistently positive coeffecient of the variable $C_{67} - C_{63}$ in Table 4 is consistent with the competitive viewpoint, and must increase our doubts, however slightly, about the beneficial effects of an active deconcentration or anti-merger policy.

Table 4. [Differences in Profit Rates and Changes in Concentration Ratios.]

$$R_4 - R_1 = \quad 1.5 + .21^*C_{63} + .21(C_{67} - C_{63}) \qquad r^2 = .09$$
$$\qquad\qquad\quad (.07) \qquad\ (.42)$$

$$R_4 - R_2 = -2.9 + .12^{**}C_{63} + .37(C_{67} - C_{63}) \qquad r^2 = .06$$
$$\qquad\qquad\quad (.06) \qquad\quad (.28)$$

$$R_4 - R_3 = -3.4 + .10^{**}C_{63} + .29(C_{67} - C_{63}) \qquad r^2 = .05$$
$$\qquad\qquad\quad (.05) \qquad\quad (.24)$$

Note: *, **, respectively, 1% and 5% confidence levels.

I have presented an explanation of industry structure and profitability based on competitive superiority. The problem faced by a deconcentration or anti-merger policy was posed on the basis of this explanation. Is there a danger that such a policy will produce more inefficiency than it eliminates? The data presented suggest that this danger should be taken seriously.

Notes

1. A detailed discussion of the implicit notion of team production that underlies these arguments can be found in Alchian and Demsetz (1972).

2. For a discussion of the social costs that might be incurred by deconcentration, especially in the context of scale economics, see McGee (1971).

3. This statement is incorrect if a deconcentration or anti-merger policy causes firms to adopt socially less efficient methods of colluding than would be adopted in the absence of such a policy.

4. Since firms are segregated by absolute size, for some industries the R_3 firms

will be relatively large. A better test could be secured by contrasting the rates of return for the 1% largest and 10% smallest firms in each industry. But the data do not allow such a comparison. However, see footnote 6 for the result of a similar type of adjustment.

5. On the margin of output, however, these large firms need not have an advantage over small firms, just as fertile land has no advantage over poor land for producing marginal units. The failure of the large firms to become more dominant in these industries suggests the absence of such advantage.

6. Three adjustments in procedure and in variables were undertaken to analyze certain problems in the data and the theory.

1. It is believed by some that the profits of firms, and especially of small firms, are hidden in administrative wages. To check on the possibility that this phenomenon might have accounted for the data relationships shown above, the data were recalculated after adding back to profits all administrative salaries of firms in the R_1 asset size class. Although this increased very slightly the rates of return for this asset size class, as, of course, must be the case, no correlation between concentration and rate of return was produced. In fact, rates of return so calculated were virtually perfectly correlated with the rates of return shown above for this asset size.

2. The asset size categories used to calculate the above data are uniform over all industries. Some industries, however, had no firms in the largest asset size category, and these were dropped from the sample. An alternative method was used to check on the impact of this procedure. For each industry, the largest asset size class was redefined so as to include some firms in every industry. The mechanics of the procedure was to categorize asset sizes more finely and choose the largest three size categories containing some observations for each industry. These were then counted as the larger firms in each industry, and the rate of return for these firms was then compared to those firms contained in the three smaller asset size categories containing some observations. The unweighted average difference between large firm rate of return, R_L, and small firm rate of return, R_S, compared with industry concentration is shown below. This table is consistent with the text tables.

C_{63}	$R_L - R_S$
0–20%	6.4%
20–30	9.4
30–40	7.0
40–50	7.0
50–60	12.8
over 60	14.0

3. The efficiency argument suggests that for a given degree of industry concentration, measured by the four firm concentration ratio, the greater the difference between the sizes of the largest firms and the sizes of the smallest firms, the larger will be the disparity between R_4 and R_1. A linear regression of $R_4 - R_1$ on C_{63} and the average size of firms in the R_4 class yields a positive but not highly significant coefficient for the variable "average asset size of firms in the R_4 class." Also, there was a small reduction in the significance of the coefficient of C_{63}.

Learning from Organizational Economics

In the best of all possible worlds, this concluding chapter would present a fully integrated model of organizational economics which draws on the theories and concepts that have been presented. As several of the articles in this collection have suggested, however, we do not live in the best of all possible worlds. Rather, we inhabit a world of imperfect information, uncertainty, bounded rationality, and chance. Only after years of refining and testing will it be possible to fully evaluate the models that have been presented here. Only then will it be possible to develop a single integrated theoretical framework. This, of course, is the appropriate objective of several lifetimes of academic research. It cannot, therefore, be the objective of this concluding chapter.

Rather than focusing on a general theoretical integration, this chapter has more modest but nonetheless important objectives. First, we point to other areas in organizational economics that for one reason or another were not included among the readings selected for this book. Second, we point to some broad ideas and concepts that organization theorists could profitably learn from organizational economics. Third, we discuss some ideas and concepts taken from organization theory and behavior that seem likely to be important to organizational economists. We then develop a list of specific research questions that organizational economics will probably need to address if the integration between organization theory and organizational economics envisioned in the Introduction to this book is to take place. Finally, we return to the three business examples with which we began the Introduction and discuss the implications that organizational economics has for managers in these real world settings.

What Was Left Out?

Given the impossibility of complete coverage, our effort has focused on presenting those selections that are connected most closely to issues with which organization theorists are currently struggling and that are currently acknowledged to be, or seem likely to become, classics in the field. In an attempt to fulfill the objective of creating a map to the organizational economics literature, we will briefly consider some of the other major pieces of this literature that have not received their full share of attention here. Those interested in these areas of research will find these brief introductions helpful.

Property Rights Economics

Perhaps the most important literature omitted from the readings in this book is the property rights economics literature. This literature is alluded to several times in the readings included in this book (Jensen and Meckling, 1976a; Alchian and Demsetz, 1972). However, because it is less directly applicable to organizational analysis, we decided not to include readings in this area of research. It nevertheless deserves careful consideration.

In the introduction to readings on asymmetric information and opportunism, it was suggested that the most basic process studied by any brand of economics, including organizational economics, is the buying and selling relationship. The property rights literature focuses on this most basic of economic processes by asking the question, "What is it that is being bought and sold"? The answer to this question turns out to be property rights. A property right is the right of an individual or group of individuals to receive all the benefits and to absorb all the costs associated with the productive activity of a good, service, or process, including their right to sell or give these rights to another party. Thus, when a firm buys a machine, it is not actually paying for the machine per se, but rather the right to obtain the services and output of the machine and the associated right to do what they would like with that output, including selling it or selling the machine.

This is precisely the same concept of ownership that Alchian and Demsetz (1972) employ to discuss the property rights of the residual claimants of firms. Applying the property rights question in an organizational context generates a whole host of interesting questions. For example, who does own the modern corporation? Although in principal stockholders are the residual claimants on a firm's income, stockholders rarely exercise the control we typically associate with ownership (Jensen and Meckling, 1976a). Debt holders, at least in the United States, are limited in the amount of control they can exercise on a firm (Ouchi, 1984). Other possible owners of the firm might include its customers, its suppliers, its employees, or perhaps even the society at large. Much of this literature considers the implications that different ownership schemes might have for the behavior of firms in an economy.

Similar questions can be asked about who owns the jobs in a company: the company (if so, then who owns the company?), the person currently occupying the job, the union, or perhaps no one at all? Who owns the tenured faculty spots in a university: the professor, the university, the students, the public at large? Does it make any difference in terms of the behavior of incumbents who owns a person's job?

To investigate these questions, property rights economists have attempted to answer the question of why systems of private property rights may have emerged in the first place. Moreover, given an institutional framework that includes private property rights, these same economists have considered what happens (and what should happen) when the property rights of two or more parties conflict.

Some of the most important insights yet developed about why systems of private property rights would ever emerge are found in Demsetz's (1967) discussion of the development of property rights among the Montagnes Indians in Quebec during the late 1600s and early 1700s. Demsetz begins by noting that the central function of private property rights is to "internalize externalities." That is, private property rights assure that those who own these rights directly experience as many of the benefits and as much of the harm of the exchanges in which they engage as possible. With private property rights in place, for example, those who overfarm a plot of ground suffer the costs of that overfarming directly. These costs are not borne by neighbors, the community, or society at large. Similarly, those that manage a plot of land in ways that maximize its productivity also enjoy directly all the benefits of that productivity. Private property rights individualize the consequences of economic activity.

Demsetz then goes on to argue that property rights develop only when the benefits and costs of an exchange are large enough to be of general economic concern. Thus, prior to fur trading, there was no need among the Montagnes Indians to divide hunting grounds into privately owned parcels, because the possibility that these grounds would be overhunted was remote. With the development of the fur trade, however, overhunting became a real possibility. In order to force those who engaged in overhunting to bear the costs of their actions, private property rights emerged, the tribal hunting grounds were partitioned, and hunting was restricted to the parcel owned by the hunter. In this manner, the consequences of overhunting, including possible starvation, were borne by the person who did the overhunting, and by no one else.

Whereas Demsetz investigates the conditions which lead to the development of systems of private property rights, Coase's (1960) seminal article addresses the question of how conflicts between individuals with inconsistent property rights are and should be resolved. Coase begins with what appears to be a very simple question: Is it possible to rely on market forces to resolve conflicts between different economic actors, where the actions of one has harmful effects on the others? Coase argues that if there are no costs to using the market, then market-mediated conflicts between firms will generate the same allocation of economic resources as they would if those conflicts were efficiently mediated through the courts or in some other way. Under the condition of zero transaction costs, efforts to assign liability are misguided, since the market will efficiently adjust the value of the property rights controlled by all those involved in a conflict.

But of course, as many of the authors in this book point out, there are costs associated with using markets. Moreover, these costs can be significant. How, in these circumstances, will it be possible to resolve conflicts among different economic actors? Since one cannot rely on the market, Coase investigates two other possible mechanisms: the firm and the government. In doing so, Coase, like many other organizational economists, implicitly sees organizations and markets as alternative means of organizing economic exchanges. But Coase adds another alternative governance mechanism, the government. In this, Coase follows closely the work of John Commons (1934) and Lindblom (1977).

By focusing additional attention on the government as a means of governing transactions between economic actors, these authors establish another important connection between organizational economics and organization theory, a connection that focuses on the broader social context in which organizations find themselves. How firms find legitimacy within that context, and thus help ensure their survival, is a question of some concern to institutionalists like Zucker (1977) and Meyer and Rowan (1977).

Exit, Voice, and Loyalty

Another important area in organizational economics that has not been included in this book begins with Hirschman's seminal work *Exit, Voice, and Loyalty* (1970). Hirschman's book is short and can be easily read. Moreover, it is best read as a package of interrelated ideas and thus is not easily included in a book of readings like this one.

Exit, Voice, and Loyalty offers a fascinating look at the behavioral options facing managers in firms in decline. For Hirschman, when a firm is experiencing financial or operational problems, employees have three basic options. First, they can leave. This is exit. Exit from a firm implies going out into the job market, changing firms, and absorbing what can be very high switching costs. Second, employees can try to improve the firm's performance by pointing up problems, communicating those problems to those in charge, and attempting to implement needed changes. This is voice. The study of voice is, in many ways, the study of participative management.

However, when exit is too costly and when voice is not possible—either because it is not sanctioned by the firm or because changing what is wrong with the firm is impossible—employee options are greatly limited. They cannot leave, and they cannot change the current situation. What is left is loyalty. Hirschman discusses in some detail what loyalty is like and what implications loyalty has for the behavior of individuals within a firm.

For organization theorists, Hirschman's simple three-category description of employee behavior is simultaneously oversimplified and very insightful. On the one hand, actual employee behavior in the setting studied by Hirschman is extremely varied and reflects idiosyncratic personalities and environments. On the other hand, Hirschman's typology reminds us that, although there are numerous differences in detail, the basic options are not that diverse. It also reminds organization theorists who would focus only on voice through participative management that both firms and employees have other options when managing decline.

Market Signaling

Still another organizational economic area of significant interest to organization theorists, but not included in this book, is the now growing market signaling literature. Much of this literature is highly technical and mathematical in nature, and does not fit within the parameters that were established for this anthology.

The reference work in this area is by Spence (1973, 1974a). The idea of signaling was originally developed in the context of the labor market and thus is closely associated with literature on human capital (Becker, 1964) and implicit labor contracts (Azariadis, 1975; Azariadis and Stiglitz, 1983). However, market signals exist in a wide variety of markets, so this research has implications beyond the employment relation.

Spence (1973) begins with the simple observation that a potential employee's underlying native intelligence, creativity, and dedication, although very difficult to observe and measure directly, are nevertheless very important in predicting the value of that potential employee for the firm. Because it is important that these qualities be communicated, both to the firm evaluating potential employees and to individuals of high quality looking for good jobs, potential employees will invest in what Spence calls "market signals.'' A market signal is simply an investment made by a potential employee that conveys some information about any of that individual's difficult to observe underlying traits and characteristics. To qualify as a market signal, the investment made by potential employees must somehow be correlated with these underlying attributes. Thus, for example, under the assumption that native intelligence is usually correlated with the probability of obtaining a degree from a first-rate university, obtaining a diploma from such a school becomes a market signal, communicating information about the native intelligence of those with the diploma.

Notice that the analysis focuses not on the substance of the education per se, but on the point that obtaining a "high-status" education is usually correlated with a person's native intelligence. Spence is able to isolate a wide variety of market signals, some of which communicate information about the underlying traits of prospective employees even though they may violate commonly held values about what one should and should not consider when making employment choices.

The direct implications of market signaling theory for organization theory in analyses of the employment relation and of careers are quite clear. But market signals are important in other contexts as well. Indeed, Porter's (1980) analysis of sending strategic signals to forestall the competitive actions of other firms is subject to similar kinds of analyses. For example, firms can signal their intention to severely retaliate against new entrants by keeping excess manufacturing capacity on line and available. In any case, in order for an investment to be a market signal, it must be associated with some underlying, but not directly observable, organizational trait, attribute, or intention. A firm's strategic intent may be just one example of such unobservable organizational attributes.

Contestable Markets

One final area in organizational economics that has been omitted from this collection of readings is contestable market economics (Baumol, Panzar, and Willig, 1982). Though still in relative infancy, contestable market economics may have important implications for strategic theories of organizational behavior.

The key concept in these arguments is that firms, in competitive settings, respond not only to current and actual behavior of competitors, but to the anticipated behavior of competitors. So far, this view has been developed in considering why a firm enjoying a current monopolistic situation might refrain from acting like a monopolist. Such a firm maintains a low profile since open monopolistic behavior would cause other firms to enter its market, increase competition, and drive returns to a normal level. Anticipated entry, therefore, disciplines the monopolist.

In the context of organization theory, this focus on anticipated behavior pushes the role of competition in constraining firm actions one step beyond current work. Now, instead of firms being constrained simply by the actual behavior of others, they are constrained by the actions others might take. Management systems designed to anticipate the responses of others to a firm's own strategy thus become an important component of a firm's overall strategic management efforts. Competition in a world of actual and anticipated corporate strategy quickly leads one to adopt a game theory approach to analyzing strategic behavior (Schelling, 1960). For these reasons, game theory and related models may come to have an important impact on the field of strategy over the next decade.

Learning from Organizational Economics

Throughout the presentation of current research and thinking in organizational economics, efforts have been made to point to specific ideas and concepts that organizational economists have developed that can be of direct use to organization theorists working on a variety of different problems. But much of what organization theorists can learn from organizational economics has less to do with specific applications of concepts or models, and more to do with a way of thinking about organizations and about organizational phenomena. Incorporating these ways of thinking into organization theory is likely to have as important an impact on organization theory as would incorporating any particular model or concept taken from organizational economics. We next consider three specific aspects of this economic way of thinking and their implications for organization theory.

Equilibrium Analysis

Much of the research that has been presented here adopts an equilibrium form of reasoning. Equilibrium reasoning has a soiled reputation among many organization theorists, because this form of reasoning is often associated with the abstractions of neoclassical price theory. Organization theorists might question spending so much time and energy attempting to characterize intra- and interorganizational equilibria when it is obvious that real organizations are never in such states.

But, in many ways, this question misses the point about equilibrium reasoning. First, equilibrium reasoning is not the same as neoclassical price theory. One does not need to assume perfect information, zero transaction costs, homogeneous products and firms, and so on in order to use equilibrium reasoning. Rather, the focus is on underlying processes within and between organizations and on the stable state to which those processes will evolve if left alone. In this sense, Akerlof's (1970) model of the Lemons Principle is a classic equilibrium argument, since he is able to isolate some simple processes (withholding information to exploit asymmetries) and the stable state these processes would generate if left alone (the disappearance of markets). Akerlof's model is clearly not a perfect competition model, but it nevertheless applies equilibrium forms of reasoning.

Second, the criticism that equilibrium arguments waste intellectual energy describing results that will never exist misses the importance of such arguments in suggesting why these states never develop. In fact, the strength of the equilibrium form of reasoning rests in its ability to highlight the reasons why equilibrium states do not actually develop. In the case of the Lemons Principle, we learn from equilibrium analysis the kinds of institutional mechanisms that must be put in place in order for markets with qualitative uncertainty to exist. In this way, the reasons behind firms, product guarantees, and product reputations, and their essential attributes, are all revealed. Without knowing the kinds of transaction problems these institutional mechanisms are supposed to resolve, it is not possible to explain why these mechanisms, or why any mechanisms, would develop.

A final strength of equilibrium analyses lies in their inherently dynamic form. Equilibrium analysis does not stop at: the actions of firm A engender the actions of firm B. Rather, it tells us that the actions of A lead to the actions of B, which in turn lead to more responses by A (and by other firms, C and D), and so on. This multistage dynamic stands in contrast to what is seen in most organization theory models, where behavior A leads to behavior B, and that is the end of it. This limitation in the reasoning used by most organization theorists has already been pointed out in the case of resource dependence theory (Pfeffer and Salancik, 1978), where an equilibrium analysis of resource dependence logic suggests that industries characterized by any uncertainty will be dominated by a small number of large, vertically integrated firms. Since this is not the case in most industries, the question that resource dependence theory should ask but has yet to is: why not? What constraints face firms seeking to reduce their dependence to zero? What constraints prevent the equilibrium that is the result of following resource dependence logic to its conclusion?

The Transaction as the Unit of Analysis

In organization theory and organizational behavior, there is a widespread belief that research on organizations needs to go forward on multiple levels of analysis simultaneously. The levels of analysis cited most commonly are the individual, the group, intergroup relations, the organization, interorganizational relations, and, finally, organization-environment relations. The discipline bases of these units of analysis also increase in scope from psychology to social psychology to sociology and political science. Recently, anthropology has begun to reemerge as an important discipline in understanding intergroup and organizational phenomena.

While research conducted at multiple levels of analysis is not unknown, it is nevertheless relatively rare. The reasons for this are clear. Each level of analysis has associated with it different disciplines, although they overlap to some extent. The theoretical content of these disciplines is typically based on different sets of assumptions and beliefs. Developing single frameworks to deal with multilevel phenomena requires at least a partial integration of theories based on different disciplines. Such "general social theories" tend to be very abstract indeed, often divorced from the empirical reality. Perhaps the best example of the pitfalls of such multilevel general social theories can be found in the highly abstract, and no longer influential, work of Talcott Parsons (1951). Thus, rather than fall subject to these abstractions, research in organization theory has tended to retreat to single levels of analysis, only rarely venturing forth to multiple levels and then only in a tentative way.

Much of the theory of organizational economics overcomes the liabilities of multiple levels of analysis by positing the existence of only one appropriate level: the transaction. A transaction, as defined by Williamson (1981), is simply an exchange between technologically separable entities. In this way, the definition of a transaction is closely related to exchange theory as it has been developed in sociology and social psychology (Blau, 1964; Homans, 1958). And even though the language is not used universally among organizational economists, such concepts as "the nexus of contracts" and "interspecific human capital" as used by property rights, agency, and transaction-costs theorists all build on this single unit of analysis.

Organizational sociologists, in particular, are likely to find the abandonment of multiple levels of analysis particularly troubling, since they often see in this abandonment the destruction of their discipline. Ever since Durkheim (1966), sociologists have specialized in arguing that there is something distinctly different about sociological phenomena, that it requires a separate unit of analysis for explanation.

Adoption of the transaction as the single unit of analysis in organization theory would have important implications for research and teaching in the field. Many old and familiar concepts suddenly disappear. For example, there is no such thing as an "organizational boundary," at least as it has been defined; that is, there is no longer a clear inside and outside to a firm. Some economic exchanges occur between separate legal entities but are long-lasting and cooperative. What meaning does the concept of a boundary have for these exchanges?

By implication, then, there is no such thing as an "organizational environment." Rather, firms face hundreds of microenvironments for each of the different transactions in which they engage. Some of these may be uncertain and complex, while others may be certain and simple. Overall characterizations of environments as uncertain or turbulent or complex or simple become meaningless in this context. Also, there is no such thing as an "organization's structure," at least as this concept traditionally has been used. Rather, exchanges are governed in a wide variety of ways, using competition or cooperation, rules or trust, and bureaucracies or clans, all simultaneously. Obviously, characterizing a structure as centralized or decentralized when it might be both simultaneously is misleading.

All this is not to suggest that macroorganizational analyses are impossible when using the transaction as the unit of analysis. Indeed, Williamson's (1975) M-form hypothesis is just such an analysis. However, by adopting the transaction as the unit of analysis, careful attention must be focused on important questions about: the process of aggregating individual transactions into bundles of transactions to discuss groups; aggregating groups to discuss intergroup relations (that is, transactions between groups); aggregating even further to focus on firms and firm structure; and, finally, aggregating transactions to the point where interfirm relations can be discussed. In other words, adopting the transaction as the unit of analysis, and then proceeding to conduct a macroanalysis of organizations necessitates multiple levels of analysis and cross-discipline research.

The Concept of Organization

Finally, organizational economists have been able to point to a fundamental ambiguity at the heart of organization theory. This ambiguity lies in what does and does not constitute organization. For organizational economists, an event or process is organized if it exhibits regular patterns and structures. Thus, market exchanges, because they exhibit such regular patterns, are organized social events, subject to study and analysis (Hirshleifer, 1980). Also, the structure of events inside firms can be organized and is subject to similar forms of analysis (Hoenack, 1983).

For organization theorists, on the other hand, organization is typically meant to include activities within and between what might be called firms (both for profit and nonprofit) and within and between government bureaucracies. This concept of organization is much more narrow and restrictive than what would be accepted by organizational economists.

One of the liabilities of adopting this narrow definition of organization is that it unrealistically restricts the range of phenomena that can be studied by organization theorists. One of the common themes running throughout organizational economics is comparing the efficiency characteristics of a hierarchy to those of a market in governing specific economic transactions. In this sense, hierarchies, markets, and intermediate market forms are specific alternatives among which managers can choose when deciding how to govern transactions. In organization theory, several of these alternatives are often omitted. Research is artificially restricted to considering one of several types of hierarchical responses. Markets and quasi-market alternatives are thereby excluded, perhaps prematurely.

There is, of course, a political and value laden side to including markets as transaction governance mechanisms within a broader redefined organization theory. Indeed, the neoconservative political leanings of many economists are well known (Friedman, 1970). Indeed, the organization theorist's emphasis on hierarchical governance may reflect underlying value preferences for the use of centralized control to resolve economic exchange problems or a preference for exposing the abuse of power in hierarchies. Nevertheless, as Williamson (1975) and others have shown, it is possible to separate the value and political questions from the efficiency questions of transaction governance mechanisms.

Perhaps organization theorists balk at generalizing the definition of the concept of organization to include market and quasi-market phenomena out of fear of academic incursions by economists into their protected domain. Without this broader definition, organization theory becomes just part of a general framework for analyzing economic transactions, a specialty that focuses on the more behavioral aspects of exchange. Perhaps this is appropriate. Perhaps organization theory will ultimately find itself integrated into this larger framework, its distinctiveness lost. Is this a bad thing? If, after all, the nature of the phenomena being studied requires this integration, is it not appropriate to attempt to accomplish it?

Learning from Organization Theory

But the learning between organizational economics and organization theory has not been one-way. Organization theory has had and continues to have important implications for organizational economics. Incorporating these points of view into organizational economics almost certainly will improve the analyses, explanations, and predictions of organizational economists.

Organizational Influences on Rational Decision Making

One of the most important contributions of organization theory to organizational economics has been recognition of the extrarational aspects of decision making. For most organizational economists, decision making is characterized by boundedly rational—but intentionally rational—utility maximizing information collectors and analyzers. While this is a description of decision making that applies in some settings, including perhaps the making of certain investment decisions, it is certainly not complete. For example, it probably does not describe how organizational economists, themselves, make a large number of decisions about their lives or careers.

Organization theorists also acknowledge bounded rationality and self-interest (Simon, 1961); but organizational research has shown that so-called rational decision making is affected by many other factors. These include the age and sex of those making decisions (Elder, 1975; Kanter, 1977), the nature of intergroup conflicts in an organization (Alderfer, 1977), the number and types of individuals making a decision (Kanter, 1977), the abilities of senior managers to encourage open discussion (Ouchi, 1981; Vroom and Yetton, 1973), and a host of other factors. Note that these factors do not create a situation in which individuals make irrational decisions, but rather a situation in which that which is rational changes in stable and predictable ways. That is, what is rational for a woman in a large organization may not be rational for a man in that same organization. What is rational when one is twenty-five is not rational, perhaps, at age thirty or at midlife. The level of open discussion that is rational in a participatively managed firm may not be rational in an autocratically managed firm.

Including these other factors in describing decision making by organization participants will almost certainly improve the predictive capabilities of economic models. It is also likely to substantially alter the structure of those models and introduce a level of complexity and subtlety that has yet to be characteristic of organizational economics.

Empirical Research

The other major tradition in organization theory that should influence organizational economists lies in the role and use of empirical research. Organization theory is characterized by a rich tradition of both qualitative and quantitative research. Beginning with the Hawthorne studies (Roethlisberger and Dickson, 1939), this work has not only been used to test theories deductively, but also to develop concepts and ideas inductively. The number of qualitatively rich descriptions of actual organizational processes has been and continues to be a resource pool of empirical phenomena against which many theories in organization behavior and theory have been judged (Christensen and others, 1982).

In organizational economics, quantitative and qualitative empirical research has been the exception rather than the rule. Indeed, the ratio of empirical papers to nonempirical papers in this collection of readings (1:14) is probably not much different from that found in organizational economics journals.

On the one hand, this lack of empirical research suggests a strong theoretical focus among organizational economists, a focus which certainly can be applauded. It also reflects a level of confidence in theory that organization theorists would probably find overstated. On the other hand, this paucity of empirical research leaves much of the ultimate potential of this approach unexamined. There is, within organizational economics, a large number of interesting ideas. Whether they help explain actual organizational phenomena unfortunately remains a largely unanswered question.

The relative lack of empirical work in organizational economics has at least two causes. First, empirical work in microeconomics generally has not received the attention it warrants. Organizational economists have continued this theoretical focus. Second, and perhaps more important, the use of the transaction as the unit of analysis by many organizational economists greatly complicates empirical analyses. A firm very well may be a ''legal fiction'' or a ''nexus of contracts,'' but data are collected and available at the firm level. Thus, tests of transaction level predictions are difficult. It is interesting to note, however, that most of the current empirical research in organizational economics, including Walker and Weber (1984), Barney (1986), and others has been conducted by organization theorists, with the important exception of Teece and his associates (Armour and Teece, 1978; Monteverde and Teece, 1982), marketing specialists, and other noneconomists. This suggests that, despite the difficulty of empirical work in this area, the paucity of such work done by economists reflects their interests and tastes as much as it does the difficulty of the research.

Some Unanswered Issues in Organizational Economics

As is suggested by our discussion of nonrational factors in decision making and the lack of empirical work, there are unresolved questions and issues in organizational economics that ultimately must be addressed if the integration between organization theory and organizational economics is to proceed. Some of these issues are considered below.

Firm Differences. It is a truism of organization theory that different firms are different. Research in the economics of strategy also suggests that firms are different and that these differences are important in explaining competitive behavior and the evolution of an industry. However, within organization theory and organizational economics, there is no vocabulary for describing these differences. Numerous authors, including Chamberlin (1933), cite examples of differences, but no one has developed a typology of differences that can be applied in deriving strategies that different firms should employ. Such a typology must be more than just a list of examples of differences; it must be based on a theoretical discussion of what constitutes an important difference between firms, and which classes of organizational traits are likely to have such differences.

Aggregation Logic. In our discussion of the use of the transaction as the unit of analysis, we suggested that the more macroanalytic levels of analysis must pay special attention to questions of aggregation. The importance of this concept is perhaps best exemplified by the work of Schelling (1971, 1978), who analyzes the macroscopic results of aggregating microphenomena. To suggest that aggregation can lead to some surprising results is clearly an understatement. For example, in a simulation of race relations in a community, Schelling (1978) is able to show that relatively nonracist attitudes at the level of the individual can end up generating almost completely segregated communities.

Despite the importance of aggregation questions when using the transaction as the unit of analysis, work in organizational economics has yet to specify fully the ways in which transaction governance mechanisms aggregate to become organizational structures. Williamson (1975) presents a typology of transaction governance mechanisms and a typology of organizational structures but does not develop a logic that connects these two typologies.

Types of Opportunism. A great deal of research in organizational economics turns on the concept of opportunism, Williamson's (1975) notion of "self-disbelieved behavior." However, even casual reflection suggests that there are different kinds of opportunism and that they may have different implications for organizational behavior.

Organizational economists have isolated at least three types of opportunism: adverse selection (Akerlof, 1970; Spence, 1974a), moral hazard (Arrow, 1962; Jensen and Meckling, 1976a), and holdup (Becker, 1962; Klein, Crawford, and Alchian, 1978; Williamson, 1975). Adverse selection is a type of opportunism that develops before two parties have actually begun an economic exchange. In this setting, opportunism takes the form of misrepresenting one's background, interests, or capabilities in an attempt to obtain more favorable terms in an exchange. The term *adverse selection* is adopted from the insurance markets (Arrow, 1962) and can develop when one party to an exchange has information about its background, interests, capabilities, and other characteristics (that is, its type) that the other party cannot obtain without cost. This informational asymmetry creates an incentive for individuals with informational advantages to misrepresent their type. Thus, some parties to an exchange can represent themselves opportunistically as something (for example, high-quality, honest, high-ability, low-risk) that they are not. In so doing, they can attempt to secure more favorable terms in the exchange being negotiated.

Whereas adverse selection is precontractual opportunism that exploits asymmetric information about *future* performance, moral hazard is postcontractual opportunism that exploits asymmetric information about *current* performance. Moral hazard arises in an exchange relationship when one party cannot directly observe the other's actions, and where efforts to determine these actions are both costly and subject to error. In such settings, parties to an exchange have a strong incentive not to meet agreed upon performance standards or to shirk their responsibilities in other ways, since they know that in so doing, they may receive a level of compensation greater than that which is justified by their performance. To avoid such exploitation in an exchange, parties subject to moral hazard will engage in costly monitoring activities in an attempt to gauge more accurately the performance of exchange partners.

Finally, the presence of assets and investments with a value specific to an exchange creates additional incentives for opportunism. This form of opportunism is called holdup (Klein, Crawford, and Alchian, 1978). As before, specific investments are any investments of personnel or physical capital that have much greater value in the current transaction than they would in any other transaction (Williamson, 1979). For example, once a firm makes investments in an employee that are specific to that firm (that is, their value in other firms is almost zero), through on-the-job and other training experiences, then the employee has an incentive to exploit these investments by threatening to terminate the employment relation (Becker, 1962).

Requiring that the employee make specific investments in the firm only transfers the incentive for opportunism from the employee to the employer. The employer can now appropriate the employee's specific investment by threatening to terminate the employment relation. Absent a mechanism or governance device to instill some sort of trust between parties to an exchange with specific investments, no such specific investment would be made, and the transaction would not occur.

While these kinds of opportunism have been isolated, their implications for organizational behavior have yet to be fully explored. In particular, the types of governance mechanisms appropriate for resolving different forms of opportunism have not been spelled out. Rather, many different devices, some of them hierarchical, some relying on market forces, and some intermediate between the market and hierarchy, have been specified as solutions to all three types of opportunism. If all these governance mechanisms can help resolve all these types of opportunism, then how much insight into organizational phenomena can the distinction between these types of opportunism provide?

Typology of Governance. Finally, in the introduction to Chapter Three, it was posited that one of the great strengths of organization economic research on organization structure was that this research was done using the language and vocabulary of managers. This common language, it was suggested, greatly facilitated the development of implications for managerial action from this research.

The use of this managerial vocabulary in the study of organizational structure stands in marked contrast to the vocabulary used by organizational economists to study transaction governance mechanisms. Williamson's (1975) original distinction between a market and a hierarchy is similar to managerial distinctions, but when it comes to intermediate forms of governance, enormous ambiguities arise. Where managers speak of joint ventures, licensing arrangements, and franchises, most organizational economists talk about complete contingent claims contracts (Williamson, 1979), clan-assisted market relations (Barney and Ouchi, 1984), and relational contracting (Williamson, 1979). Nor is this simply a problem of different individuals using different terms when describing the same phenomena. The correspondence between these two languages is not clear. Thus, for example, some joint ventures might be clan-assisted markets, while others might be bureaucratically assisted markets.

This lack of correspondence between the typologies of managers and the typologies of organizational economists may partially explain the paucity of empirical work in organizational economics. Until a correspondence between these two vocabularies is established, it will be difficult to know how to test theories developed using an organizational economic vocabulary with data collected on phenomena defined by a managerial vocabulary.

Management Implications of Organizational Economics

Finally, we turn to perhaps the greatest challenge of organizational economics: deriving implications for management practice. Many have suggested that such an objective is inappropriate for any research on organizational phenomena, that the purpose of such research is and should be description and explanation, not application (McKelvey, 1982). Our view is different. For us, the question of application is simply another aspect of testing a theory, for, if nothing else, application is at least a type of quasi-experimental examination of a theory (Campbell and Stanley, 1963). While it may be that not all theories of organization can be applied, our view is that those that can be, should be.

Perhaps the best way to begin to outline some of the managerial implications of organizational economics is to return to the three business examples with which we began the first chapter, and to see what insights different organizational economic models might have generated for these managers.

In the first example, a group vice-president was considering the costs and benefits of centralized manufacturing in his group. The work of both Coase and Williamson suggests that this manager's search for synergy is an appropriate one, for if no synergies existed among the business units in his group, then there would be no clear advantage to owning these business units. If bringing them under a hierarchy offered no advantage, he would be better simply to invest in them across the market by owning stock. Williamson's M-form hypothesis suggests that the problems facing this group vice-president in attempting to balance the independent needs of different business units against the collective needs of the group are typical in M-form companies and that care must be taken to manage that balancing act over time.

While transaction-cost theory suggests that the search for synergies is an appropriate one, it does not tell this group vice-president whether or not centralized manufacturing is the right synergy to try to exploit. To answer this question, the group vice-president would have to turn to the economic theories of strategy presented in this book. First, he would have to evaluate the long-term potential of the division facing Japanese competition by considering that division's unique competitive capabilities (Chamberlinian competition) and its environmental competitive opportunities (industrial organization, or IO, competition). After determining the potential of this division, he would then have to decide whether transferring capital from other divisions, often done in M-form companies, would maximize the wealth of the firm's stockholders. He would have to consider too the impact on his personal career. How these trade-offs might be made, and what their impact would be on a firm's cost of capital and relations with stockholders, could be analyzed using Jensen and Meckling's agency theory.

In the second example, the entrepreneurial managers of a new firm are concerned about retaining and motivating their engineers, and about the relationship of their efforts in this area to financing their firm's growth. Jensen and Meckling's agency theory suggests that if these managers engage in activities to motivate managers that are contrary to the interests of outside investors (in this case the venture capitalists), then the venture capitalists will effectively raise their cost of capital in subsequent rounds of financing. Thus, these managers cannot feel free to give equity to their engineers in large amounts. On the other hand, since the engineers form the core of the firm's distinctive competence (Chamberlinian competition), failing to retain these engineers would likely hurt the future of firm performance, and this would also be reflected in a firm's cost of capital.

Some sort of equity arrangement with the engineers does have its advantages. Most important, this would reduce whatever agency costs exist between the engineers, managers, and venture capitalists, since all their financial futures would depend on the performance of the firm's stock. With a strong equity position, Alchian and Demsetz's argument suggests engineers could act as their own "owners," thereby substantially reducing the problems of shirking typical of team production. Such an equity-sharing plan would also lead to a reduced cost of capital for the firm in the next round of financing.

In the final example, managers in a participatively managed

firm were struggling to understand the source of a 20 percent cost disadvantage vis-à-vis a major competitor. The industrial organization theory of strategy suggests that their efforts to look beyond the management practices of their competitors to their relationships with capital sources and other suppliers is appropriate, since the IO model suggests that such relationships can give firms competitive advantages. In particular, close relations between a firm and its capital sources should lead to lower costs of capital for a firm, because close relations between these parties can reduce residual, monitoring, and bonding agency costs. This could be reflected either in a lower cost of debt or a higher debt-to-equity ratio.

The degree of vertical integration characteristic of this competitor is also a potential source of cost advantage. If a competitor has put a more efficient governance device in place to manage a particular transaction, other business factors being equal, firms without that governance solution will be at a disadvantage. The transaction-cost work of both Williamson and Coase suggests that the objective attributes of these transactions may have changed, perhaps as a result of changes in technology, suggesting that new governance mechanisms might be appropriate. If the new transactions are characterized by less specific investment or less uncertainty, for example, vertical disintegration might be appropriate.

These three examples are only suggestive. But they do indicate, at the very least, that organizational economic concepts can sometimes be used to help inform managers in real business situations. As this field develops and, in particular, as organizational economics is more fully integrated into organization theory, the breadth of this applicability will certainly increase.

Final Remarks

Thus, this is organizational economics: a collection of ideas and models, with the potential to be integrated, to guide managerial action, and to inform organization theory and behavior but only just beginning to realize its potential. As this field continues to develop, the many threads of ideas presented here will begin to weave themselves around empirical regularities in organizations, ultimately becoming the cloth out of which the next generation of theories about organizations and organizational phenomena will be cut. The next decade will bring not only confrontations between this new way of thinking about firms and the more traditional models in organization theory but also collaboration leading to insights and theoretical progress.

References

Aharoni, Y. *The Foreign Investment Decision.* Cambridge, Mass.: Division of Research, Harvard Graduate School of Business Administration, 1966.

Akerlof, G. A. "The Market for 'Lemons': Qualitative Uncertainty and the Market Mechanism." *Quarterly Journal of Economics,* 1970, *84*, 488–500.

Alchian, A. "Uncertainty, Evolution and Economic Theory." *Journal of Political Economy,* 1950, *58*, 211–221.

Alchian, A. "The Basis of Some Advances in the Theory of Management of the Firm." *Journal of Industrial Economics,* 1965, *14*, 30–41.

Alchian, A. "Corporate Management and Property Rights." In *Economic Policy and the Regulation of Securities.* Washington, D.C.: American Enterprise Institute, 1968.

Alchian, A. "Some Implications of Recognition of Property Right Transaction Costs." Paper presented at the First Interlaken Conference on Analysis and Ideology, Switzerland, June 1974.

Alchian, A., and Allen, W. R. *Exchange and Production: Theory in Use.* Belmont, Calif.: Wadsworth, 1969.

Alchian, A., and Demsetz, H. "Production, Information Costs, and Economic Organization." *American Economic Review,* 1972, *62*, 777–795.

Alchian, A., and Kessel, R. A. "Competition, Monopoly and

the Pursuit of Pecuniary Gain.'' In *Aspects of Labor Economics*. Princeton, N.J.: National Bureau of Economic Research, 1962.

Alderfer, C. P. ''Improving Organizational Communication Through Long-term Intergroup Intervention.'' *Journal of Applied Behavioral Science*, 1977, *13*, 193–210.

Alland, A. *Evolution and Human Behavior*. Garden City, N.Y.: Natural History Press, 1967.

Allen, R.G.D. *Mathematical Analysis for Economists*. London: Macmillan, 1938.

Allen, S. A. ''Corporate Divisional Relationships in Highly Diversified Firms.'' In J. W. Lorsch and P. R. Lawrence (eds.), *Studies in Organizational Design*. Homewood, Ill.: Irwin, 1970.

American Petroleum Institute. *Basic Petroleum Data Book: Petroleum Industry Statistics*. Washington, D.C.: American Petroleum Institute, 1975.

Anderson, O. W., and Feldman, J. J. *Family Medical Costs and Insurance*. New York: McGraw-Hill, 1956.

Andrews, K. R. *The Concept of Corporate Strategy*. New York: Dow Jones-Irwin, 1971.

Angell, F. J. *Insurance: Principles and Practices*. New York: Ronald Press, 1957.

Angyal, A. ''A Logic of Systems.'' In F. E. Emery (ed.), *Systems Thinking*. Middlesex, England: Penguin Books Ltd., 1969.

Ansoff, H. I., and Brandenberg, R. G. ''A Language for Organizational Design.'' *Management Science*, 1971, *17*, 705–732.

Ansoff, I. *Corporate Strategy*. New York: McGraw-Hill, 1965.

Ardrey, R. *African Genesis*. New York: Atheneum, 1961.

Ardrey, R. *The Social Contract*. New York: Atheneum, 1970.

Armour, H. O., and Teece, D. J. ''Organization Structure and Economic Performance: A Test of the Multidivisional Hypothesis.'' *Bell Journal of Economics*, 1978, *9*, 106–122.

Arrow, K. J. ''Economic Welfare and the Allocation of Resources for Invention.'' In *The Rate and Direction of Inventive Activity*. Princeton, N.J.: Princeton University Press, 1962.

Arrow, K. J. ''Uncertainty and Medical Care.'' *American Economic Review*, 1963, *53*.

Arrow, K. J. ''Control in Large Organizations.'' *Management Science*, 1964a, *10*, 397–408.

Arrow, K. J. "The Role of Securities in the Optimal Allocation of Risk Bearing." *Review of Economic Studies*, 1964b, *31*, 91–96.

Arrow, K. J. *Aspects of the Theory of Risk Bearing*. Helsinki, Finland: Yrjo Jahnssonin Saatio, 1965.

Arrow, K. J. *Essays in the Theory of Risk Bearing*. Amsterdam: North-Holland, 1971.

Arrow, K. J. *The Limits of Organization*. New York: Norton, 1974.

Ashenfelter, O., and Johnson, G. "Unionism, Relative Wages, and Labor Quality in U.S. Manufacturing Industries." *International Economic Review*, 1972, *13*, 488–508.

Atkinson, T. R. "Trends in Corporate Bond Quality." In *Studies in Corporate Bond Finance*. New York: National Bureau of Economic Research, 1967.

Atwood, J., and Kobrin, P. *Integration and Joint Ventures in Pipelines*. Research Study No. 5. Washington D.C.: American Petroleum Institute, 1977.

Azariadis, C. "Implicit Contracts and Underemployment Equilibria." *Journal of Political Economy*, 1975, *83*, 1183–1202.

Azariadis, C., and Stiglitz, J. E. "Implicit Contracts and Fixed Price Equilibria." *Quarterly Journal of Economics*, 1983, *148*, 1–22.

Babbage, C. *On the Economy of Machinery and Manufacturers*. New York: A. M. Kelley, 1832.

Bagehot, W. *Physics and Politics*. East Norwalk, Conn.: Appleton-Century-Crofts, 1875.

Bain, J. S. *Barriers to New Competition*. Cambridge, Mass.: Harvard University Press, 1956.

Bain, J. S. *Industrial Organization*. (2nd ed.) New York: Wiley, 1968.

Bain, J. S. *Essays on Price Theory and Industrial Organization*. Boston: Little, Brown, 1972.

Barney, J. B. "Theory Z, Institutional Economics, and the Theory of Strategy." In P. Kleindorfer (ed.), *The Management of Productivity and Technology in Manufacturing*. New York: Plenum, 1985.

Barney, J. B. "The Organization of Capital Acquisition." Unpublished manuscript, Graduate School of Management, University of California, Los Angeles, 1986.

Barney, J. B. "Organizational Culture: Can It Be a Source of Sustained Competitive Advantage?" *Academy of Management Review*, forthcoming (a).

Barney, J. B. "Strategic Factor Markets: Expectations, Luck, and the Theory of Strategy." *Management Science*, forthcoming (b).

Barney, J. B. "Types of Competition and the Theory of Strategy." *Academy of Management Review*, forthcoming (c).

Barney, J. B. and Ouchi, W. G. "Information Cost and the Organization of Transaction Governance." Unpublished manuscript, Graduate School of Management, University of California, Los Angeles, 1984.

Barzel, Y. "Measurement Cost and the Organization of Markets." Unpublished paper, 1979.

Bass, F. M., Cattin, P., and Wittink, O. R. "Fire Effects and Industry Effects in the Analysis of Market Structure and Profitability." *Journal of Marketing Research*, 1978, *15*, 3–10.

Batt, F. R. *The Law of Master and Servant*. New York: Pitman, 1929.

Baumol, W. J. *Business Behavior, Value and Growth*. New York: Macmillan, 1959.

Baumol, W. J., Panzar, J. C., and Willig, R. P. *Contestable Markets and the Theory of Industry Structure*. San Diego, Calif.: Harcourt Brace Jovanovich, 1982.

Beaver, W., Kettler, P., and Scholes, M. "The Association Between Market Determined and Accounting Determined Risk Measures." *Accounting Review*, 1970, *45*, 654–682.

Becker, G. S. *The Economics of Discrimination*. Chicago: University of Chicago Press, 1957.

Becker, G. S. "An Economic Analysis of Fertility." In *Demographic and Economic Change in Developed Countries*. Princeton, N.J.: Princeton University Press, 1960.

Becker, G. S. "Investment in Human Capital: A Theoretical Analysis." *Journal of Political Economy*, 1962, *70*, 9–44.

Becker, G. S. *Human Capital*. New York: Columbia University Press, 1964.

Becker, G. S. "A Theory of the Allocation of Time." *Economic Journal*, 1965, *75*, 493–517.

Becker, G. S. "Crime and Punishment: An Economic Approach." *Journal of Political Economy*, 1968, *76*, 169–217.

Becker, G. S. "A Theory of Marriage: Part I." *Journal of Political Economy*, 1973, *81*, 813–846.

Becker, G. S. "A Theory of Social Interactions." *Journal of Political Economy*, 1974, *82*, 1063–1093.

Becker, G. S. "Altruism, Egoism, and Genetic Fitness: Economics and Sociobiology." *Journal of Economic Literature*, 1976, *14*, 817–827.

Becker, G. S., and Stigler, G. J. "Law Enforcement, Corruption, and Compensation of Enforcers." Paper presented at the Conference on Capitalism and Freedom, Oct. 1972.

Becker, G. S., and Stigler, G. J. "Law Enforcement, Malfeasance, and Compensation of Enforcers." *Journal of Legal Studies*, 1974, *3*, 1–18.

Beer, S. "The Aborting Corporate Plan: A Cybernetic Account of the Interface Between Planning and Action." In E. Jantsch (ed.), *Perspectives on Planning*. Paris, 1969.

Ben-Porath, Y. *The F-Connection: Families, Friends, and Firms and the Organization of Exchange*. Jerusalem, Israel: The Hebrew University of Jerusalem, Report No. 29/78, 1978.

Benston, G. "The Impact of Maturity Regulation on High Interest Rate Lenders and Borrowers." *Journal of Financial Economics*, 1977, *4*.

Berhold, M. "A Theory of Linear Profit Sharing Incentives." *Quarterly Journal of Economics*, 1971, *85*, 460–482.

Berle, A. A., and Means, G. C. *The Modern Corporation and Private Property*. New York: Macmillan, 1932.

Biggadike, R. "Entry, Strategy, and Performance." Unpublished doctoral dissertation, Graduate School of Business Administration, Harvard University, 1976.

Billet, L. "The Just Economy: The Moral Basis of the Wealth of Nations." *Review of Social Economy*, 1976, *34*, 295–316.

Black, F., Miller, M. H., and Posner, R. A. "An Approach to the Regulation of Bank Holding Companies." Unpublished paper, Department of Economics, University of Chicago, 1974.

Black, F., and Scholes, M. "The Pricing of Options and Corporate Liabilities." *Journal of Political Economy*, 1973, *81*, 637–654.

Blau, P. M. *Bureaucracy in Modern Society*. New York: Random House, 1956.

Blau, P. M. *The Dynamics of Bureaucracy: A Study of Interpersonal Relations in Two Government Agencies*. Chicago: University of Chicago Press, 1963.

Blau, P. M. *Exchange and Power in Social Life*. New York: Wiley, 1964.

Bork, R. H. "Vertical Integration and the Sherman Act: The Legal History of an Economic Misconception." *University of Chicago Law Review*, 1954, *22*, 157–196.

Bork, R. H. "Vertical Integration and Competitive Processes." In J. F. Weston and S. Pelzman (eds.), *Public Policy Toward Mergers*. Pacific Palisades, Calif.: Goodyear, 1969.

Boulding, K. E. *A Reconstruction of Economics*. New York: Wiley, 1950.

Boulding, K. E. *Conflict and Defense*. New York: Harper & Row, 1962.

Bower, J. L. *Managing the Resource Allocation Process*. Cambridge, Mass.: Division of Research, Graduate School of Business Administration, Harvard University, 1970.

Bower, J. L. "Management Decision Making in Large Diversified Firms." Unpublished paper, Harvard University, 1971.

Bowman, W. S. *Patents and Antitrust Law: A Legal and Economic Appraisal*. Chicago: University of Chicago Press, 1973.

Branch, B. "Corporate Objectives and Market Performance." *Financial Management*, 1973, 24–29.

Brown, A. *Organization: A Formulation of Principles*. New York: Hibbert Printing, 1945.

Buchanan, D. H. *The Development of Capitalist Enterprise in India*. Fairfield, N. J.: Kelley, 1966.

Buchanan, J. M. *The Demand and Supply of Public Goods*. Skokie, Ill.: Rand McNally, 1968.

Buchanan, J. M., and Tullock, G. *The Calculus of Consent*. Ann Arbor: University of Michigan Press, 1962.

Buse, A. "Goodness of Fit in Generalized Least Squares." *The American Statistician*, 1973, *27*, 106–108.

Buzzell, R. D., Gale, B. T., and Sultan, R. G. M. "Market Share: A Key to Profitability." *Harvard Business Review*, 1976, *53*, 97–106.

Cairns, M. B. *The Law of Tort in Local Government*. London: Shaw, 1954.

Calabresi, G. "Transaction Costs, Resource Allocation, and

Liability Rules: A Comment." *Journal of Law and Economics*, 1968, *11*, 67–74.

Campbell, D. T., and Stanley, J. C. *Experimental and Quasi-Experimental Designs for Research*. Skokie, Ill.: Rand McNally, 1963.

Canes, M. E. "A Model of a Sports League." Unpublished doctoral dissertation, University of California, Los Angeles, 1970.

Canes, M. E. "A Theory of the Vertical Integration of Oil Firms." Unpublished manuscript, American Petroleum Institute, 1976.

Cannon, J. T. *Business Strategy and Policy*. San Diego, Calif.: Harcourt Brace Jovanovich, 1968.

Carlton, D. W. "Contracts, Price Rigidity, and Market Equilibrium." *Journal of Political Economy*, 1979a, *87*, 1034–1062.

Carlton, D. W. "Vertical Integration in Competitive Markets Under Uncertainty." *Journal of Industrial Economics*, 1979b, *27*, 189–209.

Cartwright, D., and Zander, A. (eds.). *Group Dynamics: Research and Theory*. New York: Row, Peterson, 1960.

Caves, R. E. "Industrial Organization, Corporate Strategy, and Structure: A Survey." *Journal of Economic Literature*, 1980, *18*, 64–92.

Caves, R. E., and Murphy, W. F., II. "Franchising: Firms, Markets, and Intangible Assets." *Southern Economic Journal*, 1976, *42*, 572–586.

Caves, R. E., and Porter, M. E. "From Entry Barriers to Mobility Barriers: Conjectural Decisions and Contrived Deterence to New Competition." *Quarterly Journal of Economics*, 1977, *91*, 241–262.

Caves, R. E., Porter, M. E., and Spence, A. M. *Competition in the Open Economy*. Cambridge, Mass.: Harvard University Press, 1980.

Chamberlin, E. H. *The Theory of Monopolistic Competition*. Cambridge, Mass.: Harvard University Press, 1933.

Chamberlin, E. H. "New Frontiers in Economic Thought: Discussion." *American Economic Review*, 1946, *36*, 139–142.

Chandler, A. D. *Strategy and Structure: Chapters in the History of the American Industrial Enterprise*. Cambridge, Mass.: MIT Press, 1962.

Chandler, A. D. *The Visible Hand.* Cambridge, Mass.: Harvard University Press, 1977.

Chandler, A. D., and Daems, H. *Managerial Hierarchies.* Cambridge, Mass.: Harvard University Press, 1980.

Charnov, E. L. "Optimal Foraging: The Marginal Value Theorem." *Theoretical Population Biology,* 1976, *9,* 126–143.

Charnov, E. L., and Krebs, J. R. "The Evolution of Alarm Calls: Altruism or Manipulation." *American Naturalist,* 1975, *109,* 107–121.

Cheung, S. N. *The Theory of Share Tenancy.* Chicago: University of Chicago Press, 1969.

Christensen, C. R., and others. *Business Policy.* Homewood, Ill.: Irwin, 1982.

Churchill, N. C., Cooper, W. W., and Sainsbury, T. "Laboratory and Field Studies of the Behavioral Effects of Audits." In C. P. Bonini and others (eds.), *Management Controls: New Directions in Basic Research.* New York: McGraw-Hill, 1964.

Clark, J. B. *Distribution of Wealth.* London: Macmillan, 1899.

Clark, J. M. *Economics of Overhead Costs.* Chicago: University of Chicago Press, 1923.

Coase, R. H. "The Nature of the Firm." *Economica,* 1937, *4,* 386–405.

Coase, R. II. "The Federal Communications Commission." *Journal of Law and Economics,* 1959, *2,* 1–40.

Coase, R. H. "The Problem of Social Cost." *Journal of Law and Economics,* 1960, *3,* 1–44.

Coase, R. H. "Discussion." *American Economic Review,* 1964, *54,* 194–197.

Coase, R. H. "Durability and Monopoly." *Journal of Law and Economics,* 1972, *15,* 143–150.

Coase, R. H. "Adam Smith's View of Man." *Journal of Law and Economics,* 1976, *19,* 529–546.

Cody, M. L. "Optimization in Ecology." *Science,* 1974, *183,* 1156–1170.

Cohen, R. "Altruism: Human, Cultural or What?" *Journal of Social Issues,* 1972, *2,* 39–54.

Comanor, W. S., and Wilson, T. A. *Advertising and Market Power.* Cambridge, Mass.: Harvard University Press, 1974.

Commons, J. R. *Institutional Economics.* Madison: University of Wisconsin Press, 1934.

Copeland, T., and Weston, J. F. *Financial Theory and Corporate Policy.* Reading, Mass.: Addison-Wesley, 1979.

Cowling, K. "On the Theoretical Specification of Industrial Structure-Performance Relationships." *European Economic Review*, 1976, *8*, 1.

Cox, A. "The Legal Nature of Collective Bargaining Agreements." *Michigan Law Review*, 1958, *57*, 1–36.

Crozier, M. *The Bureaucratic Phenomena.* Chicago: University of Chicago Press, 1964.

Cyert, R. M., and Hedrick, C. L. "Theory of the Firm: Past, Present, and Future: An Interpretation." *Journal of Economic Literature*, 1972, *10*, 398–412.

Cyert, R. M., and March, J. G. *A Behavioral Theory of the Firm.* Englewood Cliffs, N.J.: Prentice-Hall, 1963.

Dahlman, C. J. "The Problem of Externality." *Journal of Law and Economics*, 1979, *22*, 141–162.

Darby, M. R., and Karni, E. "Free Competition and the Optimal Amount of Fraud." *Journal of Law and Economics*, 1973, *16*, 67–88.

Darling, M. *Punjabi: Peasant in Prosperity and Debt.* (3rd ed.) Oxford: Oxford University Press, 1932.

Darwin, C. *On the Origin of Species.* London: J. Murray, 1859.

Dawes, H. "Labour Mobility in the Steel Industry." *Economic Journal*, 1934, *44*, 84–94.

Day, R. H. "Adaptive Processes and Economic Theory." In R. H. Day and T. Graves (eds.), *Adaptive Economic Models.* Orlando, Fla.: Academic Press, 1975.

De Alessi, L. "Private Property and Dispersion of Ownership in Large Corporations." *Journal of Finance*, 1973, *26*, 939–956.

Debreu, G. *Theory of Value.* New York: Wiley, 1959.

de Chazeau, M. G., and Kahn, A. H. *Integration and Competition in the Petroleum Industry.* New Haven, Conn.: Yale University Press, 1959.

Demsetz, H. "Toward a Theory of Property Rights." *American Economic Review*, 1967, *57*, 347–359.

Demsetz, H. "Information and Efficiency: Another Viewpoint." *Journal of Law and Economics*, 1969, *12*, 1–22.

Demsetz, H. "Industry Structure, Market Rivalry, and Public Policy." *Journal of Law and Economics*, 1973, *16*, 1–9.

Demsetz, H. "On Thinking Like an Economist." *Paleobiology*, 1975, *1*, 216–220.

Denenberg, H. S., and others. *Risk and Insurance*. (2nd ed.) Englewood Cliffs, N.J.: Prentice-Hall, 1964.

Denning, A. *Freedom Under the Law*. London: Stevens, 1949.

Diamond, P. A. "The Role of a Stock Market in a General Equilibrium Model with Technological Uncertainty." *American Economic Review*, 1967, *57*, 759–776.

Dickerson, D. D. *Health Insurance*. Homewood, Ill.: Irwin, 1959.

Dobb, M. *Capitalist Enterprise and Social Progress*. London: G. Routledge, 1926.

Dobb, M. *Russian Economic Development Since the Revolution*. London: Labour Research Department, 1928.

Dobzhansky, T. *Mankind Evolving*. New Haven, Conn.: Yale University Press, 1962.

Downs, A. *An Economic Theory of Democracy*. New York: Harper & Row, 1957.

Drucker, P. F. "The New Markets and the New Capitalism." *Public Interest*, 1970, *21*, 44–79.

Durbin, E.F.M. "Economic Calculus in a Planned Economy." *Economic Journal*, 1936, 676–690.

Durbin, J., and Watson, G. S. "Testing for Serial Correlation in Least Squares Regression." *Biometrika*, 1950, *37*, 409–428.

Durham, W. H. "Resource Competition and Human Aggression, Part I: A Review of Primitive War." *Quarterly Review of Biology*, 1976, *51*, 385–407.

Durkheim, E. *The Division of Labor in Society*. (G. Simpson, trans.) New York: Free Press, 1933.

Durkheim, E. *The Rules of the Sociological Method*. (8th ed.) New York: Free Press, 1966.

Elder, G. H., Jr. "Age Differentiation and Life Course." In A. Inkeles, J. Coleman, and N. Smelser (eds.), *Annual Review of Sociology, 1975*. Vol. 1. Palo Alto, Calif.: Annual Review, 1975.

Elfreth, W. H. *Patents, Copyrights, and Trademarks.* New York: Baker, Voorhis, 1918.

Ely, R. T. *Monopolies and Trusts.* New York: Macmillan, 1917.

Ely, R. T. *Outlines of Economics.* (5th ed.) New York: Macmillan, 1930.

Emery, J. C. *Organizational Planning and Control Systems: Theory and Technology.* New York: Macmillan, 1969.

Enke, S. "On Maximizing Profits: A Distinction Between Chamberlin and Robinson." *American Economic Review,* 1951, *41,* 566–578.

Evans, J. L., and Archer, S. H. "Diversification and the Reduction of Dispersion: An Empirical Analysis." *Journal of Finance,* 1968, *23,* 761–768.

Fama, E. F. "Efficient Capital Markets: A Review of Theory and Empirical Work." *Journal of Finance,* 1970a, *25,* 383–417.

Fama, E. F. "Multiperiod Consumption—Investment Decisions." *American Economic Review,* 1970b, *60,* 163–174.

Fama, E. F. "Ordinal and Measurable Utility." In M. C. Jensen (ed.), *Studies in the Theory of Capital Markets.* New York: Praeger, 1972.

Fama, E. F. *Foundations of Finance.* New York: Basic Books, 1976.

Fama, E. F. "Agency Problems and the Theory of the Firm." *Journal of Political Economy,* 1980, *88,* 288–307.

Fama, E. F., and Jensen, M. C. "Agency Problems and Residual Claims." *Journal of Law and Economics,* 1983a, *26,* 327–349.

Fama, E. F., and Jensen, M. C. "Organizational Forms and Investment Decisions." Working paper no. MERC 83–03, Managerial Economics Research Center, University of Rochester, 1983b.

Fama, E. F., and Jensen, M. C. "Separation of Ownership and Control." *Journal of Law and Economics,* 1983c, *26,* 301–325.

Fama, E. F., and Miller, M. *The Theory of Finance.* New York: Holt, Rinehart & Winston, 1972.

Feller, D. E. "A General Theory of the Collective Bargaining Agreement." *California Law Review,* 1973, *61,* 663–857.

Feller, W. *An Introduction to Probability Theory and Its Applications.* New York: Wiley, 1950.

Feller, W. "On Fitness and the Cost of Natural Selection." *Genetic Research*, 1967, *9*, 1–16.

Fellner, W. J. *Competition Among the Few*. Fairfield, N.J.: Kelley, 1985 (Originally published 1949.)

Fischer, S. "Long-Term Contracting, Sticky Prices, and Monetary Policy: Comment." *Journal of Monetary Economics*, 1977, *3*, 317–323.

Fisher, I. *Elementary Principles of Economics*. New York: Macmillan, 1912.

Fisher, R. A. *The Genetic Theory of Natural Selection*. (Rev. ed.) New York: Dover, 1958.

Flaherty, T. "Industry Structure and Cost-Reducing Investment: A Dynamic Equilibrium Analysis." Unpublished doctoral dissertation, Department of Economics, Carnegie-Mellon University, 1976.

Frankel, P. H. "Integration in the Oil Industry." *Journal of Industrial Economics*, 1953, *1*, 201–215.

Franko, L. G. "The Growth and Organizational Efficiency of European Multinational Firms: Some Emerging Hypotheses." *Collogues international aux C.N.R.S.*, 1972, *549*, 335–366.

Frech, H. E. "Biological Externalities and Evolution: A Comment." *Journal of Theoretical Biology*, 1973, *39*, 699–672.

Fredlund, M. C. "Wolves, Chimps, and Demsetz." *Economic Inquiry*, 1976, *14*, 279–290.

French, J. P., and Raven, B. "The Bases of Social Power." In D. Cartwright (ed.), *Studies in Social Power*. Ann Arbor: University of Michigan Press, 1960.

Friedman, L. M. *Contract Law in America*. Madison: University of Wisconsin Press, 1965.

Friedman, M. *Essays in Positive Economics*. Chicago: University of Chicago Press, 1953.

Friedman, M. "The Optimum Quantity of Money." In *The Optimum Quantity of Money and Other Essays*. Hawthorne, N.Y.: Aldine, 1969.

Friedman, M. "The Social Responsibility of Business Is To Increase Its Profits." *New York Times Magazine*, Sept. 13, 1970.

Friedman, M., and Savage, L. "The Utility Analysis of Choices

Involving Risks." *Journal of Political Economy*, 1948, *56*, 279–397.

Fruhan, W. E., Jr. *The Fight for Competitive Advantage*. Cambridge, Mass.: Division of Research, Graduate School of Business, Harvard University, 1972.

Fruhan, W. E., Jr. *Financial Strategy*. Homewood, Ill.: Irwin, 1979.

Fukuzawa, H. "Cotton Mill Industry." In V. B. Singh (ed.), *Economic History of India, 1857–1956*. Bombay, India: Allied, 1965.

Fuller, L. L. "Collective Bargaining and the Arbitrator." *Wisconsin Law Review*, 1963, *3*, 3–46.

Fuller, L. L. *The Morality of Law*. New Haven, Conn.: Yale University Press, 1964.

Furobotn, E. G., and Pejovich, S. "Property Rights and the Behavior of the Firm in a Socialist State." *Zeitschrift für Nationalökonomie*, 1970, *30*, 431–454.

Furobotn, E. G., and Pejovich, S. "Property Rights and Economic Theory: A Survey of Recent Literature." *Journal of Economic Literature*, 1972, *10*, 1137–1162.

Gadgil, M., and Bossert, W. H. "Life-Historical Consequences of Natural Selection." *American Naturalist*, 1970, *104*, 1–14.

Galai, P., and Masulis, R. W. "The Option Pricing Model and the Risk Factor of Stock." *Journal of Financial Economics*, 1976, *3*, 53–82.

Gale, B. T. "Market Share and Rate of Return." *Review of Economics and Statistics*, 1972, *54*, 412–423.

Gale, C. J. *Gale on Easements*. (13th ed.) London: Sweet & Maxwell, 1959. (Originally published 1840.)

Galenson, W., and Odaka, K. "The Japanese Labor Market." In H. Patrick and H. Rosovsky (eds.), *Asia's New Giant*. Washington, D.C.: Brookings Institution, 1976.

Garver, F. B., and Hansen, A. H. *Principles of Economics*. Boston: Ginn, 1928.

General Motors Corporation. *Sixteenth Annual Report*, year ended December 31, 1924. Detroit, Mich.: General Motors Corporation, 1924.

Ghiselin, M. T. *The Economy of Nature and the Evolution of Sex*. Berkeley: University of California Press, 1974.

Goldberg, V. "Toward an Expanded Economic Theory of Contract." *Journal of Economic Issues*, 1976a, *10*, 45–62.

Goldberg, V. "Regulation and Administered Contracts." *Bell Journal of Economics*, 1976b, *7*, 426–448.

Goldberg, V. "Pigou on Complex Contracts and Welfare Economics." Unpublished manuscript, 1979.

Goldschmidt, H. J., Mann, H. M., and Weston, J. F. *Industrial Concentration: The New Learning.* Boston: Little, Brown, 1974.

Gordon, D. F. "A Neoclassical Theory of Keynesian Unemployment." *Economic Inquiry*, 1974, *12*, 431–459.

Green, J. G. "Vertical Integration and Assurance of Markets." Discussion paper no. 383, Institute of Economic Research, Harvard University, 1974.

Grinyer, P. H., Yasai-Ardekani, M., and Al-Bazzaz, S. "Strategy, Structure, and Financial Performance in 48 United Kingdom Companies." *Academy of Management Journal*, 1980, *23*, 193–220.

Grossbard, A. "Economic Analysis of Polygyny: The Case of Maiduguri." *Current Anthropology*, 1976, *17*, 701–707.

Gustafson, W. E. "Periodicals and Books." In M. Hall (ed.), *Made in New York*. Cambridge, Mass.: Harvard University Press, 1959.

Haar, C. M. *Land-Use Planning: A Casebook on the Use, Misuse and Re-use of Urban Land.* Boston: Little, Brown, 1959.

Hakansson, N. H. "The Superfund: Efficient Paths Toward a Complete Financial Market." Unpublished paper, 1974a.

Hakansson, N. H. "Ordering Markets and the Capital Structures of Firms With Illustrations." Working paper no. 24, Institute of Business and Economic Research, University of California, Berkeley, 1974b.

Haldane, J. B. S. "The Cost of Natural Selection." *Journal of Genetics*, 1957, *55*, 511–524.

Hall, M., and Weiss, L. "Firm Size and Profitability." *Review of Economics and Statistics*, 1967, *49*, 319–331.

Halsbury, H. S. G. *Law of England.* (3rd ed.) London: Butterworth, 1952.

Hamilton, W. D. "The Genetical Evolution of Social Behavior." *Journal of Theoretical Biology*, 1964, *7*, 1–16.

Hamilton, W. F., and Moses, M. A. "An Optimization Model for Corporate Financial Planning." *Operations Research*, 1973, *21*, 677–692.

Hannan, M. T., and Freeman, J. "The Population Ecology of Organizations." *American Journal of Sociology*, 1977, *82*, 929–964.

Hansmann, H. B. "The Role of Nonprofit Enterprise." *Yale Law Journal*, 1980, *89*, 835–901.

Harper, F. V., and James, F. *The Law of Torts*. Indianapolis: Bobbs-Merrill, 1956.

Harrigan, K. R. "Strategies for Declining Business." Unpublished doctoral dissertation, Harvard University, 1979.

Hashimoto, M. "Wage Reduction, Unemployment, and Specific Human Capital." *Economic Inquiry*, 1975, *13*, 485–504.

Hatten, K. J. "Strategic Models in the Brewing Industries." Unpublished doctoral dissertation, Purdue University, 1974.

Hatten, K. J., and Schendel, D. "Heterogeneity Within an Industry: Firm Conduct in the US Brewing Industry, 1952–1971." Working paper 76–26, Graduate School of Business Administration, Harvard University, 1976.

Havighurst, H. C. *The Nature of Private Contract*. Evanston, Ill.: Northwestern University Press, 1961.

Hayek, F. A. "The Trend of Economic Thinking." *Economica*, 1933, 121–137.

Hayek, F. A. "The Use of Knowledge in Society." *American Economic Review*, 1945, *35*, 519–530.

Hayes, R. H., and Abernathy, W. J. "Managing Our Way to Economic Decline." *Harvard Business Review*, July–Aug. 1980.

Heckerman, D. G. "Motivating Managers to Make Investment Decisions." *Journal of Financial Economics*, 1975, *2*, 273–292.

Heflebower, R. B. "Observations on Decentralization in Large Enterprises." *Journal of Industrial Economics*, 1960, *9*, 7–22.

Henderson, B. *Henderson on Strategy*. New York: Mentor, 1979.

Henderson, H. D. *Supply and Demand*. London: Nisbet, 1922.

Henry, R. S. *This Fascinating Railroad Business*. Indianapolis: Bobbs-Merrill, 1942.

Herman, E. S. "Conflict of Interest in the Savings and Loan Industry." In I. Friend (ed.), *A Study of the Savings and Loan Industry*. Washington, D.C.: U.S. Government Printing Office, 1969.

Herman, E. S. *Corporate Control, Corporate Power.* Twentieth Century Fund Study. New York: Cambridge University Press, 1981.

Hickson, D. J., Pugh, D. S., and Pheysey, D. "Operations Technology and Organization Structure: An Empirical Reappraisal." *Administrative Science Quarterly*, 1969, *14*, 378–397.

Hickson, D. J., and others. "A Strategic Contingencies Theory of Intraorganizational Power." *Administrative Science Quarterly*, 1971, *16*, 216–227.

Hidy, R. W., and Hidy, M. E. *History of Standard Oil Company (New Jersey): Pioneering in Big Business 1882–1911.* New York: Harper & Row, 1955.

Himmelfarb, G. *Darwin and the Darwinian Revolution.* Garden City, N.Y.: Doubleday, 1959.

Hirschman, A. O. *Exit, Voice, and Loyalty.* Cambridge, Mass.: Harvard University Press, 1970.

Hirshleifer, J. "On the Theory of Optimal Investment Decisions." *Journal of Political Economy*, 1958, *66*, 329–352.

Hirshleifer, J. *Investment, Interest, and Capital.* Englewood Cliffs, N.J.: Prentice-Hall, 1970.

Hirshleifer, J. "Shakespeare vs. Becker on Altruism: The Importance of Having the Last Word." *Journal of Economic Literature*, 1977a, *15*, 500–501.

Hirshleifer, J. "Economics from a Biological Point of View." *Journal of Law and Economics*, 1977b, *20*, 1–52.

Hirshleifer, J. *Price Theory and Applications.* (2nd ed.) Englewood Cliffs, N.J.: Prentice-Hall, 1980.

Hoenack, S. A. *Economic Behavior Within Organizations.* New York: Cambridge University Press, 1983.

Hofer, C. W., and Schendel, D. *Strategy Formulation: Analytical Concepts.* St. Paul, Minn.: West, 1978.

Hofstadter, R. *Social Darwinism in American Thought.* (Rev. ed.) Boston: Beacon Press, 1955.

Homans, G. C. "Social Behavior as Exchange." *American Journal of Sociology*, 1958, *63*, 597–606.

Homans, G. C. *Social Behavior: Its Elementary Forms.* San Diego, Calif.: Harcourt Brace Jovanovich, 1961.

Horngren, C. *Cost Accounting: A Managerial Emphasis.* Englewood Cliffs, N.J.: Prentice-Hall, 1982.

Houthakker, H. S. "Economics and Biology: Specialization and Speciation." *Kyklos*, 1956, *9*, 181–189.

Hunt, M. S. "Competition in the Major Home Appliance Industry, 1960–1970." Unpublished doctoral dissertation, Graduate School of Business Administration, Harvard University, 1972.

Huntington, E. *Mainsprings of Civilization*. New York: Wiley, 1945.

Hurdle, G. "Leverage, Risk, Market Share, and Profitability." *Review of Economics and Statistics*, 1974, *56*, 478–485.

Huxley, J. S. *The Living Thoughts of Darwin*. (Rev. ed.) New York: Longmans, Green, 1958.

Iacocca, L. A., and Novak, W. *Iacocca: An Autobiography*. New York: Bantam Books, 1984.

Jay, A. *Corporation Man*. New York: Random House, 1971.

Jelinek, M., Smircich, L., and Hirsch, P. "Introduction: A Code of Many Colors." *Administrative Science Quarterly*, 1983, *28*, 331–338.

Jensen, M. C. "Risk, the Pricing of Capital Assets, and the Evaluation of Investment Portfolios." *Journal of Business*, 1969, *42*, 167–247.

Jensen, M. C. "Capital Markets: Theory and Evidence." *Bell Journal of Economics and Management Science*, 1972, *3*, 357–398.

Jensen, M. C. "Tests of Capital Market Theory and Implications of the Evidence." Working paper series no. 7414, Graduate School of Management, University of Rochester, 1974.

Jensen, M. C. "Organization Theory and Methodology." *Accounting Review*, 1983, *50*, 319–339.

Jensen, M. C., and Long, J. B. "Corporate Investment Under Uncertainty and Pareto Optimality in the Capital Markets." *Bell Journal of Economics and Management Science*, 1972, *3*, 151–174.

Jensen, M. C., and Meckling, W. H. "Theory of the Firm: Managerial Behavior, Agency Costs and Ownership Structure." *Journal of Financial Economics*, 1976a, *3*, 305–360.

Jensen, M. C., and Meckling, W. H. "Can the Corporations Survive?" Working paper no. PPS76-4, Center for Research in Government Policy and Business, University of Rochester, 1976b.

Jensen, M. C., and Meckling, W. H. "On the Labor-Managed

Firm and the Code Termination Movement.'' Unpublished manuscript, University of Rochester, 1977.

Jensen, M. C., and Meckling, W. H. ''Rights and Production Functions: An Application to Labor-Managed Firms and Code Termination.'' *Journal of Business*, 1979, *52*, 469–506.

Johnson, A. S. *Introduction to Economics.* Lexington, Mass.: Heath, 1909.

Johnston, J. *Econometric Methods.* New York: McGraw-Hill, 1972.

Jones, E. *The Trust Problem in the United States.* New York: Macmillan, 1921.

Jones, G. R. ''Transaction Costs, Property Rights, and Organizational Culture: An Exchange Perspective.'' *Administrative Science Quarterly*, 1983, *28*, 454–467.

Joskow, P. L. ''Commercial Impossibility, the Uranium Market, and the Westinghouse Case.'' *Journal of Legal Studies*, 1977, *6*, 119–176.

Kadiyala, K. R. ''A Transformation Used to Circumvent the Problem of Autocorrelation.'' *Econometrica*, 1968, *36*, 93–96.

Kagel, J. H., and others. ''Experimental Studies of Consumer Demand Behavior Using Laboratory Animals.'' *Economic Inquiry*, 1975, *13*, 22–38.

Kaldor, N. ''A Classificatory Note on the Determinateness of Equilibrium.'' *Review of Economic Studies*, 1934, *1*, 122–136.

Kamien, M., and Schwartz, N. ''Timing of Innovations Under Rivalry.'' *Econometrica*, 1972, *44*, 43–60.

Kanter, R. *Men and Women of the Corporation.* New York: Basic, 1977.

Kasper, D. M. ''Managing in the Regulated Environment.'' Working paper no. 79–26, Graduate School of Business Administration, Harvard University, 1979.

Kessler, F., and Stern, R. H. ''Competition, Contract, and Vertical Integration.'' *Yale Law Journal*, 1959, *69*, 1–130.

Keynes, J. M. *Essays in Biography.* San Diego, Calif.: Harcourt Brace Jovanovich, 1933.

Kindleberger, C. P. *Economic Development.* New York: McGraw-Hill, 1958.

Klein, B. ''The Competitive Supply of Money.'' *Journal of Money, Credit, and Banking*, 1974, *6*, 423–454.

Klein, B., Crawford, R. G., and Alchian, A. A. "Vertical Integration, Appropriable Rents and the Competitive Contracting Process." *Journal of Law and Economics*, 1978, *21*, 297–326.

Klein, B., and Leffler, K. "The Role of Price in Guaranteeing Quality." *Journal of Political Economy*, 1981, *89*, 615–641.

Klein, B., and McLaughlin, A. "Resale Price Maintenance, Exclusive Territories, and Franchise Termination: The Coors Case." Unpublished manuscript, University of California, Los Angeles, 1978.

Klein, W. H. "Legal and Economic Perspectives on the Firm." Unpublished paper, University of California, Los Angeles, 1976.

Kmenta, J. *Elements of Econometrics.* New York: Macmillan, 1971.

Knickerbocker, F. T. *Oligopolistic Reaction and Multinational Enterprise.* Cambridge, Mass.: Division of Research, Graduate School of Business, Harvard University, 1973.

Knight, F. H. "Cost of Production and Price over Long and Short Periods." *Journal of Political Economy*, 1921, *29*, 332.

Knight, F. H. *Risk, Uncertainty, and Profit.* New York: Harper & Row, 1964. (Originally published 1933.)

Kraus, A., and Litzenberger, R. "A State Preference Model of Optimal Financial Leverage." *Journal of Finance*, 1972, *28*, 911–922.

Kuhn, T. *The Structure of Scientific Revolutions.* Chicago: University of Chicago Press, 1970.

Kurz, M. "Altruistic Equilibrium." Stanford University Institute for Mathematical Studies in Social Science and Economics, no. 156, 1975.

Lancaster, K. J. "A New Approach to Consumer Theory." *Journal of Political Economy*, 1966, *74*, 132–157.

Lanchester, F. W. *Aircraft in Warfare*, 1916.

Lawrence, P. R., and Lorsch, J. W. *Organization and Environment: Managing Differentiation and Integration.* Cambridge, Mass.: Graduate School of Business Administration, Harvard University, 1967.

Learned, E. P., Christensen, C. R., Andrews, K. R., and Guth, W. *Business Policy.* Homewood, Ill.: Irwin, 1969.

Leff, A. A. "Contract as a Thing." *American University Law Review*, 1970, *19*, 131.

Leff, N. H. "Industrial Organization and Entrepreneurship in the Developing Countries: The Economic Groups." *Economic Development and Cultural Change*, 1978, *26*.

Leontiades, M. "Rationalizing the Unrelated Acquisition." *California Management Review*, 1982, *24*, 5-14.

Levy, M. J. "Contrasting Factors in the Modernization of China and Japan." In S. Kuznets and others (eds.), *Economic Growth: Brazil, India, Japan*. Durham, N.C.: Duke University Press, 1955.

Lewis, A. W. *The Theory of Economic Growth*. Homewood, Ill.: Irwin, 1955.

Lewontin, R. C. "Evolution: The Concept of Evolution." *International Encyclopedia of Social Science*, 1968, *5*.

Lewontin, R. C. "The Units of Selection." *Annual Review of Ecology and Systematics*, 1970, *1*, 1-35.

Lindblom, C. E. *Politics and Markets*, New York: Basic, 1977.

Lintner, J. "Security Prices, Risk and Maximal Gains from Diversification." *Journal of Finance*, 1965, *20*, 587-616.

Lippman, S., and Rumelt, R. "Uncertain Imitability: An Analysis of Interfirm Differences in Efficiency Under Competition." *Bell Journal of Economics*, 1982, *13*, 418-438.

Llewellyn, K. N. "What Price Contract? An Essay in Perspective." *Yale Law Journal*, 1931, *40*, 704-751.

Lloyd-Davies, P. "Risk and Optimal Leverage." Unpublished paper, University of Rochester, 1975.

Long, J. B. "Wealth, Welfare, and the Price of Risk." *Journal of Finance*, 1972, *27*, 419-433.

Long, J. B. "Discussion." *Journal of Finance*, 1974, *29*, 485-488.

Lorenz, K. *On Aggression*. (M. Wilson, trans.) San Diego, Calif.: Harcourt Brace Jovanovich, 1966.

Lowry, S. T. "Bargain and Contract Theory in Law and Economics." *Journal of Economic Issues*, 1976, 10, 1-22.

Lucas, R. E. "Some International Evidence on Output-Inflation Tradeoffs." *American Economic Review*, 1973, *63*, 326-334.

Luce, R. D., and Raiffa, H. *Games and Decisions*. New York: Wiley, 1957.

Lustgarten, S. R. "The Effect of Buyer Concentration in Manufacturing Industries." *Review of Economics and Statistics*, 1975, *57*, 125-132.

Luthans, F. *Organizational Behavior: A Modern Behavioral Approach to Management.* New York: McGraw-Hill, 1973.

Macaulay, S. "Non-Contractual Relations in Business: A Preliminary Study." *American Sociological Review*, 1963a, *28*, 55–66.

Macaulay, S. "The Use and Nonuse of Contracts in the Manufacturing Industry." *Practical Lawyer*, 1963b, *9*, 13–40.

McGee, J. S. *In Defense of Industrial Concentration.* New York: Praeger, 1971.

McGregor, D. *The Human Side of Enterprise.* New York: McGraw-Hill, 1960.

Macgregor, D. H. *Industrial Combination.* London: G. Bell, 1906.

Machlup, F. "Theories of the Firm: Marginalist, Behavioral, Managerial." *American Economic Review*, 1967, *57*, 1–33.

Machlup, F., and Taber, M. "Bilateral Monopoly, Successive Monopoly, and Vertical Integration." *Economica*, 1960, *27*, 101–119.

McKelvey, W. *Organizational Systematics: Taxonomy, Evolution, and Classification.* Los Angeles: University of California Press, 1982.

McManus, J. C. "The Cost of Alternative Economic Organizations." *Canadian Journal of Economics*, 1975, *8*, 334–350.

MacMillan, I. *Strategy Formulation: Political Concepts.* St. Paul, Minn.: West, 1978.

McNaughton, S. J., and Woolf, L. L. *General Ecology.* New York: Holt, Rinehart & Winston, 1973.

Macneil, I. R. "The Many Futures of Contract." *Southern California Law Review*, 1974, *47*, 691–816.

Macneil, I. R. "Contracts: Adjustment of Long-Term Economic Relations Under Classical, Neoclassical, and Contract Law." *Northwestern University Law Review*, 1978, *72*, 854–906.

Malmgren, H. B. "Information, Expectations and the Theory of the Firm." *Quarterly Journal of Economics*, 1961, *75*, 399–421.

Manne, H. G. "The 'Higher Criticism' of the Modern Corporation." *Columbia Law Review*, 1962, *62*, 399–432.

Manne, H. G. "Mergers and the Market for Corporate Control." *Journal of Political Economy*, 1965, *73*, 110–120.

Manne, H. G. "Our Two Corporate Systems: Law and Economics." *Virginia Law Review*, 1967, *53*, 259–284.

Manne, H. G. "The Social Responsibility of Regulated Utilities." *Wisconsin Law Review*, 1972, *5*, 995-1009.

March, J. G., and Simon, H. A. *Organizations*. New York: Wiley, 1958.

Marris, R. *The Economic Theory of Managerial Capitalism*. Glencoe, Ill.: Free Press, 1964.

Marshall, A. *Principles of Economics*. (2nd ed.) London: Macmillan, 1891.

Mason, E. S. "Price and Production Policies of Large-Scale Enterprises." *American Economic Review*, 1939, *29*, 61-74.

Mason, E. S. *The Corporation in Modern Society*. Cambridge, Mass.: Harvard University Press, 1960. (Originally published 1959.)

Mayr, E. "The Emergence of Evolutionary Novelties." In S. Tax and C. Calendar (eds.), *Evolution After Darwin: The Evolution of Life*. Chicago: University of Chicago Press, 1960.

Meade, J. E. *The Controlled Economy*. London: Allen and Unwin, 1971.

Meckling, W. H. "Values and the Choice of the Model of the Individual in the Social Sciences." *Schweizerische Zeitschrift für Volkswirtschaft*, 1976.

Mehta, M. M. *Structure of Indian Industries*. Bombay, India: Popular Book Depot, 1955.

Merton, R. C. "The Theory of Rational Option Pricing." *Bell Journal of Economics and Management Science*, 1973, *4*, 141-183.

Merton, R. C. "On the Pricing of Corporate Debt: The Risk Structure of Interest Rates." *Journal of Finance*, 1974, *29*, 449-470.

Merton, R. C., and Subrahmanyam, M. G. "The Optimality of a Competitive Stock Market." *Bell Journal of Economics*, 1974, *5*, 145-170.

Meyer, J. W., and Rowan, B. "Institutional Organizations: Formal Structure as Myth and Ceremony." *American Journal of Sociology*, 1977, *83*, 340-363.

Miles, R. H. *Macro Organizational Behavior*. Santa Monica, Calif.: Goodyear, 1980.

Mill, J. S. *Principles of Political Economy*. Book V. East Norwalk, Conn.: Appleton-Century-Crafts, 1884.

Miller, M. H., and Modigliani, F. "Some Estimates of the Cost

of Capital to the Electric Utility Industry, 1954–1957." *American Economic Review*, 1966, *56*, 333–391.

Mintz, S. W. "Pratik: Haitian Personal Economic Relations." In G. Foster and others (eds.), *Peasant Society: A Reader*. Boston: Little, Brown, 1967.

Mishnan, E. J. "The Meaning of Efficiency in Economics." *The Bankers Magazine*, 1960, *189*, 482–495.

Modigliani, F., and Miller, M. H. "The Costs of Capital, Corporation Finance, and the Theory of Investment." *American Economic Review*, 1958, *48*, 261–297.

Modigliani, F., and Miller, M. H. "Corporate Income Taxes and the Cost of Capital: A Correction." *American Economic Review*, 1963, *53*, 433–443.

Mollenhoff, C. "Presidential Guile." *Harpers*, June 1973, pp. 38–42.

Monsen, R. J., and Downs, A. "A Theory of Large Managerial Firms." *Journal of Political Economy*, 1965, *73*, 221–226.

Monteverde, K., and Teece, D. J. "Supplier Switching Costs and Vertical Integration." *Bell Journal of Economics*, 1982, *13*, 206–213.

Morris, D. *The Naked Ape*. New York: McGraw-Hill, 1967.

Morse, P. M., and Kimball, G. E. *Methods of Operation Research*. New York: Wiley, 1951.

Mueller, W. F., and Hamm, L. G. "Trends in Industrial Market Concentration, 1947–1970." *Review of Economics and Statistics*, 1974, *56*, 511–520.

Myers, S. C. "A Note on the Determinants of Corporate Debt Capacity." Unpublished manuscript, Graduate School of Business Studies, London School of Economics, 1975.

Nelson, P. "Information and Consumer Behavior." *Journal of Political Economy*, 1970, *78*, 311–329.

Nelson, P. "Advertising as Information." *Journal of Political Economy*, 1974, *82*, 729–754.

Nelson, R. R., and Winter, S. G. "Neoclassical vs. Evolutionary Theories of Economic Growth: Critique and Prospectus." *Economic Journal*, 1974, *84*, 886–905.

Nelson, R. R., and Winter, S. G. *An Evolutionary Theory of Economic Change*. Cambridge, Mass.: Harvard University Press, 1982.

Nerlove, M. "Household and Economy: Toward a New Theory of Population and Economic Growth." *Journal of Political Economy*, 1974, *82*, S200–S218.

Nevins, A. *John D. Rockefeller: The Heroic Age of American Enterprise.* New York: Scribner's, 1940.

Newman, H. H. "Strategic Groups and The Structure/Performance Relationship: A Study with Respect to the Chemical Process Industries." Unpublished doctoral dissertation, Harvard University, 1973.

Newman, H. H. "Strategic Groups and the Structure/Performance Relationship." *Review of Economics and Statistics*, 1978, *56*, 58–66.

Nicholson, A. J. "The Role of Population Dynamics in Natural Selection. "In S. Tax and C. Calendar (eds.), *Evolution After Darwin.* Chicago: University of Chicago Press, 1960.

Olson, M. *The Logic of Collective Action.* Cambridge, Mass.: Harvard Economic Studies, Harvard University Press, 1965.

Orr, D. "The Determinants of Entry: A Study of the Canadian Manufacturing Industries." *Review of Economics and Statistics*, 1974, *56*, 58–66.

Ouchi, W. G. "Markets, Bureaucracies, and Clans." *Administrative Science Quarterly*, 1980, *25*, 124–141.

Ouchi, W. G. *Theory Z.* Reading, Mass.: Addison-Wesley, 1981.

Ouchi, W. G. *The M-Form Society.* Reading, Mass.: Addison-Wesley, 1984.

Park, R. E. "Estimation with Heteroscedastic Terms." *Econometrica*, 1966, *34*, 888.

Parsons, T. *The Social System.* New York: Free Press, 1951.

Pejovich, S. "The Firm, Monetary Policy, and Property Rights in a Planned Economy." *Western Economic Journal*, 1969, *7*, 193–200.

Pennings, J. M. *Interlocking Directorates: Origins and Consequences of Connections Among Organizations' Boards of Directors.* San Francisco: Jossey-Bass, 1980.

Penrose, E. T. "Biological Analogies in the Theory of the Firm." *American Economic Review*, 1952, *42*, 804–819.

Penrose, E. T. "Biological Analogies in the Theory of the Firm." *American Economic Review*, 1953, *43*, 603–609.

Penrose, E. T. *The Theory of the Growth of the Firm.* New York: Wiley, 1958.

Perrow, C. *Complex Organizations: A Critical Essay.* Glenview, Ill.: Scott, Foresman, 1972.

Peters, T., and Waterman, R. H. *In Search of Excellence.* New York: Harper & Row, 1982.

Peterson, S. "Corporate Control and Capitalism." *Quarterly Journal of Economics*, 1965, *79*, 1–24.

Pfeffer, J., and Cohen, Y. "Determinants of Internal Labor Markets in Organizations." *Administrative Science Quarterly*, 1984, *29*, 550–572.

Pfeffer, J., and Leong, A. "Resource Allocation in United Funds: An Examination of Power and Dependence." *Social Forces*, 1977, *55*, 775–790.

Pfeffer, J., and Salancik, G. R. *The External Control of Organizations: A Resource Dependence Perspective.* New York: Harper & Row, 1978.

Pigou, A. C. "Some Aspects of the Housing Problem." In B. S. Rowntree and A. C. Pigou (eds.), *Lectures on Housing.* Manchester, England: Manchester University Press, 1914.

Pigou, A. C. *The Economics of Welfare.* (4th ed.) London: Macmillan, 1932. (Originally published 1920.)

Pigou, A. C. *A Study in Public Finance.* (3rd ed.) London: Macmillan, 1947. (Originally published 1929.)

Plant, A. "Trends in Business Administration." *Economica*, Feb. 1932, pp. 45–62.

Polanyi, M. *Personal Knowledge: Towards a Post Critical Philosophy.* London: Routledge, 1962.

Porter, M. E. "Consumer Behavior, Retailer Power, and Manufacturer Strategy in Consumer Goods Industries." Unpublished doctoral dissertation, Harvard University, 1973.

Porter, M. E. "Consumer Behavior, Retailer Power, and Performance in Consumer Goods Industries." *Review of Economics and Statistics*, 1974a, *56*, 419–431.

Porter, M. E. *Note On the Structural Analysis of Industries.* Case no. 9-376-054. Boston: Intercollegiate Case Clearing House, 1974b.

Porter, M. E. *Interbrand Choice, Strategy, and Bilateral Market Power.* Cambridge, Mass.: Harvard Economic Studies, Harvard University Press, 1976a.

Porter, M. E. "Please Note Location of Nearest Exit: Exit Barriers and Planning," *California Management Review*, 1976b, *19*, 21–33.

Porter, M. E. "Market Structure, Strategy Formulation, and Firm Profitability: The Theory of Strategic Groups and Mobility Barriers." In J. Cady (ed.), *Marketing and the Public Interest*. Cambridge, Mass.: Marketing Science Institute, 1978.

Porter, M. E. "How Competitive Forces Shape Strategy." *Harvard Business Review*, 1979a, *57*, 137–156.

Porter, M. E. "The Structure Within Industries and Companies' Performance." *Review of Economics and Statistics*, 1979b, *61*, 214–227.

Porter, M. E. *Competitive Strategy: Techniques for Analyzing Industries and Competitors*. New York: Free Press, 1980.

Porter, M. E. "The Contributions of Industrial Organization to Strategic Management." *Academy of Management Review*, 1981, *6*, 609–620.

Porter, M. E., and Caves, R. E. "Barriers to Exit." In R. T. Mason and D. Qualls (eds.), *Essays in Industrial Organization in Honor of Joe S. Bain*. Cambridge, Mass.: Ballinger, 1976.

Porter, M. E., and Spence, A. M. "The Capacity Expansion Process in a Growing Oligopoly: The Case of Corn Wet Milling." Unpublished manuscript, Graduate School of Business Administration, Harvard University, 1978.

Preston, L. E. "Corporation and Society: The Search for a Paradigm." *Journal of Economic Literature*, 1975, *13*, 434–453.

Prindle, R. *Patents as a Factor in Manufacturing*. New York: The Engineering Magazine, 1908.

Prosser, W. L. *Handbook of the Law of Torts*. St. Paul, Minn.: West, 1955.

Pugel, T. A. *International Market Linkages and U.S. Manufacturing: An International Perspective*. Cambridge, Mass.: Ballinger, 1978.

Radner, R. "Equilibre de marchés á terme et au compatant en cas incertitude." *Cashiers économetric*, 1967, *12*.

Rapoport, A. *Fights, Games, and Debates*. Ann Arbor: University of Michigan Press, 1960.

Rapport, D. J. "An Optimization Model of Food Selection." *American Naturalist*, 1971, *105*, 575–588.

Rapport, D., and Turner, J. E. "Economic Models in Ecology." *Science*, 1977, *195*, 367–378.

Rehnquist, W. "Remarks of Mr. Justice Rehnquist." Miami, Fla.: The Adversary Society, Baron di Hirsch Meyer Lecture, School of Law, University of Miami, 1978.

Report of the Committee on the Distribution of Income and Levels of Living, Part I. Government of India, Planning Commission, Feb. 1964, p. 44.

Richardson, L. F. "Variation of the Frequency of Fatal Quarrels with Magnitude." *Journal of American Statistical Analysis*, 1948, *43*, 523–546.

Riley, J. G. "Information, Screening, and Human Capital." *American Economic Review*, 1976, *66*, 254–260.

Riley, P. "A Structurationist Account of Political Culture." *Administrative Science Quarterly*, 1983, *28*, 414–437.

Robbins, L. C. *An Essay on the Nature and Significance of Economic Science*. London: Macmillan, 1932.

Robertson, D. H. *Control of Industry*. London: Nisbet, 1936.

Robertson, D. H. *Lectures on Economic Principles*. London: Staples Press, 1957.

Robinson, E.A.G. *The Structure of Competitive Industry*. London: Nisbet, 1931.

Robinson, E.A.G. "The Problem of Management and the Size of the Firm." *Economic Journal*, 1934, 242–257.

Robinson, J. *Economics Is a Serious Subject*. Cambridge, Mass.: Heffer, 1932.

Robinson, J. *Economics of Imperfect Competition*. London: Macmillan, 1933.

Roethlisberger, F. J., and Dickson, W. J. *Management and the Worker*. Cambridge, Mass.: Harvard University Press, 1939.

Rogers, E. S. *Goodwill, Trade-Marks and Unfair Trading*. Chicago: Shaw, 1914.

Ross, S. A. "The Economic Theory of Agency: The Principal Problem." *American Economic Review*, 1973, *63*, 134–139.

Ross, S. A. "The Economic Theory of Agency and the Principle of Similarity." In M. D. Balch and others (eds.), *Essays on Economic Behavior Under Uncertainty*. Amsterdam: North-Holland, 1974a.

Ross, S. A. "Options and Efficiency." Working paper no. 3-74, Rodney L. White Center for Financial Research, University of Pennsylvania, 1974b.

Rosse, J. N. *Estimation and Prediction with Complex Heteroscedasticity*.

Studies in Industry Economics, no. 75. Stanford, Calif.: Department of Economics, Stanford University, 1977.

Rubin, P. H. "The Theory of the Firm and the Structure of the Franchise Contract." *Journal of Law and Economics*, 1978, *21*, 223–234.

Rubinstein, M. "A Discrete-Time Synthesis of Financial Theory, Parts I and II." Working papers nos. 20, 21. Institute of Business and Economic Research, University of California, Berkeley, 1974.

Rumelt, R. P. *Strategy, Structure, and Economic Performance*. Cambridge, Mass.: Division of Research, Graduate School of Business Administration, Harvard University, 1974.

Salmond, J. W. *The Law of Torts*. (12th ed.) London: Sweet & Maxwell, 1947. (Originally published 1907.)

Salop, S. C. "Strategic Entry Deterrence." *American Economic Review*, 1979, *69*, 335–338.

Salter, A. *Allied Shipping Control*. Oxford, England: Clarendon Press, 1921.

Samuelson, P. *Foundations of Economic Analysis*. Cambridge, Mass.: Harvard University Press, 1946.

Schelling, T. C. *The Strategy of Conflict*. Cambridge, Mass.: Harvard University Press, 1960.

Schelling, T. C. "Dynamic Models of Segregation." *Journal of Mathematical Sociology*, 1971, *1*, 143–186.

Schelling, T. C. *Micromotives and Macrobehavior*. New York: Norton, 1978.

Schendel, D., and Patton, G. R. "A Simultaneous Equation Model of Corporate Strategy." Graduate School of Business, Purdue University, 1977. (Mimeographed.)

Scherer, F. M. *Industrial Market Structure and Economic Performance*. Skokie, Ill.: Rand McNally, 1970.

Schmalensee, R. "Entry Deterrence in the Ready-to-Eat Breakfast Cereal Industry." *Bell Journal of Economics*, 1978, *9*, 305–327.

Schmidt, P., and Strauss, R. P. "The Effects of Unions on Earnings and Earnings on Unions: A Mixed Logic Approach." *International Economic Review*, 1976, *17*, 204–212.

Schultz, T. W. *The Economic Value of Education*. New York: Columbia University Press, 1964.

Schumpeter, J. A. *The Theory of Economic Development*. Cambridge, Mass.: Harvard University Press, 1934.

Schumpeter, J. A. *Capitalism, Socialism, and Democracy*. (3rd ed.) New York: Harper & Row, 1950.

Scitovsky, T. "A Note on Profit Maximization and Its Implications." *Review of Economic Studies*, 1943, *11*, 57–60.

Scott, B. R. "The Industrial State: Old Myths and New Realities." *Harvard Business Review*, 1973, *51*, 133–149.

Seager, R. *Principles of Economics*. New York: Holt, Rinehart & Winston, 1917.

Selznick, P. *Leadership in Administration: A Sociological Interpretation*. New York: Harper & Row, 1957.

Selznick, P. *TVA and the Grass Roots: A Study in the Sociology of Formal Organizations*. Berkeley: University of California Press, 1966. (Originally published 1949.)

Shapiro, S., Schlesinger, E. R., and Nesbitt, R. L. *Infant, Perinatal, Maternal, and Childhood Mortality in the United States*. U.S. Department of Health, Education, and Welfare. Washington, D.C.: U.S. Government Printing Office, 1968.

Sharpe, W. F. "Capital Asset Prices: A Theory of Market Equilibrium Under Conditions of Risk." *Journal of Finance*, 1964, *19*, 425–442.

Shepherd, W. G. "The Elements of Market Structure." *Review of Economics and Statistics*, 1972, *54*, 25–37.

Shove, G. F. "The Imperfection of the Market: A Further Note." *Economic Journal*, 1933, 113–125.

Shubik, M. "A Curmudgeon's Guide to Microeconomics." *Journal of Economic Literature*, 1970, *8*, 405–434.

Silver, M., and Auster, R. "Entrepreneurship, Profit, and Limits on Firm Size." *Journal of Business*, 1969, *42*, 277–281.

Simmel, G. *Conflict*. (K.H. Wolff, trans.) New York: Free Press, 1955.

Simon, H. A. "A Behavioral Model of Rational Choice." *Quarterly Journal of Economics*, 1955, *69*, 99–118.

Simon, H. A. "Theories of Decision-Making in Economics and Behavioral Science." *American Economic Review*, 1959, *49*, 253–283.

Simon, H. A. *Administrative Behavior*. (2nd ed.) New York: Wiley, 1961.

Simon, H. A. "The Architecture of Complexity." *Proceedings of the American Philosophical Society*, 1962, *106*, 467–482.

Skinner, G. W. "Marketing and Social Structure in Rural China." In G. Foster and others (eds.), *Peasant Society: A Reader*. Boston: Little, Brown, 1967.

Smiley, R. "The Economics of Tender Offers." Unpublished doctoral dissertation, Department of Economics, Stanford University, 1973.

Smith, A. *An Inquiry into the Nature and Causes of the Wealth of Nations*. (Cannan ed.) New York: Modern Library, 1937. (Originally published 1776.)

Smith, C. "Option Pricing: A Review." *Journal of Financial Economics*, 1976, *3*, 1-52.

Smith, J. M. "Group Selection and Kin Selection." *Nature*, 1964, *201*, 1145-1147.

Smith, K. V., and Schreiner, J. C. "A Portfolio Analysis of Conglomerate Diversification." *Journal of Finance*, 1969, *24*, 413-429.

Smith, V. L. "Experimental Economics: Induced Value Theory." *American Economic Review*, 1976, *66*, 274-279.

Sowell, T. *Knowledge and Decisions*. New York: Basic Books, 1980.

Speck, F. G. "The Basis of American Indian Ownership of Land." *Old Penn Weekly Review*, Jan. 16, 1915, pp. 491-495.

Spence, A. M. "Job Market Signalling." *Quarterly Journal of Economics*, 1973, *87*, 355-374.

Spence, A. M. *Market Signalling: Informational Transfer in Hiring and Related Screening Processes*. Cambridge, Mass.: Harvard University Press, 1974a.

Spence, A. M. "Competitive and Optimal Responses to Signals: An Analysis of Efficiency and Distribution." *Journal of Economic Theory*, 1974b, *7*, 296-315.

Spence, A. M. "Entry Capacity Investment and Oligopolistic Pricing." *Bell Journal of Economics*, 1977, *8*, 534-544.

Spence, A. M. "Investment Strategy and Growth in a New Market." *Bell Journal of Economics*, 1979, *10*, 1-9.

Spence, A. M. "The Learning Curve and Competition." *Bell Journal of Economics*, 1981, *12*, 49-70.

Stephen, J. F. *A General View of the Criminal Law of England*. London: Macmillan, 1890.

Stettler, H. P. *Auditing Principles*. Englewood Cliffs, N.J.: Prentice-Hall, 1977.

Stigler, G. J. "The Division of Labor is Limited by the Extent of the Market." *Journal of Political Economy*, 1951, *59*, 185–193.

Stigler, G. J. *The Theory of Price*. New York: Macmillan, 1952.

Stigler, G. J. "The Economics of Scale." *Journal of Law and Economics*, 1958, *1*, 54–71.

Stigler, G. J. "Information and the Labor Market." *Journal of Political Economy*, 1962, *70*, 94–105.

Stigler, G. J. *The Theory of Price*. (3rd ed.) New York: Macmillan, 1966.

Stigler, G. J. "A Note on Profitability, Competition, and Concentration." In *The Organization of Industry*. Homewood, Ill.: Irwin, 1968.

Stiglitz, J. E. "Some Aspects of the Pure Theory of Corporate Finance: Bankruptcies and Takeovers." *Bell Journal of Economics*, 1972, *3*, 458–482.

Stiglitz, J. E. "The Theory of 'Screening': Education and the Distribution of Income." *American Economic Review*, 1975, *65*, 283–300.

Stonebreaker, R. J. "Corporate Profits and Risks of Entry." *Review of Economics and Statistics*, 1976, *58*, 33–39.

Street, H. *The Law of Torts*. London: Butterworth, 1959.

Sultan, R.G.M. *Pricing in the Electrical Monopoly*. Vols. 1 and 2. Cambridge, Mass.: Division of Research, Graduate School of Business Administration, Harvard University, 1974.

Summers, C. W. "Collective Agreements and the Law of Contracts." *Yale Law Journal*, 1969, *78*, 525–575.

Taira, K. *Economic Development and the Labor Market in Japan*. New York: Columbia University Press, 1970.

Taussig, F. W. *Principles of Economics*. (3rd ed.) New York: Macmillan, 1921.

Teece, D. J. "Vertical Integration and Divestiture in the U.S. Oil Industry." In E. J. Mitchell (ed.), *Vertical Integration in the Oil Industry*. Washington, D.C.: American Enterprise Institute for Public Policy Research, 1976.

Telser, L. G., and Higinbotham, H. N. "Organized Futures Markets: Costs and Benefits." *Journal of Political Economy*, 1977, *85*, 969–1000.

Temin, P. "Modes of Economic Behavior: Variations of Themes of J. R. Hicks and Herbert Simon." Working paper no. 235,

Department of Economics, Massachusetts Institute of Technology, 1979.

Thompson, E. A. "Nonpecuniary Rewards and the Aggregate Production Function." *Review of Economics and Statistics*, 1970, *52*, 395–404.

Thompson, J. D. *Organizations in Action*. New York: McGraw-Hill, 1967.

Thorelli, H. G. (ed.). *Strategy + Structure = Performance*. Bloomington: Indiana University Press, 1977.

Tichy, N. *Managing Strategic Change*. New York: Wiley, 1983.

Tiger, L., and Fox, R. *The Imperial Animal*. New York: Holt, Rinehart & Winston, 1971.

Tinker, H. *South Asia: A Short History*. New York: Praeger, 1966.

Tinter, G. "The Pure Theory of Production Under Technological Risk and Uncertainty." *Econometrica*, 1941a, *9*, 305–311.

Tinter, G. "The Theory of Choice Under Subjective Risk and Uncertainty." *Econometrica*, 1941b, *9*, 298–304.

Tinter, G. "A Contribution to the Nonstatic Theory of Production." *Studies in Mathematical Economics and Econometrics*. Chicago: University of Chicago Press, 1942.

Trivers, R. L. "The Evolution of Reciprocal Altruism." *Quarterly Review of Biology*, 1971, *46*, 35–57.

Trivers, R. L. "Parental Investment and Sexual Selection." In B. Campbell (ed.), *Sexual Selection and the Descent of Man, 1871–1971*. Chicago: Aldine, 1972.

Trivers, R. L. "Parent-Offspring Conflict." *American Zoologist*, 1974, *14*, 249–264.

Trivers, R. L., and Hare, H. "Haplodiploidy and the Evolution of the Social Insects." *Science*, 1976, *191*, 249–261.

Trivers, R. L., and Willard. "Natural Selection of Parental Ability to Vary the Sex Ratio of Offspring." *Science*, 1973, *179*, 90–102.

Tullock, G. "Biological Externalities." *Journal of Theoretical Biology*, 1971, *33*, 565–576.

Ulrich, P., and Barney, J. B. "Perspectives in Organizations: Resource Dependence, Efficiency, and Population." *Academy of Management Review*, 1984, *9*, 471–481.

Usher, A. P. *Introduction to the Industrial History of England*. Boston: Houghton Mifflin, 1920.

Uyterhoeven, H.E.R., Ackerman, R. W., and Rosenblum, J.W. *Strategy and Organization*. (Rev. ed.) Homewood, Ill.: Irwin, 1977.

Van de Ven, A. "Three R's of Administrative Behavior: Rational, Random, and Reasonable." Unpublished manuscript, School of Management, University of Minnesota, 1982.

Vaughn, M. *The Economics of Our Patent System*. New York: Macmillan, 1927.

Veblen, T. *The Theory of Business Enterprise*. New York: Scribner's, 1927. (Originally published 1904.)

von Neumann, J., and Morgenstern, O. *The Theory of Games and Economic Behavior*. Princeton, N.J.: Princeton University Press, 1953.

Vroom, V., and Yetton, P. *Leadership and Decision Making*. Pittsburgh, Penn.: University of Pittsburgh Press, 1973.

Wachter M. L., and Williamson, O. E. "Obligational Markets and the Mechanics of Inflation." *Bell Journal of Economics*, 1978, *9*, 549-572.

Waddington, C. H. *The Nature of Life*. New York: Atheneum, 1961.

Walker, G., and Weber, D. "A Transaction Cost Approach to Make-or-Buy Decisions." *Administrative Science Quarterly*, 1984, *29*, 373-391.

Ward, B. "Cash or Credit Crops." In G. Foster and others (eds.), *Peasant Society: A Reader*. Boston: Little, Brown, 1967.

Warner, J. B. "Bankruptcy Costs, Absolute Priority, and the Pricing of Risky Debt Claims." Unpublished paper, Department of Economics, University of Chicago, 1975.

Weber, M. "Bureaucracy." In H. H. Gerth and C. W. Mills (eds.), *From Max Weber: Essays in Sociology*. New York: Oxford University Press, 1946.

Weber, M. *The Theory of Social and Economic Organization*. (A. M. Henderson and T. Parsons, trans.) New York: Free Press, 1947.

Weick, K. *The Social Psychology of Organizing*. Reading, Mass.: Addison-Wesley, 1969.

Weiss, L. W. "The Concentration-Profits Relationship and Antitrust." In H. J. Goldsmith and others (eds.), *Industrial Concentration: The New Learning*. Boston: Little, Brown, 1974.

Westerfield, R. "A Note on the Measure of Conglomerate Diversification." *Journal of Finance*, 1970, *25*, 904-914.

Weston, J. F. "Diversification and Merger Trends." *Business Economics*, 1970, *5*, 50–57.

Whinston, G. "A Note on Perspective Time: Goldberg's Relational Exchange, Repetitiveness, and Free Riders in Time and Space." Unpublished paper, 1978.

White, H. J. "Monopolistic and Perfect Competition." *American Economic Review*, 1936.

Wilkins, A. L., and Ouchi, W. G. "Efficient Cultures: Exploring the Relationship Between Culture and Organizational Performance." *Administrative Science Quarterly*, 1983, *28*, 468–481.

Williams, G. C. *Adaptation and Natural Selection*. Princeton, N.J.: Princeton University Press, 1966.

Williams, G. L. *Liability for Animals*. Cambridge, Mass.: Harvard University Press, 1939.

Williamson, H. F., and Daum, A. R. *The American Petroleum Industry*. Evanston Ill.: Northwestern University Press, 1959.

Williamson, O. E. *The Economics of Discretionary Behavior: Managerial Objectives in a Theory of the Firm*. Englewood Cliffs, N.J.: Prentice-Hall, 1964.

Williamson, O. E. *Corporate Control and Business Behavior*. Englewood Cliffs, N.J.: Prentice-Hall, 1970.

Williamson, O.E. "The Vertical Integration of Production: Market Failure Considerations." *American Economic Review*, 1971, *61*, 112–113.

Williamson, O.E. *Markets and Hierarchies: Analysis and Antitrust Implications*. New York: Free Press, 1975.

Williamson, O. E. "Franchise Bidding for Natural Monopolies—In General and with Respect to CATV." *Bell Journal of Economics*, 1976, *7*, 73–104.

Williamson, O. E. "Transaction-Cost Economics: The Governance of Contractual Relations." *Journal of Law and Economics*, 1979, *22*, 233–261.

Williamson, O. E. "The Modern Corporation: Origins, Evolution, Attributes." *Journal of Economic Literature*, 1981, *19*, 1537– 1568.

Williamson, O. E., and Bhargava, N. "Assessing and Classifying the Internal Structure and Control Apparatus of the Modern Corporation." In K. Cowling (ed.), *Market Structure and Corporate Behavior: Theory and Empiricial Analysis of the Firm*. London: Gray-Mills, 1972.

Williamson, O. E., and Ouchi, W. G. "The Markets and Hierarchies Perspective: Origins, Implications, Prospects." In A. Van de Ven and W. F. Joyce (eds.), *Assessing Organization Design and Performance*. New York: Wiley, 1981.

Wilson, D. S. "A Theory of Group Selection." *Proceedings of the National Academy of Science*, 1975, *72*, 143–152.

Wilson, E. O. *Sociobiology*. Cambridge, Mass.: Harvard University Press, 1975.

Wilson, E. O. "Biology and the Social Sciences." *Daedalus*, 1977, *106* (2), 127–140.

Wilson, E. O., and Bossert, W. H. *A Primer of Population Biology*. Stanford, Conn.: Sinauer Associates, 1971.

Wilson, R. "On the Theory of Syndicates." *Econometrica*, 1968, *36*, 119–132.

Wilson, R. *La Decision: Agregation et dynamique des orders de preference*. Paris: Editions du Centre National de la Recherche Scientifique, 1969.

Windfield, P. H. *Torts*. (6th ed.) London: Sweet & Maxwell, 1954.

Winter, S. G. "Economic Natural Selection and the Theory of the Firm." *Yale Economic Essays*, 1964, *4*, 225–272.

Winter, S. G. "Satisficing, Selection, and the Innovating Remnant." *Quarterly Journal of Economics*, 1971, *85*, 237–261.

Winter, S. G. "Optimization and Evolution in the Theory of the Firm." In R. H. Day and T. Graves (eds.), *Adaptive Economic Models*. Orlando, Fla.: Academic Press, 1975.

Wolfe, A. B. "Competitive Costs and the Rent of Business Ability." *Quarterly Journal of Economics*, 1924, *39*, 39–69.

Woods, D. H. "Improving Estimates That Involve Uncertainty." *Harvard Business Review*, 1966, *44*, 91–98.

Wynne-Edwards, V. C. *Animal Dispersion in Relation to Social Behavior*. Edinburgh, Scotland: Oliver & Boyd, 1962.

Zeckhauser, R. "Risk Spreading and Distribution." Discussion paper no. 10, Kennedy School, Harvard University, 1972.

Zucker, L. "The Role of Institutionalization in Cultural Persistence." *American Sociological Review*, 1977, *42*, 726–743.

Name Index

Subject Index